To Libby .

from

Mum . Dad   (English)
"Russetts"   16th May 1983

Mrs Beeton's
COOKERY FOR ALL

Mrs Beeton's
COOKERY FOR ALL

Ward Lock Limited · London

First published in Great Britain in 1982
by Ward Lock Limited, 82 Gower Street,
London WC1E 6EQ, a Pentos Company.

Edited by Susan Dixon
Designed by Andrew Shoolbred
Line drawings by Sue Sharples
Food photography by Sue and John Jorgenson

Text filmset in Photina
by Jolly & Barber Limited, Rugby
Printed in Great Britain by
Jolly & Barber Limited, Rugby

British Library Cataloguing in Publication Data

Beeton, *Mrs*
  Mrs Beeton's cookery for all.
  1. Cookery
  I. Title
  641.5   TX651

ISBN 0-7063-6135-0

CONTENTS

Weights, Measures, Temperatures
and other Basic Information   7

First-Course Dishes   14

Stuffings, Garnishes and Accompaniments   42

Main Courses   60

Sauces, Gravies, Marinades and Butters   200

Vegetables, Pasta and Rice   234

Puddings, Desserts and Ices   274

Breads, Cakes, Biscuits,
Icings, Fillings and Decorations   338

Pastry Making and Pastry Goods   401

Home Freezing   429

Index   443

Contributors

Maggie Black; British Poultry Federation; British Turkey Federation; Maître Jean Conil – Principal, Academy of Gastronomy; Mrs Carolyn Cheek Deynel MA – American Women's Club, London; J. Audrey Ellison BSc, FSFST, FAHE, FRSH – food consultant and writer; Flour Advisory Bureau; Shirley Hislop; Mrs Joyce Hughes BSc, MAHE – consultant home economist; Patricia Jacobs; Peter Lackington – Youngs Seafoods Ltd; Barbara Logan MHEA – consultant home economist; Moya Maynard; Barbara Morrison FAHE – consultant home economist; Mary Norwak – cookery writer; Gabor Oliver – managing director, Cheeses from Switzerland Ltd; Miss Joan Peters – consultant home economist; Jennie Reekie.

The publishers would also like to thank the following people and companies for their valuable assistance:
Jane Atkinson; FMC Ltd; Meat and Livestock Commission; Judy Ridgway; Christopher G. Smith BA, MCHIMA.

WEIGHTS, MEASURES, TEMPERATURES AND OTHER BASIC INFORMATION

Metric quantities are easy to weigh and measure; all you need are weighing scales giving metric quantities, a metric measuring jug, and a set of metric measuring spoons for small quantities.

Metric Units used in Cookery

Weight	gram	(g)		*Length*	millimetre	(mm)
	kilogram = 1000g	(kg)			centimetre	(cm)
Capacity	millilitre	(ml)			metre = 1000mm	(m)
	centilitre	(cl)			100cm	
	decilitre	(dl)		*Temperature*	degree Celsius	(°C)
	litre = 1000ml	(litre)			(Centigrade)	
	100cl					
	10dl					

Measuring by Weight
Spring balance and loose weight metric scales are available in various sizes and designs. Those calibrated in 10g divisions for small amounts and 25g or 50g for larger amounts are the most useful.

Measuring by Capacity

Using a metric jug
Measuring jugs are available in 500ml, 1 litre and 2 litre sizes calibrated in divisions of 50ml, 100ml and 200ml, and sometimes, in decimals or fractions of a litre.

Using metric measuring spoons
These spoons are used for measuring small quantities of both dry and liquid ingredients, and are available in sets containing the following sizes:

    *1.25ml
    2.5ml
    5ml
    10ml
    15ml
    *20ml

* *These two spoons are not as widely available as the others and are not used in the recipes in this book*

Metric spoons are described by capacity rather than as teaspoons, dessertspoons or tablespoons; this avoids confusion with domestic spoons which vary considerably.

Guide to spoon measures

This table gives 10g, 15g, 25g and 40g quantities of many common ingredients which you may find easy to measure using standard spoons. Results are, however, only approximate as measuring is not as accurate as weighing. The quantities for dry ingredients refer to full spoons levelled with a knife edge.

	Spoons equivalent to			
Ingredient	10g approx	15g approx	25g approx	40g approx
almonds, ground	2 × 10ml	3 × 10ml	5 × 10ml	5 × 15ml
butter, margarine, lard	1 × 15ml	2 × 10ml	2 × 15ml	3 × 15ml
chocolate, grated	3 × 15ml	4 × 15ml	6 × 15ml	9 × 15ml
cocoa	2 × 10ml	2 × 15ml	4 × 15ml	6 × 15ml
cornflour, custard powder	2 × 10ml	3 × 10ml	3 × 15ml	7 × 10ml
desiccated coconut	2 × 15ml	3 × 15ml	5 × 15ml	8 × 15ml
drinking chocolate	3 × 5ml	4 × 5ml	4 × 10ml	7 × 10ml
flour, unsifted	2 × 10ml	3 × 10ml	3 × 15ml	5 × 15ml
gelatine	2 × 10ml	5 × 5ml	3 × 15ml	6 × 10ml
golden syrup, clear honey, black treacle, molasses, corn syrup, maple syrup, etc	1 × 10ml	1 × 15ml	1 × 15ml	2 × 15ml
ground rice	1 × 15ml	2 × 10ml	4 × 10ml	4 × 15ml
jam (eg raspberry)*	1 × 10ml	1 × 15ml	2 × 10ml	2 × 15ml
mixed peel	1 × 15ml	2 × 10ml	2 × 15ml	4 × 15ml
oats, rolled	2 × 15ml	3 × 15ml	5 × 15ml	7 × 15ml
rice	1 × 15ml	2 × 10ml	2 × 15ml	5 × 10ml
salt	1 × 10ml	3 × 5ml	2 × 10ml	7 × 5ml
sugar – granulated, caster	5 × 2.5ml	2 × 10ml	2 × 15ml	3 × 15ml
sugar – Demerara	5 × 2.5ml	2 × 10ml	2 × 15ml	3 × 15ml
sugar – soft brown	1 × 15ml	2 × 10ml	2 × 15ml	5 × 10ml
sugar – icing	1 × 15ml	3 × 10ml	3 × 15ml	7 × 10ml
Crumbs				
breadcrumbs, fresh white	3 × 15ml	7 × 10ml	7 × 15ml	12 × 15ml
bread raspings, dried white breadcrumbs	2 × 10ml	3 × 10ml	3 × 15ml	7 × 10ml
plain sponge cake crumbs	2 × 15ml	3 × 15ml	5 × 15ml	8 × 15ml
crispbread, oatcake, digestive biscuits, cornflake crumbs	2 × 15ml	3 × 15ml	4 × 15ml	7 × 15ml
dried yeast	5 × 2.5ml	2 × 10ml	2 × 15ml	3 × 15ml
Cheese				
Cheddar, coarsely grated	2 × 10ml	2 × 15ml	3 × 15ml	5 × 15ml
finely grated	1 × 10ml	1 × 15ml	4 × 15ml	5 × 15ml
Parmesan, grated	3 × 10ml	4 × 10ml	4 × 15ml	6 × 15ml
soft paste or soft (without rind)	1 × 10ml	1 × 15ml	5 × 5ml	4 × 10ml

* *varies according to how much whole fruit jam contains*

Cookware

The size of cookware varies from manufacturer to manufacturer, so sizes given in recipes should be treated as approximations only. The following range of measurements will help you select the appropriate-sized piece of cookware:

Dimension

Metric	imperial equivalent	Metric	imperial equivalent
2cm	¾ inch	25cm	10 inches
5cm	2 inches	30cm	12 inches
7cm	2¾ inches	35cm	14 inches
10cm	4 inches	40cm	16 inches
15cm	6 inches	45cm	18 inches
20cm	8 inches	50cm	20 inches

Capacity

Metric	imperial equivalent	Metric	imperial equivalent
125–150ml	¼ pint	750–900ml	1½ pints
250–300ml	½ pint	1 litre–1.25 litres	1¾–2 pints
375–450ml	¾ pint	1.4–1.75 litres	3 pints
500 (0.5 litre)–600ml	1 pint	1.8–2 litres	4 pints
625–700ml	1¼ pints	3 litres	6 pints

Dimension is used most frequently to describe the length of straight edge tins or the diameter of round cookware. Height and depth are used where they are particularly important.

Capacity measurements apply largely to pans, ovenproof dishes, bowls, moulds, and basins, and soufflé or pie dishes. The exact equivalent depends on the other ingredients in the recipe.

Note Some cookware, such as loaf tins, can also be described by the average weight of the contents, the most common weights being 1kg (2lb) and 500g (1lb).

Temperatures

Oven temperatures

°C	°F	Gas mark	Oven heat
70	150		
80	175		
100	200		
110	225	¼	very cool
120	250	½	very cool
140	275	1	very cool
150	300	2	cool
160	325	3	warm
180	350	4	moderate
190	375	5	fairly hot
200	400	6	fairly hot
220	425	7	hot
230	450	8	very hot
240	475	9	very hot
260	500		
270	525		
290	550		

Deep fat frying temperatures

These are basic guidelines only, since the temperature depends so much on the thickness of the food to be cooked, whether more is added during frying, whether it is frozen, etc.

Using a thermometer

Temperatures are given for the principal types of food to be deep fried, and should be used as a guide for all similar recipes.

VEGETABLES, PASTA AND CEREALS

	°C	Approx. frying time (minutes)		°C	Approx. frying time (minutes)
Potatoes			Other vegetables		
chips			(raw)		
cook from raw	185	4–6	sliced and coated	175–180	2–3
final browning	190	1–2	sliced uncoated	175–180	1–2
small cut			Other vegetables		
cook from raw	185	3	(parboiled)		
final browning	190	1	in batter	175–180	3–4
potato puffs			Onion rings		
cook from raw	175	soft	dipped in milk	180–185	2–3
second cooking	190	well puffed	and flour		
game chips, potato ribbons	190	3	Parsley	190	5–10 secs
croquettes	190	4–5	Crisp noodles	175–180	2–3
with choux pastry	190	golden-brown			

	°C	Approx. frying time (minutes)		°C	Approx. frying time (minutes)
FISH AND SHELLFISH			Fish, whole		
Fish fillets, thin			sole 250–350g	170–175	5–6
in batter or breadcrumbed	175–180	3–5	smelts, sprats	180–185	1–2
			whitebait	190–195	$\frac{1}{2}$–1
goujons (eg plaice)	175	2–3	whiting 250–300g	170–175	6–8
Fish portions, thick			Fish cakes, croquettes, rissolettes	175–180	2–3
in batter or breadcrumbed	170–175	3–5	Shellfish (eg scampi, oysters)	175–180	2–3

	°C	Approx. frying time (minutes)		°C	Approx. frying time (minutes)
MEAT AND POULTRY					
Cooked meat and poultry			Poultry/Game portions		
croquettes, etc	175–180	2–4	breadcrumbed		
cutlets	175–180	2–5	large	160–165	8–12
fritters, other batters	175–180	2–4	small	175–180	6–10
kromeskies, rissoles, pancakes, etc	180–185	3–4	cooked in batter	175–180	4–7

Note Sausages, hamburgers and similar raw meat items are better shallow fried as they exude animal fat which contaminates the frying medium.

DAIRY FOODS AND EGGS	°C	Approx. frying time (minutes)	SWEET ITEMS	°C	Approx. frying time (minutes)
Scotch Eggs	170–175	5–6	Fruit fritters		
egg croquettes	175–180	2–3	in batter		
choux fritters, meringues	170–175	6–7	apple	175–180	3–4
			other fruits	180–185	2–3
			Doughnuts	185–190	3–4

Bread Test

The other method of testing the temperature of deep fat or oil is by lowering a 2cm square of day-old thickly sliced bread into the hot fat as follows:

To reach temperature of	Bread turns brown in:
160°C	2 minutes
170°C	1½ minutes
180°C	1 minute
190°C	½ minute

Egg Grading Systems

The European Economic Community (EEC) has two grading systems.

The first is based on weight, and ranges between Grade 1 and Grade 7:

Grade 1 – 70g and over   Grade 5 – 50g–54g
Grade 2 – 65g–69g   Grade 6 – 45g–49g
Grade 3 – 60g–64g   Grade 7 – below 45g
Grade 4 – 55g–59g

Eggs of Grades 1 and 2 correspond approximately to the old-style large eggs, Grades 3 and 4 to standard eggs, Grades 5 and 6 to medium eggs, and Grade 7 to small and extra small eggs.

The second grading system, based on quality, ranges between Grade A and Grade C. Grade A eggs are fresh, with clean unstained shells, sound texture, and a good shape. The egg content should have no visible blemish or discoloration when tested. The yolk should be positioned centrally and defined clearly. The white should be translucent with the two parts visible. The air space should not exceed 5mm in depth.

Some packs containing Grade A eggs have a red band, with the word 'Extra' around them. This means superior quality with air cells of less than 4mm in depth at the time of packing, which itself has been less than 7 days. In addition, they will have come from a producer from whom the packer collects at least twice a week. (Once a week is sufficient for other eggs.) The shopkeeper is expected to remove this band if the eggs have not been sold within 7 days.

Grade B are second quality eggs which have been downgraded because they may have enlarged air cells, indicating age, or they may have been stored or refrigerated.

Grade C eggs are only suitable for manufacturers. They are neither graded by weight nor available in retail shops.

Convenience Foods – Chart of Storage Life

Food	Method of production/ packaging	Storage life (unopened)	Food	Method of production/ packaging	Storage life (unopened)
Baby food	Bottled	12–18 months	Ham, sterilized, below 900g	Canned	2–3 years
	Canned	1–2 years	Jams and marmalades	Bottled	2 years
Bread	Dried mix	6 months, 1 month if opened		Canned	2 years
	Pre-baked loaf	6 months	Jellies	Crystals	12–18 months
Cake decorations	Packeted	6 months		Tablets	1 year
Cakes	Dried mix	6 months, 1 month if opened	Meat products	Vacuum packed	Date stamped
			Meat products, processed	Bottled	2 years
Carbonated drinks	Canned	6–12 months	Meat products, solid packed	Canned	5 years
Casserole mixes	Dried mix	18 months			
Cheeses	Tube	1 year	Milk products	Canned	1 year
	Vacuum packed	Date stamped		Dried	6 months
Coatings	Dried mix	1 year	Pasta	Dried	2 years
Coffee, liquid	Bottled	1 year	Pasta, cook-in sauces	Canned	2 years
Coffee, instant	Jars	1 year	Pastes	Bottled	6 months
	Packeted	1 year		Canned	1 year
Desserts	Dried mix	18 months		Tube	1 year
Dessert toppings	Bottled	1 year	Pastry mixes	Dried mix	6 months, 1 month if opened
	Canned	1 year			
	Dried mix	18 months			
Fish in brine	Bottled	9–12 months	Pâtés	Bottled	6 months
Fish in oil	Canned	5 years		Canned	2 years
Fish in sauce	Canned	2 years	Pickles	Bottled	2 years
Flavourings, alcohol base	Bottled	5 years	Porridge oats	Packeted	1 year
Flavourings, non-alcoholic	Bottled	18 months	Raising agents	Dried	6 months
Flours	Packeted	6–9 months	Rice	Canned	2 years
Fruit juices	Bottled	1 year		Dried	2 years
	Canned	2 years	Sauces	Bottled	6 months
	Carton	Date stamped		Canned	2 years
	Concentrated, frozen	6 months		Dried mix	18 months
	Dried mix	18 months	Seasonings	Dried mix	6 months
Fruit pie fillings	Canned	1–2 years*	Soups	Canned	2 years
Fruits	Bottled	1 year		Dried mix	6–12 months
	Canned	1–2 years	Stock cubes	Dried mix	1 year
	Dried	2 years	Stuffings	Dried mix	1 year
Gelatine	Leaf	6–12 months	Sugars	Packeted	5 years
	Powdered	6–12 months	Textured vegetable protein (TVP)	Dried	5 years
Gravies	Canned	1–2 years	Vegetables	Canned	2 years***
	Dried mix	1 year		Dried	1–2 years
Ham, pasteurized, above 900g	Canned	6 months, refrigerated**	Vegetables in brine or water	Bottled	2 years
			Yeast extracts	Bottled	2 years
			Yeast granules	Dried	1 year

*Rhubarb and prunes should be kept for 1 year only, and gooseberries, plums, blackberries and blackcurrants for 18 months

**This is an exception to the general guide that cans should not be stored in the refrigerator

***New potatoes should only be kept for 18 months

Metric/Imperial Equivalents

25g=0.875oz	500g=1.1lbs	1kg=2.2lbs
25ml=0.875fl oz	500ml=0.88 pint	1 litre=1.76 pints

The figures above link metric and imperial quantities exactly. As these are very inconvenient to use, the following approximate conversions should be used to convert British imperial recipes to metric, if the following points are borne in mind:

1) The fundamental proportions in metric recipes are the same as imperial ones, so that a rich pastry will use half fat to flour in both metric and imperial versions.
2) *Always* convert all ingredients, solid and liquid.
3) *Never* use both metric and imperial in the same recipe.
4) Using the 25g/ounce equivalent you will decrease all quantities by approximately 10% when converting imperial quantities to metric. When using small quantities, the reduction will be insignificant, so existing cookware can still be used and the baking time will be the same. For large recipe quantities, smaller tins and shorter baking times will be needed.

Note If you wish to convert metric measures to imperial ones, remember that metric measures based on the 25g/ounce give 10% more of any goods weighed in oz/lb than the equivalent gram/kg.

WEIGHT		CAPACITY	
Metric	*Approx. imperial equivalent*	*Metric*	*Approx. imperial equivalent*
10–15g	½oz	25ml	1 fl oz
25g	1oz	50ml	2 fl oz
50g	2oz	125–150ml	¼ pint (5 fl oz/1 gill)
75g	3oz	250–300ml	½ pint
100–125g	4oz	375–450ml	¾ pint
150–175g	6oz	500–600ml	1pt (20 fl oz)
200–250g	8oz	750–900ml	1½ pints
300–375g	12oz	1–1.25 litres	1¾–2 pints
400–500g	1lb	1.4–1.75 litres	3 pints
600–750g	1½lb		
800–1000g (1kg)	2lb		
1.5kg	3lb		

Where alternative metric figures are shown, the weight or capacity used depends on the type of recipe, and the proportion of other ingredients. For large-scale recipes such as those for breads or jams, the larger figure is more suitable. For ½oz, 10g or 15g may be selected according to the importance of the ingredient in the recipe.

FIRST-COURSE DISHES

Artichoke Salad
6 helpings

6 globe artichokes   vinaigrette sauce

Boil or steam the artichokes. Trim the bases so that they stand upright. When cold, trim off the tips of the leaves, if liked. Place the artichokes on individual dishes and serve the vinaigrette sauce separately.

Artichokes are generally served as a starter by themselves.

Dressed Artichoke Bases or Fonds
6 helpings

12 small cooked **or** canned artichoke   200g macédoine of cooked vegetables
  bases   (p54)
2–3 gherkins   125ml mayonnaise
1 × 15ml spoon capers

Garnish
strips of canned pimento   4–6 sliced stuffed olives

Trim the artichokes neatly. Chop the gherkins finely and mix with the capers, vegetables, and enough mayonnaise to moisten. Fill the hollow parts of the artichoke with the mixture. Arrange on a serving plate and spoon the remaining mayonnaise over the vegetables. Garnish with the pimento and olives.

Note Artichoke bases are the round fleshy parts of the artichoke found under the hairy choke.

VARIATION

The stuffing mixture is also good as a filling for avocado pears. Use the quantities above to fill 4 halved pears, to serve four.

Avocado Pears Vinaigrette
4 helpings

2 large, firm, ripe avocado pears   vinaigrette sauce
2 × 15ml spoons lemon juice

Make sure the pears are firm but ripe, and are not discoloured. If they show any signs of over-ripeness such as being soft or blackened, use them for a cooked dish.

Halve the pears lengthways and remove the stones. Brush the halved pears with lemon juice immediately to prevent discoloration. Serve 1 half pear per person, cut side uppermost on a small plate, with a special avocado spoon, stainless steel or silver teaspoon or a grapefruit spoon. Serve the vinaigrette sauce separately.

Avocado Pears with Prawns or Avocado Royale
4 helpings

2 × 15ml spoons olive oil
2 × 15ml spoons distilled vinegar
a pinch each of salt and pepper
a little mixed French mustard
  (not Dijon)
2 large avocado pears

a pinch of sugar (optional)
½ clove of garlic (optional)
100g peeled prawns, fresh, frozen **or**
  canned
crisp lettuce leaves

Garnish
lemon wedges

Blend the oil, vinegar, and seasonings together. Halve and stone the pears, and brush all over with a little of the dressing. Add the sugar and crush and add the garlic to the remaining dressing, if used. Toss the prawns in this; then spoon into the pear halves. Place on crisp lettuce leaves. Garnish with lemon wedges.
Note Frozen prawns should be squeezed gently before using to get rid of any excess moisture.

Celeriac in Mustard Dressing
4 helpings

450g **or** 1 medium-sized celeriac
3 × 2.5ml spoons salt
3 × 2.5ml spoons lemon juice
4 × 15ml spoons French mustard

3 × 15ml spoons boiling water
100ml olive oil **or** as needed
2 × 15ml spoons white vinegar
salt and pepper

Garnish
2 × 15ml spoons chopped mixed herbs
  or parsley

Peel the celeriac, and cut it into matchsticks. Toss the sticks in a bowl with the salt and lemon juice, and leave to stand for 30 minutes. Rinse in a strainer under cold running water, drain well, and pat dry. Put the mustard into a warmed bowl, and very gradually whisk in the boiling water. Then whisk in the oil drop by drop as when making mayonnaise (p222), using enough to make a thick sauce. Whisk in the vinegar in the same way. Season with salt and pepper. Fold in the celeriac matchsticks, cover loosely with a cloth, and leave in a cool place for several hours or overnight. Sprinkle the herbs over the dish before serving.

Crudités

These are small raw or blanched vegetables, cut up or grated, and served as a first course with an oil and vinegar dressing, French dressing or a dip. They are usually arranged in a decorative pattern on a large flat dish or tray, from which people help themselves. Suitable items to include are:

 1) apples (cubed, dipped in lemon juice)
 2) black or green olives
 3) carrots (cut into matchsticks)
 4) cauliflower florets (blanched)
 5) celery (raw or blanched, sliced thinly)
 6) courgettes (unpeeled, cut into matchsticks)
 7) cucumber (cubed or sliced thickly)
 8) fennel (raw or blanched, sliced thinly)
 9) green or red pepper (cut in rings or strips)
10) radishes (small, whole)
11) spring onions
12) tomatoes (thin wedges, slices, or if small, halved)

Soured Cream Dip for Crudités

3–4 helpings

$\frac{1}{2}$ clove of garlic
1 × 15ml spoon chilli sauce
1 × 5ml spoon creamed horseradish
1 × 15ml spoon Worcestershire sauce

$\frac{1}{2}$ × 2.5ml spoon dry mustard
a pinch of Cayenne pepper
1 × 5ml spoon lemon juice
250ml soured cream

Crush the garlic. In a small basin, combine all the ingredients. Chill for 2–3 hours to allow the flavours to develop.

Serve with crudités or with cream crackers or potato crisps.

Cucumber in Soured Cream

4 helpings

3 cucumbers
salt
1 × 5cm piece fennel stem **or** 1 thick
   slice of the bulb
1 hard-boiled egg yolk

pepper
150ml soured cream
1 × 10ml spoon cider vinegar **or**
   white wine vinegar

Slice the cucumbers very thinly, sprinkle with the salt; then leave for 30 minutes. Drain and pat dry. Slice the fennel thinly. Crumble the egg yolk coarsely and mix it with the fennel. Just before serving, sprinkle the cucumber with pepper, mix the soured cream with salt and the vinegar, and pour it over the cucumbers. Sprinkle with the fennel and egg.

Note This can also be served with meat rissoles, fish cakes, grilled meat or fried fish.

Eggs Courtet
4 helpings

4 tomatoes (75g each approx)	salt and pepper
4 eggs	25g butter
4 × 15ml spoons milk	150ml aspic jelly

Garnish
chopped parsley

Cut the tomatoes in half and scoop out the centres. Leave upside-down to drain. Beat the eggs, milk, salt, and pepper together lightly. Melt the butter in a small pan, add the beaten egg, reduce the heat and cook gently, stirring all the time, until the eggs are just set and creamy. Fill the tomato cups with the eggs and leave until cold.

Melt the aspic jelly; then chill it until at setting point but still liquid. Coat each filled tomato half with jelly. Chill the remaining jelly until set; then chop it roughly. Serve the tomato cups surrounded by the chopped jelly on a platter of salad, and garnish with parsley.

Eggs Rémoulade
4 helpings

4 hard-boiled eggs	1 × 2.5ml spoon anchovy essence
4 × 15ml spoons thick mayonnaise	

Garnish

tomato	4 crisp lettuce leaves
gherkin	

Cut the eggs in half lengthways. Pat dry with kitchen paper. Mix together the mayonnaise and anchovy essence. Turn the eggs, cut side down and coat the white outside with the mayonnaise mixture. Arrange small pieces of tomato or gherkin on top. Place 2 egg halves, cut side down, on each lettuce leaf.

Stuffed Russian Eggs
6 helpings

6 hard-boiled eggs	oil
1 × 100g jar lumpfish roe	vinegar
3 × 15ml spoons mayonnaise	salt and pepper
2–3 even-sized tomatoes	chopped parsley

Garnish
chopped parsley

Cut the eggs in half lengthways, remove the yolks, and trim a small slice off the rounded side of each half white to make them stand firmly. Fill with lumpfish roe. Rub the yolks through a sieve, blend with the mayonnaise, and using a forcing bag with a star nozzle, pipe the mixture on to the stuffed egg whites. Cut the tomatoes into slices, and season with oil, vinegar, salt, and pepper. Sprinkle with chopped parsley. Serve the eggs on the slices of tomato and garnish with extra chopped parsley.

Grapefruit
4 helpings

2 large firm grapefuit
white **or** brown sugar

4 × 10ml spoons medium-dry sherry
(optional)

Decoration
2 maraschino **or** glacé cherries

angelica (optional)

Choose sound, ripe fruit and wipe them. Cut them in half crossways, and remove the pips. Snip out the cores with scissors. With a stainless steel knife (preferably with a saw edge) or a grapefruit knife, cut round each half between the flesh and the pith, to loosen the flesh. Cut between the membranes which divide the segments, but leave the flesh in the halved skins as if uncut. Sweeten to taste with sugar, or, if preferred, pour 1 × 10ml spoon sherry over each half grapefruit, and serve sugar separately. Decorate the centre of each half fruit with a halved cherry and with angelica, if liked. Chill before serving. Serve 1 half fruit per person.

Spiced Grapefruit
4 helpings

2 large grapefruit
25g softened butter

25–50g brown sugar
$\frac{1}{2}$–1 × 5ml spoon ground mixed spice

Decoration
4 glacé or maraschino cherries

Cut the grapefruit in half crossways and prepare as in the recipe for Grapefruit. Spread the butter over the grapefruit and sprinkle with the sugar and spice. Put under a hot grill for 4 minutes, or in a fairly hot oven at 200°C, Gas 6, for 10 minutes. Decorate with the cherries and serve at once.

Herring Rolls
4 helpings

4 salted **or** rollmop herrings
2 hard-boiled eggs
8 anchovy fillets

25g butter
Cayenne pepper
lemon juice

Garnish
8 lemon slices
4–6 sliced gherkins

1 small diced beetroot
chopped parsley

If using salted herrings, soak them in cold water for several hours, then fillet, and remove all the bones. If using rollmop herrings, divide each into 2 fillets. Separate the egg yolks and whites. Chop the anchovy fillets and egg yolks finely, and mix them with the butter and pepper. Spread most of the anchovy mixture on the herring fillets and roll up firmly. Spread the remaining mixture thinly on the round ends of each roll. Chop the egg whites finely and use to coat the spread end of the rolls. Sprinkle with lemon juice and garnish with lemon slices, gherkins, beetroot, and parsley.

Kipper Mousse
4 helpings

600g kipper fillets
1 small onion
50g butter
50ml Velouté sauce (p211)
250ml mayonnaise
15g gelatine

75ml dry white wine
250ml double cream
salt and black pepper
lemon juice
butter for greasing

Garnish
lemon slices

parsley sprigs

Skin the kipper fillets and cut into 2–3cm pieces. Skin the onion and slice it finely. Fry the fish and onion gently in the butter for 7 minutes. Mix in the Velouté sauce and mayonnaise. Pound, or process in an electric blender to make a smooth purée. Soften the gelatine in the wine in a small heatproof container. Stand the container in hot water and stir until the gelatine dissolves. Add it to the purée and mix very thoroughly. Blend in the cream and season to taste. Add a squeeze of lemon juice. Spoon into a lightly buttered soufflé dish or oval pâté mould and chill for 2 hours. Serve from the dish, or turn out the mousse on to a serving dish and garnish with lemon slices and parsley sprigs.

Serve with hot toast and lemon slices.

Liver Pâté
Makes 700g (approx)

200g calf's **or** pig's liver
200g poultry livers
1 small onion
100g very lean ham **or** bacon
75g butter
a few gherkins (optional)

1–2 hard-boiled eggs
salt and pepper
1–2 × 5ml spoons dried mixed herbs
butter for greasing
melted clarified butter (p232)

Remove any skin and tubes from the livers. Skin the onion. Chop the liver, onion, and ham or bacon into small pieces. Melt the butter in a pan and cook the meats and onion for 5–6 minutes. Mince finely twice or process in an electric blender to make a smooth paste. Chop the gherkins, if used, and the hard-boiled eggs and add to the liver mixture together with the seasoning and herbs. Put into an ovenproof terrine or similar dish and cover with buttered greaseproof paper. Stand the dish in a pan of hot water which comes half-way up the sides. Bake in a moderate oven at 180°C, Gas 4, for about 30 minutes.

When cooked, either cover immediately with a layer of clarified butter and leave to cool, then chill before serving; or place under a light weight (p20) and cover with clarified butter as soon as cold. Serve the pâté in the dish in which it has been cooked, or cut into slices and place on a bed of crisp lettuce.

Serve with hot dry toast or brown bread rolled sandwiches.

Weighting and Cooling a Pâté

If a pâté needs to be weighted, first cut a piece of stout card to fit the top of the dish, inside the rim, and cover it with foil. Place this cover over the dish and put a weight on top, eg a can of fruit, a large stone, flat iron or brick. A light weight should be used first, especially if there is any melted fat round the sides of the pâté which may well up and spill over if a heavy weight is used. As the dish cools, the pressure can be increased by substituting or adding a heavier weight. The heavier the weight, the more solid or condensed the pâté will be.

Cool the pâté by standing the dish in a pan of iced or very cold water which comes half-way up its sides, for between 12–24 hours, or as indicated in the recipe. Leave on a cold surface such as a stone slab or floor, or a metal table, in a cool place. Remove the weight, take out of the water, cover with clingfilm, and chill in a refrigerator or very cool place to allow the flavours to blend and mature. Pâtés should be eaten as soon as possible, so should not be stored for very long.
Note Whether or not a pâté needs to be weighted, any melted fat should be removed from the sides before serving.

Melon

Melon makes a refreshing starter throughout the year. The varieties most often used are the Cantaloup, honeydew, Ogen, Charentais, and watermelon. Melon should always be served lightly chilled, but it should not be too cold or it loses its delicate flavour.

To serve a large Cantaloup or honeydew melon, cut it in half lengthways, then cut into segments and remove the seeds with a spoon. Serve 1 segment per person; a large melon should supply 8 segments.

Serve the melon with the flesh attached to the skin, or cut the flesh from the skin with a sharp knife but leave the skin underneath the melon segment. The melon flesh can then also be cut into small pieces which are easier to eat.

Smaller melons, such as Ogen and Charentais, should just be cut in half crossways, and the pips scooped out with a spoon. They serve 2 people as a rule, although they can be cut into quarters, to serve four.

Watermelon should be cut into suitably sized segments. Small spoons should be provided for removing the seeds, as well as knives and forks for cutting up the melon.

Ripe melons may not require any sugar, but sugar can be served separately, with chopped stem ginger or ground ginger, or with lemon or lime.

Melon with Parma Ham

This is a more elaborate dish using paper-thin slices of Parma or other smoked ham. For each person, serve 3 loosely rolled sices of ham arranged in a line alternately with 7 × 2cm sticks of firm, ripe, green-fleshed melon.

Mixed Hors d'Oeuvre Wheel
4–6 helpings

6–8 anchovy fillets
150g liver pâté
100–150g Cucumber in Soured Cream
  (p16)
2 medium-sized red-skinned dessert
  apples
lemon juice
75g black and stuffed green olives

200g Celeriac in Mustard Dressing
  (p15)
2 medium-sized carrots
oil
4 **or** 6 Stuffed Russian Eggs, using
  2 **or** 3 whole eggs (p17)
grated orange rind
salt and pepper

Garnish
parsley sprigs

Use a large, flat, round hors d'oeuvre wheel. Drain the anchovy fillets and wind them round the black olives using cocktail sticks, if necessary. Arrange with the stuffed olives in the centre. Cut the pâté in neat slices, 1 per person. Prepare the cucumber and soured cream but keep the fennel and egg garnish aside. Core and cube the apples and sprinkle with lemon juice. Prepare the celeriac for serving. Grate the carrots and mix with a little oil. Prepare the Russian Eggs.

Arrange all these ingredients in triangular sections on the wheel. Sprinkle the cucumbers with their fennel and egg garnish, and the carrots with grated orange rind and seasoning. Garnish with parsley sprigs.

Offer small spoons for people to help themselves. Serve slices of dark rye bread separately.

Note Instead of a wheel a 25–30cm platter with a small dish in the centre, can be used.

Mrs Beeton's Dressed Whitebait
3–4 helpings

50g flour
salt and pepper
100g whitebait

milk
fat for deep frying
Cayenne pepper

Garnish
parsley sprigs

lemon wedges

Season the flour with salt and pepper. Wash the whitebait, dip in the milk, and coat with flour, by shaking them together in a tea-towel or plastic bag. Make sure that the fish are separate. Heat the fat (p10), and fry the fish in small batches until crisp. Check that the fat is at the correct temperature before putting in each batch. When all the fish are fried, sprinkle with salt and Cayenne pepper. Serve immediately, garnished with parsley and lemon wedges, with thinly cut brown bread and butter.
Note Whitebait are eaten whole.

Platter of Pork Meats

Choose 4–6 varieties of bought sausage and other pork meats, ready to eat, allowing 100–125g per person. Arrange them in a decorative pattern on a bed of lettuce leaves. Serve with small forks, and offer rolled sandwiches of dark rye bread or pumpernickel.

Some suitable meats to offer are, for instance:

1) salami
2) thin slices of Italian raw smoked ham, loosely rolled
3) cooked British sausages, thinly sliced diagonally
4) very small slices of cooked pork fillet
5) thin slices or 2cm cubes of pickled pork or pork luncheon meat

Potted Beef

Makes 550g (approx)

500g raw lean beef	butter for greasing
a blade of mace	75g butter
a pinch of ground ginger	salt and pepper
2 × 15ml spoons beef stock	melted clarified butter (p232)

Wipe the meat and trim off any fat and gristle. Cut the meat into small cubes. Put it in an ovenproof casserole with the mace, ginger, and stock. Cover tightly with buttered greaseproof paper and foil. Bake in a cool oven at 150°C, Gas 2, for 3–3½ hours until the meat is very tender. Remove the mace. Mince the meat twice, then pound it well with the butter and any meat juices left in the casserole to make a smooth paste. Season with salt and pepper. Turn into small pots and cover with clarified butter. Leave until the butter is firm.

Note When sealed with clarified butter, this meat will keep for at least a week in a refrigerator or for 2 days in a cool place.

Potted Shrimps or Prawns

Makes 500g (approx)

200g unsalted butter	½ × 2.5ml spoon ground mace
400g cooked, peeled shrimps or prawns	½ × 2.5ml spoon ground cloves
½ × 2.5ml spoon ground white pepper	melted clarified butter (p232)

Melt the butter in a pan and heat the shellfish very gently, without boiling, with the pepper, mace and cloves. Turn into small pots with a little of the butter. Leave the remaining butter until the residue has settled, then pour the butter over the shellfish. Chill. When firm, cover with clarified butter. Store in a refrigerator for not more than 48 hours before use.

Prawn Cocktail
4 helpings

4 lettuce leaves
200g peeled prawns
5 × 15ml spoons mayonnaise
1 × 15ml spoon concentrated tomato
   purée **or** tomato ketchup

a pinch of Cayenne pepper **or** a few
   drops Tabasco sauce
salt (optional)
1 × 5ml spoon chilli vinegar **or**
   tarragon vinegar (optional)

Garnish
4 shell-on prawns

Shred the lettuce leaves. Place a little shredded lettuce at the bottom of 4 glass dishes.
Put the prawns on top. Mix the mayonnaise with the tomato purée or ketchup and
add a pinch of Cayenne pepper or a few drops of Tabasco sauce. Season with salt and
vinegar if required. Pour the mayonnaise over the prawns and garnish each dish
with an unshelled prawn.
   Serve with rolled brown bread and butter.

Russian Salad
4 helpings

1 small cooked cauliflower
3 boiled potatoes
2 tomatoes
50g ham **or** tongue (optional)
3 gherkins
a few lettuce leaves
4 × 15ml spoons peas

2 × 15ml spoons diced cooked carrot
2 × 15ml spoons diced cooked turnip
50g peeled prawns **or** shrimps
   (optional)
salt and pepper
3 × 15ml spoons mayonnaise

Garnish
1 small diced cooked beetroot
50g smoked salmon, cut into strips
   (optional)

4 olives
1 × 15ml spoon capers
4 anchovy fillets (optional)

Break the cauliflower into small sprigs. Peel and dice the potatoes. Skin, de-seed, and
dice the tomatoes. Cut the ham or tongue into small strips, if used. Chop the gherkins
and shred the lettuce leaves. Put the vegetables, meat, and fish, if used, in layers in a
salad bowl, sprinkling each layer with salt, pepper, and mayonnaise. Garnish with
the remaining ingredients.
Note If using Russian Salad as part of a mixed hors d'oeuvre or for stuffing items such
as eggs, omit the lettuce and garnish, and mix all the ingredients together lightly.

Salad Niçoise
4–6 helpings

250g French beans
2 hard-boiled eggs
3 tomatoes
1 large lettuce
1 clove of garlic

225g canned tuna
50g black olives
4 × 15ml spoons French dressing
salt and pepper

Garnish
50g canned anchovy fillets

Boil or steam the beans until just tender. Cut the eggs into quarters. Skin and quarter the tomatoes. Wash the lettuce and dry thoroughly. Skin and crush the garlic, and drain and flake the tuna. Line a large salad bowl with the lettuce leaves. Put the beans, eggs, tomatoes, garlic, tuna, most of the olives, and the dressing into a bowl and toss lightly. Season to taste. Pile into the centre of the salad bowl and garnish with the remaining olives and the anchovy fillets before serving.

Smoked Mackerel Pâté
Makes 450g (approx)

2 shallots
25g clarified butter (p232)
75g concentrated tomato purée
1 × 5ml spoon soft light brown sugar
juice of $\frac{1}{2}$ lemon
8 crushed peppercorns
1 × 5ml spoon chopped fresh basil

$\frac{1}{2}$ × 2.5ml spoon dried tarragon
a few drops Tabasco sauce
400g skinned smoked mackerel fillets
75ml double cream
additional melted clarified butter
　(p232) for sealing

Skin and chop the shallots very finely. Melt the clarified butter in a pan and cook the shallots gently until softened. Add the purée, sugar, lemon juice, peppercorns, and herbs, and cook gently for 4–5 minutes to make a sauce. Add the Tabasco sauce, remove from the heat and leave to cool. Process the sauce, mackerel, and cream in an electric blender or pound to a smooth paste. Turn into a suitable dish or mould and leave to cool. Cover with clarified butter. Leave until the butter is firm.

Serve with hot dry toast.

Taramasalata
4 helpings

100g smoked cod's roe
1 clove of garlic
2 × 15ml spoons lemon juice

4 × 15ml spoons olive oil
2 × 15ml spoons cold water
freshly ground black pepper

Skin the roe and garlic. Pound them in a mortar with the lemon juice until smooth. Add small amounts of oil and water alternately until the mixture is completely blended. Season to taste with black pepper, and serve with pita bread.

Mixed Hors D'Oeuvre Wheel (p21)

TOP Platter of Pork Meats (p22)

LEFT Kipper Mousse (p19)

RIGHT Eggs Courtet (p17)

Consommé Royale (p32)

RIGHT Marinated Roast Beef (p106), with Yorkshire Puddings, Roast Potatoes, Demi-Glace Sauce and Horseradish Cream

LEFT Lamb's Liver and Bacon (p139)

TOP RIGHT Brains in Black Butter (p151) and BELOW Sautéed Kidneys (p140)

Roast Savoury Loin of Pork (p155) with Red Cabbage and Apple Sauce

Crown Roast of Lamb with Saffron Rice (p130)

SOUPS

Stocks

Brown Stock (Beef stock)
Makes 1.5 litres (approx)

500g beef **or** veal marrow bones
500g lean shin of beef
1.5 litres cold water
1 × 5ml spoon salt
1 medium-sized onion (100g approx)

1 medium-sized carrot (50g approx)
1 stick of celery (50g approx)
bouquet garni (see **Note**)
1 × 2.5ml spoon black peppercorns

Ask the butcher to chop the bones into manageable pieces. Wipe them thoroughly. Trim off any fat and cut the meat into small pieces. Put the bones and meat in a roasting tin in a hot oven at 220°C, Gas 7, for 30–40 minutes to brown, turning them occasionally.

Put the browned bones and meat in a large saucepan with the water and salt. Prepare and slice the vegetables. Add them to the pan with the bouquet garni and peppercorns. Heat slowly to boiling point, skim well, and cover the pan with a tight-fitting lid. Reduce the heat and simmer very gently for 4 hours. Strain through a fine sieve and leave to cool. When cold, remove any fat from the surface.

Note To make a *bouquet garni*, tie together 3 parsley stalks, 1 sprig of thyme and 1 bay leaf, and tie in a square of muslin or cheesecloth. Alternatively tie 1 × 10ml spoon mixed dried herbs and 1 bay leaf in muslin. Vary the herbs and add spices as liked.

General Household Stock
Makes 1 litre (approx)

1kg cooked **or** raw bones of any meat
   or poultry, cooked **or** raw meat
   trimmings, giblets, and bacon rinds
500g onions, carrots, celery, and leeks

salt
1 bay leaf
4 black peppercorns

Break or chop the bones into manageable pieces. Wipe thoroughly. Prepare and slice the vegetables, retaining a piece of brown onion skin if a brown stock is required. Put the bones and meat trimmings into a saucepan. Cover with cold water and add 1 × 2.5ml spoon salt for each litre of water used. Heat slowly to simmering point. Add the other ingredients. Simmer, uncovered, for at least 3 hours. Strain and cool quickly by standing the pan in chilled water. When cold, skim off the fat. If the stock is not required at once, keep it cold. Use within 24 hours, or within 3 days if kept in a refrigerator. Reboil before use.

White Stock
Makes 2 litres (approx)

1kg knuckle of veal
1 medium-sized onion (100g approx)
1 stick of celery (50g approx)
2 litres cold water
1 × 10ml spoon salt

1 × 10ml spoon white vinegar **or**
   lemon juice
1 × 2.5ml spoon white peppercorns
a small strip of lemon rind
1 bay leaf

Chop the knuckle into manageable pieces. Scrape the bones, trim off any fat, and wipe the bones thoroughly. Prepare and slice the onion and celery. Put the bones in a large pan with the cold water, salt, and vinegar or lemon juice. Heat to boiling point and skim. Add the vegetables and the other ingredients. Bring back to the boil, cover, reduce the heat, and simmer gently for 4 hours. Strain the stock through a fine sieve and cool it quickly by standing the pan in chilled water. When cold, skim off the fat. Store as for General Household Stock (p25).

Chicken or Game Stock
Makes 1 litre (using 1 litre water)

1 medium-sized onion (100g approx)
1 stick of celery (50g approx)
carcass of 1 chicken **or** game bird,
   including the giblets

cleaned feet of bird (optional)
1 × 10ml spoon salt
4 white peppercorns
bouquet garni

Prepare and slice the vegetables. Break or chop the carcass into manageable pieces. Put the carcass, giblets, and feet, if used, in a large saucepan, cover with cold water, and add the salt. Heat to boiling point. Draw the pan off the heat and leave to stand for 2–3 minutes, then skim off any fat. Add the vegetables, peppercorns, and bouquet garni. Re-heat to boiling point, cover, reduce the-heat, and simmer very gently for 3–4 hours. Strain the stock through a fine sieve and cool it quickly by standing the container in chilled water. When cold, skim off the fat. Store as for General Household Stock (p25).

Fish Stock
Makes 1 litre (using 1 litre water)

bones, skin, and heads from filleted fish
   or fish trimmings **or** cod's **or** other
   fish heads **or** any mixture of these
1 × 5ml spoon salt

1 small onion (50g approx)
1 stick of celery (50g approx)
4 white peppercorns
bouquet garni

Break up the bones and wash the fish trimmings, if used. Prepare and slice the vegetables. Put the bones, fish trimmings or heads in a saucepan and cover with cold water. Add the salt. Heat to boiling point. Add the vegetables, the peppercorns, and bouquet garni. Cover, and simmer gently for 40 minutes. Strain the stock through a fine sieve.

Note If cooked for longer than 40 minutes, fish stock tastes bitter. It does not keep unless frozen, and should be made only as required.

Vegetable Stock
Makes 2 litres (approx)

2 large carrots (200g approx)
2 medium-sized onions (200g approx)
3 sticks celery (150g approx)
2 tomatoes (100g approx)
25g butter **or** margarine
2 litres boiling water
1 × 2.5ml spoon yeast extract

bouquet garni
1 × 5ml spoon salt
6 black peppercorns
a blade of mace
outer leaves of 1 lettuce **or** ¼ small
    cabbage (100g approx)

Slice the carrots, onions, and celery thinly and chop the tomatoes. Melt the fat in a large saucepan and fry the carrots, onions, and celery for 5–10 minutes until the onions are golden-brown. Add the tomatoes and fry for a further minute. Add the water and the rest of the ingredients, except the lettuce or cabbage. Cover, and simmer for 1 hour. Shred the lettuce or cabbage, and add to the pan. Simmer for a further 20 minutes. Strain through a fine sieve. Use the same day, if possible, or cool quickly and store in a refrigerator for up to 2 days.

Thin Soups

Beef Broth
4–6 helpings

1 medium-sized carrot (50g approx)
1 small turnip (50g approx)
1 medium-sized onion (100g approx)
1 clove of garlic (optional)
25g butter **or** margarine
1 litre brown **or** general household
    stock (p25)

1 × 2.5ml spoon salt
½ small cabbage (250g approx)
a sprig of parsley
a few chives
salt and pepper
grated nutmeg
6 thin slices French bread

Prepare the carrot, turnip, and onion, and slice them thinly. Skin and crush the garlic, if used. Melt the fat in a large saucepan, add the vegetables, cover, and fry gently for 10 minutes. Heat the stock to boiling point and add to the vegetables in the pan with the salt. Cover and simmer for 30 minutes.

Meanwhile, shred the cabbage and chop the parsley and chives. Add the cabbage to the broth, cover, and simmer for a further 20 minutes. Season to taste with salt, pepper, and a little nutmeg. Add the parsley and chives. Keep over very low heat while toasting the bread slices until golden. Put one in each soup bowl or cup and pour the broth over them.

Serve with grated cheese, if liked.

Beef Tea
2 helpings

400g shin, flank **or** skirt of beef   1 × 2.5ml spoon salt
500ml water

Wipe the meat and trim off all visible fat; cut into 2cm cubes. Put the meat into an ovenproof casserole or basin, and add the water and salt. Cover the container with a saucer or lid, and cook in a very cool oven, 140°C, Gas 1, for 3 hours.

Strain the liquid through muslin or a fine sieve, and allow to cool. Skim any fat from the top. Re-heat, without boiling, and serve as a light soup or beverage, with toast or dry biscuits.

VARIATION
To the basic ingredients, add the following thinly sliced vegetables: 1 small carrot, ⅓ small turnip, and 1 small onion. Add them to the meat and water, with a few sprigs of parsley and 2 bay leaves, and continue cooking as in the basic recipe.
Note Beef tea can be stored in a refrigerator for 2 days. If this is not possible, it must be freshly made each time it is wanted.

Chicken Broth
8 helpings

1 small boiling fowl (1.5kg approx) **or**   1 stick of celery (50g approx)
   1 chicken carcass with some flesh   ½ × 2.5ml spoon ground pepper
   left on it   a blade of mace
giblets of the bird   bouquet garni
1.5–2 litres water   a strip of lemon rind
1 × 5ml spoon salt   25g long-grain rice (optional)
1 medium-sized onion (100g approx)   1 × 15ml spoon chopped parsley
2 medium-sized carrots (100g approx)

Joint the boiling fowl or break up the carcass bones, and wash the giblets. Put them into a large saucepan and cover with the cold water. Add the salt, and heat slowly to simmering point. Cut the onion in half, and dice the carrots and celery. Add the vegetables to the pan with the pepper, mace, bouquet garni, and lemon rind. Cover, and simmer gently for 3–3½ hours if using a raw boiling fowl, or for 1½ hours if using a chicken carcass. Strain the broth through a colander. Skim off the fat.

Return the broth to the pan and re-heat to simmering point. Wash the rice, if used, and sprinkle it into the broth. Cover, and simmer for a further 15–20 minutes until the rice is cooked.

Some of the meat can be chopped finely and added to the broth, the rest can be used in made-up dishes, eg a fricassée. Just before serving the broth, re-season if required, and add the chopped parsley.

Hotch Potch
8 helpings

1kg scrag and middle neck of lamb
  or mutton
1.25 litres water
1 × 10ml spoon salt
bouquet garni
1 medium-sized carrot (50g approx)
1 small turnip (50g approx)
6 spring onions

1 small cabbage (100g approx)
100g shelled young broad beans or
  runner beans
100g cauliflower florets
150g shelled peas
salt and pepper
1 × 15ml spoon chopped parsley

Wipe the meat and trim off any excess fat. Remove the meat from the bone and cut the meat into small pieces. Put the bone and meat into a large saucepan, add the water, and heat very slowly to simmering point. Add the salt and the bouquet garni, cover, and simmer very gently for 30 minutes.

Meanwhile, cut the carrot and turnip into 5mm dice and the spring onions into thin rings; shred the lettuce and runner beans, if used. Add the carrot, turnip, and spring onions to the pan, cover, and simmer for 1½ hours. Add the rest of the vegetables to the soup, cover, and simmer for a further 30 minutes. Season to taste. Skim off the fat and remove the bouquet garni and the bones. Add the chopped parsley just before serving.

Note The vegetables can be varied according to the season.

Scots or Scotch Broth
4–6 helpings

500g scrag end of neck of mutton
1 × 5ml spoon salt
1 litre cold water
50g pearl barley
2 medium carrots

2 leeks
1 small turnip
1 stick of celery
pepper
1 × 10ml spoon chopped parsley

Wipe and trim the meat, and cut into 2cm pieces. Put into a deep pan with the bones, salt, and cold water. Heat gently to simmering point. Blanch the barley. Add to the pan, cover, and simmer gently for 2 hours. Prepare the vegetables, setting aside one whole carrot and cutting the rest into 5mm dice. Add them to the broth, cover, and simmer for another hour. Grate the whole carrot and add it to the broth 20 minutes before serving. Skim the fat. Remove the bones. Season to taste with pepper and add the chopped parsley just before serving.

Veal Broth
4–5 helpings

1 knuckle of veal (600–750g approx)	1 leek **or** medium-sized onion
1.5 litres water	(100g approx)
1 × 10ml spoon lemon juice	1 stick of celery (50g approx)
3 × 2.5ml spoons salt	bouquet garni
25g pearl barley **or** rice	a strip of lemon rind
2 medium-sized carrots (100g approx)	4 white peppercorns
1 small turnip (50g approx)	1 × 10ml spoon chopped parsley

Wipe the knuckle and put it into a pan with the water. Heat slowly to simmering point, and add the lemon juice and salt. Blanch the pearl barley or rice and add it to the pan. Cover, and simmer gently for 2 hours. Cut the vegetables into 5mm dice. After the broth has simmered for 2 hours, add the vegetables, bouquet garni, lemon rind, and peppercorns. Cover, and simmer for a further hour. Lift out the knuckle of veal. Remove all the meat from the bone and cut it into 5mm dice. Strain the broth through a colander and return it to the pan; keep hot. Remove the bouquet garni, lemon rind, and peppercorns from the vegetables. Return the meat and vegetables to the broth and add the parsley. Re-season if required. Re-heat before serving.
Note The bone can be used again for stock.

Calf's Foot Broth
4–6 helpings

1 calf's foot	salt and pepper
1.5 litres water	egg yolks
2–3 strips lemon rind	milk

Wash the foot thoroughly. Put it into a large saucepan with the water, heat to simmering point, cover, and simmer gently for 3 hours. Strain through a colander or a sieve into a basin and leave to cool. When cold, skim the fat. Re-heat the broth with the lemon rind until sufficiently flavoured. Remove the lemon rind. Season to taste. For each 250ml broth, allow 1 egg yolk and 4 × 15ml spoons milk. Beat together the egg yolks and milk with a fork until well blended. Beat into a little hot soup, and fold into the rest of the soup. Stir over low heat until thickened. Do not allow the broth to boil or it will curdle. Serve hot.

Consommé
Makes 1 litre (approx)

100g lean shin of beef
125ml water
1 small onion (50g approx)
1 small carrot (25g approx)
1 small stick of celery (25g approx)

1.25 litres cold brown stock (p25)
bouquet garni
$\frac{1}{2}$ × 2.5ml spoon salt
4 white peppercorns
white and crushed shell of 1 egg

Shred the beef finely, trimming off all the fat. Soak the meat in the water for 15 minutes. Prepare the vegetables. Put the meat, water, and the rest of the ingredients into a deep saucepan, adding the egg white and shell last. Heat slowly to simmering point, whisking all the time, until a froth rises to the surface. Remove the whisk, cover, and simmer the consommé very gently for $1\frac{1}{2}$–2 hours. Do not allow to boil or the froth will break up and cloud the consommé. Strain slowly into a basin through muslin or a scalded jelly bag. If necessary, strain the consommé again. Re-heat, re-season if required, and serve plain or with a garnish (see below).

Consommé Brunoise
4–6 helpings

1 litre consommé
1 × 2.5ml spoon lemon juice

1 × 15ml spoon sherry (optional)

Garnish
1 × 15ml spoon finely diced carrot
1 × 15ml spoon finely diced turnip

1 × 15ml spoon finely diced green leek
1 × 15ml spoon finely diced celery

Cook the diced vegetables for the garnish very carefully in boiling salted water until just tender. Drain and rinse the vegetables; then put them into a warmed tureen.

Meanwhile, heat the consommé to boiling point and add the lemon juice and sherry, if used. Pour the hot consommé over the diced vegetables, and serve.

Consommé Julienne
4–6 helpings

1 litre consommé

Garnish
1 × 15ml spoon julienne carrot
1 × 15ml spoon julienne turnip

1 × 15ml spoon julienne leek

Cook the vegetables for the garnish separately in boiling salted water until just tender. Drain and rinse them, then put them into a warmed tureen.

Meanwhile, heat the consommé to boiling point. Pour the hot consommé over the vegetables, and serve.

Consommé with Rice
4–6 helpings

1 litre consommé (p31)

Garnish
25g Patna rice

Cook the rice in boiling salted water until just tender. Rinse and drain. Heat the consommé to boiling point, add the rice, and heat through.

Consommé Royale
4–6 helpings

1 litre consommé (p31)

Garnish (Royale Custard)
1 egg yolk   butter for greasing
salt and pepper
1 × 15ml spoon white stock (p26)
  or milk **or** cream

Mix the egg yolk, seasoning, and stock or milk or cream. Strain into a small greased basin and cover with buttered greaseproof paper or foil. Stand the basin in a pan of simmering water and steam the custard for about 8 minutes or until firm. Leave until cold and turn out. Cut into thin slices and then into tiny fancy shapes. Rinse the custard shapes in hot water, and drain.

Heat the consommé to boiling point and add the custard garnishes just before serving.

Iced Consommé (Consommé Frappé)
6 helpings

1 litre brown stock (p25) **or** chicken   1 × 15ml spoon (approx) dry sherry
  stock (p26) made with veal bones   ice (optional)

Garnish
chopped parsley, chives, and tarragon   finely chopped hard-boiled egg white
  or chervil   small squares of skinned tomato
finely diced raw cucumber

Make the stock with veal bones to give a firmer jelly when it is iced. Clear the stock as for Consommé (p31). Season it carefully before cooling the consommé. When cool, add the sherry. Chill in a refrigerator, or in a bowl surrounded by ice, for 1–2 hours. The chilled consommé should be a soft jelly. Just before serving, whip the jelly lightly with a fork so that it is not quite solid. Serve in chilled soup bowls with one of the above garnishes.

Note Canned consommé can also be served iced. Check that it will 'jelly' by chilling it. Heat the canned consommé until liquid. Add a little dissolved gelatine, if necessary. Check the seasoning, leave to cool, then add sherry to taste. Chill, and serve as above.

Thick Soups

Butter Bean Soup

6 helpings

150g butter beans
1 litre water **or** general household stock
  (p25)
a few bacon scraps **or** rinds **or** a
  bacon bone
1 medium-sized onion (100g approx)
2 sticks celery

½ small turnip (25g approx)
1 medium-sized potato (100g approx)
1 × 10ml spoon bacon fat
bouquet garni
a blade of mace
250ml milk
salt and pepper

Wash the beans. Heat the water or stock to boiling point, pour it over the beans, and leave to soak overnight. Chop the bacon, if used. Prepare and slice the vegetables. Heat the bacon fat in a deep saucepan, add the bacon or bone, and vegetables, and fry gently for 10 minutes. Add the soaked beans and the liquid, the bouquet garni, and mace. Heat to boiling point, cover, and simmer for 2 hours or until the beans are quite soft. Remove the bouquet garni and bone, if used, and rub the vegetables and cooking liquid through a sieve, or process in an electric blender. Return to a clean pan and add the milk. No starch thickener other than the potato should be needed. Re-heat and season to taste.

VARIATIONS

Dried Pea Soup

Substitute 150g dried, whole or split peas for the butter beans, and add a sprig of mint or a little dried mint.

Haricot Bean Soup

Substitute 150g haricot beans for the butter beans.

Lentil Soup

Substitute 150g red or brown lentils for the butter beans, and add 50g carrot to the flavouring vegetables.

Split Pea and Ham Soup

Substitute 150g split peas for the butter beans, and add a ham or bacon bone to the soup.

Cow-Heel Soup
4–6 helpings

1 cow-heel
1.5 litres water
1 medium-sized onion (100g approx)
1 large carrot (100g approx)
1 stick of celery
bouquet garni

salt and pepper
25g fine tapioca **or** sago
1 × 5ml spoon lemon juice
a pinch of grated nutmeg
1 × 15ml spoon chopped parsley

Scrape and clean the cow-heel. Put in a saucepan, cover with cold water, and heat slowly to boiling point to blanch. Pour off the water. Divide the cow-heel into pieces. Put in a large saucepan with the water and heat to boiling point. Prepare the vegetables and cut into 5mm dice. Add to the pan with the bouquet garni. Cover, and simmer for $3\frac{1}{2}$ hours. Remove the cow-heel and strain the soup. Remove some meat from the bone and cut into 5mm dice. Season the soup to taste. Re-heat to boiling point and sprinkle in the tapioca or sago. Cook until the grain is quite clear and soft. Add the pieces of meat, the lemon juice, nutmeg, and parsley.

Cream of Chicken Soup
4–6 helpings

25g cornflour
125ml milk
1 litre chicken stock (p26)
50g cooked chicken
salt and pepper

1 × 5ml spoon lemon juice
a pinch of grated nutmeg
2 egg yolks
2 × 15ml spoons single cream

Blend the cornflour with a little of the milk. Heat the stock to boiling point and stir into the blended cornflour. Return the mixture to the pan and re-heat to boiling point, stirring all the time. Reduce the heat, cover, and simmer for 20 minutes. Cut the chicken into 5mm dice and heat these in the soup. Season to taste, and add the lemon juice and nutmeg. Beat the yolks with the rest of the milk and the cream; beat in a little hot soup, and fold into the rest of the soup. Heat until it thickens, but do not allow it to boil.

Fisherman's Hot Pot

4 helpings

50g white cabbage
100g leek
250g potatoes
100g onions
25g red pepper
2 slices white bread
50ml cooking oil
25g butter
250g cod **or** other white fish fillets
  (see **Note**)

150ml Muscadet **or** other dry white
  wine
1 litre water
50g concentrated tomato purée
1 chicken stock cube
bouquet garni
1 clove of garlic
salt and pepper

Garnish
1 × 15ml spoon chopped parsley

Shred the cabbage, slice the leek and potatoes, chop the onion and pepper. Remove the crusts from the bread, cut into 1cm cubes, and dry in the oven for 10 minutes.

Heat the oil and butter in a large saucepan, add the vegetables, cover, and cook gently for 7–8 minutes; do not let them colour. Skin the fish, cut them into 3cm cubes, and fry for 3 minutes with the vegetables, turning them over to firm the surface of the cubes. Pour in the wine, water, and tomato purée. Crumble in the stock cube. Skin and crush the garlic. Add the bouquet garni and garlic, and season to taste. Heat to simmering point and simmer for 20 minutes. Discard the bouquet garni. Pour into a soup tureen and sprinkle with the chopped parsley.

Serve with sippets of bread (p48).

Note Any white fish can be used for the hot pot, eg haddock, hake, whiting, ling, etc.

Giblet Soup

4 helpings

2–3 sets chicken giblets **or** 1 set of
  turkey **or** goose giblets
1 litre water
1 medium-sized onion (100g approx)
1 medium-sized carrot (50g approx)
1 stick of celery
bouquet garni

1 clove
a small blade of mace
6 black peppercorns
1 × 5ml spoon salt
25g butter **or** margarine
25g flour

Prepare the giblets if required (p173). Put them in a saucepan and add the cold water. Heat gently to simmering point. Prepare the vegetables and either leave them whole or chop coarsely. Add them to the pan with the bouquet garni, spices, peppercorns, and salt. Cover, and simmer for 2½ hours. Strain the stock. Melt the fat in a saucepan, stir in the flour, and brown very slowly, stirring all the time. Gradually add the stock and stir until boiling. Boil for 5 minutes, stirring all the time. Dice the best pieces of giblets finely and add to the soup. Re-season if required. Re-heat and serve.

Kidney Soup
4 helpings

200g ox kidney	1 stick of celery
25g plain flour	1 litre general household stock (p25)
25g dripping **or** lard	bouquet garni
1 medium-sized onion (100g approx)	6 black peppercorns
1 large carrot (100g approx)	salt
1 small turnip (50g approx)	a little extra stock **or** cold water

Skin, core, and cut the kidney into small pieces. Coat with flour. Keep any remaining flour to thicken the soup at the end. Heat the fat in a large saucepan. Fry the kidney lightly until just browned, then remove from the pan. Prepare and slice the vegetables. Fry them in the fat for about 5 minutes until they begin to brown. Drain off any excess fat. Add the stock, bouquet garni, and seasoning. Heat to boiling point, cover, reduce the heat, and simmer gently for 2 hours.

Remove the bouquet garni and strain the soup. Reserve a few pieces of kidney for the garnish. Purée the rest of the kidney and add to the soup. Blend any remaining flour with a little stock or water, add it to the soup, and stir until boiling. Reduce the heat and simmer for 5 minutes. Chop the reserved kidney pieces and add to the soup. Re-season if required.

Note Kidney Soup can be served with Herb Dumplings (p50).

Liver Soup
4 helpings

1 medium-sized carrot (50g approx)	$\frac{1}{2} \times 2.5$ml spoon yeast **or** meat extract
1 medium-sized onion (100g approx)	salt and pepper
25g butter **or** margarine	2 tomatoes (100g approx)
25g flour	200g calf's, ox **or** lamb's liver
1 litre general household stock (p25)	1×5ml spoon lemon juice
a blade of mace	

Prepare and slice the carrot and onion. Melt the fat in a large saucepan, and fry the vegetables until they begin to brown. Add the flour, and fry gently until browned, stirring occasionally. Gradually add the stock and stir until boiling. Add the mace, yeast or meat extract, and seasoning. Cover, reduce the heat and simmer the soup for 1 hour.

Meanwhile, skin and chop the tomatoes. Add to the soup, cover, and continue simmering for another 30 minutes. Rub the soup through a fine sieve. Remove the skin and tubes from the liver, and mince or chop it finely. Whisk it into the soup with the lemon juice. Re-heat the soup and simmer until the liver just loses its red colour. Re-season if required.

Minestrone
4–6 helpings

75g butter beans **or** haricot beans
2 rashers streaky bacon, without rinds
1 clove of garlic
1 leek
1 onion
2 carrots
50g French beans
3 sticks celery
2 potatoes

150g white cabbage
25g butter
1 bay leaf
1 × 10ml spoon concentrated tomato
   purée
1.25 litres white stock (p26)
salt and pepper
50g pasta rings

Garnish
grated Parmesan cheese

Soak the beans overnight in cold water. Drain thoroughly. Chop the bacon. Skin and crush the garlic. Slice the leek, onion, carrots, and French beans, chop the celery, dice the potatoes, and shred the cabbage. Fry the bacon in a saucepan for 2–3 minutes, add the garlic and butter, and fry for 2–3 minutes. Add all the vegetables and cook for 3–4 minutes. Add the bay leaf, tomato purée, stock, salt, and pepper. Heat to boiling point, cover, then simmer for 45–50 minutes. Add the pasta rings and cook for a further 6–8 minutes.

Serve hot, garnished with grated Parmesan cheese.

Mulligatawny Soup
4 helpings

400g lean mutton, rabbit, stewing veal
   or shin of beef
1 medium-sized onion (100g approx)
1 small cooking apple (100g approx)
25g butter **or** margarine
2–3 × 15ml spoons curry powder
25g plain flour
1 litre water

1 large carrot (100g approx)
½ small parsnip (50g approx)
bouquet garni
1 × 2.5ml spoon lemon juice
1 × 2.5ml spoon salt
½ × 2.5ml spoon black treacle **or**
   extra lemon juice

Trim off any fat and cut the meat into small pieces. Prepare the onion and apple and chop them finely. Melt the fat in a deep saucepan and fry the onion and apple quickly for 2–3 minutes. Add the curry powder, cook gently for 2 minutes, then stir in the flour. Gradually add the water and stir until boiling. Add the meat. Prepare and slice the carrot and parsnip, and add to the pan with the bouquet garni, lemon juice, and salt. Simmer until the meat is very tender. This will take 2 hours for rabbit, 3 hours for stewing veal and mutton, and 4 hours for shin of beef.

Taste the soup, and add black treacle or more lemon juice to obtain a flavour that is neither predominantly sweet nor acid. Strain the soup. Dice some of the meat finely, add to the soup and re-heat.

Serve with boiled long-grain rice.

Oxtail Soup
4–6 helpings

1 oxtail
25g beef dripping
1 medium-sized onion (100g approx)
1 large carrot (100g approx)
1 turnip (25g approx)
1 stick of celery

1 litre water **or** general household stock
   (p25)
1 × 5ml spoon salt
bouquet garni
6 black peppercorns
25g plain flour

Wash, trim off any fat, and joint the tail. Heat the dripping in a saucepan. Add half the jointed tail and fry until the meat is browned. Lift out the meat and reserve the fat in the pan. Prepare and slice the vegetables. Fry in the hot dripping until golden-brown, then remove. Put all the oxtail and the fried vegetables into a deep saucepan. Add the water or stock, and heat very slowly to boiling point. Add the salt, bouquet garni, and peppercorns. Cover, and simmer very gently for 3–4 hours.

Meanwhile, stir the flour into the dripping in the saucepan and fry gently until golden-brown. Strain the soup. Remove all the meat from the bones. Return some of the smaller pieces of meat and any small slices of carrot to the soup. Whisk in the browned flour. Re-heat the soup to boiling point, whisking all the time. Re-season if required.

Prawn Bisque
4–6 helpings

100g butter
250g cooked shelled prawns
25g flour
750ml fish stock (p26) in which
   prawn shells have been cooked
125ml white wine
125ml court bouillon (p75)

1 egg yolk
125ml single cream **or** milk **or**
   half cream and half milk
salt and pepper
lemon juice
a pinch of grated nutmeg

Melt 25g of the butter in a saucepan. Add the prawns, and toss over gentle heat for 5 minutes. Pound the prawns, gradually working in another 50g of the butter. Rub the pounded prawn and butter mixture through a sieve, or process briefly in an electric blender. Melt the remaining 25g butter in a deep saucepan. Stir in the flour and cook gently for 1–2 minutes. Strain the fish stock and gradually stir it into the flour with the wine and court bouillon. Heat to boiling point. Mix the egg yolk with the cream or milk or both. Season the soup and add lemon juice and nutmeg to taste. Whisk the prawn butter into the soup, at just below boiling point, adding a small pat at a time. Add the egg yolk and cream mixture and stir over low heat, without boiling, to thicken the egg.

White Fish Chowder
4 helpings

125ml dry white wine	75g leek
1 litre of water	75g carrot
bouquet garni	50g butter
salt and pepper	50g flour
400g skinned coley fillets **or** other	1 × 5ml spoon turmeric
coarse-fleshed white fish	3 × 15ml spoons chopped parsley

Put the wine, water, bouquet garni, and seasoning in a pan and poach the fish gently in the liquid until tender. Meanwhile, prepare and dice the leek and carrot. Strain the soup into a clean pan. Remove the bouquet garni and cut the fish into 1.5cm cubes. Return the pan to the heat and heat to simmering point. Cream the butter and flour to a smooth paste, then add it gradually to the soup, whisking in each addition. Stir in the turmeric. Add the diced vegetables and simmer gently for 7 minutes. Add the fish and the parsley. Simmer for a further 5 minutes. Serve hot with crusty bread.

Vegetable Soup *Basic recipe*
4 helpings

500g vegetables (approx)	salt and pepper
15–25g butter, margarine **or** other fat	125ml milk
500ml–1 litre white stock (p26) **or**	2 × 10ml spoons thickening (flour,
general household stock (p25)	cornflour, ground rice, tapioca, **or**
bouquet garni **or** flavouring herbs	potato) for each 500ml puréed soup
lemon juice	cold stock, water **or** milk

For Cream of Vegetable Soup
add
4–8 × 15ml spoons single cream
   and/or 1 egg yolk

Prepare and chop the vegetables. Melt the fat in a deep saucepan, add the vegetables, and fry gently for 5–10 minutes without browning them. Add the stock, bouquet garni or herbs, lemon juice, and seasoning to taste. Heat to boiling point, reduce the heat, and simmer gently until the vegetables are quite soft. Do not overcook.

Remove the bouquet garni. Purée the vegetables and liquid by either rubbing through a fine sieve, or by processing in an electric blender. Add the milk, measure the soup, and return it to a clean pan. Weigh the thickening in the correct proportion and blend it with a little cold stock, water or milk. Stir it into the soup. Bring to the boil, stirring all the time, and cook for 5 minutes. Re-season if required. Serve with croûtons (p48), Melba or fairy toast (p51).

Note To make a cream of vegetable soup, remove the pan from the heat after the soup has been thickened and leave to cool slightly. Add a little of the hot soup to the single cream (which can replace some of the milk in the main recipe) and egg yolk, if using, and beat well. Whisk the mixture into the rest of the soup. Return the soup to gentle heat and re-heat, without boiling, stirring all the time.

Green Pea Soup
4 helpings

600g green peas in the pod
1 medium-sized onion (100g approx)
a few spinach leaves
1 × 10ml spoon butter
500ml white stock (p26)
a sprig of mint
a few parsley stalks

2 × 10ml spoons cornflour for each
    500ml puréed soup
cold stock, water **or** milk
salt and pepper
sugar
a few drops green food colouring
    (optional)

For Cream of Green Pea Soup
add
4 × 15ml spoons single cream (see
    Method)

Garnish
a few shelled peas

4 × 15ml spoons chilled whipping
    cream

Shell the peas and wash half the pods. Trim off any hard parts. Skin and slice the onion. Wash the spinach leaves and chop them roughly. Melt the butter in a deep saucepan, add the washed pods and onion, and fry very gently for 10 minutes. Add the stock and heat to boiling point. Add the peas, spinach leaves, and herbs. Simmer for 10–20 minutes or until the peas are just cooked. Proceed as for Vegetable Soup (p39). Season to taste with salt, pepper, and sugar; add the colouring, if liked. Stir in the cream, if used, at boiling point, off the heat.

Meanwhile, cook the peas for the garnish in boiling salted water until just tender. Whip the cream until stiff. Add the cooked peas and blobs of whipped cream to the soup just before serving.

Hot Vichyssoise Cream Soup
4 helpings

250g leeks, white parts only
250g potatoes
25g butter
500ml white stock (p26)

salt and pepper
125ml milk
4–8 × 15ml spoons single cream

Make as for Vegetable Soup (p39). No thickening is required.
VARIATION
Iced Vichyssoise
Make as above but chill the soup well before serving it.

Italian Tomato Soup
4 helpings

600g fresh tomatoes
1 × 15ml spoon olive oil
500ml white stock (p26)
1 clove of garlic
a sprig of parsley
a pinch of dried basil

a pinch of dried marjoram
salt and pepper
2 × 10ml spoons ground rice
4 × 15ml spoons single cream
   (optional)
1 egg yolk (optional)

Chop the tomatoes finely to shorten their cooking time. Proceed as for Vegetable Soup (p39), but cook the tomatoes in the stock for 5 minutes only before sieving them.

Note This soup can be iced if it is not thickened. Sprinkle in 4 × 10ml spoons finely sieved brown breadcrumbs before chilling it.

STUFFINGS, GARNISHES, AND ACCOMPANIMENTS

STUFFINGS OR FORCEMEATS

Breadcrumbs (to make)

Soft breadcrumbs: Remove the crusts from white or brown bread that is at least 1 day old. Either process in an electric blender, or grate coarsely. Alternatively, rub through a wire sieve, or between the palms of the hand until fine crumbs are obtained.
Note Soft crumbs can be stored in a clean polythene bag or sealed polythene container for 2 to 3 days in a refrigerator, or up to 3 months in a freezer. Frozen breadcrumbs remain separate and the required quantity can be removed from the container easily.

Dried breadcrumbs: Prepare soft breadcrumbs and dry them slowly without colouring in a very cool oven, or in a warm place, until thoroughly dry.
Note Dried breadcrumbs can be stored in an airtight jar or tin for 2–3 weeks in a cool place. However, they develop a strong stale taste if kept longer.

Browned breadcrumbs (raspings): Put crusts or any pieces of stale bread in a moderate oven, 180°C, Gas 4, and bake them until golden-brown and crisp. Crush with a rolling-pin or process in an electric blender. These crumbs are not used for stuffings, but for coating croquettes, fish cakes, rissoles, etc or for covering *au gratin* dishes.
Note They can be stored in an airtight jar or tin for 2–3 weeks in a cool place. Like dried breadcrumbs, they develop a strong stale taste if kept longer.

Buttered breadcrumbs: Lightly fork 125g soft breadcrumbs with 25g melted butter. When the crumbs have absorbed the fat, spread them on a baking sheet and dry them without browning, in a very cool oven, 110°C, Gas ¼. Buttered crumbs can be used as they are for coating meat, fish or croquettes, or for covering *au gratin* dishes.

To use in place of soft crumbs, soak buttered crumbs in a little hot water (100g buttered crumbs to 5 × 15ml spoons water) for 5 minutes. Soaked buttered crumbs can be used for bread sauce and stuffings.
Note Buttered crumbs keep better and longer than either soft crumbs or raspings (unless these are frozen). They can be stored in an airtight container in a cool place for up to 2 months.

Apricot Stuffing

Enough for 1 boned joint of pork or a 2.5kg duck; double the quantity will stuff a 4–5kg goose

75g dried apricots
75g boiled long-grain rice **or** soft
 white breadcrumbs
25g butter
1 × 2.5ml spoon salt
1 × 2.5ml spoon ground pepper

a pinch each of dried thyme, ground
 mace and grated nutmeg
1 stick celery **or** 50g green pepper
white stock (p26) **or** water from
 soaked apricots

Soak the apricots overnight in cold water. Drain and reserve the liquid. Chop the apricots and mix with the rice or breadcrumbs. Melt the butter and stir it into the stuffing with the seasoning, herbs, and spices. Prepare the celery or green pepper, chop finely, and add to the mixture. Moisten the stuffing with a little stock or water reserved from the soaked apricots.

Use as above, or for roast chicken, turkey, guineafowl, and lamb.

Basic Herb Stuffing or Forcemeat

Enough for a 1.5–2kg chicken, a boned joint of veal or eight 75g thin fish fillets; use double the quantity for the neck end of a 5–6kg turkey

50g shredded suet **or** margarine
100g soft breadcrumbs
a pinch of grated nutmeg
1 × 15ml spoon chopped parsley
1 × 5ml spoon chopped fresh mixed
 herbs

grated rind of ½ lemon
salt and pepper
1 egg

Melt the margarine, if using. Mix the breadcrumbs with the suet or margarine. Add the nutmeg, herbs, and lemon rind. Season, beat the egg until liquid, and stir into the mixture to bind it.

Use as above, or for vegetables. Alternatively, form the mixture into 12 or 16 balls, and bake in a moderate oven at 180°C, Gas 4, for 15–20 minutes, or fry in deep or shallow fat until golden.

VARIATIONS

Thyme and Parsley Stuffing

Substitute 1 × 5ml spoon thyme for the mixed herbs and omit the grated nutmeg.

Ham Stuffing

Mince or shred 100g lean ham or bacon, and add to the breadcrumbs before mixing with the fat. Use a little milk or chicken stock with the egg to bind the mixture if necessary.

Use for veal, poultry or rabbit. When made with suet, the stuffing can also be used for hare.

For further **variations**, see over.

Prawn or Shrimp Stuffing

Enough for four 450g whole fish, 6 fish cutlets or eight 75g thin fish fillets

Add 100g prawns or shrimps to the breadcrumbs before mixing with the fat. Chop large prawns roughly, leave small fish whole. Add a little milk with the egg, if necessary, to bind.

Glazed Forcemeat Balls

Brush the balls with egg wash before baking them.

Crumbed Forcemeat Balls

Coat the balls with beaten egg yolk; then roll in dried or browned breadcrumbs before baking or frying them.

Nut Forcemeat Balls

Coat the balls with beaten egg yolk; then roll in finely chopped or ground nuts before baking them.

Chestnut Stuffing

Enough for the neck end of a 5–6kg turkey; half the quantity will stuff a 1.5kg chicken

800g chestnuts **or** 500g shelled **or**
  canned chestnuts (approx)
125–250ml stock
50g butter

salt and pepper
a pinch of ground cinnamon
1 × 2.5ml spoon sugar

Make a slit in the rounded side of chestnuts in their shells and bake or boil them for 20 minutes. Remove the shells and skins while hot. Put the chestnuts in a pan with just enough stock to cover them. Heat to boiling point, reduce the heat, cover, and stew until the chestnuts are tender. Drain and reserve the stock. Rub the chestnuts through a fine wire sieve into a bowl. Add the butter, seasoning, cinnamon, and the sugar. Stir in enough stock to make a soft stuffing.

Chicken Giblet Stuffing

Enough for a 2kg chicken or the neck end of a 5–6kg turkey

1 set of chicken giblets
1 medium-sized onion
100g soft white breadcrumbs
50g butter **or** margarine
1 × 15ml spoon chopped parsley

1 × 2.5ml spoon dried mixed herbs
grated rind of ½ lemon
salt and pepper
1 egg

Prepare the giblets if required. Skin the onion and slice it thickly. Put into a saucepan with the giblets, cover with water, heat to boiling point, reduce the heat, and simmer for 45 minutes or until the giblets are cooked. Strain, and reserve 125ml of the cooking liquid; use the rest to make a gravy, soup or sauce.

Pick all the meat off the neck bones, and cut out the lining of the gizzard; chop or mince the flesh of all the giblets. Soak the crumbs in the reserved stock to moisten them. Melt the butter or margarine, and mix together with the giblets, breadcrumbs, herbs, and lemon rind. Season to taste. Beat the egg until liquid and stir into the stuffing mixture.

Use as above, or for pasta (eg cannelloni) or vegetables such as peppers.

VARIATION

Turkey Giblet Stuffing

Substitute turkey giblets for chicken giblets, and use double the quantity of bread-crumbs, stock, and butter or margarine.

Fish Forcemeat

Enough for twelve 75g thin fish fillets, 8 fish cutlets or 4 whole fish weighing 350–450g

1 egg
100g panada, using fish stock (p26)
　or milk
salt and pepper

200g raw white fish, without skin or
　bone
grated rind and juice of ½ lemon

Beat the egg until liquid. Add it gradually to the cooled panada, beating well after each addition. Season to taste. Flake the fish and beat it into the panada. Add the grated lemon rind and juice to taste.

Use as above, or for vegetables.

Flour Panada *Basic recipe*

125ml water, stock or milk
25g butter

25g plain flour
salt and pepper

Put the liquid and butter in a small pan, and heat to boiling point. Sift the flour and add to the pan, stirring briskly with a wooden spoon. Continue to stir over heat until the panada forms a stiff ball and leaves the sides of the pan clean. Season to taste. Spread the panada on a plate, and when cool, use to bind savoury pancake fillings and croquette mixtures.

Prune and Apple Stuffing

Enough for 1 boned joint of pork or a 2.5kg duck; double the quantity will stuff a 4–5kg goose

100g prunes
4 × 10ml spoons long-grain rice or
　125g cooked rice
1 large cooking apple
50g shredded almonds

50g shredded suet or butter
salt and pepper
grated rind and juice of ½ lemon
1 egg

Soak the prunes overnight in cold water. Drain off the liquid. Cook the rice in boiling salted water until tender; then drain. Stone and chop the prunes. Peel, core, and chop the apple roughly, and mix together with the prunes, rice, apple, almonds, and suet or butter. Season to taste and add the lemon rind and juice. Beat the egg until liquid and mix into the stuffing to bind it.

Rice Stuffing
Enough for a 2kg chicken

50g long-grain rice **or** 150g cooked rice
1 chicken liver
1 small onion
50g seedless raisins
50g ground almonds

25g butter
2 × 15ml spoons chopped parsley
a sprig of thyme
salt and pepper
1 egg

Cook the rice in boiling salted water until just tender; then drain. Remove the skin and tubes, and chop the liver. Skin the onion and chop it finely. Mix together with the rice, liver, raisins, and almonds. Mash in the butter with a fork. Add the herbs, and season to taste. Mix well. Beat the egg until liquid and mix into the stuffing to bind it.

Use for roast chicken, other meats, fish or vegetables.

Sage and Onion Stuffing
Enough for a 2.5kg duck; double the quantity will stuff a 4–5kg goose

2 small onions
4 young sage leaves **or**
    1 × 2.5ml spoon dried sage
100g soft white breadcrumbs

50g butter **or** margarine
salt and pepper
1 egg (optional)

Skin the onions and slice them thickly. Put them in a pan with a little water and parboil. Drain and chop the onions finely. Scald the fresh sage leaves, if used, and chop them finely. Mix together with the onions and breadcrumbs. Melt the butter or margarine, add to the stuffing, and season to taste. Mix together thoroughly. If the stuffing is to be shaped into balls, beat the egg until liquid and add enough to the stuffing to bind it.

Use as above, or for pork.

Sausage-meat Stuffing
Enough for a 1.5–2kg chicken; triple the quantity will stuff a 5–6kg turkey

liver of the bird to be stuffed
500g pork sausage-meat
50g soft white breadcrumbs
1 × 15ml spoon chopped parsley

1 × 5ml spoon dried mixed herbs
1 egg
salt and pepper

Remove the skin and tubes, and chop the liver finely. Mix together with the sausage-meat and breadcrumbs, Add the herbs. Beat the egg until liquid and mix into the stuffing to bind it. Season to taste.

GARNISHES AND ACCOMPANIMENTS

Anchovy Fillets
Well-drained anchovy fillets are used to garnish pizzas and some salads.

Apple Slices (fried)
4 helpings

2 large cooking apples
sugar (optional)
flour for coating

salt and ground black pepper
fat for shallow frying

Peel and core the apples and cut each apple into 4 round slices. Discard the rounded ends. Sprinkle the slices with a little sugar if very sour. Season the flour with salt and pepper and coat the slices quickly before they discolour. Heat a little fat in a frying pan and fry the slices gently, turning once, until golden and just tender but not yet soft.

Use as a garnish for any fried or grilled pork dish.

Aspic Jelly
Makes 1 litre (approx)

1 litre brown stock (p25) **or**
   white stock (p26)
125ml white wine **or** 4 × 15ml spoons
   white wine and 4 × 15ml spoons
   dry sherry (for use with red meats
   or game)

2 × 15ml spoons white wine vinegar
40–50g gelatine
bouquet garni
whites and crushed shells of 2 eggs

Leave the stock to cool completely, if necessary. Skim off the fat. Put into a scalded enamel or tin-lined (not aluminium) pan with the rest of the ingredients. Stir with a scalded whisk until the gelatine softens; then bring almost to boiling point whisking all the time. Remove the whisk and leave for a few minutes. Let the liquid rise to the top of the pan, and remove from the heat.

Strain the crust and liquid very gently into a basin through muslin or a scalded jelly bag; do not break the crust as it acts as an extra filter. If it is cloudy, strain again to obtain a sparklingly clear jelly.

Note It is possible, but seldom economic or practical today, to make the jellied stock with 2 calf's feet or 500g cracked veal knuckles and 100g pork rind, instead of using the gelatine. The long, slow boiling of the large quantity of stock needed to make 1 litre of jellied stock is costly and time consuming.

Bacon Rashers

These can be fried or grilled and served as they are. The rinds can be removed before cooking if a plain garnish is required, but the rashers curl and look more decorative if the rinds are left on. The bacon should be cooked until crisp.

Uncooked rashers are used to line a terrine to form a 'jacket' for certain pâtés. They can also be wrapped round prunes, then cooked and served as a garnish for hot savoury dishes. Long, narrow strips of bacon can be wrapped in spirals round food such as sausages, and cooked with them. Small, narrow strips of bacon can be used to bard the surface of a piece of meat for a decorative effect.

Bacon Rolls (fried or grilled)

Cut the rinds off the rashers of streaky bacon, if required. Roll up each rasher. If frying, secure the outer end with a wooden toothpick inserted along each roll. If grilling, thread the rolls on short skewers. Put in a dry frying pan or under moderate grilling heat, and fry or grill for 3–5 minutes, turning frequently, until crisp.

Crumbled Cooked Bacon

Crisp bacon makes an excellent garnish if it is crumbled finely and evenly. It can then be scattered over any meat or vegetable dish, or combined with grated cheese, browned breadcrumbs or hard-boiled egg yolk.

Bread Croûtons

Cut bread slices into 5mm–1cm dice and fry in deep or shallow fat until golden-brown. Alternatively, butter a 5mm thick slice of crustless bread, cut into dice, and place, buttered side up, in a shallow tin. Bake in a moderate oven at 180°C, Gas 4, until golden-brown and crisp.

Serve hot in a separate dish or sprinkle over any kind of soup.

Crescents of Fried Bread

Remove the crusts, and cut each slice of bread into crescents. Fry in shallow fat until golden-brown. Use to garnish blanquettes or fricassées and various fish dishes.

Sippets or Toasted Croûtons

Toast thin slices of bread until crisp and golden. Cut into triangles, 'fingers' or small dice. Serve hot, separately, with thick soups.

Celery Curls

Wash a young tender stick of celery and cut it into 5cm lengths. Slice lengthways into very fine strips, or shred by drawing the pieces lengthways over a coarse grater or mandoline. Put the shreds into very cold water (iced if possible) and leave for 30 minutes. Drain the curls thoroughly, first in a colander and then on soft kitchen paper. Use chiefly for garnishing plates of cocktail snacks or for mixed hors d'oeuvres and salads. Can also garnish hot dishes containing celery.

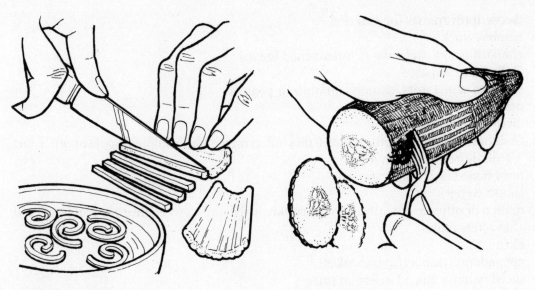

Making celery curls   *Scoring cucumber with a fork*

Cucumber (sliced)

Peel or score lengthways with the prongs of a fork or with a canelling knife. Slice thinly on to a plate. Sprinkle with salt and leave for 30 minutes with the plate slightly tilted. Drain off the liquid.

Thinly sliced cucumber, laid in overlapping lines, is used to garnish a great many cold dishes and salads. It is the classic garnish or accompaniment for cold poached salmon.

Cold Horseradish Cream

Makes 150ml (approx)

125ml double cream
2 × 15ml spoons fresh grated
  horseradish
1 × 15ml spoon white wine vinegar **or**
  lemon juice

1 × 10ml spoon caster sugar
½ × 2.5ml spoon made English mustard
salt and pepper

Whip the cream lightly until semi-stiff. Carefully fold in the other ingredients. Chill until ready to use.

Serve with beef.

Accompaniments for Curries

bombay duck

chapatti (small, flat cake of unleavened bread)

chilli sauce or paste

chopped salted nuts, usually almonds or peanuts

desiccated coconut

diced fresh pineapple

fresh or dried dates or other dried fruits (often mixed with chopped apple or other tart
fruit dipped in lemon juice)

hard-boiled eggs cut in sections

lemon wedges

mango or other fruit chutney (a sharp-flavoured and a sweet chutney can be offered
as alternatives)

okra

poppadoms (thin, crisp pancakes)

sliced banana dipped in lemon juice

sliced cucumber

sliced cucumber in soured cream

sliced tomato sprinkled with oil, vinegar, and chopped chives or mint

small strips of red and green sweet peppers

thick natural yoghurt or curd cheese

thin rings of finely sliced raw onion

Apart from rice, certain accompaniments for curries have become traditional and
a selection of those listed here is usually served with curries in Europe, even though
they may not form part of Eastern cuisines.

Serve them in small dishes or bowls, placed on the table so that diners can help
themselves.

Most of these accompaniments are also served with Indonesian, Malaysian and
other South East Asian curries and similar dishes such as *satés*; also with grain-based
dishes such as the Indonesian *ryjsttavel* (rice table).

Dumplings *Basic recipe*
Makes 16 (approx)

100g self-raising flour	salt and pepper
50g shredded suet	

Mix together the flour, suet, and seasoning to taste. Bind with enough cold water to
make a soft smooth dough. With floured hands, divide the dough into 16 portions
and roll into balls. Drop into simmering salted water, stock, soup or into a stew, and
simmer for 15–20 minutes.

Serve with the liquid or with boiled meat, stew or vegetables.

VARIATIONS

Herb Dumplings

Add 25g finely grated onion and 1 × 2.5ml spoon chopped fresh herbs to the flour
and suet.

Meat Dumplings
Add 2 × 15ml spoons finely minced or puréed meat to the flour and fat, and bind the dumplings with the meat stock instead of water.

Soya Dumplings
Substitute 1 × 15ml spoon soya flour for 1 × 15ml flour, and add 1 × 2.5ml spoon dried mixed herbs.

Fairy Toast
Bake very thin slices of bread in a cool oven at 150°C, Gas 2, until golden and very crisp. Serve hot, separately, with most soups.

Melba Toast
Toast thin slices of white bread, then split carefully through the middle and toast the untoasted surfaces under a hot grill, or bake in a cool oven until crisp and golden. Serve with any hot soup.

Pulled Bread
Break apart a fresh French loaf, pull out the inside, and dry in a very cool oven until pale golden and crisp. Serve with soup or pâté.

Fleurons of Puff Pastry
Roll out the pastry, 5cm thick, and cut out circles with a 6cm cutter. Move the cutter half-way across the circle and cut it again, making a half moon and an almond shape. Lay the half moon shapes on a baking sheet, brush the tops with egg wash, and bake in a fairly hot oven at 200°C, Gas 6, for 8–10 minutes. Roll out and re-cut the almond shapes, or bake and serve them as small biscuits.

Use to garnish dishes in a white or creamy sauce.

Fried Onion Rings
Skin an onion and slice thinly. Dip the rings in egg white, or milk and flour, and fry in a little fat, until golden-brown and crisp. Add to a thick soup just before it is served or serve with grilled or fried meat dishes.

Raw Onion Rings
Thin rings of sliced, raw onion, sometimes lightly blanched, can garnish a number of salads and spicy savoury dishes.

Grated Hard Cheese
Serve separately with Minestrone (p37) and other mixed vegetable soups. Can also be sprinkled over the soup just before it is served. Finely grated Parmesan is usually served with these soups.

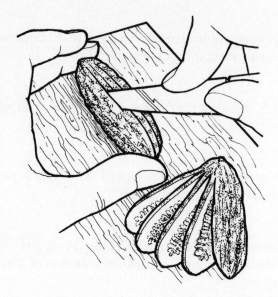

Making gherkin fans

Gherkin Fans

Make about 6 cuts from the top almost to the base of each gherkin, taking care not to cut right through the base. Spread the gherkins out carefully into fan shapes, with the base as a hinge.

Use to garnish cocktail snacks and salads.

Hard-boiled Egg

Crumbled or sieved hard-boiled egg yolk makes an attractive, colourful garnish sprinkled over hot or cold dishes. When sprinkled over a vegetable salad, it is known as a Mimosa salad.

It can be mixed with about half its quantity of fried breadcrumbs, crumbled, crisply fried bacon, grated hard cheese or finely chopped fresh parsley.

Whole hard-boiled eggs, sliced or cut into wedges, make an attractive garnish for many salads. Run cold water over the eggs as soon as their cooking time is up, and before shelling them, to prevent a dark line developing round the yolk.

Herbs

Fresh herbs, chopped and sprinkled over a dish, are one of the simplest yet most attractive garnishes. They should be chopped and put on the dish just before it is served, so that their aroma and flavour are at their strongest. No addition is needed except perhaps a few grains of salt or 1–2 drops of lemon juice. Chives are particularly good for their fresh sharp flavour. Use chopped basil, marjoram, mint, parsley or thyme. The feathery sprays of dill and fennel make a delicately attractive garnish.

Dried herbs have little appeal as a garnish and should not be substituted for fresh herbs.

Julienne Vegetables

Finely shred vegetables into strips about 2–3cm in length. Use as required.

Lemon, Orange or Grapefruit Baskets

Take a clean lemon, orange or grapefruit and, with a sharp knife, cut out almost a whole quarter segment. Leave a strip of rind wide enough for the handle (about 5mm) and then cut out the corresponding segment on the other side. Carefully cut out the pulp from the handle and then remove the pulp from the lower half.

Alternatively, proceed as for Tomato Lilies (p59); then cut out the flesh from each half. Fill with any cold savoury or sweet mixture which has lemon, orange or grapefruit in its flavouring.

Note For melon and pineapple baskets and containers, see p305.

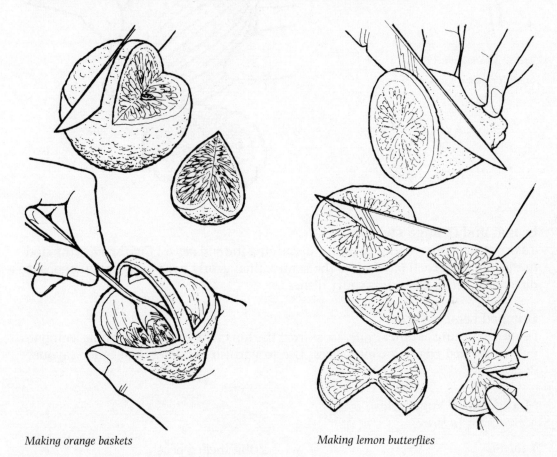

Making orange baskets   *Making lemon butterflies*

Lemon Butterflies

Take a clean lemon and, with a sharp knife, cut it into thin slices, discarding the end pieces. Depending on the size of 'wings' required and the size of the lemon, cut the slices either into halves or quarters. Cut through the rind in the middle of each piece and gently pull into 2 wings without breaking into 2 pieces. A piece of parsley may be placed in the centre to represent the 'butterfly's' body.

Lemon 'butterflies' can garnish both savoury and sweet dishes. They are served on breadcrumbed, fried or grilled meats, such as veal escalopes, and on several fish dishes.

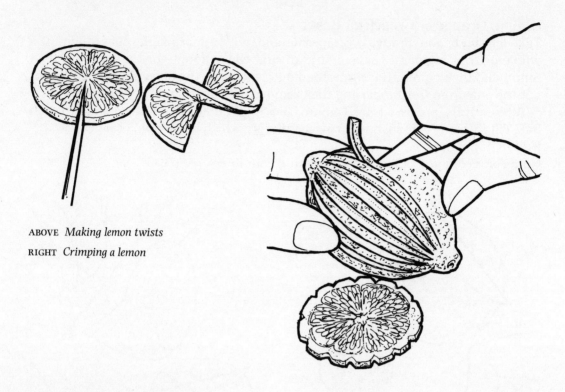

ABOVE *Making lemon twists*

RIGHT *Crimping a lemon*

Lemon and Orange Twists

Take a clean lemon, and slice thinly, discarding the end pieces. Cut through the rind in the middle of each piece up to the centre, then gently twist each half in opposite directions. Use to garnish savoury dishes.

Crimped Lemon Slices

Using a canelling or other knife, score from the top to the bottom of a whole lemon to give a serrated edge. Cut into slices. Use to garnish escalopes and other savoury dishes.

Macédoine of Vegetables

Makes 500g (approx)

1 turnip	200g shelled peas
100g carrot	750ml water
200g potatoes	1 × 5ml spoon salt
a few runner beans	3–4 × 15ml spoons butter
a few cauliflower florets	pepper

Prepare all the vegetables. Cut the turnip, carrot, and potatoes into 1cm dice. Cut the beans into 1cm diamond shapes. Bring the water to the boil, and add the salt. Put in the turnip and carrots, and boil for 3 minutes. Add the beans, and boil for another 3 minutes; then add the remaining vegetables. Boil for 5–10 minutes until the vegetables are tender but not broken. Drain thoroughly and toss in the butter. Season to taste, and use as a border or in small piles round a dish of meat. Serve hot.

Meat Glaze

This can be made from any strong, dark, meat stock made with lean meat and bones. It is strained, then boiled steadily until syrupy. When cooled, it should set like a rich, shiny, brown jelly. If the stock has been made without bones, gelatine is sometimes added to make it set, but it lacks the clarity of flavour of reduced bone stock and it does not keep as well.

Meat glaze is used to augment and improve the flavour of gravy and sauces, and it is sometimes added to vegetables for the same purpose. It can also be brushed over meats, such as roast beef or tongue, or over a galantine or pâté to improve its appearance, although it will not give it an aspic coating.

Meat Glaze (made with gelatine)

Makes 150ml (approx)

4 × 15ml spoons gelatine
125ml cold water
1 × 5ml spoon beef extract **or** yeast
  extract

a few grains onion salt (optional)
a few drops dry sherry (optional)
1–2 drops gravy browning (optional)

Using a metal spoon, stir the gelatine into the cold water in a heatproof container. Stand the container in a pan of hot water and stir until dissolved; then stir in the extract and chosen flavouring. Add gravy browning if a darker colour is wanted. Brush the glaze at once, while still hot, over cold meats, galantines or pâtés. If it starts to set in ridges or lumps while brushing, replace the bowl in hot water to keep it warm.

Note Do not store the glaze for more than 48 hours. Keep covered in a refrigerator.

Other Glazes

1) *Hot meat and poultry:* Brush very lightly with butter or oil just before serving.
2a) *Crackling on roast pork:* Brush with apricot glaze (p396) or smooth apricot jam 7–10 minutes before the end of the cooking time. Return to the oven to finish cooking and to set the glaze.
  b) Melted, cooled redcurrant jelly can be used in the same way; so can clear honey flavoured with lemon juice or mixed English mustard.
  c) Sieved fine-cut marmalade is sometimes used as a glaze and can be flavoured with whisky.
  d) A fruit syrup glaze, eg from canned fruit, has less colour than a jam glaze, but gives a clear crisp coating.
  e) If a non-sweet glaze is wanted for the crackling, brush with lightly salted butter or oil, with a little extra salt added. Raise the oven heat for a short time so that the crackling is, in effect, 'fried'.
3) *Frothing:* Dredge meat or poultry with flour and baste thoroughly with its cooking juices or with fat, shortly before the end of the cooking time. Return to the oven at a high heat to give a well-browned glazed appearance.
4) *Glazes for Pastry:* See p407.

Mint Sauce
Makes 125ml (approx)

4 × 15ml spoons chopped fresh mint
1 × 10ml spoon sugar

1 × 15ml spoon boiling water
2 × 15ml spoons vinegar

Put the mint into a sauce-boat. Sprinkle with the sugar. Add the boiling water, and stir until the sugar dissolves; then add the vinegar. Leave the sauce for 1–2 hours for the flavours to infuse.

Serve with roast lamb.

Mushroom Slices
Slice mushrooms thinly and fry gently in a little butter for a few minutes, until softened. Add to thick soups.

Parsley (fried)
Unless the parsley is very dirty, do not wash it before frying as parsley is difficult to dry and the moisture causes the fat to bubble and spit, which can be dangerous. Allow 4 good sprigs of parsley for each person and cut off the main stalks. Heat a pan of deep oil or fat (p10), place the parsley sprigs in the frying basket and put it into the pan. Remove from the pan immediately the hissing noise stops. Drain and serve.

Use to garnish grilled or fried fish and steaks.

Pasta
Pasta, such as macaroni and tagliatelli, can be added, in short lengths, to thin soups. Cook the pasta separately so that the soup is not clouded. Add the hot, drained pasta to the soup just before it is served.

Potatoes
Whole boiled potatoes are so often used to garnish fish dishes that they are called 'fish potatoes'. Boiled new potatoes topped with butter and chopped parsley are a common garnish for fish, white meats, poultry, and rabbit.

Potatoes Parisienne
4–6 helpings

1kg potatoes
25g butter
1 × 15ml spoon oil
$\frac{1}{2}$ × 2.5ml spoon salt
3 × 15ml spoons softened butter

3 × 15ml spoons finely chopped fresh mixed herbs (parsley, chives, tarragon)
pepper

Peel the potatoes and cut into small, round balls, using a potato ball scoop. Dry in a clean cloth. Heat the butter and oil in a frying pan large enough to hold all the potatoes in 1 layer. Put in the potatoes and coat evenly in the fat. Fry them gently until the potatoes are a light golden colour all over. Reduce the heat, sprinkle with the salt and cover the pan. Continue frying very gently for 12–15 minutes, shaking the pan frequently, until the potatoes are tender. Drain off the fat. Raise the heat and shake the potatoes in the pan until sizzling. Remove from the heat, add the softened butter and herbs, season well with pepper, and roll the potatoes round the pan until coated with herbs. Arrange round a meat dish or serve separately in a warmed dish. **Note** Carrots, turnips, and similar vegetables can be cooked in the same way as the potatoes.

Duchesse Potatoes
Makes 500g (approx)

500g old potatoes	a little grated nutmeg (optional)
25g butter **or** margarine	butter **or** margarine for greasing
1 egg **or** 2 egg yolks	a little beaten egg for brushing
salt and pepper	(optional)

Prepare the potatoes, and boil or steam them. Drain thoroughly, and sieve. Beat in the fat and egg or egg yolks. Season to taste with salt and pepper and add the nutmeg, if used. Spoon the mixture into a piping bag fitted with a large rose nozzle and pipe rounds of potato on to a greased baking tray or round the edge of a heatproof serving dish. Brush with a little beaten egg, or leave plain for a white border. Bake in a fairly hot oven at 200°C, Gas 6, for about 15 minutes or until the potatoes are a good golden-brown. Transfer to a serving dish if necessary.

Alternatively, form the potato into a long, narrow roll with your hands and, using as little flour as possible, arrange the roll on a serving dish or baking sheet in the shape you want. Glaze it with beaten egg, if liked, and bake as above.

Use to garnish fish and meat dishes in sauces. A border of creamed potato is often used to garnish fish dishes in scallop shells and *au gratin* dishes.

Prawns
Cooked shelled prawns are often scattered over a hot fish dish or cold fish salad. Unshelled prawns may be arranged round the edge of a hot dish, eg, Sweet and Sour Prawns (p89). Use 1 unshelled prawn to garnish an individual dish such as fish cooked *au gratin* and presented in a scallop shell. Unshelled prawns also make an attractive garnish for a cold fish dish such as a prawn cocktail or a salad.

Many dishes for sole are garnished with prawns.

Rice
Dry boiled rice can be added to soup just before it is served, or it can be cooked in the soup. In this case, it should be added about 15 minutes before the end of the cooking time.

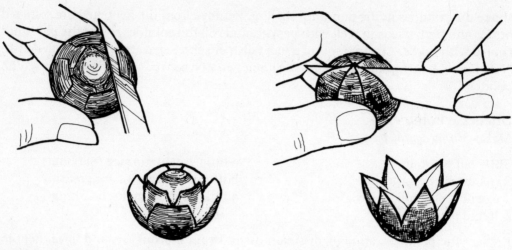

Making radish roses   *Making radish water lilies*

Radish Roses

Wash the radishes, cut off the stalks and a very thin slice of the root end. Cut thin petals from the root to the stem, taking care not to cut right through; then place the radishes in cold water (preferably iced) until they open out like roses.

Radish Water Lilies

Wash the radishes and cut off the stalks and the roots. Make 4–6 cuts from the root to the stem, taking care not to cut right through. Place in cold water (preferably iced) and leave until the radishes open out like lilies.

Sharp Sauce (hot or cold)
Makes 200ml (approx)

1 shallot
2 hard-boiled egg yolks
4 anchovies
1 × 2.5ml spoon made English mustard

1 × 10ml spoon vinegar
1 × 5ml spoon chopped capers
salt and pepper
caster sugar

For a Cold Sauce
125ml single cream

For a Hot Sauce
125ml thin gravy (p229)

Skin and chop the shallot finely. Rub the egg yolks through a sieve. Pound the shallot, egg yolks, and anchovies together to form a paste. Add the mustard, vinegar, and capers, and blend together.

For a cold sauce, whip the cream until it forms soft peaks, and fold it carefully into the other ingredients.

For a hot sauce, heat the gravy to boiling point and add to the other ingredients. Return to the pan and heat to just below boiling point.

Serve with roast or grilled meats, or grilled or baked fish.

Spiced Pears, Peaches or Apricots
4 helpings

2 (fresh or canned) pears **or** peaches
   or 8 apricots
25g butter

1×15ml spoon soft light brown sugar
$\frac{1}{2} \times 2.5$ml spoon ground cinnamon
$\frac{1}{2} \times 2.5$ml spoon grated nutmeg

Peel the pears, if using fresh ones, cut in half and remove the cores. Halve fresh peaches or apricots and remove the stones. If using canned fruit, drain off the syrup. Arrange the fruit, cut side up, in a shallow tin. Place a small nut of butter in each hollow and sprinkle lightly with the brown sugar, cinnamon, and nutmeg. Bake in the oven for 5–10 minutes with the joint.

Serve with baked ham or with roast pork.

Tomatoes
Small, whole baked tomatoes, halved, baked or grilled tomatoes, or sliced, grilled or fried tomatoes are often used as a garnish for grilled and fried meat dishes, especially a mixed grill, kebabs or chops. They are also used to garnish grilled chicken or game birds.

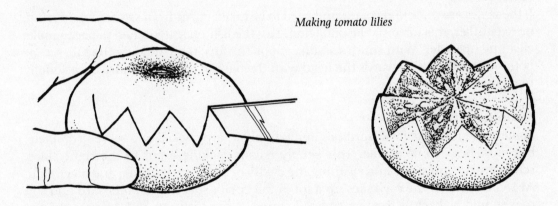

Making tomato lilies

Tomato Lilies
Take a clean, firm tomato and, using a sharp knife, halve it by making a series of zigzag cuts. When you have gone right round the tomato, gently pull the halves apart. Alternatively, use a potato peeler to make the zigzag cuts.

Besides being a decorative way of presenting tomatoes as part of a large salad, small cherry tomatoes made into 'lilies' can also garnish hot or cold sliced meats.

Watercress
Wash, dry, and break into small sprigs. Keep in a polythene bag in a refrigerator until needed. Add to thick soups, especially chicken or vegetable purée soups, just before serving. Use also to garnish cold poultry.

MAIN COURSES

FISH AND SHELLFISH

Preparing Fish

Except for small round fish, most fish caught by commercial fishermen are gutted at sea. Only fish such as herrings, mackerel, and red mullet have to be gutted by the fishmonger or in the kitchen.

Scaling Fish

If the scales are thick and coarse and need to be taken off, eg from sea bream, herring, or red mullet, this job must be done first. Lay the fish on soft kitchen paper to make cleaning up easier. With sharp scissors, cut off the fins; then, holding the tail, scrape both sides of the fish towards the head with the back of the knife. Rinse occasionally to remove the loose scales.

Cleaning Fish

Some small fish, like fresh sardines and whitebait, are cooked and served complete, but most have to be gutted. This simply means making a cut in the right place, removing the intestines and cleaning the cavity of blood, membrane, and black skin. At some seasons, the roe takes up a lot of the cavity space, and both hard and soft roes should be kept as they make good eating. After cleaning, lightly rinse the cut area with cold water and pat dry.

Flat fish: Place the fish, dark skin up, on soft kitchen paper and locate the gill cover, positioned just behind the head. Make a deep cut from the centre line of the fish out to the fin just at the rear of the gill opening. Remove the intestines, but if the fish is to be cooked whole, leave the roe in place. To complete the cleaning, trim the 'frill' fins and tail back to the body. You can cut off the heads of plaice and lemon sole, but the head of a Dover sole is normally left on.

Large round fish: Cut the belly lengthways, from the gills to a point about two-thirds the length of the fish from the head. Remove the entrails, saving the roe if required, rinse thoroughly, and pat dry.

Small round fish: Clean most white fish and trout as described above. It is usual to remove mackerel heads before preparing, which makes cleaning easier. Herring are different because the entrails to be disposed of are minimal. So just make a downward cut behind the gills and pull the head back; then clean the area before rinsing. Leave the roe in place if grilling or cooking whole.

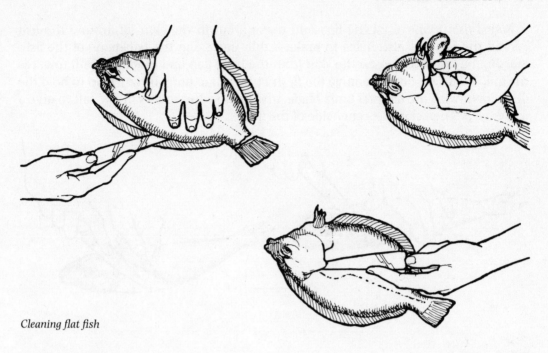

Cleaning flat fish

Skinning Fish

Removing the skin from a slippery fish can be tricky and it may be simpler to cook the fish first. Dover soles should have at least the dark skin removed because it is coarser than that of lemon sole or plaice.

Flat fish: Lay the fish on a wooden board, white side down. With a sharp knife or scissors cut the 'frill' fin and tail back to the fish, if not already done, and scrape the tail end until the skin starts to lift. It is then easy to free a piece of skin; now slip the thumb or the end of a round-bladed knife under it and loosen the skin from the flesh, working towards the head. When enough has been loosened like this, pull it off from the tail to head end. Repeat the process on the white side if required.

Work cautiously on soft-skinned fish, so as not to tear the flesh.

Skinning flat fish

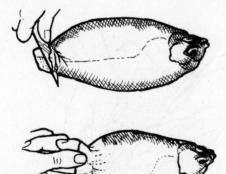

Round fish: Remove all the fins and make a cut in the skin all around the fish behind the head. It also helps to make a thin cut along the backbone of the fish. Starting on one side, loosen the skin from the belly flap and gradually pull towards the tail. Take care not to remove the flesh at the same time. It may help to hold the flesh down with the flat of a knife blade, and to dip your fingers in dry salt to give a firmer grip. Then skin the other side of the fish.

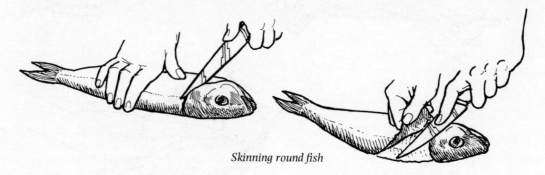

Skinning round fish

Filleting Fish

Filleting means removing the flesh in two or four whole slices from the head and central bone structure. The head, bones, and skin of white fish are the basis for natural fish stock and should not be thrown away. If the fishmonger is filleting the fish, always ask him for the bones and trimmings. You have paid for them, and are entitled to them.

Flat fish: Lay the fish on a flat surface with its tail towards you. With a sharp, pointed knife, make a cut down the centre of the back right down to the backbone, from just behind the head to the tail. Then, turning the knife so that it lies flat against the bones, cut the flesh free from the bone, using the bone structure as a guide. Cut and loosen the fillet all the way to the edge of the fish and lift free.

Repeat the process with the other top fillet; then turn the fish over, and remove the two fillets from the other side in the same way.

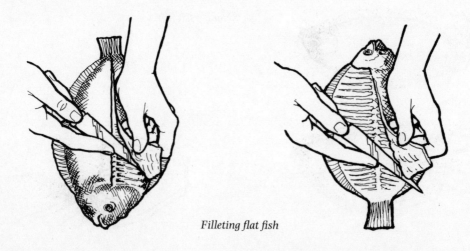

Filleting flat fish

Round fish: Lay the gutted fish on its side and cut round behind the head. Then insert the point of the knife into the back of the fish, just behind the head, and cut right down the backbone all the way to the tail. Keeping the knife flat, and pressed against the rib bones, slice the fillet free along the length of the fish. Turn the fish over and remove the second fillet in the same fashion. Rinse, check for bones, and cut off the fins.

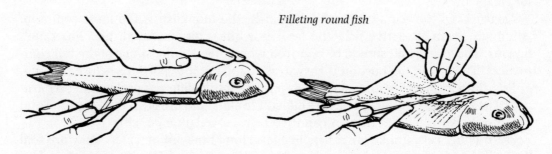

Filleting round fish

Boning Fish

Herring, mackerel or trout: Remove the head and cut the belly right to the tail. Open the fish flat, and set aside the roe; then place the fish, skin side up, on a board and press both sides of the backbone all the way down the fish. Turn over and pull the backbone clear, cut off end of bone and tail. Rinse and check for any remaining bones. For boning sprats, see p69.

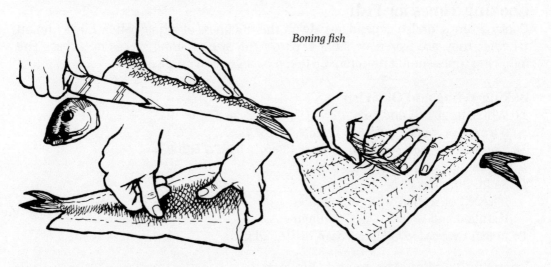

Boning fish

Other Specialized Preparations

Skate: Fish other than the two main types may require a more specialized filleting technique. For instance, when preparing skate or any of the other rays, only the 'wings' are used for cooking. The skate wings are cut from either side of the backbone and cooked whole or cut into portions, depending on size; skate bones are large and pliable, so there is no need to fillet the wings. However, the dark skin is a problem and the sharp hooks embedded in the skin should be carefully cut out after skinning. Skate carry a good deal of natural slime and this should be scrubbed off first; then nick out the flesh along the thick side, just under the skin, to provide a purchase point. Use a strong pair of pliers to grip the skin and pull it off in one piece.

Dogfish or tope: These members of the shark family present the same sort of problem. The fish has a soft boned (cartilaginous) structure so there is no need to fillet it. The skin, however, is very tough and needs to be removed before cooking. Gut the fish as for round fish and remove the fins and tail. To skin, follow the method described for eel (below).

Monkfish: Of the remaining soft-boned fish, the monkfish is the most common. Although an unattractive fish, the flesh is white, close-textured, and has much flavour. The large head should be removed where the definite shape of the tail commences. The meaty tail portion is easy to skin and cut into portions before cooking.

Eels: Both fresh-water and conger eels pose a slightly different problem in preparation. The larger sea-water species are difficult to skin, and are best cooked gutted and cut into steaks or fillets. The skin can then be removed after cooking.

Fresh-water eels, unlike other fish, live for a long time out of water. They are sold live, killed at the point of sale, and then skinned if necessary. If large, hang the eel up by a string round the 'neck', and make a cut through the skin all round the eel, just behind the head. Loosen the skin with a knife and pull the skin downwards over the tail. If small, just secure the head, and proceed in the same way. Clean the eel after skinning and cut into sections across the body before cooking. The very small young eels called elvers can, however, be cooked whole.

Cooking Times for Fish
Cooking times for fish depend largely on the thickness of whole fish or fillets and on whether they are frozen or stuffed, or on the size of small pieces or cubes. The following times should therefore be taken as a general guide only.

Baking White and Oily Fish
1) Whole large fish and cuts   *25–35 minutes per 500g*
   If frozen or stuffed   *35–45 minutes per 500g*
2) Small whole fish, steaks, and thick fillets   *15–20 minutes*
   If frozen or stuffed   *20–30 minutes*
3) Small thin fillets   *8–12 minutes*
   If frozen or stuffed   *15–20 minutes*
   If stuffed and rolled   *20–30 minutes*

Treat fish *wrapped in foil* like frozen or stuffed fish.

Frying and Grilling White and Oily Fish
1) Thin fillets and pieces, and kebab cubes
   Coated and deep fried   *5–10 minutes*
   Coated and shallow fried   *10–15 minutes*
   Uncoated and shallow fried   *5–10 minutes*
   Grilled   *7–8 minutes*
2) Steaks and thick whole fish or pieces
   Grilled   *10–15 minutes*

Poaching White and Oily Fish
1) Small thin fillets and portions   *3–5 minutes*
2) Medium and thick fillets   *6–10 minutes*
3) Steaks and thick portions and small whole fish *8–15 minutes*
4) 700g–1kg whole fish or cut   *8–15 minutes*
5) 1.8–2.6kg   *15–18 minutes*
6) Larger fish   *5–12 minutes per 500g*

These times are also suitable for smoked fish. Allow 5–8 minutes extra if the fish is frozen, stuffed or rolled. Allow 5–10 minutes extra for *steaming* fish.

Stewing White and Oily Fish
1) Cubes and thick small pieces of coarse fish *8–10 minutes*
2) Cubes and thick small pieces of soft fish   *4–7 minutes*

Casseroling White and Oily Fish
1) Thick whole fish, thick cuts and steaks   *20–30 minutes*
2) Thin whole fish, fillets   *15 minutes (approx)*
Allow 5–8 minutes extra if the fish is frozen.

Types of Fish
The supply of fish varies with weather conditions and the seasons. However, many white fish, and some others, are interchangeable in cooking; so if the particular fish you want is scarce or expensive, you can easily substitute another.

Bream (Red Fish, Ocean Perch)
This delicately flavoured white fish gives a deep fillet when large, or can be cooked whole when small. Cook like other white sea fish.

   Fresh-water bream are deep-bodied, with a reddish tinge to the scales. Soak in salt water for 30–45 minutes; then cook as for other river fish.

Brill
In season all the year, but reaches its best condition from April to July. Good flavour, but not as firm as turbot. Soak well in salted water; then cook like carp, but handle the soft flesh carefully.

Carp
A fresh-water fish, at its best from November to January. There are several types, but the common carp (scales all over), and mirror carp (olive colour and isolated large scales) are most valued for the table. The fish should be cleaned, soaked in salt water, and rinsed in vinegar and water before cooking. Cook as for other river fish.

Catfish (Wolf-fish, Rock-fish)
The wolf-fish, a variety of catfish, commonly sold in the UK under the name of rock-fish, has a large head, with strong jaws and striped body. The flesh is pinkish white with a small amount of bone. Bake or grill with a sprinkling of lemon juice.

Cod

Cod is available everywhere, wet or frozen. Smoked fillets and roe are also popular. Cod has firm, flaky white flesh, and can be cooked in all the accepted ways for white fish. Take care not to overcook.

Coley (Saithe)

A close relation of cod but has darker coloured skin and flesh. In cooking, the fish turns white and can be used as an alternative to cod and haddock. Available everywhere, wet or frozen.

Dab

A smaller member of the plaice family, in season all year round. Gut, trim fins, and fry or grill whole. Larger dabs can be cooked like plaice.

Dogfish (Huss, Flake, Tope)

Available all the year. It is most popular in batter and deep fried but is even better grilled, baked or in kebabs, soups, and fish stock, because of its firm flesh.

Eel

Fresh-water eels are olive in colour, with very rich, oily flesh. Though always in season, they are less good in summer. Available live from specialist fishmongers, also cooked and jellied. Because of their fat content, eels are excellent smoked for eating raw. Unsmoked eels are poached and sauced, baked or grilled, and are an essential ingredient in continental fish hot-pots, chowders, and cotriades.

Conger eel, a sea-water fish, can grow up to 3 metres in length. Dark-grey in colour, the medium-sized ones are best for eating. Can be used in recipes for monkfish or dogfish, or instead of freshwater eels in most recipes.

Grey Mullet

Best from July to February. Clean and soak in several changes of salt water before cooking. Cook like mackerel or red mullet.

Gudgeon

Gut the fish and remove gills, dip in egg and breadcrumbs and deepfry. Serve whole, 3–4 per person depending on size.

Gurnet (Gurnard)

These colourful fish can be grey, red or yellow, depending on the type. They are easily identified by their large angular bony heads. The red-coloured fish is the best for eating, and is available at good fishmongers. Most seasonable from July to April. Cook whole or filleted. Try poaching in court bouillon and serving cold with mayonnaise.

Haddock

In season all year round, but best from November to February. Available everywhere, wet or frozen. Cook wet fish gently to appreciate its sweet, fresh flavour.

Finnan haddock are either split or left on the bone; they are lightly cold smoked. They have a delicious, mild flavour. *Smoked haddock cutlets* (boned), unlike finnan haddock, have been dyed and quite heavily smoked. *Arbroath smokies* are headless and hot smoked, so can be eaten cold or heated in the oven.

Poach smoked fish in half milk and half water, and serve with a generous pat of plain or savoury butter.

Hake
This fish belongs to the same family as haddock and cod, but it has a longer, slimmer shape. In best condition from June to January when it is quite widely available from fishmongers, especially those in the west and south western areas of the country.

Frozen hake usually comes from South Atlantic fishing grounds, and has a drier, more fibrous texture than the silver hake from more northerly waters.

Halibut
A very large flat fish, rich in vitamins A and D. Widely available from fishmongers as whole fish (up to 1.5kg, it is called chicken halibut) or in steaks from larger fish. The pre-sawn frozen steaks of Pacific halibut make a good alternative to the Atlantic ones. Both types are available fresh and frozen.

Greenland halibut is grey-brown with rather more watery flesh than the Atlantic or Pacific fish. This has led to it being called 'mock' halibut.

Herring
This excellent fish is found in many guises, and it also provides both hard and soft roes. It can be split, boned, and cold smoked to produce a *kipper*. Most kippers are now in fact, salted and dyed to give a pleasant traditional taste and tint. (Uncoloured kippers are also available though.) Kippers are also sold as cutlets, with the head and backbone removed, or as fillets.

Bloaters are ungutted herrings lightly smoked. They must be cooked as soon as they are purchased. *Buckling* are the same fish hot smoked, and can be used as an alternative to smoked trout without further cooking.

Red herrings are heavily smoked and salted, but are rarely seen in Britain, most of them being exported. They need long soaking before cooking.

Herrings are also available in various sauces and continental styles. *Matjes herrings* are preserved in a light brine, *Bismarck herrings* in a marinade of white wine and vinegar with onions and juniper berries, and the most popular preserved herrings, *rollmops*, are packed with gherkins and onions in a vinegar marinade.

Herrings are oily fish and a little mustard or horseradish sauce helps to offset the richness. They can be grilled, baked or fried without adding fat.

Ling
This is another member of the cod family, with a distinctive elongated body and an underchin barbel. Fairly widely available, and in best condition from September to May. Cook as for other white fish.

Mackerel

Available everywhere wet or frozen; at its best in the winter and spring. Grill, souse, or stuff and bake *en papillote.*

Smoked mackerel is also widely available either as whole fish or fillets; it is popular in salads and as a pâté. It is available hot smoked and therefore cooked and ready to eat, or cold smoked and vacuum packed.

Kippered mackerel is cold smoked and needs cooking, like kippers. Like herring, the flesh is savoury and rich, so horseradish, mustard or some other piquant condiment or side dish should be served with the fish.

Megrim

Closely related to brill and turbot. Cook in the same ways.

Monkfish

As a rule only the tail of this strange-looking fish is seen on the fishmonger's slab. The firm white meat is delicious and can be cooked in all the ways suggested for halibut or turbot; it is excellent eaten either hot or cold.

Perch

A fresh-water fish, olive-green with vertical black stripes. Has a large spiny dorsal fin with a sting. Good eating quality although bony. Fillet and poach in court bouillon; then remove skin and scales. Alternatively, fillet, skin, and cook *à la meunière.*

Pike

A large, fierce fresh-water fish. Medium-sized fish of up to 3kg are best for cooking. Gut and remove the head, tail, and fins; then soak for 5–6 hours in salt water. Rinse in vinegar before poaching in court bouillon or fish stock. The flesh breaks easily, making it good for quenelles (p83). Alternatively, grill long fillets with bacon.

Plaice

Easily recognized flat fish with dark coloured upperside dotted with orange spots. Widely available as whole fish or fillets, wet or frozen; when frozen, plaice are often sold ready-prepared in breadcrumbs or sauced. In best condition from May to January. The flesh is white and distinctive in flavour; it should not be overcooked. Frozen prepared fish or fillets are suitable for deep or shallow frying, steaming or poaching, and for baked dishes with a sauce.

Salmon

For appearance and flavour, the salmon is the king of all fish. Its deep red flesh turns pink when cooked. Frozen Pacific salmon is less expensive than European fresh salmon, and with careful defrosting and cooking makes an attractive, more economical alternative. Poach salmon whole in court bouillon, cook *en papillote*; poach, grill or fry steaks or cutlets cut across the fish.

Smoked salmon is the cold smoked fillet or flank of the fish, either Atlantic or Pacific, the latter being cheaper. Slice very thinly and serve with lemon wedges, Cayenne pepper, and brown bread and butter. Alternatively, form thicker slices into cornets and secure with cocktail sticks, if necessary. Smoked salmon can also be served on canapés.

Canned salmon, containing Pacific fish, is a useful standby, but because the fish is already cooked, its culinary uses are restricted.

Salmon Trout (Sea Trout)
Since it has the colour of salmon and the texture of trout, the salmon trout has the attributes of both fish, and can truly be called the finest fresh-water fish. At its best in spring and summer, and available from most good fishmongers. When *rainbow trout* (see trout) are sea-farmed and fed on shellfish, the flesh turns pink, making an acceptable, cheaper alternative to true salmon trout.

Sardines
Fresh sardines make a stylish first course when grilled or floured and shallow fried. There is no need to gut or head the fish. Cook through and serve 4–5 fish per person with lemon wedges.

Canned small sardines in oil from Spain, Portugal or France are a delicacy in their own right. The best quality packs use good olive oil, and the sardines are allowed to mature in the can. Serve with lemon and a crisp green salad or as part of a mixed hors d'oeuvre platter.

Skate
Only the wings are eaten, the best part being the fleshier centre cut. The flesh is firm and delicate with a simple, soft bone formation. It is available everywhere from fishmongers. Portions of the wing can be deep or shallow fried, or used in the classic Skate in Black Butter (p85).

Sole (Dover)
The finest flat fish of all. The 'tear drop' shape of this fish differentiates it from distant relations like *lemon sole*. Available everywhere, wet or frozen, but always relatively expensive. Has firm white flesh, with a succulent flavour, easy to separate from bones. Remove the dark skin; then grill, cook *à la meunière*, or use in any of the recipes on pp86–87.

Sole (Lemon)
Widely available wet and frozen, comes between Dover sole and plaice in flesh, texture, and flavour, and is a pleasant alternative to either. Fry or poach fillets, or cook whole to retain the natural juices.

Sprats
Bright little silvery fish widely available during the winter months. Can be grilled, deep-fried or home-smoked. Allow 500g for 3 portions. Cut off the head and split the fish by running the thumbnail down the belly to the tail. Open out and pull the backbone out starting at the head end.

Commercially smoked sprats are also available and make a good first course.

Brisling are small sprats canned and ready to serve in the same way as sardines.

Trout (Rainbow)

With the advance of modern fish farming, trout is now as popular as some of the better-known sea fish. It can be cooked plainly *à la meunière*, yet also lends itself well to more elaborate cooking and to various sauces. Gut and remove the gills before cooking. Grilled, baked (especially *en papillote*), poached, or fried *à la meunière*, the fish is easy to bone, and with good presentation adds style to any meal.

Turbot

A large flat fish, available most of the year. Rated next to Dover sole for quality of flesh. Large fish must be sliced into cutlets, but the smaller (chicken turbot) fish can be foil-wrapped and cooked whole with butter and seasoning. Serve with a savoury herb butter or a shrimp sauce, or serve grilled cutlets with Maître d'Hôtel butter (p232) or Béarnaise sauce (p214).

Whitebait

These are the fry (young fish) of herring and sprats. Certainly the smallest fish eaten, but with a long gastronomic history and always a fashionable dish. Caught in several large estuaries round British coasts, the bulk of the catch is now frozen because the little fish deteriorate quickly. They should be floured and deep fried whole.

Whiting

Another member of the great cod family. The flesh is white, flaky, very soft, and tender. Available everywhere, the gutted and headed fish can be egg and bread-crumbed before frying. Opened and with the backbone removed, the whiting can be grilled or poached in milk with seasoning and is an easily digested dish suitable for invalids.

Blue whiting are slimmer and less well fleshed than the true whiting; these fish are caught in deep water. The flesh is darker though quite pleasant when cooked. Cut off the head, gut, and skin; then fry. As the fish are small, allow 2–3 per portion.

Types of Shellfish

Cockle

Rarely sold uncooked. However, if supplies are available, keep alive for 24 hours in sea water to clear sand from the intestine, and wash in several changes of water; then boil in salt water for 5–6 minutes until the shells open. Cool, and discard the shells; eat with salad or in a mixed fish dish.

Shelled cockle meat is quite widely available loose or in frozen packs, and canned or bottled. Fresh or frozen cockles are better than canned or bottled ones for cooked dishes because they are vinegar-free. Wash well before cooking to remove any particles of grit.

Crab

Available live, cooked or as frozen crabmeat, crabs are plentiful. Choose a crab by weight rather than size, and if bought ready-cooked make sure that the shell is fresh and dry, and the legs and claws tight against the body.

British crabs produce white meat from the claws and legs and spicy brown meat from inside the main shell. Frozen or canned crab packs usually contain foreign *Pacific King* crab or the smaller *Atlantic Queen* crab. Both are closer to spider crabs which have large legs containing good white meat, but have very little meat in the body.

Crabmeat has many uses from conventional salad dishes to seafood flans, stuffings, and soups. The brown meat (the liver and roe) of the female is particularly good as a flavouring for sauces or savoury butters.

To cook a live crab: Choose a good-sized heavy crab and kill it either by piercing it through the shell above the mouth, or by drowning it in tepid fresh water for 2 hours. It is wise to kill the crab before boiling it to prevent water entering the body.

Place in a large pan of boiling water containing 2 × 15ml spoons of salt per litre. Boil for 3 minutes, then lower the heat and simmer for a further 25 minutes; remove and leave to cool.

To pick and dress a cooked crab: Turn the crab on its back. Male crabs have a slim flap on the underside, the females have a broader one. Twist off the legs and claws. Press firmly on the 'crown' where the legs join the body, and remove in one piece. Discard the grey finger-like gills and pick out the meat. Remove the meat from the main shell, keeping dark meat and pink coral separate from the white meat. Crack the claws and legs with nutcrackers or a clean hammer, and pick out the white meat. The crab should give 25–30% of its total cooked weight in meat; males usually give more white meat.

Scrub and dry the main shell inside and out, and break off the undershell to the dark line around the perimeter. Flake the white meat from the legs and claws. Cream together the darker meat, liver and coral, and add 2 × 15ml spoons of fresh brown breadcrumbs and a little seasoning. Mix thoroughly and fill both ends of the shell. Place the white meat in the centre.

Lobster

Available all year round, the most popular sizes range between 500g and 1.5kg in weight. When live they should feel heavy for their size and be lively when picked up. The dark shells turn bright red on being cooked; if buying a ready-cooked lobster look for a dry, firm shell and tightly curled tail. Lobsters are often dressed and eaten cold with mayonnaise, but there are also many superb hot lobster dishes; many of them call for the meat to be prepared, then returned to the shell for presentation.

To boil a lobster: There are several methods of cooking a live lobster. The simplest is to half-fill a suitably sized pan with salt water (2 × 15ml spoons salt per litre), bring the water to the boil and drop the lobster in quickly. Place a lid on the pan and weight it down; then lower the heat to keep the water just under boiling point. Cook for 15–20 minutes, depending on the lobster's size.

An alternative method is to put the live lobster into cool, salted water or court bouillon, and bring to the boil, then to cook as described. Perhaps a less harrowing method is to drown the lobster by leaving it in tepid fresh water for 2–3 hours before cooking.

After cooking, allow the lobster to cool, then place on a cutting board with the tail spread behind. Take a large, sharp, broad-bladed knife and insert the point in the

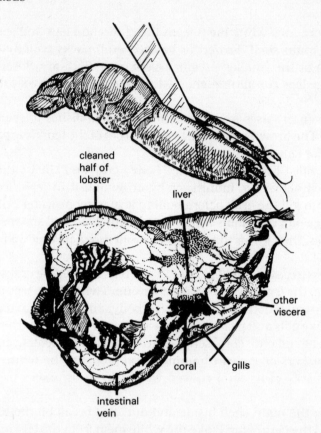

cleaned
half of
lobster

liver

other
viscera

coral   gills

intestinal
vein

middle of the head. Lower the blade of the knife and cut through the shell, along the centre line, splitting the shellfish into 2 equal parts. Pull out the intestinal tract that runs from the head to the tail and clear out the head cavity. Remove the sponge-like gills also. The dark, mustard-coloured meat is the liver and is good for flavouring sauces. The pink coral sometimes found in the female is also valuable for lobster butter, a luxurious accompaniment for grilled fish.

To dress a lobster to eat cold: Place the half lobster, cut side up, on a suitable plate. Crack the claws and arrange them round the half-shell. (Offer a suitable thin fork or lobster pick to get all the meat out of them.) Garnish the half lobster by filling the head cavity with Russian salad (p23) and serve chilled with mayonnaise and salad. A half lobster is generally thought enough for a single portion as a first course.

Mussels

These under-valued, black bivalve molluscs are abundant around northern European coastlines. If you collect them personally, make sure that it is in a pure water area. They are of better quality when there is an 'R' in the month. Mussels are farmed commercially in carefully selected sea-water areas. Buy from a reliable dealer, and make sure that the mussels have tightly closed shells. This shows that they are alive. Mussel meat can also be bought frozen, bottled or canned; the frozen ones are better for cooked and mixed seafood dishes since they have not been preserved in salt or vinegar. When adding any cooked shellfish, but particularly mussels, to a recipe, cook for as short a time as possible, to avoid making them tough.

To prepare mussels: Wash the mussels in several changes of clean water; then scrape off the byssus threads (the beard), found near the hinge of the two shells, using a sharp knife. These threads are the anchors which hold the shellfish to the rocks. Check again that each mussel is tightly shut before cooking. For the basic cooking, follow the Moules Marinière recipe (p89) as it produces a valuable bonus of delicious mussel liquor.

Prawns

For cocktails, salads, and cold dishes, shell-on or peeled cold-water prawns are best. The warm-water prawns are more suitable for cooked dishes and curries, and are usually cheaper.

Nearly all prawns sold in Britain, whether shell-on or peeled, are imported ready-cooked; they are sold widely, fresh or in frozen packs. Always allow a reasonable defrosting time; never defrost quickly in water. The best method is to sprinkle the prawns lightly with salt and then to defrost them on a plate overnight in a refrigerator.

Both shell-on and peeled prawns are used in a great many recipes for cooked and cold dishes, and garnishes.

King Prawns: These larger prawns come from various warm water fishing areas round the world. All supplies in Britain are frozen raw, headless, but with the shells. Packs of 1kg contain 16–20 prawns, depending on size. King prawns should be marinated before cooking, and their size and texture then make them well suited to grilling or barbecuing. If the prawns are wanted for a cold dish, poach in fish stock and allow to cool in the liquid. Chill well before serving.

Crystal Prawns: These come from Middle East or Far East fishing grounds. The large whole prawns are sold ready-cooked, and are pink to orange in colour. Defrost overnight in a refrigerator.

Scallops

When buying scallops on the half shell, always ask for the deep shells to hold the many 'scalloped' cooked fish dishes, for example the well-known Coquilles St Jacques (p90).

Large scallops can be bought frozen all year round, but fresh only from November to March. The scallop is very tender, with a high natural liquid content, and great care should be taken when cooking. Just let the shellfish turn from translucent to solid white over a low heat in a little white wine or seasoned milk; if they must be heated in a sauce, add them at the last possible moment to prevent toughening and shrinkage.

Queen Scallops: These smaller versions are usually sold shelled and frozen. Cook in the same way as larger scallops, using minimal heat. Queen scallops are excellent dipped in batter or egg and breadcrumbs, and briefly deep fried.

Scampi

These are often referred to as Dublin Bay Prawns. They are closely related to lobster and crawfish, but do not change colour when cooked. Widely distributed from Iceland to the Mediterranean, they are popular everywhere.

Scampi (from Italian *scampo*) is, properly, the term for the tail meat from shellfish de-headed at sea, and is most often fried. However, the whole shellfish can be poached, and then served cold or grilled.

Scampi flesh is sweet and tender, but deteriorates quickly, so most supplies are frozen. Like scallops, scampi should be cooked briefly. In dishes using a sauce, the defrosted shellfish should be added at the last moment to prevent overcooking.

Shrimps

Smaller and rounder-bodied than prawns, shrimps are caught in shallow sandy water and turn from grey to pinkish-brown when cooked in salted water. They must be boiled alive to have the characteristic springy curled shape.

Peeled shrimps have a particularly good and sweet shellfish flavour, and are used in mixed sea-food dishes, as stuffings or fillings, in sauces, and as a garnish.

Fresh shell-on shrimps are widely available and so are frozen and potted shrimps.

Pink Shrimps: These are smaller relatives of a certain type of prawn. They are slim in body like cold-water prawns but the size of brown shrimps. They are caught in the same areas, and turn pink when boiled. Very colourful for display. Use like brown shrimps.

Squid (Ink Fish, Calamares)

Before cooking, cut off the heads (eyes) and tentacles, remove the transparent central 'bone' and pull out the dark coloured ink sac at the same time. Wash and pull off any visible outer skin.

Squid is well suited to stuffing; it is also good thinly sliced (body and tentacles), coated, and deep fried. Alternatively, slice and poach in a little white wine or seasoned milk, chill and mix with peeled prawns, cockles, mussels, and white crabmeat as a seafood salad.

Whelks and Winkles

Whelks are boiled in salt water and shelled before sale. The firm, cream-coloured flesh can be eaten with vinegar or in a mixed seafood hors d'oeuvre. It can also be minced or diced for adding to stuffings, sauces, and soups.

The whelk and winkle are the only shellfish which need steady boiling in salted water for 5–10 minutes. Wash in several changes of fresh water beforehand, and allow the shellfish to cool in the boiling liquid.

The winkle has a flat black cover to the shell opening and this should be discarded before removing the shellfish entire with a pin or needle. They can make an interesting contribution to a mixed shellfish platter.

Basic Recipes for Cooking Fish

In the following recipes the fish are assumed to be gutted and filleted where required.

Court Bouillon (for salmon, salmon trout, and other whole fish)

water
500ml dry white wine **or** dry cider to
   each litre water
2 × 15ml spoons white wine vinegar to
   each litre water
2 large carrots

2 large onions
2–3 sticks celery
parsley stalks
1 bouquet garni to each litre water
a few peppercorns
salt and pepper

Put the liquids in a large pan. Slice the carrots and onions, chop the celery, and crush the parsley stalks. Add to the liquid with the remaining ingredients. Simmer for 30 minutes, leave to cool, then strain and use as required.

Basic Recipe for Grilling Fish

fish fillets
salt and pepper
1 × 5ml spoon chopped gherkins
   (optional)
1 × 5ml spoon chopped capers
   (optional)

2 × 10ml spoons salad oil
1 × 10ml spoon white wine vinegar **or**
   lemon juice

Garnish
chopped parsley

Remove the rack of the grill pan. Wipe the fish and season it with salt and pepper. Mix the gherkins and capers, if used, with the oil and vinegar. Heat the grill to give a medium cooking heat. Snip or slash the skin of the fish to prevent curling, if necessary. Lay it in the bottom of the grill pan, skin side up. Pour most of the liquid mixture over it. Grill, basting frequently. Turn the fish over and pour the remaining liquid over it. Grill for about another 5 minutes. Calculate the total grilling time from the table on p64. Sprinkle with chopped parsley and serve immediately.

Note Use gherkins and capers for fairly large thick fillets and for most river fish. Thin, delicately flavoured fillets can be grilled with just a sprinkling of lemon juice instead of vinegar.

Basic Recipe for Poaching Fish

1 small whole fish **or** fillets
juice of ½ lemon

court bouillon (p75)

Garnish
lemon wedges

parsley sprigs

Allow 100–150g fish for each helping. Clean a whole fish inside, rinse the cavity and wipe both inside and outside dry. Cut off the fins. Wipe fillets, if used. Sprinkle the fish or fillets with a little lemon juice.

Put the fish into a large, deep frying pan, and add enough court bouillon to cover 1–2cm of the pan depth when the fish is in it. Cover with a spatterproof lid or a plate, and poach gently, with the liquid barely shivering. Calculate the cooking time from the table on p65. Lift out the cooked fish gently with a broad slice, drain, and slide it on to a warmed serving dish. Garnish with lemon wedges and parsley sprigs.

Steaming Fish

This is a good way to cook fish without fat, yet without making it too moist. It also avoids any risk of overcooking small thin fillets. It is useful for those on a light diet, or for precooking fish which will be finished in a sauce or served cold.

Take a plate which fits neatly on top of a saucepan, half fill the pan with water and heat until it boils; then reduce the heat so that the water only simmers. Place the plate on the saucepan and, if wished, warm a knob of butter on the plate until it melts, and add just a little water, wine, milk or lemon juice. Add any seasoning required; then put the prepared fish fillet on the plate and cover with another plate. See the table on p65 for cooking times. Serve with a little of the liquid.

Basic Recipe for Baking Fish

1 whole fish
salt and pepper
butter for greasing

water **or** fish stock (p26) (optional)
50g butter

Wash the cleaned fish inside and out and pat dry. Season with salt and pepper and place in a well-greased baking dish. Add enough water or stock to cover 5mm of the dish, if desired. Dot with small pieces of butter. Cover loosely with greased paper and bake in a fairly hot oven at 190°C, Gas 5. Calculate the cooking time from the table on p64.

Basic Recipe for Deep Frying Fish in Batter

fish fillets
flour for coating

salt and pepper
oil **or** fat for deep frying

Batter
100g plain flour
$\frac{1}{2} \times 2.5$ml spoon salt

1 egg
125ml milk

Make the batter first. Sift the flour and salt into a bowl. Make a well in the centre of the flour and add the egg and a little of the milk. Gradually work in the flour from the sides, then beat until smooth. Stir in the rest of the milk.

Cut the fish into serving portions, if required; the pieces should all be of a similar size. Season the flour with salt and pepper. Dry the pieces of fish well and coat in the flour. Stir the batter well and dip the pieces of fish into it. Heat the oil or fat (p10) and fry until golden-brown. Drain on soft kitchen paper and serve immediately.
Note Do not use a basket when frying fish in batter as it will stick. Use a perforated spoon or broad slice to lift it out.

For Fish and Chips use the basic recipe above with any suitable fish, eg cod, haddock or plaice, and the recipe for potato chips on p261.

Basic Recipe for Shallow Frying Fish

small whole fish **or** fish fillets
flour for coating
salt and pepper

1 egg
dry white breadcrumbs for coating
fat for shallow frying

Garnish
lemon wedges

Cut the fish into serving portions, if required. Season the flour with salt and pepper and beat the egg lightly. Coat the fish with flour, then dip in the egg, and coat with breadcrumbs. Heat the fat in a frying pan and fry the fish, turning once, for the time given in the table on p64, until the coating is golden-brown. Serve immediately with lemon wedges.
Note Fry the flesh side of fillets first, and the skin side afterwards.

Basic Recipe for Frying Fish (à la meunière)

small whole fish **or** fish fillets
flour for coating
salt and pepper

50g butter
1×10ml spoon chopped parsley
juice of $\frac{1}{2}$ lemon

Trim off the fins if necessary, rinse the fish, and dry well with soft kitchen paper. Season the flour with salt and pepper and coat the fish with the flour. Heat the butter in a frying pan. When foaming, place the fish in the pan. Cook gently for the time given in the table on p64, turning once. When the fish is golden-brown and cooked through, arrange on a serving dish and keep hot. Season the butter left in the pan and heat until it is nut-brown. Add the parsley and lemon juice, pour over the fish, and serve at once.

Recipes for Sea and River Fish

Brill and Potato Mornay
6 helpings

800g potatoes
75g butter
600g brill fillets
salt and pepper

juice of 1 lemon
500ml cheese sauce (p201)
50g Cheddar cheese

Boil the potatoes in their skins and keep them hot. Use a little of the butter to grease a shallow oven-to-table baking dish and a sheet of greaseproof paper. Lay the fish in the buttered dish, season with salt and pepper, dot with butter, and sprinkle with lemon juice. Cover the dish with the sheet of buttered greaseproof paper and bake in a moderate oven at 180°C, Gas 4, for 15 minutes. Meanwhile, make the cheese sauce. Peel the potatoes, cut into rounds, and cover the fish with them in a neat pattern. Pour the cheese sauce over the fish, then grate the cheese, and sprinkle it evenly on top. Brown under the grill.

Golden Grilled Cod
4 helpings

4 cod cutlets **or** steaks (2cm thick
    approx)

margarine for greasing

Topping
50g mild Cheddar **or** Gruyère cheese
25g soft margarine

2 × 15ml spoons milk (optional)
salt and pepper

Garnish
grilled tomatoes

watercress sprigs

Trim and rinse the fish and pat dry. Place the fish in a greased shallow flameproof dish and grill under moderate heat for 2–3 minutes on one side only. Meanwhile, grate the cheese and cream the margarine with it. Work in the milk, a few drops at a time, if used, and season to taste.

Turn the fish over, spread the topping on the uncooked side, and return to the grill. Reduce the heat slightly and cook for 10–12 minutes until the fish is cooked through and the topping is golden-brown. Serve garnished with grilled halved tomatoes and watercress sprigs.

Cod à la Maître d'Hôtel
5–6 helpings

800g cod fillets (cold leftovers can be
used)
100g butter
2 × 15ml spoons chopped onion

1 × 15ml spoon chopped parsley
juice of ½ lemon
salt and pepper

Poach the cod if required, and remove the skin when cool. Separate the flesh into large flakes. Melt the butter in a saucepan, add the onion, and fry for 2–3 minutes without browning. Add the fish and sprinkle it with the chopped parsley, lemon juice, and a good pinch of salt and pepper. Cook over low heat for 5 minutes, stirring gently all the time.

Serve with boiled potatoes.

Fish Mousse
4 helpings

50g onion
1 celery stick
250ml milk
1 bay leaf
3–4 peppercorns
500g haddock **or** cod fillets
25g butter

25g flour
grated rind and juice of ½ lemon
1 × 15ml spoon chopped parsley
salt and pepper
1 × 10ml spoon gelatine
2 × 15ml spoons water
125ml double cream

Garnish
125ml aspic jelly
watercress leaves

thin strips of lemon rind

Slice the onion and celery thickly. Put into a pan with the milk, bay leaf, peppercorns and fish. Bring to the boil slowly, cover, and draw off the heat for 10 minutes. Lift out the fish, remove any skin or bones, and flake the flesh. Strain the milk.

Melt the butter, stir in the flour, and cook for 1–2 minutes. Add the flavoured milk gradually. Bring to the boil and cook for 1–2 minutes, stirring all the time. Remove from the heat and stir in the flaked fish, lemon rind and juice, chopped parsley, and a generous amount of salt and pepper.

Soften the gelatine in the water in a small heatproof basin. Stand the basin in a pan of hot water and stir until it has dissolved. Add a little of the fish mixture, stir, then mix into the rest. Stir in well. Put in a cool place.

When it is on the point of setting, whip the cream until it forms soft peaks and fold in until evenly distributed. Put into an 800ml dish, level the top, and chill until set.

Spoon sufficient liquid aspic jelly on to the mousse to cover it by 2mm. When the aspic has set, arrange the watercress and lemon rind cut into shapes on top, and spoon over enough liquid jelly to cover the garnish. Leave to set.

Note Fish mousses can be made more piquant by substituting 100ml home-made mayonnaise (p222) for the double cream and adding 2 × 15ml spoons double cream, lightly whipped.

Fish Cakes
4 helpings

300g cooked white fish (cod, haddock, coley, etc)
500g cold boiled potatoes
25g butter
2 × 15ml spoons cream

1 × 15ml spoon finely chopped parsley
salt and pepper
flour for coating
fat for shallow frying

Flake the fish and remove all the bones. Mash the potatoes until smooth, and mix in the butter and cream. Add the flaked fish and parsley, and season to taste. Divide the mixture into 8 portions, and shape into flat, round cakes. Season the flour, and dip each cake in it. Shallow fry in butter or oil for 6–8 minutes, turning once.

VARIATION

Instead of coating with flour, dip each cake in beaten egg, coat in breadcrumbs, and deep fry (p10) until crisp and golden-brown.

Kedgeree
4 helpings

150g long-grain rice
400g smoked haddock
100ml milk
100ml water
50g butter

1 × 15ml spoon curry powder
salt and pepper
Cayenne pepper
2 hard-boiled eggs

Garnish
1 × 15ml spoon chopped parsley

butter

Boil the rice for 12 minutes and drain thoroughly. Keep warm. Poach the haddock in equal quantities of milk and water in a covered pan for 4 minutes. Remove from the pan and drain. Remove the skin and tail, and break up the fish into fairly large flakes. Melt half the butter in a saucepan. Blend in the curry powder and add the flaked fish. Warm the mixture through. Warm the rice in the rest of the butter. Season both the fish mixture and the rice with salt, pepper, and a few grains of Cayenne pepper. Chop the hard-boiled eggs coarsely. Add them to the fish and combine the mixture with the rice. Pile on a heated dish and sprinkle with chopped parsley. Dot with butter and serve immediately.

Cooking time 25 minutes (approx)

Hake with Sweet and Sour Sauce
3–4 helpings

400g hake fillets
1 green pepper

cornflour for coating
oil for deep frying

Marinade
2 spring onions
1 × 15ml spoon medium-dry sherry

2 × 15ml spoons soy sauce
1 × 15ml spoon chopped ginger root

Sauce
6 × 15ml spoons pineapple juice
2 × 5ml spoons cornflour
2 × 15ml spoons soy sauce
1 × 15ml spoon medium-dry sherry

1 × 5ml spoon white wine **or** malt
  vinegar
1 × 5ml spoon cooking oil
1 × 227g can pineapple pieces

Skin the fillets if necessary. Cut the fish into 2cm cubes. Chop the spring onions. Mix together the sherry, soy sauce, ginger, and spring onions; marinate the fish in this mixture for 1–2 hours. De-seed and chop the green pepper finely.

Make the sauce. Mix the pineapple juice with the cornflour. When blended, add all the other sauce ingredients except the pineapple pieces. Bring to the boil, stirring all the time, reduce the heat, and simmer for 3 minutes.

Drain the fish and roll in cornflour. Heat the oil (p10) and fry the fish until well and evenly browned. Dry the fish with soft kitchen paper. Place in a warmed serving dish and sprinkle with the chopped green pepper. Add the pineapple pieces to the sauce, heat through, and pour the sauce over the fish.

Scalloped Halibut
4 helpings

butter for greasing
100g Gruyère cheese
250ml Mornay sauce (p208)
100g mushrooms
400g halibut

500ml court bouillon (p75)
400g soft white breadcrumbs
400g creamed potato
25g butter

Grease lightly 4 deep scallop shells or other suitable oven-to-table individual dishes. Grate the cheese and add half to the Mornay sauce. Clean and slice the mushrooms. Poach the fish in the court bouillon for 10 minutes, add the mushrooms for the last 5 minutes. Leave to cool; then remove the bones from the fish and flake the flesh. Divide the fish and mushrooms between the shells or dishes and cover with the sauce. Mix together the remaining cheese and breadcrumbs and sprinkle over the dishes. Pipe the creamed potato around the rims. Dot with the butter and bake in a fairly hot oven at 190°C, Gas 5, for 15–20 minutes.

Herrings with Mustard Sauce
4 helpings

4 herrings
2 × 5ml spoons lemon juice
salt and pepper
1 × 10ml spoon dry mustard
2 egg yolks

50g butter
2 × 15ml spoons double cream
1 × 15ml spoon chopped capers
1 × 15ml spoon chopped gherkin

Scale the herrings, cut off the heads, and bone the fish. Sprinkle the flesh with lemon juice and season well. Grill, using moderate heat, for 3–5 minutes on each side. Keep hot. Put the dry mustard and egg yolks in a basin and whisk over a pan of hot water until creamy. Divide the butter into small pieces, and whisk into the sauce one by one. When the sauce thickens, remove from the heat and stir in the cream. Add the finely chopped capers and gherkin. Season well. Serve the sauce hot with the herrings.

Jugged or Poached Kippers
4 helpings

4 kippers

Garnish (optional)
4 pats chilled Maître d'Hôtel butter
  (p232)

Put the kippers, tail end up, in a tall, heatproof jug. Pour boiling water over the whole fish except the tails. Cover the jug with a cloth, and leave to stand for 5 minutes. Tilt the jug gently over a sink, and drain off the water. Do not try to pull the kippers out by their tails. Serve them on warmed plates, topped with pats of Maître d'Hôtel butter, if liked.

Grilled Kippers
4 helpings

4 kippers

4 × 5ml spoons butter **or** margarine

Garnish
4 pats chilled butter

chopped parsley

Lay the kippers flat, skin side up, on the grill pan base (not on the rack). Grill under medium heat for 3 minutes. Turn, dot each kipper with 1 × 5ml spoon butter or margarine, and grill for another 3 minutes. Serve on warmed plates, topped with pats of chilled butter and sprinkled with parsley.

Mackerel with Gooseberry Sauce
4 helpings

flour for coating
salt and pepper
8 mackerel fillets

50g butter
25g parsley (approx)
juice of 1 lemon

Sauce
400g gooseberries
50ml dry still cider

25g butter
1 × 15ml spoon caster sugar

Make the sauce first. Wash and prepare the gooseberries, and poach in the cider and butter until tender. Sieve to make a smooth purée. Add the sugar. Put into a saucepan and put to one side.

Meanwhile, season the flour with salt and pepper. Dip the fish fillets in the flour. Heat the butter in a frying pan and fry the fillets gently for 5–7 minutes, turning once. Remove them, arrange on a serving plate and keep hot. Reserve the butter in the pan. Chop the parsley.

Heat the gooseberry sauce and keep hot. Add the remaining butter to the pan, and heat until light brown. Add the lemon juice and chopped parsley, and pour this over the fish.

Serve the gooseberry sauce separately.

Pike Quenelles (Quenelles de Brochet)
4–6 helpings

400g pike fillets
4–5 egg whites
500ml double cream

salt and pepper
a pinch of grated nutmeg
1 litre court bouillon (p75)

Skin the fillets if necessary. Dice the fish finely, add the egg whites, and process in an electric blender to a smooth purée. Rub the mixture through a sieve. Whip the cream to the same consistency as the fish purée. Fold it in lightly but thoroughly. Season the mixture with salt, pepper and nutmeg, and chill in the refrigerator for several hours.

Heat the court bouillon until just simmering. Shape the chilled fish mixture into quenelles with warmed rounded dessertspoons, and gently lower into the liquid. Simmer for 8–10 minutes. Drain with a perforated spoon.

Serve immediately with 500ml of either hot Aurora (p208) or Mushroom (p202) Sauce.

Plaice Portugaise
4 helpings

2 shallots	butter for greasing
300g tomatoes	8 plaice fillets (75g each approx)
25g butter	100ml medium-dry white wine
100g button mushrooms	salt and pepper

Skin and slice the shallots. Skin, de-seed, and chop the tomatoes and fry in the butter with the shallots. Add the mushrooms and heat gently for 4–5 minutes. Pour into a buttered oven-to-table baking dish. Fold each fillet into three, skin side in, and lay on the tomato mixture. Pour over the wine, season, and cover loosely. Bake in a fairly hot oven at 190°C, Gas 5, for 25 minutes. Bast the fish with the mixture before serving.

Goujons of Plaice
6 helpings

12 plaice fillets (100g each approx)	100ml milk
flour for coating	oil **or** fat for deep frying
salt and pepper	

Garnish

fried parsley (p56)	lemon wedges

Cut the fillets lengthways into short strips 3–4cms wide. Season the flour with salt and pepper. Dip the fish in the milk and coat with the flour, shaking off any excess. Heat the oil (p10) and fry the strips until golden-brown. Serve hot on a dish, garnish with fried parsley and lemon wedges, and serve with Tartare Sauce (p209).

Stuffed Whole Plaice
4 helpings

4 small plaice (300g each approx)	25g butter

Stuffing

100g mild Cheddar cheese	1 × 10ml spoon mixed dried herbs
50g soft white breadcrumbs	juice of ½ lemon
1 × 5ml spoon dry mustard	2 × 15ml spoons beaten egg
salt and pepper	

Garnish

lemon wedges	parsley sprigs

Make a cut down the centre of the entire length of the fish as for filleting. Loosen the flesh from the bone on each side of the cut, but do not detach it. Make the stuffing. Grate the cheese and mix with the crumbs, together with the mustard, seasoning, herbs, lemon juice, and beaten egg. Raise the 2 loose flaps of the fish and fill the pockets with the stuffing. Place the fish in a buttered oven-to-table baking dish, dot with the rest of the butter, and cover loosely with foil. Bake in a fairly hot oven at 190°C, Gas 5, for 20–30 minutes. Garnish with lemon wedges and parsley sprigs.

Grilled Salmon Steaks

clarified butter (p232) for brushing   salt and pepper
1 salmon steak per person (150–200g
    each approx)

Garnish
Maître d'Hôtel butter (p232)

Melt the butter. Season each salmon steak well with salt and pepper. Brush liberally
with melted butter. Grill, using moderate heat, for 4–5 minutes on each side, turning
once. Serve garnished with Maître d'Hôtel butter.

Poached Salmon

1 salmon (1.6–3.2kg)   3–4 litres (approx) court bouillon
                        (p75)

Weigh the fish to determine the cooking time (see p65), if it is to be served hot. Put
the fish into a fish kettle and pour over the court bouillon. Bring gently to the boil. If
the salmon is to be served cold, simmer for 5 minutes, then leave to cool in the
cooking liquid before draining. If the fish is to be served hot, bring the liquid to
boiling point, reduce the heat and simmer for the required time. Drain and skin.

Hot salmon can be served with Hollandaise Sauce (p217).

Cold salmon is served glazed with fish fumet or aspic jelly, and garnished with a
line of cucumber slices along each side of the fish.

Allow about 150g salmon per helping.

Skate in Black Butter
3–4 helpings

1–2 skate wings (800g approx)   2 × 15ml spoons capers
1 litre court bouillon (p75)   2 × 10ml spoons chopped parsley
25g butter   75ml wine vinegar
salt and pepper

Rinse and dry the skate and cut it into serving portions. Put the fish in a deep frying
pan and cover with the court bouillon. Bring to the boil, reduce the heat, cover, and
simmer for 15–20 minutes. Lift out the fish, drain on soft kitchen paper, and gently
scrape away the skin. Place in an ovenproof dish and keep hot.

To make the black butter, pour off the stock, put in the butter and heat until it is a
rich golden-brown colour. Spoon it quickly over the fish, season with salt and pepper, and scatter the capers and chopped parsley over the fish. Add the vinegar to the
pan, heat quickly, and pour over the dish. Serve immediately.

Fillets of Sole Bonne Femme
4 helpings

8 lemon sole fillets
butter for greasing
150g mushrooms
1 shallot
1 × 10ml spoon chopped parsley

salt and pepper
125ml dry white wine
125ml Velouté sauce (p211)
25g butter

Put the fish in a greased oven-to-table baking dish. Clean and slice the mushrooms. Skin and slice the shallot. Sprinkle them over the fish, add the parsley, and season well. Add the wine and cover the dish loosely with greased paper or foil. Bake in a moderate oven at 180°C, Gas 4, for 20 minutes.

Remove the fish and keep hot. Strain the liquid into a clean saucepan and boil it rapidly until reduced by half. Stir in the hot Velouté sauce and the butter. As soon as the butter has melted, pour the sauce over the fillets, and place under a hot grill until lightly browned. Serve at once.

Sole Colbert
6 helpings

6 Dover soles
2 eggs
100g flour
salt and pepper
soft white breadcrumbs

fat for deep frying
200g Maître d'Hôtel butter (p232)
2 × 5ml spoons finely chopped
 tarragon
2 × 15ml spoons meat glaze (p55)

Garnish
fried parsley (p56)

lemon wedges

Remove the dark skin of the fish. Cut down the backbone on the skinned side and slice under the flesh, following the bones to make a pocket on each side. Cut the backbone in 3 places with sharp scissors, to allow removal after cooking.

Beat the eggs until liquid. Season the flour with salt and pepper. Coat the fish with flour, then with egg and breadcrumbs. Heat the fat and deep fry the fish (p10) until golden-brown. Drain, then remove the bone where cut and arrange on a serving dish. Keep hot. Mix together the Maître d'Hôtel butter, tarragon, and meat glaze to make Colbert butter. Fill the pockets of the fish with the Colbert butter. Serve immediately, garnished with fried parsley and lemon wedges.

Sole Véronique
4 helpings

4 large lemon sole fillets
2 shallots
50g button mushrooms
parsley sprigs
1 bay leaf
salt and pepper
125ml dry white wine

125ml water
100g small white grapes
25g butter
2 × 15ml spoons flour
125ml milk
juice of $\frac{1}{2}$ lemon
2 × 15ml spoons single cream

Garnish
fleurons of puff pastry (p51)

chopped parsley

Lay the fillets in a shallow ovenproof dish. Skin and chop the shallots and clean and chop the mushrooms. Sprinkle them over the fish. Add the herbs, season well, and pour the wine and water over the dish. Cover and bake in a fairly hot oven at 190°C, Gas 5, for 15 minutes.

Meanwhile, peel and de-pip the grapes. Drain the fish, and keep it hot. Reserve the cooking liquid, and reduce it to half by boiling uncovered. Melt the butter and stir in the flour. Cook for 2–3 minutes without colouring. Add the cooking liquid and milk gradually, stirring all the time, and heat the sauce until it thickens. Stir in the grapes, saving a few to garnish the dish. Add the lemon juice and cream. Pour over the fish, garnish with the reserved grapes, the fleurons and parsley, and serve immediately.

Trout with Almonds
4 helpings

4 trout
100g butter
salt and pepper
juice of $\frac{1}{2}$ lemon

50g flaked blanched almonds
125ml double cream
3 egg yolks

Garnish
parsley sprigs

Clean the trout and remove the fins. Melt the butter in a grill pan under medium heat. Lay the trout in the pan, season, and sprinkle with lemon juice. Grill for 5 minutes, and then turn the fish. Sprinkle the trout with most of the almonds, spread the rest at the side of the pan, and continue grilling for a further 3–5 minutes until the trout are tender and the almonds are browned. Drain the trout and almonds on soft kitchen paper. Put the almonds to one side.

Mix the cream with the egg yolks and put into a small pan with any juices from the grill pan. Heat gently, stirring well, until thickened; do not let the mixture boil. Lay the trout on a serving dish, and spoon the cream sauce over them. Garnish with the reserved almonds and with parsley.

Recipes for Shellfish

Crab Au Gratin
4 helpings

400g white crabmeat
100g Gruyère cheese
25g butter
25g plain flour

250ml milk
salt and pepper
50g soft white breadcrumbs
grated Parmesan cheese

Garnish
2 sliced tomatoes

parsley sprigs

Flake the crabmeat. Grate the cheese. Make a roux with the butter and flour, add the milk gradually, and stir until the sauce thickens. Season well. Add the crabmeat and the Gruyère cheese and stir into the sauce. Re-season if required. Put the mixture into empty crab shells or an ovenproof dish, and sprinkle with the breadcrumbs and Parmesan cheese. Brown under the grill for 2–3 minutes. Garnish with slices of tomato and parsley sprigs.

Lobster Thermidor
4 helpings

2 shallots
3 × 15ml spoons butter
150ml dry white wine (approx)
1 × 5ml spoon chopped tarragon
1 × 5ml spoon chopped chervil
200ml Béchamel sauce (p207)

125ml double cream
2 × 15ml spoons French mustard
2 × 15ml spoons grated Parmesan
  cheese
salt and pepper
2 cooked lobsters (pp71–72)

Garnish
watercress sprigs

Skin and finely chop the shallots. Melt the butter and fry them gently until soft. Add the wine and herbs and boil, uncovered, until the liquid is reduced by half; then add the Béchamel sauce. Remove from the heat. Stir well, and mix in the cream, mustard, and half the cheese. Season well and put to one side.

Split the lobsters in half lengthways. Remove the meat from the claws and body and chop coarsely. Mix with most of the sauce, keeping a little sauce separate to complete the dish; return the sauced lobster meat to the shells. Place the shells on a flat dish, cut side up, and coat the surface of the shellfish with the remaining sauce. Sprinkle with the rest of the cheese and brown in a fairly hot oven at 200°C, Gas 6, for 10–15 minutes. Garnish with watercress sprigs and serve very hot.

Moules Marinière
4–6 helpings

1.6kg live mussels
1 onion
1 carrot
1 stick of celery
bouquet garni

125ml water
125ml white wine
25g butter
1 × 15ml spoon flour
pepper

Garnish
chopped parsley

Scrub and beard the mussels, making sure that all are tightly closed, and put them into a large pan. Peel and slice the vegetables and tuck them among the mussels with the bouquet garni. Pour the water and wine over the mussels and place over moderate heat. Leave until the liquid boils up over them. Shake the pan 2 or 3 times and draw to one side.

Blend the butter and flour together into a smooth beurre manié and put to one side. Strain the liquid from the pan of mussels, through muslin, into a smaller pan. Keep the mussels warm. Add the butter and flour mixture to the liquid in small pieces, whisking well. Heat until boiling, then season well with pepper. Put the mussels into a deep dish and pour the cooking liquid over them. Sprinkle with chopped parsley.

Serve with pieces of crusty bread.
Cooking time 10–15 minutes

Sweet and Sour Prawns
4 helpings

200g peeled prawns
1 × 15ml spoon medium-dry sherry
salt and pepper
2 onions
2 green peppers
2 × 15ml spoons oil

125ml chicken stock
1 × 227g can pineapple pieces
1 × 15ml spoon cornflour
2 × 15ml spoons soy sauce
125ml white wine vinegar
75g sugar

Garnish
unpeeled prawns

Marinate the prawns in the sherry for 30 minutes and season well. Skin the onions and de-seed the green peppers. Slice them into rings. Heat the oil in a saucepan and fry the onions and peppers gently until tender. Add the stock, and drain; then add the pineapple. Cover and cook for 3–5 minutes. Blend the cornflour, soy sauce, vinegar, and sugar together, and add to the mixture. Stir until thickened. Add the prawns, and cook for 1 minute.

Serve hot on boiled rice garnished with prawns.

Coquilles St Jacques Mornay
4 helpings

1 small onion
400g scallops
salt and pepper
1 bay leaf
50ml dry white wine
75ml water
juice of $\frac{1}{2}$ lemon
25g butter
25g flour

125ml milk
75ml single cream
butter for greasing
200g mashed potatoes
3 × 15ml spoons dry white
  breadcrumbs
4 × 15ml spoons grated Parmesan
  cheese

Skin and slice the onion. Wash the scallops and place in a pan with the sliced onion, seasoning, and bay leaf. Pour the wine, water, and lemon juice over them. Poach gently for 5 minutes. Strain off the liquid and put to one side with the scallops.

Melt the butter in a pan, then stir in the flour. Blend in the liquid strained from the scallops, and stir over gentle heat until the sauce starts to thicken. Add the milk and simmer for 2–3 minutes. Stir in the cream. Slice the scallops and divide between 4 lightly greased scallop shells or suitable small flameproof dishes. Coat with the sauce. Pipe the mashed potato around the edge of each shell. Sprinkle lightly with the breadcrumbs and Parmesan cheese. Bake in a fairly hot oven at 200°C, Gas 6, for 10–15 minutes.

Fried Scampi
2 helpings

flour for coating
salt and pepper

225g peeled scampi
oil **or** fat for deep frying

Batter
1 egg
100g plain flour
salt

1 × 15ml spoon cooking oil
2–3 × 15ml spoons milk

Garnish
lemon wedges

Season the flour with salt and pepper in a plastic bag and toss the scampi in the flour. Separate the egg. Mix the flour, salt, oil, egg yolk, and milk to a stiff batter. Just before cooking, whisk the egg white until stiff and fold it into the batter. Heat the oil (p10). Dip the scampi in the batter and fry, a few at a time, until golden-brown. Drain, and serve garnished with lemon wedges.

Offer Tartare Sauce (p209) separately.

MEAT

Methods of Cooking Meat

Roasting

Method 1 – Quick roasting: The meat is cooked in a very hot oven, 230°C, Gas 8, for about 10 minutes to sear or brown the outside of the meat and seal in the juices. The temperature is then reduced to fairly hot, 190°C, Gas 5, to finish the cooking. (See Meat Roasting Chart on page 92.) This method preserves the full flavour of prime joints. However, it is not very suitable for a small joint because it will shrink.

Method 2 – Slow roasting: The meat is cooked in a warm or moderate oven, 160°–180°C, Gas 3–4, for a longer time. (See Meat Roasting Chart on page 92.) This method is best suited to the poorer quality roasting joints and small joints, since it causes less shrinkage and provides a more tender joint.

Whichever roasting method is used, any joint must be weighed in order to calculate its cooking time. Both its size and shape influence this also. The larger the joint, the shorter the time per kg; joints on the bone cook faster than boned ones because the bone conducts heat more quickly than muscle fibres. Roasting in foil also affects the cooking time (see below).

The cooking times given in the Meat Roasting Chart are, therefore, only approximate. If you roast varied types of joints, it is worth investing in a meat thermometer which registers the internal temperature of the meat and takes a great deal of the guesswork out of roasting times. The meat thermometer should be inserted into the thickest part of the meat before it is cooked, taking care that it does not touch bone or fat as they will affect the reading. When the right temperature is reached, the joint is cooked. A meat thermometer is particularly useful for calculating the cooking time for beef according to whether you want the meat to be lightly cooked, still pink inside (known as 'rare'), or fully cooked ('well-done').

Where a meat thermometer is not available, a good indication of readiness is the colour of the juice which seeps out of the meat when a skewer is pushed into the centre and withdrawn. The juice from a well-done joint or piece of meat will be colourless, juice from a rare joint will be pinkish-red, and there will be various shades of pink in between.

Joints for roasting should be placed, fat side up, on a wire rack in a shallow roasting tin. If the outside covering of fat varies in thickness, then the thickest part should be uppermost. A rib, cooked on the bone, should be prepared by the butcher so that it will stand upright. A rolled piece of beef should be slightly flattened on one side so that it will stand level. It is advisable to rub a lean joint with dripping or lard before putting it in the oven. Place the roasting tin in the centre of the oven so that air circulates round it freely. During roasting, enough fat should come from the meat to baste it naturally. However, basting the joint from time to time will give an improved flavour and moistness.

Roasting in foil or clear plastic roasting bags is popular, mainly because it keeps the oven cleaner. It is also particularly beneficial when roasting slightly tough joints because the moist heat tenderizes the meat; when roasting small joints of 1.5kg or less, it reduces the shrinkage and any drying out. When using foil, the joint should be wrapped loosely in it and the edges sealed; this does away with the need to baste the joint during cooking. However, it is advisable to remove the foil for the last 15–30 minutes of cooking time to brown the surface of the joint. Foil deflects the heat, and so the oven temperature should be raised by 10°–20°C or by one Gas mark; alternatively the cooking time should be increased.

Follow the manufacturer's instructions when using clear plastic roasting bags. The bag need only be removed when the joint has finished cooking since the meat browns whilst in the bag.

Meat Roasting Chart

Meat	Method 1 – Quick Roasting 230°C, Gas 8, reducing to 190°C, Gas 5, after 10 mins	Method 2 – Slow Roasting at 160°–180°C, Gas 3–4	Meat thermometer temperatures
Beef (with bone)	15 minutes per 0.5kg plus 15 minutes extra	25 minutes per 0.5kg plus 25 minutes extra	rare – 60°C
Beef (without bone – rolled)	20 minutes per 0.5kg plus 20 minutes extra	30 minutes per 0.5kg plus 30 minutes extra	medium – 68°–70°C well-done – 75°–77°C
Lamb (with bone)	20 minutes per 0.5kg plus 20 minutes extra	25 minutes per 0.5kg plus 25 minutes extra	80°–82°C
Lamb and Mutton (without bone – rolled)	25 minutes per 0.5kg plus 25 minutes extra	30 minutes per 0.5kg plus 30 minutes extra	
Mutton (with bone)	20–25 minutes per 0.5kg plus 25 minutes extra	30–35 minutes per 0.5kg plus 35 minutes extra	
Veal (with bone)	25 minutes per 0.5kg plus 25 minutes extra	30 minutes per 0.5kg plus 30 minutes extra	80°–82°C
Veal (without bone – rolled)	30 minutes per 0.5kg plus 30 minutes extra	40 minutes per 0.5kg plus 30 minutes extra	
Pork (with bone)	25–30 minutes per 0.5kg plus 25–30 minutes extra	35 minutes per 0.5kg plus 35 minutes extra	85°–88°C
Pork (without bone – rolled)	35 minutes per 0.5kg plus 35 minutes extra		

Note The above cooking times are approximate. The exact time will depend on the form and thickness of the joint, its age and condition, and its preparation.

Grilling

Grilled meat is cooked by radiant heat under a hot grill, usually preheated. It is an ideal cooking method for small, tender cuts, and other items: prime steak, chops, sausages, liver, kidney, bacon and gammon rashers or steaks, if you do not want to use much fat. The meat is only lightly brushed with oil or fat before placing it under the grill; this prevents the high heat from drying the meat out. The grill bars or grid must also be greased to prevent the meat sticking to them. The meat is cooked on one side until it is lightly browned. It is then turned over (using a palette knife and spoon to avoid piercing the meat and letting its juices run out) to brown the other side quickly. The heat is reduced, if necessary, after browning, to allow the meat time to cook through. Beef is usually cooked using high heat throughout, while other meats are cooked more slowly.

Frying

Frying is used for the same cuts of meat as grilling. Frying times are the same as grilling times. In addition, some meats, notably mutton, lamb and veal, are often coated with egg and breadcrumbs before frying.

Meat is almost always shallow fried. Use just enough fat and/or oil to cover the base of the pan. Dripping can be used for beef, or lard for pork; butter gives the best flavour to other meats. Add the meat to the hot (but not smoking) fat or oil. Fry it over high heat, turning once only, again taking care not to puncture the surface. For thick cuts, the heat should be reduced considerably after the outside has been seared and the cooking continued until the meat is well-done.

For cooking times, see the Chart below and the Steak Grilling and Frying Chart on p107.

Grilling and Frying Chart

Cuts	Approx cooking time	Cuts	Approx cooking time
Beef		*Bacon and Gammon*	
Steaks	see Chart, p107	*Bacon chops*	10–15 minutes
		Bacon rashers (thin)	5 minutes
Lamb and Mutton		*Gammon steaks*	10–15 minutes
Chops (loin and chump)	8–15 minutes		
Cutlets	7–10 minutes	*Offal*	
		Kidney	5–10 minutes
Veal		*Liver (1cm thick)*	8–10 minutes
Cutlets	12–15 minutes		
Escalopes (beaten and crumbed)	7–10 minutes	*Sausages*	
		Large	10–15 minutes
Pork		*Chipolata*	7–10 minutes
Chops (loin, chump and spare rib)	15–20 minutes		

Pot-roasting

This is best for smaller and less tender joints of meat. The meat is browned all over in hot fat in a deep, heavy-based pan. It is then put on a wire rack or a bed of root vegetables in the pan, covered with a tight-fitting lid and cooked slowly over low heat or in a warm oven, 160°C, Gas 3, for 45 minutes per 0.5kg or until tender.

Braising

This method combines pot-roasting and stewing. The meat is browned all over in hot fat. It is then placed on a bed of fried vegetables called a mirepoix (see p269), in a casserole or heavy-based pan. Stock or water is added to cover the vegetables. The casserole or pan is covered with a tight-fitting lid and the meat cooked slowly over low heat or in a warm oven, 160°C, Gas 3, for 2–3 hours or until tender.

Casseroling and Stewing

These are long, slow, moist methods of cooking suitable for tougher cuts of meat. Solid cuts or small pieces of meat are browned quickly in hot fat and then cooked in liquid, with vegetables, in a pan covered with a tight-fitting lid or in a heatproof casserole over gentle heat; or they are cooked in a warm oven, 160°C, Gas 3, for $1\frac{1}{2}$–4 hours until tender.

Boiling

This is a moist method of cooking whole joints, but a rather more tender cut is used for boiling than for stewing. The meat is totally or almost covered with stock or water. Herbs, spices, seasonings, and onions may be added for extra flavour. The liquid is heated to boiling point, skimmed well, then reduced to simmering point until the meat is tender. A little of the liquid may be served with the meat, and the rest used as a basis for a sauce, to make broth or, where suitable, as a general stock.

Using Dripping and Other Meat-flavoured Fat

This makes an appetizing spread on hot toast. It can also be used for flavouring vegetables, for making plain cakes (p363) and in various other ways, especially if it is cleared, or clarified. Hard fat or suet cut off raw meat can also be used if all skin and gristle are removed. This can be done by melting (rendering) the fat.

To Clarify Fat

To clean fat which has been used for cooking meat, eg for frying, put the fat into a large saucepan and add about the same volume of cold water. Heat very gently until the water begins to boil, removing the scum as it rises. Allow to simmer for about 5 minutes, then strain into a bowl and leave the fat to cool and solidify. Remove the fat in one piece, dry it on soft kitchen paper and scrape away the sediment from underneath. Heat the fat very gently until all bubbling ceases, to drive off any water.

To Render Fat or Suet

Cut the fat into small pieces, and heat very gently in a frying pan or in a cool oven, 150°C, Gas 2, until the fat has melted and the pieces of tissue or skin are quite crisp. While hot, strain the fat through a fine metal strainer into a clean basin, pressing the pieces of tissue and skin against the strainer to extract all the fat. The crispy bits left are called by different names in different parts of the UK, eg mammocks, scraps, scratchings or scruggins, and are used sometimes in old recipes. When crushed, they make a good topping for baked meat or vegetable dishes.

Carving

Carving is an acquired skill requiring practice and a really sharp knife. A sharp knife is essential since it can be used lightly and is always under control. Carving knives should be sharpened before use either with a hone, steel, patent sharpener or an oil-stone. When a knife fails to produce a good edge with a domestic sharpener, take it to an ironmonger or send it to the manufacturer for regrinding.

Note Some modern, stainless steel knives have a hollowed-out grooved blade; these seldom require sharpening.

Sharpening a Carving Knife

Hold the steel in your left hand (if you are right-handed), with your thumb on top of the handle. Hold the carving knife in your right hand. Angle both the steel and the knife upwards. Place the heel of the blade on the handle end of the steel, almost flat against it, and draw the blade sharply along the steel with a stroking movement.

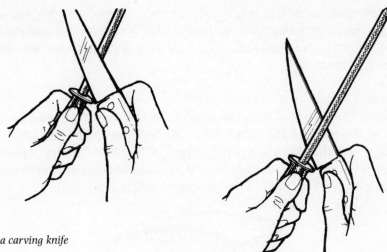

Sharpening a carving knife

Repeat, but start with the blade *under* the steel, and sharpen the other side of the knife. Go on doing this, alternately holding the knife on top of the steel and under it, until the knife has a sharp, tapered, cutting edge. About 6 strokes on each side should be enough to sharpen any good quality knife.

Carving knives can also be sharpened on a fine oil-stone or carborundum stone. First dip the stone in water, then sharpen the knife as above.

Another method of using an oil-stone, which may be easier, is to lay the knife almost flat on the stone, with the cutting edge towards you. Draw the knife along the stone, away from you; then turn the knife over, lay it on the far end of the stone and draw it towards you. Repeat several times.

How to Carve

A knife should be used in the same way as a saw, ie drawn back and forth through the meat. Never try to push even a sharp knife through meat without using a sawing movement. If the knife is sharp, keep the backward and forward movements long and light, and the knife will cut through the meat quickly and smoothly. Try to hold the knife slanted at the same angle all the way through the joint, and to make each slice equally thick when cutting slices of meat from a partly carved joint.

When cutting slices from the top of a rolled joint which is standing on end, always try to cut from right to left (if you are right-handed), not towards you, so that there is no danger of the knife slipping and cutting you. Protect the left hand by using a proper carving fork with a thumb guard. A modern carving dish studded with small, sharp prongs which hold the joint steady can be a great help.

Boned and rolled joints rarely present carving problems since the bones have already been removed, so a beginner learning to carve should start on them. When carving rolled joints, leave some strings and skewers in place until you have carved down to them and then only remove the one which impedes further carving. Anyone who carves meat on the bone should, however, know how the bones lie in the meat, and where the knuckle ends are.

Meat is usually carved across the grain or run of muscle in the UK, because this makes it more tender to cut and eat. The thickness of the slices varies with each type of meat. In general, carve thin slices of beef from a boneless joint and thicker slices from fillet or sirloin. Carve moderately thick slices of pork and veal, and still thicker slices of lamb and mutton.

Beef

Joints on the bone are carved from the outside fat towards the bone after making a vertical cut at the edge of the chine bone. At the base bone, the knife is turned parallel with it and the slices are gently eased off the bone. When dealing with a sirloin or ribs, try to carve the outside rib muscles first as these are better eaten really hot. Save the least cooked meat in the centre for eating cold.

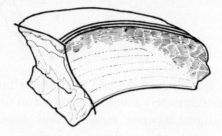

Carving a joint on the bone

Brisket of beef on the bone: The joint should be cut in even slices across the whole width of the joint, across the bones.

Ribs of beef: Loosen the meat from the ribs by inserting the knife between the meat and bones. Cut thin slices off the sides, starting at the thick end and carving through to the thin end.

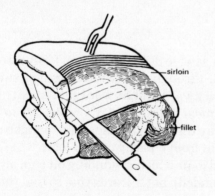

LEFT *Carving rib of beef*

BELOW *Carving the fillet*

Sirloin of beef: A sirloin is carved on the bone. First cut out the fillet or undercut. Carve it into a suitable number of slices. It is best eaten hot. Then turn the sirloin over, so that it rests on the bone, and carve the meat across the width of the joint and straight down towards the blade of the bone. These slices are cut thicker than slices from a boneless joint.

Round of beef: Use a thin-bladed and very sharp knife. Cut a thick slice first from the outside of the joint, at its top, leaving the surface smooth; then carve thin, even slices to leave a level-topped joint.

RIGHT *Carving an unpressed beef tongue*
BELOW *Carving a round of beef*

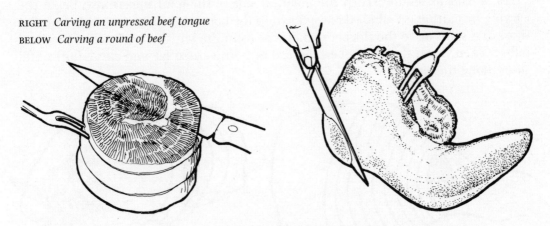

Beef tongue (pressed): Carve thinly across the top, parallel to the round base.

Beef tongue (unpressed): Cut across the tongue at the thickest part, all the way through it. Cut out and serve a fairly thick slice. Continue carving in this way towards the tip of the tongue until all the best meat on the upper side has been served. The fat which lies around the root of the tongue can be turned over, sliced, and served.

Lamb and Mutton

Mutton and, to a lesser extent, lamb, should always be served as quickly as possible and on very hot plates. This is because the flavour of mutton is soon lost, and because lamb and mutton fat have a higher melting point than other animal fats. On a cold plate, they solidify, leaving semi-solid fat which coats the palate, producing a 'furry' or diminished sense of taste.

Forequarter of lamb: When carving a forequarter of lamb, first separate the shoulder from the breast. To do this, raise the shoulder, into which the fork should be firmly

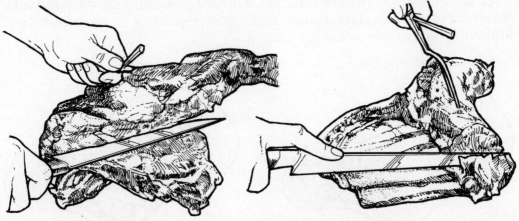

Raising the shoulder from the breast   *Carving cutlets from the ribs*

fixed. It will then come away easily by cutting round the outline of the shoulder and slipping the knife beneath it. The main part of the joint is then turned over and served as cutlets carved from the ribs. The shoulder can be served cold later.

Leg of lamb or mutton: Turn the meatiest side of the joint uppermost. Begin the carving by cutting a V-shaped piece down to the bone close to the knuckle end. Cut slices at a slant up to the thicker end. Those from the knuckle end will be the most fully cooked. Turn the joint over, discard any unwanted fat and carve horizontal slices along the leg.

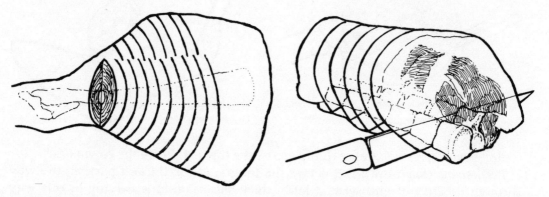

Carving a leg of lamb or mutton

Carving a loin of lamb or mutton

Loin of lamb or mutton: Loin, and other similar pieces, should be well-jointed before cooking. Ask the butcher to chine or saw it across the blade parts of the bone or to chop it through the joints for serving in cutlets. If this has not been done, use an old knife and knock the blade through between the joints where they are separated by white discs of gristle, before trying to carve. Carve the loin downwards, in thick slices or in chops, following the natural division of the bones. If boned and rolled, the loin can be carved in thinner slices, like any other boned and rolled joint.

Saddle of lamb or mutton: There are two ways of carving a saddle, either by carving the slices at right angles to the backbone (spine), or by cutting the slices parallel to it.

For the first method, cut down one side of the spine, and then slip the knife under the meat and cut slices at right angles to the spine, separating the meat from them. Repeat this on the other side of the spine.

Cutting down one side of the spine

Cutting slices at right angles to the spine

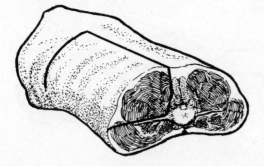
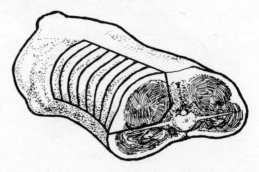

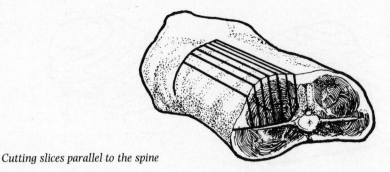

Cutting slices parallel to the spine

For the second method, cut down each side of the spine and separate the meat from the rib bones as in the first method. Make a cut, parallel to the spine a few centimetres up from the lower edge of the meat, then cut slices off downwards parallel to the spine and the cut line. This can be done in the kitchen; the slices can then be put back in place for serving at the table.

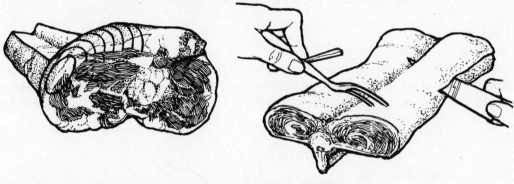

Carving the chops at the chump end   *Slicing the fillet*

To finish both methods, carve the chops at the chump end from each side in turn, slanting the knife towards the centre of the joint.

Turn the joint over and slice the fillet along the length of the joint.

Shoulder of lamb or mutton: Before cooking, insert a sharp knife and ease the meat away from the whole surface of the bladebone, to make carving easier. Turn the joint over, if necessary, so that the thickest part is on top. When cooked, carve a vertical slice at the narrow end of this bladebone right down to the bone. Then carve thick

Carving thick slices along the length of the bladebone

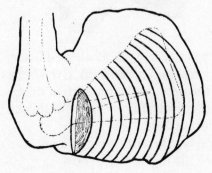

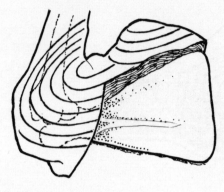

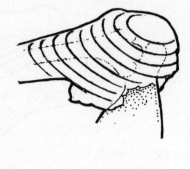

Carving the shank in horizontal slices along the shank bone

Carving the remaining meat

slices along the length of the bladebone until all the shoulder meat on top has been carved, leaving only the shank of the foreleg. Carve this in horizontal slices along the shank bone until all the meat has been cut from the top of the joint. Turn the joint over, and carve the remaining meat in horizontal slices.

Veal

Breast of veal: A breast of veal consists of two parts – the rib bones and the gristly brisket. Separate these first by passing the knife sharply through the centre of the joint. Then cut off each rib bone and serve it. The brisket can be served by cutting pieces from the centre part of the joint. If the veal is boned and stuffed, carve it by cutting downwards across the end of the rolled joint.

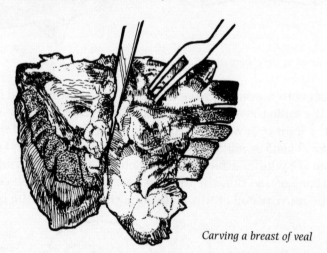

Carving a breast of veal

Calf's head: A calf's head is nearly always boned before serving, and is then cut into slices like any other boned and rolled joint. If the bones have not been removed, cut strips from the ear to the nose, and with each of these serve a piece of the throat sweetbreads, cut in a half-moon shape from the throat. The tongue and brains should be served on a separate dish.

Fillet of veal: The carving of this joint is very like that of a round or roll of beef. A stuffing is inserted between the flap and the meat.

Loin of veal: As in the case of a loin of lamb, the careful jointing of a loin of veal greatly lessens the difficulty in carving it. Ask the butcher to do this. When properly jointed, there should be little difficulty in separating the chops from each other. Each helping should include a piece of the kidney and kidney fat.

Pork and Cured Pig Meat

When carving a joint with crackling, first take off a small section of crackling, but only enough to serve one or two people. Cut it into serving portions.

Leg of pork: This joint, a favourite with many people, is easy to carve. Having removed some of the crackling, begin to carve by cutting a V-shaped piece down to the bone close to the knuckle end. Cut slices at a slant up to the thicker end, as when carving a leg of lamb.

Loin of pork: Like a loin of lamb, a loin of pork must be properly chined before roasting, and the crackling must be scored. Ask the butcher to do both. Cut through the cooked meat between the bones into neat, even chops. A boned and rolled loin of pork can be carved in thinner slices, but remove more of the crackling first to make carving easier.

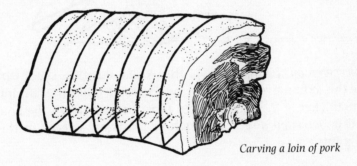

Carving a loin of pork

Hand and spring of pork: Using a sharp, thin-bladed knife, remove the rib bones from the underside and the crackling from the top.

Carve the meat from each side of the bone in downward slices until the bone is reached. Turn the joint over and carve the rest of the meat across the grain.

Removing the rib bones   *Carving the meat from each side of the bone*

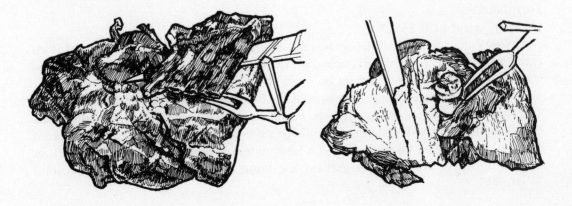

Suckling-pig: A suckling-pig seems, at first sight, an elaborate dish to carve. Like poultry, it is mainly jointed rather than sliced. It is usually prepared by splitting it in half lengthways; the head is then separated from the body. Detach the shoulders from the carcass in the same way as a shoulder is separated from a forequarter of lamb. Then take off the hind legs; the ribs are then ready to be cut up and may be served as 2 or 3 helpings.

Whole gammon or ham: Turn the meatiest side of the joint uppermost. Using a very sharp and thin knife, begin carving at the knuckle end. Make a V-shaped cut into one side of the joint, down to the bone. Take out the slice of meat. Then take thin slices down the side of the joint. Repeat this on the other side of the joint until all the gammon or ham has been carved.

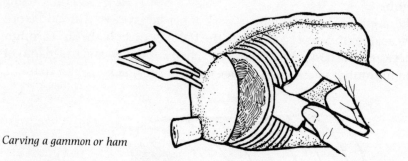

Carving a gammon or ham

Middle gammon: Using a sharp, thin knife, cut thin slices through to the bone. Because this joint narrows towards the bone end, make the cuts into the joint opposite the bone thicker at the outside, then taper them towards the bone.

Note All pot-roasted and braised whole joints are carved in the same way as the roasted joints above.

Beef

Beef Cuts

Cuts of beef vary considerably in different parts of Great Britain. Those described are the most widely used British cuts, but they are by no means standard and reference is made to some of the other terms used. The cuts will be better understood from the diagram opposite.

Forequarter
(Average weight 66.25kg)

1) *Shin* comes from the foreleg, has much gristle, and is relatively cheap. It is an excellent soup meat and when cooked on the bone provides a good, jellied stock and is ideal for making brawn. (Av wt boneless shin 2–2.5kg)

2) *Brisket* is the muscular extension of the belly of the animal towards the chest. The boned and rolled joint can also be bought cut up into smaller joints and is best pot-roasted or braised. It is also available salted, ready for boiling. Brisket is an economical, yet well-flavoured joint which, when properly cooked, is little fattier than sirloin. (Av wt whole brisket on the bone 9–13.5kg; Av wt boneless joint 7–10.5kg)

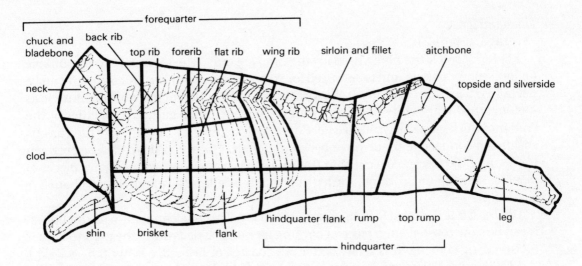

3) *Flank* is also from the belly of the animal. It is a cheaper cut which deserves wider recognition. It provides a more fatty joint than brisket and is ideal for pot-roasting, braising or boiling. It is sometimes salted or pickled before being boiled, for pressed beef. (Av wt 1–2.25kg)

4) *Flat rib* comes from between the flank and foreribs. Like the forerib, this joint should be slowly roasted. (Av wt 5kg)

5) *Wing rib* is a rib joint cut from between the forerib and sirloin. It is one of the most expensive cuts and is particularly good when roasted. (Av wt 2–6kg)

6) *Forerib* is merely an extension of the sirloin, but it requires slower cooking at a lower temperature than the sirloin because the muscles of the live animal were more fully exercised. The forerib can be bought either on the bone, or boned and rolled. (Av wt on the bone 1.4–2.6kg; Av wt boneless 1–2kg)

7) *Top rib* along with the *back rib* is also known as middle rib or thick ribs or leg-of-mutton cut, and comes from the ribs between the foreribs and shoulders. In other words, it is an extension of the foreribs. The joint is often divided into two (top and back ribs) and partly boned and rolled which makes it easier to carve. There is less bone in these joints than in forerib joints and they are very good when slow roasted or pot-roasted. (Av wt 7–11.5kg)

8) *Chuck* and *bladebone* are similar types of beef; the meat is removed from the bone and sold as chuck steak for braising, stewing, and as fillings for puddings and pies. Though sold for stewing, chuck steak needs a shorter cooking time than any other cut of stewing meat. Many butchers cut blade of beef into dice and mix it with chopped kidney, ready for filling puddings and pies. Chuck is known in the north of England as a chine, and in Scotland the chuck and blade together is known as a shoulder. (Av wt boneless chuck – 4.5kg; Av wt boneless bladebone – 3kg)

9) *Clod* or *front chest* and

10) *Sticking* or *neck* of the animal provide meat suitable for casseroling or stewing. These cuts contain less connective tissue than the shin or leg and less marbling fat than chuck steak and bladebone. Both clod and sticking are usually cheap. There is, however, a little wastage due to gristle. (Av wt clod (de-fatted) – 4.5kg; Av wt sticking – 3.5kg)

Hindquarter
(Average weight 71.5–72kg)

11) *Leg of beef* is the name used for the hind leg only. The leg meat is only suitable for long, slow cooking and is best used for stews, casseroles, pies, and soups. It can be cut in two ways. Cut in strips, it shows clearly the structure of the working muscle as it is sheathed with white or transparent connective tissue gathered together at the ends into thick pieces of white gristle. Cut in slices, it reveals 'lines' where the various sheaths of connective tissue have been cut across. There is little to choose between the leg and the foreleg, except that the leg is larger and so provides bigger pieces of meat for stewing. In Scotland, the leg and shin are called the hough. (Av wt boneless leg – 4kg)

12) *Topside* is the muscle of the inside of the leg. This is a lean joint without bones. It can be slow roasted but a piece of barding fat must be tied round the joint to keep it moist during cooking. It is really better pot-roasted or braised. (Av wt 8.5–8.75kg)

13) *Silverside* is the muscle of the outside of the thigh and buttock. It is common for this joint to be roasted but it is best suited to salting and boiling, as in the past (Av wt boneless silverside – 5.5kg)

14) *Top rump* or *thick flank* is the muscle of the front of the thigh, which is usually cut into 2 joints and barded with fat. This makes an acceptable joint for slow roasting or, better still, for moist cooking such as pot-roasting. It may also be sold sliced, ready for frying or braising. (Av wt boned and trimmed 5.25–5.5kg)

15) *Aitchbone* is the cut lying over the rump bone. It is a large joint on the bone which can be roasted or braised. Can be boned and cut into smaller joints. Not cut very often nowadays. (Av wt on the bone – 5.4kg)

16) *Rump* is the joint next to the sirloin and is one of the commonest cuts for frying and grilling. In Scotland rump steak is sometimes called 'pope's eye'. Although not as tender as fillet, it is preferred by many people for its fuller flavour. The meat should be close-grained and should have about 5mm fat on the outside edge and no gristle. (Av wt boned and trimmed rump 8.25–8.5kg)

17) *Sirloin* (which properly includes the fillet) is the traditional joint for roast beef. It is tender and full of flavour, but is also the most expensive joint. It is often sold without the fillet which makes it slightly cheaper. Sirloin is also sold sliced as steaks for grilling or frying. (Av wt sirloin with bone and fillet – 12.25kg)

18) *Fillet* is found on the inside of the sirloin bone, and fillet and sirloin may be boned and rolled together to provide a luxury roast. If the sirloin is bought on the bone, the fillet can be removed for roasting by itself in the piece, or for slicing into fillet steaks, which are the most tender steaks for grilling or frying. (Av wt fillet 1.5–2.25kg)

19) *Hindquarter flank* is the belly of the animal, which provides a cheap and delicious joint for pot-roasting, braising or boiling. It is, however, rather fatty. It is not suitable for dry heat cooking methods. (Av wt with bone – 6.25kg)

Steaks
Several terms are used for various types of beef steaks. They are not new terms and some have already been mentioned.

Fillet (undercut) is a lean and boneless piece lying below the ribs of the sirloin. It is the most expensive steak meat and is usually sliced for grilling or frying. The tiny flecks of fat running through the meat are evidence that the steak will grill or fry well. Fillet steak can be served in several ways and under several names.

Tournedos is a slice from the fillet, weighing about 125–150g, usually 2cm thick and a neat round shape. It is sometimes tied to preserve its shape.

Châteaubriand is a piece of fillet enough for 2 people, ideally about 4cm thick and cut from the centre of the fillet. A popular and delicious steak. Its average weight is 250g.

Rump is the best flavoured steak, particularly good for grilling and frying. It is not as tender as fillet steak but has a good texture. This steak should have about 5mm fat on the outside edge.

Sirloin (contre-fillet) provides tender steaks with a good flavour. However, the texture is not as good as fillet or rump. Sirloin, like fillet, is cut in several ways and served under several names.

Porterhouse is a thick steak about 2–2.5cm thick, cut from the wing end (thick end) of the sirloin. Excellent for grilling.

T-bone is a steak cut through the sirloin so that it contains, on one side at least, the T-shaped loin bone. It has 2 'eyes', that of the loin meat and that of the fillet.

Entrecôte is a sirloin steak without the undercut (fillet) and without the bone. In other words, it is the eye meat of the loin cut into steaks. Each steak is usually cut 2–3cm thick.

Minute steak is a very thin steak from the upper part of the sirloin or occasionally from the fillet, weighing 125–150g without any trimmings or fat.

Roasted and Baked Dishes
Roast Beef *Basic recipe*

a joint of beef suitable for roasting
salt and pepper

beef dripping (25g per 0.5kg meat approx)

Select the method of roasting, ie quick or slow roasting (p91). Weigh the meat to calculate the cooking time (p92). Wipe, trim, and tie the meat into a neat shape. Place the joint, fat side up, on a wire rack if available, in a shallow roasting tin. Season the meat, and rub or spread it with the dripping. Place the roasting tin in the oven and cook for the required time.

Transfer the cooked meat to a warmed serving dish, remove any string and secure with a metal skewer if necessary. Keep hot. Drain off the fat from the roasting tin and make a gravy from the sediment in the tin, if liked.

Serve with Yorkshire Pudding (pp191–92) and Cold Horseradish Cream (p49) if using traditional accompaniments.

Marinated Roast Beef
6–8 helpings

750g–1kg fillet **or** boned sirloin **or** topside of beef
fat for greasing

2 × 5ml spoons meat glaze (p55)
250ml Demi-glace sauce (p211)

Marinade

2 × 15ml spoons olive oil
1 × 15ml spoon lemon juice **or** vinegar
1 × 5ml spoon chopped onion
1 × 5ml spoon chopped parsley

a pinch of dried mixed herbs
a pinch of ground cloves
a pinch of ground pepper
$\frac{1}{2}$ × 2.5ml spoon salt

Make the marinade first by mixing all the ingredients together. Wipe, trim and tie the meat into a neat shape. Place the meat in a bowl, pour the marinade over and leave it to soak for 2–3 hours, turning and basting frequently.

Cut a sheet of foil large enough to form a parcel round the meat, and grease it well. Lay the foil in an ovenproof dish with sides so that it forms a container, and place the meat in the centre of it; use the marinade also. Fold the foil round the meat and seal the edges to form a parcel. Roast the beef in a fairly hot oven, 190°C, Gas 5, for 1 hour for fillet, and 1$\frac{1}{2}$ hours for sirloin or topside. Open the foil for the last 15 minutes of the cooking time to let the meat brown. Lift out the meat, place it on a warmed serving dish and remove the string. Brush with Demi-glace Sauce. If liked, a little of the sauce can also be poured round the dish, the rest being served separately.

Serve with Cold Horseradish Cream (p49), as well as the Demi-glace Sauce.

Fillet of Beef en Croûte
6 helpings

750g–1kg fillet of beef
ground pepper
25g butter
1 × 15ml spoon oil
100g button mushrooms
1 × 5ml spoon fresh mixed herbs, chopped

1 × 5ml spoon chopped parsley
450g prepared puff pastry (p412)
flour for rolling out
beaten egg for glazing

Wipe, trim, and tie the meat into a neat shape. Season with pepper. Heat the butter and oil in a large pan, add the fillet and brown it quickly all over. Reserve the fat in the pan and draw it off the heat. Transfer the fillet to a roasting tin and roast it in a very hot oven, 230°C, Gas 8, for 10 minutes. Remove the fillet, and leave it to get cold.

Meanwhile, clean and slice the mushrooms. Sauté them in the remaining oil and butter in the pan for 2–3 minutes. Remove from the heat, add the herbs, and leave to cool.

Roll out the puff pastry on a lightly floured surface to make a rectangle large enough to enclose the fillet. Put the mushroom mixture on one half of the pastry. Lay the beef on top of the mushroom mixture. Wrap the pastry round the beef to form a neat parcel, sealing the edges well. Place the parcel on a baking tray with the cut edges underneath. Decorate with leaves cut from the pastry trimmings and brush the pastry with the beaten egg. Bake in a hot oven, 220°C, Gas 7, for 20–30 minutes, or until the pastry is well-browned. Serve hot or cold.

Steaks
Steak Grilling and Frying Chart

	Fillet	Tournedos	Châteaubriand	Rump	Sirloin	Porterhouse	T-bone	Entrecôte	Minute
Thickness of meat	2cm	2–3cm	4cm	2cm	2–2.5cm	4–5cm	4–5cm	2–3cm	1cm
Helpings	1	1	2	4	1	2	2–3	1	1
Cooking times (in minutes):									
Rare	6	6–7	15–17	6–7	5	7–8	7–8	5	1–1.5
Medium rare	7	8	18–20	8–10	6–7	9–12	9–12	6–7	2–3
Well-done	8	9–10	21–24	12–14	9–10	14–16	14–16	9–10	4–5

Grilled Steak *Basic recipe*

150–200g steak per person
oil **or** melted butter

freshly ground pepper

Garnish
Maître d'Hôtel butter (p232)

Wipe the steaks and trim off any excess fat. Beat each steak lightly on both sides with a cutlet bat or rolling-pin. Brush with oil or melted butter and, if possible, leave for 1 hour before cooking.

Season with pepper. (Do not salt steaks before grilling because it makes the juices run.) Heat the grill to a high heat and oil the grid, or brush with melted butter. Place the meat on the grid and cook under the grill until the steak has browned lightly on one side. Turn the meat over, using a palette knife or spoons. Grill quickly to brown the other side. If the steaks are required medium rare or well-done, lower the grid or the grill heat and continue cooking as required (see Steak Grilling Chart above). Serve at once with a pat of Maître d'Hôtel butter on the top of each helping.

Serve with chipped potatoes, grilled mushrooms, and/or grilled tomatoes, and a sprig of watercress.

Fried Steaks *Basic recipe*

150–200g steak, 2cm thick, per
  person
freshly ground pepper
1 × 15ml spoon oil, dripping **or** butter
  (approx)

a pinch of onion salt (optional)
1–2 × 5ml spoons flour for gravy
  (optional)
100ml boiling water (optional)

Garnish
Maître d'Hôtel **or** other savoury butter
  (p232)

Wipe the steaks and trim off any excess fat. Beat each steak lightly on both sides with a cutlet bat or rolling-pin. Season with pepper. (Do not salt steaks before frying because it makes the juices run.) Heat a thick, heavy frying pan on full heat until hot. Add enough oil, dripping or butter just to cover the bottom of the frying pan and, when hot, put in the prepared steaks. Keep on full heat until they are well-browned on one side; then turn them over with a palette knife or spoons, and brown the other side. Reduce the heat if necessary to complete the cooking time (see Chart on p107). Serve at once garnished with a pat of Maître d'Hôtel or other butter.

If serving gravy with the steak, drain any fat from the frying pan, keeping back the sediment. Add a pinch of ground black pepper and onion salt, and stir in the flour. Gradually add the water, and stir until boiling. Skim and strain the gravy.

Serve with chipped potatoes, grilled mushrooms and/or grilled tomatoes, and a sprig of watercress.

Steak au Poivre
4 helpings

4 steaks (fillet **or** sirloin **or** entrecôte,
  150–200g each)
2 × 10ml spoons whole black and
  white peppercorns, mixed

1 clove of garlic
4 × 15ml spoons olive oil
50g unsalted butter

Garnish
50g herb butter (p232)

Wipe the steaks and trim off any excess fat. Crush the peppercorns coarsely in a mortar or in a paper or polythene bag using a rolling-pin. Skin and cut the garlic in half and rub the steaks on both sides with the garlic. Brush each steak on both sides with 1 × 15ml spoon of olive oil. With the heel of your hand, press the crushed peppercorns into the surface of the meat on each side.

Heat the butter in a frying pan and fry the steaks over high heat for 1 minute on both sides until sealed and browned. Reduce the heat and fry the steaks for 4–5 minutes for rare, 7 minutes for medium-rare, and 9 minutes for well-done steaks, turning them 2 or 3 times. Remove with a palette knife or spoons, and place on a warmed serving dish. Garnish with pats of herb butter and serve at once.

Tournedos Rossini
4 helpings

4 tournedos steaks (175g each approx)	50ml Madeira **or** dry Marsala
4 slices white bread	75ml brown stock (p25)
50g butter	100ml Espagnole sauce (p210)
1 × 15ml spoon cooking oil	salt and freshly ground black pepper
50g unsalted butter	

Garnish

4 rounds good quality liver pâté (5mm thick)	4 × 5ml spoons chilled butter
4 small flat mushrooms	sprigs of watercress

Wipe, trim, and tie the tournedos into a neat shape. Cut 4 rounds from the bread slices, a little wider than the tournedos' bases. Heat the butter and oil in a large, deep frying pan, and fry the bread rounds over moderate heat until light gold and crisp on both sides. Transfer them to a warmed serving dish and keep warm under buttered paper.

Put half the unsalted butter into the pan. Pat the tournedos dry, add them to the pan, raise the heat, and fry the steaks quickly, turning as required, until they are well seared and browned all over but rare inside. Remove them with a palette knife or spoons. Place them on the fried bread rounds and keep warm.

Lower the heat and stir the wine and stock quickly into the pan, scraping up all the drippings. Simmer for 3 minutes, then stir in the sauce and simmer until reduced to the desired consistency.

Meanwhile, heat the remaining 25g unsalted butter in a small frying pan, and turn the pâté slices and mushrooms in it for 2–3 minutes over high heat, until the mushrooms are soft and the pâté is lightly browned but not melted.

Place a slice of pâté on each tournedos and cap it with a mushroom, gill side down. Garnish the top of each mushroom with 1 × 5ml spoon chilled butter. Serve at once, with the sauce in a warmed sauceboat. Garnish the dish with watercress and offer a peppermill of black pepper with the steaks.

Fondue Bourguignonne

150g good quality fillet **or** rump steak
per person
garlic (optional)

salt and freshly ground black pepper
oil for deep frying

Sauces

Agro-dolce sauce (p213)
Béarnaise sauce (p214)
Curry mayonnaise (p222)
Hollandaise sauce (p217)

Cold Horseradish cream (p49)
Tartare sauce (p224)
Tomato mayonnaise (p223)

In the kitchen, wipe the meat and remove any excess fat. Cut the meat into 2cm cubes. Grate or mince a little garlic, if used, and season the meat with the garlic and with salt and pepper. Choose and prepare 4–5 of the sauces. Fill the fondue pot one-third full of oil, and heat it to 190°C. If possible, have a second pot of oil heating so that the first pot, in use on the dining table, can be replaced when it cools. Carry the first pot carefully to the table.

At the table, light the spirit lamp or burner, and put the pot on the trivet. If using an electric table cooker, fill it one-third full of oil, set the thermostat, and heat it up at the table itself. Bring the meat and the sauces to the table, arrange the sauces round the fondue pot in the centre, and place a dish of meat and two long-handled forks in front of each diner. The diner spears a piece of meat on a fork, dips it into the hot oil and holds it there until cooked. After cooking, he transfers the meat to the second, cold fork and dips it into one or other of the sauces before eating.

This dish is given much of it character by the side dishes served with it. Choose accompaniments from among the following: beetroot sliced in vinegar, chopped celery, chopped nuts, cocktail onions, cucumber in soured cream or thick yoghurt sprinkled with dill, green salad with French dressing, sliced gherkins, sliced potato in French dressing, sliced tomato with chives and French dressing. French bread and butter should also be served.

VARIATION
Substitute pork fillets for fillet or rump steak. Cook for at least $2\frac{1}{2}$ minutes per cube to ensure it is fully cooked through.

Braised, Casseroled, Stewed and Boiled Dishes
Mrs Beeton's Beef à la Mode
4 helpings

2 rashers back bacon (100g approx)	75ml port
1kg thick flank of beef (see **Note**)	salt and pepper
100ml red wine vinegar	

Seasoning

1 clove	1 sprig of fresh thyme **or** a good pinch
4 black peppercorns	of dried thyme
3 allspice berries	1 bay leaf
3 sprigs parsley	

Mirepoix

1 medium-sized onion (100g approx)	½ turnip (50g approx)
2 sticks celery	50g clarified dripping (p232)
1 medium-sized carrot (50g approx)	250ml water

Cut the bacon into strips 2cm wide crossways, including lean and fat in each strip. Wipe the meat and make deep slits in the flesh with a sharp-pointed knife. Make the same number of slits as strips of bacon.

Make the seasoning mixture. Pound the clove, peppercorns, and allspice berries in a mortar. Chop the parsley and thyme finely and crumble the bay leaf finely. Mix the ingredients together to make 1 × 5ml spoon seasoning.

Dip the bacon strips in the vinegar, then coat them with about one-third of the seasoning mixture. Insert 1 bacon strip into each slit in the meat. Rub the meat all over with the remaining seasoning and tie the meat into a neat shape.

Prepare the vegetables for the mirepoix. Slice the onion and celery, and chop the carrot and turnip. Melt the dripping in a flameproof casserole or stewpan. Add the onion and fry gently until softened and golden-brown. Add the celery, carrot, and turnip. Place the meat on the vegetables. Pour the vinegar and water gently over the vegetables, then cover the pan closely. Heat to boiling point, reduce the heat, and simmer very gently for 1 hour 40 minutes. Turn the meat over after 40 minutes cooking time, and again after a further 30 minutes.

When cooked, transfer the meat to a warmed serving dish and keep hot. Strain the cooking liquid into a pan, skim off the fat, and add the port. Heat gently to boiling point. Taste, and season if required. Remove the strings from the meat and pour a little of the sauce over the meat. Serve the rest separately in a warmed sauce-boat.

Note Thick flank or top rump, as it is often called, is usually sold with extra fat tied round it. In this recipe the weight of the meat is without the added fat.

Beef Olives
4 helpings

500g rump **or** chuck steak
100g basic herb stuffing (p43)
3 × 15ml spoons dripping
1 large onion (200g approx)
3 × 15ml spoons plain flour

625ml general household **or** brown
    stock (p25)
1 tomato
1 medium-sized carrot (50g approx)
1 × 15ml spoon Worcestershire sauce
salt and pepper

Wipe, trim, and flatten the slices of meat with a cutlet bat or rolling-pin. Cut the meat into 4 slices. Divide the stuffing into 4 portions. Spread 1 portion on each slice of meat, roll up tightly and tie securely with fine string or cotton.

Heat the dripping in a large saucepan and fry the beef olives, turning them frequently until browned. Transfer to a warmed dish and keep hot. Skin and slice the onion, and fry in the fat until golden-brown. Remove with a perforated spoon and keep hot with the beef olives. Add the flour to the fat, stir, and cook until golden-brown. Draw the pan off the heat and gradually stir in the stock. Return to the heat and stir until boiling, then reduce the heat and simmer for 5 minutes. Skin the tomato, scrape the carrot, and slice them. Return the beef olives and onion to the pan. Add the tomato, carrot, Worcestershire sauce, and seasoning to taste. Cover the pan with a tight-fitting lid and simmer for $1\frac{1}{2}$–2 hours; or cook in a moderate oven, 180°C, Gas 4, for $1\frac{1}{2}$ hours.

Remove the strings from the beef olives, and serve the meat arranged in a row on a bed of mashed potatoes. Strain the sauce and pour it over the beef olives.

Carbonnade of Beef *Basic recipe*
6 helpings

700g stewing steak (chuck, blade, skirt
    or thin flank)
50g dripping
2 large onions (400g approx)
1 clove of garlic
1 × 15ml spoon plain flour
250ml beef stock **or** water
375ml brown ale
salt and pepper

bouquet garni
a pinch of grated nutmeg
a pinch of light soft brown sugar
1 × 5ml spoon red wine vinegar
6 thin slices from a French bâton loaf
1 × 15ml spoon French mustard **or**
    1 × 15ml spoon English mustard
    mixed with vinegar to taste

Wipe the meat and trim off any excess fat. Cut the meat into 3–4cm cubes. Heat the dripping in a large pan. Fry the meat quickly until browned on all sides. Transfer to a casserole and keep warm. Skin and slice the onions and fry them in the fat in the pan until lightly browned. Skin and crush the garlic, add it to the onions and fry gently for 1 minute. Pour off any excess fat. Sprinkle the flour over the onion and garlic and cook, stirring until just beginning to brown. Gradually stir in the stock or water, and the ale. Add the salt and pepper, bouquet garni, nutmeg, sugar, and vinegar. Heat to boiling point and pour the liquid over the meat in the casserole. Cover, and cook in a warm oven, 160°C, Gas 3, for $1\frac{1}{2}$–2 hours.

When cooked, remove the bouquet garni, spread the slices of bread with mustard, and press them well down into the gravy. Return the casserole, uncovered, to the oven, for about 15 minutes to allow the bread to brown slightly. Serve from the casserole.

Boeuf Bourguignonne
4−6 helpings

600g chuck steak	2 rashers bacon, without rinds
250ml red wine	3 × 15ml spoons oil
½ × 2.5ml spoon black pepper	12 small onions **or** shallots
1 × 2.5ml spoon salt	12 button mushrooms
bouquet garni	25g flour
1 small onion	salt and pepper
1 small carrot	250ml beef stock (approx)
2 cloves garlic	

Garnish

sippets of fried bread	chopped parsley

Wipe the steak and cut it into 2cm cubes. Put it in a basin, pour the wine over it, and add the pepper, salt, and bouquet garni. Prepare and finely slice the onion and carrot. Skin and crush the garlic. Add these to the meat and wine, cover, and leave to marinate for about 6 hours.

Cut the bacon into small pieces. Heat most of the oil in a frying pan, add the bacon, and fry lightly, then remove and put to one side. Fry the onions or shallots and the mushrooms in the oil for 3−4 minutes, then remove and put to one side. Drain the meat, reserving the marinade, and pat dry on soft kitchen paper. Season the flour with salt and pepper and coat the meat in the flour. Add a little more oil to the frying pan and fry the meat until sealed all over. Put into a 1.5 litre ovenproof casserole. Stir in the bacon, onions, and mushrooms. Strain the marinade over the meat and add about 250ml stock. Cover, and cook in a warm oven, 160°C, Gas 3, for about 2 hours. Season to taste. Serve garnished with the sippets and chopped parsley.

Beef Stroganoff
4 helpings

500g fillet of beef
1 onion
3 × 10ml spoons vegetable oil
salt and pepper

1 × 10ml spoon flour
250ml soured cream
1 × 10ml spoon Piquant sauce (p206)

Garnish
chopped fennel **or** parsley

Wipe and trim the meat, cut into small slices, and beat well with a cutlet bat or rolling-pin. Cut into fine slivers. Skin and slice the onion finely. Heat the oil, and fry the onion until softened. Add the sliced meat, season to taste, and fry for 5–6 minutes, stirring slowly with a fork. Sprinkle the meat with the flour, stir, and cook for 2–3 minutes. Add the soured cream, stir, and cook for a further 2–3 minutes. Add the Piquant sauce and salt to taste. Sprinkle with chopped fennel or parsley.

Serve with fried potatoes.

Brown Stew
6 helpings

700g stewing steak (chuck, blade **or** neck)
1 large onion (200g approx)
2 large carrots (200g approx)
1 large turnip (100g approx)
25g dripping

3 × 15ml spoons plain flour
750ml general household **or** brown stock (p25) **or** water
salt and pepper
bouquet garni

Wipe the meat and trim off any excess fat. Cut the meat into neat pieces 2–3cm thick. Prepare the vegetables; then slice the onion and carrots, and dice the turnip.

Heat the dripping in a stewpan. Put in the meat, and fry quickly until browned on all sides. Take the meat out of the pan, and put in the onion. Reduce the heat, and fry the onion gently until lightly browned. Stir in the flour and cook slowly until it turns a rich brown colour. Gradually add the stock or water, and heat to boiling point, stirring all the time. Add the seasoning and bouquet garni. Return the meat to the pan, cover with a tight-fitting lid, and simmer for $1\frac{1}{2}$ hours. Skim off any fat on the surface. Add the carrot and turnip, replace the lid and simmer for another hour or until the meat and vegetables are tender. Again skim off any fat. Re-season if required, and remove the bouquet garni before serving.

Note If preferred, the stew can be cooked in a warm oven, 160°C, Gas 3, for $1\frac{1}{2}$–2 hours. Add the carrot and turnip for the last hour of cooking.

Exeter Stew
6 helpings

700g chuck steak **or** blade **or** neck of beef
3 × 10ml spoons dripping
3 medium-sized onions (300g approx)

3 × 15ml spoons plain flour
625ml water
1 × 5ml spoon vinegar
salt and pepper

Savoury Parsley Balls

100g plain flour
½ × 2.5ml spoon baking powder
4½ × 15ml spoons shredded suet
1 × 15ml spoon finely chopped parsley

1 × 2.5ml spoon dried mixed herbs
1 × 5ml spoon salt
1 × 2.5ml spoon ground pepper
1 egg **or** 3 × 15ml spoons milk

Wipe the meat and trim off any excess fat. Cut the meat into 5cm cubes. Heat the dripping in a stewpan and fry the meat in it until browned on all sides. Remove the meat and put to one side. Skin and slice the onions. Put them in the pan, and fry gently until light brown. Add the flour, and cook, stirring until browned. Mix in the water and stir until boiling. Reduce the heat to simmering point. Add the vinegar and seasoning to taste. Return the meat, cover and simmer gently for 1½ hours.

To make the parsley balls, sift the flour and baking powder into a bowl. Add the suet, herbs, salt and pepper, and mix together. Beat the egg, if used, until liquid and bind the dry ingredients together with the beaten egg or milk to form a stiff dough. Divide the dough into 12 equal pieces and roll each into a ball.

Heat the stew to boiling point and drop in the balls. Reduce the heat and simmer for a further 30 minutes with the pan half-covered. Pile the meat in the centre of a warmed serving dish, pour the gravy over it and arrange the balls round the base.

Beef Creole
6–8 helpings

1kg topside **or** rump **or** brisket of beef
1 × 5ml spoon salt
1 × 5ml spoon ground pepper
75g streaky bacon, without rinds

500g onions
500g tomatoes
1 green pepper (125g approx)
a little beef stock **or** water (optional)

Wipe, trim, and tie the meat into a neat shape, if necessary. Season with salt and pepper. Lay the rashers in the bottom of an ovenproof casserole. Place the meat on the bacon. Skin and slice the onions and tomatoes. De-seed and slice the pepper. Cover the meat with the vegetables. Cover the casserole with a tight-fitting lid and cook in a warm oven, 160°C, Gas 3, for about 2½ hours, until the meat is tender. Lift out the meat, remove the string, and cut the meat into slices. Arrange the slices on a warmed serving dish and keep hot.

Rub the onions, tomatoes, and pepper through a sieve into a saucepan and re-heat to form a sauce, thinning with a little stock or water, if necessary. Pour the sauce round the beef slices.

Boiled Beef with Vegetables and Dumplings *Basic recipe*
8–10 helpings

1–1.25kg brisket **or** silverside **or**
  aitchbone of beef
1 × 5ml spoon salt
3 cloves
10 peppercorns

bouquet garni
3 medium-sized onions (300g approx)
4 large carrots (400g approx)
2 small turnips (100g approx)

Suet Dumplings
200g self-raising flour
100g suet

$\frac{1}{2}$ × 2.5ml spoon salt

Weigh the meat and calculate the cooking time, allowing 25 minutes per 0.5kg plus 20 minutes over. Wipe, trim, and tie the meat into a neat shape with string, if necessary. Put the meat into a large stewpan, cover with boiling water, and add the salt. Bring to the boil again and boil for 5 minutes to seal the surface of the meat. Reduce the heat to simmering point, and skim. Add the cloves, peppercorns, and bouquet garni. Cover the pan and simmer for the rest of the calculated cooking time.

Meanwhile, prepare the vegetables and cut them into serving-sized pieces. About 45 minutes before the end of the cooking time, add the vegetables to the meat and re-heat to simmering point.

Prepare the dumplings. Mix the flour, suet, and salt in a bowl. Add enough cold water to make a fairly stiff dough. Divide this mixture into walnut-sized pieces and roll them into balls. Drop them into the pan with the beef, so that they simmer for the final 20–30 minutes of the cooking time. Keep the pan covered and turn the dumplings over once during this time.

To serve, remove the bouquet garni. Take out the dumplings and vegetables with a perforated spoon, and arrange them as a border on a large warmed serving dish. Remove any strings from the meat, skewer if necessary, and set it in the centre of the dish. Serve some of the liquid separately in a sauce-boat.

Note When adding the dumplings, make sure they have plenty of room to swell. If the pan is very full, it is better to cook them separately in stock.

Pastry and Minced Dishes
Mrs Beeton's Steak Pie
6 helpings

600g lean stewing steak (chuck, blade or neck)	250ml beef stock **or** water (approx)
3 × 15ml spoons plain flour	flaky (p411) **or** rough puff (p412) pastry using 100g flour **or** shortcrust
1 × 5ml spoon salt	pastry (p407) using 200g flour
½ × 2.5ml spoon ground pepper	flour for rolling out
2 medium-sized onions (200g approx)	beaten egg **or** milk for glazing

Wipe the meat and trim off any excess fat. Cut the meat into 1–2cm cubes. Mix the flour with the salt and pepper in a bag or deep bowl. Toss the cubes of meat in the seasoned flour and put them in a 1 litre pie dish, piling them higher in the centre. Skin and chop the onions, and sprinkle them between the pieces of meat. Pour in stock or water to quarter-fill the dish.

Roll out the pastry on a lightly floured surface and use to cover the dish. Trim the edge, knock up with the back of a knife and flute the edge. Make a small hole in the centre of the lid, and decorate round with leaves of pastry. Make a pastry tassel or rose to cover the hole after baking, if liked. Brush the pastry with the beaten egg or milk.

Bake the pie in a very hot oven, 230°C, Gas 8, until the pastry is risen and light brown. Bake the tassel or rose blind, if made. Reduce the oven heat to moderate, 180°C, Gas 4, and, if necessary, place the pie on a lower shelf. Cover with greaseproof paper to prevent the pastry over-browning, and continue cooking for about 2 hours until the meat is quite tender when tested with a skewer. Heat the remaining stock and pour in enough to fill the dish by funnelling it through the hole in the pastry. Insert the pastry tassel or rose, if made, and serve.

VARIATIONS
Steak and Kidney Pie
Follow the recipe for Steak Pie, but add 2 sheep's or 150g ox kidneys. Skin, core, and cut the kidneys into slices before mixing with the steak and onions.

Steak and Mushroom Pie
Follow the recipe for Steak Pie, but add 100g mushrooms, cleaned and sliced, to the meat in the pie dish.

Steak and Potato Pie
Follow the recipe for Steak Pie, but add about 300g potatoes. Slice the meat and dip in seasoned flour. Prepare and slice the potatoes thinly. Place a layer of sliced potatoes on the bottom of the pie dish, season, and cover with a layer of meat. Add a little of the chopped onion. Repeat the layers of potato, meat, onion, and seasoning until the dish is full. Add enough stock or water to fill one-third of the dish. Proceed as for Steak Pie.

Steak Pudding
6 helpings

600g stewing steak (chuck, blade **or** neck)
3 × 15ml spoons plain flour
1 × 5ml spoon salt
½ × 2.5ml spoon ground pepper

suet crust pastry (p408) using
    200g flour
flour for rolling out
fat for greasing
3 × 15ml spoons beef stock **or** water

Wipe the meat and trim off any excess fat. Cut the meat into 1cm cubes. Mix the flour with the salt and pepper in a bag or deep bowl. Toss the cubes of meat in the seasoned flour.

Reserve one-quarter of the pastry for the lid. Roll out the rest on a lightly floured surface so that it is 1cm larger than the top of a greased 750ml basin, and 5mm thick. Press well into the basin to remove any creases. Half fill the basin with the prepared meat and add the stock or water; then add the rest of the meat. Roll out the pastry reserved for the lid to fit the top of the basin. Dampen the edges, place the lid in position, and seal. Cover with greased greaseproof paper or foil.

Place the basin in a steamer, or on a saucer in a pan with water coming half-way up the basin's sides. Steam, or half-steam, for 3–3½ hours, topping up the steamer or pan with boiling water when it is reduced by a third. Serve from the basin or turn out on to a warmed serving dish. Serve with a thin beef gravy.

VARIATION
Steak and Kidney Pudding
Follow the recipe for Steak Pudding, but add 2 sheep's kidneys or 150g ox kidney. Cut the meat into thin slices about 8 × 5cm. Dip them in the seasoned flour. Skin, core, and cut the kidneys into thin slices a little smaller than the meat. Dip them in the seasoned flour. Place a slice of kidney on each slice of meat, roll up tightly, and place the rolls on end in the pastry-lined basin. Proceed as for Steak Pudding.

Cornish Pasties
Makes 6

300g chuck steak **or** blade of beef
1 large potato (150g approx)
1 small onion (50g approx)
salt and pepper
2 × 15ml spoons water **or** beef stock

shortcrust pastry (p407) using
    200g flour
flour for rolling out
beaten egg **or** milk for glazing
    (optional)

Wipe the meat and trim off any excess fat. Cut the meat into 5mm dice. Prepare and dice the potato; skin and chop the onion finely. Mix together the meat, potato, onion, and add seasoning to taste. Add the water or stock to moisten.

Divide the pastry into 6 portions. Roll each portion on a lightly floured surface into a circle 12–14cm in diameter (approx). Trim the edges neatly. (A saucer or small plate can be used to cut the rounds.) Divide the meat filling into 6 portions and pile one portion on one half of each circle of pastry. Dampen the edges of the pastry and fold over to cover the mixture. Press the edges of the pastry together. Turn the pasties so that the sealed edges are on the top. Flute the sealed edges with the fingers. Brush with beaten egg or milk, if liked. Place the pasties on a baking tray. Bake in a hot oven, 220°C, Gas 7, for about 10 minutes, then reduce the heat to moderate, 180°C, Gas 4, and cook for 30–40 minutes.

Sea Pie
6 helpings

600g stewing steak (chuck, blade **or** neck)
3 × 15ml spoons plain flour
2 × 5ml spoons salt
½ × 2.5ml spoon ground pepper
1 medium-sized onion (100g approx)

1 large carrot (100g approx)
2 small turnips (100g approx)
brown stock (p25) **or** water to cover
suet crust pastry (p408) using
    200g flour
flour for rolling out

Wipe the meat and trim off any excess fat. Cut the meat into thin slices about 5cm square. Mix the flour with the salt and pepper in a bag or deep bowl. Toss the pieces of meat in the seasoned flour. Skin and slice the onion and dice the carrot and turnips. Put the meat and vegetables into a pan. Heat to boiling point just enough stock or water to cover the meat and vegetables and pour into the pan. Re-heat, cover with a tight-fitting lid, and simmer very gently for about 1½ hours.

Roll out the pastry on a lightly floured surface to a round a little smaller than the top of the stewpan. Place the pastry on top of the meat and vegetables. Cover with the pan lid and continue cooking for 1 hour. Cut the pastry into portions and serve with the meat.

Minced Beef *Basic recipe*
4–5 helpings

1 large onion (200g approx)
1 clove of garlic
2 × 15ml spoons oil
500g raw minced beef
salt and pepper

250g canned tomatoes
1 × 15ml spoon chopped parsley **or**
    1 × 5ml spoon dried parsley
a pinch of dried mixed herbs
1 bay leaf

Skin and chop the onion and garlic. Heat the oil in a stewpan. Add the onion and garlic, and fry gently until softened. Add the minced meat and fry until browned, stirring all the time. Season, and add the tomatoes and herbs. Stir well, and heat to boiling point. Reduce the heat and simmer, uncovered, for about 30 minutes, stirring from time to time.

Serve with vegetables, pasta or rice, or use as a filling for green peppers, baked potatoes, etc.

Note Minced beef from the butcher may be prepared from coarse cuts and trimmings or from good quality braising or stewing steak. The price is often the only indication of the quality. If you want to be certain of the type of meat, buy the cut first, then ask the butcher to mince it, or mince it yourself.

Hamburgers *Basic recipe*
4 helpings

500g raw blade **or** chuck steak, minced
2 × 5ml spoons grated onion (optional)
freshly ground black pepper
coarse salt

4 × 5ml spoons butter
Tabasco sauce
Worcestershire sauce
lemon juice

Garnish
chopped parsley

chopped chives

Mix together the minced beef and onion, if used, and season with pepper. Shape the meat lightly into 4 flat round cakes about 1cm thick. Sprinkle a thin layer of salt in a cold frying pan. Place the frying pan over high heat and put in the patties. Cook for about 5 minutes until well browned underneath. Turn the patties over and cook to the degree of rareness wanted. For a rare hamburger, cook for 1–2 minutes only, lowering the heat to medium after 30 seconds. When cooked, top each patty with 1 × 5ml spoon butter, and sprinkle with Tabasco and Worcestershire sauce and lemon juice. Transfer to a warmed serving dish, pour any pan juices over them, and serve garnished with parsley and chives.

VARIATIONS

1) Add 1 × 2.5ml spoon salt, a pinch of paprika and 2 × 15ml spoons double cream to the meat mixture. Brush the pan lightly with melted bacon fat instead of using salt. Brown the patties on both sides over high heat, then reduce the heat and cook slowly as required.

2) Prepare the patties as for variation 1. Wrap each in a rasher of bacon secured with a toothpick before cooking.

3) After cooking the patties as for the basic recipe, transfer them to a warmed serving dish but omit the sauces and lemon juice. Instead, add to the pan 50ml red wine or soured cream or 2 × 15ml spoons sherry or brandy; swill round, scraping up the pan juices, and pour the sauce over the patties.

4) Prepare the patties as for the basic recipe. Brush them lightly with melted butter, then grill under high heat for 5 minutes. Lower the heat and cook the second side for 1–2 minutes, or longer for well-done patties. Season and garnish as for the basic recipe.

5) Prepare and cook the patties and serve on buttered toast seasoned with the pan juices.

6) Garnish each cooked hamburger with a fried onion ring and 1 × 5ml spoon tomato ketchup or chutney instead of parsley and chives.

7) Split 4 round soft dinner rolls in half horizontally. Prepare the patties as for the basic recipe, brush lightly with butter, then grill them on one side only. Place them on the bottom halves of the rolls, cooked side down, then grill the second side. Top each with a fried onion ring and 1 × 5ml spoon tomato ketchup or chutney and replace the top halves of the rolls.

Beef Galantine
6–8 helpings

200g lean bacon, without rinds
500g chuck steak **or** blade of beef,
 minced
150g soft white **or** brown breadcrumbs
salt and pepper

1 egg
125ml brown stock (p25)
margarine **or** lard for greasing
2 × 15ml spoons raspings (p42) **or**
 1 × 15ml spoon meat glaze (p55)

Garnish
125ml chopped aspic jelly

Mince the bacon. Put into a bowl with the meat, breadcrumbs and seasoning to taste, and mix together well. Beat the egg until liquid, add the stock, and stir into the meat mixture to bind. Shape the mixture into a short, thick roll, wrap it in greased greaseproof paper, wrap in a scalded pudding cloth, and secure the ends. Steam for $2\frac{1}{2}$–3 hours or, if preferred, boil gently in stock for about 2 hours.

When cooked, remove the meat, unwrap it, and then roll it up tightly in a clean dry cloth. Press the roll between 2 plates until cold. When cold, remove the cloth and roll the meat in the raspings, or brush all over with melted meat glaze. Garnish with aspic jelly.

Spaghetti Bolognese
4 helpings

75g unsmoked streaky bacon, without
 rinds
1 medium-sized onion
1 medium-sized carrot
$\frac{1}{2}$ stick celery
200g lean beef mince
100g chicken livers
15g butter
1 × 15ml spoon olive oil

1 × 15ml spoon concentrated tomato
 purée
125ml dry white wine
salt and pepper
a pinch of grated nutmeg
200ml beef stock
300g spaghetti
a knob of butter

Chop the bacon into small pieces. Prepare and chop finely the onion, carrot, and celery. Break down any lumps in the mince with a fork. Cut the chicken livers into small shreds. Heat the butter and oil in a saucepan, and cook the bacon gently until brown. Add the vegetables and fry until tender and browned. Stir in the mince, and turn it until browned all over. Add the chicken livers and continue cooking for 3 minutes, turning the livers over to brown them. Mix in gradually the tomato purée and then the wine. Season with salt, pepper, and nutmeg. Lower the heat so that the sauce just simmers. Stir in the stock, cover the pan, and simmer for 30–40 minutes or until the sauce is the desired consistency. Meanwhile, boil the spaghetti as directed. Drain it and pile on a warmed serving dish. Pour the sauce over the spaghetti. Top with a knob of butter and serve Parmesan cheese separately.

Shepherd's Pie (Cottage Pie)
4–6 helpings

600g lean beef mince
2 medium-sized onions
25g dripping
1 × 15ml spoon flour
150ml strong beef stock
salt and freshly ground black pepper

700g potatoes
a pinch of grated nutmeg
milk
1–2 × 15ml spoons butter (optional)
butter for greasing

Break up any lumps in the meat with a fork. Skin and slice the onions. Melt the dripping in a saucepan, and fry the onions until softened but not coloured. Stir in the flour, and cook gently for 1–2 minutes, stirring all the time. Gradually add the stock, without letting lumps form, and stir until boiling. Reduce the heat, and simmer for 2–3 minutes until the sauce thickens. Stir in the mince, cover the pan, and simmer for 20 minutes. Season well, replace the lid, and simmer for 10 minutes longer or until the mince is cooked through and tender.

Meanwhile, prepare the potatoes and boil them in salted water until tender. Mash them until smooth with a seasoning of salt, pepper, nutmeg, enough milk to make them creamy, and butter if liked. Put the meat and sauce into a greased pie dish or shallow oven-to-table baking dish. Cover with the potato, smooth the top, then flick it up into small peaks or score a pattern on the surface with a fork. Bake for 10–15 minutes in a hot oven, 220°C, Gas 7, until browned on top. Serve hot.

Beef Croquettes
4 helpings

250g cooked beef
25g cooking fat
25g finely chopped onion
25g flour
150ml beef stock
salt and pepper
1 × 5ml spoon chopped parsley

1 × 5ml spoon any bottled savoury
  sauce
flour for dusting
2 eggs
50g dry white breadcrumbs
oil **or** fat for deep frying

Remove any fat, skin or gristle, and mince the meat. Melt the fat in a large frying pan and fry the onion for 2–3 minutes. Stir in the stock and bring to the boil, stirring all the time. Cook for 2 minutes until the sauce thickens. Add the meat, seasoning, parsley, and sauce. Stir over the heat for a moment. Turn the mixture on to a plate, level the surface, cover with a second plate, and leave to cool completely.

When cold, divide into 8 equal-sized portions. On a floured surface, form into neat cork or roll-shaped pieces. Beat the eggs until liquid. Scatter the crumbs on a sheet of greaseproof paper. Dip each croquette into the egg, brushing it all over to make sure it is evenly covered, then roll it in the crumbs until it is completely covered. Press the crumbs on lightly. Heat the fat (p10). Coat each croquette a second time. Fry in the hot fat, a few at a time, until crisp and browned all over. Drain well. Keep the first batches hot while cooking the rest.

Note The filling should have a soft creamy texture, contrasting with the crisp coating.

Offal Dishes
Baked Stuffed Ox Heart
6 helpings

1 ox heart
150g sage and onion stuffing (p46)
  or basic herb **or** ham stuffing (p43)
50–75g dripping

25g flour
500ml strong general household **or**
  brown stock (p25)

Wash the heart thoroughly under running water or in several changes of cold water. Cut off the flaps and lobes, and remove any gristle. Cut away the membranes which separate the cavities inside the heart and see that it is quite free from blood inside. Soak in cold water for 30 minutes. Drain and dry the heart thoroughly and fill it with the stuffing. Sew up the top with fine string or cotton, or skewer securely.

Heat the dripping in a roasting tin, and put in the heart. Baste well and bake in a warm oven, 160°C, Gas 3, for 3 hours. Baste frequently and turn it occasionally. When tender, remove the string, cotton or skewer, place the heart on a warmed serving dish and keep hot. Pour off most of the fat from the baking tin, retaining about 1 × 15ml spoon of the sediment. Stir in the flour and cook until browned. Gradually add the stock and stir until boiling. Boil for 3 minutes. Pour a little round the heart and serve the rest separately.

Serve redcurrant jelly with the heart if stuffed with basic herb stuffing; serve Cranberry Sauce (p215) if it is stuffed with ham or sage and onion stuffing.

Liver Hot Pot
6 helpings

650g ox liver
25g flour
salt and pepper
100g streaky bacon, without rinds
3 large onions

900g–1kg potatoes
3 × 2.5ml spoons dried sage
beef stock **or** water to cover
dripping

Garnish
chopped parsley

Remove the skin and tubes, and cut the liver into 5mm slices. Season the flour with salt and pepper in a bag or bowl, and toss the liver slices in it. Cut the bacon into small squares. Skin the onions and slice them thinly. Prepare and slice the potatoes.

Place alternate layers of liver, bacon, onion and potatoes in a pie dish or casserole, sprinkling each layer with a little sage and seasoning. End with a thick layer of potatoes. Pour in just enough stock or water to cover the contents of the dish, cover with a lid, and cook in a moderate oven, 180°C, Gas 4, for about 2 hours. Remove the lid 30 minutes before serving, dot the top of the dish with dripping, and leave to cook, uncovered, to brown the potatoes. Sprinkle with parsley, and serve from the dish.

Kidney in Italian Sauce

4 helpings

500g ox kidney
3 × 15ml spoons plain flour
1 × 2.5ml spoon salt
pepper
1 small onion (50g approx)
3 × 10ml spoons beef dripping

25g butter **or** margarine
375ml general household **or** brown
  stock (p25)
100g mushrooms
1–2 × 15ml spoons sherry (optional)

Garnish
100g cooked green peas

Skin, core, and cut the kidney into slices about 1cm thick. Season the flour with the salt and a generous pinch of pepper in a bag or bowl and toss the kidney in it until well-coated. Skin and chop the onion. Heat the dripping in a sauté pan and fry the kidney quickly on both sides. Add the onion, reduce the heat, cover, and fry gently for 20 minutes.

Meanwhile, melt the butter or margarine in a saucepan. Stir in the flour left after coating the kidney and cook until a nut-brown colour. Gradually add the stock and stir until boiling. Reduce the heat and simmer for 5 minutes. Drain the kidney and onion from the fat, add them to the sauce, half cover the pan and simmer for about 45 minutes. Clean and slice the mushrooms and add them to the pan with the sherry, if used, and extra seasoning, if liked. Simmer for a further 15 minutes. Serve hot, garnished with green peas.

Mrs Beeton's Stewed Ox Cheek

6 helpings

1 boned ox cheek
2 medium-sized onions (200g approx)
2 large carrots (200g approx)
1 turnip (50g approx)
12 peppercorns
2 cloves
bouquet garni

2 × 5ml spoons salt
2 × 10ml spoons butter **or** margarine
4 × 10ml spoons plain flour
2–3 × 15ml spoons sherry (optional)
2 × 5ml spoons lemon juice
salt and pepper

Garnish
diced **or** julienne strips of cooked carrot
  and turnip

Wash the ox cheek well in cold water. Soak for at least 12 hours in salted water, changing the water 2 or 3 times; then wash it well in warm water. Cut the cheek into convenient-sized pieces. Put them into a stewpan and cover with cold water. Heat to boiling point and skim well. Prepare the vegetables and slice them thickly. Add to the pan with the peppercorns, cloves, bouquet garni, and salt. Re-heat to boiling point, reduce the heat, cover with a tight-fitting lid, and simmer very gently for 1½–2 hours, or until the meat is tender, keeping it just covered with liquid the whole time.

When cooked, strain the liquid from the meat into a measuring jug. Put the meat

to one side. Melt the butter or margarine in a saucepan, stir in the flour and cook over gentle heat until lightly browned. Gradually add 625ml of the reserved liquid and stir until boiling; reduce the heat and simmer for 10 minutes. Add the sherry, if used, the lemon juice, and seasoning to taste. Add the pieces of meat to the sauce, and re-heat briefly. Serve on a warmed dish, and garnish with the carrot and turnip.
Note The rest of the cooking liquid will make an excellent soup stock.

Boiled Ox Tongue
9–12 helpings

1 fresh ox tongue (2kg approx)
1 medium-sized onion
1 medium-sized carrot

1 turnip
bouquet garni
6 black peppercorns

Hot Garnish
boiled sprigs of cauliflower **or**
    Brussels sprouts

Cold Garnish
chopped parsley

savoury butter (optional) (p232)

Weigh the tongue, then wash it thoroughly. Soak for 2 hours. Drain and put in a large pan. Cover with cold water, heat to boiling point, then drain thoroughly.

Return to the pan and cover a second time with fresh cold water. Prepare and dice the vegetables. Add to the pan with the bouquet garni and peppercorns. Heat to boiling point, cover with a tight-fitting lid, reduce the heat and simmer gently, allowing 30 minutes per 0.5kg plus 30 minutes over. When cooked, lift out the tongue and plunge it into cold water. Drain. Remove the skin carefully, and the small bones at the root of the tongue, together with any excess fat, glands, and gristle.

To serve hot: Garnish the tongue with sprigs of cauliflower or Brussels sprouts.

To serve cold: **(1)** Place the tongue on a board and stick a fork through the root and another through the top to straighten it. Leave to cool completely, then trim. Glaze with meat glaze (p55) or aspic jelly and garnish with parsley. Decorate with rosettes of a smooth savoury butter, if liked.

(2) Bend and roll the tongue into a round shape and press it into a deep round cake tin, just big enough to hold it (18cm in diameter approx). Spoon over a little of the strained stock in which the tongue was cooked to fill up the crevices. Put a flat plate on the tongue and then a heavy weight. Leave to set, then turn out and serve in slices.

Braised Oxtail
4−6 helpings

1.5kg oxtail	salt and pepper
50g beef dripping	bouquet garni
2 medium-sized onions (200g approx)	2 cloves
25g plain flour	1 blade of mace
500ml water **or** beef stock	juice of ½ lemon

Garnish

fried bread croûtons   diced **or** julienne strips of cooked carrot and turnip

Wash the oxtail, dry it thoroughly, and trim off any excess fat. Cut into joints, if not already jointed by the butcher, and divide the thick parts in half.

Heat the dripping in a stewpan. Fry the pieces of oxtail until browned all over, then remove them from the pan and put to one side. Skin and slice the onions. Fry them slowly in the fat until browned. Stir in the flour and cook for 1−2 minutes. Gradually add the water or stock, then add the seasoning, bouquet garni and spices, and stir until boiling. Return the pieces of oxtail to the pan, cover with a tight-fitting lid, reduce the heat, and simmer gently for 2½−3 hours. Remove the meat and arrange it on a warmed serving dish. Add the lemon juice to the sauce and re-season if required. Strain the sauce and pour it over the oxtail. Garnish with the bread croûtons, carrot and turnip.

Mrs Beeton's Boiled Marrow Bones
2 pieces of marrow bone per helping

marrow bones (150g approx each)   flour

Choose marrow bones from the leg or shin. Ask your butcher to saw them across into pieces 7cm long or do it yourself. Shape the thick ends by chopping them so that the bones will stand upright. Mix some flour to a stiff paste with water, and plaster this paste over the open end of each bone to seal in the marrow. Tie each bone in a floured cloth.

Stand the bones upright in a deep saucepan containing enough boiling water to come half-way up the bones. Cover the pan with a tight-fitting lid, reduce the heat, and simmer gently for about 1½ hours. Refill the pan with boiling water, if necessary. When cooked, remove the bones from the cloths and scrape off the paste. Fasten a paper napkin round each one and serve with a pointed teaspoon to extract the marrow.

Serve with Melba or hot dry toast and a seasoning of pepper.

Tripe and Onion
4 helpings

500g dressed tripe
500ml milk
salt and pepper

3 medium-sized onions (300g approx)
25g butter **or** margarine
25g flour

Garnish
1 × 15ml spoon chopped parsley

toasted croûtons

Wash the tripe and cut it into pieces 5cm square (approx). Put into a stewpan, pour over the milk and, if necessary, add some water to cover. Add salt and pepper to taste. Skin and chop the onions. Add them to the pan. Heat to boiling point, cover with a tight-fitting lid, reduce the heat and simmer gently until the tripe is tender (the length of time should be suggested by the butcher).

Knead the butter or margarine and flour together until evenly blended, and add it in small pieces to the contents of the pan. Stir until smooth, then continue cooking for another 30 minutes. Serve the tripe on a warmed dish and garnish with chopped parsley and toasted croûtons.

Lamb and Mutton

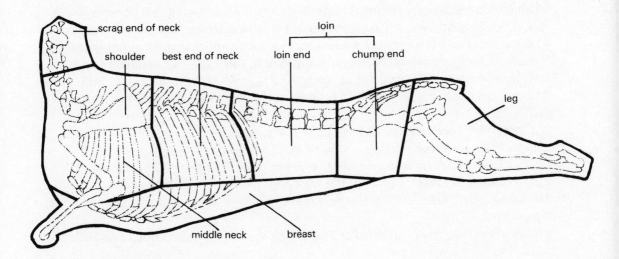

Lamb and Mutton Cuts
English lamb and mutton and most imported, chilled and frozen lamb and mutton are usually cut in a similar way to beef, ie into sides and quarters before jointing. As with beef, cuts vary in different parts of Great Britain. The diagram above shows the most usual ones.

1) *Leg* or hind limb, also known as gigot in Scotland, is an excellent roasting joint on the bone or boned, stuffed and rolled. The leg is often divided into fillet and shank end. Leg is leaner (tougher and slightly drier) than the shoulder (forelimb) and is also more expensive. (Av wt leg of lamb – 2kg; Av wt leg of mutton – 2.5kg)

2) *Loin* can be roasted whole on the bone or boned, stuffed, and rolled. However, it is usually divided into loin end and chump end, and is cut into loin chops and chump chops (see below). (Av wt loin of lamb – 1.5kg; Av wt loin of mutton – 2kg)

3) *Saddle* is the whole loin from both sides of the animal, left in one piece. (Av wt saddle of lamb – 3.5kg; Av wt saddle of mutton – 4.5kg)

4) *Best end of neck* can be roasted on the bone or boned, stuffed, and rolled. It is often sold as chops or cutlets for grilling and frying. These chops or cutlets are sometimes served as noisettes which are prepared by removing the backbone (chine bone) and trimming away some of the meat at the rib end. Two best ends of neck are used to make a Crown Roast (p130) or Guard of Honour (pp131–32). (Av wt best end of neck of lamb – 1kg; Av wt best end of neck of mutton – 2.5kg)

5) *Breast* is the most economical cut for roasting or braising and for tasty stews. Because of its high fat content it is best roasted with a stuffing to which no fat has been added so that much of the lamb fat is absorbed, making it a more palatable dish. (Av wt breast of lamb – 675g; Av wt breast of mutton – 1kg)

6) *Shoulder* is an economical roast on the bone or boned, stuffed, and rolled. It is fattier than the leg and is more moist after roasting. It is often divided into two smaller cuts: the blade or best end and the knuckle end. Both are ideal for roasting, braising, and casseroling. In Scotland, shoulder is not cut as a separate joint. The entire forequarter is usually divided in half, boned and rolled, then cut into smaller rolled joints. (Av wt shoulder of lamb – 1.75kg; Av wt shoulder of mutton – 2.5kg)

7) *Middle neck* is usually cut into chops for casseroles and stews. It is possible to cut 2 or 3 chops for grilling or frying from the meat closest to the best end of neck.

8) *Scrag end of neck* is a very economical cut for stews and soups. To avoid splinters of bone, look for scrag which has been cut into neat rings and not chopped roughly. (Av wt middle neck and scrag end of lamb – 0.75kg; Av wt of mutton – 1.5kg)

9) *Lamb chops* are cut from the loin or from the leg. Good for grilling, frying or braising.

> *Chump:* 4–6 per carcass. (Av wt 125–150g each)
> *Loin:* 6 (approx) per carcass. (Av wt 100–150g each)
> *Neck (cutlet with rib bone removed):* 4–6 per cut. (Av wt 75–125g each)
> *Leg (chops or cutlets):* Cut from the fillet end. (Av wt 100–150g each)

10) *Lamb cutlets* are cut from the best end of neck. 4–6 per carcass. (Av wt 75–150g each)

Mutton chops and cutlets are thicker and weigh more than lamb chops and cutlets.

Roasted and Baked Dishes
Roast Leg of Lamb or Mutton *Basic recipe*

a leg of lamb **or** mutton   oil **or** fat for basting
salt and pepper

Select the method of roasting, ie quick or slow roasting (p91). Weigh the joint to calculate the cooking time (p92). Wipe the meat. Place on a wire rack, if available, in a shallow roasting tin. Season the meat, and either pour over it a little oil or rub it with a little fat. Place the roasting tin in the oven, and cook for the required time.

Transfer the cooked meat from the oven to a warmed meat dish, and keep hot. Prepare a gravy, if liked, from the sediment in the roasting tin.

Serve roast leg of lamb with Mint Sauce (p56), and roast leg of mutton with Onion Sauce (p203) and redcurrant jelly.

Stuffed Roast Shoulder of Lamb or Mutton

6–10 helpings

a shoulder of lamb **or** mutton	150–200g basic herb (p43) **or**
salt and pepper	sage and onion (p46) stuffing
	dripping

Remove all the bones from the meat. Wipe the meat and trim off any skin and excess fat. Flatten the meat with a cutlet bat or rolling-pin. Season the inner surface of the meat well with salt and pepper and spread on the stuffing. Roll it up and tie securely with fine string.

Weigh the meat to calculate the cooking time, allowing 30 minutes per 0.5kg plus either 30 minutes over for lamb, or 35 minutes over for mutton. Heat the dripping in a roasting tin, put in the meat, and baste with the dripping. Cover the roasting tin and roast in a moderate oven, 180°C, Gas 4, until tender. Baste occasionally during the cooking time.

Serve on a warmed dish with lamb gravy (p229) or Foundation Brown Sauce (p204).

Lamb Cutlets en Papillotes

6 helpings

6 lamb cutlets	1 × 10ml spoon chopped parsley
4–6 slices cooked ham	salt and pepper
1 medium-sized onion (100g approx)	grated rind of $\frac{1}{2}$ lemon
25g flat **or** button mushrooms	oil **or** butter for greasing
1 × 10ml spoon oil **or** butter	

Wipe and trim the cutlets neatly. Cut 12 small rounds of ham just large enough to cover the round part of the cutlet. Prepare the onion and mushrooms and chop finely. Heat the oil or butter in a small pan, and fry the onion until tender and lightly browned. Remove from the heat and stir in the mushrooms, parsley, salt and pepper to taste, and the grated lemon rind. Leave to cool.

Cut out 6 heart-shaped pieces of strong white paper or double thickness grease-proof paper or foil large enough to hold the cutlets. Grease them well with oil or butter. Place a slice of ham on half of each paper or foil, and spread on top a little of the cooled onion mixture. Then arrange the cutlet, a little more of the onion mixture, and a round of ham in layers on top. Fold over the paper or foil and twist the edges well together. Lay the cutlets in a greased baking tin and cook in a fairly hot oven, 190°C, Gas 5, for 30 minutes. Arrange the cutlets in the paper or foil on a warmed serving dish.

Foundation Brown Sauce (p204) or gravy can be served separately.

Crown Roast of Lamb with Saffron Rice
6 helpings

2 best ends of neck of lamb (6 cutlets each)

oil for brushing
salt and pepper

Saffron Rice
1 stick of celery (50g approx)
1 medium-sized onion (100g approx)
500ml chicken stock
$\frac{1}{2} \times 2.5$ml spoon powdered saffron
50g butter

150g long-grain white rice
4×15ml spoons dry white wine
25g blanched almonds
2 dessert apples (250g approx)
50g frozen green peas

Ask the butcher to prepare the crown roast or prepare it as follows. Wipe the meat. Remove the fat and meat from the top 4–5cm of the thin ends of the bones and scrape the bone ends clean. Slice the lower half of each best end of neck between each bone, about two-thirds up from the base. Trim off any excess fat. Turn the joints so that bones are on the outside and the meat is on the inside, and sew the pieces together with a trussing needle and fine string. The thick ends of the meat will be the base of the crown, so make sure they stand level.

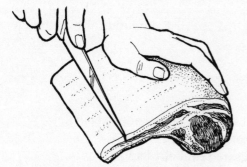

Removing the fat and meat from the bone ends

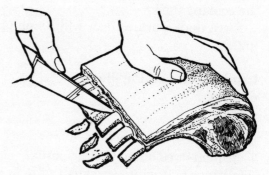

Scraping the bone ends clean

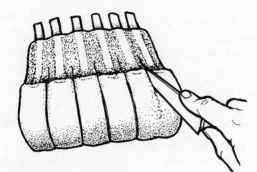

Slicing between each bone

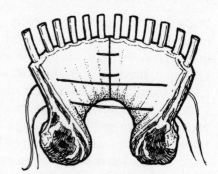

Sewing pieces to form a crown roast

Place the prepared crown roast in a roasting tin. Brush it with oil and season well with salt and pepper. Wrap a piece of foil round the top of each cutlet bone to prevent it from scorching. Cook in a fairly hot oven, 190°C, Gas 5, for $1\frac{1}{4}$–$1\frac{1}{2}$ hours.

About 30 minutes before the end of the cooking time, make the saffron rice. Prepare and chop the celery and onion. Heat the chicken stock in a saucepan with the powdered saffron. Heat 25g of the butter in a saucepan and fry the celery and onion gently until softened but not browned. Wash the rice, stir it into the vegetables and cook for 1–2 minutes. Pour on the wine and cook gently until the rice has absorbed it. Add 250ml of the hot stock and cook, uncovered, stirring occasionally, until almost all the liquid is absorbed. Pour the remaining stock into the rice and cook gently until it has been completely absorbed and the rice is just tender. Chop the almonds and peel, core, and dice the apples. Remove the rice from the heat and add the almonds, diced apple, peas, and butter. Cover the pan with a tight-fitting lid, and leave to cook in its own steam until the peas are thawed and heated through, and the roast is ready.

When cooked, place the crown roast on a warmed serving dish. Remove the foil from the cutlet bones. Fill the hollow centre of the roast with the hot saffron rice. Top each cutlet with a cutlet frill and serve. Any extra rice can be served separately.

Guard of Honour
6 helpings

2 best ends of neck of lamb (6–7 cutlets each)

2×15ml spoons oil

Stuffing

1 small onion (50g approx)
50g mushrooms
25g butter **or** margarine
100g soft white breadcrumbs
1×15ml spoon chopped parsley

grated rind of 1 lemon
salt and pepper
1 egg
a little milk

Gravy

1×15ml spoon plain flour
250ml vegetable stock (p27)

salt and pepper
gravy browning (optional)

Garnish

sprigs of parsley

Ask the butcher to chine the joints. Remove the fat and meat from the top 5cm of the thin end of the bones and scrape the bone ends clean. Wipe the meat and score the fat with a sharp knife in a lattice pattern. Place the joints together to form an arch.

Make the stuffing. Prepare the onion and mushrooms. Melt the butter or margarine in a frying pan and fry the onion gently for 5 minutes until softened but not browned. Mix together the fried onion, mushrooms, breadcrumbs, parsley, lemon rind, and seasoning to taste. Beat the egg until liquid and add it to the stuffing with enough milk to bind it together. Stuff the cavity of the Guard of Honour.

Close the joints together at the top, by criss-crossing the bones. Cover the bones with foil to prevent them from scorching. Heat the oil in a baking tin and put in the Guard of Honour. Bake in a fairly hot oven, 190°C, Gas 5, for $1\frac{1}{4}$–$1\frac{1}{2}$ hours or until the lamb is tender. When cooked, transfer the lamb to a warmed serving dish, and allow to rest in the turned-off oven.

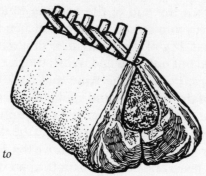

*Best ends of neck placed together to
form an arch*

Meanwhile, make the gravy. Pour off most of the fat from the roasting tin. Stir in the flour, and cook gently for a few minutes. Gradually add the stock and stir until boiling. Reduce the heat and simmer for 2 minutes. Season to taste and add gravy browning if liked. Pour into a warmed gravy-boat.

Remove the foil from the bones of the Guard of Honour and replace with cutlet frills. Garnish with sprigs of parsley.

Grilled and Fried Dishes
Grilled Lamb or Mutton Cutlets or Chops *Basic recipe*
6–8 helpings

6–8 lamb **or** mutton cutlets **or** chops   oil for brushing
salt and pepper

Garnish (optional)
pats of any savoury butter (p232)

Choose plump cutlets or chops with the nut of meat 2–2.5cm thick so that they will not curl up when grilled. Wipe and trim the cutlets or chops into a neat shape. Season with salt and pepper and brush them all over with oil. Cook on the grid or base of the grilling pan, turning once or twice; keep well-brushed with oil. Cutlets require 7–10 minutes in all, and chops require 8–15 minutes, according to their thickness. When cooked, the cutlets or chops should be well-browned with crisp fat on the outside, and slightly pink on the inside when cut. Garnish with pats of any savoury butter, if liked. The ends of the cutlet bones can be covered with cutlet frills before serving.

Suitable accompaniments are green peas, baby carrots, new, creamed or chipped potatoes, and lamb gravy (p229) or Demi-glace Sauce (p211).

Lamb Shish Kebab
6 helpings

1kg boned lean lamb, preferably
  from the leg

6 firm tomatoes
3 small green peppers

Marinade
1 large onion (200g approx)
$1\frac{1}{2} \times 15$ml spoons olive oil
3×15ml spoons lemon juice

5×5ml spoons salt
1×2.5ml spoon ground black pepper

Wipe the meat and trim off any excess fat. Cut the meat into 2cm cubes.

Make the marinade. Skin the onion and slice it thinly. Put it in a deep bowl. Sprinkle the olive oil, lemon juice, salt and pepper over the onion slices. Add the meat and stir well to coat the pieces of meat thoroughly. Marinate the meat at room temperature for several hours, turning it occasionally.

Remove the lamb from the marinade and drain thoroughly. Cut the tomatoes crossways into slices. Cut the green pepper into chunks and remove the membranes and seeds. Thread tomato slices, meat, and chunks of pepper on each skewer. Grill the skewers of meat and vegetables under high heat, or over a charcoal fire, turning the skewers occasionally, until the vegetables are well-browned and the lamb is done to taste. For pink lamb, allow about 10 minutes; for well-done lamb, allow about 15 minutes. Slide the lamb and vegetables off the skewers on to warmed individual plates.

Serve with boiled rice.

Fried Lamb or Mutton Cutlets or Chops *Basic recipe*
6–8 helpings

6–8 lamb **or** mutton cutlets **or** chops
salt and pepper
1×15ml spoon plain flour
1 egg
6×15ml spoons dried white
  breadcrumbs

2×15ml spoons oil
25g butter
250ml Fresh Tomato sauce (p216)

Garnish
200g cooked green peas

Wipe and trim the cutlets and scrape clean about 2cm of the thin end of the bones, or wipe and trim the chops neatly. Season well on both sides. Dust lightly with the flour. Beat the egg until liquid and brush the cutlets or chops all over with the beaten egg; then coat them lightly with the crumbs.

Heat the oil and butter together in a frying pan and fry the meat until golden-brown on both sides and cooked through; this takes 7–10 minutes for cutlets and 8–15 minutes for chops, depending on their thickness. Drain thoroughly. Arrange the fried cutlets or chops on a warmed serving dish, and garnish with the peas. Pour some of the tomato sauce round and serve the rest separately.

Note The cutlets or chops can be fried without the egg and breadcrumb coating.

Noisettes of Lamb Jardinière

6 helpings

1kg boned best end of neck of lamb	500g creamed potatoes
salt and pepper	250ml lamb gravy (p229) **or**
2 × 15ml spoons oil for grilling **or** frying	Demi-glace sauce (p211)

Garnish

2 × 15ml spoons diced green beans	2 × 15ml spoons diced turnip
2 × 15ml spoons diced carrot	2 × 15ml spoons diced celery

Wipe the meat. Roll it up and tie it with fine string at 2–3cm intervals. Cut through the roll between the string to make noisettes. Season the noisettes on both sides. Either brush them with oil and grill for 6–7 minutes, turning once or twice, or heat the oil in a frying pan and fry them, turning once or twice, until cooked through and browned on both sides.

At the same time, cook each vegetable for the garnish separately in boiling salted water until tender. Drain and mix together.

Spoon or pipe the hot creamed potatoes in a border on a warmed serving dish and arrange the noisettes on top. Garnish with the vegetables, pour a little of the hot gravy or Demi-glace sauce round the noisettes, and serve the rest in a warmed sauce-boat.

Casseroled, Braised and Boiled Dishes
Lancashire Hot Pot

6 helpings

1kg middle neck of lamb **or** mutton	fat for greasing
3 sheep's kidneys	salt and pepper
1kg potatoes	250ml general household stock (p25)
1 large onion (200g approx)	25g lard **or** dripping

Wipe the meat, cut it into neat cutlets, and trim off any excess fat. Skin, core, and slice the kidneys. Prepare the potatoes, slice half of them, and cut the rest into chunks or in half, if small, for the top of the casserole. Skin and slice the onion.

Put a layer of potatoes in the bottom of a greased, large, deep casserole. Arrange the cutlets on top, slightly overlapping each other, and cover with the kidneys and onion. Season well. Arrange the remainder of the potatoes (halves or chunks) neatly on top. Pour in the hot stock. Melt the lard or dripping and brush it over the top layer of potatoes. Cover the casserole with a tight-fitting lid and bake in a moderate oven, 180°C, Gas 4, for about 2 hours or until the meat and potatoes are tender. Remove the lid, increase the oven temperature to hot, 220°C, Gas 7, and cook for another 20 minutes or until the top layer of potatoes is brown and crisp. Serve from the casserole.

Irish Stew
4–6 helpings

1kg middle neck **or** scrag end of neck
  of lamb **or** mutton
2 large onions (400g approx)
1kg potatoes

salt and pepper
water **or** general household stock
  (p25) as required

Garnish
2 × 15ml spoons chopped parsley

Wipe the meat, cut it into neat cutlets or pieces, and trim off any excess fat. Skin the onions and slice them thinly; prepare and slice the potatoes. In a stewpan, place layers of meat, onions, and potatoes, adding seasoning between each layer, and finishing with a layer of potatoes. Add enough water or stock to come half-way up the meat and vegetables. Cover the pan with a lid, heat to simmering point, and simmer gently for 2½ hours. Alternatively, cook the stew in a casserole, covered with a lid, in a fairly hot oven, 190°C, Gas 5, for 2–2½ hours. Serve garnished with chopped parsley.

Curried Lamb
6 helpings

650–700g lean leg **or** loin of lamb
50g dripping
2 medium-sized onions (200g approx)
1 clove of garlic (optional)
2–3 × 5ml spoons curry powder
25g ground rice
1 cooking apple (150g approx)
25g tamarind **or** mango chutney
1 × 10ml spoon plum jam

1 × 10ml spoon desiccated coconut
6 black peppercorns
4 allspice berries
Cayenne pepper
salt
50g concentrated tomato purée
675ml white **or** chicken stock (p26)
lemon juice (optional)

Wipe the meat and cut it into 2cm cubes. Heat the dripping in a stewpan and fry the meat lightly, then put the meat to one side. Skin and slice the onions thinly, and skin and crush the garlic, if used. Fry the onion and garlic in the fat until pale golden. Add the curry powder and ground rice, and fry for 6 minutes. Peel, core, and chop the apple. Add the apple and the rest of the ingredients, except the lemon juice, to the pan. Heat to boiling point, stirring all the time. Return the meat to the pan, cover with a tight-fitting lid, and simmer gently for about 1½ hours, stirring frequently. Lift the meat out on to a warmed serving dish. Add the lemon juice, if used, to the sauce and re-season if required. Strain the sauce over the meat.

Serve in a border of plain boiled rice and serve extra rice separately.

Braised Lamb or Mutton Provençale
8–12 helpings

a leg **or** shoulder **or** loin of lamb
  or mutton

fat for greasing
meat glaze (p55)

Stuffing

50g lean ham
50g pork **or** veal
6 button mushrooms
1 shallot
1 egg

50g soft white breadcrumbs
1 × 5ml spoon chopped parsley
1 × 2.5ml spoon dried mixed herbs
1 × 2.5ml spoon grated lemon rind
salt and pepper

Mirepoix

2 medium-sized onions (200g approx)
2 medium-sized carrots (100g approx)
1 turnip (75g approx)
2 sticks celery (100g approx)

75g dripping
bouquet garni
10 black peppercorns
1 litre beef stock (approx)

Provençale Sauce

500ml foundation brown sauce (p204)
1 tomato (50g approx)
1 small onion (50g approx)
2 large mushrooms (25g approx)

25g butter **or** margarine
1 × 2.5ml spoon chopped parsley
1 × 2.5ml spoon lemon juice

Garnish

baked tomatoes

baked mushrooms

Wipe the meat. Bone it, or ask the butcher to do it for you.

Make the stuffing. Mince the meat. Prepare the mushrooms and shallot and chop them. Beat the egg until liquid. Mix together all the stuffing ingredients. Press the mixture lightly into the cavity left by the bone and sew up the opening.

Prepare the vegetables for the mirepoix and slice them thickly. Heat the dripping in a large stewpan and fry the vegetables gently for 3–5 minutes. Add the bouquet garni and peppercorns. Pour in enough stock to come three-quarters of the way up the vegetables. Place the meat on top. Lay a piece of greased greaseproof paper on top of the pan, greased side down, and cover with a tight-fitting lid. Cook over low heat for 2 hours for lamb or 2½ hours for mutton, basting frequently and making up the volume of stock as it reduces.

Transfer the meat to a baking tin and cook in a fairly hot oven, 200°C, Gas 6, for another 30 minutes, basting with a little stock as needed.

Meanwhile, strain the braising liquid from the stewpan and use it to make the brown sauce if not already made. Prepare and slice the tomato, onion, and mushrooms. Melt the butter or margarine in a saucepan. Add the vegetables and chopped parsley, half cover and cook gently for 15–20 minutes. Add the brown sauce to this mixture and simmer for another 10 minutes. Season carefully and strain through a sieve. Re-heat without boiling, add the lemon juice, and keep hot.

When cooked, transfer the meat to a warmed serving dish. Brush with warm meat glaze. Garnish with baked tomatoes and mushrooms. Serve the sauce separately.

Boiled Leg of Lamb or Mutton with Caper Sauce
8–10 helpings

a leg of lamb (2kg approx) **or** a small
  leg of mutton (2.5kg approx)
1 × 5ml spoon salt
10 black peppercorns
2 medium-sized onions (200g approx)

4 medium-sized carrots (200g approx)
2 turnips **or** 1 large parsnip
  (100g approx)
1–2 leeks
375–500ml Caper sauce (p202)

Wipe the meat and trim off any excess fat. Put the meat in a large stewpan with the salt, peppercorns, and enough cold water to cover. Heat to boiling point. Skim, reduce the heat, cover the pan with a tight-fitting lid, and simmer over gentle heat for 2½–3 hours or until the meat is tender.

Meanwhile, prepare the vegetables and leave whole if small, or cut into large neat pieces. Add the vegetables 45 minutes before the end of the cooking time. When cooked, drain the meat and vegetables from the cooking liquid. Place the meat on a warmed serving dish, coat with the Caper sauce, and arrange with the vegetables.

Pastry and Minced Dishes
Lamb Pie
4–6 helpings

1kg best end **or** middle neck **or** breast
  of lamb
salt and pepper
1–2 sheep's kidneys
stock **or** water

shortcrust pastry (p407) using
  150g flour **or** puff pastry (p412)
  using 100g flour
flour for rolling out

Wipe the meat and remove the fat and bones. Boil the bones to make stock for the gravy. Cut the meat into 2cm cubes and put them in a 750ml pie dish. Sprinkle each layer with salt and pepper. Skin, core, and slice the kidneys thinly. Add them to the meat in the pie dish. Half fill the dish with stock or water. Roll out the pastry on a lightly floured surface and use to cover the dish. Make a hole in the centre of the lid for the steam to escape. Bake in a moderate oven, 180°C, Gas 4, for 1½–2 hours, until the meat is tender (test with a skewer).

Strain the liquid off the bones. Season it to taste. Just before serving, pour enough of this gravy stock through the hole in the centre of the pie to fill the dish.

Lamb or Mutton Pudding
5–6 helpings

500g lean lamb **or** mutton
3 × 15ml spoons plain flour
salt and pepper
1–2 sheep's kidneys
suet crust pastry (p408) using
  250g flour

flour for rolling out
fat for greasing
3 × 15ml spoons general household
  stock (p25) **or** water

Follow the directions for Steak and Kidney Pudding (p118).

Cumberland Mutton Pies
6 helpings

300g lean mutton
1 medium-sized onion (100g approx)
1 × 10ml spoon dripping
100g mushrooms
1 × 10ml spoon chopped parsley
a pinch of dried thyme
salt and pepper

shortcrust pastry (p407) using
　　300g flour
flour for rolling out
6 × 10ml spoons general household
　　stock (p25)
beaten egg **or** milk for glazing

Wipe and mince the meat. Skin and chop the onion. Heat the dripping in a pan and fry the onion lightly. Remove the onion and mix it with the mutton. Clean and chop the mushrooms, and add them to the meat with the parsley, thyme, and seasoning to taste.

Roll out half the pastry on a lightly floured surface, and cut out 6 circles to line 6 small round tins or saucers. Divide the mixture between the tins. Add to each 1 × 10ml spoon stock to moisten. Roll out the rest of the pastry and cut out 6 lids for the pies. Dampen the edges of the pies, put on the lids and seal well. Brush with beaten egg or milk. Make a hole in the lid of each pie to allow steam to escape. Bake in a moderate oven, 180°C, Gas 4, for 40–45 minutes.

Lamb or Mutton Roll
6 helpings

650g lean lamb **or** mutton
200g ham **or** bacon
1 × 2.5ml spoon finely chopped onion
3 × 15ml spoons soft white
　　breadcrumbs
1 × 5ml spoon chopped parsley
½ × 2.5ml spoon dried mixed herbs
a pinch of grated nutmeg
1 × 2.5ml spoon grated lemon rind

salt and pepper
1 egg
2 × 15ml spoons chicken stock (p26)
　　or lamb gravy (p229)
1 × 15ml spoon plain flour **or**
　　beaten egg and 2 × 15ml spoons
　　breadcrumbs
2 × 15ml spoons dripping

Wipe the lamb or mutton. Finely chop or mince all the meat. Put in a bowl and mix it well with the onion, breadcrumbs, herbs, nutmeg, and grated lemon rind. Season to taste. Beat the egg until liquid, and add it with the stock or gravy to moisten the mixture. Shape it into a short thick roll. Wrap the roll in foil or several thicknesses of greaseproof paper to keep it in shape and to protect the meat. Bake in a moderate oven, 180°C, Gas 4, for 1½ hours.

Remove the foil or paper and lightly dredge the roll with the flour, or brush it with the beaten egg and coat it with breadcrumbs. Heat the dripping in a baking tin and place the roll in the tin. Baste well and return it to the oven for a further 30 minutes until browned.

Serve with gravy.

Note Under-cooked cold lamb or mutton can be used. The roll should then be cooked for only 1 hour before browning it.

Moussaka
4 helpings

1 medium-sized aubergine
salt
1 large onion
1 clove of garlic
2 medium-sized tomatoes
2 × 15ml spoons olive oil
500g raw lamb **or** beef, minced
pepper

1 × 10ml spoon chopped parsley
150ml dry white wine
300ml milk
1 egg
2 egg yolks
a pinch of grated nutmeg
75g Kefalotiri **or** Parmesan cheese
fat for greasing

Cut the aubergine into 1cm slices, sprinkle them with salt and put to one side on a large platter to drain. Chop the onion, grate the garlic, and skin, de-seed, and chop the tomatoes. Heat the olive oil, add the onion and garlic, and sauté gently until the onion is soft. Add the minced meat and continue cooking, stirring with a fork to break up any lumps in the meat. When the meat is thoroughly browned, add salt, pepper, parsley, and the tomatoes. Mix well, and add the white wine. Simmer the mixture for a few minutes to blend the flavours, then remove from the heat.

In a basin, beat together the milk, egg, egg yolks, salt, and a good pinch of grated nutmeg. Grate the cheese, add about half to the egg mixture, and beat again briefly.

Grease a 20 × 10 × 10cm oven-to-table baking dish. Drain the aubergine slices and pat dry with soft kitchen paper. Place half in the bottom of the casserole and cover with the meat mixture. Lay the remaining aubergine slices on the meat and pour the milk and egg mixture over them. Sprinkle the remaining cheese on top. Bake in a moderate oven, 180°C, Gas 4, for 30–40 minutes, until the custard is set and the top is light golden-brown. Serve from the dish.

Offal Dishes
Lamb's Liver and Bacon
4–6 helpings

500g sheep's **or** lamb's liver
50g flour
salt and pepper

250g back bacon rashers, without
  rinds
400ml brown stock (p25)

Garnish
sprigs of parsley

Remove the skin and tubes, and cut the liver into 1cm thick slices. Season the flour with salt and pepper. Dip each slice of liver in the seasoned flour. Cook the bacon rashers in a frying pan. Transfer the bacon to a warmed dish and keep hot. Fry the slices of liver lightly and quickly in the fat from the bacon until browned on both sides, without hardening or over-cooking them. Transfer the liver to a warmed serving dish, arrange the bacon around it and keep hot.

Drain off all but about 1 × 10ml spoon of fat, stir in the remaining seasoned flour and cook until browned. Gradually add the stock and stir until boiling. Re-season if required. Garnish the liver and bacon with sprigs of parsley and serve the sauce separately.

Sautéed Kidneys
4 helpings

4 sheep's **or** lamb's kidneys
1 small onion
50g butter
1 × 5ml spoon chopped parsley

125ml foundation brown sauce (p204)
salt and pepper
4 slices fried bread

Garnish
chopped parsley

Skin and core the kidneys, and slice them very thinly. Skin the onion, and chop it finely. Melt the butter in a frying pan, and fry the onion until just golden-brown. Add the kidney slices and parsley. Stir, and turn over in the fat for 2–3 minutes until very lightly fried. Add the brown sauce, and season to taste. Bring the sauce just to the boil. Pour the mixture on to a warmed serving dish. Cut the slices of fried bread into triangles, and arrange around the edge of the dish. Garnish with chopped parsley, and serve at once.

Lamb's Fry
6 helpings

650–700g lamb's fry (liver, heart,
    lights, melts, sweetbreads)
1 small onion (50g approx)
1 small carrot (25g approx)
bouquet garni
salt and pepper
1 × 15ml spoon lemon juice

1 egg
4–6 × 15ml spoons soft white
    breadcrumbs
75g dripping **or** lard
25g plain flour
1 × 5ml spoon finely chopped parsley

Garnish
6 grilled bacon rolls (p48)

Prepare the fry as for Fried Pig's Fry (p160). Prepare the onion and carrot, and slice them thinly. Put the fry, onion, carrot, and bouquet garni into a stewpan and cover with cold water. Heat to boiling point, reduce the heat, cover the pan, and simmer gently for about 30 minutes. Allow the meat to cool in the stock. When cold, strain and reserve the stock, and divide the meat into 2 portions.

Cut 1 portion of the meat into thin slices. Season with salt and pepper. Sprinkle with the lemon juice. Beat the egg until liquid and coat the slices with beaten egg and then with the breadcrumbs, and put to one side. Dice the rest of the meat.

Melt 25g of the dripping or lard in a saucepan. Stir in the flour and cook for 3 minutes. Gradually add 250ml of the strained stock and stir until boiling. Season to taste. Add the diced meat and parsley. Cover the pan and keep hot without boiling. Heat the remaining 50g dripping or lard in a frying pan. Fry the breadcrumbed slices of fry quickly on both sides until browned. Drain thoroughly.

Pile the diced meat and sauce from the saucepan into the centre of a warmed serving dish. Arrange the slices of fried meat round the outside and garnish with the bacon rolls.

Brains on Toast
6 helpings

3 sheep's **or** lamb's brains
salt and pepper
1 hard-boiled egg

25g butter
1 × 5ml spoon chopped parsley

Soak the brains in lightly salted cold water for 30 minutes to remove all traces of blood; then cut off any membranes. Wash thoroughly but very gently. Tie the brains in muslin. Heat a pan of water to boiling point, add 1 × 2.5ml spoon of salt and the brains, and cook gently for 15 minutes.

Drain the brains and remove them from the muslin. Chop the brains and the egg roughly. Melt the butter in a pan, add the brains and egg, and heat through. Season to taste and add the parsley.

Serve hot on buttered toast.

Note This recipe can also be used for calf's or pig's brains.

Sweetbreads Bourgeoise
6 helpings

3 pairs lamb's sweetbreads
   (650–675g approx)
25g butter **or** margarine
white **or** chicken stock (p26)
   to cover
salt and pepper

2 × 15ml spoons peas
2 × 15ml spoons diced turnip
2 × 15ml spoons diced carrot
250ml foundation brown (p204)
   or Espagnole (p210) sauce

Soak the sweetbreads in cold water for 1–2 hours to remove all the blood. Drain, and put them in a pan with cold water to cover. Heat to boiling point and pour off the liquid. Rinse the sweetbreads under cold water. Remove the black veins and as much as possible of the membranes which cover them.

Heat the butter or margarine in a saucepan and toss the sweetbreads in it. Then barely cover them with the stock. Season to taste with salt and pepper. Heat to simmering point, cover the pan, and cook gently for 45 minutes–1 hour, until tender. Transfer to a warmed dish and keep hot.

Prepare the vegetables and cook them separately in boiling salted water until just tender. Drain, and add them to the hot brown or Espagnole Sauce. Divide the sweet-breads between 6 soup bowls and pour the sauce over them. Serve very hot.

Boiled Sheep's Head *Basic recipe*
3–5 helpings

a sheep's head
salt
2 medium-sized onions (200g approx)

2 medium-sized carrots (100g approx)
10 black peppercorns
bouquet garni

Garnish
1 × 10ml spoon chopped parsley

Ask the butcher to split the head if not already done. Remove the brains and put to one side. Snip off any remaining hairy bits of skin, scrub the teeth and jaw bones with salt and scrape the bones from the nostrils. Rinse the head and soak it in cold water. Add 1 × 15ml spoon salt to each litre of water. Put the brains in the water with the head and soak them for 30 minutes to remove all traces of blood; then cut off any membranes. Wash thoroughly but very gently. The brains can be used separately or tied in muslin, cooked for part of the time with the head, and used with the meat of the head.

Cover the head with cold water, heat to boiling point, and pour the water away. Cover the head with fresh cold water. Prepare the onions and carrots and add them to the pan with 2 × 5ml spoons salt, the peppercorns, and bouquet garni. Heat to boiling point, reduce the heat, cover the pan with a tight-fitting lid, and simmer gently for 2 hours until the meat is tender.

If the brains are not to be used separately, tie them in muslin and add them to the pan for the last 10–15 minutes of the cooking time. Remove the head and brains, if cooked, from the pan and put to one side until they are cool enough to handle. Strain the liquid into a clean pan. Reserve a little for serving with the meat. Alternatively, reserve 375ml to make brain sauce (p201) to serve with the meat.

Put the head on a board. Remove and slice the meat from the bones. Strip the skin from the tongue, remove the small bones at the root, together with the excess fat and gristle. Remove the brains from the muslin. Slice the tongue and the brains, if they are to be served with the meat. Re-heat the meats in the strained stock in the pan. Season to taste.

Serve garnished with chopped parsley and with either the reserved stock or brain sauce.

Note A calf's head can be prepared in the same way.

Boiled Sheep's or Lamb's Tongues

4 helpings

2 sheep's **or** 4 lamb's tongues
500ml general household stock (p25)
salt and pepper
25g butter

1 × 15ml spoon plain flour
1 × 15ml spoon capers (optional)
1 × 15ml spoon dry sherry (optional)

Soak the tongues in cold salted water for 1 hour, then drain them. Place them in a pan, cover with cold water and heat to boiling point. Pour off the water, and dry the tongues.

Put them in the pan, cover with stock, and season with salt and pepper. Heat to boiling point, reduce the heat, cover the pan with a tight-fitting lid and simmer for about 2 hours until tender. Drain, and reserve 250ml stock. Strip the skin and remove the small bones at the root of the tongue, together with the excess fat and gristle. Divide the sheep's tongues lengthways into three, and the lamb's tongues lengthways in half. Transfer to a warmed dish and keep hot.

Melt the butter in a saucepan. Stir in the flour and cook for 3 minutes. Gradually add the seasoned stock and stir until boiling, then reduce the heat and simmer for 2 minutes. Season to taste. Chop and add the capers, and the sherry, if used; then add the sliced tongues and re-heat.

Serve hot in a border of cooked spaghetti, creamed potatoes or chopped spinach.

Veal

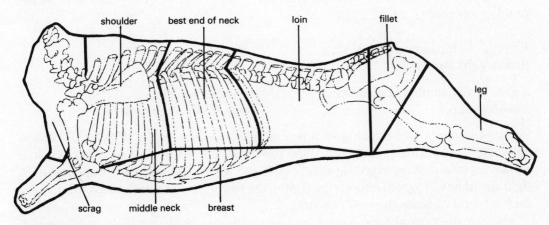

Veal Cuts

Veal is cut in the same way as lamb and the cuts are usually described by the same names. See diagram above.

Taking an average carcass weight of 22kg, the approximate weights of the cuts are as follows:

1) *Leg* is a large and expensive joint. The hind knuckle or shin is removed at the knee joint or boned and used for pie veal. The rest of the leg can be roasted on the bone. Because of the continental method of cutting a leg of veal lengthways along the muscles, escalopes are usually taken from the topside (cushion) of veal or *noix*.

This cut (escalope) gives solid slices of meat cut across the grain, which do not curl in cooking. British butchers do not usually cut a leg in this way, so escalopes are often cut from the fleshy part of the leg, and must be snipped at the edges to prevent curling. They should be cut 1cm thick, and beaten out to 5mm thick, then left to regain resilience before cooking. (Av wt boneless leg – 3.5kg)

2) *Fillet* is the most expensive of the veal cuts. Usually cut into fillet steaks or escalopes but can be larded and roasted whole. (Av wt bobby calves 225–300g; Av wt veal calves – 900g)

3) *Loin* is suitable for roasting as a joint on the bone or as a boned, stuffed and rolled joint. It can also be cut into loin chops, suitable for grilling and frying. The end of the loin closest to the leg is often called the chump end. (Av wt 1.5–1.75kg)

4) *Best end of neck* is suitable for roasting or braising. Also available cut into cutlets for grilling, frying or baking. (Av wt – 1kg)

5) *Breast* when boned, stuffed and roasted is a most tasty and economical cut of veal. (Av wt – 675g)

6) *Shoulder* (also called Oyster of Veal after the fore knuckle has been removed) is suitable for roasting on the bone or boned and rolled. (Av wt – 2.5kg)

7) *Middle neck* and

8) *Scrag* are economical cuts, but there is a high proportion of bone. Middle neck is usually sold in cutlets for braising or stewing or is boned for pie veal. Scrag is mainly sold for boiling, stewing or casseroles. (Av wt both joints – 1.5kg)

9) *Cutlets* are obtained from the best end of neck. 6 per carcass. (Av wt – 175g each)

10) *Chops* from the loin (with or without kidney) can be cut to any size, so the number varies. (Av wt – 225g each)

Roasted, Grilled and Fried Dishes
Roast Veal *Basic recipe*

a joint of veal suitable for roasting
salt and pepper

grated lemon rind
strips of bacon **or** pork fat

Choose the method of roasting, ie quick or slow roasting (p91). Weigh the joint to calculate the cooking time (p92). Wipe the meat. Place the joint on a wire rack, if available, in a shallow roasting tin. Season the meat well with salt, pepper, and a light sprinkling of grated lemon rind. Cover the top of the joint with strips of bacon or pork fat, and cook for the required time.

Transfer the cooked meat from the oven to a warmed serving dish and keep hot. Prepare gravy from the sediment in the roasting tin.

Serve roast veal with basic herb stuffing or forcemeat balls (p43) and with bacon rolls (p48) and lemon wedges.

Honey-Glazed Ham with Pineapple (p166)

Galantine of Chicken (p185)

RIGHT (above) Spatchcocked Chicken (p178) and (below) Stuffed Chicken Legs (p183)

LEFT Golden Grilled Cod (p78)

BELOW Sweet and Sour Prawns (p89)

RIGHT Stuffed Whole Plaice (p84)

Sole Véronique (p87)

RIGHT (above) Stacked Omelets (p196) filled with prawns, mushrooms and tomatoes
and (below) Steak and Kidney Pie (p117)

Savoury Soufflé (pp196–8)

Grilled Veal Cutlets
6 helpings

600–700g best end **or** middle neck
  of veal, cut into cutlets
1 egg
salt and pepper
dried white breadcrumbs for coating

a little melted butter **or** oil
375ml Italian (p208) **or** Fresh
  Tomato (p216) **or** Demi-glace (p211)
  sauce

Garnish
sprigs of parsley

slices of lemon

Wipe and trim the cutlets. Beat the egg lightly until liquid and season to taste. Brush the cutlets with the beaten egg and coat with breadcrumbs, pressing them on well; then brush the cutlets carefully with a little melted butter or oil. Place them on the rack of a grill pan and cook under a hot grill for about 10–15 minutes, basting occasionally with more melted butter or oil to prevent the breadcrumbs burning, until the cutlets are golden-brown on both sides and cooked through. Arrange them on a warmed serving dish and garnish with parsley and slices of lemon. Pour some of the chosen sauce round the cutlets and serve the rest separately.

Fried Veal Cutlets
6 helpings

600–700g best end **or** middle neck
  of veal, cut into cutlets
1 egg
2 × 15ml spoons milk
1 × 5ml spoon chopped parsley
½ × 2.5ml spoon dried thyme
1 × 2.5ml spoon grated lemon rind

salt and pepper
1 × 10ml spoon melted butter
dried white breadcrumbs for coating
butter **or** oil and butter for frying
375ml Fresh Tomato (p216),
  Demi-glace (p211) **or** Piquant (p206)
  sauce

Garnish
sprigs of parsley

slices of lemon

Wipe and trim the cutlets. Beat the egg and milk together and mix with the parsley, thyme, lemon rind, seasoning, and melted butter. Brush the cutlets with the egg mixture and coat with breadcrumbs, pressing them on well.

Heat the butter or oil and butter mixture in a frying pan, and fry the cutlets over moderate heat, turning once, until golden-brown on both sides; then reduce the heat and cook more slowly for 10–15 minutes in all. Remove the cutlets from the pan and drain thoroughly. Arrange on a warmed serving dish. Garnish with sprigs of parsley and lemon slices.

Serve with Fresh Tomato Sauce, Demi-glace Sauce or Piquant Sauce.

Escalopes of Veal (Wiener Schnitzel)
6 helpings

6 thin escalopes of veal (13 × 8cm approx)	1 egg
plain flour	2–3 drops oil
salt and pepper	dried white breadcrumbs for coating
	butter **or** oil and butter for frying

Garnish

6 crimped lemon slices (p54)	1 × 15ml spoon chopped parsley

Wipe the meat. Season the flour with salt and pepper. Dip the escalopes in the seasoned flour. Beat the egg until liquid with the oil. Brush the escalopes with the egg mixture and coat with breadcrumbs, pressing them on well. Heat the butter or mixture of oil and butter in a large frying pan. Put in the escalopes and fry over moderate to gentle heat for 7–10 minutes, turning them once only.

Remove the escalopes and place them, overlapping slightly, on a warmed, flat serving dish. Garnish the middle of each escalope with a crimped slice of lemon sprinkled with parsley.

VARIATION

Holstein Schnitzel

Cook as for Wiener Schnitzel, but serve with a fried, poached or chopped hard-boiled egg. Garnish with small heaps of chopped gherkin and beetroot, whole capers, whole green olives, and drained anchovy fillets. Place a crimped slice of lemon or 'lemon butterfly' (p53) on the schnitzel, and pour a little Beurre Noisette (p214) over the schnitzel before serving.

Parisian Veal
3–4 helpings

300g fillet of veal	1 × 10ml spoon finely chopped onion
salt and pepper	200ml Madeira sauce (p211)
1 × 15ml spoon olive oil	1 × 5ml spoon chopped parsley

Garnish

potatoes Parisienne (p56)	fried bread croûtons

Wipe, trim, and cut the meat into 3 or 4 slices 1cm thick (approx). Season each slice well. Heat the oil in a frying pan and fry the fillets gently, turning once until lightly browned on both sides. Add the onion and continue frying gently until the onion is transparent. Add the sauce, cover the pan loosely, and cook gently for about 30 minutes until the meat is tender. Add the chopped parsley and arrange on a warmed serving dish. Garnish with potatoes Parisienne and bread croûtons.

Braised, Stewed and Steamed Dishes
Stuffed Breast of Veal
6 helpings

a thick end of breast of veal
  (1kg approx)
salt and pepper
300g pork **or** beef sausage-meat
1 large onion (200g approx)
1 large carrot (100g approx)
½ turnip (25g approx)

bouquet garni
6 black peppercorns
white stock (p26) **or** water to cover
butter for greasing
225g short-grain rice
50g grated Parmesan cheese
meat glaze (p55) (optional)

Garnish
slices of lemon

Remove all bones and tendons from the meat. Wipe, and tie into a neat shape. Season well. Spread the sausage-meat evenly over the inner surface of the meat, roll up and tie securely with fine string. Prepare and slice the vegetables. Put them with the bones and trimmings in a large pan. Add the bouquet garni, peppercorns, salt and pepper, and enough stock or water to cover the vegetables. Place the meat on top, cover with buttered greaseproof paper and a tight-fitting lid. Heat to boiling point, reduce the heat and simmer gently for about 2½ hours. Baste occasionally and add more stock or water if necessary. Transfer to a warmed dish and keep hot.

Strain off the liquid and make it up to 750ml with stock or water. Put the stock in a pan and bring to the boil. Wash the rice and cook it in the stock until the stock is absorbed. Season to taste and stir in the cheese. Place the rice in a layer on a warmed serving dish and put the meat on top. Brush the meat with glaze, if used, and garnish with slices of lemon.

Stewed Rolled Breast of Veal
6 helpings

1.25–1.5kg breast of veal
salt and pepper
200g basic herb stuffing (p43)

1.5–2 litres white **or** chicken stock
  (p26)
250ml slightly thickened gravy (p230)

Garnish
6 fried bacon rolls (p48)

slices of lemon

Wipe and bone the meat, and flatten it with a cutlet bat or rolling-pin. Season, and spread with a thin layer of stuffing. Roll up the meat and skewer or tie it securely. Form the rest of the stuffing into balls for frying. Heat enough stock to cover the rolled meat in a large saucepan. When boiling, place the meat in it, re-heat to boiling point, and skim. Cover the pan with a tight-fitting lid, reduce the heat, and simmer gently for about 3 hours.

Place the veal on a warmed serving dish, remove the skewers or string, and pour a little gravy over it if liked. Garnish with the bacon rolls, forcemeat balls, and lemon slices. Serve the rest of the gravy separately.

Steamed Veal
6 helpings

600–800g topside leg of veal
salt and pepper
3 sticks celery (150g approx)
25g butter

25g plain flour
250ml milk
1–2 egg yolks
1–2 × 5ml spoons lemon juice

Garnish (optional)
6 grilled bacon rolls (p48)

sprigs of cooked cauliflower

Wipe, trim, and tie the veal into a neat shape. Season well. Wash the celery and cut it into 2cm lengths. Put the meat and celery in the top of a steamer. Steam for $1\frac{1}{2}$–2 hours or until tender.

When the veal is nearly ready, melt the butter in a small saucepan. Stir in the flour and cook for 2–3 minutes over low heat, stirring well. Do not allow to brown. Gradually add the milk and any liquid in the steamer and stir until boiling. Reduce the heat and simmer for 5 minutes. Remove the pan from the heat. Beat the egg yolks in a bowl and stir into them a little of the hot sauce. Return the egg yolk mixture to the rest of the sauce in the pan, stirring well. Add the lemon juice and season to taste. Place the veal on a warmed serving dish, remove the string, and pour the sauce over the meat. Garnish, if liked, with bacon rolls and sprigs of cooked cauliflower.

Pastry and Minced Dishes
Veal and Ham Pie
6–8 helpings

puff (p412) **or** flaky (p411) pastry
    using 100g flour
500g fillet, breast or neck of veal
250g ham
salt
1 × 2.5ml spoon pepper
1 × 2.5ml spoon mixed herbs

1 × 2.5ml spoon ground mace
grated rind of 1 lemon
well-flavoured, cooled and jellied stock
    (pp25–27), as required
2 hard-boiled eggs
flour for rolling out
beaten egg for glazing

Prepare the pastry and leave to stand in a cool place. Cut the veal and ham into 1cm cubes, and add the seasoning and flavourings. Heat the stock until melted and mix a small amount in with the meat. Slice the hard-boiled eggs. Put half the meat mixture into a 500ml pie dish, cover with the sliced eggs and add the remaining meat. Moisten with the stock, but do not overfill the dish with liquid.

Roll out the pastry on a lightly floured surface, and cut it to fit the top of the pie dish. Dampen the edges of the dish with water. Use some of the trimmings to line the rim of the dish. Dampen the pastry rim, lift the top crust into position, and seal the edge. Make a hole in the centre of the pie, decorate with pastry leaves, and brush with beaten egg. Bake in a hot oven, 220°C, Gas 7, for 15 minutes, then reduce the heat to moderate, 180°C, Gas 4, and bake for $1\frac{1}{2}$ hours. Remove the pie from the oven, make a second hole in the crust and pour in a little more stock. Leave to cool thoroughly, preferably overnight, in a refrigerator.

Serve cold with salads.

Pot Pie of Veal
6 helpings

500g lean pie veal
200g salt (pickled) pork
salt and pepper
white (p26) **or** general household (p25)
    stock to cover

500g potatoes
puff **or** rough puff pastry (p412) using
    150g flour
flour for rolling out
beaten egg **or** milk for glazing

Wipe the veal and cut it into 3–5cm cubes, and the pork into thin strips. Place the veal and pork in layers in a 1.5 litre pie dish, seasoning each layer well with salt and pepper. Fill the dish three-quarters full with stock. Cover with a lid and cook in a moderate oven, 180°C, Gas 4, for 1½ hours.

Meanwhile, prepare and parboil the potatoes in salted water. Drain, and slice thickly. Remove the meat from the oven and cool slightly. Add extra stock to the dish to bring it back to its original level, if necessary. Arrange the potatoes evenly on top of the meat. Roll out the pastry on a lightly floured surface to cover the top of the pie dish. Brush with the beaten egg or milk. Make a hole in the centre to let the steam escape. Bake in a very hot oven, 230°C, Gas 8, for 10–15 minutes until the pastry is set, then reduce the heat to fairly hot, 190°C, Gas 5, and cook for 25–30 minutes. Add more hot stock through the hole in the top to fill the pie.

Raised Veal, Pork, and Egg Pie
6 helpings

hot water crust pastry (p410) using
    400g flour
400g pie veal
400g lean pork
25g plain flour
1½ × 5ml spoons salt
½ × 2.5ml spoon ground pepper

3 hard-boiled eggs
2 × 15ml spoons water
beaten egg for glazing
125ml (approx) well-flavoured, cooled
    and jellied stock **or** canned
    consommé

Line a 20cm round pie mould with three-quarters of the pastry, or use a round cake tin to mould the pie as described on pp410–11. Use the remaining quarter for the lid.

Cut the meat into small pieces, removing any gristle or fat. Season the flour with salt and pepper, and toss the meat in it. Put half into the pastry case and put in the whole eggs. Add the rest of the meat and the water. Put on the lid, brush with beaten egg, and make a hole in the centre to let steam escape. Bake in a very hot oven, 230°C, Gas 8, for 15 minutes. Reduce the heat to very cool, 140°C, Gas 1, and continue cooking for 2½ hours. Remove the greaseproof paper or mould for the last 30 minutes of the cooking time and brush the top and sides of the pastry with beaten egg.

Heat the stock or consommé until melted and, when the pie is cooked, funnel it through the hole in the lid until the pie is full. Cool completely before serving.

Note If preferred, the ingredients can be made into 6 individual pies. Slice the eggs.

Veal and Ham Pudding
6 helpings

600–800g lean pie veal
150g ham **or** bacon **or** salt (pickled)
   pork
suet crust pastry (p408) using
   200g flour
flour for rolling out

fat for greasing
salt and pepper
4 × 15ml spoons general household
   stock (p25)
375ml thickened gravy (p230)

Garnish
chopped parsley

Wipe the veal and cut it into small neat pieces. Cut the ham, bacon or pork into narrow strips. Reserve one-quarter of the pastry for the lid. Roll out the rest on a lightly floured surface so that it is 1cm larger than the top of a greased 1 litre basin, and 5mm thick. Press well into the basin to remove any creases. Fill with alternate layers of veal and ham, bacon or pork, seasoning each layer well. Add the stock when the basin is half full. Roll out the reserved pastry to fit the top of the basin. Dampen the edges, place the lid in position, and seal. Cover with a round of greased greaseproof paper, then cover tightly with foil.

Place the basin in a steamer, or on a saucer in a pan with water coming half-way up the basin's sides. Steam, or half steam the pudding for 3 hours, topping up the steamer or pan with boiling water when it is reduced by a third.

Remove the foil and paper from the pudding when ready. Serve in the basin, garnished with chopped parsley. Serve the gravy separately.

Fricadelles of Veal
4–6 helpings

500g boned lean veal (see **Note**)
75g white bread
50ml milk
200g shredded suet
1 × 5ml spoon grated lemon rind
a pinch of grated nutmeg
salt and pepper

3 eggs
750ml white stock (p26) **or** salted
   water
soft white breadcrumbs for coating
oil for deep frying
375ml foundation brown sauce (p204)

Garnish
slices of lemon   chopped parsley

Wipe and trim the meat. Cut the crusts off the bread. Soak the bread in the milk for 5 minutes, and then squeeze it as dry as possible and rub out any lumps. Mince the veal. Mix it with the bread, suet, lemon rind, nutmeg, and salt and pepper. Beat two of the eggs until liquid, and stir into the veal mixture. Shape into balls about the size of a large walnut. Bring the stock or salted water to the boil in a pan. Drop the balls into it and cook for 6 minutes. Drain, and dry thoroughly.

Beat the remaining egg until liquid. Coat the balls with beaten egg, then with breadcrumbs. Heat the oil (p10) and fry the fricadelles until golden-brown. Drain, and add them to the brown sauce in a saucepan. Heat to simmering point and simmer very gently for 30 minutes. Serve in the sauce, garnished with lemon and chopped parsley.

Note If the meat is boned by the butcher, make sure he gives you the bones. These, together with the meat trimmings, can be used to make the white stock and the brown sauce.

Offal Dishes
Brains in Black Butter (Cervelles au Beurre Noir)
4 helpings

2 sets calf's brains	bouquet garni
salt	flour for dusting
1 × 5ml spoon lemon juice	ground pepper
1 small onion	2 × 15ml spoons butter
1 litre water	butter for greasing
2 × 15ml spoons white wine vinegar	

Black Butter

4 × 15ml spoons butter	2 × 15ml spoons capers (optional)
1 × 15ml spoon white wine vinegar	

Garnish
sprig of parsley

Soak the brains for 30 minutes in lightly salted cold water sharpened with the lemon juice to remove all traces of blood. Meanwhile, skin and halve the onion, and put it in a saucepan with the water, vinegar, and bouquet garni. Heat to simmering point and simmer for 30 minutes. Leave the stock to cool.

Drain the brains, and cut off any membranes. Wash thoroughly but very gently. Put the brains into the stock, heat slowly to simmering point, and poach for 20 minutes. Drain thoroughly, and put into very cold water to cool. Drain again and pat dry. Season the flour with salt and pepper, and dust the brains with it. Heat the 2 × 15ml spoons butter in a frying pan, and fry the brains lightly, turning them over, until just browned on all sides. Put them in a shallow serving dish, and keep them warm under buttered paper.

Take any bits of brain out of the frying pan, add the butter for the Black Butter and heat until golden-brown. Add the vinegar, and let it boil up. As soon as it foams, pour the mixture over the brains, adding the capers, if used. Serve at once, garnished with a sprig of parsley.

Calf's Liver with Savoury Rice
6 helpings

500g calf's liver
1 medium-sized onion (100g approx)
2 cloves garlic (optional)
40g butter **or** margarine
150g Patna rice
375ml well-flavoured white stock
   (p26)

salt and pepper
$\frac{1}{2}$–1 × 2.5ml spoon powdered saffron
plain flour
butter **or** oil for frying
250ml foundation brown sauce (p204)
juice of $\frac{1}{2}$ lemon
butter for greasing

Garnish
6 baked **or** fried bacon rolls (p48)
        paprika

Remove the skin and tubes, and cut the liver into thin slices. Skin the onion and garlic cloves, if used, and chop them finely. Heat 25g of the butter or margarine in a pan and sauté the onion and garlic without colouring for 2–3 minutes. Wash the rice and add it to the pan. Mix well and cook for about 3 minutes. Add the stock, salt and pepper to taste, and the saffron. Cover the pan, and cook for 30–45 minutes over gentle heat, or in a moderate oven, 180°C, Gas 4, until the rice is tender and has absorbed all the stock. Add the remaining butter or margarine, mix well, and press into a border mould. Put to one side until set.

    Season some flour with salt and pepper and dip the slices of liver in it. Heat a little butter or oil in a frying pan and fry the liver, turning once, until browned and cooked through. Drain thoroughly. Heat the brown sauce in a saucepan to boiling point, add the lemon juice and the liver, and heat through. Turn the rice on to a warmed dish, cover with buttered greaseproof paper, and heat in a warm oven, 160°C, Gas 3, for 10–12 minutes. Place the liver and sauce in the centre of the mould, and garnish with the bacon rolls and paprika.

Braised Veal Sweetbreads
6 helpings

3 pairs veal sweetbreads
1 small onion (50g approx)
1 small carrot (25g approx)
$\frac{1}{2}$ small turnip (25g approx)
25g butter **or** margarine
bouquet garni
6 black peppercorns

salt
white (p26) **or** general household (p25)
   stock to cover
butter for greasing
1 slice of white bread 5cm thick
fat **or** oil for frying

Prepare the sweetbreads (p141). Press between 2 plates until quite cold.

    Prepare and slice the vegetables. Melt the fat in a flameproof casserole, and fry the vegetables for about 10 minutes. Add the bouquet garni, peppercorns, salt to taste, and enough stock almost to cover the vegetables. Place the sweetbreads on top of the vegetables, cover with buttered greaseproof paper, and heat to boiling point. Baste the sweetbreads well, cover the casserole and cook in a moderate oven, 180°C, Gas 4, for about 1 hour. Add more stock, if necessary, and baste occasionally.

Meanwhile, cut a croûte from the slice of bread and fry it in shallow fat or oil, turning once, until golden-brown on both sides. Drain thoroughly. Place the croûte on a warmed serving dish and serve the sweetbreads on top.

Note Use the stock and vegetables for soup.

Calf's Foot Jelly
3–4 helpings

1 calf's foot	1 egg white and shell
1 litre water	a pinch of ground cinnamon
salt and pepper	2 cloves
pared rind and juice of 1 large lemon	25ml dry sherry (optional)

Cut the foot into convenient-sized pieces to fit into a stewpan. Wash and blanch them by putting them in the stewpan, covering with cold water and heating to boiling point, then skimming and draining.

Put the pieces back in the pan with 1 litre water, and add salt and pepper to taste. Heat to boiling point, cover with a tight-fitting lid, reduce the heat, and simmer gently for 3–4 hours, removing any scum which rises. Strain, and measure the stock. If more than 500ml, return to the pan and boil until reduced to 500ml. Leave to cool completely, then remove any fat.

Return the stock to the pan with the lemon rind and juice, egg white and shell, cinnamon, and cloves. Heat to simmering point and simmer for 10 minutes, then allow to stand for 10 minutes. Strain through a fine sieve or jelly bag. Stir in the sherry, if used. Store in a refrigerator or very cool place.

Pork

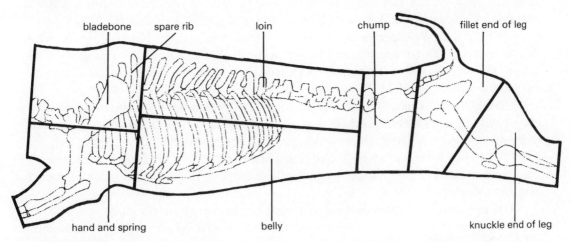

Pork cuts
English and Scottish cuts of pork vary considerably. Those noted below are the most widely used English cuts. See also the diagram above.

1) *Leg* is a succulent and popular roasting joint. In Scotland a leg is known as a gigot. Often divided into fillet end and knuckle end, and used as follows (p154):

Fillet end: The top of the leg which is ideal for roasting or for slicing into steaks for grilling and frying. (Av wt – 2.5kg)

Knuckle end: The lower half of the leg which can be roasted whole or boned and stuffed. (Av wt – 2.5kg)

2) *Loin* is a popular roast on the bone or boned, stuffed and rolled. It is often divided into loin and chump chops. (Av wt – 4–5.5kg)

Tenderloin is the lean cut found on the inside of the loin bone. It is sometimes called 'pork fillet' but it must not be confused with 'fillet end' from the leg. Ideal for roasting, braising, grilling, and frying. (Av wt 0.5–2.5kg)

3) *Belly* (also called draft or flank pork) is suitable (fresh or pickled) for braising, stewing or boiling. Sliced belly is a very economical cut for grilling and frying. Thick end of belly can make an economical and tasty roast, particularly when stuffed. (Av wt 1.5–2.25kg)

4) *Bladebone* is a roasting joint, tasty when boned and stuffed. It is also ideal for boiling, either fresh or pickled. (Av wt 1.75–2kg)

5) *Spare rib* is almost a parallel cut to the middle neck of lamb. It is a lean and economical roasting joint with little top fat. Meat from this cut makes the best filling for home-made pork pies. It can also be cut into spare rib chops. (Av wt 2.75–3.25kg)

6) *Spare ribs* (American-style) are cut from the belly and are removed in 1 sheath or slab, leaving the meat between the sections of rib bones. (They may also be sold under the name of pork rib bones.) They are usually barbecued. Chinese-style spare ribs are cut from the rib cage and have little meat on them. They are served roasted or braised in a sweet-sour sauce. (Av wt 2.7–3.2kg; Av wt Chinese – 2.3kg)

7) *Hand* and *spring* is cut from the foreleg of the pig and, in bone structure, is similar to knuckle half shoulder of lamb. It is a large economical roasting joint. However, it is often too large for a small family, so it is sometimes sold divided into hand and shank. The hand can be boned and roasted or boiled. The shank is most suitable for casseroles and stews. (Av wt hand and spring 3–3.25kg)

In Scotland, a shoulder of pork includes hand and spring, blade and ribs. The shoulder is usually cut in half, and boned and rolled. The amount required is cut to order. The shank end of the foreleg is called the hough end. The hand and spring, minus the shank, is called the runner.

8) *Head:* The pig carcass is usually delivered to the butcher with the head on, so a pig's head is easier to obtain than a sheep's or ox head. The head contains a considerable quantity of meat, plus the tongue and brain. (Av wt 1.75–2kg)

9) *Trotters* or *pettitoes* can be boiled, then boned, crumbed, and fried or fricasséed. The stock is used to make aspic jelly or jellied stock. (Av wt trotter – 200g; Av wt pettitoe – 150g)

10) *Chops* are thick slices of meat cut from the loin or spare rib joints.

Chump: First 2–3 chops cut from the end of loin where the leg is removed. Chump chops are large and meaty and are good for grilling, frying or baking. (Av wt 200–300g each)

Middle loin: Sometimes sold with the kidney and, occasionally, with the tenderloin (fillet). All cut from the loin. (Av wt 125–300g each)

Fore loin: Similar to neck of lamb chops. (Av wt 125–175g)

Spare rib: Cut from spare rib; grill, fry or braise. (Av wt 125–175g)

Roasted, Fried and Grilled Dishes
Roast Pork *Basic recipe*

a joint of pork on the bone suitable for roasting	salt and pepper
	oil **or** fat for basting

Ask the butcher to score the rind in narrow lines, or do it yourself with a sharp knife. Select the method of roasting, ie quick or slow roasting (p91). Weigh the joint to calculate the cooking time (p92). Wipe the meat. Place the joint on a rack in a shallow roasting tin. Season the meat with salt and pepper and pour over a little oil or rub it with a little fat. Rub some salt into the scored rind to produce crisp crackling. Place the roasting tin in the oven, and cook for the required time.

If liked, brush the joint with apricot jam or glaze or with syrup from canned peaches, 10 minutes before the end of the cooking time. Alternatively, sprinkle the rind with brown sugar mixed with a little dry mustard. These mixtures give a sweeter crisp crackling.

Transfer the cooked meat to a warmed meat dish and keep hot. Prepare the gravy from the sediment in the roasting tin.

Serve roast pork with sage and onion stuffing (p46) and apple sauce.

Roast Savoury Loin of Pork

6–7 helpings

1.5kg loin of pork on the bone	a pinch of dry mustard
1 × 15ml spoon finely chopped onion	glaze (p55) (optional)
1 × 2.5ml spoon dried sage	125ml apple sauce
1 × 2.5ml spoon salt	250ml thickened gravy (p230)
½ × 2.5ml spoon freshly ground pepper	

Ask the butcher to chine the pork and score the rind in narrow lines, or do it yourself with a sharp knife. Wipe the meat. Mix the onion with sage, salt, pepper, and mustard. Rub the mixture well into the surface of the meat. Roast the pork in a hot oven, 220°C, Gas 7, for 10 minutes, then reduce the heat to moderate, 180°C, Gas 4, for the rest of the calculated cooking time, allowing 30 minutes per 0.5kg plus 30 minutes over. About 30 minutes before serving, cover with glaze, if liked, and continue cooking to crisp the crackling. Serve hot apple sauce and gravy separately.

Fried Pork Chops *Basic recipe*
6 helpings

6 chump **or** middle loin **or** fore loin **or**
  spare rib pork chops
ground pepper
dried sage

1 × 15ml spoon oil **or** butter **or** lard
salt
1 × 15ml spoon plain flour
250ml general household stock (p25)

Wipe the chops and trim off any excess fat. Sprinkle each chop with pepper and sage. Heat the fat in a frying pan. Add the chops and fry until sealed and browned on the underside. Turn with a palette knife and continue to fry until the other side is browned. Reduce the heat and continue to fry, turning once or twice, until the meat is cooked through. The total frying time is 15–20 minutes, or longer for thick chops. Transfer the chops to a warmed serving dish, sprinkle with salt, and keep hot.

Pour the fat from the pan, reserving the sediment. Stir in the flour, and cook. Gradually add the stock and stir until boiling. Season to taste. Serve the gravy separately in a sauce-boat.

VARIATION

Fried Pork Chops with Peaches

Follow the recipe for Fried Pork Chops until the chops are cooked through. Arrange the fried chops on a warmed serving dish and keep hot. Pour off the fat and sediment from the frying pan and reserve for making gravy, if liked. Melt 25g butter and add 6 drained, canned peach halves. Fry gently until golden on both sides. Top each chop with a peach half, cut side down. Garnish with mustard and cress. If serving gravy, make it as for Fried Pork Chops.

Grilled Pork Chops *Basic recipe*
6 helpings

6 chump **or** middle loin **or** fore loin
  or spare rib pork chops
2 × 15ml spoons oil **or** melted butter
ground pepper
dried sage
dried marjoram

caster sugar
salt
1 × 15ml spoon plain flour
250ml general household stock (p25)
125ml apple sauce

Wipe the chops and trim off any excess fat. Brush the grill rack with oil or melted butter and place the chops on it. Brush the upper surface of the chops with oil or melted butter and sprinkle with pepper, sage, marjoram, and sugar. Cook under a hot grill until one side is lightly browned. Draw off the heat and turn the chops over with a palette knife and spoon. Brush the second side with oil or melted butter and sprinkle with pepper, herbs, and sugar. Return to the heat and brown quickly. Reduce the heat and grill until the chops are cooked through. The total grilling time is 15–20 minutes for loin and spare rib chops, a little longer for the larger chump chops. Arrange the chops on a warmed serving dish, sprinkle with salt and keep hot.

Pour the fat from the grill pan and scrape the sediment into a small pan. Stir in the flour, then gradually add the stock and stir until boiling. Season to taste. Serve the gravy and hot apple sauce separately.

VARIATION
Grilled Pork Chops with Apple Slices
Follow the recipe for Grilled Pork Chops. When cooked, transfer the chops to a warmed serving dish and keep hot. Peel, core, and cut 6 slices (1cm thick) of a sharp apple. Put on to the grill rack, brush with the fat in the pan, and brown lightly on both sides. Place 1 apple slice on each chop and garnish with sprigs of parsley.

Braised and Casseroled Dishes
Braised Pork *Basic recipe*
8–10 helpings

a bladebone **or** a spare rib joint of pork (2kg approx)
50g lard **or** 3 × 15ml spoons cooking oil
1 large onion (200g approx)
2 large carrots (200g approx)
1 clove of garlic
125ml dry cider
125ml general household stock (p25)
bouquet garni
salt and pepper

Wipe and trim the meat. Weigh it to calculate the cooking time. Heat the lard or oil in a large, deep frying pan and fry the joint, turning often, until browned all over. Remove the meat and put to one side. Prepare and slice the onion and carrots. Skin and crush the garlic. Add the vegetables and garlic to the pan and fry gently for 5 minutes. Pour in the cider and stock and add the bouquet garni. Return the meat to the pan and season well with salt and pepper. Heat to boiling point, cover the pan, reduce the heat, and simmer gently, allowing 35 minutes per 0.5kg meat. Turn the meat occasionally. When cooked, transfer to a warmed serving dish.

Strain the liquid from the pan, skim off the fat, re-heat, and serve in a sauce-boat.

Pork Fillets Stuffed with Prunes
6 helpings

100g prunes
800g fillet of pork
2 small cooking apples (200g approx)
50g butter **or** margarine
100ml boiling water
200ml single cream
salt and pepper
2 × 10ml spoons butter (approx)

Soak the prunes in cold water overnight, or cover them with boiling water and soak for 2 hours. Wipe the fillets and trim off any skin and fat, then slice them down the middle almost but not quite right through. Drain and stone the prunes; peel, core and slice the apples. Put the prunes and apple slices into the slits in the fillets, press the fillets back into shape, and tie them with thin string.

Heat the butter or margarine in a large pan, put in the fillets and brown them all over. Add the boiling water, 100ml of the cream, and salt and pepper to taste. Cover the pan, and cook gently for 30 minutes. Transfer the fillets to a warmed serving dish, remove the string, and keep hot. Add the rest of the cream to the pan, whisk well, then add a little cold butter. Pour the sauce over the fillets and serve hot.

Pork and Apple Hot Pot
4 helpings

4 loin **or** spare rib chops
1 medium-sized cooking apple
   (200g approx)
1 medium-sized onion (100g approx)
50g lard **or** oil

100g mushrooms
fat for greasing
1 × 2.5ml spoon dried sage **or** savory
500g potatoes
salt and pepper

Garnish
chopped parsley

Wipe the chops and trim off any excess fat. Prepare the apple and onion and slice them thinly. Heat the lard or oil in a pan and fry the apple and onion until golden-brown. Clean and slice the mushrooms.

Grease a casserole and put the mushrooms in the bottom. Lay the chops on the mushrooms and cover with the apple and onion. Sprinkle the herb over the top. Prepare the potatoes and cut them into 1.5cm cubes. Top the casserole with the potatoes and brush them with the fat remaining in the pan. Season with salt and pepper. Pour in enough water to come half-way up the meat and vegetables. Cover the pan with a tight-fitting lid and cook in a moderate oven, 180°C, Gas 4, for $1\frac{1}{2}$ hours. Remove the lid 30 minutes before the end of the cooking time to allow the potatoes to brown. Garnish with chopped parsley and serve from the casserole.

Pastry Dishes and Offal
Raised Pork Pie
6 helpings

400g pork bones (approx)
1 small onion
salt and pepper
150ml cold water **or** stock

hot water crust pastry (p410) using
   250g flour
500g lean pork
$\frac{1}{2}$ × 2.5ml spoon dried sage
beaten egg **or** milk for glazing

Put the pork bones in a saucepan. Skin and chop the onion finely. Add it to the pan with salt, pepper, and the water or stock. Cover the pan, heat to simmering point, and simmer for 2 hours. Leave to cool until jellied.

Line a 1kg pie mould with three-quarters of the pastry, or use a round cake tin to mould the pie as described on pp410–11, keeping it about 5mm thick. Use the remaining quarter for the lid. Wipe and dice the pork. Season with salt, pepper, and sage. Put into the prepared pie crust and add 2 × 15ml spoons of the jellied stock. Put on the lid, brush with beaten egg or milk, and make a hole in the centre to allow steam to escape. Bake in a hot oven, 220°C, Gas 7, for 15 minutes. Reduce the heat to moderate, 180°C, Gas 4, and cook the pie for a further $1\frac{1}{2}$ hours. Remove the greaseproof paper or mould for the last 30 minutes of the cooking time and brush the top and sides of the pastry with egg or milk.

When cooked, remove from the oven and cool. Warm the remaining jellied stock and funnel it through the hole in the lid until the pie is full. Cool for 2 hours until the stock sets.

Pork Sausage-meat *Basic recipe*
Makes 650–700g

450g lean pork (see **Note**)
1 slice of dry white bread
200g hard pork fat
1 × 2.5ml spoon ground mace **or**
  allspice

freshly ground black pepper
a pinch of dried thyme
25g dry white breadcrumbs
1 × 5ml spoon salt (see **Note**)

Wipe the meat. Remove the crusts from the bread. Mince the pork very finely together with the fat and bread. Season thoroughly with the spice, pepper, and thyme. Mix in the breadcrumbs, and add salt as needed. Use as required.
Note Cured pork can be used instead of fresh pork but the salt must be used sparingly or not at all.

Braised Pig's Liver
6–8 helpings

1kg pig's liver in 1 piece
200g streaky bacon, without rinds
8 small carrots (200g approx)
1 medium-sized onion (100g approx)
1 clove

bouquet garni
1 × 5ml spoon salt
freshly ground pepper
100ml dry white wine **or** dry cider
chicken stock to cover

Remove the skin and tubes, but leave the liver whole. Put 100g of the bacon rashers in the bottom of a casserole and place the liver on top. Prepare the vegetables and press the clove into the skinned onion. Add the carrots, onion, and bouquet garni to the casserole, and season with salt and pepper. Pour the wine or cider over them. Add enough stock to come to the top of the liver. Put the rest of the bacon on top of the liver. Cover the casserole with a lid and bake in a moderate oven, 180°C, Gas 4, for about 45 minutes or until the liver is cooked through. Transfer the liver and bacon to a warmed serving dish and keep hot.

Strain the sauce into a clean pan. Bring to the boil over high heat until the sauce is reduced by half. Pour the sauce over the liver, and serve hot.
Note Lamb's or calf's liver can be cooked in the same way.

Fried Pig's Fry
6 helpings

800–900g pig's fry (sweetbreads,
   heart, liver, lights, melts)
salt
1 small onion (50g approx)

flour for coating
ground pepper
1 × 5ml spoon dried sage
fat for shallow frying

Prepare the sweetbreads (p141) and the heart (p123). Remove the skin and tubes of the liver. Lights need no preparation. Trim excess fat and skin off the melts.

Put the fry in a saucepan with just enough water to cover it. Salt lightly. Skin and add the onion. Heat to boiling point, skim, reduce the heat, and simmer for 30 minutes. Drain, dry thoroughly, and cut all the meats into thin slices. Season the flour with salt, pepper and sage, and use it to coat the slices lightly. Heat the fat in a frying pan, put in the slices, and fry gently, turning once, until browned on both sides.

Serve with a well-flavoured thickened gravy or with fried apple slices (p47) and crab-apple jelly.

Faggots or Savoury Ducks
4–6 helpings

800g pig's liver **or** fry (sweetbreads,
   heart, liver, lights, melts)
100g fat belly of pork
2 medium-sized onions (200g approx)
a pinch of dried thyme
1 × 2.5ml spoon dried sage
a pinch of dried basil (optional)

salt and pepper
a pinch of grated nutmeg
1 egg
100g soft white breadcrumbs
caul fat **or** flour, as preferred
fat for greasing

Prepare the liver or fry as for Fried Pig's Fry. Slice the liver or fry and pork belly. Skin and slice the onions. Put the meat and onions in a saucepan with just enough water to cover them. Heat to boiling point, cover the pan, reduce the heat, and simmer for 30 minutes. Strain off the liquid and reserve it for the gravy.

Mince the meat and onions finely. Add the herbs, salt, pepper, and nutmeg. Beat the egg until liquid and stir it in. Mix in enough breadcrumbs to make a mixture which can be moulded. Divide it into 8 equal portions and shape them into round balls. Cut squares of caul fat, if used, large enough to encase the balls and wrap each ball in a piece of fat. Alternatively, roll each ball in flour. Lay the faggots side by side in a greased baking tin. Cover the tin loosely with foil. Bake in a moderate oven, 180°C, Gas 4, for 25 minutes. Remove the foil and bake for 10 minutes to brown the tops of the faggots.

Serve hot, with a thickened gravy made from the cooking liquid or with Fresh Tomato Sauce (p216).

Fried Pig's Kidneys
4 helpings

4 pig's kidneys
2 small onions (100g approx)
50g butter **or** oil
salt and pepper
2 × 15ml spoons mushroom ketchup

1 × 10ml spoon chopped parsley
1 × 10ml spoon plain flour
125ml general household (p25) **or**
  chicken (p26) stock

Skin, core, and cut the kidneys into thin slices. Skin and chop the onions finely. Heat the butter or oil in a frying pan and fry the onions until lightly browned. Add the kidney slices, seasoning, and mushroom ketchup. Toss gently over heat for 3–4 minutes. Add the parsley and lift out on to a warmed serving dish. Sprinkle the flour into the pan and cook until browned. Gradually add the stock and stir until boiling. Re-season if required. Pour the sauce round the kidney slices and serve hot.

Pork Brawn
10–12 helpings

½ pig's head
400g shin of beef on the bone
1 × 5ml spoon salt
2 medium-sized onions (200g approx)
4 cloves

2 small carrots (50g approx)
½ × 2.5ml spoon ground mace
6 black peppercorns
bouquet garni
salt and pepper

Ask the butcher to remove the hair, eye and snout, and to chop the half head into 2 or 3 manageable pieces and the shin beef bone in half crossways. Remove the brains and tongue from the head and use these for another dish. Scald and clean the ear and wash the head well in cold water. Soak the head meat in salted water for 2 hours, changing the water 3 or 4 times. Drain thoroughly.

Put all the meat and the salt in a large pan. Skin the onions, and press 2 cloves in each. Scrape the carrots. Add the onions and carrots to the pan with the mace, peppercorns, and bouquet garni. Cover with cold water. Heat to boiling point, skim carefully, cover with a lid, reduce the heat, and simmer gently for 2–3 hours until the meat is tender.

Lift the meat out of the stock and drain thoroughly. Reserve the stock in the pan. Remove all the meat from the bones, trimming off the skin and fat, and dice the meat finely. Put the meat in a wetted mould, basin or cake tin.

Return the bones to the pan of stock. Bring the stock to the boil and boil rapidly, uncovered, to reduce it by about half. Strain the stock and season to taste. Pour just enough stock over the meat to cover it. Stir gently to distribute the meat evenly. Allow to cool. Cover, and leave in a refrigerator or cold place until set. Turn out to serve.

VARIATION

A pickled head can be bought from a butcher which gives additional flavour to brawn. Treat in the same way as the unpickled head, but reduce the cooking time to 1½–1¾ hours.

Fricasséed Pig's Trotters or Pettitoes
4–6 helpings

4 pig's trotters **or** 8 pettitoes (see **Note**)
100g pig's liver
100g pig's heart (1 small **or**
  ½ large heart)
white stock (p26) to cover
½ small onion (25g approx)
1 blade of mace

6 white peppercorns
salt and pepper
a thin strip of lemon rind
25g butter **or** margarine
1 × 15ml spoon flour
1 × 15ml spoon single cream **or** milk

Wash the trotters or pettitoes thoroughly in salted water. Remove the skin and tubes from the liver and prepare the heart (p123). Put the trotters or pettitoes, liver and heart in a large pan and cover with stock. Skin the onion and add it with the mace, peppercorns, salt and pepper to taste, and lemon rind. Heat to boiling point, cover the pan with a tight-fitting lid, reduce the heat, and simmer for 1 hour. Remove the liver and heart, chop them finely, and put to one side. Allow the trotters or pettitoes to continue cooking for another 1–2 hours until the meat can be easily removed from the bones. (Pettitoes may take less time to cook than trotters.) Lift out the trotters or pettitoes, split them open, remove the bones and cut the meat into neat pieces. Put to one side with the liver and heart. Strain the stock and measure 250ml.

Melt the butter or margarine in a saucepan. Stir in the flour and cook for 2–3 minutes. Gradually add the 250ml stock, stir until boiling, and cook for 2–3 minutes. Season to taste. Add the meat. Heat through and stir in the cream or milk. Turn at once into a warmed dish and serve very hot.

Note Pig's trotters are the feet and leg up to the knuckle of a pig. Pettitoes are the same as trotters but taken from a suckling-pig and, therefore, smaller.

Bacon, Gammon and Ham

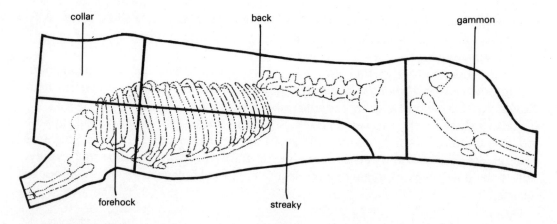

Bacon Pig Cuts
Cuts vary in different parts of Great Britain. The following are the most usual ones. See also the diagram above.

1) *Forehock* can be cooked whole. It bakes well or can be boiled (Av wt – 3.5kg) It can be cut into three smaller joints.

Butt: The leanest end of the forehock, usually boiled. (Av wt – 1.7kg)

Small hock: Not recommended as a joint. Remove the bone, and casserole or mince the meat. (Av wt – 1.3kg)

Fore slipper: Fat but good taste, usually boiled. Forehock joints are cheaper than gammon because their muscle structure is less regular. (Av wt – 0.5kg)

2) *Streaky* is usually divided into smaller cuts (Av wt – 3.7kg)

Top streaky can be boned and boiled or cut into thin rashers for frying or grilling (Av wt – 2.5kg)

Prime streaky can be boiled in a piece or cut into rashers for frying or grilling. (Av wt – 2.5kg)

Thin streaky is sliced to make crisp small rashers or bacon rolls. (Av wt – 0.7kg)

3) *Back* is usually divided into smaller cuts (Av wt – 8.7kg)

Flank is sliced and can be served with liver and kidneys. Economical. (Av wt – 1.2kg)

Long back and *oyster* are sliced for grilling or frying. (Av wt – 1.2kg)

Short back is cut into prime rashers for grilling or frying. (Av wt – 2.3kg)

Back and ribs can be boiled in a piece or cut into lean, economical rashers. (Av wt – 3kg)

Top back can be boiled or braised or cut into bacon chops. (Av wt – 1kg)

4) *Collar* can be bought whole and is most suitable for boiling. (Av wt – 3.6kg) It is often divided into smaller cuts.

Prime collar is a good boiling joint whole or cut into smaller joints. (Av wt – 2.7kg)

End collar is economical. Skin and press after boiling or baking. (Av wt – 0.9kg)

5) *Head* can be boiled for brawn or cooked whole for an occasion. (Av wt half head – 3kg)

6) *Chap* is the lower jaw and cheek of a pig. Boiled for Bath Chap. (Av wt 350–450g)

7) *Gammon* can be divided into four cuts. (Av wt 6.5–8kg)

Gammon slipper is a small, lean joint for boiling. (Av wt – 0.7kg)

Gammon hock is boiled or parboiled and then baked. Very good cold. High proportion of bone. (Av wt – 2kg)

Middle gammon is the best joint for boiling. Can be sliced into rashers for grilled gammon with eggs, etc. (Av wt – 2.3kg)

Corner gammon is a lean joint for boiling or for cutting into rashers for grilling. (Av wt – 1.8kg)

Cooking Bacon, Gammon and Ham

Cured pig meat which has been dried or smoked must generally be boiled before it can be used. After boiling, it can be used hot, but it is often reboiled or baked before it is served. Home-cured bacon, if very salty, can be soaked for 30 minutes in cold water or covered in boiling water and allowed to stand for 1 minute.

The small, family-sized bacon, gammon and ham joints in the shops have either been precooked before being cut, or they have been cut with special instruments which do not tear or spoil the meat.

A whole raw gammon or ham weighs at least 6.5kg and may weigh as much as 10kg. It is possible to cook a whole, bought or home-cured raw gammon or ham at home, but only given certain conditions. These are:

1) The whole gammon or ham can be boiled, par-boiled or baked, in 1 piece and in a very large container in both cases. An average joint measures about 56×30×13cm and so a boiling pan and an oven of at least this size, is needed if the joint is to be baked.

2) There are several hours available in which to cook the gammon or ham. A solid fuel cooker cuts the fuel costs.

3) There is a hook or similar appliance, hanging above the cooker, to suspend the joint in its cooking pot. During the initial boiling, the knuckle end of the gammon or ham should be out of the water for the first part of the cooking time, otherwise it will cook before the bulkier part of the meat, and will be sodden and partly wasted through shrinkage.

An economic factor to be considered before boiling a bought or home-cured raw gammon or ham is the wastage. An average-sized joint will lose up to 1kg during its first boiling. In a joint smaller than 6.5kg, the ratio of bone to meat is too high to make it economic to cure the joint. These smaller joints are, therefore, normally used as fresh meat.

Because a gammon or ham can vary so much in size, in the ratio of bone to meat, in the uses to which the meat is put, and on the thickness of the slices cut, it is impossible to give an average number of helpings per joint. As a rule, cold meat can be cut more thinly than hot meat.

Fried Bacon

rashers of back, streaky **or** long cut
   bacon **or** thin slices from any
   suitable bacon joint

Cut the rinds off the bacon rashers to prevent the bacon curling. Heat a frying pan for 1–2 minutes, then lay the rashers or slices in the pan in 1 layer. Cook until the fat is becoming transparent and the underside of the bacon is lightly browned. Turn the rashers or slices over with tongs or a palette knife, and fry the second side to the preferred degree of crispness. The total frying time is 3–4 minutes. Drain thoroughly. Serve quickly before the fat congeals.

Grilled Bacon

rashers of back, streaky **or** long cut
   bacon **or** thin slices from any
   suitable bacon joint **or** thick slices
   or steaks from a joint **or** gammon
   steaks

Cut the rinds off the bacon rashers or snip them at intervals to prevent the bacon curling. Heat the grill for 1–2 minutes. Lay the rashers, slices or steaks on the grill rack or pan in 1 layer. Place under the grill, and cook for 2–3 minutes until the fat is bubbling and the meat is beginning to brown. Turn the bacon or gammon over with tongs or a palette knife, reduce the heat and continue cooking to the degree of crispness preferred (for rashers and slices) or until thoroughly heated and cooked through (for steaks). The total grilling time is 4–8 minutes. Drain thoroughly. Serve quickly before the fat congeals.

Boiled Bacon *Basic recipe*

any bacon joint suitable for boiling
cider (optional)
sugar (optional)
ginger root (optional)
4 cloves (optional)

1 onion (optional)
6–8 black peppercorns (optional)
1 bay leaf (optional)
2–3 juniper berries (optional)

Garnish (optional)
raspings (p42)   Demerara sugar

A bought or home-cured bacon joint will probably need soaking for 1–12 hours before cooking, depending on the saltiness of the meat. Packaged and similar joints do not need soaking as a rule. They can be put into a pan, covered with boiling water, then drained.

Weigh the joint and measure its thickness. Calculate the cooking time according to the thickness of the joint. As a guide, allow 30 minutes per 0.5kg meat plus 30 minutes over for any joint more than 10cm thick, eg cook a 1kg joint for $1\frac{1}{2}$ hours. Do not undercook the meat, but on no account cook it fast or it will shrink and be tough.

Scrape the underside and rind before boiling any bacon joint. Choose a pan large enough to hold the meat comfortably with a little space to spare, especially if boiling more than 1 joint at a time. Add enough cold, fresh water to cover the meat, or use a mixture of cider and water, if preferred. Add sugar, ginger root or other spices, if liked (see **Note**). Cloves can be pressed into a whole onion, or tied in a square of muslin with the peppercorns, bay leaf and juniper berries, if preferred. Heat to simmering point, then simmer steadily for the calculated time. Test for tenderness by piercing the meat, near the bone if it has one, with a skewer.

Alternatively, shorten the cooking time by 15 minutes, and let the meat lie in the hot cooking liquid, off the heat, for 30 minutes. This gives an easier, firmer joint to carve.

Lift out the joint, pat dry, place it on a board and remove the rind. It should come off easily, in one piece. Coat the skinned area thoroughly with raspings, mixed with a little Demerara sugar, if liked. Serve hot or cold.

As a rule, the cooking liquid is too salty to use for stock.

Note Optional spices include coriander seeds, cumin seeds, allspice berries, a blade of mace, small pieces of nutmeg, or a whole, small, red chilli pepper.

Boiled Ham

a raw ham **or** gammon

Garnish
raspings (p42)   Demerara sugar

To ensure that the ham is sweet before cooking, insert a sharp knife close to the bone; when withdrawn, it should not give off any unpleasant odour or be slimy.

If the ham or gammon has been hung for a long time, and is very dry and salty, soak it for 24 hours at least, changing the water every 6–8 hours. For most hams, about 12 hours soaking or less is enough.

Drain; then weigh the ham and calculate the cooking time after soaking the ham (see Boiled Bacon p165). Clean and trim off any 'rusty' parts. Put the ham into a boiling pot big enough to hold it, but keep the knuckle end out of the water. Add enough cold water to cover the joint when laid flat, and cover the pan with a cloth to prevent undue evaporation. Heat to simmering point and simmer gently until tender or until parboiled, if to be baked after boiling. Do not let the water level sink below the surface of the ham when it is laid flat. Top up the pot with boiling water when required. Calculate the cooking time for the knuckle end on the thickness of the meat, and lay the ham flat in the pot to cook it (usually for about three-quarters of the total cooking time).

When cooked, lift out the ham and remove the rind. If to be eaten hot, immediately cover the skinned side with equal quantities of raspings and Demerara sugar. If to be eaten cold, put it back in its cooking liquid until cold, then drain, and cover the ham with the raspings and sugar mixture. If the ham is to be reboiled or baked, leave the coating until ready to serve.

Honey-glazed Ham with Pineapple
8–10 helpings

1.5–2kg parboiled York **or**
  Virginia ham
500ml dry cider

4 × 5ml spoons softened butter
1 × 15ml spoon double cream

Garnish
1 × 5ml spoon mixed English mustard
3 × 15ml spoons stiff honey
a good pinch of ground cloves

1 × 226g can pineapple chunks
  or rings
maraschino cherries
sprigs of watercress

Put the ham in a baking tin with the cider. Cover the tin tightly with foil. Bake the ham in a moderate oven, 180°C, Gas 4, for 30 minutes.

Meanwhile, mix together the mustard, honey, and cloves for the glaze. Drain the pineapple, reserving the juice. Cut pineapple rings into cubes, if used. Halve the cherries.

When the ham is baked, remove the foil and pour off the cider into a measuring jug. Remove the rind. Score the fat in a pattern of 4–5cm squares, then brush it all over with the mustard and honey glaze. Place pineapple pieces and halved cherries, cut side down, in alternate squares on the ham. Brush over with a little more glaze. Bake, loosely covered with the foil, in the oven for 20–30 minutes until the glaze is set.

Meanwhile, measure the cider and make it up to 500ml with the reserved pineapple juice, if required. Heat to simmering point in a saucepan. Stir in the butter, in small pieces, and melt. Simmer until well reduced and flavoured. Remove from the heat, and stir in the cream. Pour the sauce into a warmed sauce-boat and keep warm.

Place the ham on a carving dish and garnish with watercress. Serve the sauce separately.

Ham Slices with Fruit
3 main-course or 6 light first-course or supper helpings

6 ham **or** gammon slices **or** steaks (1cm thick approx)	75g soft white breadcrumbs
	200ml pineapple juice
150g soft light brown sugar	

Garnish

3 apples	75g margarine

Remove the rind from the ham or gammon and snip the fat at intervals to prevent curling. Put the slices or steaks in a frying pan with a very little water, heat to simmering point, and simmer for 10 minutes, turning them once. Drain. Lay the slices or steaks in an overlapping layer in a large, shallow, ovenproof baking dish. Mix together the sugar and breadcrumbs, and spread it over the slices or steaks, then trickle the pineapple juice over them. Bake, uncovered, in a moderate oven, 180°C, Gas 4, for 25 minutes.

Meanwhile, peel, core, and cut the apples into rings, 2cm thick (approx). Melt the margarine in a frying pan, and fry the rings until tender but not soft. Decorate the cooked dish with the apple rings, and serve at once.

VARIATIONS

1) *Apricots:* Soak 100g dried apricots in hot water for 20 minutes, then spread them over the prepared ham, and bake. Use the apricot water with the juice of an orange instead of the pineapple juice.

2) *Pineapple:* Spread 6 pineapple slices (canned or fresh) over the ham and breadcrumbs, add the pineapple juice, and bake for 20 minutes. Add the sugar, dot with butter, and continue baking for 15 minutes until the pineapple is glazed.

3) *Bacon chops:* Substitute chops for slices to make a more substantial meal. Fry the chops until browned on both sides, then continue as above.

Gammon Steaks with Marmalade
4 helpings

4 medium-sized gammon steaks
ground pepper
1 small onion
1 × 5ml spoon butter **or** margarine

4 × 15ml spoons medium-cut orange
  marmalade
2 × 5ml spoons vinegar

Garnish
chopped parsley

Remove the rind from the gammon steaks and snip the fat at intervals to prevent curling. Place on a grill rack and season with pepper to taste. Cook under a moderate grill, turning once, for 10–15 minutes depending on the thickness of the steaks. When cooked, transfer the steaks to a warmed serving dish and keep hot.

Skin the onion and chop it finely. Melt the fat in a pan and cook the onion gently for 5 minutes without browning it. Draw the pan off the heat and stir in the marmalade and vinegar, with any fat and juices left in the grill pan. Return to the heat and heat to boiling point, to reduce slightly.

Spoon the sauce over the gammon steaks. Garnish with chopped parsley and serve at once.

POULTRY

Preparing Poultry for Cooking

Trussing
The object of trussing a bird is to make it look attractive and to secure the stuffing.

The easiest way to truss is with a large needle and stout thread. Needles designed specifically for trussing can be bought at most shops selling kitchen equipment.

Put the uncooked bird on its back, and hold the legs together to form a V-shape pointing towards the neck end. Insert the threaded needle into one leg, just above the thigh bone; pass it through the body and out at the same point the other side. Leave a good length of thread on either side.

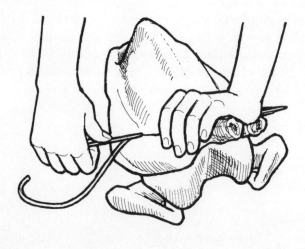

Turn the bird breast downwards and carry the thread through the elbow joint of the wing on each side.

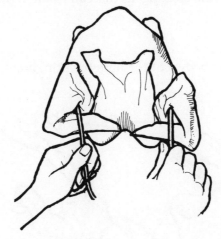

Twist the end of the wing under the neck to hold the flap of skin in place; tie the ends of the thread together, not too tightly.

Loop the thread over the ends of the drumsticks and draw them together, tying off round the 'parson's nose'. To make this easier, a slit may be cut in the flesh above the original vent cut and the 'parson's nose' pushed through.

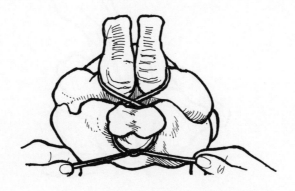

When the bird is trussed, the skin should still be complete if possible, to prevent any loss of fat from the bird during cooking, as this can result in over-dry and unpalatable meat.

Jointing

Pull the leg away from the body; cut through the skin; break leg from body at joint; cut through the joint.

Cut the thigh from the drumstick at the joint.

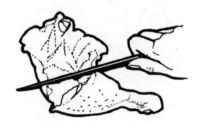

Cut the breast meat straight down to the wing joint; break the joint and cut so that the piece of breast meat and the wing are all in one piece.

With a heavy knife, cut down the back of the carcass, from vent to neck end.

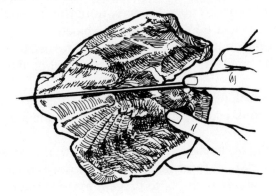

Cut the breast into two or four pieces, according to size.

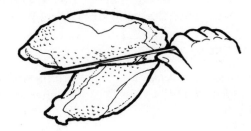

Cut off the pinions (extreme tips) of the wings (these can be cooked with the giblets); remove all small bones.

Boning
See Stuffed Boned Duck (p188).

Skinning
Loosen skin at the neck end exposing the wishbone. Using the fingertips and working under the skin, gradually loosen the skin from both sides of the breastbone. Slit the skin carefully along the length of the breastbone.

With a tugging movement and a firm grip, pull the skin off thigh and wing joints. Use a sharp knife if necessary to separate skin where it adheres to the bone. Chop away the last two sections of the wing joints and the last leg joint on the drumstick. Pull off the last remaining skin.

General Instructions for Roasting Whole Birds
Chickens, capons, and small turkeys: Traditionally, chicken is stuffed at the neck end with forcemeat or other stuffing, or just with fresh herbs; turkey with basic forcemeat, or chestnut stuffing in the crop and sausage-meat in the body. Nowadays however, the stuffing is almost always put into the body cavity; and only a large turkey for a festive dinner has 2 stuffings.

Put the bird in a roasting tin, preferably on a trivet or upturned saucer, and brush with melted fat or oil. Cover the breast with streaky bacon, if liked, or with foil. Cook for 20 minutes per 500g and 20 minutes over, until the thickest parts of the thigh, when pricked, give out a clear liquid without any blood.

The bird can be roasted on its side to start with and turned over half-way through the cooking to keep the breast moist. The final cooking should be breast side upper-most.

When the bird is cooked, place it on a warmed serving dish and keep hot. Serve with the traditional or other accompaniments (see p173) and gravy made with giblet stock if possible.

Large turkeys: Stuff the neck end and body cavity with the chosen stuffings. Place in a roasting tin and prepare as for smaller birds. (The bird can also be started on its side if liked.) Cover the breast with foil to prevent excess browning. This should be removed for the last 30 minutes – 1 hour.

For birds which are fully stuffed, cook for 15–20 minutes in a fairly hot oven, 200°C, Gas 6, then reduce to moderate, 180°C, Gas 4, and cook until tender. For unstuffed birds or ones with only the neck stuffed, cook in a warm oven, 160°C, Gas 3, until tender.

Approximate cooking times:

weight	unstuffed or with neck end only stuffed, at 160°C, Gas 3	fully stuffed, at 180°C, Gas 4 (after 20 mins at 200°C, Gas 6)
2.5 kg	$2\frac{1}{2}$–3 hrs	$2\frac{1}{2}$–3 hrs
2.75–3.5 kg	3 –$3\frac{1}{4}$ hrs	3 –$3\frac{3}{4}$ hrs
3.5–4.5 kg	$3\frac{1}{2}$–4 hrs	$3\frac{3}{4}$–$4\frac{1}{2}$ hrs
4.5–5.5 kg	4 –$4\frac{1}{2}$ hrs	$4\frac{1}{2}$–5 hrs
5.5–13.5 kg	20 mins per 500g + 20 mins	20 mins per 500g + 20 mins

Ducks: These are usually, although not always, stuffed before roasting. They are normally roasted in a fairly hot oven, 190°–200°C, Gas 5–6, allowing 15–20 minutes per 500g for a young bird, 20–25 minutes per 500g for an older one, a few minutes longer if fully stuffed. Allow about 300g stuffing for an average-sized bird.

The skin of a duck is sometimes pricked all over with a fork before roasting to en-courage the fat to run, and some cooks pour boiling water over the bird to encourage this further. The bird is roasted on a trivet with buttered paper over the breast. An average-sized bird takes 1–$1\frac{1}{2}$ hours.

Geese: These are generally stuffed, and are usually roasted in a moderate oven, 180°C, Gas 4, for 20–25 minutes per 500g, although this may vary slightly with the age and size of the bird. A buttered paper is put over the breast instead of bacon; apart from this, it is roasted like turkey. An average-sized bird, when stuffed, takes 2–$2\frac{1}{2}$ hours to roast. Allow 1.3–1.5kg stuffing for a 4–4.5kg goose.

Guinea-fowl can be treated either like chicken or like pheasant.

Roasting in Foil

This is a more convenient and cleaner method of roasting poultry than open roasting, since the bird is completely enclosed in foil and no basting is required; the juices are kept within the parcel and can be poured off and used for gravy, leaving the roasting tin clean. Use a piece of foil large enough to enclose the bird. Put the foil in the roasting tin, place the bird on top, and fold up the foil to enclose the bird, making a loose parcel. Open the foil for the last 15–20 minutes of the cooking time, to brown the bird.

Cook in a hot oven, 220°C, Gas 7, for approximately the following times:

Chicken up to 1.75kg   30–35 mins per 500g
                  1.75–3.5kg   25 mins per 500g
Turkey over 3.75kg   23 mins per 500g

For ducks, allow 10 minutes per 500g more than the times shown on p172, and for geese, 20 minutes extra per 500g when roasting in foil.

Preparing Giblets for Cooking

The giblets usually kept and used are the liver, heart, neck, and gizzard. If bought from a poulterer or obtained with a frozen bird they are ready prepared for cooking. If using giblets from a bird bought before eviscerating, cut the small greenish gall-bladder away from the liver, taking care not to break it; it will give the giblets a very bitter flavour. Cut any small sinews from the liver, and cut excess fat off the heart and gizzard. Break the neck into 2 or 3 pieces (a turkey neck into 4 or 5 pieces). Rinse the giblets in cold water briefly if necessary, then use them as the recipe directs.

Note Once the bones and meat have been removed, the skin of the neck of larger birds is sometimes used to contain a stuffing mixture in the same way as sausage skins.

What to Serve with Roasted Poultry

Any stuffing, sauce, garnish, and vegetable can be served with a plainly cooked bird, but some trimmings are traditional because they have proved particularly good. Duck and goose, which are fatty and strongly flavoured, need a drier stuffing than chickens, and a thickened, less sharp gravy. The following are the traditional accompaniments to serve with roasted birds:

Roast Chicken
1) Thin gravy (p229)
2) Basic herb stuffing (p43)
3) Bacon rolls (p48)
4) Bread sauce (p215)
5) Watercress to garnish

Roast Turkey
1) Thickened gravy (p230)
2) For the crop: chestnut stuffing (p44) or basic herb stuffing (p43)
3) For the body: sausage-meat stuffing (p46)
4) Bacon rolls (p48)
5) Grilled chipolata sausages
6) Bread sauce (p215) or cranberry sauce (p215)

Roast Duck
1) Thickened gravy (p230)
2) Sage and onion stuffing (p46)
3) Apple sauce (p213) or cranberry sauce (p215) or Cumberland sauce (p216)
4) Watercress to garnish

Roast Goose
1) Thickened gravy (p230)
2) Sage and onion stuffing (p46)
3) Apple sauce (p213)

Carving
Good carving, skilfully done, can make a bird much more economical.

Chicken, Small Turkey, Capon
Insert a carving fork firmly in the breast of the bird. On each side, make a downward cut with a sharp knife between the thigh and the body, then turn the blade outward so that the joint is exposed. Cut it through with either poultry shears or a sharp carving knife. Put the legs to one side.

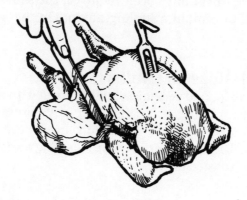

With the fork still inserted in the breast, remove the wings by cutting widely, but not too deeply, over the adjacent part of the breast, to give the wing enough meat without depriving the breast of too much flesh.

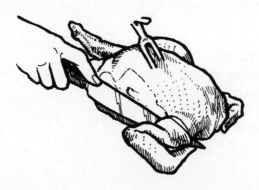

The breast of a large fowl can be sliced from the carcass as a whole.

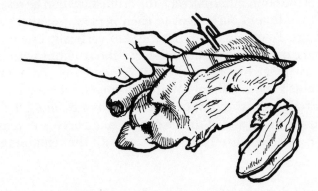

Alternatively, it can be separated from the back by cutting through the rib bones with poultry shears or a sharp knife. The breast of a small bird is detached from the carcass whole, thus providing two portions.

Carve the brown meat off the legs, if liked, working downwards in thin slices, following the direction of the bone. Serve some breast and some dark meat to each person.

To complete the carving of a large bird whose breast and back have been separated, place the back on the dish with the rib bones facing downwards; press the knife firmly across the centre of it, and raise the neck end at the same time with the fork to divide the back into two pieces.

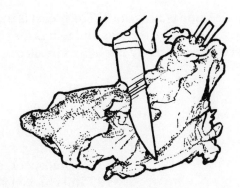

Remove the two 'oysters' (choice morsels of dark-coloured flesh) from the shallow hollows beside the thigh sockets. To do this, the tail part of the back must be stood on end and held firmly with the fork.

Large Turkey

Holding the bird steady with one carving fork, use a second one to bend each leg outward and downward, exposing the joint. Cut it through with poultry shears or a sharp carving knife. Put the legs to one side. Remove the wings in the same way. Do not take off any breast meat with the wing joints.

Carve the breast meat on the carcass, cutting downwards, parallel with the breast-bone.

The legs (thighs and drumsticks) should be carved downwards in thin slices, following the direction of the bone. Alternatively, the drumsticks can be reserved for another meal. Serve both white and dark meat to each person, together with a portion of each of the stuffings. To obtain these, slit the skin vertically down the centre of the vent and neck ends, open out the slits and serve the stuffings with a spoon.

When the breast meat has been cleared, remove any remaining stuffing to a warmed plate. Detach the wishbone. With the knife or shears, cut horizontally all round the bird through the thinnest part of the rib bones, and lift off the top part of the carcass. Turn the back part of the bird over, and carve any remaining meat off the back and sides parallel with the bone. Serve with the remaining stuffings.

Duck

Cut off the legs, and then the wings with a little breast meat attached to each. The breast is carved in quite thick, wedge-shaped slices: make the first cut down along the breastbone, and, with the blade of the knife slanted slightly towards the centre, make a series of cuts down the breast, parallel to the first cut. Remove the slices by cutting upwards towards the breastbone.

Duckling

To split the bird in half, cut down along the breastbone. Use poultry shears to cut through the bone. To divide each half into leg and wing portions, cut between the ribs so that some breast meat is attached to each joint.

Goose

Goose can be carved in the same way as duck. The breast is the best part. If the bird is large, carve only the breast and save the legs and wings for cold or re-heated dishes. **Note** A boned and stuffed bird is usually cut across in slices.

Chickens

Roast Chicken
4–6 helpings

1 roasting chicken	1 × 15ml spoon plain flour
oil **or** fat for basting	275ml chicken stock
salt and pepper	gravy browning
2–3 rashers streaky bacon (optional)	

Truss the chicken if liked. Put the oil or fat in a roasting tin and place for a few minutes in a fairly hot oven, 190°C–200°C, Gas 5–6. Remove from the oven. Place the chicken in the roasting tin, on a trivet if liked. Baste, sprinkle with salt and pepper, and place the bacon rashers, if used, over the breast. Cover the breast with a piece of foil or buttered greaseproof paper, if liked. Return the tin to the oven and cook the bird for the recommended time (p172), until tender. (Prick the thigh to test for tenderness; if there is any trace of blood, the chicken is not cooked.) The bacon and foil or greaseproof paper should be removed 10–15 minutes before serving, to allow the breast to brown.

When cooked, place the chicken on a hot carving dish, remove trussing strings or skewers, and keep hot. Pour out and discard the excess fat from the tin, keeping back the sediment for gravy. Sprinkle in the flour, stir well with a metal spoon, and add the stock gradually. Bring to the boil and boil for 2–3 minutes. Season to taste, add a little gravy browning, and strain into a hot sauce-boat.

Serve with chicken accompaniments (p173).

Roast Chicken with Honey and Almonds
4–6 helpings

1 roasting chicken	50g blanched almonds
½ lemon	a pinch of powdered saffron (optional)
salt and pepper	2 × 15ml spoons oil
3 × 15ml spoons honey	

Truss the chicken. Rub all over with the cut lemon, then sprinkle with salt and pepper. Line a roasting tin with a piece of foil large enough to cover the bird and to meet over the top. Put the bird on the foil, and rub it all over with honey. Slice the almonds and sprinkle them and the saffron, if used, over the bird. Pour the oil over the bird very gently. Wrap it completely in the foil, keeping it clear of the skin. Seal by folding over the edges. Roast in a moderate – fairly hot oven, 180°–190°C, Gas 4–5, for about 1½ hours until tender. Unwrap the foil for the last 10 minutes to allow the breast to brown.

Grilled Chicken Joints
1 helping

1 breast and wing **or** leg of chicken	1 × 15ml spoon butter
salt and pepper	

Garnish
Maître d'Hôtel butter (p232) **or**
   sauce (p202)

Remove the pinion from the wing, if used, and any excess skin. Trim away the bone end while still keeping the joint in a neat shape. Season it lightly with salt and pepper. Melt the butter and brush it over the chicken. Grill under high heat, turning 2 or 3 times during grilling to ensure even cooking. It should take 10–15 minutes to cook, depending on size.

Serve with a little Maître d'Hôtel butter or sauce.

Spatchcocked Chicken
2 helpings

1 spring chicken	salt and pepper
25g butter	

Garnish

bacon rolls (p48)	parsley sprigs

Split the bird in half, cutting through the back only. Flatten out the bird, removing the breastbone if necessary. Break the joints and remove the pinions from the wings, to make flattening easier. Use skewers to keep it in shape while cooking.

Melt the butter and brush it on both sides of the chicken; season lightly. Grill for 20 minutes, or until cooked. Brush the chicken with more butter and turn while grilling to ensure even cooking. Remove the skewers when done.

Serve garnished with bacon rolls and parsley sprigs, and accompanied by Tartare Sauce (p209) or Piquant Sauce (p206).

Chicken Kiev
4 helpings

4 chicken breast and wing joints	1 egg
salt and pepper	100g soft white breadcrumbs (approx)
flour for coating	fat **or** oil for deep frying

Butter Filling

finely grated rind of $\frac{1}{2}$ lemon	salt and freshly ground black pepper
1 × 15ml spoon chopped parsley	2 small cloves garlic
100g softened butter	

Garnish

lemon wedges	parsley sprigs

Make the butter filling first. Work the lemon rind and parsley thoroughly into the butter, and season to taste. Crush and work in the garlic. Form the butter into a roll, wrap in clingfilm and chill.

To prepare the chicken, cut off the wing pinions. Turn the joints, flesh side up, and cut out all bones except the wing bone which is left in place. Do not cut right through the flesh. Flatten out the boned meat, cover with greaseproof paper, and beat lightly with a cutlet bat or heavy knife. Cut the seasoned butter into 4 long pieces and place one on each piece of chicken. Fold the flesh over the butter to enclose it completely, and secure with wooden cocktail sticks. The wing bone should protrude at one end of each cutlet. Season the flour with salt and pepper and roll each piece of chicken in it. Beat the egg lightly on a plate. Roll or dip the chicken in the egg, coating each cutlet completely; then roll each in the breadcrumbs. Heat the fat or oil (p10) and deep fry 2 cutlets at a time until they are golden-brown and cooked through. Drain thoroughly and keep hot while frying the remaining two. Place the cutlets on a warmed serving dish with the bones overlapping in the centre. Remove the cocktail sticks and garnish with lemon wedges and parsley before serving.

Braised Chicken with Chestnuts and Sausages
4–6 helpings

1 chicken
salt and pepper
flour for coating
3 × 15ml spoons oil
1 onion

3 rashers streaky bacon, without rinds
150ml chicken stock **or** water
25g flour
25g butter

Stuffing

450g chestnuts
250ml chicken stock (approx)
50g ham
100g fine soft white breadcrumbs
grated rind of 1 lemon

salt and pepper
a few sprigs parsley
25g butter
1 egg

Garnish

450g fried chipolata sausages

lemon slices

Make the stuffing first. Remove the shells and skins of the chestnuts. Place the cleaned nuts in a saucepan, just cover with stock, and bring to the boil. Cover, reduce the heat until the liquid is only just boiling, and cook for about 1 hour or until the nuts are tender. Drain and mash them or put them through a fine sieve. Chop the ham finely. Mix the nuts, ham, breadcrumbs, and lemon rind together, and season with salt and pepper. Chop the parsley finely. Melt the butter slowly, and add the chopped parsley. Beat the egg until liquid. Mix all the ingredients for the stuffing together well. Stuff the bird with the mixture, and truss it.

Season the flour and roll the bird in it. Heat the oil in a large, heavy-bottomed flameproof casserole or pan with a lid. Fry the bird on all sides until lightly browned, then remove it. Skin and slice the onion, and cut the bacon into strips. Fry the onion and bacon lightly in the pan. Place a trivet or inverted saucer in the pan and place the chicken on it. Pour in the stock or water. Cover the pan, bring to the boil, then lower the heat until the liquid is just simmering. Cook for about 1½ hours, or until the chicken is tender. Add a little more stock if necessary before the end of the cooking time.

Remove the chicken. Sieve the pan juices or process in an electric blender. Knead the flour and butter into a beurre manié for the sauce. Heat the juices, then remove from the heat and add the beurre manié in small balls, stirring all the time. Return to the heat and stir until the mixture boils. Cook for a few minutes, then season to taste.

Garnish with fried sausages and lemon slices. Offer the sauce separately.

Chicken Casserole
6 helpings

1 chicken **or** 6 small chicken joints	50g mushrooms
salt and pepper	25g shallots
25g flour	50g butter **or** fat
125g streaky bacon, without rinds	500ml chicken stock

Joint the chicken. Season the flour, and dip the joints in it. Cut the bacon into strips 1cm wide, slice the mushrooms, and skin and chop the shallots. Heat the fat in a flameproof casserole and fry the bacon, mushrooms, and shallots gently. Add the chicken joints and fry them until golden on all sides, turning them as required.

Add enough hot stock just to cover the chicken pieces. Simmer for $1-1\frac{1}{2}$ hours or until tender. Re-season if required. Serve from the casserole.

Chicken Chasseur
4–6 helpings

1 roasting chicken	25g onion **or** shallot
salt and pepper	175g button mushrooms
25g flour	150ml dry white wine
1 × 15ml spoon cooking oil	275ml chicken stock
50g butter	1 sprig each of fresh tarragon, chervil,
3 tomatoes **or** 1 × 15ml spoon concentrated tomato purée	and parsley

Divide the chicken into 8 serving portions. Season the flour with salt and pepper, and use to dust the portions. Heat the oil and butter in a frying pan, and fry the chicken pieces until tender and browned all over, allowing 15–20 minutes for dark meat (drumsticks and thighs), 10–12 minutes for light meat (breast and wings). When tender, remove from the pan, drain on soft kitchen paper, and transfer to a warmed serving dish. Cover loosely with buttered paper and keep hot.

Skin and chop the tomatoes if used, and the onion or shallot. Put the onion or shallot into the pan, in the fat in which the chicken was cooked, and fry gently without colouring. Meanwhile, slice the mushrooms, add them to the pan, and continue frying until they are tender. Pour in the wine, and add the chopped tomatoes or the tomato purée and the stock. Stir until well blended, then simmer gently for 10 minutes. Chop the herbs and add most of them to the sauce. Season to taste.

Pour the sauce over the chicken, sprinkle with the remaining herbs, and serve very hot.

Coq au Vin
4–6 helpings

1 chicken with giblets
bouquet garni
salt and pepper
125g belly of pickled pork **or**
   green bacon rashers
175g button mushrooms
125g button onions
1 clove of garlic

50g unsalted butter
1 × 15ml spoon oil
2 × 15ml spoons brandy
575ml Burgundy **or** other red wine
2 × 5ml spoons concentrated
   tomato purée
25g butter
25g plain flour

Garnish
croûtes of fried bread

chopped parsley

Joint the chicken. Place the giblets in a saucepan, cover with water, and add the bouquet garni, salt, and pepper. Cook gently for 1 hour to make 275ml stock.

Remove the rind from the belly of pork or bacon rashers. Clean the mushrooms if necessary, skin the onions, and skin and crush the garlic. Heat the 50g butter and the oil in a flameproof casserole, add the pork or bacon, and the onions, and cook slowly until the fat runs and the onions are lightly coloured. Remove them to a plate.

Brown the chicken lightly all over in the same fat, then pour off any surplus fat. Warm the brandy, set alight, and pour it over the chicken. When the flame dies down, add the wine, stock, pork or bacon, onions, mushrooms, garlic, and tomato purée. Cover with a lid and cook over low heat, or in a cool oven, 150°C, Gas 2, for 1 hour or until the chicken is tender.

Remove the chicken to a serving dish and keep hot. Using a perforated spoon, remove the onions, bacon, and mushrooms, and arrange over the chicken. Simmer the liquid until reduced by about one-third. Meanwhile, make a beurre manié by kneading together the 25g butter and flour. Lower the heat of the liquid to below boiling point and gradually whisk in the beurre manié in small pieces. Continue to whisk until the sauce thickens. Pour it over the chicken. Arrange croûtes of fried bread round the dish and sprinkle with chopped parsley.

Poultry Hot Pot
4–6 helpings

1 boiling fowl with giblets
3 rashers streaky bacon, without rinds
salt and pepper
nutmeg

2 onions
2 carrots
275ml chicken stock
3 × 10ml spoons flour

Garnish
2 × 15ml spoons chopped parsley

Joint the fowl and remove the skin. Place the joints, with the liver and heart, in a casserole or saucepan with a tight-fitting lid. Cut the bacon into strips, and add with the salt, pepper, and nutmeg. Prepare and slice the onions and carrots, and add with the stock. Cover, then either cook in a fairly hot oven, 190–200°C, Gas 5–6, or simmer for about 2–2½ hours until tender. Blend the flour with a little water, add some of the chicken stock, and return to the pan. Stir it in, and cook until thickened. Serve sprinkled with parsley.

Boiled rice makes a good accompaniment.

Mrs Beeton's Chicken or Fowl Pie
6–8 helpings

1 chicken **or** boiling fowl with giblets
250ml water
1 onion
salt and pepper
bouquet garni
1 blade of whole mace
chicken fat **or** margarine for greasing
1 × 2.5ml spoon grated nutmeg
1 × 2.5ml spoon ground mace

6 slices lean cooked ham
150g basic herb forcemeat (p43) **or**
    250–300g sausage-meat
3 hard-boiled eggs
150–200ml water
flour for dredging
puff pastry (p412) using 150g flour
beaten egg for glazing

Skin the chicken or fowl and cut it into small serving joints. Put the leftover bones, neck, and gizzard into a small pan with the water. Split the onion in half and add it to the pan with the seasoning, bouquet garni, and mace. Half cover and simmer gently for about 45 minutes until the liquid is well reduced and strongly flavoured. Put to one side.

Grease lightly a 1.5 litre pie dish or oven-to-table baking dish. Put a layer of chicken joints in the bottom. Season lightly with salt, pepper, nutmeg, and ground mace. Cover with a layer of ham, then with forcemeat or sausage-meat; re-season. Slice the eggs, place a layer over the forcemeat, and season again. Repeat the layers until the dish is full and all the ingredients are used, ending with a layer of chicken joints. Pour 150–200ml water into the dish and dredge lightly with flour.

Roll out the pastry on a lightly floured surface to the same shape as the dish but 3cm larger all round. Cut off the outside 2cm of the pastry. Lay the pastry strip on the rim of the dish. Dampen the strip and lay the lid on top. Knock up the edge, trim, and use any trimmings to decorate the crust with pastry leaves. Make a pastry rose and put to one side. Brush the pastry with the beaten egg. Make a small hole in the centre of the pie. Bake in a hot oven, 220°C, Gas 7, for 15 minutes to set the pastry, then reduce the temperature to moderate, 180°C, Gas 4, and cover the pastry loosely with greaseproof paper. Bake for $1-1\frac{1}{4}$ hours if using forcemeat, for $1\frac{1}{2}-2$ hours if using sausage-meat. Bake the pastry rose with the pie for the final 20 minutes but bake it blind. Test whether the joints are cooked through by running a small heated skewer into the pie through the central hole. It should come out clean with no trace of blood or smell of raw meat on it.

Just before the pie is cooked, re-heat the stock and strain it. When the pie is cooked, pour the stock in through the central hole, and cover with the pastry rose. Serve hot or cold.

Note For serving cold the joints can be boned. In this case sausage-meat should be used. Add the bones to the saucepan when making stock, and use a smaller dish. The cooking time will be the same.

Stuffed Chicken Legs
4 helpings

4 cooked drumsticks
salt and Cayenne pepper
1×15ml spoon vegetable oil
2×15ml spoons soft white
    breadcrumbs
1×2.5ml spoon mixed herbs

1×5ml spoon chopped parsley
1 small onion
1×2.5ml spoon grated lemon rind
1 egg
4 gammon rashers
fat for greasing

Garnish
parsley sprigs

Season each drumstick with salt and Cayenne pepper and moisten with oil. Mix the breadcrumbs, herbs, and finely chopped parsley in a basin. Skin, blanch, and chop the onion finely and add it to the basin together with the lemon rind. Moisten the mixture with the egg. Spread each gammon rasher with this stuffing, and wrap one rasher around each drumstick. Tie or skewer the rasher securely in place. Put the drumsticks on a greased baking tray and cook in a moderate oven, 180°C, Gas 4, for 20 minutes; then cover them with foil, and cook for a further 20 minutes. Garnish with parsley sprigs.

Serve at once on trimmed slices of hot buttered toast.

Chicken Rissoles
4 helpings

100g cooked chicken
50g cooked ham **or** tongue
25g button mushrooms
25g butter
25g flour
150ml chicken stock
1 × 15ml spoon double cream

salt and pepper
shortcrust (p407) **or** rough puff (p412)
    pastry using 200g flour
flour for rolling out
oil **or** fat for deep frying
1 egg
fine dry white breadcrumbs for coating

Chop the chicken and ham finely. Chop the mushrooms. Melt the butter gently in a fairly large pan, add the mushrooms and cook for 1–2 minutes. Stir in the flour, add the stock gradually, and bring to the boil, stirring all the time. Cook for 1–2 minutes. Add the meat, cream, and seasoning. Leave to cool completely between 2 plates.

Roll out the pastry very thinly on a lightly floured surface, and cut into eight 12cm rounds. Divide the filling between the rounds, dampen the edges, and fold over to form half circles. Press the edges together and seal firmly. Heat the fat (p10). Beat the egg until liquid. Coat the rissoles with the beaten egg and breadcrumbs. Fry in the fat until golden-brown on both sides. Drain well.

Chaudfroid of Chicken
6 helpings

6 cooked chicken joints
125ml aspic jelly
375ml mayonnaise

lettuce leaves
3 sticks celery
2 hard-boiled eggs

Garnish
stoned olives **or** gherkins

tomato wedges **or** slices

Remove the skin, excess fat, and bones from the chicken joints, keeping the pieces in neat shapes. Melt the aspic jelly, and leave to cool. Just before it reaches setting point, while still tepid, add half the mayonnaise, and whisk in. Blend to a smooth consistency. Place the chicken joints on a wire cooling tray and coat with the mayonnaise sauce as soon as it reaches a good coating consistency. Arrange the lettuce leaves on a serving dish and place the chicken joints on top. Prepare and chop the celery, slice the eggs, and arrange these round the chicken. Spoon the remaining mayonnaise over the celery and egg. Garnish with the olives or gherkins and the tomatoes.

Chicken Mayonnaise
6 helpings

1 cold cooked chicken **or** 6 cooked
   chicken joints

275ml aspic jelly
425ml mayonnaise

Garnish
pickled walnuts

pieces of red and green pepper

Joint the whole chicken, if used; remove the skin, excess fat, and as much bone as possible, and trim the joints to a neat shape. Melt the aspic jelly. When almost cool, blend 150ml of it carefully into the mayonnaise. Beat well to blend thoroughly. Place the pieces of chicken on a wire cooling rack, and when the sauce is a good coating consistency, coat the pieces, using a large spoon. Cut the pickled nuts and the pieces of red and green pepper into attractive shapes for garnishing, dry well on soft kitchen paper, and stick on the chicken with dabs of half-set mayonnaise. Melt the remaining aspic jelly again if necessary; cool until it is on the point of setting, and use to coat the chicken thinly.

Galantine of Chicken
8–10 helpings

1 cooked boiling fowl
salt and pepper
100g ham **or** tongue
2 hard-boiled eggs
6 mushrooms
10–15g pistachio nuts **or** almonds

450g sausage-meat
750ml chicken stock (approx)
1 chicken stock cube
500ml White Chaudfroid sauce (p218)
125ml aspic jelly

Garnish
chopped pimento
strips of lemon rind

sliced hard-boiled egg

Cut down the back of the fowl, then remove all the bones neatly. Spread out the boned bird like a spatchcocked chicken (p178), distributing any loose pieces of meat evenly over the surface. Season well. Cut the ham or tongue into 1 × 3cm strips, slice the eggs, and chop the mushrooms. Blanch, skin, and chop the nuts. Spread 225g of the sausage-meat on the bird. Arrange the ham or tongue, egg slices, mushrooms, and nuts on top. Season well, then cover with the remaining sausage-meat.

    Lift the 2 halves of the bird, and bring them together so that it is as near its original shape as possible. Wrap the bird in foil. Heat the chicken stock and add the cube. Put in the chicken in foil, and simmer gently for $2\frac{1}{2}$ hours. Allow to cool slightly in the stock. Remove and drain. Tighten the foil to allow for any shrinkage while cooking. Press the 'parcel' between 2 large plates or boards and leave until quite cold.

    Unwrap, remove the skin, and wipe away any excess grease. Spoon the Chaudfroid sauce over the chicken. Chop the aspic coarsely and place round the chicken. Garnish in a decorative pattern with the pimento, lemon rind, and egg.

Turkey

Mrs Beeton's Roast Turkey

1 turkey
450g basic herb forcemeat (p43)
500g–1.5kg seasoned sausage-meat

2–3 rashers fat bacon
fat for basting

Stuff the neck of the bird with basic forcemeat and put the sausage-meat inside the body. Truss, and lay the bacon rashers over the breast. Roast in a hot oven, 220°C, Gas 7, for 15–20 minutes, then reduce the heat to moderate, 180°C, Gas 4. (For the overall cooking time see p172.) Baste frequently. About 20 minutes before serving, remove the bacon to allow the breast to brown. Remove the trussing string. Serve on a hot dish.

Serve with the traditional accompaniments (p173) and with roast potatoes and Brussels sprouts.

Note A 6kg bird will just fit comfortably into an oven with an interior capacity of 0.07 cubic metres (42 × 40 × 40cm). If the oven is smaller than this, or if one wishes to cook a larger bird, it can sometimes be done by removing the legs and cooking them separately. In any recipe for a whole roast turkey, the quantity of stuffing and the accompaniments should be adapted to fit the size of the bird.

The breast meat of a large turkey may become dry before the legs are cooked. To avoid this problem, remove the legs either before roasting the bird or when the breast is cooked, and use them for another meal.

The quantity of stuffing required will vary to some extent with the type of stuffing. One uses less of a light fluffy stuffing which needs room to swell than of a dense stuffing such as sausage-meat. As a very general guide, 700g sausage-meat and 450g basic forcemeat will stuff an average-sized (6kg) turkey.

Turkey Loaf
6–8 helpings

50g long-grain rice
225g cooked turkey meat
4 rashers streaky bacon, without rinds
salt and pepper
1 egg

25g (approx) thyme and parsley
   stuffing mix
grated rind of ½ lemon
1 × 5ml spoon paprika
fat for greasing

Cook the rice in boiling salted water for 10 minutes. Mince the turkey and the bacon rashers, and mix with the salt, pepper, and egg. Drain the rice and add to the turkey mixture. Mix thoroughly.

Make up the stuffing according to the directions on the packet. Add the lemon rind and paprika. Mix well. Place half the turkey mixture in a greased tin, and spread with stuffing; cover with the remaining turkey mixture. Cook in a fairly hot oven, 190°C, Gas 5, for 35 minutes. Serve hot or cold.

Goose and Duck

Roast Goose with Fruit Stuffing and Red Cabbage
6–8 helpings

350g prunes
1 goose with giblets
1.5 litres water
½ lemon

salt and pepper
450g cooking apples
1 × 15ml spoon redcurrant jelly

Red Cabbage
1.5kg red cabbage
50g butter
50g Demerara sugar

75ml water
75ml malt **or** cider vinegar
salt and pepper

Soak the prunes overnight. Remove the giblets from the goose and simmer them in 1.5 litres water until the liquid is reduced by half. Weigh the goose and calculate the cooking time at 20 minutes for every 500g. Remove the excess fat usually found around the vent. Rinse the inside of the bird, then rub the skin with lemon. Season with salt and pepper. Remove the stones from the prunes and chop the flesh. Peel and core the apples and chop them roughly. Mix with the prunes and season to taste. Stuff into the body of the bird. Place in a very hot oven, 230°C, Gas 8, reduce the temperature immediately to moderate, 180°C, Gas 4, and cook for the calculated time.

Meanwhile, prepare the red cabbage, shred finely. Melt the butter in a large flame-proof casserole. Add the sugar and cabbage and stir well. Add the water, vinegar, and seasoning, cover and cook in the bottom of the oven for about 2 hours, stirring occasionally.

When the goose is cooked, drain off the excess fat, retaining the juices in the pan. Add the redcurrant jelly and stir until it melts.

Serve the gravy and red cabbage separately.

English Roast Duck
4–5 helpings

1 duck
sage and onion stuffing (p46)
fat for basting

3 × 10ml spoons flour
275ml stock
salt and pepper

Fill the duck with sage and onion stuffing, and truss for roasting. Heat the fat and baste the duck well. Roast in a fairly hot oven, 190–200°C, Gas 5–6, covered with buttered paper, for 1–1½ hours or until tender, basting frequently. Uncover for the last 30 minutes. Keep the duck hot. Pour off the fat from the roasting tin, sprinkle in the flour, and brown it. Stir in the stock, simmer for 3–4 minutes, season, and strain. Remove the trussing string from the duck.

Serve hot with traditional accompaniments (p174).

Roast Duck with Orange
4–5 helpings

1 duck	3 × 10ml spoons flour
basic herb forcemeat (p43)	275ml stock
fat for basting	salt and pepper

Garnish

1 large orange	1 × 15ml spoon brandy

Truss and roast the duck as for English Roast Duck (p187), but use basic forcemeat instead of sage and onion stuffing. Meanwhile, pare the rind of the orange and remove all the pith. Cut the orange into segments, discard the membranes, and soak the segments in the brandy. Cut the rind into thin strips, boil in a little water for 5 minutes, then drain. Heat the orange segments gently in the brandy. Serve the cooked duck with the strips of rind and hot orange segments as a garnish.

Stuffed Boned Duck
6–8 helpings

100g onion	1 egg
25g butter **or** margarine	50g peanuts
100g long-grain rice	225g ham
275ml chicken stock	50g seedless raisins
1 bay leaf	1 duck
salt and pepper	2 × 15ml spoons corn oil
1 small red pepper	

Skin and chop the onion finely. Melt the butter or margarine, and fry the onion without browning. Stir in the rice and cook until it is translucent. Pour on the stock, add the bay leaf, salt and pepper, and cook for 12–15 minutes or until the rice is tender and the stock has been absorbed. Drain if necessary, and remove the bay leaf.

Wash the pepper, remove the membranes and seeds. Place in cold water, bring to the boil, and cook for 5 minutes. Drain well and cool under cold water. Beat the egg until liquid. Chop the peanuts coarsely. Mince the ham, raisins, pepper, peanuts, and rice together, add the egg, and stir in. Add salt and pepper.

Remove any trussing string from the duck. Use a small pointed knife to loosen and remove the wishbone. Slit the skin right along the backbone. Ease the flesh away from the bones either side of the backbone and down as far as the leg joints. Place the breast meat flat, skin side down, on a board. At the leg joints, cut the sinew joining them to the body; then, holding the leg firmly, gradually scrape and push the flesh away from the bones. Remove the bones. Repeat the process on the other leg. Cut away the first 2 joints of the wing, scrape the flesh down so that the bones can be pulled out. Repeat the process on the other wing. Continue carefully cutting away the flesh from the breastbone, being careful not to puncture the skin. Carefully remove the breastbone. If serving the duck hot, cover the bones with water, cook, and make stock for the gravy.

Put the stuffing in the body of the bird, make it a good shape, and sew the skin together. Heat the oil in a roasting tin in a fairly hot oven, 190–200°C, Gas 5–6. Place the duck in the tin, breast side up, and baste with the hot oil. Cook for 1–1½ hours. Serve hot or cold.

Note The above directions for boning can be followed for any poultry or game bird.

MISCELLANEOUS

Beer Batter
Makes 375ml (approx)

100g plain flour
a pinch of salt
1 egg

1 × 15ml spoon oil **or** cool
    melted butter
250ml light beer

Sift the flour and salt into a bowl. Make a well in the centre of the flour, and add the egg and oil or butter. Stir in half the beer, gradually working the flour down from the sides. Beat vigorously until the mixture is smooth and bubbly. Stir in the rest of the beer. Let the batter rest for about 30 minutes to allow the beer froth to settle.

Use for savoury dishes such as Toad-in-the-hole.

Toad-in-the-hole
4 helpings

500g skinless sausages
25g cooking fat **or** dripping

375ml beer batter

Heat the oven to hot, 220°C, Gas 7. Cut each sausage into 3 pieces. Put the sausages and fat into a 17 × 27cm baking tin and heat in the oven for 5 minutes. Pour the batter round the sausages quickly, and bake for 30–35 minutes until brown and well-risen.

Serve cut into 4 pieces, with gravy.

Note 500g sausage-meat can be used instead, rolled into 8 sausage shapes on a floured board.

Coating Batter (1)
Makes 250ml (approx)

100g plain flour
$\frac{1}{2} \times 2.5$ml spoon salt
1×15ml spoon cooking oil **or**
   melted butter

125ml water **or** milk and water
2 egg whites

Sift the flour and salt into a bowl. Make a well in the centre of the flour and add the oil or butter and some of the liquid. Gradually work in the flour from the sides, then beat well until smooth. Stir in the rest of the liquid. Just before using, whisk the egg whites until stiff. Give the batter a final beat and fold in the egg whites lightly.

Alternatively, use an electric blender. Put the water and oil into the goblet. Add the flour and salt and blend until smooth. Just before using, whisk the egg whites until stiff in a separate bowl. Give the batter a quick mix, then pour it down the sides of the bowl containing the egg whites. Fold the egg whites into the mixture lightly.

This makes a crisp, light batter suitable for fruit fritters, small fish fillets, and kromeskies.

Note The egg yolks can be added to the flour but then only 100ml liquid should be added. This makes a thicker, richer batter.

Coating Batter (2)
Makes 175ml (approx)

100g plain flour
$\frac{1}{2} \times 2.5$ml spoon salt

1 egg
125ml milk

Sift the flour and salt into a bowl. Make a well in the centre of the flour, and add the egg and a little of the milk. Gradually work in the flour from the sides, then beat until smooth. Stir in the rest of the milk. Just before using, stir well.

Alternatively, use an electric blender. Put the milk and egg into the goblet. Add the flour and salt and blend until smooth.

This makes a firmer batter suitable for fish fillets, fish and meat cakes, and meat.

Coating Batter (3)
Makes 175ml (approx)

100g plain flour
$\frac{1}{2} \times 2.5$ml spoon salt
1×15ml spoon oil **or** melted butter

125ml warm water
1×5ml spoon baking powder

Sift the flour and salt into a bowl. Make a well in the centre of the flour, and add the oil or butter and a little of the water. Gradually work in the flour from the sides, then beat until smooth. Stir in the rest of the water. Alternatively, use a blender. Make in the same way as Batter (2). Just before using, sprinkle on the baking powder and give the batter a final beat. Use as for Batter (2).

Coating Batter (4)
Makes 400ml (approx)

125ml milk
25g butter
1 × 5ml spoon dried yeast **or** 10g fresh
   yeast

$\frac{1}{2}$ × 2.5ml spoon caster sugar
100g plain flour
a pinch of salt

Warm the milk and butter until the butter melts. Do not let it get hot. Mix the yeast and sugar into the milk. Leave for 15 minutes in a warm place until frothy.

Put the flour and salt into a bowl, make a well in the centre, and pour in the yeast and milk. Gradually work in the flour from the sides to form a thick batter, the consistency of double cream. Cover and leave to stand in a warm place for 30–35 minutes, until the mixture doubles in size.

This makes a crisp, well-flavoured batter, suitable for meat and fish.

Basic Thin Batter (for puddings and pancakes)
Makes 375ml (approx)

100g plain flour
$\frac{1}{2}$ × 2.5ml spoon salt

1 egg
250ml milk

Sift the flour and salt into a bowl, make a well in the centre and add the egg. Stir in half the milk, gradually working the flour down from the sides. Beat vigorously until the mixture is smooth and bubbly. Stir in the rest of the milk. Use as below, and for pancakes (pp192–93).

Note Half milk and half water can be used. Some cooks claim this gives a lighter batter.

VARIATIONS
Baked Batter Pudding
Heat the oven to hot, 220°C, Gas 7. Put 25g cooking fat or 25ml oil into a 17 × 27cm baking tin. Heat in the oven for 15 minutes. Pour in the batter quickly and bake for 30–35 minutes, until brown and well risen.

Serve immediately, cut into squares, either with a savoury sauce or gravy, or as an accompaniment to roast beef, sausages or braised vegetables. The batter can also be served as a sweet pudding; sprinkle with sugar and serve with jam.

Yorkshire Pudding
Plain baked batter is eaten most often as Yorkshire Pudding. It is the traditional British accompaniment to roast beef. In the north of England, the meat is roasted on a grid placed in the meat tin. Thirty minutes before the meat is cooked, the joint is basted for the last time, and then the batter is poured into the meat tin below the grid, where it cooks in the meat dripping. The pudding is served either with the meat or, more traditionally, as a first course with gravy.

Very often Yorkshire Pudding is cooked in a separate tin, using beef dripping for the flavour; the tin is placed on the shelf above the meat, and cooked as in the basic Baked Batter Pudding.

For another **variation**, see over.

Individual Yorkshire Puddings

These should be baked in deep individual patty tins. Put a small knob of lard (about 1 × 5ml spoon) in each tin. Place in a preheated oven, 220°C, Gas 7, until the fat is smoking hot. Half fill the tins with basic thin batter and bake for at least 20–25 minutes, depending on the depth of the tins. The puddings will rise high above the tins, and will be almost hollow shells. Do not underbake or they will collapse when taken out of the oven.

Plain Pancakes *Basic recipe*
Makes 8 pancakes

Prepare a basic thin batter (p191). Pour it into a jug. Heat a little cooking fat or oil in a clean 18cm frying pan or omelet pan. Pour off any excess fat or oil, as the pan should only be coated with a thin film of grease. Stir the batter and pour in 2–3 × 15ml spoons batter, just enough to cover the base of the pan thinly. Tilt and rotate the pan to make sure that the batter runs over the whole surface evenly. Cook over moderate heat for about 1 minute until the pancake is set and golden-brown underneath. Make sure the pancake is loose by shaking the pan, then either toss it or turn over with a palette knife or fish slice. Cook the second side for about 30 seconds until golden. Slide out on to a warmed plate so that the first side fried will be on the outside when the pancake is rolled up or folded.

Repeat until all the batter has been used, greasing the pan when necessary.

VARIATIONS
Rich Pancake Batter

Add 15g butter, melted and cooled, or 1 × 15ml spoon oil, and an egg yolk to the batter. Alternatively, add 1 whole extra egg.

Cream Pancake Batter

Use 150ml milk and 50ml single cream instead of 250ml milk. Add 2 eggs and 25g cooled butter. The mixture should only just coat the back of a spoon as the pancakes should be very thin. For sweet pancakes, 1 × 15ml spoon brandy can be added and 2 × 15ml spoons caster sugar.

Savoury Pancakes *Basic recipe*

Add salt and pepper to a basic thin batter (p191). Make the consistency a little thicker by using slightly less liquid than for sweet pancakes.

Savoury pancakes are usually rolled round a thick filling and arranged in an oven-proof dish. They are then heated in a moderate oven at 180°C, Gas 4, for 30 minutes if they have a cold filling and for 20 minutes if the filling is hot. Alternatively, pancakes with hot fillings can be browned lightly under the grill.

VARIATIONS
Beef Pancakes

Brown 500g minced beef in 2 × 15ml spoons oil. Add 2 × 5ml spoons chopped parsley, 4 × 15ml spoons cooked rice, 1 × 15ml spoon grated onion, salt and pepper, a pinch of herbs, and 125ml beef stock. Simmer for 5 minutes until the stock is absorbed. Fill the pancakes, sprinkle with 25g grated cheese and re-heat. (Cheddar, Cheshire, Lancashire or a mixture of Gruyère and Parmesan can be used.)

Cheese Pancakes

Add 50g grated strong cheese to 375ml thick white sauce (p200). Fill the pancakes, sprinkle with 25g grated hard cheese and 1 × 15ml spoon chopped parsley. Dot with butter and re-heat.

Chicken Pancakes

Mix 100g minced cooked chicken, 50g finely chopped red or green pepper, 50g grated onion, salt and pepper. Fill the pancakes and arrange in a dish. Mix 1 × 15ml spoon concentrated tomato purée with 125ml soured cream, pour over the pancakes, sprinkle with 1 × 15ml spoon grated cheese and re-heat.

Curried Turkey Pancakes

Fry 50g chopped onion in 50g fat for 5 minutes, until tender. Add 1 × 5ml spoon curry powder and cook for 1 minute. Stir in 25g flour and 250ml chicken stock to make a sauce. Add 300g chopped cooked turkey and 1 × 15ml spoon cream. Fill the pancakes, sprinkle with 25g grated cheese and re-heat.

Smoked Haddock Pancakes

Poach 300g smoked haddock fillets in a little water for 10–15 minutes. Drain and flake the fish. Make 250ml white sauce (p200). Add the fish and 2 chopped hard-boiled eggs, 1 × 5ml spoon chopped capers, 1 × 15ml spoon chopped parsley, 2 × 15ml spoons lemon juice, salt and pepper. Fill the pancakes, sprinkle with 25g grated cheese and re-heat.

Spinach Pancakes

Cook 300g frozen spinach and drain well. Add 200g cottage cheese, 3 lightly beaten eggs, 50g grated strong cheese, 100ml double cream, a pinch of ground nutmeg, salt and pepper. Fill the pancakes. Sprinkle with 25g grated cheese and re-heat.

Macaroni Cheese (Macaroni Au Gratin)
3–4 helpings

125g long **or** elbow cut macaroni	salt and pepper
500ml foundation white sauce (p200)	25g butter
100g Cheddar cheese	

Break long macaroni into 2cm pieces. Cook in boiling salted water as directed; then drain well. Meanwhile, heat the white sauce and grate the cheese. Mix together in a pan the macaroni, sauce, 75g of the cheese, and season to taste. Heat thoroughly for 1–2 minutes, and put the mixture in a greased 700ml pie dish. Sprinkle with the remaining cheese, and dot with the rest of the butter. Grill for 2–4 minutes to melt and brown the cheese. Alternatively, bake in a hot oven, 220°C, Gas 7, for 20 minutes.

Pizza con Mozzarella
Makes two 25cm pizze

Dough

15g fresh yeast
125ml warm water
a few grains caster sugar
175g strong white flour

1 × 2.5ml spoon salt
3 × 2.5ml spoons olive oil (approx)
polenta (cornmeal) for dusting
oil for greasing

Filling

150ml Salsa Pomodoro (p217)
200g Mozzarella cheese
4 black olives
4 anchovy fillets

4 × 15ml spoons olive oil
3 × 15ml spoons grated Parmesan
    cheese

Make the dough. Blend the yeast into a little of the warm water with the sugar, then stir in the remaining water. Leave in a warm place until frothy. Sift the flour and salt into a bowl. Pour in the yeast mixture and oil. Work into a dough and knead well until smooth and elastic. Dust lightly with flour and place in a lightly oiled polythene bag. Leave in a warm place for 1½ hours or until doubled in size. Knock back the dough and divide into two equal portions. Knead lightly. Roll out each portion on a board dusted with polenta into a circle 25cm in diameter and about 5mm thick. Heat the oven to very hot, 230°C, Gas 8.

Pinch up the edge of each dough circle to make a low rim. Pour half the Salsa Pomodoro into each pizza. Crumble half the Mozzarella cheese over the sauce. Halve and stone the olives. Place 2 anchovy fillets in the form of a cross on each pizza, and place the halved olives, cut side down, in the spaces between them. Trickle half the oil over each pizza, and sprinkle the Parmesan cheese on top. Bake on a lightly greased baking sheet for 5 minutes. Reduce the temperature to fairly hot, 200°C, Gas 6, and bake for a further 5 minutes until the dough is lightly browned and the cheese has melted. Serve at once.

Plain Omelet *Basic recipe*
1 helping

2 eggs
salt and pepper
1 × 15ml spoon water

1 × 15ml spoon unsalted butter **or**
    margarine

Break the eggs into a basin, season with salt and pepper, add the water, and beat lightly with a fork. Place the pan over gentle heat and when it is hot, add the butter or margarine. Tilt the pan so that the whole surface is greased lightly. Do not over-heat or let the butter brown. Without drawing the pan off the heat, pour the beaten eggs on to the hot fat. Leave to stand for 10 seconds; then with the back of the prongs of a fork, or with a spatula, draw the mixture gently from the sides to the centre as it sets and let the liquid egg from the centre run to the sides. Repeat this once or twice more, as necessary. Do not stir round, or it will become scrambled eggs. In about 1 minute, the egg will have set softly. Leave it to cook for a further 4–5 seconds until it is golden underneath. Remove the pan from the heat. Loosen the edges by shaking the pan or using a round-bladed knife. Tilt the pan slightly towards you, and as the omelet slides up the side of the pan towards the handle, use a palette knife or spatula to fold this third of the omelet towards the centre. Raise the handle of the pan, slide the omelet up the side furthest from the handle, and fold over the opposite third, also towards the centre.

Change your grip on the pan so that your hand is underneath the handle and it runs across the palm between the thumb and forefinger. Hold the plate in the other hand, and with a quick movement, tip the omelet on to it, folded sides underneath.

Filled Omelets

Any plain omelet can be filled. Some flavourings are added to the beaten eggs and some are added to the omelet just before it is folded.
Add to the beaten eggs one of the following:

Cheese Omelet
Grate 50g cheese and mix 40g with the eggs; sprinkle the rest over the omelet just before serving it.

Omelette Fines Herbes
Add 1 × 2.5ml spoon chopped tarragon, 1 × 2.5ml spoon chopped chervil, 1 × 5ml spoon chopped parsley, and a few chopped chives or 1 × 5ml spoon mixed dried herbs.

Fish Omelet
Add 50g flaked cooked fish.

Ham or Tongue Omelet
Add 50g chopped meat and 1 × 5ml spoon chopped parsley.

Onion Omelet
Chop 25g onion and sauté in butter in a saucepan until tender, ie about 5 minutes.

Put one or more of the following into the centre of the omelet before folding. Fold in half, rather than in thirds.

Bacon Omelet
Chop 2 rashers of rindless bacon; fry in a saucepan until crisp.

Mushroom Omelet
Clean and slice 50g mushrooms and cook in butter, in a saucepan, until soft.

Omelette Provençale
Mix together 1 skinned and chopped tomato, a little garlic, 50g finely chopped onion, 1 × 15ml spoon chopped parsley, a little chopped fresh tarragon, salt and pepper. Sauté in a little butter for 5 minutes, until the onion is tender.

Tomato Omelet

Peel and chop 1–2 tomatoes and fry in a little butter for 5 minutes, until soft and pulpy. Add $\frac{1}{2} \times 15$ml spoon chopped parsley.

If a 3-egg omelet is filled with a substantial filling it will make 2 helpings. Omelets of this type are:

Chicken Omelet

Chop 50g cooked chicken and heat gently in a little white sauce.

Prawn and Mushroom Omelet

Melt 25g butter, and sauté 25g chopped mushrooms; remove from the butter, and keep hot. Make a sauce using the butter, 3×10ml spoons flour, and 125ml milk. Add the mushrooms and 50g coarsely chopped prawns. Re-heat and season before filling the omelet.

Stacked Omelets

These serve four or more people. Make up three or four types of filling, such as shrimps mixed with a little cream, chopped mushrooms fried with onions, and grated cheese. Make a plain omelet and slide it on to a plate standing over hot water. Top with a filling. Make a second omelet and lay it over the first. Top with another type of filling. Repeat, allowing at least 1 omelet per person. To serve, cut the stack into wedge-shaped pieces.

Savoury Soufflé *Basic recipe*
4–6 helpings

50g butter	salt and pepper
5×15ml spoons flour	4 eggs
250ml milk	1 egg white

Heat the oven to fairly hot, 190°C. Gas 5, or put a steamer on to heat. Prepare the soufflé dish (p197). Melt the butter in a pan, stir in the flour, and cook slowly for 2–3 minutes, stirring all the time. Add the milk gradually and beat until smooth. Cook for another 1–2 minutes, still stirring all the time. Remove the pan from the heat and beat hard until the sauce comes away from the sides of the pan cleanly. Put into a bowl, season well, and add any flavouring (see variations). Separate the eggs and beat the yolks into the mixture one by one. Whisk all the egg whites until stiff. Using a metal spoon, stir 1 spoonful into the mixture and then fold in the rest until evenly distributed. Put into 1 prepared 800ml or 6×200ml dishes. Bake in the centre of the oven for 30–35 minutes, until well risen and browned; or cover with greaseproof paper and steam for 1 hour until just firm to the touch.

Serve immediately with hot buttered toast.

To Prepare a Soufflé Dish or Tin

Cut a strip from two thicknesses of greaseproof paper or vegetable parchment 8cm taller than the dish and long enough to go right round the dish with an overlap. Tie the paper round the dish with string. If the dish has sloping sides or a projecting rim, secure the paper above and below the rim with gummed tape or pins. Make sure that the paper is uncreased and forms a neat round shape. Grease the inside of the dish and paper collar for a hot soufflé with clarified butter or oil. Oil the inside of the collar for a cold soufflé. When the soufflé is ready for the table, ease the paper away from its sides with the blade of a knife.

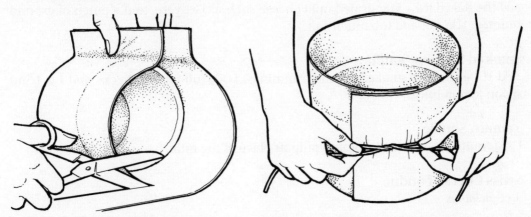

Cutting a strip to go round a soufflé dish with an overlap

Tying the paper round the dish with string

Preparing a soufflé dish can be tricky, and it is not essential to use a paper collar. A soufflé can be baked without one, although it will not rise as much as when a collar is used. A cold soufflé can be set in a dish big enough to hold all the mixture.

If a paper collar is used, put any of the following hot soufflés into an 800ml dish; otherwise use a 1 litre dish. Use a paper collar if the recipe tells you to prepare a soufflé dish before making the soufflé.

VARIATIONS

Asparagus Soufflé

Cook 200g frozen asparagus according to the directions on the packet or drain 200g canned asparagus. Chop it, and fold into the savoury soufflé mixture.

Cheese Soufflé

Reduce the flour to 25g and add 100–150g grated Cheddar cheese or 75–100g grated Parmesan and Gruyère cheese, and $\frac{1}{2} \times 2.5$ml spoon dry mustard or a pinch of Cayenne pepper.

Chicken Soufflé

Add 200g cooked minced chicken, 25g chopped sautéed onion, 2×15ml spoons lemon juice, and 1×5ml spoon chopped parsley.

For further **variations,** see over.

Ham or Ham and Tongue Soufflé
Make a sauce using 125ml stock and 125ml tomato juice. Add 150g minced meat, 1 × 10ml spoon chopped parsley, grated nutmeg, and Cayenne pepper.

Salmon Soufflé
Add 150g cooked salmon to 100ml Béchamel sauce (p207).

Smoked Haddock Soufflé
Cook 200g smoked haddock in the milk. Use the milk to make the sauce and then add the flaked fish, 50g grated mild cheese such as Gruyère, and a pinch of ground nutmeg. (Do not add too much salt.)

Smoked Salmon Soufflé
Add 100g chopped smoked salmon trimmings, 100g full-fat soft cheese, and 1 × 15ml spoon lemon juice.

Tomato Soufflé
Use tomato juice or fresh tomato pulp in place of the milk.

Swiss Cheese Fondue
4–6 helpings

300–450g white bread
250–350g Emmental cheese
500–750g Gruyère cheese
1 clove of garlic
350ml light dry white wine
2 × 5ml spoons fresh lemon juice
   (approx)

1 × 10ml spoon cornflour **or**
   potato flour
1 × 15ml spoon Kirsch
white pepper and grated nutmeg

In the kitchen, cut the bread into 2cm cubes, providing about 75g per person. Put into a basket.

To make the fondue, grate the cheeses. Cut the garlic clove in half, and rub the cut sides over the inside of a *caquelon* or casserole. Warm the wine in the casserole and add lemon juice to taste. Add the cheese in 15ml spoonfuls and bring slowly to the boil, stirring all the time with a whisk. Blend the cornflour or potato flour with the Kirsch to make a smooth paste. Add in 5ml spoonfuls to the cheese mixture, stirring with a figure of eight movement, until the mixture is smooth, thick, and creamy. Season to taste with the pepper and nutmeg. Transfer to the dining table with the basket of bread.

At the table, place the *caquelon* or casserole on a lit burner or hotplate, and eat immediately. Each diner serves himself from the *caquelon* or casserole by spearing bread cubes on a long-handled fork, and dipping them into the fondue mixture.

Plain green salad and Kirsch are the only accompaniments traditionally served with a fondue, although wine can be served instead of Kirsch.

Cooking time in kitchen 30 minutes (approx)

Scotch Eggs
4 helpings

250g sausage-meat
1 × 15ml spoon flour
1 egg
2 × 5ml spoons water

salt and pepper
4 hard-boiled eggs
50g soft white breadcrumbs
oil for deep frying

Garnish
parsley sprigs

Divide the sausage-meat into 4 equal pieces. On a lightly floured surface, roll each piece into a circle 12cm in diameter. Beat the egg with the water. Season the remaining flour with salt and pepper and toss the hard-boiled eggs in it. Place an egg in the centre of each circle of sausage-meat and mould evenly round the egg, making sure it fits closely. Seal the joins with the beaten egg and pinch well together. Mould each Scotch egg into a good shape, brush it all over with beaten egg, and then toss it in the breadcrumbs, covering the surface evenly. Press the crumbs well in. Put enough oil to cover the Scotch eggs into a deep pan and heat it (p11). Fry the eggs until golden-brown. Drain them on soft kitchen paper. Cut in half lengthways and garnish each half with a small piece of parsley.

Serve hot with Fresh Tomato Sauce (p216) or cold with salad.

Note As the sausage-meat is raw, it is important that the frying should not be hurried.

Welsh Rarebit
4 helpings

100–150g Cheddar cheese
25g butter **or** margarine
1 × 15ml spoon flour
75ml milk **or** 3 × 15ml spoons milk
    and 2 × 15ml spoons ale **or** beer

1 × 5ml spoon French mustard
a few drops Worcestershire sauce
salt and pepper
4 slices bread
butter for spreading

Grate the cheese. Melt the fat in a pan, and stir in the flour. Cook together for 2–3 minutes, stirring all the time; do not let the flour colour. Stir in the milk and blend to a smooth, thick mixture; then stir in the ale or beer, if used, the mustard and Worcestershire sauce. Add the cheese little by little, stir in, and season to taste. Remove from the heat as soon as well blended. Remove the crusts from the bread and toast lightly on both sides. Butter one side well and spread the cheese mixture on the buttered sides. Grill briefly, if liked, using high heat, to brown the surface of the cheese mixture. Serve immediately.

Note The term *rarebit* is generally considered as synonymous with *rabbit.*

VARIATIONS
Buck Rarebit
Make as for Welsh Rarebit, but top each slice with a poached egg. Serve at once.

Yorkshire Rarebit
Make as for Welsh Rarebit, but add 4 rashers of cooked bacon, without rinds.

SAUCES, GRAVIES, MARINADES AND BUTTERS

SAUCES

English Foundation Sauces

Foundation White Sauce *Basic recipe*
Makes 500ml coating or pouring sauce

Coating Sauce

50g butter **or** margarine
50g plain flour

500ml milk **or** fish stock (p26) **or**
    white stock (p26) **or** a mixture of
    stock and milk
salt and pepper

Pouring Sauce

35g butter **or** margarine
35g plain flour

500ml liquid as for coating sauce
salt and pepper

1) *Roux Method*

Melt the fat in a saucepan, add the flour and stir over low heat for 2–3 minutes, without allowing the mixture (roux) to colour. Draw the pan off the heat and gradually add the liquid, stirring all the time. Return to moderate heat, and stir until the sauce boils and has thickened. Reduce the heat, and simmer for 1–2 minutes, beating briskly. (This helps to give the sauce a gloss.) Season to taste.

2) *Beurre Manié Method*

Knead the fat and flour, or work them together with a fork or spoon until they are blended smoothly. Heat the liquid in a saucepan and, when at just below boiling point, gradually whisk in the kneaded butter and flour in small pieces. Continue to whisk the sauce until it boils, by which time all the beurre manié must be smoothly blended in. Season to taste.

3) *All-in-one Method*

Put the fat, flour, and liquid in a saucepan. Whisk over moderate heat until the sauce comes to the boil. Reduce the heat and cook for 3–4 minutes, whisking all the time, until the sauce has thickened, and is smooth and glossy. Season to taste.

Note A coating sauce should coat the back of the spoon used for stirring. A pouring sauce should barely mask the spoon and should flow freely.

Sauces based on Foundation White Sauce

A foundation white sauce made by any of the three methods above can be used as the basis of many other savoury sauces. The quantities of the ingredients in the following recipes are for adding to 250ml Foundation White Sauce of either coating or pouring consistency. In most cases, this will give about 250ml completed sauce, the extra ingredients making up the small quantity lost by evaporation.

Anchovy Sauce

250ml foundation white sauce (p200)
  made with fish stock (p26) **or**
  half milk and half fish stock

1–2 × 5ml spoons anchovy essence
½ × 2.5ml spoon lemon juice
1–2 drops red colouring

Heat the sauce, if necessary; then stir in the anchovy essence to taste. Add the lemon juice and stir in enough red colouring to tint the sauce a dull pink.
  Serve with fish.

Brain Sauce

1 set of sheep's brains
1 large onion (200g approx)
250ml white stock (p26)
250ml foundation white sauce (p200)
  made with white stock

1 × 2.5ml spoon lemon juice
1 × 10ml spoon chopped parsley
salt and pepper (optional)

Prepare the brains (p141). Skin and slice the onion. Put in a saucepan with the brains. Add the stock. Heat to boiling point, cover, reduce the heat and simmer gently for 30 minutes. Strain off the stock. Heat the sauce, if necessary. Chop the onion and brains. Add them to the white sauce with the lemon juice and parsley. Stir well, and re-season if required.
  Serve with steamed or boiled meats.

Cheese Sauce

75g Cheddar cheese **or** other hard
  cheese
250ml foundation white sauce (p200)
  made with milk **or** half milk and
  half white stock

a pinch of dry English mustard
a pinch of Cayenne pepper
salt and pepper

Grate the cheese finely. Heat the sauce to boiling point, then remove the pan from the heat. Add the grated cheese, mustard, Cayenne pepper, and seasoning to taste. Stir well. Do not reboil the sauce; use at once.
  Serve with vegetables, fish, ham, poultry, eggs or pasta.

Caper Sauce (1) (white)

250ml foundation white sauce (p200) made with white stock (p26) **or** half milk and half white stock

1 × 15ml spoon chopped capers
1 × 5ml spoon vinegar in which the capers were pickled

Heat the sauce, if necessary. Add the capers and vinegar, and stir well.
Serve with boiled mutton or fish.

Herb Sauce

250ml foundation white sauce (p200) made with milk

1–2 × 15ml spoons chopped fresh mixed herbs (parsley, chives, tarragon, sorrel, thyme, marjoram, and savory)

Heat the sauce, if necessary. Add the herbs and simmer for 5 minutes.
Serve with fish, poultry, veal or eggs.

Hot Horseradish Sauce

250ml foundation white sauce (p200) made with milk **or** half milk and half white stock

2 × 15ml spoons grated horseradish
1 × 5ml spoon vinegar
1 × 2.5ml spoon sugar

Heat the sauce, if necessary. Add the horseradish, vinegar, and sugar, and stir well.
Serve with beef, trout, mackerel or herring.

Maître d'Hôtel Sauce

juice of $\frac{1}{2}$ lemon
250ml foundation white sauce (p200) made with milk

2 × 15ml spoons finely chopped parsley
25g butter

Strain the lemon juice. Heat the sauce, if necessary, and add the lemon juice and parsley. When heated to just below boiling point, whisk the butter into the sauce, adding a small pat at a time.
Serve with fish, poultry or vegetables.

Mushroom Sauce (white)

50–100g button mushrooms
15–25g butter

250ml foundation white sauce (p200) made with milk

Clean the mushrooms and slice them thinly. Melt the butter in a pan, add the mushrooms, and cook gently for 15–20 minutes. Heat the sauce, if necessary. Stir the mushrooms and their cooking juices into the sauce.
Serve with most fish and meat entrées, poultry, ham, egg, and vegetable dishes.

Onion Sauce (1) (white)

2 medium-sized onions (200g approx)
250ml foundation white sauce (p200)
   made with half milk and half liquid
   in which onions were cooked

a few drops lemon juice

Skin and chop the onions. Put them in a saucepan and cover with salted water. Heat to boiling point, reduce the heat, and simmer for 10–15 minutes until softened. Drain thoroughly, and reserve the liquid to make the white sauce. Stir the onion into the sauce. Add the lemon juice.

   Serve with lamb or mutton, rabbit or tripe.

Parsley Sauce

250ml foundation white sauce (p200)
   made with white or fish (p26) stock
   or half milk and half stock

1–2 × 15ml spoons chopped parsley
25g butter

Heat the sauce, if necessary. Add the parsley and heat to just below boiling point. Whisk the butter into the sauce, adding a small pat at a time.

   Serve with fish, lamb or mutton, or light dishes such as quenelles or vegetables.

Savoury Lemon Sauce

juice and rind of 1 lemon
250ml foundation white sauce (p200)
   made with milk or half milk and
   half white stock (p26) or half milk
   and half fish stock (p26)

1–2 × 15ml spoons single cream
   (optional)
1 × 15ml spoon chopped parsley
   (optional)
1 × 2.5ml spoon sugar (optional)

Add the lemon rind to the milk or stock which is to be used to make the sauce, and simmer for 10 minutes. Strain the liquid and use it to make the white sauce. Carefully stir the lemon juice and the cream, if used, into the hot sauce. Do not reboil. Stir in the parsley and sugar, if used.

   Serve with fish, chicken or rabbit.

Sorrel Sauce (white)

100g sorrel leaves
15g butter
250ml foundation white sauce (p200)
   made with half milk and half
   vegetable stock (p27)

a small pinch grated nutmeg
2 × 15ml spoons single cream
   (optional)

Wash and chop the sorrel. Melt the butter in a saucepan, add the sorrel, and cook gently for 5 minutes. Rub through a fine nylon sieve. Heat the sauce, if necessary. Whisk the sorrel purée into the sauce at boiling point. Add the nutmeg, and stir in the cream, if used. Do not reboil.

   Serve with veal or poultry; without the cream, it can be served with goose.

White Wine Sauce

250ml foundation white sauce (p200)
   made with white **or** fish (p26) stock
4 × 15ml spoons white wine

1–2 egg yolks
juice of $\frac{1}{2}$ lemon
25g butter
salt and pepper

Heat the sauce, if necessary, add the wine and simmer for 10 minutes. Blend the egg yolks and lemon juice together. Whisk the butter into the sauce at just below boiling point, adding a small pat at a time. Draw the pan off the heat, and mix a little of the sauce with the egg yolk mixture. Beat this mixture into the rest of the sauce. Re-heat the sauce, stirring carefully, without allowing it to boil. Season to taste.
   Serve with fish or white meat.

Foundation Brown Sauce *Basic recipe*
Makes 300ml (approx)

1 small carrot
1 medium-sized onion (100g approx)
25g dripping **or** lard

25g plain flour
500ml general household stock (p25)
salt and pepper

Prepare and slice the carrot and onion. Melt the dripping or lard in a saucepan. Fry the carrot and onion slowly until the onion is golden-brown. Stir in the flour, reduce the heat, and cook the flour very gently until it is also golden-brown. Draw the pan off the heat and gradually add the stock, stirring all the time to prevent lumps forming. Return to moderate heat and stir the sauce until boiling. Reduce the heat, cover, and simmer for 30 minutes. Strain the sauce. Season to taste.
Note For extra flavour, add mushroom trimmings or a piece of celeriac to the carrot and onion. For extra colour add a piece of brown onion skin, a little gravy browning, meat or vegetable extract before the sauce is simmered.

Sauces based on Foundation Brown Sauce
The quantities of the ingredients in the following recipes are for adding to 300ml Foundation Brown Sauce. In most cases, this will give about 300ml completed sauce, the extra ingredients making up the small quantity lost by evaporation.

Bordelaise Sauce

1 medium-sized carrot (100g approx)
2 small onions (100g approx) **or**
   2 shallots (25g approx)
1 clove of garlic
150ml general household stock (p25)
6 black peppercorns
1 bay leaf
a sprig of thyme

a few parsley stalks
a sprig of tarragon
150ml red **or** white wine
300ml foundation brown sauce
lemon juice
Cayenne pepper
1 × 5ml spoon chopped fresh chervil
1 × 5ml spoon chopped parsley

Prepare and chop the carrot and onions or shallots. Skin and crush the garlic. Put the stock, vegetables, garlic, peppercorns, bay leaf, thyme, parsley stalks, and the tarragon into a small saucepan. Heat slowly to simmering point and simmer until the liquid is reduced to a sticky consistency. Add the wine. Re-heat, and cook until the liquid is reduced slightly. Add the brown sauce and heat to boiling point. Strain the sauce. Add the lemon juice and Cayenne pepper to taste. Stir in the chervil and parsley just before serving.

Serve with beef, pork, ham or duck.

Caper Sauce (2) (brown)

1 small onion (50g approx) **or** 1 shallot
   (15g approx)
300ml foundation brown sauce (p204)
1 × 15ml spoon capers
1 × 5ml spoon vinegar in which
   capers were pickled

1 × 5ml spoon anchovy essence
Cayenne pepper
lemon juice

Skin and chop the onion or shallot. Add to the brown sauce and simmer for 10 minutes; then strain it. Halve the capers, and add to the sauce with the caper vinegar, essence, Cayenne pepper, and lemon juice to taste. Re-heat the sauce.

Serve with steak, kidneys or fish.

Italian Sauce (1) (brown)

a bunch of parsley stalks
a sprig of thyme
1 bay leaf
4 shallots (50g approx)
6 mushrooms (50g approx)
1 × 15ml spoon olive oil

4 × 15ml spoons general household
   stock (p25)
4 × 15ml spoons white wine (optional)
300ml foundation brown sauce (p204)
salt and pepper

Tie the herbs in a small square of cotton or muslin. Prepare and chop the shallots and mushrooms. Heat the olive oil in a small saucepan, and fry the chopped vegetables very gently for 10 minutes. Add the stock, wine, if used, and the herbs. Heat to boiling point, reduce the heat, and simmer gently until reduced by half. Add the brown sauce. Re-heat and simmer gently for 20 minutes. Remove the herbs. Season to taste.

Serve with fish or meat.

Onion Sauce (2) (brown)

300ml foundation brown sauce (p204)
   made with 2 medium-sized onions
   (200g approx) and omitting the
   carrot
a pinch of grated nutmeg

1 × 5ml spoon wine vinegar
1 × 2.5ml spoon made English **or**
   French mustard
salt and pepper

Prepare the sauce in the usual way, but do not strain it. Add a little grated nutmeg, the vinegar, and mustard. Season to taste.

Serve with beef or offal.

Pepper Sauce (Poivrade Sauce)

2 shallots (25g approx)
a sprig of thyme
1 bay leaf
12 black peppercorns

4 × 15ml spoons red wine
2 × 15ml spoons wine vinegar
300ml foundation brown sauce (p204)
freshly ground pepper

Skin the shallots and chop them finely. Put into a saucepan with the herbs, pepper-corns, wine, and vinegar. Heat to boiling point, reduce the heat, and simmer until the liquid is reduced by half. Heat the sauce, if necessary. Strain the liquid into the brown sauce. Season to taste with pepper.

Serve with roast or grilled beef or game.

Piquant Sauce

1 small onion (50g approx) **or**
  2 shallots (25g approx)
25g mushrooms
1 bay leaf
a blade of mace
2 × 15ml spoons vinegar

300ml foundation brown sauce (p204)
1 × 15ml spoon capers
1 × 15ml spoon gherkins
1 × 10ml spoon mushroom ketchup
1 × 2.5ml spoon sugar (optional)

Skin the onion or shallots and chop finely. Clean the mushrooms and chop coarsely. Put the onion or shallots, bay leaf, mace, and vinegar in a saucepan. Heat to boiling point, reduce the heat and simmer for 10 minutes. Heat the sauce, if necessary. Add the onion mixture and the mushrooms to the brown sauce, and simmer for about 15 minutes until the mushrooms are softened.

Meanwhile, halve the capers and chop the gherkins. Remove the bay leaf and mace from the sauce, and add the capers, gherkins, mushroom ketchup, and sugar, if used. Re-heat if required.

Serve with pork, mutton or vegetables.

Reform Sauce

2 mushrooms (15g approx)
a little brown stock (p25)
6 cocktail gherkins
15g cooked tongue

white of 1 small hard-boiled egg
300ml Pepper sauce
2 × 15ml spoons port
1 × 15ml spoon redcurrant jelly

Clean the mushrooms, then poach them in a little stock. Drain. Shred the mush-rooms, gherkins, tongue, and egg white. Heat the sauce, if necessary. Add the port and redcurrant jelly to the Pepper sauce; then add the shredded ingredients. Re-heat the sauce.

Serve with lamb cutlets.

Robert Sauce

1 small onion (50g approx)
15g butter
½ × 2.5ml spoon made English mustard

1 × 2.5ml spoon sugar
4 × 15ml spoons white wine
300ml foundation brown sauce (p204)

Skin and chop the onion. Melt the butter in a saucepan, add the onion, and fry until golden-brown. Stir in the mustard, sugar, and wine, and simmer for 10 minutes. Add the brown sauce. Re-heat, and simmer for a further 10 minutes.

Serve with roast or grilled beef, lamb or mutton, pork or goose.

French Foundation Sauces

Béchamel Sauce (French Foundation White Sauce) *Basic recipe*
Makes 500ml (approx)

1 small onion (50g approx)
1 small carrot (25g approx)
a piece of celery (15g approx)
500ml milk
1 bay leaf
a few parsley stalks
a sprig of thyme
salt

1 clove
6 white peppercorns
a blade of mace
50g butter
50g flour
4 × 15ml spoons single cream
   (optional)

Prepare the vegetables and heat gently to simmering point with the milk, herbs, salt, and spices. Cover with a lid, and stand the pan in a warm place on the cooker to infuse for 30 minutes. Do not allow to boil. Strain the milk.

Melt the butter in a saucepan, add the flour, and stir until smooth. Cook over gentle heat, without allowing it to colour, for 2–3 minutes, stirring until the mixture (roux) begins to bubble. Draw the pan off the heat, and gradually add the flavoured milk, stirring to prevent lumps forming. Return to moderate heat and bring the sauce to the boil, stirring all the time. When the sauce has thickened, simmer for 3–4 minutes, beating briskly. (This helps to give the sauce a gloss.) Re-season if required. If cream is used, add it to the sauce just at boiling point, and remove from the heat immediately. Do not let the sauce reboil.
Note This sauce can be made with half white stock (p26) and half milk; it will have a good flavour, but will be less creamy in texture.

Sauces based on Béchamel Sauce
The quantities of the ingredients in the recipes which follow on pp208–9 are for adding to 125ml or 250ml Béchamel Sauce. In most cases, this will give about 125ml or 250ml completed sauce, the extra ingredients making up the small quantity lost by evaporation.

Aurora Sauce

250ml Béchamel sauce (p207) made
  from fish stock (p26)
2 × 15ml spoons concentrated
  tomato purée **or** 1 × 15ml spoon
  sieved, canned pimento

paprika
2 × 15ml spoons single cream
  (optional)

Heat the sauce, if necessary. Carefully stir the tomato purée or sieved pimento into the sauce. Add paprika to taste and the cream, if used. Re-heat the sauce without allowing it to boil.
    Serve with eggs, chicken or fish.
Note This sauce can also be made from Velouté Sauce based on fish stock (p26). Serve with fish.

Italian Sauce (2) (white)

2 shallots (25g approx)
50g button mushrooms
1 × 15ml spoon butter
50ml Béchamel sauce (p207)
50ml dry white wine (optional)

125ml chicken stock
salt and pepper
lemon juice
1 × 10ml spoon chopped parsley
2 × 15ml spoons single cream

Prepare the shallots and mushrooms and chop them finely. Melt the butter in a saucepan. Add the vegetables and cook very gently for 10 minutes. Stir in the sauce, wine, if used, and stock. Heat to simmering point, and simmer steadily until the mushrooms are softened and the sauce is reduced to a creamy consistency. Season with salt and pepper and add lemon juice to taste. Stir in the parsley. Just before serving, stir in the cream.
    Serve with chicken, veal or fish.

Mornay Sauce

250ml Béchamel sauce (p207)
1 egg yolk
40g grated Parmesan and Gruyère
  cheese, mixed

4 × 15ml spoons single cream
  (optional)
a few grains Cayenne pepper

Cool the sauce, if necessary. Stir a little into the yolk, and blend together. Add to the rest of the Béchamel Sauce. Heat the sauce gently, stirring carefully, to cook the egg yolk; do not let it boil. Stir the cheeses into the sauce. Add the cream, if used, and season with Cayenne pepper.
    Serve with fish, chicken, ham, eggs or vegetables.

Savoury Cream Sauce

250ml Béchamel sauce (p207)
Cayenne pepper
salt
lemon juice
4 × 15ml spoons single cream

Heat the sauce, if necessary. Add Cayenne pepper, salt, and lemon juice to taste. Heat to just below boiling point, then stir in the cream. Do not allow the sauce to boil. Use at once.

Serve with chicken, veal, fish or delicately flavoured vegetables.

Soubise Sauce

200g onions
40g butter
1–2 × 15ml spoons white stock (p26)
250ml Béchamel sauce (p207)
salt and pepper
sugar
grated nutmeg

Skin and slice the onions. Heat 15g of the butter in a saucepan. Add the onions and enough stock to moisten them. Cook gently until tender. Sieve the onions. Add the onion purée to the Béchamel sauce and re-heat. Season with salt and pepper, and add sugar and nutmeg to taste. When heated to boiling point, whisk the rest of the butter into the sauce, adding a small pat at a time. Do not allow the sauce to reboil. Use at once.

Serve with fish, poultry or vegetables.

Tartare Sauce (1) (hot)

250ml Béchamel sauce (p207)
1–2 egg yolks
1 × 15ml spoon single cream
1 × 5ml spoon chopped gherkins
1 × 15ml spoon chopped capers
1 × 10ml spoon chopped parsley
lemon juice **or** white wine vinegar

Cool the sauce, if necessary. Mix the egg yolks and cream, and stir in a little of the sauce. Add this to the rest of the sauce. Heat the sauce gently, without boiling, to cook the egg yolk. Stir the gherkins, capers, and parsley into the sauce. Add lemon juice or vinegar to taste. Use at once.

Serve with salmon or other fish.

Espagnole Sauce (French Foundation Brown Sauce) *Basic recipe*

Makes 350ml (when using tomato purée and omitting the sherry); makes 500ml
(when using tomato pulp and sherry)

1 small onion (50g approx)
1 small carrot (25g approx)
50g mushrooms **or** mushroom
    trimmings
50g lean raw ham **or** bacon
50g butter
50g flour
500ml brown stock (p25)

bouquet garni
6 black peppercorns
1 bay leaf
125ml tomato pulp **or** 1 × 15ml spoon
    concentrated tomato purée
salt
4 × 15ml spoons sherry (optional)

Prepare and slice the vegetables. Chop the ham or bacon into small pieces. Melt the butter in a saucepan and fry the ham or bacon for 2–3 minutes. Add the vegetables, and fry very slowly for 8–10 minutes until golden-brown. Add the flour and stir until smooth. Cook over gentle heat, stirring frequently, for about 10 minutes or until the flour is a rich brown colour. Draw the pan off the heat and gradually add the stock, stirring all the time to prevent lumps forming. Add the bouquet garni, peppercorns, and bay leaf. Return to moderate heat and stir until boiling. Half cover the pan, reduce the heat and simmer the sauce gently for 30 minutes. Add the tomato pulp or concentrated tomato purée. Simmer the sauce for a further 30 minutes. Rub through a fine nylon sieve. Season to taste with salt. Add the sherry, if used. Re-heat the sauce before serving.

VARIATION

Substitute 1 large tomato for the mushrooms. Add the vegetables and flour to the ham or bacon in the saucepan and fry them together for 10 minutes. Add 1 × 10ml spoon mushroom ketchup with the stock instead of using tomato pulp or purée. Makes 425ml sauce.

Sauces based on Espagnole Sauce

The quantities of the ingredients in the following recipes are for adding to 250ml Espagnole Sauce. In most cases, this will give about 250ml completed sauce, the extra ingredients making up the small quantity lost by evaporation.

Bigarade Sauce

½ Seville orange
juice of ½ lemon
250ml Espagnole sauce
4 × 15ml spoons red wine (optional)

1 × 5ml spoon redcurrant jelly
salt
Cayenne pepper
sugar

Pare the orange rind and cut into neat, thin strips, Put them in a saucepan and cover with a little cold water. Heat to simmering point and cook until just tender. Drain. Squeeze the juice from the orange. Add to the Espagnole Sauce with the orange rind and lemon juice. Re-heat the sauce. Stir in the wine, if used, and the redcurrant jelly. Add salt, Cayenne pepper, and sugar to taste.

Serve with roast duck, goose, wild duck, pork or ham.

Demi-Glace Sauce

125ml juices from roast meat **or**
   125ml bone stock (p25) and
   1 × 5ml spoon beef extract **or** meat
   glaze (p55)

250ml Espagnole sauce (p210)

Add the meat juices, stock or meat glaze to the sauce. Bring to the boil and boil until the sauce is well reduced. Skim off any fat.
   Serve with meat, poultry or game.

Madeira Sauce

250ml Demi-glace sauce
4 × 15ml spoons Madeira

salt and pepper
1 × 5ml spoon meat glaze (p55)

Heat the sauce, if necessary. Add the Madeira, and simmer together until well reduced. Season to taste. Add the meat glaze and stir until dissolved. Strain the sauce.
   Serve with meat, poultry or game.

Velouté Sauce (French Foundation Fawn Sauce) *Basic recipe*
Makes 500ml (when using 100ml cream)

50g butter
6 button mushrooms **or**
   25–50g mushroom trimmings
12 black peppercorns
a few parsley stalks
50g flour

500ml white stock (p26) (fish,
   vegetable or meat)
salt and pepper
lemon juice
4–8 × 15ml spoons single cream

Melt the butter in a saucepan, and add the mushrooms, peppercorns, and parsley stalks. Cook gently for 10 minutes. Add the flour, and stir over gentle heat for 2–3 minutes, without allowing it to colour. Draw the pan off the heat and add the stock gradually, stirring well to prevent lumps forming. Return to gentle heat and heat the sauce to simmering point, stirring all the time. Simmer for 3–4 minutes. Rub the sauce through a sieve. Season to taste with salt and pepper, and add lemon juice to taste. Re-heat the sauce to boiling point and stir in enough cream to give the desired flavour and consistency. Do not reboil. Use at once.
   Serve with meat, poultry, fish or vegetables.

Sauces based on Velouté Sauce
The quantities of the ingredients in the recipes which follow on p212 are for adding to 250ml Velouté Sauce. In most cases, this will give about 250ml completed sauce, the extra ingredients making up the small quantity lost by evaporation.

Bercy Sauce

2 shallots (25g approx)
4 × 15ml spoons white wine
250ml Velouté sauce (p211) made
  with fish stock (p26) **or** chicken
  stock (p26)

25g butter
1 × 10ml spoon chopped parsley

Skin and chop the shallots. Put into a small saucepan with the wine, and cook until the wine is reduced by half. Add the sauce, and re-heat without allowing it to boil. Whisk in the butter, adding a small pat at a time. Add the parsley to the sauce.
    Serve with fish or meat.

Ravigote Sauce (hot)

250ml Velouté sauce (p211)
1 × 15ml spoon wine vinegar
grated nutmeg

sugar
salt and pepper
25g Ravigote butter (p232)

Heat the sauce, if necessary. Add the vinegar, nutmeg, sugar, and seasoning to taste. When heated to just below boiling point, whisk in the Ravigote butter, adding a small pat at a time. Do not allow the sauce to boil. Use at once.
    Serve with meat, boiled fish or poultry.

Suprême Sauce

250ml Velouté sauce (p211)
2–4 × 15ml spoons single cream
1 egg yolk
15–25g butter

grated nutmeg
lemon juice
salt and pepper

Cool the sauce, if necessary. Mix the cream and egg yolk, using the larger quantity of cream for a rich sauce. Stir a little of the cooled sauce into the cream and yolk mixture. Add this to the rest of the Velouté sauce. Heat the sauce gently, stirring carefully to thicken the egg yolk; do not let it boil. Whisk in the butter, adding a small pat at a time. Add nutmeg, lemon juice, and seasoning to taste. Use at once.
    Serve with any meat, poultry, fish or vegetables.
Note Adjust the proportions of cream, butter, and seasoning in this classic sauce to give the flavour and richness you want.

Other Savoury Sauces

Agro-Dolce (Bitter-sweet Sauce)
Makes 250ml (approx)

1 onion
1 carrot
1 clove of garlic (optional)
1 bay leaf
6 black peppercorns
1 × 15ml spoon olive oil

125ml red wine
75ml wine vinegar
50g sugar
2 × 15ml spoons water
125ml good thin gravy (p229)

Sweetening

1 × 5ml spoon chopped mint
1 × 5ml spoon finely shredded candied
   orange peel

1 × 10ml spoon chopped nuts
1 × 10ml spoon sultanas
1 × 15ml spoon grated bitter chocolate

Prepare and chop the onion and carrot. Skin and crush the garlic, if used. Put them into a saucepan with the bay leaf, peppercorns, and oil, and cook very gently, half-covered, for 15–20 minutes. Drain off the oil, and add the wine and vinegar. Simmer gently for 30 minutes; remove the bay leaf and peppercorns.

Put the sugar and water into a separate pan. Heat gently until the sugar has dissolved, then boil rapidly, without stirring, until the sugar becomes a golden caramel. Remove from the heat immediately. Stir into the wine mixture with the gravy. Add any one, or a mixture, of the sweetening ingredients to taste.

Serve with braised meat or vegetables.

Apple Sauce
Makes 375ml (approx)

500g apples
2 × 15ml spoons water
15g butter **or** margarine

rind and juice of ½ lemon
sugar

Peel, core, and slice the apples. Put them into a saucepan with the water, fat, and lemon rind. Cover, and cook over low heat until the apple is reduced to a pulp. Beat until smooth, rub through a sieve, or process in an electric blender. Re-heat the sauce with the lemon juice and sugar to taste.

Serve hot or cold with roast pork, duck or goose.

Note Apple sauce is also excellent served as a sweet sauce with ginger pudding.

Béarnaise Sauce
Makes 200ml (approx)

1 shallot **or** 25g onion
1 × 15ml spoon chopped fresh tarragon
1 × 15ml spoon chopped fresh chervil
a small piece of bay leaf
4 peppercorns

4 × 15ml spoons wine **or** tarragon
  vinegar
2 egg yolks
100g softened butter
salt and pepper

Prepare and chop the shallot or onion finely. Put in a saucepan with the herbs. Crush the peppercorns and add with the vinegar. Bring to the boil, and boil gently until reduced by half. Leave to cool, then strain. Heat the sauce in a basin placed in a pan of hot water to avoid boiling the sauce. Whisk in the yolks, one at a time. Stir until thickened. Whisk in the butter, adding a small pat at a time. It should be as thick as mayonnaise. Season to taste.

Serve the sauce, lukewarm, as soon as possible. Keep warm, if necessary, over hot water and re-whisk before serving. This sauce is thicker and sharper in flavour than Hollandaise Sauce.

Serve with steaks, shellfish or grilled fish, poultry or eggs.

Black Butter (Beurre Noir)
Makes 200ml (approx)

150g butter
2 × 15ml spoons chopped parsley

1 × 15ml spoon chopped capers
1 × 10ml spoon vinegar (approx)

Heat the butter in a saucepan until nut-brown but not burned. Add the parsley and capers. Pour into a heated container. Heat the vinegar in the same pan and mix it with the butter.

Serve poured over brains, fish, and some vegetables.

Note Use also with eggs. Omit the parsley and capers.

VARIATION

Brown Butter (Beurre Noisette)
Heat the butter until a light hazelnut colour. Add lemon juice to taste.

Serve poured over eggs, brains, skate, soft roes, or various vegetables.

Meunière Butter

butter
chopped parsley

a few drops lemon juice
salt and pepper

Heat the butter to a light hazelnut colour. Add the parsley, lemon juice, and seasoning to taste. Use sizzling hot.

This butter is used mainly for cooking fish or other ingredients, but it can be made and served separately.

Bread Sauce
Makes 250ml (approx)

1 large onion (200g approx)
250ml milk
2 cloves
a blade of mace
4 peppercorns
1 allspice berry

1 bay leaf
50g dried white breadcrumbs
1 × 15ml spoon butter
salt and pepper
2 × 15ml spoons single cream
    (optional)

Skin the onion. Heat the milk very slowly to boiling point with the spices, bay leaf, and onion. Cover the pan and infuse over gentle heat for 30 minutes. Strain the liquid. Add the breadcrumbs and butter to the flavoured milk. Season to taste. Heat the mixture to just below simmering point and keep at this temperature for 20 minutes. Stir in the cream, if used.

Serve with roast chicken or turkey.

Celery Sauce
Makes 250ml (approx)

6 large sticks celery
250ml water
25g butter **or** margarine
25g plain flour

salt and pepper
1–2 drops lemon juice
1–2 × 15ml spoons single cream
    (optional)

Wash the celery and cut into short lengths. Heat the water to boiling point, add the celery, reduce the heat, cover, and simmer for 20 minutes or until the celery is softened. Drain, and reserve the liquid. Rub the celery through a fine nylon sieve, or process in an electric blender and then sieve. Measure the purée and make it up to 250ml with the reserved liquid.

Melt the fat in a saucepan and add the flour. Stir over gentle heat, without allowing the flour to colour, for 2–3 minutes, or until the mixture begins to bubble. Draw the pan off the heat and gradually stir in the celery purée. Return to moderate heat and bring the sauce to the boil, stirring all the time to prevent lumps forming. When it has thickened, simmer for 3–4 minutes, beating vigorously. Season to taste. Remove from the heat, and stir in the lemon juice and the cream, if used.

Serve with lamb, mutton or rabbit.

Cranberry Sauce
Makes 300ml (approx)

125ml water
150g sugar

200g cranberries

Put the water and sugar in a saucepan and stir over gentle heat until the sugar dissolves. Add the cranberries, and cook gently for about 10 minutes until they have burst and are quite tender. Leave to cool.

Serve with roast turkey, chicken or game.

Chestnut Sauce
Makes 375ml (approx)

200g chestnuts
375ml chicken **or** white stock (p26)
a pinch of ground cinnamon
a small strip of lemon rind

25g butter
salt and pepper
75ml single cream (optional)

Make a slit in the rounded side of the shells of the chestnuts, and boil or bake them for 15–20 minutes. Remove the shells and skins while hot. Put the chestnuts in a saucepan with the stock, cinnamon, and lemon rind. Heat to simmering point, and simmer gently for 30 minutes or until the chestnuts are very tender. Remove the lemon rind. Rub the chestnuts and the liquid through a sieve, or process in an electric blender. Return the purée to the pan, add the butter, and season to taste. Heat gently for 2–3 minutes. Stir in the cream, if used, just before serving.

Serve with roast chicken or turkey.

Cumberland Sauce
Makes 250ml (approx)

grated rind and juice of 1 orange
grated rind and juice of 1 lemon
75ml water
75ml port
2 × 15ml spoons vinegar

100g redcurrant jelly
$\frac{1}{2}$ × 2.5ml spoon made English mustard
salt
a pinch of Cayenne pepper

Put the orange and lemon rind into a small saucepan with the water and heat to simmering point. Simmer gently for 10 minutes. Add the port, vinegar, redcurrant jelly, and mustard, and heat gently until the jelly melts. Add the orange and lemon juice to the pan with the seasoning. Simmer for 3–4 minutes.

Serve hot or cold with roast duck, mutton or ham.

Fresh Tomato Sauce
Makes 500ml (approx)

1 medium-sized onion
1 clove of garlic (optional)
1 rasher of streaky bacon, without
  rinds
750g tomatoes

2 × 15ml spoons olive oil
salt and pepper
a pinch of sugar
1 × 5ml spoon chopped fresh basil
  (optional)

Skin the onion and chop it finely. Skin and crush the garlic, if used. Chop the bacon rasher. Skin and chop the tomatoes. Heat the oil in a saucepan, and fry the onion, garlic, and bacon over gentle heat for 5 minutes. Add the rest of the ingredients, cover, and simmer gently for 30 minutes. Rub through a sieve or process in an electric blender until smooth. Re-heat and re-season if required.

Serve with meat, some fish, and pasta.

Salsa Pomodoro (Tomato Sauce)
Makes 750ml (approx)

250g tomatoes
50g red pepper
50g lean bacon, without rinds
50g bacon fat
50g onion
1 clove of garlic
25g plain flour

50g concentrated tomato purée
300ml chicken stock
salt and pepper
1 × 10ml spoon thick honey
150ml sweet red vermouth (optional)
1 × 15ml spoon chopped herbs,
    eg oregano, basil, rosemary, mint

Skin and de-seed the tomatoes and chop them coarsely. De-seed the pepper. Mince the bacon. Heat the fat in a large pan and sauté the bacon for 2 minutes. Chop the onion, garlic, and pepper. Add them to the bacon, and cook gently for 5 minutes, turning with a spoon. Sprinkle in the flour; stir it in, and add the tomato purée. Cook for 3 minutes. Add the chopped tomatoes, and stir in the chicken stock. Bring to the boil, reduce the heat, and simmer gently for 30 minutes. Season well. Just before serving, stir in the honey, and the vermouth, if liked. Sprinkle with the herbs.

Hollandaise Sauce
Makes 125ml (approx)

2 × 15ml spoons white wine vinegar
2 × 15ml spoons water
4 peppercorns
a small piece of bay leaf
2 egg yolks

100g softened butter
salt and pepper
Cayenne pepper
lemon juice (optional)

Put the vinegar and water into a small saucepan. Crush the peppercorns and add to the pan with the bay leaf. Bring to the boil, and continue boiling gently until the liquid is reduced by half. Leave to cool. Strain the liquid into a double boiler or a basin over a pan of hot water to avoid boiling the sauce. Whisk in the egg yolks, one at a time. Cook until the mixture is thick, whisking all the time. Whisk in the butter, adding a small pat at a time. The sauce should be just thick enough to hold its shape. Each addition must be thoroughly worked in before the next is added. Season lightly with salt, pepper, and Cayenne pepper. Add a little lemon juice, if liked, to give a slightly piquant flavour.

Note A Hollandaise Sauce with a more delicate flavour can be made by using 1 × 15ml spoon strained lemon juice and 1 × 15ml spoon water instead of the reduced vinegar.

VARIATION

Mousseline Hollandaise Sauce
Just before serving, fold in 2–3 × 15ml spoons lightly whipped double cream. Re-season if required.

Fruit Curry Sauce
Makes 500ml (approx)

½ small onion (25g approx)
½ cooking apple (100g approx)
1 banana (150g approx)
6 seedless raisins
1 tomato (50g approx)
25g butter **or** margarine

1 × 5ml spoon desiccated coconut
50g flour
1 × 10ml spoon curry powder
salt
500ml vegetable stock (p27)
lemon juice

Prepare the onion and apple, and chop them finely. Slice the banana. Chop the raisins. Skin and chop the tomato. Melt the fat in a saucepan, add the vegetables and fruit, and fry gently for 5 minutes. Add the coconut, flour, curry powder, and salt to taste, and stir well. Stir in the stock. Heat to simmering point, cover, and simmer gently for 20 minutes. Add lemon juice to taste.

Serve with vegetables or eggs.

Raisin Sauce
Makes 400ml (approx)

75g soft dark brown sugar
25g flour
1 × 15ml spoon dry English mustard
salt and pepper

350ml boiling water
50ml vinegar
50g seedless raisins
25g butter

Mix the dry ingredients in the top of a double saucepan or in a basin placed over simmering water. Stir in the boiling water and the vinegar gradually to prevent lumps forming. Cook slowly for 15–20 minutes. Add the raisins, and continue to cook for 5 minutes. Beat in the butter, a small pat at a time. Use at once.

Serve with hot ham dishes.

White Chaudfroid Sauce
Makes 375ml (approx)

250ml Béchamel sauce (p207)
125ml aspic jelly
1 × 10ml spoon gelatine
salt and pepper

1 × 5ml spoon white wine vinegar
   or lemon juice
1 × 15ml spoon double cream

Cool the Béchamel Sauce until tepid. Melt the aspic jelly in a basin placed over hot water. Add the gelatine to the melted aspic. Continue to stir over heat until the gelatine dissolves. Cool the aspic jelly until tepid, then fold it into the sauce. Season to taste. Add the vinegar or lemon juice. Rub the sauce through a fine sieve. Fold in the cream. Leave the sauce to cool completely but use while still liquid. Use the sauce to mask poultry, veal or fish served *en chaudfroid*.

Brown Chaudfroid Sauce
Make as for White Chaudfroid Sauce, substituting Espagnole Sauce (p210) for Béchamel Sauce
   Use for masking beef, mutton or game

Fawn Chaudfroid Sauce
Make as for White Chaudfroid Sauce, substituting Velouté Sauce (p211) for Béchamel Sauce.
   Use for masking lamb, veal or poultry.

Green Chaudfroid Sauce
Make as for White Chaudfroid Sauce, using 1 × 15ml spoon spinach purée (p264) or green colouring with the Béchamel Sauce.
   Use for masking veal or poultry.

Tomato Chaudfroid Sauce
Make as for White Chaudfroid Sauce, substituting Fresh Tomato Sauce (p216) for Béchamel Sauce.
   Use for masking fish, veal, poultry or lamb.

Salad Dressings and Sauces

Aïoli
Makes 200ml (approx)

4–6 cloves garlic **or** 4 shallots
1 egg yolk
a pinch of salt
125ml olive oil

1 × 15ml spoon lemon juice **or** wine
   vinegar
1 medium-sized potato
a pinch of Cayenne pepper

Crush the garlic or shallots and pound to a smooth pulp. Add the egg yolk and salt; then proceed as for mayonnaise (p222). Cook the potato for 20 minutes in enough boiling salted water to cover it. Drain, rub through a sieve, and leave to cool. Gradually work the sauce into the potato, beating thoroughly. Season to taste with Cayenne pepper.
   Serve with salads, vegetables, fish or meat.

Cold Mousseline Sauce
Makes 150ml (approx)

2 × 15ml spoons double cream

125ml mayonnaise (p222)

Whip the cream lightly until it holds its shape, then fold into the mayonnaise.
   Serve with fish.

Green Mousseline Sauce
Fold 1 × 15ml spoon of cooked spinach purée into the mayonnaise with the cream.

Cream Salad Dressing
Makes 100ml (approx)

1 × 2.5ml spoon made English mustard
½ × 2.5ml spoon salt
½ × 2.5ml spoon caster sugar

4 × 15ml spoons double cream
1 × 15ml spoon malt **or** wine vinegar
1 × 5ml spoon tarragon vinegar

Mix the mustard, salt, and sugar together. Stir in the cream. Add the vinegars, drop by drop, beating the mixture all the time.

English Salad Dressing or Cream *Basic recipe*

Use the ingredients below in the proportions of:

1 hard-boiled egg yolk
½ × 2.5ml spoon mixed English
　mustard
1 × 5ml spoon Worcestershire sauce
　or to taste
salt and pepper
a pinch of caster sugar

1 × 10ml spoon cider **or**
　white wine vinegar
1 × 15ml spoon olive oil
2 × 15ml spoons double cream **or**
　evaporated milk prepared for
　whipping

Sieve the egg yolk. Work into it gradually the seasonings, vinegar, and oil. Whip the cream or evaporated milk lightly, and fold into the mixture. Use at once.

Epicurean Sauce
Makes 500ml (approx)

½ cucumber
salt
4 × 15ml spoons aspic jelly **or** good
　stock and 1 × 2.5ml spoon gelatine
1 × 15ml spoon tarragon vinegar
4 × 15ml spoons double cream

125ml mayonnaise (p222)
2 gherkins
1 × 10ml spoon chutney
1 × 5ml spoon anchovy essence
pepper
sugar

Peel and dice the cucumber. Cook in 5mm depth of salted water until tender, or steam. Sieve, or process in an electric blender to make a smooth purée. If using stock and gelatine, sprinkle the gelatine over the stock in a basin and leave for 5 minutes to soften. Stand the basin over a pan of hot water and leave until the gelatine dissolves. Allow to cool. Stir the cucumber purée and the vinegar into the stock or aspic jelly. Whip the cream until it holds its shape, then fold it into the mayonnaise. Finely chop the gherkins and any large pieces in the chutney. Fold into the mayonnaise with the anchovy essence, and finally fold in the aspic jelly and cucumber mixture. Season with salt and pepper and add sugar to taste.
　Serve with fish salads, asparagus or globe artichokes.

Evaporated Milk Dressing
Makes 100ml (approx)

4 × 15ml spoons unsweetened
   evaporated milk
1 × 15ml spoon malt **or** wine vinegar

$\frac{1}{2}$ × 2.5ml spoon made mustard
a good pinch of caster sugar
$\frac{1}{2}$ × 2.5ml spoon salt

Whisk the milk until it forms soft peaks. Beat in the vinegar, drop by drop, then the mustard, sugar, and salt.

French Dressing *Basic recipe*

Use the ingredients below in the proportions of:

2–3 × 15ml spoons olive oil
salt and freshly ground black pepper
a pinch of dry English mustard
   (optional)

a pinch of caster sugar (optional)
1 × 15ml spoon wine vinegar

Mix together the oil and seasonings. Add the vinegar gradually, stirring all the time with a wooden spoon so that an emulsion is formed. Alternatively, put all the ingredients into a small screw-topped jar, and shake vigorously until well blended.

The standard basic French dressing is made with oil, salt and pepper and vinegar alone, but it can be varied in other ways, eg
1) Use $\frac{1}{2}$ × 2.5ml spoon French or mixed English or German mustard instead of dry mustard.
2) Use white wine instead of some of the vinegar.
3) Use lemon juice instead of some or all of the vinegar.
4) In recipes which contain grapefruit or orange, use grapefruit or orange juice instead of the vinegar.
5) Add a little skinned garlic, crushed without salt, to the basic ingredients.
Note French dressing keeps well, so a large quantity can be made and stored in a screw-topped jar or bottle in a cool place. Shake well before use.

Vinaigrette Sauce
Makes 100ml (approx)

4 × 15ml spoons French dressing
1 × 5ml spoon finely chopped gherkin
1 × 2.5ml spoon finely chopped chives
   or shallot

1 × 2.5ml spoon finely chopped parsley
1 × 5ml spoon finely chopped capers
1 × 2.5ml spoon finely chopped
   tarragon **and/or** chervil

Mix all the ingredients together and leave for at least 1 hour before using for the flavours to blend.

Mayonnaise *Basic egg and oil sauce*
Makes 300ml (approx)

2 egg yolks
1 × 2.5ml spoon dry English mustard
1 × 2.5ml spoon salt
pepper

2 × 15ml spoons white wine vinegar,
tarragon vinegar, **or** lemon juice
250ml oil, preferably either olive **or**
corn oil

Blend the egg yolks with the mustard, salt, pepper, and 1 × 15ml spoon of the vinegar or lemon juice in a basin. Using either a balloon whisk, a wooden spoon, or an electric blender, beat in the oil very gradually, drop by drop, until about half of it has been added and the mixture looks thick and shiny. At this stage, the oil can be added in a slow thin stream. Add the remaining vinegar or lemon juice when all the oil has been incorporated.

If the mayonnaise curdles while making, beat a fresh egg yolk in another basin and beat the mixture into this gradually, 1 × 5ml spoonful at a time.

To store the mayonnaise, put it into a basin or jar, cover, and store in the least cold part of the refrigerator; if the mayonnaise becomes too cold, it will separate.
Note For the best results, all the ingredients should be at room temperature. If the eggs are used straight from the refrigerator, the mayonnaise is much more likely to curdle.

Cooked Mayonnaise
Makes 300ml (approx)

1 × 5ml spoon caster sugar
1 × 2.5ml spoon salt
1 × 2.5ml spoon dry mustard
a pinch of pepper
1 × 15ml spoon corn **or** vegetable oil

3 egg yolks
4 × 15ml spoons wine vinegar
1 × 5ml spoon tarragon vinegar
250ml milk **or** single cream

Mix the sugar, salt, mustard, and pepper. Stir in the oil, then the egg yolks. Beat well. Add the vinegars gradually and finally the milk or cream. Turn into the top of a double boiler, or into a basin placed over a pan of gently simmering water. Cook the sauce, stirring all the time until it thickens. Do not allow the sauce to boil or it will curdle. Remove from the heat and leave to cool, stirring frequently to prevent a skin forming. Re-season if required when cold.

Curry Mayonnaise
Makes 125ml (approx)

1 clove of garlic
125ml mayonnaise

1 × 2.5ml spoon curry powder

Crush the garlic and fold it into the mayonnaise with the curry powder.

Serve with cold meat or fish; this sauce is particularly good with cold chicken.

Green Mayonnaise
Makes 150ml (approx)

25g mixed leaves of watercress,
   spinach, chervil, tarragon, parsley,
   and chives

salt
125ml mayonnaise (p222)

Cook the leaves in a very little boiling salted water until just tender. Drain thoroughly and sieve, or process in an electric blender to a smooth purée. Fold into the mayonnaise just before serving. Do not add the purée to the mayonnaise too early or it will lose its colour.
   Serve with fish and fish salads.

Tomato Mayonnaise
Makes 150ml (approx)

2 × 15ml spoons thick fresh tomato
   purée **or** 1 × 10ml spoon
   concentrated tomato purée **or**
   2 × 10ml spoons tomato ketchup

125ml mayonnaise (p222)

Fold the tomato purée or ketchup into the mayonnaise.
   Serve with meat or fish or shellfish salads.

VARIATION
Add a few drops of Worcestershire sauce.

Remoulade Sauce
Makes 125ml (approx)

1 × 5ml spoon French mustard
1 × 5ml spoon chopped capers
1 × 2.5ml spoon chopped parsley

1 × 2.5ml spoon chopped tarragon
1 × 2.5ml spoon chopped chervil
125ml mayonnaise (p222)

Fold the mustard, capers, and herbs into the mayonnaise. Leave the sauce to stand for at least 1 hour before serving for the flavours to blend.
   Serve with grilled meat or fish, or with salads.

Roquefort Salad Cream
Makes 375ml (approx)

200ml soured cream
100ml mayonnaise (p222)
2 × 15ml spoons grated onion

2 × 15ml spoons mild white vinegar
50g Roquefort cheese
1 clove of garlic

Combine the cream, mayonnaise, onion, and vinegar in a bowl or the goblet of an electric blender. Crumble the cheese, and add it to the mixture. Split the garlic clove and rub a salad bowl thoroughly with the cut sides. Discard the garlic. Whisk or blend the other ingredients until smooth. Use over a green salad placed in the bowl. **Note** If to be stored, rub the garlic clove round the inside of the storage container before putting in the dressing. Store chilled.

Soured Cream Dressing
Makes 125ml (approx)

125ml soured cream
salt and pepper
1 × 5ml spoon French mustard **or**
  1 × 2.5ml spoon made English
  mustard

a pinch of caster sugar
milk **or** top of the milk
  (optional)

Stir the cream, then add the seasoning, mustard, and sugar. If liked, the dressing can be thinned down with a little milk or top of the milk.

VARIATION
Yoghurt Dressing
Use thick natural yoghurt instead of soured cream.

Soured Cream Cooked Dressing
Makes 250ml (approx)

1 × 10ml spoon flour
1 × 10ml spoon sugar
1 × 5ml spoon dry mustard
1 × 5ml spoon salt
a pinch of Cayenne pepper

1 egg yolk
3 × 15ml spoons white vinegar
1 × 15ml spoon melted butter
125ml soured cream

Put all the dry ingredients into the top of a double boiler or in a basin over a pan of hot water. Add the egg yolk and vinegar, and beat well. Cook gently for 7–8 minutes, stirring all the time. Add the butter. Remove from the heat and leave to cool. Fold into the soured cream before serving.

Tartare Sauce (2)
Makes 150ml (approx)

1 × 5ml spoon each of
  chopped gherkins
  chopped olives
  chopped capers
  chopped parsley
  chopped chives

125ml mayonnaise (p222)
½ × 2.5ml spoon French mustard
1 × 10ml spoon wine vinegar **or**
  lemon juice

Fold the chopped ingredients into the mayonnaise with the mustard, then add the vinegar or lemon juice. Leave the sauce to stand for at least 1 hour before serving for the flavours to blend.

Serve with grilled or fried fish and meat.

Thousand Islands Dressing
Makes 300ml (approx)

250ml mayonnaise (p222)
1 × 15ml spoon chopped parsley
1 × 15ml spoon finely chopped capers
1 × 15ml spoon finely chopped olives

1 × 15ml spoon finely chopped pickles
1 × 15ml spoon lemon juice
tomato juice

Put the mayonnaise into a basin, add the solid ingredients and lemon juice, and mix well. Stir in enough tomato juice to make a dressing of pouring consistency.

Sweet Sauces

Sweet Cornflour Sauce or Sweet White Sauce *Basic recipe*
Makes 250ml (approx)

2 × 10ml spoons cornflour
250ml milk

1–2 × 15ml spoons sugar
vanilla essence **or** other flavouring

1) *Blended Method*
Blend the cornflour to a smooth, thin paste with a little of the cold milk. Put the rest of the milk in a saucepan and heat to boiling point. Stir the boiling milk into the blended cornflour. Return to the pan and stir until boiling. Reduce the heat and cook for 3 minutes. Add the sugar and flavouring to taste.

2) *All-in-one Method*
Put the cornflour, milk, and sugar in a medium-sized saucepan. Whisk over moderate heat until the sauce comes to the boil. Reduce the heat, and cook for 2–3 minutes, whisking all the time, until the sauce is thickened and smooth.

Note If the sauce must be kept hot for a short time, cover with wet greaseproof paper and a lid. Just before serving, beat again to remove any lumps.

VARIATIONS
The following ingredients can be added to 250ml hot Sweet Cornflour Sauce:

Almond Sauce
Add 1–2 × 10ml spoon ground almonds to the cornflour when blending to a paste with the milk. Add 2–3 drops of almond essence, and vanilla essence to taste after the sauce has been cooked.

Brandy Sauce
Add 1–2 × 15ml spoons brandy.

Chocolate Sauce (1)
Add 1 × 15ml spoon cocoa powder and 1 × 15ml spoon sugar dissolved in 1 × 15ml spoon boiling water.

For further **variations,** see over.

Coffee Sauce

Add 1 × 10ml spoon instant coffee dissolved in 1 × 10ml spoon boiling water **or** 1 × 15ml spoon coffee essence.

Ginger Sauce

Add 1 × 10ml spoon ground ginger and 50g finely chopped crystallized ginger (optional).

Lemon or Orange Sauce (1)

Add the grated rind of half an orange or lemon and a drop of orange or yellow colouring (optional).

Rich Sauce

Add 1 egg yolk and 2 × 15ml spoons cream. Re-heat the sauce but do not boil.

Rum Sauce

Add 1–2 × 15ml spoons rum.

Sweet Spice Sauce

Add 1 × 5ml spoon mixed spice **or** grated nutmeg.

Vanilla Sauce

Add ½ × 2.5ml spoon vanilla essence and a drop of yellow colouring (optional).

Sweet Arrowroot Sauce *Basic recipe*
Makes 175ml (approx) using 125ml liquid

125–250ml water	100g sugar, golden syrup **or** honey
thinly pared rind of lemon **or** other flavouring	lemon juice
	2 × 5ml spoons arrowroot

Put the water in a pan and add the lemon rind or other flavouring. Heat to boiling point, reduce the heat, and simmer gently for 15 minutes. Remove the lemon rind, if used. Add the sugar, syrup or honey. Re-heat to boiling point and boil for 5 minutes. Add lemon juice to taste. Blend the arrowroot with a little cold water until smooth and stir into the hot liquid. Heat gently for 1–2 minutes, stirring all the time until the arrowroot thickens.

VARIATIONS

Lemon Sauce (2)

Make as above, using 125ml water, the rind of half a lemon and the juice of 2 lemons.

Rich Lemon Sauce

Add a small glass of sherry and an egg yolk when the sauce is just below boiling point. The sauce must not be allowed to boil once the egg yolk has been added.

Orange Sauce (2)

Make as in the basic recipe, using 125ml water, the rind of half an orange and the juice of 1 orange instead of the lemon rind and juice.

Crème Anglaise (1) (Egg Custard Sauce)
Makes 300ml (approx)

250ml milk
a few drops vanilla essence **or** a strip
    of lemon rind

3 egg yolks
50g caster sugar

Put the milk and flavouring in a pan and warm gently but do not let it boil. Beat the egg yolks and sugar together until creamy. Remove the lemon rind, if used, and add the milk. Strain the custard into a double boiler or a basin placed over a pan of simmering water. Cook, stirring all the time with a wooden spoon, until the custard thickens and coats the back of the spoon. Take care not to let the custard curdle. Serve hot or cold.

VARIATIONS
Stir 125ml lightly whipped double cream and 2 × 15ml spoons Grand Marnier into the completed sauce.

Chocolate Custard Sauce

Grate 100g plain chocolate coarsely and add to the milk with vanilla essence instead of lemon rind. Warm until the chocolate melts, stir, and add to the egg yolks. Complete the recipe as above.

Caramel Custard Sauce

Put 25g sugar and 1 × 15ml spoon water in a small pan. Heat gently until the sugar dissolves; then boil the syrup until it is golden-brown. Remove from the heat, quickly add 2 × 15ml spoons cold water, and leave in a warm place to dissolve. Add enough caramel to the finished custard sauce to give a good flavour.

Chocolate Sauce (2)
Makes 150ml (approx)

100g plain chocolate
200g sugar
125ml water

salt
1 × 2.5ml spoon vanilla essence

Break up the chocolate and put into a saucepan with the other ingredients. Stir over gentle heat until the chocolate and sugar melt and blend together.

   Serve hot over ice cream, profiteroles or stewed pears.

Note Black coffee can be substituted for water.

Jam Sauce
Makes 300ml (approx)

4 × 15ml spoons seedless jam
250ml water
sugar

lemon juice
1 × 10ml spoon arrowroot
a few drops food colouring (optional)

Put the jam and the water in a saucepan and heat to boiling point. Add sugar and lemon juice to taste. Blend the arrowroot with a little cold water until smooth. Stir into the hot liquid and heat gently until the arrowroot thickens, stirring all the time. Colour if necessary.

Serve with steamed or baked puddings, ice cream or cold cornflour desserts.

Melba Sauce
Makes 100–125ml

200g fresh raspberries
3 × 15ml spoons icing sugar

white wine (optional)

Crush the raspberries in a sieve over a heatproof bowl. Add the sugar and rub through the sieve into the bowl. Place the bowl over a pan of simmering water and stir for 2–3 minutes to dissolve the sugar. Remove from the heat, and add a little white wine if a thinner consistency is preferred. The sauce should only just coat the back of a spoon. Chill before use.

Serve over Peach Melba (p335), meringues, or any hot or cold raspberry-flavoured dessert.

Thickened Fruit Sauce *Basic recipe*

fresh fruit (damsons, plums,
   raspberries, blueberries or
   blackberries)
sugar

lemon juice
1 × 5ml spoon arrowroot for every
   250ml fruit purée
1 × 5ml spoon water

Put the fruit into a pan with a very little water. Heat to simmering point and simmer until softened. Stone the fruit, then rub through a sieve, or process in an electric blender until smooth. Measure the fruit to calculate the quantity of arrowroot needed. Pour the fruit purée back into the saucepan and add sugar and lemon juice to taste. Blend the correct quantity of arrowroot with the water. Add to the fruit purée and bring to the boil, stirring all the time until the sauce thickens.

Note Canned or bottled fruit can be used, in which case it will be unnecessary to add extra sugar.

GRAVIES

Giblet Gravy (for roast poultry)
Makes 300ml (approx)

1 set of giblets
1 medium-sized onion (100g approx)
   (optional)
400ml water

pan juices
gravy browning (optional)
salt and pepper (optional)

Prepare the giblets (p173) and skin the onion, if used. Put the giblets and the onion in a pan and cover with cold water. Heat to boiling point, cover, reduce the heat, and simmer gently for 1 hour. Pour off the fat from the tin in which the bird has been roasted, leaving any sediment. Add the liquid from the giblets and stir until boiling. Boil for 2–3 minutes. If the gravy is pale, add a few drops of gravy browning. Season to taste, if required. Strain, and serve very hot.

Note The gravy can be thickened slightly, if liked, by adding 1×5ml spoon plain flour for each 250ml giblet stock. Blend the flour with the sediment before adding the stock. Boil for 3–4 minutes.

Lamb Gravy (for roast lamb)
Makes 250ml (approx)

pan juices
1×5ml spoon plain flour
250ml hot water from vegetables **or**
   general household stock (p25)
   made with lamb meat trimmings
   and vegetables

salt and pepper (optional)
gravy browning (optional)

Make as for Thin Gravy (p229) but, after pouring off the fat, stir the flour into the pan juices. Add the hot vegetable water or stock gradually to prevent lumps forming, and stir until boiling. Season to taste, if required. If the gravy is pale, add a few drops of gravy browning. Strain, and serve very hot.

Thin Gravy (for roast beef)
Makes 250ml (approx)

pan juices
250ml hot water from cooking
   vegetables **or** beef stock

salt and pepper (optional)
gravy browning (optional)

After roasting a joint, carefully pour off the fat from the roasting tin, leaving all pan juices and sediment behind. Add the vegetable water or beef stock to the juices. Bring to the boil, stirring well until all the sediment dissolves, and boil for 2–3 minutes to reduce the liquid slightly. Season to taste. If the gravy is pale, add a few drops of gravy browning. Strain, and serve very hot.

Thickened Gravy (for roast pork and roast veal)
Makes 250ml (approx)

pan juices
1 × 15ml spoon plain flour
250ml hot water from cooking
    vegetables **or** general household
    stock (p25) made with pork meat
    trimmings and vegetables

salt and pepper (optional)

After roasting a joint, pour off most of the fat from the roasting tin leaving 2 × 15ml spoons of fat and sediment in the tin. Sift the flour over the fat and blend thoroughly with the pan juices. Stir and cook until browned. Gradually add the hot liquid, and stir until boiling. Boil for 3–4 minutes. Season to taste. Strain, and serve very hot.

Vegetable Gravy (brown)
Makes 400ml (approx)

1 medium-sized onion (100g approx)
1 small carrot (25g approx)
½ small turnip (25g approx)
25g butter **or** margarine
1 × 15ml spoon plain flour
500ml water
bouquet garni

1 × 10ml spoon vinegar
1 × 2.5ml spoon sugar
2 cloves
½ blade of mace
salt and pepper
1 × 5ml spoon Worcestershire sauce

Prepare and chop the vegetables. Melt the fat in a saucepan, add the vegetables, and fry for about 10 minutes or until well browned. Stir in the flour. Gradually add the water and stir until boiling. Add the rest of the ingredients except the sauce. Reduce the heat, cover, and simmer gently for 1 hour. Strain. Add the Worcestershire sauce and re-season if required.

MARINADES

Uncooked White Wine Marinade (for fish or white meat)
Makes 325ml (approx)

1 onion
6–10 parsley stalks
1 × 5ml spoon fennel seeds (for fish)
1 × 5ml spoon dried thyme
1 bay leaf

juice of 1 lemon
50ml salad oil
250ml white wine **or** wine mixed with
    water
salt and pepper

Skin and slice the onion and chop the parsley stalks. Tie very loosely in butter muslin with the fennel seeds, if used, and the herbs. Put the herb bag into a basin with the fish or meat and pour the liquids over them. Season to taste. Marinate for as long as required, turning over the contents of the dish occasionally.

Uncooked Red Wine Marinade (for red meat or game)
Makes 650ml (approx)

1 medium-sized onion	1 × 2.5ml spoon ground coriander
1 medium-sized carrot	(for game)
1 stick of celery	1 × 2.5ml spoon juniper berries
6–10 parsley stalks	(for game)
1 clove of garlic	salt and pepper
1 × 5ml spoon dried thyme	250ml brown stock (p25)
1 bay leaf	125ml red wine
6–8 black peppercorns	125ml water
1–2 cloves	125ml salad oil

Chop the vegetables and parsley stalks. Skin and crush the garlic. Mix the ingredients in a basin as for the uncooked white wine marinade on p230.

Cooked Red Wine Marinade (for red meat or game)
Makes 1.25 litres (approx)

1 carrot	1 × 15ml spoon salt
1 onion	250ml red wine
1 litre water	juice of 1 lemon
3 bay leaves	1 × 5ml spoon granulated sugar
12 black peppercorns	6 juniper berries (for game)

Prepare the carrot and onion and slice them thinly. Put in a saucepan with the water, bay leaves, peppercorns, and salt, and cook until the vegetables are tender.

When cooked, add the rest of the ingredients. Put the meat or game in a basin and pour the hot marinade over it. Marinate for as long as required, turning over the meat frequently. For a large piece of meat left to soak for 36 hours or longer, strain off the marinade on the second day, reboil it, and leave to cool completely; then pour it back over the meat. This can be done a second time over a 4–5 day period, if required. The marinade should not be reboiled more than twice.

BUTTERS

Anchovy Butter

50g softened unsalted butter	lemon juice
6 anchovy fillets **or** anchovy essence	pepper

Cream the butter until light. Pound the anchovy fillets, if used, to a paste or process in an electric blender with a little of the butter. Beat the anchovy and seasonings into the butter gradually. Do not over-flavour; the butter becomes stronger as it matures. Leave to stand at room temperature for at least 30 minutes before use. Press into small pots or cartons, tapping while filling to knock out all the air; alternatively, form into pats. Use at once, or cover and chill in a refrigerator. Do not freeze.

Clarified Butter

This is used when a clear butter, free from any milk solids, salt or water is required. It is used to fry white fish, chicken and veal, as it gives a light golden colour; to moisten the surface of food to be grilled; to seal potted meats; to oil moulds or baking tins; and to add to Genoese sponge mixtures.

Hot clarified butter, or as it is sometimes called, oiled or melted butter, is often served instead of sauce with fish, meat or vegetables.

To clarify butter, put the butter in a saucepan, heat it gently until it melts, then continue to heat slowly without browning, until all bubbling ceases (this shows the water has been driven off). Remove from the heat and skim off any scum that has risen to the top. Let it stand for a few minutes for any sediment to settle, then gently pour off the clear butter into a basin or jar, leaving the sediment behind. If there is a lot of sediment, it may be necessary to strain the fat through a fine sieve or muslin.

Garlic Butter

1 clove of garlic   50–75g softened butter

Skin and chop the garlic. Either pound it, grate it, or squeeze it through a garlic press. Mix well with the butter, adjusting the quantity of butter to give the flavour you prefer. Use at once, or pot and chill as for Anchovy Butter (p231). Use within 2 days.

Herb Butter

a good pinch of dried parsley   50g softened butter
a good pinch of dried thyme $\frac{1}{2} \times 2.5$ml spoon salt

Work the herbs into the butter lightly. Season to taste. Use at once, or pot and chill as for Anchovy Butter (p231).

Maître d'Hôtel Butter

2–4 large sprigs parsley   a small pinch of pepper
50g softened butter   a few drops lemon juice
salt

Blanch the parsley, and chop it finely. Work it into the butter with the seasonings and lemon juice. Use at once, or pot and chill as for Anchovy Butter (p231).

Ravigote Butter

2 × 15ml spoons mixed fresh herbs   1 small clove of garlic
   (parsley, chervil, shallot, tarragon,   25g softened butter
   chives)   salt and pepper

Chop the herbs finely. If chervil is used it should be chopped separately and not blanched. Crush the garlic clove. Tie the herbs and garlic in a small piece of muslin. Blanch in a little boiling water, then drain and squeeze dry. Work the herbs into the butter with the back of a spoon, and season to taste. Sieve. Use at once, or pot and chill as for Anchovy Butter (p231). Use within 2 days.

Brandy Butter

50g butter 2 oz   1–2 × 15ml spoons brandy
100g caster sugar 4 oz

Cream the butter until soft. Beat the sugar gradually into the butter until it is pale and light. Work in the brandy, a little at a time, taking care not to allow the mixture to curdle. Chill before using. If the mixture has separated slightly after standing, beat well before serving.

  This sauce is traditionally served with Christmas pudding and mince pies.

Note An egg white whisked until stiff can be stirred into the butter and sugar mixture to give a softer texture.

Mrs Beeton's Fairy Butter

1 × 10ml spoon orange juice   2 hard-boiled egg yolks
25g icing sugar   1 × 10ml spoon orange flower water
100g softened butter

Decoration (optional)
1 × 10ml spoon grated orange rind

Strain the orange juice, and sift the sugar. Sieve the egg yolks. Using a rotary beater, beat in the juice, orange flower water, sugar, and butter alternately until all the ingredients are blended to a smooth paste.

  To use, press the fairy butter through a sieve on to a decorative serving plate, in a pile of thin strands. Do not press them down; flick any stray strands into place with a fork. Sprinkle with grated orange rind, if liked. Serve as a rich sweet with small crisp biscuits, or on a trifle or gâteau instead of whipped cream.

Rum Butter

50g butter   2 × 15ml spoons rum
100g light soft brown sugar

Cream the butter until soft, beating in the sugar gradually. When light and creamy, work in the rum, a little at a time. Chill before using.

VEGETABLES, PASTA AND RICE

VEGETABLES

Artichokes – *Globe*

Globe artichokes are available all year round, but are generally at their cheapest in the late summer. Although the artichoke bases, or *fonds* as they are also called, are served as a vegetable side dish, whole artichokes are generally served as a starter either hot or cold.

An artichoke base is the small fleshy part of the artichoke which is left after all the leaves and the furry 'choke' (the undeveloped flower) have been removed. It is sometimes served on its own with melted butter, Hollandaise sauce (p217) or a stuffing; or it can be deep fried. Artichoke hearts, which are the centres of very small, young artichokes, are also available frozen and in cans.

To buy: Allow 1 medium to large artichoke per person or 2 small ones. When fresh, the leaves of the artichoke should be stiff and have a slight bloom on them.

To store: Artichokes should be bought as fresh as possible, but they can be stored for several days in a cool vegetable rack or larder or in the bottom of a refrigerator.

To prepare: Wash the artichokes thoroughly in cold water. Cut the stalk level with the base and trim off any very coarse outer leaves. (The tops of the outer leaves are often also trimmed with scissors which gives a more attractive appearance.) Brush the cut surface of the artichokes with lemon juice to prevent discoloration.

To boil: Put the artichokes into a pan with just enough boiling salted water to cover them; if liked, a bouquet garni can be added to the pan. Cover and cook for 30–45 minutes, depending on the size of the artichokes; cooking is complete when one of the lower leaves can be easily pulled out. Remove from the pan and turn upside down for a minute to drain thoroughly. (The 'choke' in the centre of the artichoke can be removed before serving the artichoke if liked; it is best removed with a teaspoon.) Serve the artichokes either hot with melted butter or Hollandaise sauce (p217), or cold with vinaigrette sauce or mayonnaise.

To steam: Season with salt and cook in the top of a steamer over boiling water for 40–55 minutes. Serve as for boiled artichokes

To eat: Using your fingers, pull off each leaf, dip the soft fleshy end in the melted butter, sauce or mayonnaise and suck both together. When all the leaves have been pulled off in this way, the choke will be revealed if it has not previously been removed. Cut this off and eat the base (*fond*) beneath with a knife and fork.

To deep fry: Use only the artichoke bases. Cut 6–8 artichoke bases into 3–4 pieces according to size. Coat with batter and fry as for Jerusalem artichokes.

Artichokes – *Jerusalem*

These white tubers are not, in fact, artichokes at all; they belong to the sunflower family. They are a winter vegetable and are usually available from October to April. Jerusalem artichokes can be served in a variety of ways and in particular make an excellent soup.

To buy: Allow 150–200g per person. The tubers should be hard and firm. Prime tubers are fairly regular in shape and measure about 10 × 5cm. Try to avoid buying artichokes which are very mis-shapen because they are difficult to peel and consequently cause a lot of wastage.

To store: Artichokes will store for a few weeks in a cool vegetable rack or larder.

To prepare: Wash the artichokes thoroughly, then peel thinly or scrape, and put at once into acidulated water; this helps to keep the vegetables white. Cut into slices or pieces convenient for serving just before cooking.

To boil: Cook in just enough boiling, salted, acidulated water to cover for about 20 minutes or until tender. Drain thoroughly and serve either with melted butter and seasoned with freshly ground black pepper, or with a white, Béchamel or Hollandaise sauce.

To steam: Scrub the artichokes, but leave them whole and unpeeled. Season with salt and cook in the top of a steamer over a pan of boiling water for about 40 minutes. Peel and slice them and serve as for boiled artichokes.

To roast: Parboil the artichokes, as above, for 5 minutes. Drain thoroughly. Put into hot dripping in a roasting tin, or in the tin containing a roast joint. Roll in the fat and cook in a fairly hot oven, 190°C, Gas 5, for about 1 hour, turning 2–3 times during cooking. The colour of artichokes cooked in this way is not very good but the flavour is excellent.

To stew: Heat 50g butter for every 750g–1kg artichokes. Add the peeled and sliced artichokes and season to taste; cover tightly and cook for about 30 minutes, shaking the pan from time to time. Serve in the cooking liquor or add this to a white or Béchamel sauce.

To deep fry: (Method 1) Peel and slice the artichokes very thinly and soak in acidulated water for 10 minutes. Dry thoroughly and fry in deep fat or oil (p10) until golden-brown. Drain on soft kitchen paper and season with salt and pepper.

To deep fry: (Method 2) Peel the artichokes and cut into 1cm slices. Parboil for 5 minutes, drain, and dry thoroughly. For 750g artichokes, make up a double quantity of coating batter (1) (p190). Dip the artichoke slices into the batter and fry in deep fat or oil (p10) until golden-brown, turning once during cooking. Drain thoroughly and serve very hot with fried parsley (p56).

To purée: Mash, sieve or blend steamed or boiled artichokes, and to every 1kg artichokes (weight before cooking) add 2 × 15ml spoons milk and 25– 50g butter. Season to taste with salt and pepper and serve sprinkled with plenty of chopped parsley.

Asparagus

The season for home-grown asparagus is a short one, only May and June, but imported asparagus can be bought from March to July. It is also possible to buy asparagus at other times, but from only a few shops and usually at a premium price. Asparagus can also be bought frozen and canned. It can be served in many ways, but one of the best is to boil it, and then serve it with melted butter or Hollandaise sauce (p217) as a starter.

To buy: Fresh asparagus is generally sold in bundles and is graded according to the thickness of the stem and plumpness of the buds. The heads should be tight and well formed, and the stems should not be dry and woody. Allow 6–8 medium-sized heads per person, 150–200g approx.

To store: Asparagus is best bought on the day or the day before it is needed, although it will keep for a couple of days in the bottom of a refrigerator, if necessary.

To prepare: Cut the woody parts evenly from the base of the stems. Scrape the white part of each stalk with a knife. Tie into bundles and put into cold salted water until ready to cook.

To boil: The asparagus must stand upright in the saucepan because if it lies in the water, the heads will be overcooked and will drop off before the stems are tender. It is therefore important to use a deep saucepan (it is possible to buy special asparagus pans). The water in the saucepan should come to just below the heads of the asparagus. Salt the water and bring to the boil. Stand the asparagus in a jam jar or other heatproof pot if not using an asparagus pan. Put into the water, and cover the pan with a tight-fitting lid. Cook gently until the stems are tender; this will take 14–20 minutes depending on the thickness of the stems. Drain thoroughly and serve either with melted butter, seasoned and lightly flavoured with lemon juice, or with Hollandaise sauce (p217). Asparagus can also be served cold with vinaigrette sauce.

Asparagus Points or Tips

Sometimes, the thinner stalks of asparagus, or *sprue* as they are called, are sold loose. Cut the points and the tender green parts into short pieces. Cook in a small amount of gently boiling salted water for 5–10 minutes according to their size and age. Drain thoroughly, toss in butter, and season with salt and pepper. Serve as a garnish or as a main vegetable, or use as a filling for omelets.

Note It is a mistake to add anything which will impair the delicate flavour of asparagus, but a little chopped shallot and parsley may be fried in the butter before tossing with the asparagus.

Aubergines

Aubergines, also known as *eggplants*, are obtainable all year round, but are generally at their cheapest in late summer. They are used extensively in Mediterranean cooking and, in addition to being served as a vegetable on their own (often stuffed), are an important ingredient in such well-known dishes as Ratatouille (p270) and Moussaka (p139).

To buy: Allow 100–150g per person (an average aubergine weighs about 250g). Fresh aubergines are firm to the touch and have a firm, glossy skin, whereas those that have been in the shop for some time will be slightly soft and have a rather wrinkled skin.

To store: Aubergines can be kept for several days in a cool vegetable rack or larder or in the bottom of a refrigerator.

To prepare: Aubergines are used in a variety of ways, and preparation will vary according to the dish. They can be rather bitter, and in order to avoid this, cut them into 5mm–1cm slices, sprinkle salt over the cut surfaces, and leave in a sieve for 30 minutes to 1 hour, during which time a great deal of liquid will drain off. Rinse under cold water and dry thoroughly. If the aubergines are left whole for cooking, the skin should be scored with a knife in a few places and sprinkled with salt.

Deep-fried Aubergines
4–6 helpings

600g aubergines (approx)
salt
2 eggs

soft white **or** dried white breadcrumbs
fat **or** oil for deep frying

Cut the aubergines into slices about 8mm thick. Lay the slices flat on a large dish, sprinkle with salt, and leave for 30 minutes. Rinse and dry thoroughly. Beat the eggs until liquid. Dip the aubergine slices first in the egg and then in the breadcrumbs. Press the crumbs on firmly. Heat the fat or oil (p10) and fry the aubergine slices, a few at a time, until crisp and brown. Drain thoroughly on soft kitchen paper and serve very hot.

Beans – *Broad*
Broad beans are generally available from April to September, but can also be bought in cans; frozen beans are particularly good. Fresh beans are generally shelled before cooking although very small, young beans can be cooked in their pods.

To buy: Allow 300g per person. The pods should be full and a good green colour with no black markings; do not buy beans whose pods are shrivelled and yellow.

To store: Beans are best eaten on the day or day after they are bought, but they can be kept for a few days in a cool vegetable rack or larder or in the bottom of a refrigerator.

To prepare: Shell the beans unless using very young beans. These are cooked whole in the pod, in which case top and tail the pods and remove any strings as with runner beans. Shelled beans should be covered either with clingfilm or with some of the washed pods to prevent them drying out. If the beans are very mature, they may need to be skinned after cooking as the outer skin can be tough and unpalatable.

To boil: Add the beans to about 2cm boiling salted water, cover, and cook for 15–20 minutes for young beans in their pods or young shelled beans, or for about 30 minutes for more mature beans. If liked, a few leaves of summer savory or a sprig of parsley can also be added to the water. Drain the beans thoroughly and serve either tossed in butter with chopped parsley or savory, or with a white or Hollandaise sauce.

To steam: Season the beans with salt and cook in a steamer over a pan of boiling water for about 25–45 minutes, depending on the age of the beans. Serve as for boiled beans.

Beans – *French*
There are several varieties of French bean. The commonest is the straight bean, usually about 10–15cm long with no strings, which is also known by its French

name, *haricot vert.* Other beans include kidney beans, which are more heavily podded, with the kidney-shaped bean showing through; and pea beans, or bobby beans, which also have a heavier pod but round pea-like beans. Home-grown beans are available in the summer, but imported beans are available all year round. Frozen beans are also available, both whole and sliced.

To buy: Allow 100–150g per person. Choose beans which are a good colour, appear crisp and fresh, and are of an even size.

To store: French beans should be used as fresh as possible, but they can be stored for 2–3 days in a cool, dry place or in the bottom of a refrigerator.

To prepare: Top and tail the beans and remove any strings. Leave the beans whole.

To boil: Cook the beans in the minimum of boiling salted water for 5–10 minutes or until just tender. Drain thoroughly and toss in butter. Season with black pepper, preferably freshly ground, and top with chopped summer savory or tarragon, or a little crushed garlic, if liked.

To steam: Season the beans with salt and cook in a steamer over boiling water for 10–15 minutes or until just tender. Drain and serve as for boiled beans.

Beans – *Runner*

Runner beans are the type most often found in the UK, and are available from mid-July until the end of September. They are much larger than French beans and can vary in length from 15–30cm. Frozen runner beans are also easily obtainable, both whole and ready cut.

To buy: Allow 150g per person. The beans should be a bright green colour and it should be possible to snap them in half. The long beans are just as tender as the smaller ones but, especially early in the season, the pods should not be fat; if so, the bean inside has had time to develop, and the outside of the bean is likely to be tough. Avoid buying beans which are at all discoloured or are limp or misshapen.

To store: Runner beans can be kept for 2–3 days in a cool vegetable rack or larder or in the bottom of a refrigerator.

To prepare: Top and tail the beans and remove any strings, then cut into thin, oblique slices, about 3–5cm long.

To boil: Add the beans to about 2cm boiling salted water, cover, and cook for 5–10 minutes or until just tender. Drain thoroughly. Serve tossed with butter and a little chopped savory and well seasoned with black pepper.

To steam: Season the beans with salt and cook in a steamer over a pan of boiling water for about 10–15 minutes. Drain and serve as for boiled beans.

Beans – *Dried*

Dried beans, like other pulses, have a high protein content and can be used to make excellent, nourishing, and comparatively inexpensive meals. As well as being used as a hot vegetable, or in composite dishes, they are also very good when served cold in salads. There are many varieties of dried beans and a lot of them are known by different names according to the country of origin, but in most cases, these beans are interchangeable.

Aduki or azuki beans: Small round, red beans which are used extensively in Japanese cookery for both sweet and savoury dishes.

Black-eyed peas: Despite their name, these are in fact beans, small and white in colour and similar to a haricot bean, but, at the point of attachment to the pod, they have a small black 'eye'. They are used a great deal in South American cooking.

Borlotti beans: red or mottled pink beans used in salads and stews.

Brown beans: Medium-sized, kidney-shaped beans used extensively in Mediterranean cooking.

Butter beans: Large, white, kidney-shaped beans.

Haricot beans: There are several varieties of small white beans whose shape can vary from almost round to very long and thin, according to the variety and where it is grown.

Flageolet beans: Pale green haricot beans; a very choice variety.

Lima beans: A green American bean.

Pinto beans: These are similar to red kidney beans, but are a dappled pink in colour.

Red kidney beans: Kidney-shaped beans, traditionally used in Chilli Con Carne; deep purplish red and larger than haricot beans.

Soya beans: Creamy white and almost round. They have a very high protein content and are of particular value in a vegetarian diet.

Note Red kidney beans and soya beans must then be boiled for at least 10 minutes before adding them to oven-cooked dishes.

If cooking them in a slow cooker, they should be prepared in the same way before cooking them for at least 4 hours in the slow cooker.

To buy: Allow 40–50g dried beans per person.

To prepare: Soak the beans in cold water for 6–12 hours, preferably changing the water once during this time to prevent them fermenting.

To boil: Drain the beans and put them into a pan. Cover with fresh cold salted water and bring to the boil. Cover the pan and simmer gently for $1\frac{1}{2}$–$3\frac{1}{2}$ hours until tender.

The cooking time of beans varies with the type of bean and its age; freshly dried beans need a much shorter cooking time than older ones. If preferred, the beans can be cooked in stock to improve the flavour; alternatively or in addition, a chopped onion, a peeled clove of garlic, and sprigs of fresh herbs can be added to the water.

To serve: Drain off the excess liquid, toss in a little butter, season to taste, and sprinkle with chopped parsley.

To purée: Puréed beans, especially haricot and soya beans, are used in vegetarian cooking. Drain the beans, reserving the cooking liquor, then sieve or process in an electric blender with a little of the liquor to give a smooth purée. Season to taste and add a little butter and/or top of the milk.

Boston Roast
6 helpings

300g haricot beans	1 egg
1 onion	100g soft white breadcrumbs
1 × 15ml spoon oil	salt and pepper
150g Cheddar cheese	fat for greasing
2 × 15ml spoons meat **or** vegetable stock **or** water	

Prepare and cook the beans. Drain and mash them finely. Skin and chop the onion. Heat the oil in a frying pan and fry the onion until golden-brown. Grate the cheese. Put all the ingredients into a bowl and mix well. Shape the mixture into a loaf, place in a greased baking tin, and cover with buttered greaseproof paper. Bake in a moderate oven, 180°C, Gas 4, for 45 minutes.

Serve with gravy and vegetables.

Cooking time $2\frac{1}{2}$ hours (approx)

Bean Sprouts

Bean sprouts are available in many greengrocers' shops and supermarkets or can be grown at home. They are served both raw in salads and cooked. Excellent canned bean sprouts are also obtainable.

To buy: Allow 50g bean sprouts per person. Choose crisp fresh looking bean sprouts.

To sprout beans: Use young mung beans as old ones will not sprout. Discard any discoloured or decayed beans and soak the rest in plenty of cold water. Drain and place either on damp muslin stretched over a tray or in a jar with muslin or cheese-cloth stretched over it, and placed on its side.

Pour cold water over the beans to keep them moist and tilt the container to let the water run off. Repeat twice daily for 6–8 days until the beans have sprouted and the sprouts are 4–5cm long. Keep the beans well ventilated and at a fairly warm even temperature over 18°C and, if sprouting them in the dark, bring into the light for 24 hours before use.

To store: Bean sprouts do not keep well and should preferably be eaten on the day of purchase; if not, they can be kept for a day in the bottom of a refrigerator.

To prepare: Pick over the bean sprouts, remove any withered or brown stalks and wash in cold water.

To steam: Prepare as above and season with salt. Cook in the top of a steamer over a pan of boiling water for about 5–8 minutes or until just soft. Drain and serve as soon as possible.

To stir-fry (Chinese method): Heat 2 × 15ml spoons olive, corn or soya oil in a pan. Add the bean sprouts and cook, stirring all the time, for about 5 minutes or until they are just cooked, but are still slightly crisp. Serve as soon as possible after cooking.

Beetroot

Small, young beetroots make an excellent hot vegetable as well as being good in salads. Beetroot is available all year round, but the young ones are at their best in mid-summer. At this time of year, the leaves can be used as well as the roots and these should be cooked as for spinach (pp263–64). For salads, the beetroots should be baked, boiled or steamed, or they can be bought already cooked.

To buy: Allow 100–150g per person. Uncooked beetroots should be firm, the skins smooth and unbroken, and in the summer any leaves which have been left on should look fresh. If buying cooked beetroots, avoid buying any with a wrinkled skin which does not look moist because these tend to be hard and 'woody'.

To store: Young beetroots are best cooked and eaten as soon as possible after purchase, but older ones can be stored for several weeks in a cool airy place. Cooked beetroots can be wrapped in cling-film and stored in the bottom of a refrigerator for 2–3 days.

To prepare: Raw beetroot 'bleeds' so it is important that the skin is not damaged in any way. Cut off the leaves and trim the stalks to within 2cm of the top of the root. Wash thoroughly to remove any dirt.

To boil: Cook in a large pan of boiling salted water for 45 minutes–1 hour for small beetroots, or for up to 2 hours for large, older ones. Drain thoroughly if serving hot, or allow to cool in the cooking water. To serve beetroot hot, peel off the skin and either season with pepper and top with melted butter and chopped parsley or mint, or serve with a white, parsley or caper sauce.

To steam: Season the beetroots with salt. Cook in the top of a steamer over a pan of boiling water for $1\frac{1}{2}$ hours if small, or for up to $2\frac{1}{2}$ hours if large. Serve as for boiled beetroot.

To bake: If the skin of the beetroot has been damaged in any way, seal the damaged part with a little flour and water paste. Place each beetroot in a piece of buttered greaseproof paper and enclose it completely. Bake in a moderate oven, 180°C, Gas 4, for 1 hour (for young beetroots) or for up to 2 hours for older beetroots. Serve as for boiled beetroot.

Beetroot is also excellent cooked in a pressure cooker.

Broccoli

There are three different kinds of broccoli, and this often causes confusion.

1) Many of the winter cauliflowers available are, in fact, broccoli, because the broccoli plant is much hardier than the cauliflower; this broccoli should be cooked and treated exactly like cauliflower.

2) Heads of purple sprouting and white sprouting broccoli are found in the shops at the end of the winter and in early spring. After this central head has been removed, the plant gives out leafy side shoots with a small head which are available in the late spring.

3) The third and choicest type of broccoli is the green or Italian *Calabrese* variety. Home-grown *Calabrese* is in the shops from July to December, but if imported it is available at other times of the year. *Calabrese* also freezes well and is fairly widely obtainable in this form.

To buy: Allow 100–200g per person depending on the amount of leaf and consequent wastage. The heads of both *Calabrese* and purple sprouting broccoli should be a good colour. The leaves should appear fresh, and the stalks should be firm and not limp.

To store: Purple sprouting broccoli does not store well and should be kept for only 1–2 days in a cool, dry vegetable rack or larder or in a polythene bag in the bottom of a refrigerator. *Calabrese* will keep for 2–3 days in a polythene bag in a refrigerator, but should be eaten as fresh as possible.

To prepare: Calabrese does not generally require very much preparation since it is usually separated into small heads when bought. Simply trim the stalks to within 7–10cm of the head and wash thoroughly. The whole heads of purple sprouting broccoli should be trimmed and either left whole if they are small, or broken up into smaller heads if large. The leafy side shoots should be trimmed and any tough stalks discarded. It is often neater to tie the shoots in bundles before cooking.

To boil: Cook the broccoli in the minimum of boiling salted water for 10–15 minutes or until just tender. Drain thoroughly and turn into a serving dish. Season with pepper, preferably freshly ground, and either spoon melted butter over it or serve with Hollandaise (p217) or Béarnaise (p214) sauce.

To steam: Season the broccoli with salt. Cook in the top of a steamer over a pan of boiling water for 15–20 minutes. Drain thoroughly and serve as for boiled broccoli.

Brussels Sprouts

Brussels sprouts are in season from August to March, although the flavour is generally better after the first frosts. The best sprouts to buy are the small hard ones, also known as button sprouts, since these have the best flavour and texture and freeze well. Sprout tops, when available, should be cooked as for spinach.

To buy: Allow 150–200g sprouts per person. Choose sprouts which are small, firm, and green and which do not have a great many loose outside leaves. These should also be a good green colour and not yellow or wilted.

To store: Sprouts can be kept for 1–2 days in a cool, dry vegetable rack or larder, or for 2–3 days in a polythene bag in a refrigerator, but they are best eaten as fresh as possible.

To prepare: Cut a slice off the bottom of each sprout and remove the outer leaves. Soak the sprouts for 10 minutes in cold salted water and drain thoroughly. To cook large sprouts more quickly and evenly, cut a cross in the base.

To boil: Add the sprouts, a few at a time, to the minimum of boiling salted water so that the water does not leave the boil. Cook for 7–10 minutes according to size or until they are just tender. Do not overcook. Drain thoroughly and season with black pepper, preferably freshly ground. Toss in melted butter or soured cream or sprinkle with a little crumbled crisply fried or grilled bacon.

The sprouts can also be boiled in stock. Prepare 750g sprouts and cook in 500ml beef stock. Drain, reserving the cooking liquor, and keep warm. Boil the cooking liquor rapidly until it is reduced to a thin glaze. Pour over the sprouts and serve as soon as possible.

To steam: Season the sprouts with salt. Cook in the top of a steamer over a pan of boiling water for about 15 minutes or until the sprouts are just tender. Drain and serve as for boiled sprouts.

To braise: Parboil the sprouts in boiling salted water for 5 minutes. Fry a chopped onion in 25g butter until it is just soft. Pour 500ml stock over it, season, and simmer for 5 minutes. Add the sprouts and simmer for a further 10 minutes.

Cabbage

There are many varieties of cabbage, but the most common are:

1) the Savoy
2) the pale green, hard or 'white' (Dutch) cabbage
3) red cabbage
4) spring and summer cabbage.

To buy: Allow 200g per person. Always choose cabbages that are crisp and a good colour. They should never be limp with yellow edges; this indicates that they were picked some time ago and so probably lack both flavour and valuable vitamin C.

To store: Apart from red and white cabbage, which can be stored for some time, it is inadvisable to store cabbage for more than a few days. It should be kept in a cool, dry vegetable rack or larder. If only part of a cabbage is needed, wrap the rest and store in the bottom of a refrigerator.

To prepare: Remove the coarse outer leaves and trim off the stem. Cut the cabbage into half, cut out the hard part of the stalk, then cut into quarters. Spring and summer cabbage is usually left in quarters, but other varieties are generally finely shredded. This should not be done until shortly before the vegetable is to be cooked because mineral salts and vitamin C are rapidly lost. Wash the cabbage well in cold water; a little salt added to the water helps to draw out any small insects which may be between the leaves. Drain in a colander.

To boil: Add the cabbage, a little at a time, to boiling salted water so that the water does not leave the boil. Cover the pan and cook for 5–12 minutes or until the cabbage is just tender but not soggy; do not overcook. Drain thoroughly and season with a little pepper, preferably freshly ground, and any other flavouring desired; grated nutmeg or a few caraway seeds are popular. Toss in butter just before serving.

To steam: Season the cabbage with salt and cook in the top of a steamer over boiling water for 5–12 minutes or until just tender. Serve as for boiled cabbage.

To braise: Parboil wedges of cabbage for 10 minutes. Drain and dry thoroughly. Fry a chopped onion and carrot in a little lard or dripping. Add a bouquet garni and place the cabbage on top. Pour over just enough beef stock to cover the cabbage and cook for 1 hour. Remove from the pan with a perforated spoon and serve.

Stuffed Cabbage Leaves
4 helpings

8 large cabbage leaves	fat for greasing

Sauce

juice from the canned tomatoes	2 × 10ml spoons cornflour
1 × 15ml spoon concentrated tomato purée	a pinch of sugar
	salt and pepper

Stuffing

1 medium-sized onion	1 × 15ml spoon Worcestershire sauce
1 × 15ml spoon oil	½ × 2.5ml spoon dried mixed herbs
400g minced beef	1 × 15ml spoon chopped parsley
1 × 400g can tomatoes	salt and pepper
1 × 10ml spoon cornflour	

Remove the thick centre stems from the cabbage leaves, blanch in boiling water for 2 minutes, and drain thoroughly.

To make the stuffing, skin and chop the onion finely. Heat the oil in a pan and fry the onion gently for 5 minutes. Add the beef and cook, stirring until the beef has browned. Drain the tomatoes and reserve the juice. Add the tomatoes to the meat mixture. Blend the cornflour with the Worcestershire sauce and stir into the meat mixture with the herbs and seasoning. Cover and simmer for 20 minutes, stirring occasionally.

Divide the stuffing between the cabbage leaves and roll up, folding over the edges of the leaves to enclose the meat completely. Place in a greased, shallow, ovenproof dish, cover with foil, and bake in a fairly hot oven, 190°C, Gas 5, for 20 minutes.

Prepare the sauce while the cabbage leaves are cooking. Blend the reserved juice from the tomatoes with the tomato purée and make up to 250ml with water. Blend the cornflour with 1 × 15ml spoon of the sauce. Pour the rest of the sauce into a pan and bring to the boil. Pour in the blended cornflour and bring to the boil, stirring all the time, until the sauce has thickened. Add the sugar and season to taste. Pour the sauce over the cabbage leaves just before serving.

Cooking time 1 hour (approx)

Red Cabbage

Red cabbage can be cooked as for ordinary green cabbage but is more usually braised gently for about 1½ hours until very tender.

Carrots

Carrots are a most useful vegetable since they are used extensively as a flavouring for all kinds of soups, casseroles, and sauces. They are available throughout the year, although young carrots, which have the best flavour for serving as a vegetable, are usually only obtainable during the late spring and summer. Frozen young carrots are also available, and both young and old carrots can be bought in cans.

To buy: Allow 100–150g per person. The tops of young carrots should appear fresh and green, and the carrots should be of an even size. If the head of the carrot is green, however, the carrot is insufficiently mature. Older carrots should be firm and smooth and not broken or pitted. Care should be taken when buying prepacked carrots because they are sometimes not in prime condition and can be slimy.

To store: For the maximum flavour, young carrots should be eaten as fresh as possible, preferably on the day they are bought, although they can be stored for 1–2 days in a cool, dry vegetable rack or larder. Older carrots can be kept for several weeks, provided they are in a cool, dry place.

To prepare: Young carrots need only to be topped and tailed and scrubbed with a stiff brush. More mature carrots need to be either scraped with a knife or thinly peeled, depending on age. Young carrots should be left whole, but older carrots should be sliced and cut into strips or fancy shapes.

To boil (conservation method): Carrots should be cooked in the minimum of water to give the best flavour and to preserve all the vitamins. For 600g carrots, melt 25g butter or margarine in a heavy-based pan. Add the carrots and cook very gently for 10 minutes, shaking the pan frequently so that the carrots do not stick to the bottom. Pour over approximately 100ml boiling salted water, cover the pan, and cook the carrots gently for a further 10–15 minutes depending on their age. Serve the carrots with the cooking liquor and sprinkle them liberally with chopped parsley, mint, chervil or marjoram, and a little lemon juice, if liked. The carrots can also be served with a parsley sauce or 1–2 × 15ml spoons cream can be added to the carrots in the pan just before serving.

To steam: Young carrots are particularly good steamed. Season with salt and cook in the top of a steamer over boiling water for 10–30 minutes, depending on the age of the carrots. Serve as for boiled carrots.

To deep fry: This is suitable for old carrots. Parboil the carrots for 5 minutes, drain, and dry thoroughly. Coat with batter and fry as for Jerusalem artichokes.

To purée: Older carrots make a good purée and can be mixed with an equal quantity of puréed potatoes. Cook the carrots as above and sieve, mash or process in an electric blender together with the cooking liquor. Add 25g butter, season with salt and pepper, preferably freshly ground, and add a little cream or top of the milk, if liked, Sprinkle with chopped parsley before serving, or add a little grated orange rind for a more unusual flavour.

Cauliflower

Cauliflower is one of our most useful green vegetables because it is available throughout the year. Served with a cheese sauce, cauliflower is a popular and substantial supper dish, but it is also excellent as a side vegetable or when used for soup. Some supermarkets also sell prepacked cauliflower florets, and these can be a good buy because there is no waste. Frozen cauliflower florets are also available.

To buy: Allow 100g per person if buying florets, but 150g per person if buying a whole cauliflower. The head or curds of the cauliflower should be a good creamy white and should have no marks or blemishes. The leaves round the cauliflower should be a good green colour and should not appear yellow or wilted.

To store: Cauliflower will keep for 2–3 days in a cool, dry vegetable rack or larder, or in a refrigerator. To save space in a refrigerator it is usually easier to divide the head into florets first.

To prepare: Fresh florets should simply be washed in cold salted water. Whole cauliflower should be trimmed of most of the outside leaves and the stalk cut so that the cauliflower will stand upright. To ensure the stalk cooks quickly, either make a cross in the base, or cut out the first 2cm of the stalk with an apple corer. Soak the whole cauliflower for 10 minutes in salted water before cooking to draw out any insects.

To boil: Florets should be cooked in the minimum of boiling salted water for 8–10 minutes, or until just tender; they should then be drained. Put a whole cauliflower head, stalk down, in 2cm boiling salted water in a large pan, season with salt, and bring back to the boil. Cover, and cook over fairly high heat for about 15 minutes or until tender. Cauliflower should never be overcooked. Drain thoroughly and place on a serving dish with the head uppermost. Season with pepper, preferably freshly ground black pepper, and spoon over some melted butter and chopped chives or parsley; alternatively, sprinkle with crumbled, fried or grilled bacon or chopped and lightly fried almonds; or pour a white or light cream sauce over the cauliflower.

To steam: Steaming is particularly good for cauliflower florets. Season with salt and cook in the top of a steamer over boiling water for 15 minutes for florets, or for up to 40 minutes for a large, whole head. Do not overcook. Drain thoroughly and serve as for boiled cauliflower.

To deep fry: Divide the cauliflower into florets and parboil for about 8 minutes. Drain and dry thoroughly. For a medium-sized cauliflower or 600g florets, make up a double quantity of coating batter (1) (p190) and coat and fry as for Jerusalem artichokes. Serve deep-fried cauliflower with Tartare sauce (p209).

Cauliflower Cheese
4 helpings

1 medium-sized firm cauliflower	a pinch of dry mustard
2 × 15ml spoons butter **or** margarine	a pinch of Cayenne pepper
4 × 15ml spoons flour	salt and pepper
200ml milk	25g fine dry white breadcrumbs
125g grated Cheddar cheese	

Prepare the cauliflower. Put the head in a saucepan containing enough boiling salted water to half-cover it. Cover the pan, and cook gently for 20–30 minutes until tender. Drain well, reserving 175ml of the cooking water. Break the head carefully into sections, and place in a warmed ovenproof dish. Keep warm under greased greaseproof paper.

Melt the fat in a medium-sized pan, stir in the flour, and cook for 2–3 minutes, stirring all the time, without letting the flour colour. Mix together the milk and reserved cooking water, and gradually add to the pan, stirring all the time to prevent lumps forming. Bring the sauce to the boil, lower the heat, and simmer until thickened. Remove from the heat, and stir in 100g of the cheese, with the mustard and Cayenne pepper. Season to taste. Stir until the cheese is fully melted, then pour the sauce over the cauliflower. Mix the remaining cheese with the breadcrumbs, and sprinkle them on top. Place in a hot oven, 220°C, Gas 7, for 7–10 minutes, to brown the top. Serve at once.

Note A mixture of 2 × 15ml spoons grated Cheddar cheese and 1 × 15ml spoon grated Parmesan cheese can be used for sprinkling, if liked, or 1–2 crumbled, crisply fried rashers of streaky bacon.

Celeriac

This large swede-like root has a flavour very like that of celery and can be used in the same way for flavouring soups, stews, and casseroles. It can also be used raw, shredded, in salads. For a more delicate flavour it can be blanched in acidulated water for 2 minutes before shredding. Celeriac is available from October to April.

To buy: Allow 150g celeriac per person. The root should be firm to the touch and not caked in too much mud and earth.

To store: Celeriac, like other root vegetables, will keep well for several weeks in a cool, dry place.

To prepare: Celeriac can be cooked either whole or cut into slices 1cm thick. Unfortunately, celeriac is not easy to peel because it is rather knobbly. Wash it first in cold water to remove all the mud and earth. If it is to be cooked in slices, slice and then peel it; if it is to be cooked whole, peel thickly with a small sharp knife. As soon as the celeriac has been peeled, it should be put into acidulated water to preserve the colour.

To boil: Cook the whole or sliced celeriac in boiling, salted, acidulated water for 25–30 minutes for sliced celeriac, or for 45 minutes–1 hour for whole celeriac. Drain thoroughly, season with pepper, preferably freshly ground, and either spoon melted butter and/or a squeeze of lemon juice over it, or serve with a white, cheese or Hollandaise sauce.

To steam: Season the celeriac with salt and toss in lemon juice to preserve the colour. Cook in the top of a steamer over boiling water for 30–35 minutes if sliced or for 1–1½ hours if whole.

To bake: Cut the celeriac root in half lengthways without peeling it. Heat 5mm depth of bacon fat or dripping in a roasting tin. Put the celeriac into the fat, cut side down, and bake in a moderate oven, 180°C, Gas 4, for 1–1½ hours. The celeriac is cooked when a skewer pierces it easily. Turn it cut side up for serving, and cut in wedges as with melon.

To shallow fry: Cut the celeriac into slices and parboil for 10 minutes. Drain and dry thoroughly. Fry in some butter or margarine until they are golden-brown. Drain thoroughly, sprinkle with chopped parsley, and serve as soon as possible.

To deep fry: Cut the celeriac into slices and parboil for 10 minutes. Drain and dry thoroughly. Coat in batter and fry as for Jerusalem artichokes.

To purée: Boil or steam the celeriac, drain, and then sieve, mash or process in an electric blender. Because it has a very strong flavour, celeriac purée is best mixed with an equal quantity of potato purée. Season with salt and pepper and add a good knob of butter and a little cream or top of the milk.

Celery

Celery is generally served braised as a side vegetable, but is also used extensively as a flavouring in soups, stews, and casseroles (for which the tough outer stalks can be used), as well as raw in salads, or with cheese. Celery is available all year round, although the best home-grown celery comes in November after the first frosts. Celery hearts (the tender inner part of the vegetable), are also available in cans.

To buy: Allow 1 small head per person if braising or half a head if boiling, steaming or frying. The celery should be crisp and white, without too many thick outer stalks.

To store: Celery can be kept for 2–3 days in a cool, dry vegetable rack but is best separated into stalks and stood in a jug of cold water to keep it crisp and fresh. Outer celery stalks, which you may wish to reserve for flavouring, can be kept for several days in a polythene bag in a refrigerator until they are required.

To prepare: Remove the outer stalks of the celery and put on one side to use as flavouring. Either separate the celery into stalks or leave the head whole. Wash or wipe the celery if required. Leave the stalks whole, or cut in half lengthways if very wide. Cut the whole head or the stalks crossways into halves or quarters.

To boil: Cut the celery stalks into 2cm pieces and cook in the minimum of boiling salted water for 15–20 minutes or until just tender. Drain, season with pepper, preferably freshly ground, and spoon over some melted butter or a white or cheese sauce.

To steam: Cut the celery stalks into 2cm pieces and season with salt. Cook in the top of a steamer over boiling water for 20–30 minutes until tender. Drain and serve as for boiled celery.

To deep fry: Cut the celery into 2cm pieces and parboil for 5 minutes. Drain thoroughly. Coat in batter and fry as for Jerusalem artichokes.

To braise: Trim the celery, but leave it whole. For 4 small heads of celery make a mirepoix (p269) and add enough stock to half-cover the vegetables. Bring to the boil and place the celery on top. Baste some of the stock over the celery. Cover the pan with a piece of greaseproof paper or foil and then with the lid. Cook over gentle heat for 1½ hours or until the celery is very tender, basting with the stock from time to time. Remove the celery from the pan with a perforated spoon and place in a serving dish. Drain the cooking liquor into a small pan and add 1 × 5ml spoon meat glaze (p55), if available. Boil the liquor rapidly until it is reduced to a thin glaze, and then pour it over the celery. The mirepoix can be served as a separate vegetable dish, sprinkled with chopped parsley.

Chicory

People sometimes confuse chicory with endive because its French name is *endive*. Chicory is, however, a clump of fleshy white leaves with yellow tips, widely used raw in salads. It is also served as a side vegetable and is available from September to May.

To buy: Allow 1 large or 2 small heads per person (75–100g approx). Buy chicory which looks fresh and has no withered stems. The ends should be yellow, not green; green ends tend to be very bitter.

To store: Chicory can be kept for 2–3 days in a cool, dry vegetable rack or larder, or for up to a week in a polythene bag in the bottom of a refrigerator.

To prepare: Cut a slice off the base and remove a few outer leaves. Wash thoroughly in cold water. To reduce the bitterness, first blanch the chicory for 5 minutes in boiling water, and then drain and cook as required. Do not leave chicory standing once it has been cut because it tends to discolour.

To boil: Blanch the chicory as above. Cook in a very little boiling salted water for

15–20 minutes or until just tender. Drain thoroughly and season with pepper. Spoon a little melted butter over it or serve with a white or cheese sauce.

To braise: Blanch the chicory as above. Cook as for braised celery.

Courgettes

Courgettes, or *zucchini* as they are also called, are small vegetable marrows, produced by using special strains of seed. They are available all year round, but are generally at their cheapest and best from June to September. Besides being served as a side vegetable, they are also excellent stuffed and served hot or cold as a main course or starter.

To buy: Allow 100–150g per person. Courgettes vary considerably in size from almost finger thickness and length, to 4–5cm in diameter and 25cm long. If they are too thick, however, the flavour will not be as good. The courgettes should be a good green colour, firm to the touch, and not limp.

To store: Courgettes can be kept for several days in a cool, dry vegetable rack or larder.

To prepare: Very small courgettes can be cooked whole. Simply trim off each end, and wash in cold water. Larger courgettes should be trimmed at either end and cut into 1–2cm slices; or they can be trimmed, and then sliced after cooking. To remove some of the excess liquid from slightly older courgettes, especially if frying, place them in a colander, sprinkle with salt, and leave for 30 minutes. Drain and dry thoroughly.

To boil: Cook the courgettes in the minimum of boiling salted water for about 10 minutes or until just tender. Drain thoroughly, season with pepper, and spoon melted butter and some chopped parsley, thyme or tarragon over them. Courgettes can also be served with a white, parsley, or cheese sauce or topped with crisply fried or grilled and roughly chopped or crumbled bacon.

To steam: Courgettes are generally best left whole for steaming. Season with salt and cook in the top of a steamer over a pan of boiling water for 10–20 minutes, depending on the size of the courgettes, until they are just tender. Drain and cut into slices, if large. Serve as for boiled courgettes.

To bake: Leave the courgettes whole and parboil for 5 minutes in boiling salted water. Drain thoroughly. For 500g courgettes, melt 50g butter in an ovenproof dish. Add the courgettes, roll in the butter and season with salt and pepper. Bake for 25 minutes in a fairly hot oven, 190°C, Gas 5.

To shallow fry: Cut the courgettes into slices. For 500g courgettes, melt 50g butter in a frying pan and fry a little chopped onion, if liked, until golden. Add the sliced courgettes and fry until golden-brown, turning frequently. Drain and serve topped with chopped tarragon, thyme or parsley.

To deep fry: Cut the courgettes into slices and parboil for 5 minutes. Drain and dry thoroughly. Coat in batter and fry as for Jerusalem artichokes.

To stew: Cut the courgettes into slices. For 500g courgettes, melt 50g butter in a pan, add the sliced courgettes, and season. Cover the pan and cook over gentle heat for 10–15 minutes, shaking the pan frequently to prevent the courgettes sticking to the bottom. Sprinkle with chopped herbs before serving in the cooking liquor.

Cucumber

Cucumbers are usually eaten raw in salads or pickled, but they are extremely useful as a side vegetable, and this is a particularly good way of using the outdoor or ridge cucumbers. Cucumbers should not be boiled because they contain a very high percentage of water; they should be either steamed or fried.

To buy: Allow 150–200g per person, or one-third of a large cucumber. Make sure the cucumbers are firm and the skin is not tough and wrinkled.

To store: Cucumbers keep for several days in a cool vegetable rack or larder or in a refrigerator.

To prepare: Hot-house cucumbers can be peeled or not, according to taste, but the skin contains much of the flavour and minute amounts of the substances which help the body to digest the cucumber flesh. Outdoor cucumbers generally have a rather tough skin, and these should be peeled. Slice the cucumber or leave whole.

To steam: Either cut the cucumber into slices 5cm thick or leave whole. Season and place in the top of a steamer over a pan of boiling water for 10 minutes, if sliced, or for up to 20 minutes, if whole. Drain thoroughly and cut into slices if the cucumber has been left whole. Season with pepper, preferably freshly ground, and serve topped with melted butter and chopped herbs (dill, tarragon, parsley, mint), with a plain white or cheese sauce with chopped tarragon, dill or celery seed added, or with Hollandaise sauce (p217).

To bake: Cut the cucumbers into 5cm pieces. Put in an ovenproof dish and cover. Dot the cucumber with butter and sprinkle with a few chopped herbs, if liked. Bake in a fairly hot oven, 190°C, Gas 5, for 30 minutes.

To fry: Cut the cucumbers into slices 2cm thick. Steam as above for 5 minutes, drain, and dry thoroughly. Dredge the cucumber slices lightly with flour and fry them in butter or margarine until golden-brown, turning frequently. Drain thoroughly, season with salt and pepper, and serve at once.

Endive

Endive, pronounced in the English way, should not be confused with chicory which is known in France as *endive*. Endive is a green vegetable, resembling a curly lettuce, which is generally used in winter salads. It is in season from November to March.

To buy: Allow 1 small or half a large endive per person. Choose endive with a good yellow heart and not too many discoloured, tough outer leaves.

To store: Endive is best stored for 2–3 days in a polythene bag in the bottom of a refrigerator.

To prepare: Cut off the stumps and discard any tough, discoloured outer leaves. The very centre of the endive can be removed and served as a salad. Wash the endive thoroughly in plenty of cold water to remove any dirt, grit, and sand. Because endive tends to be bitter, blanch it for 10 minutes in boiling water and drain thoroughly.

To braise: Blanch the endive as above. Cook as for braised celery.

Fennel

The bulbous Florence fennel can be used raw in salads or braised; it has a slight aniseed flavour. The part eaten is the swollen stem base, although the leaves can be used in soups and make an attractive feathery garnish for salads.

To buy: Allow 1 small bulb (about 150g) per person. Choose clean white fennel on which any leaf tips are still fresh and green.

To store: Fennel can be stored for 2–3 days in a cool, dry vegetable rack or larder or in the bottom of a refrigerator.

To prepare: Remove the coarse outer sheaths and trim the stalks.

To deep fry: Parboil the fennel for 10 minutes. Drain, dry thoroughly, and cut into slices. Dip the slices in batter and fry as for Jerusalem artichokes. Drain thoroughly and serve with lemon juice.

To braise: Parboil the fennel in boiling salted water for 5 minutes. Drain thoroughly and cook as for braised celery.

Kohlrabi

Kohlrabi, although a root, is really a swollen-stemmed cabbage. It has a flavour between that of a turnip and a swede, and is in season from July to April.

To buy: Allow 150g per person. Choose kohlrabi which is a good purple colour with a smooth skin. Avoid large kohlrabi because it has a coarse flavour, and reject any on which the skin is shrivelled or the leaves are withered.

To store: Kohlrabi does not store well and should be used as soon as possible after buying or picking.

To prepare: Kohlrabi can either be thinly peeled and sliced or diced before cooking, or it can simply be washed, trimmed, and cooked in the skin, which preserves the maximum flavour.

To boil: Cook in boiling salted water for 30 minutes–1 hour, depending on size. Drain and peel if cooked in the skin. Serve Kohlrabi either seasoned with pepper, preferably freshly ground, and with melted butter, or with a cream or Hollandaise sauce.

To steam: Season with salt and cook in the top of a steamer over a pan of boiling water for 45 minutes–1½ hours depending on size. Drain and serve as for boiled kohlrabi.

To braise: Parboil the kohlrabi for 5 minutes. Drain, peel, and cut into quarters. Cook as for braised celery.

Leeks

Leeks are in season from August to May and as well as being served as a vegetable are also used extensively to flavour soups and casseroles. They can also be served cooked and cold, or blanched and raw in salads.

To buy: Allow 150–200g leeks per person. Choose leeks that are of an even size with fresh-looking green tips and a firm white stem.

To store: Leeks can be kept for 2–3 days in a cool, dry vegetable rack or larder.

To prepare: Leeks need to be cleaned thoroughly because dirt and grit gets between the leaves. First, trim off the leaves, leaving only about 5cm of the green stem. Trim the roots and remove the outer leaves. Push the point of the knife through each leek about 5cm from the top and cut through to the top. Do this a second time, then peel back the leaves and wash the leeks thoroughly under running cold water to remove every speck of dirt. Leeks can also be cut into slices, in which case the vertical cuts are omitted; after slicing, wash thoroughly under running cold water.

To boil: Boiled leeks are apt to be watery so they must be drained thoroughly. Leave the leeks whole or cut into 2cm slices. Cook in the very minimum of boiling salted water for 10 minutes if sliced, or 20 minutes if whole. Drain thoroughly, turn into a serving dish, and season with pepper. Serve with melted butter or with a cheese or white sauce.

To steam: Leave the leeks whole or cut into slices. Season with salt and place in a steamer over a pan of boiling water for 15 minutes if sliced, or for 30 minutes if whole. Drain and serve as for boiled leeks.

To deep fry: Cut the leeks into 2cm slices. Parboil for 5 minutes. Drain and dry thoroughly. Coat in batter and fry as for Jerusalem artichokes.

To stew: Cut the leeks into slices. For every 750g leeks, melt 50g butter in a pan. Add the leeks and 1 × 15ml spoon lemon juice, salt, and pepper. Cover the pan and cook the leeks very gently, shaking the pan from time to time, for about 30 minutes or until the leeks are very tender. Serve in the cooking liquor. If liked, 3–4 chopped rashers of bacon can also be cooked with the leeks.

To braise: Leave the leeks whole. Parboil for 5 minutes. Drain and cook as for braised celery.

Baked Leek Casserole
4 helpings

8 large leeks	a few drops Worcestershire sauce
1 small onion	a few drops lemon juice
75g butter **or** margarine	a pinch of sugar
tomato juice	salt and pepper

Prepare the leeks and keep them whole. Skin the onion and chop it finely. Melt 50g of the fat and fry the leeks and onion until the leeks are just gilded and the onion is transparent. Transfer to an ovenproof casserole which will hold the leeks in 2 layers. Pour enough tomato juice into the casserole to half-cover the leeks. Stir in the Worcestershire sauce, lemon juice, and sugar. Season well. Dot with the rest of the fat. Cover the casserole securely, and bake in a fairly hot oven, 190°C, Gas 5, for 1 hour. Serve with the cooking liquor.

Note This recipe can also be used for small heads of celery.

Lentils

There are several kinds of lentils; the most common are pink or red; these form a purée as soon as they are cooked. If whole lentils are required, the green or brown variety must be used. The best (and most expensive) lentils are the black *lentilles de Puy* which come from the Auvergne in France.

Lentils are excellent served cold in salads.

To buy: Allow 50g lentils per person.

To prepare: Lentils do not need long soaking like peas and beans, but they can profitably be soaked for 1–2 hours before cooking.

To boil: Put the lentils into a pan and cover with cold water or stock. A small skinned onion, a few parsley stalks or a bouquet garni, a ham bone or a few bacon rinds can be added to give extra flavour. Bring the water to the boil and simmer gently for about 1 hour or until the lentils are quite tender. Drain and remove any herbs and flavouring. Re-season if required, and serve hot. If using the pink lentils, drain and purée them before serving.

Spiced Lentils
4–6 helpings

50g red lentils
1 litre water
1 × 2.5ml spoon sea salt **or** 1 × 5ml
  spoon table salt
1 onion
1 × 5ml spoon turmeric
1 × 5ml spoon crushed ginger root **or**
  ground ginger

3 tomatoes
2 whole cardamoms
3 × 15ml spoons cooking oil
1 × 5ml spoon crushed garlic
1 × 5ml spoon ground coriander
a pinch of chilli powder

Garnish
chopped fresh coriander leaves

finely chopped **or** grated onion

Put the lentils into a large pan and cover with the water and salt. Bring to the boil, reduce the heat, and simmer for 30–45 minutes until tender. Drain and put to one side.

Meanwhile, skin and chop the onion, and mix with the turmeric and ginger. Chop the tomatoes, and crush the cardamoms in a pestle and mortar, or grind in a coffee or nut mill. Heat the oil in a large, deep frying pan, add the onion, ginger, and turmeric, and fry gently until soft and lightly browned. Add the tomatoes and all the remaining ingredients, and fry for 3–4 minutes, stirring all the time. Remove from the heat.

Add the lentils to the mixture in the pan, and mix thoroughly to coat them with oil. Replace over moderate heat, and cook until well heated through and quite mushy. Serve very hot, sprinkled with the coriander leaves and onion.
Note Although hot and spicy, this dish is not as hot as a curry. It can be served as an accompaniment to any pasta, pulse or plainly cooked root vegetable dish, or with a green vegetable salad as a main-course dish.

Lettuce
Although generally used raw as a salad ingredient, lettuces can also be served as a cooked vegetable, provided they are well-hearted or have crisp outer leaves. Cos lettuce is particularly good.

To buy: Choose fresh, green lettuces and allow 1 small lettuce per person. Alternatively, use the outside leaves of 2 lettuces and reserve the hearts for salads.

To store: Lettuces can be kept for 1–2 days in a cool, dry vegetable rack or larder or in a polythene bag in a refrigerator.

To prepare: Remove the very outside leaves of the lettuce. Trim off the root and wash the lettuce well in plenty of cold water to remove all the dirt and sand.

To stew: For 4 lettuces, melt 50g butter or margarine in a wide pan. Add the lettuces and season with salt. Cover the pan and stew for about 30 minutes or until the lettuces are very tender. Season to taste with salt and pepper before serving.

To braise: Make each lettuce into a neat bundle by tying the loose leaf tops together with fine string. Blanch the bundles for 5 minutes in boiling salted water and drain thoroughly. Cook as for braised celery.

Mushrooms

Cultivated mushrooms are available throughout the year. There are three main types which are all grown from the same spore, the only difference being their age. The youngest mushrooms are the small round button ones in which the underneath of the mushroom touches the stalks; cup mushrooms are slightly larger and flatter but still have a lip on the underside; the larger, flat mushrooms are the oldest and have the strongest flavour. For pale sauces, it is always best to use button or cup mushrooms because the black underside of flat mushrooms will discolour a sauce.

As for wild mushrooms, field mushrooms are similar to cultivated mushrooms. They can be cooked in all the same ways and are particularly good grilled or stuffed.

Although the whole of any mushroom can be used, the stalks are sometimes removed for appearance's sake or for easier cooking (eg stuffed mushrooms) and are used separately for flavouring sauces and casseroles.

Button mushrooms are also available in cans and make a very useful standby. Button and cup mushrooms can be bought frozen.

To buy: Allow 50–75g per person. Mushrooms should look fresh and moist, and the tops should be creamy white.

To store: Mushrooms should be eaten on the day of purchase, but they can be kept for a day in the bottom of a refrigerator.

To prepare: Cultivated mushrooms should not be peeled. Simply wipe with a damp cloth, or wash if they are very dirty, and trim a slice off the stalk ends. Either leave the mushrooms whole or cut them into slices, halves or quarters, depending on their size and how you wish to serve them.

To boil: Mushrooms are not generally boiled because their flavour is better when fried, grilled or baked, but this is a good method for slimmers. Cook the mushrooms in the minimum of boiling salted water, with a good squeeze of lemon juice, for about 5 minutes. Drain thoroughly and serve seasoned with black pepper, preferably freshly ground, and sprinkled with chopped parsley or chives.

To bake: Place the mushrooms in a greased ovenproof dish and dot with butter or margarine. Season with salt and pepper and a little powdered mace, grated nutmeg or chopped lemon thyme. Cover, and bake in a fairly hot oven, 190°C, Gas 5, for 25–30 minutes. Serve the mushrooms either in the dish in which they were cooked, or transfer them to a serving dish together with all the juices.

To grill: Grilling is suitable for flat or large cup mushrooms. Remove the stalks; these can be put into the grill pan under the rack and will cook in the juices from the caps. Brush both surfaces of the mushrooms with oil or dot with butter or margarine; season with salt and pepper. Place the mushrooms on the rack of the grill pan and cook under a moderate grill for about 5 minutes or until the mushrooms are very tender, turning once, and basting with fat several times to prevent them drying out. Serve with the juices collected in the grill pan.

To fry: For every 100g mushrooms, heat 25g butter, margarine or lard, or 2 × 15ml spoons oil in a frying pan. Fry the mushrooms for about 5 minutes or until they are very tender. Season with salt and black pepper, preferably freshly ground. Serve together with the cooking liquid, and sprinkle with chopped parsley, chives or lemon thyme. A squeeze of lemon juice added to the pan will also improve the flavour.

To deep fry: Whole button mushrooms are excellent deep-fried. Using 125g mushrooms, coat in batter, and fry as for Jerusalem artichokes.

Onions

Onions are used mostly as a flavouring for sauces, soups, stews, casseroles, and stuffings, although they make an excellent vegetable dish and can be cooked in various ways. Small pickling onions, or button onions as they are also called, are available from July to October, while main-crop onions grown in the UK are in season from September to March. Imported onions are available during the summer, and Spanish onions are generally available throughout the year. These are large onions with a mild flavour which originally came from Spain, although they are now grown in many other parts of the world. Spring onions, which are a mild small onion used mainly in salads, are also available throughout the year, although they are much scarcer in winter.

To buy: When serving as a side vegetable, allow 1 large or 2 medium-sized onions (150–200g) per person. Choose onions which are firm with a smooth skin. They should not have wrinkled skins or be at all soft since this generally indicates that they are bad inside. Avoid buying onions which have already begun to sprout.

To store: Onions keep well for several months in a cool, dry vegetable rack or larder, especially in winter. If you have sufficient storage space, it can be quite economical to buy a sack of onions in the autumn, when they are generally cheaper, so that some are always to hand.

To prepare: For certain methods of cooking, onions are cooked in their skins, but they are generally skinned and either left whole, chopped, or cut into rings.

To chop an onion, first cut it in half lengthways. Lay the flat surface on a chopping board and make 3 or 4 horizontal cuts, stopping about 1cm from the root. Holding the root end, make about 6 cuts at right angles to the root, but stopping 1cm short, then cut the onion across into small pieces. To prevent onions making you cry while preparing them, either skin the onions under running cold water or skin them under water, and then place them in cold water straight away.

To boil: Skin the onions but leave them whole. If you do not like a very strong flavour, blanch the onions first by putting them into a pan of cold water. Bring to the boil, boil for 1 minute, and then drain. Cook the onions in the minimum of boiling salted water for 20–25 minutes for button onions, for 45–50 minutes for medium-sized onions, and for up to $1\frac{1}{4}$ hours for large onions. Drain the onions thoroughly and serve topped with melted butter or with a white sauce made from half milk and half stock from cooking the onions. Onions can also be boiled in their skins, which colours the cooking water pale pink and helps to preserve the nutritional value of the onion.

To bake (Method 1): Skin medium-sized or large onions, but leave them whole. Parboil in boiling salted water for 20 minutes. Drain thoroughly. Place in a shallow, greased ovenproof dish. Season with salt and pepper and dot with butter. Pour in enough milk to come half-way up the onions. Cover and bake in a moderate oven,

180°C, Gas 4, for 45 minutes–1 hour or until the onions are very tender. Serve with the cooking liquor, which can be thickened with a little cornflour or arrowroot, if liked.

To bake (Method 2): Top and tail medium-sized or large onions, but leave the skins on. Parboil, if very large, for 20 minutes; drain and dry thoroughly. Wrap each onion in a piece of well-buttered greaseproof paper and place in an ovenproof dish. Bake in a moderate oven, 180°C, Gas 4, for 1–1¼ hours. Peel the onions before serving with butter and grated nutmeg.

To bake (Method 3): Place unpeeled medium-sized to large onions on a baking tray and bake in a fairly hot oven, 200°C, Gas 6, for 1½ hours or until tender. Remove from the oven and carefully skin. Place in a serving dish and dot with butter, salt, pepper, and a little grated nutmeg, if liked.

To shallow fry: Skin the onions and cut into rings. For every 400g onions, melt 25g butter, margarine or lard, or heat 2 × 15ml spoons oil in a pan. Fry the onions gently for about 30 minutes, turning them frequently until they are golden-brown. Season well, drain, and serve hot. A little chopped thyme or sage or a few caraway seeds can also be fried with the onions.

To deep fry: Skin the onions, slice into rings, and separate. Dip the onion rings in a little milk and then toss in seasoned flour. Fry the onion rings in deep oil or fat (p10) until they are golden-brown and crisp. Drain on soft kitchen paper and serve hot. Onion rings can also be dipped in batter and fried as for Jerusalem artichokes.

To stew: Skin and blanch the onions as above. Put into a pan just large enough to hold them all upright. For 6 large onions, pour over 500ml brown stock (p25) and add a bouquet garni. Cover and simmer gently for 1½ hours. Re-season if required, and serve the onions with the cooking liquor.

To braise: Skin the onions but leave them whole. Parboil for 5 minutes. Drain thoroughly. Cook as for braised celery.

Parsnips

Parsnips are in season from September to April, but are generally better when there has been a slight frost on the ground. They are an extremely useful winter vegetable and are excellent roasted with potatoes around a joint, or puréed and served on their own.

To buy: Allow 150g parsnips per person. Choose parsnips that are firm to the touch; the skins should not appear shrivelled and wrinkled.

To store: Parsnips can be stored for several days in a cool larder or vegetable rack, but are better eaten as soon as possible after purchase.

To prepare: Peel and trim the parsnips and either cut into slices, or cut into quarters lengthways according to the method of cooking. Remove any hard core from the quarters.

To boil: Like carrots, parsnips should be cooked in the minimum of water to give the best flavour and to preserve all the vitamins. For 600g parsnips, melt 25g butter or margarine in a heavy-based pan. Add the thinly sliced parsnips and cook very gently for 10 minutes, shaking the pan frequently so that they do not stick to the bottom. Pour approximately 100ml boiling salted water over them, cover the pan, and cook the parsnips for a further 15–20 minutes or until they are very tender.

Serve with the cooking liquor and sprinkle liberally with chopped parsley or chopped lemon thyme.

To steam: Steam only young parsnips. Cut into quarters, season with salt, and steam in the top of a double saucepan over a pan of boiling water for 35 minutes or until very tender. Drain and season with black pepper, preferably freshly ground, spoon melted butter over them, and sprinkle with chopped parsley.

To roast: Cut the parsnips into quarters lengthways. Parboil in boiling salted water for 10 minutes. Drain and dry thoroughly. Heat a little dripping in a roasting tin. Add the parsnips and roll in the hot dripping or put into the dripping in a pan around a roast joint. Roast in a fairly hot oven, 190°–200°C, Gas 5–6, for 45 minutes–1 hour or until tender and golden-brown.

To deep fry (Method 1): Cut the parsnips into thin slices. Parboil for 10 minutes and drain thoroughly. Coat in batter and fry as for Jerusalem artichokes.

To deep fry (Method 2): Cut the parsnips into paper-thin slices. Dry thoroughly and fry in deep fat as for game chips (p10).

To purée: Parsnips make an excellent purée, either on their own or mixed with carrots or mashed potato. Boil or steam the parsnips as above and sieve, mash, or process in an electric blender together with the cooking liquor. Add 25g butter, season with salt and pepper, preferably freshly ground, and add a little cream or top of the milk, if wished. Sprinkle with plenty of chopped parsley before serving.

Peas

Fresh peas are in season from May to September, although imported peas can be found at other times and mange-tout peas are available most of the year. Peas freeze extremely well, and both frozen and canned peas are easily obtainable.

To buy: When buying fresh peas, allow 300–400g per person, depending on the fullness of the pods. It is not always easy to buy good, fresh peas because the majority of the best crops are bought straight from the fields by large food companies for freezing. The peas should be a good green colour and the pods should appear moist. The peas should be starting to fill the pod and, if eaten raw, should taste sweet and juicy. Do not buy peas which have been allowed to grow too large because they will be dry and unpleasant.

To store: Peas should be eaten as fresh as possible, but can be kept for 1–2 days in a cool vegetable rack or larder or in the bottom of a refrigerator.

To prepare: Shell the peas and, if preparing them in advance, cover with the washed pods to keep them moist. The pods can be kept to make soup.

To boil: The peas should be cooked in the minimum of boiling salted water. Bring a pan of salted water to the boil and add a sprig of mint or chervil and a pinch of sugar, if liked. Add the peas and cook gently for about 10 minutes or until the peas are just tender. Do not overcook peas because this toughens them. Drain thoroughly and turn into a serving dish. Season with black pepper, preferably freshly ground, and dot with butter. Serve as soon as possible after cooking.

To steam: Shell the peas and season with salt. Cook in the top of a steamer over a pan of boiling water for 15–20 minutes or until tender. Drain and serve as for boiled peas.

Mange-tout Peas

These flat pea pods are widely available throughout most of the year. The word literally means 'eat all' which is what you do; mange-tout can therefore be extremely economical because there is no wastage.

To buy: Allow 50–75g per person. Choose mange-tout that are a good green colour and appear bright and fresh.

To store: They should be eaten as fresh as possible, but can be kept for 1–2 days in the bottom of a refrigerator.

To prepare: Remove the tops and tails of the mange-tout and any strings from the sides of older pods.

To boil: Cook the mange-tout in the very minimum of boiling salted water for about 2–3 minutes or until just tender. Drain thoroughly, turn into a serving dish, and season with pepper, preferably freshly ground. Spoon plenty of melted butter over them and serve as soon as possible.

To steam: Season the mange-tout with salt and cook in the top of a steamer over a pan of boiling water for 5 minutes. Drain and serve as for boiled mange-tout.

To stew: For every 200g mange-tout, heat 50g butter in a pan. Add the pea pods, season with salt and pepper, and cover. Cook for about 5 minutes or until they are quite tender, shaking the pan frequently to prevent the peas sticking to the bottom. Serve with the juices from the pan.

Peas – *Dried*

With the popularity of deep freezing, dried green peas are not used as widely as they used to be, although they can be a useful standby. Like other pulses, such as lentils and dried beans, they have a high protein content. The following are the main types of dried peas.

Green peas: These are dried garden peas which are used mainly for soups and purées.

Green and yellow split peas: Green split peas are traditionally used for Pease Pudding (see opposite), but are also used in soups, stews, and purées.

Chick-peas or *garbanzos:* These are large round peas which are used extensively in Spanish, Greek, Middle Eastern, and American cooking.

To buy: Allow 40–50g per person.

To prepare: Soak the peas for 6–12 hours in cold water, preferably changing the water once during this time to prevent the peas fermenting.

To boil: Drain and cover with fresh cold water. Season with salt and add a chopped onion, a few parsley stalks or a bouquet garni if liked. A few bacon rinds or bacon trimmings can also be added to the cooking liquor for extra flavour. Bring the water to the boil and cook for about 2–2½ hours or until the peas are very tender.

To purée: Cook the peas as above and drain thoroughly, reserving the cooking liquor. Sieve the peas or process in an electric blender, then add enough of the cooking liquor to give a thick purée, or add a little cream or top of the milk. Season to taste. Pea purée is excellent served with grilled or fried sausages, bacon, or bacon and eggs. If liked, the pea purée can be served garnished with crisply fried or grilled bacon or bacon rinds, which have been roughly chopped or crumbled.

Pease Pudding
6 helpings

600g split peas	salt and pepper
1 small onion	50g butter **or** margarine
bouquet garni	2 eggs

Soak the peas overnight. Drain, put into a pan, and cover with fresh cold water. Skin the onion and add to the pan with the bouquet garni and seasoning. Cover and simmer the peas slowly for about 2–2½ hours or until they are tender. Drain thoroughly and sieve or process in an electric blender. Cut the fat into small pieces, beat the eggs until liquid, and add both to the pea purée with the seasoning. Beat well together. Place the mixture in a floured cloth and tie tightly. Simmer gently in boiling salted water for 1 hour. Remove from the pan, take out of the cloth, and serve very hot.

Serve with sausages or pickled pork.

Peppers
Large, sweet or bell peppers, often called pimentos, are used raw in salads and form an important part of such dishes as Ratatouille (p270). Red peppers are the sweetest, followed by yellow and then green. Red and green peppers are available all year round, but yellow ones are less easy to obtain. The very small chilli peppers, which are extremely hot, are used as a seasoning in curries and for other highly spiced dishes. As some varieties are much hotter than others, they should always be used with caution.

To buy: Choose peppers with smooth firm skins and a good bright colour.

To store: Peppers will keep for 2–3 days in a cool vegetable rack or larder or, preferably, in the bottom of a refrigerator.

To prepare: Whether the pepper is to be used raw or cooked, the membranes and seeds must first be removed. Cut a slice off the top of the pepper, and discard the membranes and seeds. If liked, the skins of the peppers can also be removed. Heat the pepper over an open flame on a fork or skewer or under a grill until the skin blackens and splits, then skin as for a tomato. To reduce the slight bitterness of green peppers, it is sometimes preferable to blanch them before use. Plunge into boiling water for 2–3 minutes. Drain, rinse in cold water, and drain again.

To fry: Slice the peppers into rings. For 400g peppers, heat 4 × 15ml spoons olive oil in a frying pan. Add the peppers and fry gently over low heat for 30 minutes or until they are very tender. Season to taste with salt and pepper and serve with the cooking liquor. A few coriander seeds can also be added with a little chopped fennel, thyme or marjoram. A crushed clove of garlic can also be added, if liked.

Potatoes
Potatoes are a staple food in the UK, and they are certainly the most versatile of all vegetables. Different varieties of potato vary considerably, some being more suitable for boiling and mashing, and others better for frying or roasting. Home-grown new potatoes are available from May to August, and imported Jersey and other continental potatoes can be found a little earlier than this. These are generally best

served boiled or steamed, although they can be sautéed or used for chips. Generally, the best potatoes to buy in the summer for chips or for roasting are Cyprus potatoes. Of the main-crop potatoes, King Edward, Redskin, Maris Piper, Pentland Hawk, and Pentland Ivory are some of the best varieties for boiling, mashing, and baking in their jackets, while Desirée and Majestic are better for roasting and frying.

To buy: Allow 150–200g per person for new potatoes and 200–250g per person for old potatoes because of the greater wastage. New potatoes should be bought as fresh as possible every few days. To test that they are fresh, make sure the skins rub off easily and the potatoes are damp to the touch. When buying main-crop potatoes from September onwards it is practical to buy in larger quantities, and, if suitable storage space is available, a large sack of potatoes can save a considerable amount of money, but the potatoes must be stored in a cool, dark place. Never buy potatoes which are green or which have been exposed to the light.

To prepare: New potatoes should, preferably, not be peeled because the maximum amount of flavour and vitamin C is found just under the skin and is lost when the potatoes are scraped or peeled. Simply wash thoroughly to remove all the dirt and mud. If the potatoes are scraped put into cold water immediately to prevent them browning. If the skin is not too thick on older potatoes, it can be left on for boiling or steaming and removed after cooking. Otherwise, older potatoes should be peeled using a small sharp knife or vegetable peeler. Small and medium-sized potatoes are generally left whole, and large potatoes are cut into halves or quarters.

To boil: Prepare the potatoes as above. Cook in the minimum of boiling salted water until just tender, about 15 minutes for small new potatoes or up to 30 minutes for larger old potatoes. Particularly when boiling larger old potatoes, do not allow the water to boil rapidly or the outsides will start to break up before the inside of the potatoes are cooked through. Drain the potatoes thoroughly, turn into a serving dish, and spoon plenty of melted butter over them. Sprinkle with chopped parsley or chives before serving.

To steam: Both new and old potatoes can be steamed, but this method is particularly good for small new potatoes. Prepare the potatoes as above, but do not peel them. Season with salt and cook in the top of a steamer over a pan of boiling water for 20 minutes for small new potatoes or up to 45 minutes to 1 hour for larger old potatoes. Peel, if liked, after cooking and serve as for boiled potatoes.

Mashed potatoes: Boil or steam old potatoes as above. Drain thoroughly and either mash with a potato masher, or sieve or beat with an electric hand mixer until smooth. To every 1kg potatoes (weight before cooking), beat in 25–50g butter or margarine, a little milk or single cream, and salt and pepper to taste. A little grated nutmeg can also be added, if liked. Turn into a serving dish and garnish with a sprig of parsley before serving.

For creamed potatoes, add more butter and cream to give a very smooth, creamy texture.

To bake: **Jacket potatoes** – Choose medium-sized to large old potatoes. Wash thoroughly, dry, and prick lightly with a fork. For a very crisp skin, brush the outside of the potatoes with oil and place on a baking tray. Bake in a fairly hot oven, 190°–200°C, Gas 5–6, for 1–1½ hours depending on the size of the potatoes. Test with a skewer to make sure the centre of the potato is cooked. Split the potatoes in half, or make a cross in the top and push with your fingers to open up the potato. Serve with plenty of butter and coarse salt, with soured cream and chopped chives or with cream cheese. Baked potatoes can also be stuffed in many ways. Baking is an excellent way of cooking potatoes if using an automatic oven.

To roast: (Method 1): Peel old potatoes and cut into even-sized pieces (halves or quarters). Parboil in boiling salted water for 5 minutes and drain thoroughly. Return the potatoes to the pan and stand over low heat for 1–2 minutes until the potatoes are quite dry. Heat a little lard or dripping in a roasting tin, add the potatoes, and turn in the fat so that they are evenly coated, or put the potatoes in the dripping around a joint of roast meat. Roast in a fairly hot to hot oven, 190°–220°C, Gas 5–7, for 40 minutes to 1 hour or until crisp and golden-brown. Baste the potatoes with some of the fat several times during cooking. The cooking time will vary according to the size of the potatoes and the oven temperature, which will depend on the type of joint being roasted. Parboiling helps to give a very crisp roast potato.

To roast (Method 2): Peel the potatoes and cut into even-sized pieces. Put into a roasting tin containing hot dripping or fat, coat evenly with fat, and roast as above for 1–1¼ hours depending on the size of the potatoes and the oven temperature.

To fry: 1) **Chips** – Peel old potatoes and cut into sticks about 1cm thick and 8cm long. *For small French fried potatoes*, cut into small sticks about 5mm thick and 5cm long. *For potato straws*, cut into matchsticks. Leave the potatoes in cold water to remove some of the excess starch before frying; then drain and dry thoroughly. Heat the oil or deep fat in a chip pan (p10), put a layer of chips in the bottom of the wire basket and lower into the pan. Fry until the chips are pale golden. Remove from the pan and drain on soft kitchen paper. Repeat this with the remaining chips. Just before serving, re-heat the oil, and fry all the chips, French fried potatoes or potato straws until they are very crisp and golden.

2) **Game chips** – Peel old potatoes and cut into very thin slices, using either a very sharp knife or a mandoline. Rinse in cold water to remove the excess starch, then dry thoroughly. Heat the deep fat or oil (p10) and fry the chips until crisp and golden. Drain well on soft kitchen paper and sprinkle with salt before serving. Serve with roast game or poultry. These chips can also be served cold and will keep for several days in an airtight tin.

3) **Potato puffs** – Peel old potatoes and cut into slices 5mm thick. Trim into neat ovals and drop into cold water. Drain and dry them. Heat the oil or deep fat in a pan (p10), put the potato slices into the bottom of the basket and cook until they begin to rise to the surface. Drain on soft kitchen paper. Just before serving, re-heat the fat (p10) and fry the potato slices until they are well puffed. Drain again, and sprinkle with salt.

4) **Potato ribbons** – Peel old potatoes and cut across into slices 1cm thick. Trim the edges so that the potatoes have a smooth edge; then, with a sharp knife or potato peeler, cut round and round, making long ribbons. Fry as for Game Chips above.

To sauté: Boil or steam old potatoes as above, until they are just tender. Drain thoroughly and cut into 8mm slices. Heat some lard or dripping in a frying pan and fry the potato slices on both sides until crisp and golden. Drain thoroughly and serve garnished with chopped parsley.

Pumpkin

Pumpkins, which belong to the same family as marrows, can be used for both sweet and savoury dishes. They are in season from July to November and are generally sold in wedges, so that you can buy as much of the pumpkin as you wish. Pumpkin purée is available in cans.

To store: A whole pumpkin will keep for a couple of weeks in a cool larder, but a cut piece of pumpkin is best used as soon as possible. It can, however, be wrapped in clingfilm and stored for 1–2 days in the bottom of a refrigerator.

To prepare: Remove the seeds from the pumpkin, peel off the skin, and, unless roasting, cut into pieces about 5cm square.

To boil: Although pumpkin can be boiled, it is really better steamed because of the very high water content. Boil in the very minimum of boiling salted water for 20–30 minutes or until tender. If cooking the pumpkin for sweet dishes, use less salt in the cooking water. Drain the pumpkin thoroughly, turn into a serving dish, and season very well with salt and freshly ground black pepper. Dot liberally with butter and serve as soon as possible.

To steam: Season the pumpkin with salt, unless using for a sweet dish. Cook in the top of a steamer over a pan of boiling water for 35–40 minutes or until it is very tender. Drain and serve as for boiled pumpkin.

To roast: Remove the seeds from the pumpkin, peel, and cut into wedges. Roll the pumpkin in the dripping round a joint of meat and roast in a fairly hot oven, 200°C, Gas 6, for 45 minutes–1 hour.

To fry: Parboil or steam the pumpkin for 10 minutes. Drain and dry thoroughly. Coat in batter and fry as for Jerusalem artichokes.

To purée: Boil or steam the pumpkin as above. Drain thoroughly, then mash or sieve and to every 1kg pumpkin (weight before cooking) beat in 25g butter or margarine and 2 × 15ml spoons cream or milk. If serving as a savoury purée, season to taste with salt and plenty of freshly ground black pepper and serve garnished with chopped parsley.

Salsify and Scorzonera

These roots, which are in season from October to May, have a delicate and unusual flavour. Salsify is a white root, resembling a long thin parsnip, whereas scorzonera has a black skin and is generally considered to have a superior flavour. The young leaves can be used in salads or they can be cooked as for spinach.

To buy: Allow 150g per person. Choose roots that are of a good size and are not shrivelled. Any leaves which have been left on the roots should appear fresh.

To store: Salsify and scorzonera can be kept in a cool vegetable rack or larder for 3–4 days.

To prepare: If possible, scorzonera should not be scraped before cooking because much of the flavour lies just below the skin. Simply scrub and cut into 5cm lengths. Drop the scorzonera quickly into acidulated water to prevent it browning. Salsify can be scraped before cooking and cut into 5cm lengths, but it must be put immediately into acidulated water.

To boil: Cook in the minimum of boiling salted water for about 30 minutes or until just tender. If liked, a little lemon juice can also be added to the cooking water to preserve the colour. Drain the salsify or scorzonera and serve, seasoned with a little pepper and with melted butter spooned over it and/or lemon juice and chopped herbs, such as parsley, dill or tarragon. Boiled salsify can also be served in a white or cream sauce.

To shallow fry: Prepare the salsify or scorzonera but do not scrape. Boil in the skins until just tender. Drain thoroughly, peel, and cut into slices 1cm thick. Heat some butter or margarine in a pan and fry the slices until golden-brown, turning several times. Season with salt and pepper and serve hot.

To deep fry: Parboil the salsify or scorzonera for 15 minutes. Drain and dry thoroughly, coat in batter and fry as for Jerusalem artichokes.

Sorrel

Sorrel is used as both a vegetable and a herb. There are several different varieties, of which wild sorrel, which has the smallest leaves, is the most bitter. Sorrel is generally served as a purée and it should be prepared, cooked, and puréed in exactly the same way as spinach. To counteract the acidity of the sorrel, a little sugar can be added while it is cooking. Sorrel is excellent served with eggs, veal or white fish.

Spinach

Spinach is in season almost throughout the year because there are both winter and summer varieties. It is an extremely valuable source of iron and is generally a particularly good vegetable to serve to invalids and convalescents. Spinach can also be eaten raw in salads. It freezes well and can be bought frozen as either leaf spinach or chopped spinach; it is also available in cans.

To buy: When cooked, spinach reduces considerably because of its very high water content, so allow 250–300g per person. Choose spinach that is a good green colour and appears fresh without any withered yellow leaves.

To store: Once picked, spinach does not keep well and should preferably be eaten on the day of purchase, but it can be kept for 1–2 days in a cool vegetable rack or larder or in the bottom of a refrigerator.

To prepare: Remove any thick stalks from the spinach. (These can be kept and cooked as a separate vegetable. Wash them and tie together in a bundle; then boil or steam as for seakale until they are tender. Drain and serve with melted butter.) Spinach must be washed thoroughly because it can be gritty; wash in at least 3 changes of cold water.

To boil (Method 1): For 1kg spinach, melt 25g butter or margarine in a pan, then add the wet spinach leaves to the pan. Season with salt and stir for a few minutes until all the leaves are limp. Cover and cook slowly for about 10 minutes or until the spinach is tender. Drain thoroughly, pressing out the water. Heat 2 × 15ml spoons cream in the pan, replace the spinach, and cook for a minute. Season to taste with salt, pepper, and nutmeg. A small, crushed clove of garlic added to spinach helps to remove some of the iron tang, and the cream can be omitted, if preferred.

To boil (Method 2): Cook the spinach in 1cm depth of boiling salted water, adding the leaves a few at a time so that the water does not leave the boil. Cover, and cook for a further 10 minutes or until tender. Drain thoroughly, pressing all the water out and serve as for boiled spinach (1).

To purée: Cook the spinach as on p263. Drain thoroughly and either chop finely, sieve or process in an electric blender. For every 1.5kg spinach, melt 25g butter or margarine in a pan with 3 × 15ml spoons cream. Stir in the chopped or sieved spinach and heat gently. Season to taste with salt, pepper and nutmeg. Alternatively, thicken 125ml of the spinach liquor with 1 × 10ml spoon cornflour, and add the sieved or chopped spinach to this panada; or add 125ml thick foundation white (p200) or Béchamel (p207) sauce to the chopped or sieved spinach. The spinach purée can be served garnished with fleurons of puff pastry (p51), sieved hard-boiled egg yolk or crescents of fried bread.

Swedes

Swedes are generally an inexpensive root vegetable, yet very good, especially when puréed. They have a similar flavour to turnips but are milder; they are in season from September to May.

To buy: Allow 200g per person. Choose swedes of a good size, but not too large: the smaller roots have a better flavour. The skin should be firm and not wrinkled.

To store: Like other root vegetables, swedes will keep for several weeks in a cool, dark place.

To prepare: Peel the swedes thickly and cut into pieces about 8cm square or into wedges.

To boil: Cook swedes in the minimum of boiling salted water for about 30 minutes or until quite tender. Drain thoroughly, return to the pan, and put over gentle heat for 1–2 minutes to dry them out. Turn into a serving dish and season with pepper, preferably freshly ground black pepper, and a little nutmeg if liked. Spoon melted butter over the swedes and garnish with chopped parsley.

To steam: Season with salt and cook in the top of a steamer over a pan of boiling water for about 40 minutes or until tender. Drain thoroughly and serve as for boiled swedes.

To purée: Swedes can be served on their own in a purée, or mixed with potatoes, turnips or carrots. Cook the swedes as above, then mash or sieve. To every 1kg swede (weight before cooking), beat in 25g butter or margarine, 1–2 × 15ml spoons cream, if liked, seasoning, and nutmeg.

Sweetcorn (Corn)

Hot, boiled corn on the cob makes an excellent starter, or can be served as a vegetable main dish. Home-grown corn is available from July to November, but imported corn can be bought at other times of the year. Frozen and canned corn is obtainable, both on the cob and as kernels.

To buy: Allow one cob per person or 100g kernels. Once corn has been picked, the sugar in the kernels converts to starch, making the vegetable tough rather than sweet and juicy; corn should therefore be eaten as soon as possible after picking. Choose only cobs on which the kernels are a pale yellow; if they are a bright yellow they are likely to be over-ripe and hard. When pressed, the kernels should exude a milky liquid. Check also that the kernels go right to the tip of the cob and do not finish half-way up.

To store: Corn should not be stored and should be cooked as quickly as possible.

To prepare: Peel off the green husks of corn and reserve some of them if boiling the cobs. Take off the silks (threads), and trim the base end. To remove the kernels from the cob, use a sharp knife, and cut off the kernels in long strips from the centre to one end, then from the centre to the other end. Any flesh and juice which remains on the cob can also be scraped off.

To boil: **1) Cobs** – Place some of the husks in the bottom of a pan. Lay the cobs on top, cover with boiling water, and cook for 5–8 minutes, or until a kernel can easily be removed from the cob. Salt should not be added to the water because this tends to toughen the corn. Drain the cobs and serve hot with salt, freshly ground black pepper, and plenty of melted butter.

2) Kernels – Corn kernels should be cooked in boiling unsalted water for 3–5 minutes or until just tender. Drain, and serve like the cobs or with a white or parsley sauce.

To steam: Place the cobs or kernels in the top of a steamer over a pan of boiling water and steam for 10–15 minutes for cobs, or 5–10 minutes for kernels.

To bake: Put the cobs into a roasting tin and just cover with milk. Bake in a fairly hot oven, 190°C, Gas 5, for 35 minutes or until a kernel can easily be removed from the cob. Drain the cobs, toss in melted butter, and place under a hot grill for 2–3 minutes before serving, seasoned with salt and pepper.

To roast: For 6 cobs, melt 50g butter in a roasting tin. Roll the cobs in this so that they are lightly coated with butter. Roast in a fairly hot oven, 190°C, Gas 5, for about 20 minutes, turning them frequently, until a kernel can easily be removed from the cob. Season with salt and pepper and serve with the butter in which they have been cooked.

Tomatoes

Tomatoes are available throughout the year, although home-grown ones are in season only from March to November. In addition to the standard round tomatoes, large Mediterranean tomatoes and small Italian plum tomatoes can be bought, both of which have an excellent flavour.

To buy: When serving as a side vegetable allow 100g, ie 1 large or 2 medium-sized tomatoes, per person. For baking and stuffing, choose tomatoes of an even size and make sure that the skins are not cracked.

To store: Tomatoes keep well for several days in a cool, dry vegetable rack or larder.

To prepare: The preparation of tomatoes depends largely on the method of cooking. To skin tomatoes, either hold each tomato on a fork over a gas flame or under a grill until the skin blackens and splits, then skin; or place the tomatoes in a basin, cover with boiling water, leave for 1 minute, and then drain and skin.

To bake: Halve the tomatoes. Brush with oil or dot with butter or margarine and season with salt and pepper. If liked, the tomatoes can be sprinkled with a little finely chopped tarragon or basil. Place in a greased ovenproof dish, cover, and bake in a moderate oven, 180°C, Gas 4, for about 20 minutes or until soft.

To grill: Halve the tomatoes, or if very small, leave whole and mark a cross in the bottom with a sharp knife. Dot with a little butter or margarine or brush with oil and season with salt and pepper. Cook under a fairly hot grill, turning once. Serve hot.

To fry: Halve the tomatoes, season with salt and pepper, and fry in hot fat for about 5 minutes, turning once. Remove from the fat with a fish slice and serve hot.

Tomato and Onion Pie

4 helpings

400g onions, preferably Spanish
50g butter
800g tomatoes
50g Cheddar cheese

fat for greasing
salt and pepper
50g soft white breadcrumbs

Skin the onions, put into a bowl, and cover with boiling water. Leave for 5 minutes, drain, dry thoroughly, and cut into slices. Melt half the butter in a pan and fry the onions until golden-brown. Skin and slice the tomatoes, and grate the cheese. Place the onions and tomatoes in alternate layers in a greased pie dish, sprinkle each layer lightly with salt and pepper and liberally with cheese and some of the breadcrumbs. Cover the whole with a layer of breadcrumbs and dot with the remaining butter. Bake in a fairly hot oven, 190°C, Gas 5, for 45 minutes.

Turnips

There are two varieties of turnip: the young summer or early turnip and the main-crop turnip. The former has a milder flavour than the main-crop vegetable. Early turnips are in season from April to July while main-crop turnips are found from August to March.

To buy: Allow 200g turnips per person. Early turnips should be a good white colour, with a hint of green and purple, and any remaining stalks should appear fresh. Older turnips should have a smooth, unwrinkled skin and be hard; do not buy turnips which appear spongy.

To store: Early turnips should be eaten as soon as possible after purchase, although they will keep for 1–2 days in a cool vegetable rack or larder. Main-crop turnips keep well for several weeks in a cool, dark place.

To prepare: Both early and main-crop turnips should be peeled thickly. Early turnips can be left whole or cut into halves or quarters; main-crop turnips should be cut into quarters or chunks about 8cm square.

To boil (Method 1): Cook the turnips in the minimum of boiling salted water for 20–30 minutes, depending on the size and age of the turnip. Drain thoroughly, turn into a serving dish, and season with pepper, preferably freshly ground, and spoon melted butter over them. Serve garnished with parsley or chopped chives. Turnips, particularly early turnips are excellent served in a cream or Béchamel sauce.

To boil (Method 2 – conservation method): For 800g turnips, heat 25g butter or margarine in a heavy-based pan. Add the turnips and cook very gently for 10 minutes, shaking the pan frequently so that the turnips do not stick to the bottom. Pour approximately 100ml boiling salted water over them, cover the pan, and cook the turnips gently for a further 15–20 minutes depending on their age. Serve the turnips with the cooking liquor and garnish with chopped parsley before serving, or serve in a sauce as in method (1). Stir 1 × 15ml spoon cream into the cooking liquor before serving.

To steam: Season the turnips with salt, and cook in the top of a steamer over a pan of boiling water for 30–40 minutes, depending on the size and age of the turnips. Drain and serve as for boiled turnips.

To purée: Boil or steam the turnips as above and drain if boiling by method (1) or steaming. If cooking by the conservation method, retain the cooking liquor. Mash or sieve the turnips and to every 1kg turnips (weight before cooking) add 25g butter or margarine, 1–2 × 15ml spoons cream or top of the milk, and seasoning.

Turnip Greens

These, when young, are a most pleasant green vegetable, very rich in vitamin C. Turnip greens should be used as soon as they are picked. The stalks should be removed and the leaves shredded and cooked as for cabbage.

Vegetable Marrow

Together with pumpkins and courgettes, vegetable marrow forms part of the *gourd* family, known in the USA as *squash*. Other varieties are sometimes available in the UK markets; they can also be grown in gardens. They include *acorn squash* which is pale coloured and a similar, though smaller shape to marrow; *crookneck squash* which is yellow and the shape of an elongated pear; *custard marrow* which has deep ribbing and is the size of a small football; and *hubbard squash* which has a rough green skin and is melon shaped. They are all cooked in the same way as marrow, the length of cooking time depending on size.

Marrows have a very high water content and are best suited to steaming or stewing. They are in season from July to October. The biggest marrow may win the local horticultural show, but the flavour of smaller marrows is far superior.

To buy: Choose marrows not more than 30cm long. This serves 3–4 people.

To store: Marrows keep well for 1–2 weeks in a cool, dry vegetable rack or larder.

To prepare: For baking and stuffing, the marrow is often halved and the skin left on, but for steaming, stewing, and baking, cut the marrow into rings, peel thickly, and remove the seeds. Cut into halves or leave as rings.

To boil: Cook in the very minimum of boiling salted water for about 10 minutes or until just tender. Drain thoroughly. A slice of slightly stale bread put in the base of the serving dish will help to absorb excess water. Turn the marrow into a serving dish, season with pepper, preferably freshly ground, and spoon plenty of melted butter over it, or serve with a white or cheese sauce.

To steam: Season the marrow with salt and cook in the top of a steamer over a pan of boiling water for about 20 minutes, depending on the size of the marrow pieces. Serve as for boiled marrow.

To bake: Cut the marrow into rings. Place in a greased ovenproof dish, season with salt and pepper, and dot with 25g butter or margarine. Cover and bake in a fairly hot oven, 190°C, Gas 5, for 45 minutes. Serve with the cooking liquor.

To stew: Melt 25g butter or margarine in a pan. Add the pieces of marrow, and season with salt and pepper and a little chopped thyme and lemon juice, if wished. Coat the pieces of marrow with the fat, cover with a lid, and cook over gentle heat for about 30 minutes, shaking the pan from time to time. Serve the marrow together with the juices in the pan, or add these to a white or cheese sauce.

To purée: Marrow can also be served as a purée. Steam as above. Drain thoroughly, and mash; then beat in 25g butter or margarine, 1 × 15ml spoon beaten egg, and 1 × 15ml spoon cream (if liked). Season with salt, pepper, and nutmeg.

Mixed Vegetable Dishes and Salads

Bubble and Squeak

dripping **or** lard

thin slices of cold roast **or** braised **or**
  boiled meat as available

1 medium-sized onion

cold mashed potatoes as available

cold, cooked green vegetables of any
  kind, as available

salt and pepper

a dash of vinegar (optional)

Heat just enough dripping or lard in a frying pan to cover the bottom. Put in the meat, and fry quickly on both sides until lightly browned. Remove, and keep hot. Skin the onion, slice it thinly, and fry until lightly browned, adding a little more fat to the frying pan if necessary. Mix together the potatoes and green vegetables, season to taste, and add to the frying pan. Stir until thoroughly hot, then add a little vinegar, if liked. Allow to become slightly crusty on the bottom. Turn out on to a warmed dish. Place the meat on top and serve.

Note The name Bubble and Squeak is often given to a dish of re-heated vegetables without meat.

Mixed Vegetables

6 helpings

750g mixed vegetables:
  parsnips, turnips, carrots, leeks,
  cauliflower **or** broad beans, peas,
  spring onions, tomatoes, new
  carrots, new turnips

25g butter **or** margarine

100–150ml boiling water

salt and pepper

Garnish

1 × 15ml spoon chopped parsley

Prepare the vegetables; then thinly slice the parsnips, turnips, carrots, and leeks, if used, splitting the slices into halves or quarters if large. Break the cauliflower into florets. Leave most of the other vegetables whole, cutting the larger carrots into thick slices, trimming the spring onions rather short, and cutting the tomatoes into wedges. Melt the fat in a heavy-based saucepan. Add the vegetables at intervals, starting with those which take the longest time to cook. Put the lid on the pan after each addition and toss the vegetables in the fat. (Do not add the tomatoes until 5 minutes before serving.) Add the boiling water and salt; use very little water with the beans and new carrots, etc. Simmer gently until the vegetables are tender. Season with pepper and serve hot, garnished with the parsley.

Note These cooked vegetables can also be used to make a salad. Leave to cool and serve either tossed in French dressing or in mayonnaise.

Cooking time

Parsnips, etc 30–35 minutes

Broad beans, etc 20–25 minutes

VARIATIONS
Mixed Vegetables with Cheese
Cook the vegetables as above and drain off any cooking liquor. Make up 375ml cheese sauce (p201), using the cooking liquor. Coat the vegetables with the sauce in a heatproof dish and sprinkle with 1 × 15ml spoon grated Cheddar cheese. Put under a hot grill to brown or into a hot oven, 220°C, Gas 7, for 10 minutes or until golden-brown.

Note This mixture can also be used to stuff peppers or marrows for a vegetarian main course.

Curried Mixed Vegetables
Cook the vegetables as above and drain off any cooking liquor. Make up 375ml Fruit Curry sauce (p218), using the cooking liquor, and simmer the sauce for at least 2 hours. Add the cooked vegetables and re-heat gently.

Serve with boiled rice and the usual curry accompaniments.

Mirepoix of Vegetables
A mirepoix is used in the base of a pan when braising meat and vegetables to give flavour. It is generally discarded after cooking, although it can be kept and served as a vegetable, or puréed and used as a base for a soup. The ingredients can be varied according to the time of year and whatever is being braised. The proportions below give a well-flavoured mirepoix. Keeping these proportions, use larger or smaller quantities of the ingredients as the individual recipes require.

2 medium-sized onions (250g approx)	25g fat bacon
1 carrot (50g approx)	15g dripping
$\frac{1}{2}$ turnip (50g approx)	

Skin and chop the onions, carrot, and turnip. Chop the bacon. Melt the dripping in a pan, add the vegetables and bacon, cover, and fry gently for 10 minutes. Use as required.

Nut Mince
6 helpings

200g shelled nuts	1 × 15ml spoon mushroom ketchup **or**
1 medium-sized onion	any similar sauce
25g margarine	375ml (approx) vegetable stock
150g dried breadcrumbs	salt and pepper

Pass the nuts through a nut mill, process them in an electric blender, or chop very finely. Skin and grate the onion. Melt the margarine in a frying pan and fry the nuts, onion, and breadcrumbs until pale golden. Stir in the ketchup and stock, adding a little extra stock if the mixture is too dry. Season to taste and simmer gently for 20–30 minutes. Serve hot.

Ratatouille
4 helpings

250g onions (approx)
1 clove of garlic
100g green pepper (approx)
200g aubergine (approx)
200g courgettes

400g tomatoes
4 × 15ml spoons olive oil
salt and pepper
1 × 2.5ml spoon coriander seeds

Garnish
1 × 15ml spoon chopped parsley

Skin the onions and slice in rings. Skin and crush the garlic. Remove the membranes and seeds from the pepper and cut the flesh into thin strips. Cut the unpeeled aubergine and courgettes into 1cm slices. Skin and chop the tomatoes roughly.

Heat 2 × 15ml spoons of the oil in a pan and gently fry the onions, garlic, and pepper for about 10 minutes. Add the remaining oil, and aubergine, and the courgettes. Cover and simmer gently for 30 minutes, stirring occasionally to prevent the vegetables from sticking to the bottom. Add the tomatoes, seasoning and coriander seeds, and simmer for a further 15 minutes. Serve hot or cold, garnished with the parsley.

Green Salads
The simplest and most usual salad is a tossed green salad, but even this must be carefully prepared. The salad consists of green leaves of one type, or a mixture such as lettuce, watercress, chicory, and endive. The leaves must be fresh and crisp, and they must be dried thoroughly or the salad will be watery and tasteless. The vegetables should be tossed in a French dressing or vinaigrette sauce just before serving with chopped herbs, such as parsley, chervil, chives, savory, and marjoram, if liked. If you like garlic, a small crushed clove can be added to the dressing; or a *châpon* of bread can be put in the salad bowl, as is often done in France. To make a *châpon*, rub a crust of French or ordinary white bread all over with crushed garlic. Place the crust in the bottom of the salad bowl with the salad vegetables on top. Pour the dressing over it and toss the bread with the salad, so that the flavour of the garlic gently permeates the whole dish. Although the bread is only meant as a flavouring, garlic addicts will enjoy eating it afterwards!

Cooked Vegetable Salads
Not only raw vegetables are used in salads, although nutritionally this is the best way to eat them so that their full vitamin and mineral content is retained. Cooked vegetables of all kinds are also excellent served in a French dressing or in mayonnaise with other herbs and seasonings added. Ideally, most vegetables should be cooked especially for the salad and tossed in the dressing while they are still warm, but very good salads can be made from cooked, leftover vegetables, particularly root vegetables.

Salads with Pulses, Pasta, and Rice

Dried pulses – peas, beans, lentils etc, make appetising salads, especially in winter when good fresh vegetables are scarce. They should be tossed in their dressing while still warm, and left to cool and marinate for at least 2–3 hours. For maximum flavour, they can be cooked in stock rather than water; fresh herbs can be added with the dressing.

For more filling and economical salads, pasta and rice provide a good basis, to which can be added a wide variety of fruits and vegetables such as peppers, celery, chicory, carrots, cooked peas, apples, oranges, dried fruit, and nuts. While good for family meals, these salads are particularly useful for buffet parties, since they are easy to prepare in large quantities and are easy to eat with a fork.

Salads with Fruit

Adding fruit to mixed salads, or using it as a salad on its own, is an American custom which is now extremely popular in the UK. Fresh fruit is preferable, but frozen or canned can be used if it is not too sweet. Fruits which discolour quickly, such as apples, pears, bananas and peaches, must be quickly dipped in lemon juice or in the dressing in which they will be served – usually mayonnaise or French dressing, to preserve their colour. Apples can be peeled, but the bright green or red skins often give an attractive colour and texture contrast to other ingredients in the salad. Citrus fruit, such as oranges and grapefruit, should be stripped of every scrap of white pith; they are then generally cut into segments or slices and the thin skin between the segments is removed. Dried fruit, such as apricots, raisins and sultanas, and nuts (usually walnuts, hazelnuts and almonds) can also be added to rice and pasta salads, coleslaw, and other mixed vegetable salads.

PASTA AND RICE

Cooking Pasta

All pasta can be cooked simply in fast-boiling, well-salted water. However, for some dishes such as lasagne, the pasta is removed after a few minutes only, when it will have just softened, and the dish is finished in the oven (*pasta al forno*).

Basic method

1) Provide 50–75g pasta (uncooked weight) per person for a first-course dish, 75–100g for a main dish.
2) Use 1 litre water and 1 × 5ml spoon table salt or 1 × 2.5ml spoon household salt per 100g pasta. The addition of 2 × 15ml spoons of oil to the cooking water will help prevent the pasta sticking together.
3) Bring the water, salt, and oil, if used, to a fast boil. Break long pasta into 15–25cm lengths. Put them into the water and push them gently below the surface as they soften. Drop round pasta shapes into the water a few at a time, and stir once. Slide large pasta such as sheets of lasagne into the water individually to prevent them sticking together. Drop bundled (folded) pasta into the water, leave for 2 minutes, then stir with a fork to separate the strands. Do not allow the water to go off the boil.

4) Cook for the appropriate time (see table below), stirring once or twice with a fork to prevent the pasta sticking to the bottom of the pan. The pasta, when cooked, should have no floury taste, but should be *al dente*, firm to the bite, apart from dishes which are also to be baked in the oven.
5) Drain into a colander; then return to the dry pan, off the heat, if making a sauce. If the pasta must wait more than 4 minutes, place it on a damp cloth in a strainer or sieve, over simmering water.

Cooking Times for Pasta

The cooking time for dried pasta depends partly on the size of the shapes and partly on the flour used. Manufacturers usually state the cooking times for their pasta on each packet, and their directions should be followed. If none are given, use the following general guide:

String or tubular and flat ribbons, eg

cappellini, vermicelli, spaghettini	5 minutes
spaghetti, tagliatelle	7–12 minutes
macaroni	12–20 minutes

Fancy shapes and short lengths, eg

shells, bows, cocks-combs	8–10 minutes

Ridged, large, eg

cannelloni, rigatoni	16–20 minutes

Stuffed

ravioli	15–20 minutes

Soup

alphabets, stars, small wheels, small rings, small shells	4–8 minutes

Cooking Rice

Everybody has their own way of cooking rice, especially boiled rice. But the differences are slight, and generally the results are the same if the preparation and cooking are done correctly.

Before cooking, wash the rice well under running cold water in a sieve or colander. This removes the loose surface starch which prevents rice drying out into separate grains when cooked. Remove also any dark or discoloured grains.

Do not overcook the rice. Something between 12–20 minutes is a basic guide, depending on the type of rice used. Test it after 10 minutes; it should be tender to the touch but still have a slight 'bite' for savoury dishes. Toss lightly with a fork before serving.

As rice almost trebles its bulk when boiled, 25–50g of dry rice is usually enough for one average helping.

Boiled Rice (white) *Basic recipe*

3–4 helpings

METHOD 1

Put 125g long-grain rice into a saucepan, pour in 375ml cold water and add 1 × 5ml spoon salt. Bring to the boil, stir once with a fork, reduce the heat, cover with a lid, and simmer for 12–15 minutes by which time the liquid should all be absorbed.

METHOD 2

Put 3 litres of water into a large saucepan, add 1 × 5ml spoon salt and bring to the boil. Sprinkle in 125g long-grain rice and stir two or three times with a fork until the water is at boiling point again. Reduce the heat so that the water is just boiling and cook for 15–18 minutes. Test for readiness after 10 minutes. Drain thoroughly before use.

Note The juice of half a lemon, added to the water, will help to keep the rice white.

Boiled Rice (brown) *Basic recipe*

4 helpings

Put 275g brown rice into a large saucepan, pour in 400ml water, and add 1 × 2.5ml spoon salt. Bring slowly to the boil. Reduce the heat, cover with a lid, and simmer gently for about 20 minutes. Do not stir. If the pan is dry, add a little more water. After 30 minutes, add a few drops more water if the rice is not yet cooked. When ready, the liquid should all be absorbed and the rice should just be beginning to stick to the bottom. Remove from the heat and let it stand, covered, for 10–15 minutes before use.

Note Brown rice keeps well for 4–5 days in a refrigerator, so it is worth cooking a fairly large quantity at one time.

PUDDINGS, DESSERTS AND ICES

HOT PUDDINGS AND DESSERTS

Milk and Custard Puddings

Large Grain Milk Puddings (eg whole or flaked rice, sago, flaked tapioca)
4–5 helpings

butter for greasing
100g grain
1 litre milk
a pinch of salt

50–75g caster sugar
15g butter (optional)
$\frac{1}{2} \times 2.5$ml spoon grated nutmeg **or**
 similar flavouring (see **Note**)

Butter a 1.75 litre pie dish. Wash the grain in cold water, and put it into the dish with the milk. Leave to stand for 30 minutes. Add the salt and sugar, and sprinkle with flakes of butter and nutmeg, if used. Bake in a cool oven at 150°C, Gas 2, for $2-2\frac{1}{2}$ hours or until the pudding is thick and creamy, and brown on the top. The pudding is better if it cooks even more slowly, for 4–5 hours.
Note If using a flavouring essence, mix it into the milk before cooking. If using dried or canned milk, reduce the grain to 75g, use the quantity of milk product to make up 1 litre, and cook at 140°C, Gas 1, for at least $3\frac{1}{2}-4$ hours.

Large Grain Milk Puddings with Eggs
6 helpings

100g grain
1 litre milk
2–3 eggs
a pinch of salt

50–75g caster sugar
flavouring (eg grated lemon rind or
 ground cinnamon)
butter for greasing

Wash the grain in cold water and put it into the top of a double boiler with the milk. Cook slowly for about 1 hour, or until the grain is tender. Remove from the heat and leave to cool slightly. Separate the eggs. Stir the egg yolks, salt, sugar and flavouring into the grain. Whisk the egg whites to the same consistency as the pudding, and fold into the mixture. Pour into a buttered 1.75 litre pie dish and bake in a warm oven at 160°C, Gas 3, for 40–45 minutes until the top is brown.

Medium and Small Grain Milk Puddings (eg coarsely ground rice, semolina or oatmeal, small sago, cornmeal)
6 helpings

1 litre milk	a pinch of salt
flavouring (eg grated lemon rind or ground cinnamon)	50–75g caster sugar
75g grain	butter for greasing (optional)

Warm the milk. Infuse any solid flavouring, if used, in the milk for about 10 minutes; then remove. Sprinkle the grain into the milk, stirring quickly to prevent lumps forming. Bring to simmering point, stirring all the time. Continue stirring, and simmer for 15–20 minutes or until the grain is transparent and cooked through. Add the salt, sugar, and any flavouring essence used.

The pudding can then be served as it is, hot or cold; alternatively, it can be poured into a well-buttered 1.75 litre pie dish, and baked in a moderate oven at 180°C, Gas 4, for 20–30 minutes until the top has browned.

Serve with stewed fruit, or with warmed jam or marmalade.

VARIATION
Medium and Small Grain Milk Puddings with Eggs
Cook the grain as above, but add the salt with the grain. Leave to cool slightly. Separate 2–3 eggs. Stir the yolks, 50–75g sugar, and any flavouring essence into the grain. Whisk the egg whites to the same consistency as the pudding, and fold into the mixture. Pour the mixture into a well-buttered 1.75 litre pie dish, and bake in a warm oven at 160°C, Gas 3, for 30–40 minutes until the top has browned.

Serve with stewed fruit, or with warmed jam or marmalade.

Powdered Grain Puddings (eg arrowroot, cornflour, custard powder, finely ground rice, fine oatmeal)
6 helpings

1 litre milk	a pinch of salt
flavouring (eg grated lemon rind or ground cinnamon)	50–75g caster sugar
65g grain	butter for greasing (optional)

Warm the milk. Infuse any solid flavouring, if used, in the milk for 30 minutes; then remove. Blend the grain with a little of the milk. Bring the rest of the milk to boiling point with the salt, and pour on to the blended paste, stirring briskly to prevent lumps forming. Return the mixture to the saucepan, heat until it thickens, and simmer for 2–3 minutes to cook the grain completely, stirring all the time. Add the sugar and any flavouring used.

The pudding can then be served as it is, hot or cold, or poured into a well-buttered 1.75 litre pie dish, and baked for 20–30 minutes in a moderate oven at 180°C, Gas 4, until the top has browned.

Serve with stewed fruit, or with warmed jam or marmalade.

For **variation**, see over.

VARIATION
Powdered Grain Puddings with Eggs
Cook the grain as in the main recipe, but do not add the flavouring or the salt. Leave to cool slightly. Separate 2–4 eggs. Stir the egg yolks, salt, sugar, and any flavourings into the grain. Whisk the egg whites to the same consistency as the pudding, and fold into the mixture. Pour into a well-buttered 1.75 litre pie dish, and bake in a warm oven at 160°C, Gas 3, for about 30 minutes until the top has browned. Sprinkle with brown sugar and/or butter flakes before baking, if liked.

Serve with stewed fruit, or with warmed jam or marmalade.

Cup or 'Boiled' Custard (Coating custard)
4 helpings or 500ml (approx)

500ml milk
4 eggs **or** 3 eggs and 2 yolks

25g caster sugar
flavouring (see below)

Warm the milk to approximately 65°C. Mix the eggs and sugar together well, and stir in the milk. Strain the custard into a saucepan or into a heatproof bowl placed over a pan of simmering water. Alternatively, use a double boiler, but make sure the water does not touch the upper pan. Cook over very gentle heat for 15–25 minutes, stirring all the time with a wooden spoon, until the custard thickens to the consistency of single cream. Stir well round the sides as well as the base of the pan or basin to prevent lumps forming, especially if using a double boiler. Do *not* let the custard boil. If it shows the slightest sign of curdling, put the pan or bowl into a bowl of cold water, or turn the custard into a clean basin and whisk rapidly.

As soon as the custard thickens, pour it into a jug to stop further cooking. Keep it warm by standing the jug in a basin of hot water. If it is to be served cold, pour into a basin and cover with a piece of dampened greaseproof paper to prevent a skin forming. When cold, pour into a serving dish.

Note A mixture of whole eggs and yolks gives a richer, smoother custard.

Flavourings
Vanilla: Add a few drops of vanilla essence with the sugar.

Lemon: Infuse strips of lemon rind in the warm milk for 30 minutes, then remove before adding the milk to the eggs.

Bay: Infuse a piece of bay leaf in the warm milk for 30 minutes, then remove before adding to the eggs.

Nutmeg or cinnamon: Sprinkle the top of the cooked custard with grated nutmeg or ground cinnamon.

VARIATIONS
Pouring Custard
Make as above but use only 3 eggs or 2 eggs and 2 yolks. The custard will thicken only to the consistency of thin single cream or top of the milk.

Rich Custard
Stir 2 × 15ml spoons double cream into the custard when it is cooling.

Simple Custard
4 helpings or 500ml (approx)

1 × 10ml spoon cornflour
500ml milk
25g caster sugar

2 eggs
flavouring (p276)

This custard will not curdle as easily as a cup custard but still keeps the delicious creamy flavour of an egg custard.

Blend the cornflour to a smooth paste with a little of the cold milk. Heat the rest of the milk and when hot, pour it on to the blended cornflour, stirring well. Return to the saucepan, bring to the boil and boil for 1–2 minutes, stirring all the time, to cook the cornflour. Remove from the heat and add the sugar. Leave to cool. Beat the eggs together lightly. Add a little of the cooked cornflour mixture, stir well, then pour into the saucepan. Heat gently for a few minutes until the egg has thickened, stirring all the time. Do not boil.

Serve hot or cold as an accompaniment to a pudding or pie.

Baked Custard
4 helpings or 500ml (approx)

500ml milk
2 eggs (for a softly set custard) **or**
   3 eggs (for a firmer custard)
25g caster sugar

fat for greasing
grated nutmeg **or** other flavouring
   (see **Note**)

Warm the milk to approximately 65°C. Mix the eggs and sugar together and stir in the milk. Strain the custard into a greased 700ml ovenproof dish. Sprinkle nutmeg on top, if used. Stand the dish in a tin containing enough hot water to come half-way up the sides of the dish, and bake in a very cool oven at 140°–150°C, Gas 1–2, for 1 hour or until the custard is set in the centre.

Note If preferred, the nutmeg can be omitted and the custard flavoured by infusing a bay leaf or thinly cut strips of lemon rind in the milk for a few minutes; they must, however, be removed before adding the milk to the eggs.

Steamed Custard
4 helpings or 500ml (approx)

500ml milk
4 eggs **or** 3 eggs and 2 yolks
25g caster sugar

fat for greasing
flavouring (p276)

Warm the milk to approximately 65°C. Mix the eggs and sugar together and stir in the milk. Strain the custard into a greased 750ml heatproof dish, cover with greased foil or oiled greaseproof paper, and steam very gently for about 40 minutes until just firm in the centre.

Serve hot or cold with fruit or Jam Sauce (p228).

Note The custard can be turned out on to a warm plate for serving, but when it is removed from the steamer, leave it to stand for a few minutes before turning it out.

Crème Anglaise (2) (Thick custard)
4 helpings or 500ml (approx)

500ml milk
a few drops vanilla essence **or** other
    flavouring (see below)

8 egg yolks
100g caster sugar

Warm the milk gently without letting it boil, and infuse any solid flavouring used;
then remove. Beat the egg yolks and sugar together until creamy. Add the milk.
Strain the custard into a double boiler or a basin placed over a pan of simmering
water. Cook, stirring all the time with a wooden spoon, for 20–30 minutes or until
the custard thickens and coats the back of the spoon. Take care not to let the custard
curdle.

Use hot, or pour into a basin and cool, stirring from time to time to prevent a skin
forming.

Flavourings
Lemon: Infuse a thin strip of lemon rind in the milk, then remove before adding the
eggs.
    Orange: Add orange rind in the same way as lemon rind.
    Liqueur: Add 1 × 15ml spoon Kirsch, curaçao or rum at the end of the cooking
time.
    Praline: Top with crushed praline (p400).
VARIATION
A simpler Crème Anglaise can be made in an ordinary saucepan without curdling
too easily. Use 6 egg yolks and blend them and the sugar with 2 × 5ml spoons
cornflour or arrowroot. Continue as above.

Apple Snow (1)
6 helpings

1kg cooking apples
pared rind of 1 lemon
75ml water
175g caster sugar

2 eggs
250ml milk
butter for greasing

Peel, core, and slice the apples into a saucepan. Add the lemon rind and water. Cover
and cook until the apples are pulped. Remove the lemon rind and beat the apple
purée until smooth. Add 100g of the sugar. Separate the eggs and beat the yolks
until liquid in a basin. Heat together the milk and 25g of the sugar and pour on to the
egg yolks. Return the mixture to the saucepan and cook, stirring all the time, until
the mixture coats the back of the spoon. Do not allow the mixture to boil. Put the
apple purée into a buttered 1 litre pie dish, pour the custard over it, and bake in a
warm oven at 160°C, Gas 3, for 30–40 minutes. Whisk the egg whites until stiff, fold
in the remaining 50g sugar and pile on top of the custard. Return to the oven and
bake for a further 10 minutes until the meringue is just set.
    Serve with Simple Custard (p277) or cream.

Banana Custard
4 helpings

500ml Coating Cup Custard (p276)   3 bananas (400g approx)

Decoration (optional)
4 × 5ml spoons crushed butterscotch
  or grated chocolate **or** browned
  flaked almonds

Make the custard. Peel and slice the bananas. Add to the custard and leave to stand for 5 minutes. Spoon into a serving dish or 4 glasses. Decorate before serving.

Bread and Butter Pudding
4 helpings

butter for greasing   a pinch of nutmeg **or** cinnamon
4 thin slices bread (100g approx)   400ml milk
25g butter   2 eggs
50g sultanas **or** currants   25g granulated sugar

Grease a 1 litre pie dish. Cut the crusts off the bread and spread the slices with the butter. Cut the bread into squares or triangles and arrange in alternate layers, buttered side up, with the sultanas or currants. Sprinkle each layer lightly with spices. Arrange the top layer of bread in an attractive pattern. Warm the milk to approximately 65°C; do not let it come near the boil. Beat together the eggs and most of the sugar with a fork and stir in the milk. Strain the custard over the bread, sprinkle some nutmeg and the remaining sugar on top, and leave to stand for 30 minutes. Bake in a moderate oven at 180°C, Gas 4, for 30–40 minutes until set and lightly browned.

Cabinet Pudding (plain)
4 helpings

fat for greasing   3 eggs
75g seedless raisins   25g caster sugar
3–4 slices white bread (100g approx)   1 × 5ml spoon grated lemon rind
400ml milk

Grease a 1 litre pudding basin and halve the raisins. Decorate the sides and base of the basin by pressing on some of the dried fruit. Chill. Remove the crusts from the bread and cut the slices into 5mm dice. Warm the milk to approximately 65°C; do not let it come near the boil. Beat the eggs and sugar together with a fork and stir in the milk. Add the lemon rind to the bread with the rest of the raisins. Strain the custard over the bread, stir, and leave to stand for 30 minutes. Pour into the prepared basin and cover with greased foil or greaseproof paper. Steam gently for 1 hour or until the pudding is firm in the centre. Remove the cooked pudding from the steamer, leave to stand for a few minutes, and turn out on to a warmed dish.

Serve with Jam Sauce (p228).

Caramel Custard
4 helpings

100g lump **or** granulated sugar
150ml water
400ml milk **or** 300ml milk and
　100ml single cream

2 eggs and 2 yolks **or** 3 eggs
25g caster sugar
a few drops vanilla essence

Prepare a thickly folded band of newspaper long enough to encircle a 13cm round cake tin or charlotte mould. Heat the tin or mould in boiling water or in the oven and wrap the newspaper round it. Prepare the caramel by heating the sugar and water together, stirring occasionally, until the sugar dissolves completely. Bring to the boil gently, and boil, without stirring, for about 10 minutes until the syrup turns golden-brown. Do not let it turn dark brown as it will have a bitter taste. Pour a little of the caramel on to a metal plate and put to one side. Pour the remaining caramel into the warmed, dry tin, tilt and turn it, holding it by the paper, until the base and sides are evenly coated. Leave until cold and set.

Warm the milk and cream to approximately 65°C; do not let it come near the boil. Beat the eggs and sugar together with a fork and stir in the milk. Add a few drops of vanilla essence. Strain the custard into the tin and cover with greased foil or grease-proof paper. Steam very gently for about 40 minutes or until the custard is firm in the centre.

Alternatively, stand the custard in a shallow tin containing enough warm water to come half-way up the sides of the dish, and bake in a very cool oven at 140°–150°C, Gas 1–2, for 1 hour.

Remove the cooked custard and leave it to stand for a few minutes, then turn it out carefully on to a warmed dish. The caramel will run off and serve as a sauce. Break up the reserved caramel by tapping sharply with a metal spoon, and decorate the top of the custard with the pieces of broken caramel.

Note Individual caramel custards can be made in four 150ml ovenproof moulds. Steam for 20 minutes, or bake for 30 minutes.

Crème Brûlée
4 helpings

1 × 15ml spoon cornflour
250ml milk
250ml single cream
a few drops vanilla essence

3 eggs
50g caster sugar
fat for greasing
ground cinnamon (optional)

Blend the cornflour to a smooth paste with a little of the milk, and bring the rest of the milk to the boil. Pour the boiling milk on to the blended cornflour, stirring well. Return the mixture to the pan, bring to the boil, and boil for 1 minute, stirring all the time. Remove from the heat and leave to cool. Beat together the cream, vanilla essence, and eggs. Stir into the cooled mixture. Whisk over low heat for about 30 minutes or until the custard thickens; do not boil. Add 25g sugar and pour into a greased 600ml flameproof dish. Sprinkle the pudding with the rest of the sugar and a little cinnamon, if used. Place under a hot grill for 10 minutes or until the sugar has melted and turned brown. Keep the custard about 10cm from the heat. Serve hot or cold.

Alternatively, bake in a fairly hot oven at 200°C, Gas 6, for about 15 minutes until the pudding is browned.

Custard Tart
4 helpings

100g shortcrust pastry (p407) using
   125g flour
flour for rolling out
250ml milk

2 eggs
50g caster sugar
a pinch of grated nutmeg

Put an 18cm flan ring on a heavy baking sheet or line an 18cm sandwich tin with foil. Roll out the pastry on a lightly floured surface and use it to line the flan ring or cake tin, taking care not to stretch the pastry. Warm the milk to approximately 65°C; do not let it come near the boil. Beat the eggs and sugar together with a fork and add the milk. Strain the mixture into the pastry case and sprinkle the top with grated nutmeg. Bake in a fairly hot oven at 190°C, Gas 5, for 10 minutes, reduce the temperature to cool, 150°C, Gas 2, and bake for a further 15–20 minutes or until the custard is just set. Serve hot or cold.

Queen of Puddings
4 helpings

75g soft white breadcrumbs
400ml milk
25g butter
2 × 5ml spoons grated lemon rind

2 eggs
75g caster sugar
fat for greasing
2 × 15ml spoons red jam

Dry the breadcrumbs slightly by placing in a cool oven for a few moments. Warm the milk with the butter and lemon rind, to approximately 65°C; do not let it come near the boil. Separate the eggs and stir 25g of the sugar into the yolks. Pour the warmed milk over the yolks, and stir in well. Add the crumbs and mix thoroughly. Pour the custard mixture into a greased 750ml pie dish and leave to stand for 30 minutes. Bake in a warm oven at 160°C, Gas 3, for 40–45 minutes until the pudding is lightly set.

Remove the pudding from the oven and reduce the temperature to 120°C, Gas ½. Warm the jam and spread it over the pudding. Whisk the egg whites until stiff, add half the remaining sugar and whisk again. Fold in nearly all the remaining sugar. Spoon the meringue round the edge of the jam and sprinkle with the remainder of the caster sugar. (The piled-up meringue and the red jam centre then suggest a crown.) Return the pudding to the oven for 40–45 minutes or until the meringue is set.

Zabaglione
4 helpings

4 egg yolks
40g caster sugar

4 × 15ml spoons Marsala (Bual) **or**
Madeira **or** sweet sherry

Put the egg yolks into a deep heatproof basin and whisk lightly. Add the sugar and wine, and place the bowl over a pan of hot water. Whisk for about 10 minutes or until the mixture is very thick and creamy. When the whisk is lifted out of the bowl, a trail of the mixture from the whisk should lie on top for 2–3 seconds. Pour the custard into individual glasses and serve at once while still warm.

Serve with Mrs Beeton's Savoy Cakes (p375).

VARIATION

Cold Zabaglione
Dissolve 50g caster sugar in 4 × 15ml spoons water, and boil for 1–2 minutes until syrupy. Whisk with the egg yolks until pale and thick. Add 2 × 15ml spoons Marsala (Bual), Madeira or sweet sherry and 2 × 15ml spoons single cream while whisking. The finely grated rind of half a lemon can be added, if liked. Chill before serving.

Soufflés, Omelets, Pancakes and Waffles

Vanilla Soufflé *Basic recipe*
4 helpings

35g butter
35g plain flour
250ml milk
4 eggs

50g caster sugar
½ × 5ml spoon vanilla essence
1 egg white
caster **or** icing sugar for dredging

Heat the oven to moderate, 180°C, Gas 4, or put the steamer on to heat. Prepare a 1 litre soufflé dish (p197). Melt the butter in a saucepan, stir in the flour and cook slowly for 2–3 minutes, without colouring, stirring all the time. Add the milk gradually and beat until smooth. Cook for another 1–2 minutes, still stirring all the time. Remove from the heat and beat hard until the sauce comes away from the sides of the pan cleanly. Cool slightly and put into a bowl.

Separate the eggs and beat the yolks into the mixture one by one. Beat in the sugar and vanilla essence. Whisk all the egg whites until stiff. Using a metal spoon, stir 1 spoonful of the whites into the mixture, then fold in the rest until evenly distributed. Put into the dish and bake for 45 minutes until well risen and browned; alternatively, cover with greased greaseproof paper and steam slowly for 1 hour until just firm to the touch.

Dredge with caster or icing sugar and serve immediately from the dish, with Jam Sauce (p228).

VARIATIONS

A hot sweet soufflé can be flavoured in many different ways. Unless otherwise stated in the variations which follow, stir in the flavouring before adding the egg yolks. Omit the vanilla essence.

Almond Soufflé

Add 100g ground almonds, 1 × 15ml spoon lemon juice, and a few drops of ratafia essence. Reduce the sugar to 40g.

Apple Soufflé

Add 125ml thick sweet apple purée, 1 × 15ml spoon lemon juice, and a pinch of powdered cinnamon. Dust with cinnamon before serving.

Apricot Soufflé

Add 125ml thick apricot purée and 1 × 15ml spoon lemon juice, if using fresh apricots. If using canned apricots (1 × 400g can makes 125ml purée) use half milk and half syrup to make the sauce. A dried apricot purée is delicious.

Coffee Soufflé

Add 2 × 15ml spoons instant coffee dissolved in a little hot water, or use 125ml strong black coffee and only 125ml milk.

Lemon Soufflé

Add the thinly grated rind and juice of 1 lemon. Serve with Lemon Sauce (p226).

Orange Soufflé

Pare the rind of 2 oranges thinly. Put in a pan with the milk and bring slowly to the boil. Remove from the heat, cover, and leave to stand for 10 minutes, then remove the rind. Make up the sauce using the flavoured milk. Reduce the sugar to 40g. Add the strained juice of half an orange.

Pineapple Soufflé

Add 125ml crushed pineapple or 75g chopped pineapple, and make the sauce using half milk and half pineapple juice.

Praline Soufflé

Dissolve 2–3 × 15ml spoons almond praline (p400) in the milk before making the sauce, or crush and add just before the egg yolks.

Raspberry Soufflé

Add 125ml raspberry purée (1 × 400g can makes 125ml purée) and 1 × 10ml spoon lemon juice.

Soufflé Ambassadrice

Crumble 2 macaroons and soak them in 2 × 15ml spoons rum with 50g chopped blanched almonds. Stir into a vanilla soufflé mixture.

Soufflé Harlequin

Make up 2 half quantities of soufflé mixture in different flavours, eg chocolate and vanilla, or praline and coffee. Spoon alternately into the dish.

For another **variation**, see over.

Strawberry Soufflé

Add 125ml strawberry purée, and make the sauce using half milk and half single cream. Add a little pink food colouring, if necessary.

Sweet Soufflé Omelet *Basic recipe*
1 helping

2 eggs
1 × 5ml spoon caster sugar
a few drops vanilla essence
2 × 15ml spoons water

1 × 15ml spoon unsalted butter **or** margarine
icing sugar for dredging

Separate the eggs. Whisk the yolks until creamy, add the sugar, vanilla essence and water, and whisk again. Whisk the egg whites until stiff and matt. Place an 18cm omelet pan over gentle heat and when it is hot add the butter or margarine. Tilt the pan so that the whole of the inside of the pan is greased. Pour out any excess. Fold the egg whites into the yolk mixture carefully until evenly distributed, using a metal spoon. Do not overmix, as it is most important not to break down the egg white foam. Pour the egg mixture into the pan, level the top very lightly, and cook for 1–2 minutes over a moderate heat until the omelet is golden-brown on the underside; the top should still be moist. (Use a palette knife to lift the edge of the omelet to look underneath.)

Put the pan under a moderate grill for 5–6 minutes until the omelet is risen and lightly browned on the top. The texture of the omelet should be firm yet spongy. Remove from the heat as soon as it is ready, as overcooking tends to make it tough. Run a palette knife gently round the edge and underneath to loosen it. Make a mark across the middle at right angles to the pan handle but do not cut the surface. Put any filling on one half, raise the handle of the pan and double the omelet over. Turn gently on to a warm plate, dredge with icing sugar and serve at once.

VARIATIONS
Soufflé omelets can have many different fillings:

Apricot Omelet

Add the grated rind of 1 orange to the egg yolks. Spread 2 × 15ml spoons warm, thick apricot purée over the omelet.

Jam Omelet

Spread the cooked omelet with 2 × 15ml spoons warmed jam.

Lemon Omelet

Add the grated rind of ½ lemon to the egg yolks. Warm 3 × 15ml spoons lemon curd with 1 × 10ml spoon lemon juice, and spread over the omelet.

Rum Omelet

Add 1 × 15ml spoon rum to the egg yolks.

Strawberry Omelet
Hull 5 ripe strawberries, and soak in a little Kirsch. Mash slightly with icing sugar. Put in the centre of the omelet.

Surprise Omelet
Put ice cream into the centre of the omelet before folding.

Sweet Pancakes *Basic recipe*
Add 2 × 5ml spoons caster sugar to a basic thin batter (p191). Cook as for Plain Pancakes (p192). Slide on to sugared paper and roll or fold as preferred.
VARIATIONS

Apple Pancakes
Mix together 250ml sweetened, thick apple purée, 50g sultanas, and a pinch of powdered cinnamon. Spoon on to the pancakes when made, and roll up. If liked, sprinkle with caster sugar, and glaze in a very hot oven or under the grill.

Apricot Pancakes
Add 1 × 15ml spoon powdered cinnamon to the batter. Soak 50g dried apricots in 4 × 15ml spoons water, and then simmer with 50g sugar and a good squeeze of lemon juice, until soft and pulpy. Add 25g almonds, lightly browned and chopped. Fill the pancakes as for Apple Pancakes.

Banana Pancakes
Mash 4 bananas with 50g softened butter, 2 × 15ml spoons sugar, and the grated rind and juice of 1 lemon. Fill the pancakes as for Apple Pancakes.

Chocolate Pancakes
Sprinkle each pancake with grated plain chocolate and dredge with icing sugar when made. Stack the flat pancakes and dredge the top one with sugar. Serve cut in wedges, with cream.

Currant Pancakes
Scatter a few currants or sultanas on each pancake as it is cooking. Allow 50g in all. Do not add to the batter as they will sink to the bottom. Serve with lemon and sugar.

Jam Pancakes
Spread the pancakes with warmed jam before rolling up.

Lemon Pancakes
Sprinkle with lemon juice, roll up, and sprinkle with caster sugar. Serve with wedges of lemon. Serve on Shrove Tuesday.

Surprise Pancakes
Spoon some ice cream into the centre of each pancake and fold it in half like an omelet. Serve with Jam Sauce (p228).

For another **variation**, see over.

Layered Pancakes

Stack the pancakes in layers, and fill each layer with the following: 100g curd cheese mixed with 1 egg yolk, 1 × 10ml spoon sugar and the grated rind of ½ lemon; warmed apricot jam; 50g finely chopped nuts mixed with 50g grated plain chocolate. Make a meringue from 2 egg whites and 100g caster sugar, and use to cover the pile of pancakes completely. Bake in a fairly hot oven at 190°C, Gas 5, for 15–20 minutes, until crisp and lightly browned. Serve cut in wedges.

Crêpes Suzette (Orange Brandy Pancakes)
4 helpings

250ml basic thin batter (p191)
1 × 15ml spoon butter

butter **or** oil for frying
50ml brandy

Filling

100g unsalted butter
75g caster sugar
grated rind and juice of 1 orange

1 × 5ml spoon lemon juice
1 × 15ml spoon liqueur (Kirsch **or** Grand Marnier)

Prepare the batter. Melt the butter, cool, and beat it into the batter. Make the filling by creaming the butter and sugar together. Beat the orange rind, lemon juice, and liqueur into the creamed mixture. Beat in enough orange juice to give a soft creamy consistency.

Make 8 very thin pancakes and keep them warm until all are cooked. Spread the filling over the pancakes, dividing it evenly between them. Fold each one in half, then in half again to make a quarter circle.

Return half the pancakes to the pan and re-heat them for 1–2 minutes. As the orange butter melts and runs out, spoon it over the pancakes. Pour in half the brandy, tip the pan to one side and increase the heat. Ignite the brandy and serve at once with the orange sauce poured over the pancakes.

Re-heat and serve the other pancakes in the same way. If you have a large enough pan, re-heat all the pancakes at once.

Waffles
Makes 8

75g butter
250g self-raising flour
½ × 5ml spoon salt

1 × 5ml spoon baking powder
2 eggs
375ml milk

Melt the butter and cool it. Sift the flour, salt, and baking powder into a bowl. Separate the eggs. Make a well in the centre of the flour. Add the egg yolks, cooled butter, and some of the milk. Gradually work in the flour from the sides and then beat well until smooth. Beat in the rest of the milk. Whisk the egg whites until stiff, and fold into the batter. It should be the consistency of thick cream.

Heat a waffle iron, pour in the batter, and cook for about 5 minutes until the steaming stops.

Serve hot with butter and golden or maple syrup.

Boiled, Steamed and Baked Puddings

Consistency of Mixture

A *dropping consistency* means the mixture should just drop from the spoon when shaken lightly.

A *soft dropping consistency* means that the mixture drops from the spoon easily.

A *slack consistency* means that it falls off the spoon almost of its own accord.

Preparing Containers

Always prepare the containers and a greased paper or foil cover before making the pudding. The inside of the container should be well greased with clarified butter or margarine, cooking fat or oil.

Note A charlotte mould, cake tin or foil container can be used instead of a pudding basin for a baked pudding. For individual puddings, small dariole moulds, ceramic cocottes or ramekins are useful.

To Line a Basin with Suet Crust

Cut off one-quarter of the pastry for the lid. Roll the remaining pastry 1cm larger than the top of the basin, and put the pastry into the greased basin. By pressing with the fingers, work evenly up the sides of the container to the top. Put in the required filling. Roll out the pastry for the lid to the same size as the top of the basin. Dampen the rim, and place it on top of the filling. Press the rim of the lid against the edge of the lining to seal the crust.

General Hints on Cooking

Steamed puddings: Only three-quarters fill the basin before putting on the pastry lid. Cover with greased paper or foil, to prevent steam getting in. Put the cover on greased side down. Either twist the edges under the rim of the basin, or tie them.

If you have a steamer, put the pudding in the perforated top part and have the water underneath boiling. If, however, a recipe calls for gentle steaming, only let the water simmer. Cover closely and steam for the time directed.

If you have no steamer, stand the pudding basin on an old saucer or plate in a saucepan, with water coming half-way up the basin's sides. Put a tight-fitting lid on the pan, and simmer gently. This method is called 'half-steaming'.

With either method, always top up the water with more boiling water when the water in the pan is reduced by a third.

After taking the pudding out of the steamer, let it stand for a few minutes to shrink and firm up before turning it out on to a dish. To turn out a steamed or boiled pudding, loosen the sides from the basin with a knife. Place the warmed serving dish upside-down over the basin and turn them over together. Do not use a plate for fruit puddings in case juice seeps out.

Boiled puddings: If you wish, you can boil a pudding in a basin covered with a floured cloth, or in a well-floured cloth only. Roly-poly puddings can be rolled in a scalded floured cloth, forming a sausage shape; tie loosely at each end, leaving room for the pudding to swell. If you use a basin, fill it completely and cover securely as for steamed puddings.

Have enough rapidly boiling water ready in a large saucepan to cover the pudding completely. Put the pudding into the fast-boiling water, and reduce the heat so that the water only simmers. Top up with boiling water when required, as above.

Let the pudding stand for a few moments after removing it from the water to let it shrink and firm up.

Baked puddings: Use a well-greased basin, pie dish, oven-to-table baking dish or a foil container with a really clean edge. Baked puddings are easier to handle if placed on a flat baking sheet in the oven.

Suet Pudding (unsweetened) *Basic recipe*
6–7 helpings

300g plain flour
$\frac{1}{2}$ × 2.5ml spoon salt
2 × 5ml spoons baking powder

150g shredded suet
cold water
flour for dusting

Sift the flour, salt, and baking powder together. Add the suet, and enough cold water to make a soft but not sticky dough. Shape into a roll. Lay the dough on a scalded, well-floured pudding cloth and roll up loosely. Tie up the ends of the cloth. Put into a saucepan of fast-boiling water, reduce the heat and simmer for $2–2\frac{1}{2}$ hours. Drain well and unwrap.

Serve sliced, with meat or gravy or with any sweet sauce.

VARIATIONS

Roly-poly Pudding
Make the suet crust as in the basic recipe. Roll out the dough into a rectangle about 5mm thick. Spread with jam almost to the edge. Dampen the edges and roll up lightly. Seal the edges. Cook as in the basic recipe.

Fruit Roly-poly
Mix into the basic recipe 150g chopped dates, currants, sultanas, raisins or figs. Shape into a roll, and cook as in the basic recipe. Drain, unwrap, slice, and serve with any custard or sweet sauce, or with warmed golden syrup and cream.

Spotted Dick
Mix into the basic recipe 150g caster sugar and 150g currants. Use milk instead of water. Shape into a roll and cook as in the basic recipe. Drain, unwrap, slice, and serve with any custard or sweet sauce, or with warmed golden syrup and cream.

Boiled Apple Dumplings
6 helpings

6 cooking apples
300g prepared suet crust pastry (p408)
flour for dusting

75g Demerara sugar
6 cloves

Core and peel the apples. Divide the pastry into 6 portions and, on a lightly floured surface, roll each into a round. Put an apple in the centre of each round of pastry and work the pastry round the apple until it almost meets at the top. Fill the core hole with sugar and stick a clove upright in the middle of each apple. Dampen the edges of the pastry, work it up to meet over the apple, and seal well, leaving the clove exposed. Tie each dumpling in a small well-floured pudding cloth. Put the dumplings into a saucepan of boiling water and boil gently for 40–50 minutes.

Drain well and serve with Apple Sauce (p213) and Pouring Cup Custard (p276).

Christmas Pudding (1) (rich boiled)
6 helpings per pudding

fat for greasing
200g plain flour
a pinch of salt
1 × 5ml spoon ground ginger
1 × 5ml spoon mixed spice
1 × 5ml spoon grated nutmeg
50g chopped blanched almonds
400g soft light **or** dark brown sugar
250g shredded suet
250g sultanas

250g currants
200g seedless raisins
200g cut mixed peel
175g stale white breadcrumbs
6 eggs
75ml stout
juice of 1 orange
50ml brandy **or** to taste
125–250ml milk

Grease four 600ml basins. Sift together the flour, salt, ginger, mixed spice, and nutmeg into a mixing bowl. Add the nuts, sugar, suet, sultanas, currants, raisins, peel, and breadcrumbs. Beat together the eggs, stout, orange juice, brandy, and 125ml milk. Stir this into the dry ingredients, adding more milk if required, to give a soft dropping consistency. Put the mixture into the prepared basins, cover with greased paper or foil, and a floured cloth. Put into deep boiling water and boil steadily for 6–7 hours, or half steam for the same length of time.

To store, cover with a clean dry cloth, wrap in greaseproof paper and store in a cool place until required. To re-heat, boil or steam for 1½–2 hours. Serve with Brandy Butter (p233) or Pouring Cup Custard (p276).

Apple Pudding (steamed)
5–6 helpings

150g cooking apples
100g shredded suet
100g stale white breadcrumbs
100g soft light brown sugar
½ × 2.5ml spoon grated nutmeg

a pinch of salt
2 eggs
125ml milk (approx)
fat for greasing

Peel, core, and chop the apples coarsely. Mix together the apples, suet, breadcrumbs, sugar, nutmeg, and salt. Beat the eggs until liquid and stir into the dry ingredients with enough milk to make a soft dropping consistency. Leave to stand for 1 hour to allow the bread to soak. If very stiff, add a little more milk. Put the mixture into a greased 1 litre basin, cover with greased paper or foil and steam for 1¾–2 hours. Serve from the basin, or leave for 5–10 minutes at room temperature to firm up, then turn out. Serve with Pouring Cup Custard (p276).

VARIATIONS
Cumberland Pudding
Use 250g apples, and substitute 200g sifted plain flour with 2 × 5ml spoons baking powder for the breadcrumbs. Add 150g currants with the flour. Reduce the sugar to 75g and the milk to 75ml. Steam in a 750ml basin. Serve turned out, dredged with soft light brown sugar.

Other Fruit Puddings
Instead of apples, use the same quantity of prepared damsons, gooseberries, greengages, plums or rhubarb.

Brown Bread Pudding
4–6 helpings

175g stale brown breadcrumbs	75g caster sugar
75g raisins	2 eggs
75g sultanas	milk
100g shredded suet	fat for greasing

Mix together all the ingredients, adding enough milk to make a dropping consistency. Leave to stand for 30 minutes. Add more milk if the pudding is too stiff, to give a dropping consistency. Put the mixture into a greased 750ml basin, cover with greased paper or foil and steam for 2½–3 hours. Serve from the basin, or leave for 5–10 minutes at room temperature to firm up, then turn out.

Serve with Pouring Cup Custard (p276) or Simple Custard (p277).

Christmas Pudding (2) (economical)
12 helpings

fat for greasing	200g shredded suet
1 cooking apple	150g mixed cut peel
100g plain flour	grated rind and juice of 1 lemon
25g self-raising flour	2 eggs
a pinch of salt	125ml milk (approx)
100g stale white breadcrumbs	1 × 5ml spoon almond essence
400g mixed dried fruit	1 × 5ml spoon gravy browning
100g soft light **or** dark brown sugar	

Grease two 600ml basins or one 1 litre basin. Peel, core, and chop the apple. Sift together the flours and salt into a bowl. Add the breadcrumbs, dried fruit, sugar, suet, peel, lemon rind, and juice. Beat together the eggs, milk, and almond essence and stir into the dry ingredients, adding more milk if required, to give a soft dropping consistency. Add the gravy browning to darken the mixture. Mix well, then put the mixture into the basins. Cover with greased paper or foil, and a floured cloth, and steam for 5 hours.

Store, re-heat and serve as for Christmas Pudding (rich boiled) (p289).

Golden Syrup Pudding
6–7 helpings

fat for greasing
3 × 15ml spoons golden syrup
150g plain flour
1 × 5ml spoon bicarbonate of soda
a pinch of salt
1 × 5ml spoon ground ginger

150g stale white breadcrumbs
100g shredded suet
50g caster sugar
1 egg
1 × 15ml spoon black treacle
75–100ml milk

Grease a 1 litre basin, and put 1 × 15ml spoon of golden syrup in the bottom. Sift together the flour, bicarbonate of soda, salt, and ginger. Add the breadcrumbs, suet, and sugar. Beat together the egg, remaining syrup, treacle, and 75ml of the milk. Stir this mixture into the dry ingredients, adding more milk if required, to make a soft dropping consistency. Put into the basin, cover with greased paper or foil and steam for 1½–2 hours. Leave for 5–10 minutes to firm up, then turn out.

Serve with warmed golden syrup and whipped cream.

Lemon Pudding
6–7 helpings

50g plain flour
a pinch of salt
1 × 5ml spoon baking powder
175g stale white breadcrumbs
100g caster sugar

100g shredded suet
grated rind and juice of 2 lemons
2 eggs
150–175ml milk
fat for greasing

Sift together the flour, salt, and baking powder. Stir in the breadcrumbs, sugar, suet, and lemon rind. Beat together the eggs, lemon juice, and about 50–75ml of the milk. Stir into the dry ingredients, adding more milk if required, to make a soft dropping consistency. Put into a greased 750ml basin, cover with greased paper or foil, and steam for 1½–2 hours. Leave for 5–10 minutes, then turn out.

Serve with Lemon Sauce (p226).

Steamed Sponge Pudding (Canary Pudding) *Basic recipe*
6 helpings

150g butter **or** margarine
150g caster sugar
3 eggs
grated rind of ½ lemon

150g plain flour
1 × 5ml spoon baking powder
fat for greasing

Work together the fat and sugar until light and creamy. Beat in the eggs gradually. Add the lemon rind. Sift together the flour and baking powder and fold lightly into the mixture. Put into a greased 750ml basin, cover with greased paper or foil and steam for 1¼–1½ hours. Leave in the basin at room temperature for 3–5 minutes, then turn out.

Serve with Pouring Cup Custard (p276) or Jam Sauce (p228).

For **variations,** see over.

VARIATIONS

1) Add to the basic recipe one of the following: 50g desiccated coconut, 150g chopped stoned dates, 150g dried fruit, 75g glacé cherries, 25g cocoa, 50g chopped preserved ginger, grated rind of 1 orange or lemon.
   Serve with Simple Custard (p277).

2) Before putting the basic mixture into the basin, put in 2 × 15ml spoons golden syrup, jam, marmalade or lemon curd. Serve with the same preserve used in the recipe.

Mrs Beeton's Bachelor's Pudding
5–6 helpings

150g cooking apples
100g stale white breadcrumbs
grated rind of ½ lemon
100g currants
75g caster sugar
a pinch of salt

½ × 2.5ml spoon grated nutmeg
2 eggs
milk
1 × 5ml spoon baking powder
fat for greasing

Peel, core, and chop the apples coarsely. Mix together the breadcrumbs, apples, grated lemon rind, currants, sugar, salt and nutmeg. Beat the eggs until liquid and add to the dry ingredients with enough milk to form a soft dropping consistency. Leave to stand for 30 minutes. Stir in the baking powder. Put the mixture into a greased 1 litre basin, cover with greased paper or foil and steam for 2½–3 hours. Leave in the basin for a few minutes, then turn out.
   Serve with Simple Custard (p277) or Vanilla Sauce (p226).

Chocolate Pudding
5–6 helpings

fat for greasing
50g plain chocolate
125ml milk
40g butter **or** margarine

40g caster sugar
2 eggs
100g stale white breadcrumbs
½ × 2.5ml spoon baking powder

Grease a 750ml basin or 6 dariole moulds. Grate the chocolate into a saucepan, add the milk and heat slowly to dissolve the chocolate. Cream together the fat and sugar. Separate the eggs and beat the yolks into the creamed mixture. Add the melted chocolate, breadcrumbs, and baking powder. Whisk the egg whites until fairly stiff and fold into the mixture. Put into the basin or moulds, cover with greased paper or foil, and steam for 1 hour for a large pudding, and 30 minutes for dariole moulds. Leave in the basin for a few minutes, then turn out.
   Serve with Chocolate Sauce (p227).

Baked Sponge Pudding *Basic recipe*
4–6 helpings

100g butter or margarine
100g caster sugar
2 eggs
150g plain flour

1 × 5ml spoon baking powder
½ × 2.5ml spoon vanilla essence
2 × 15ml spoons milk (approx)
fat for greasing

Cream the fat and sugar together until light and fluffy. Beat the eggs until liquid, then beat them gradually into the creamed mixture. Sift together the flour and baking powder, and fold them in. Add the essence and enough milk to form a soft dropping consistency. Put into a greased 1 litre pie dish and bake in a moderate oven at 180°C, Gas 4, for 30–35 minutes until well risen and golden-brown.

Serve from the dish with Pouring Cup Custard (p276) or any sweet sauce.

Note If using a pie dish it can be encircled with a pie frill before presenting at table.

VARIATIONS

Jam Sponge
Put 2 × 15ml spoons jam in the bottom of the dish before adding the sponge mixture.

Orange or Lemon Sponge
Add the grated rind of 1 orange or lemon to the creamed mixture.

Spicy Sponge
Sift 1 × 5ml spoon mixed spice, ground ginger, grated nutmeg or cinnamon with the flour.

Coconut Sponge
Substitute 25g desiccated coconut for 25g flour.

Chocolate Sponge
Substitute 50g cocoa for 50g flour.

Baked Jam Roll
6 helpings

300g plain flour
1 × 5ml spoon baking powder
a pinch of salt
150g shredded suet

flour for rolling out
200–300g jam
butter for greasing

Sift the flour, baking powder, and salt into a bowl. Add the suet and enough cold water to make a soft, but firm dough. On a lightly floured surface, roll into a rectangle about 5mm thick. Spread the jam almost to the edges, dampen the edges, and roll up lightly. Seal the edges at each end. Grease a baking sheet and place the roll on it, with the sealed edge underneath. Cover loosely with greased paper or foil. Bake in a fairly hot oven at 190°C, Gas 5, for 50–60 minutes until golden-brown.

Serve on a warm platter, sliced, with warmed jam.

Eve's Pudding
4 helpings

400g cooking apples
grated rind and juice of 1 lemon
75g Demerara sugar
1 × 15ml spoon water
fat for greasing

75g butter **or** margarine
75g caster sugar
1 egg
100g self-raising flour

Peel, core, and slice the apples thinly. Mix together with the lemon rind and juice, Demerara sugar, and water, and put into a greased 1 litre pie dish. Cream the fat and caster sugar together until light and fluffy. Beat the egg until liquid and beat into the creamed mixture. Fold in the flour lightly and spread the mixture over the apples. Bake in a moderate oven at 180°C, Gas 4, for 40–45 minutes until the apples are soft and the sponge is firm.

Serve with Pouring Cup Custard (p276) or melted apple jelly and single cream.

Fruit Puddings and Desserts

Apple Amber (1)
4 helpings

3 eggs
1 × 15ml spoon lemon juice

500ml thick apple purée
250g caster sugar (approx)

Decoration
glacé cherries

angelica

Separate the eggs. Beat the lemon juice and yolks into the apple purée with about 75g of the sugar. Turn into a 750ml baking dish, cover, and bake in a moderate oven at 180°C, Gas 4, for 15 minutes. Whisk the egg whites until they form stiff peaks. Gradually whisk in 150g of the remaining sugar, adding 1 × 5ml spoonful at a time. Pile the meringue on top of the apple mixture and sprinkle with 1 × 15ml spoon sugar. Return to the oven and bake for a further 15 minutes or until the meringue is pale golden-brown.

Serve at once with Pouring Cup Custard (p276) or single cream.

Apple Batter Pudding
4 helpings

25g cooking fat **or** oil
500g cooking apples
basic thin batter (p191)

50g sugar
grated rind of ½ lemon

Heat the oven to hot, 220°C, Gas 7. Put the fat or oil into a 17 × 27cm baking tin and heat in the oven for 5 minutes. Peel, core, and slice the apples thinly. Prepare the batter. Remove the tin from the oven, arrange the apple slices in an even layer on the bottom, and sprinkle with the sugar and lemon rind. Pour the batter over the apples and bake for 30–35 minutes until brown and well-risen.

Serve cut into 4 pieces, with golden syrup or a lemon sauce.

VARIATIONS
Apricot Batter Pudding
Just cover 100g dried apricots with water and soak until soft, preferably overnight. Put the apricots and water into a pan and simmer for 15 minutes. Drain. Heat the tin and put the apricots in an even layer on the bottom. Continue as for Apple Batter Pudding. Serve with an apricot jam sauce.

Dried Fruit Batter Pudding
Spread 50g mixed dried fruit over the bottom of the tin and sprinkle with $\frac{1}{2} \times 5$ml spoon mixed spice or ground cinnamon. Continue as for Apple Batter Pudding. Serve with a lemon sauce.

Black Cap Pudding
Grease 12 deep patty tins and divide 50g currants between them. Pour in enough batter to half-fill each tin and bake for 15–20 minutes. Turn out to serve.

Apple Charlotte
5–6 helpings

butter for greasing
400g cooking apples
grated rind and juice of 1 lemon
100g soft light brown sugar
a pinch of ground cinnamon

50–75g butter
8–10 large slices white bread,
    5mm thick
1 × 15ml spoon caster sugar

Grease a 1 litre charlotte mould or 16cm cake tin heavily with butter. Peel, core, and slice the apples. Simmer the apples, lemon rind and juice with the sugar and cinnamon until the apples soften to a thick purée. Leave to cool.

Melt the butter. Cut the crusts off the bread, and dip 1 slice in the butter. Cut it into a round to fit the bottom of the mould or tin. Fill any spaces if necessary. Dip the remaining bread slices in the butter. Line the inside of the mould with 6 slices, touching one another. Fill the bread case with the cooled purée. Complete the case by fitting the top with more bread slices. Cover loosely with greased paper or foil, and bake in a moderate oven at 180°C, Gas 4, for 40–45 minutes. For serving, turn out and dredge with caster sugar.

Serve with bramble jelly and cream.

VARIATIONS
1) Line the mould or tin with slices of bread and butter, placed buttered side out, instead of dipping bread in melted butter.
2) Instead of lining the sides of the mould or tin, arrange the purée and dipped bread in alternate layers in the mould or tin until all the ingredients are used, ending with a layer of bread.

Apple Crumble
6 helpings

600g cooking apples
100g brown sugar
50ml water
grated rind of 1 lemon
fat for greasing

75g butter **or** margarine
150g plain flour
75g caster sugar
½ × 2.5ml spoon ground ginger

Peel, core, and slice the apples. Cook with the brown sugar, water, and lemon rind in a covered pan until soft. Fill a greased 1 litre pie dish with the apples. Rub the fat into the flour until it resembles fine breadcrumbs. Add the caster sugar and ginger and stir well, sprinkle the mixture over the apples, and press down lightly. Bake in a moderate oven at 180°C, Gas 4, for 30–40 minutes until the crumble is golden-brown.

VARIATION

Instead of apples, use 600g damsons, gooseberries, pears, plums, rhubarb, or raspberries.

Baked Apples
6 helpings

6 cooking apples
filling (see below)

50g Demerara sugar
75ml water

Wash and core the apples. Cut round the skin of each apple with the tip of a sharp knife two-thirds of the way up from the base. Put into an ovenproof dish, and fill the centres with the chosen filling. Sprinkle the Demerara sugar on top of the apples and pour the water round them. Bake in a moderate oven at 180°C, Gas 4, for 45–60 minutes, depending on the cooking quality and size of the apples.

Serve with Pouring Cup Custard (p276), ice cream or with whipped cream, sweetened and flavoured with brandy.

Fillings
1) Mix together 50g Barbados or other raw sugar and 50g butter.
2) Use blackcurrant, raspberry, strawberry or apricot jam, or marmalade.
3) Chop 75g stoned dates, sultanas, raisins or currants.
4) Mix together 50g soft light brown sugar and 1 × 5ml spoon ground cinnamon.

Brown Betty
6 helpings

1kg cooking apples
fat for greasing
150g stale wholemeal breadcrumbs
grated rind and juice of 1 lemon

4 × 15ml spoons golden syrup
100g Demerara sugar
2 × 15ml spoons water

Peel, core, and thinly slice the apples. Coat a greased 1 litre pie dish with a thin layer of breadcrumbs, then fill with alternate layers of apples, lemon rind, and bread-crumbs. Heat the syrup, sugar, water, and lemon juice in a saucepan and pour over the mixture. Bake in a warm oven at 160°C, Gas 3, for 1–1¼ hours until the pudding is brown and the apple cooked.

Serve with single cream or any pouring custard (p276).

Glazed Apple Dumplings
6 helpings

300g prepared shortcrust pastry
    (p407)
flour for rolling out
½ × 2.5ml spoon ground cinnamon
50g brown sugar

6 cooking apples
12 cloves (optional)
1 × 15ml spoon milk
25g caster sugar

Divide the pastry into 6 portions. On a lightly floured surface roll each out into a round. Mix together the cinnamon and brown sugar. Peel and core the apples and put each on a round of pastry. Fill the apple cavity with the sugar mixture, and press 2 cloves into the top of each apple, if liked. Work the pastry round the apple to enclose it, moisten the edges and press well together, leaving the cloves sticking out. Place the dumplings on a baking tray. Brush them with milk and dredge with caster sugar. Bake in a fairly hot oven at 200°C, Gas 6, for 30–35 minutes or until the apples are tender.

Serve with single cream.

Fruit Fritters
Prepare the fruit as below. Dry well on soft kitchen paper. Heat deep fat or oil (p11). Test the consistency of the batter to make sure that it coats the back of a spoon. Using a skewer or fork, dip the pieces of fruit, one by one, in coating batter (1) (p190). Put a few pieces into the fat and fry, turning once, until crisp and golden. Drain the fritters well on soft kitchen paper. Keep hot in a single layer on a baking sheet in a cool oven at about 150°C, Gas 2.

Serve while hot, sprinkled with caster sugar and with a suitable fruit sauce or cream.

Apples: Peel and core 500g apples, and cut into 5mm slices. Put into water containing a little lemon juice until needed. Drain well and dry with soft kitchen paper before coating. Coat, and fry. Serve with Lemon Sauce (p226).

Apricots: Sprinkle canned apricot halves with rum and leave for 15 minutes. Coat, and fry. Serve dredged with caster sugar and cinnamon, and with custard or cream.

Bananas: Peel 4 small bananas, cut in half lengthways, then in half across. Coat, and fry. Serve with Simple Custard (p277) flavoured with rum.

Oranges: Remove the peel and pith from 4 oranges. Divide them into pieces of 2 or 3 segments each. Carefully cut into the centre to remove any pips. Coat, and fry. Serve with custard or sweetened cream flavoured with an orange-flavoured liqueur.

Pears: Peel and core 4 pears. Cut into quarters, sprinkle with sugar and Kirsch, and leave to stand for 15 minutes. Crush 4 macaroons finely, and toss the pear pieces in the crumbs. Coat, and fry. Serve with Lemon Sauce (p226) or warmed apricot jam flavoured with Kirsch.

Pineapple: Drain 1 × 566g can pineapple slices, pat dry and sprinkle with 4 × 5ml spoons Kirsch; leave for 15 minutes before coating. Coat, and fry. Serve with the pineapple juice thickened with arrowroot or cornflour.

Gooseberry Fritters
4 helpings

400g gooseberries	caster sugar
oil **or** fat for deep frying	

Batter

50g plain flour	2 eggs
a pinch of salt	3 × 15ml spoons milk
1 × 15ml spoon caster sugar	

Prepare the batter first. Sift together the flour and salt. Add the sugar. Separate the eggs. Mix the yolks and milk into the flour and beat well to form a thick batter. Prepare and dry the gooseberries. Heat the fat (p11). Whisk the egg whites until stiff and fold into the batter. Add the gooseberries. Dip a metal tablespoon in the hot fat, and then lift 3 coated gooseberries on to it. Lower them into the hot fat, without separating them. As the batter cooks, the berries will fuse together. Fry until golden-brown, turning once. Drain well. Serve sprinkled with plenty of sugar.

VARIATIONS

Hulled strawberries, stoned cherries, red and blackcurrants can be cooked in the same way. Canned fruit can also be used but it must be drained very thoroughly. Alternatively, add 50g currants to the batter instead of the gooseberries. Serve sprinkled with sugar, and with Lemon Sauce (p226).

Pineapple Upside-Down Cake

1 × 227g can pineapple rings	1 × 5ml spoon ground cinnamon
100g butter	1 × 5ml spoon ground nutmeg
275g soft dark brown sugar	2 eggs
8 maraschino **or** glacé cherries	250ml milk
450g self-raising flour	

Drain the pineapple rings, reserving the syrup. Melt 50g of the butter in a 20cm square baking tin. Add 125g of the sugar and 1 × 15ml spoon of pineapple syrup;

mix well. Arrange the pineapple rings in an even pattern in the bottom of the tin, and place a cherry in the centre of each ring.

Sift together the flour, cinnamon, and nutmeg. Beat the eggs with the remaining brown sugar. Melt the remaining butter and add to the eggs and sugar with the milk; mix into the spiced flour. Pour this mixture carefully over the fruit in the baking tin without disturbing it. Bake in a moderate oven, 180°C, Gas 4, for 45–50 minutes. Remove the tin from the oven and at once turn upside-down on to a plate; allow the caramel to run over the cake before removing the baking tin.

Serve warm with cream as a dessert, or cold for afternoon tea.

Plums with Port
6 helpings

1kg plums	150ml port
100–150g soft light brown sugar	

Cut the plums neatly in half and remove the stones. Put into a baking dish or casserole, sprinkle with the sugar (the amount required will depend on the sweetness of the plums) and pour the port on top. Cover securely with a lid or foil and bake in a cool oven at 150°C, Gas 2, for 45–60 minutes or until the plums are tender. Serve hot, or lightly chilled.

Stuffed Fresh Peaches
4–8 helpings

50g unsalted butter	125g plain **or** sponge cake crumbs
8 large peaches	2 egg whites
50g salted butter	2 drops almond essence **or** 1 × 15ml
125g caster sugar	spoon anisette liqueur
125g ground almonds	

Grease a shallow ovenproof dish with the unsalted butter. With the point of a knife, make 2 slits in the skin of each peach. Scald the fruit for 40 seconds, drain and peel. Cut in half and remove the stones carefully without spoiling the shape. Place the peaches on the dish, hollows uppermost. Melt the salted butter. Mix the sugar, ground almonds, and crumbs with most of the melted butter. Add the egg whites and essence or liqueur and beat the mixture to a creamy consistency. Using a piping bag or spoon, fill the hollow of each peach with the mixture. Brush with the remaining melted butter and bake in a moderate oven at 180°C, Gas 4, for 20 minutes.

Serve hot with Crème Anglaise (p278), ice cream or Zabaglione (p282).

COLD PUDDINGS AND DESSERTS
Cereal Sweets

Large and Whole Grain Cereal Sweets (eg rice, tapioca, barley)
Makes 1 litre (approx)

150g grain
1 litre milk
75g sugar

flavouring (p301)
25g butter

Wash the grain in cold water and put it into the top of a double boiler with the milk. Simmer gently with the lid on for $2-2\frac{1}{2}$ hours until the grain is tender and the milk almost absorbed. Stir occasionally to prevent the grain from settling on the bottom of the pan. Stir in the sugar, flavouring, and butter. Pour into a wetted 1 litre mould or basin and leave for about 2 hours to set. Turn out and serve with stewed fruit or jam.

VARIATION
Creamed Rice (1)
Fold 125ml single cream into the cooked rice.

Small and Crushed Grain Cereal Sweets (eg flaked grains, semolina, sago)
Makes 450ml (approx)

500ml milk
50g grain
1 × 10ml spoon gelatine

2 × 15ml spoons cold water
50g caster sugar
flavouring (see opposite)

Heat the milk to boiling point, sprinkle in the grain and cook gently, stirring all the time, for 15–20 minutes until soft and smooth. Soften the gelatine in the cold water in a small heatproof container, stand the container in a pan of hot water and stir until the gelatine dissolves. Stir into the mixture. Add the sugar and flavourings. Leave to cool, stirring from time to time. When tepid, pour into a wetted 500ml mould and leave for about 2 hours to set. Turn out to serve.

VARIATIONS
Blend 40g cocoa with small or powdered grain, or add 50g grated plain chocolate when the mixture is almost cooked. Extra sugar can be added if required and also a few drops of vanilla, rum or coffee essence.

Creamed Rice (2)
Whip 125–250ml double cream until thick, and fold into the mixture just before moulding. Use a 650ml mould.

Powdered Grain Cereal Sweets (eg cornflour, custard powder, ground rice, arrowroot)
Makes 1 litre (approx)

75g grain	50g sugar
1 litre milk	flavouring (see below)

Blend the grain with a little of the cold milk. Bring the rest of the milk to the boil, and pour on to the blended mixture, stirring all the time. Return the mixture to the saucepan, and bring it to simmering point, stirring all the time. Simmer for 5–10 minutes. Add the sugar and flavouring. Pour into a wetted 1 litre mould and leave for about 2 hours to set. Turn out to serve.

Note When made with cornflour, ground rice or arrowroot, and without added colouring, this basic moulded mixture is a blancmange.

VARIATIONS

Ambrosia Mould

Stir 50g melted butter and 125ml sherry into the mixture after it has come to simmering point.

Pink Coconut Mould

Stir 50g desiccated coconut, 50g melted butter, and a few drops of cochineal into the mixture after it has come to simmering point. Use a 1.25 litre mould.

Flavourings for Cereal Sweets
Flavouring essences: Almond, lemon, vanilla or coffee essence can be added to the mixture with the sugar.

Lemon or orange: The grated rind can be stirred into the cooked mixture just before moulding (large grain sweets). Alternatively, thinly cut strips of rind from 1 orange or 1 lemon can be infused in the mixture while cooking (large grain sweets), or in the milk while heating (other cereal sweets). They should be removed before mixing the milk with the grain (small and powdered grain sweets).

Peach Condé
6 helpings

1 litre cold rice pudding (p300)	125ml peach syrup from can
1 × 410g can peach halves	2 drops pink food colouring
2 × 5ml spoons arrowroot	1–2 drops yellow food colouring

Decoration
whipped cream

Divide the rice pudding between 6 sundae glasses. Drain the peaches and arrange 1 half on top of each helping of rice, cut side down. Put the arrowroot into a small saucepan and stir in the syrup. Bring to the boil, stirring all the time, and boil for about 5 minutes until it thickens and clear. Add the colouring and pour over the peaches. Leave to set. Decorate with whipped cream.

Fruit Desserts

Stewed or Poached Fresh Fruit

Apples and pears: Peel, core, and leave whole if small, quarter if large. Make a syrup with 100g sugar and 250ml water (more if the fruit is very hard) per 500g fruit. Flavour with lemon rind, cloves or cinnamon stick. Colour the syrup with cochineal, if liked, or replace some of the water with white wine or cider. Put the prepared fruit into the liquid immediately to preserve its colour; it must be completely covered by the liquid. Stew either in a saucepan or in a casserole in a moderate oven. Cooking pears may take 4–5 hours in the oven.

Currants and other soft berry fruits: Clean and prepare the fruit; remove stalks from currants. Make a syrup with 100g sugar and 125ml water per 500g fruit. Either steep the fruit in the cooled syrup and then poach very gently; or, if it is to be served cold, reduce the syrup by boiling, put the fruit into the hot syrup, and leave it to cool.

Gooseberries: Top and tail, removing a little skin from the tail end to allow the syrup to penetrate; then wash. Make a syrup with 100g sugar and 125–375ml water (depending on the hardness of the fruit) per 500g fruit. Flavour with elder-flowers, if available. Poach very gently until the skins crack.

Peaches and apricots: Peel, stone, and halve or quarter the fruit, depending on its size. Make a syrup with 100g sugar and 250ml water per 500g fruit. Flavour with almond or vanilla essence or with a few kernels from the fruit stones. Replace some of the water with white wine if liked.

Plums, greengages, and damsons: Wash the fruit, remove the stalks, and the stones if liked. Make a syrup with 100g sugar and 250ml water per 500g fruit. Flavour with lemon rind, cloves, cinnamon stick, or with a few kernels from the fruit stones. Replace some of the water with red wine, for red plums, if liked. Stew either in a saucepan or in a casserole in a moderate oven.

Rhubarb: String older garden rhubarb, but just wipe young forced fruit. Cut into 2cm lengths, lay in a casserole, and cover with soft light brown sugar. Flavour with lemon rind, root ginger or cinnamon stick. Do not add water. Cover and bake very gently, overnight if possible, in a very cool oven at 110°C, Gas $\frac{1}{4}$.

Stewed Dried Fruit (eg prunes, apricots, peaches, figs, apple rings)

Wash the fruit thoroughly in tepid water. Put it in a large bowl, cover with fresh water or cold tea, allowing 750ml liquid per 500g dried fruit, and leave to soak for 12–24 hours.

Drain, and measure out 250ml liquid (use fresh water if the fruit was soaked in tea) for cooking each 500g soaked fruit. Add sugar as required: 50–100g per 500ml liquid for apricots, peaches, apple rings; 25g per 500ml for other fruit. Add either a strip of lemon rind or a piece of cinnamon stick (for prunes), and bring to the boil. Reduce the heat, simmer for 3–4 minutes, skim, and add the fruit. Simmer until tender, then drain the fruit with a perforated spoon, and transfer to a serving bowl. Discard any solid flavourings from the syrup and boil it until it is well reduced. Pour it over the fruit and serve either hot or cold.

Alternatively, the fruit can be cooked in the liquid without any added sugar. In this case, add the sugar when the syrup is being boiled down.

Fruit Purées

Fruit purées are used for a number of fruit desserts, such as mousses (see p313) and fools. Hard fruits are generally cooked, but soft fruits such as strawberries, raspberries, peaches, mangoes or melons are simply prepared (ie hulled, peeled, and stoned), then rubbed through a fine nylon sieve, or puréed in an electric blender, and sweetened to taste. Fruit such as raspberries, which contain pips, should be sieved, not blended, to remove all the pips.

Hard fruit should be cooked in as little water as possible, About 4–5 × 15ml spoons should be enough for every 500g fruit; allow slightly less for apples and rhubarb. Put the water in a heavy-bottomed pan, add the fruit, cover, and simmer gently until the fruit is tender. When cooked, remove any stones, then sieve or purée until smooth, and sweeten to taste.

500g fresh fruit will yield about 300ml fruit purée.

Note Apples can also be baked in a moderate oven at 180°C, Gas 4, for 45 minutes–1 hour, then peeled, cored, and sieved or puréed.

Fruit Fool

6 helpings

750g fruit (approx), eg gooseberries, rhubarb, apricots, red, and black currants, raspberries, blackberries, etc

sugar
500ml thick pouring custard (p276) **or** 500ml double cream **or** 250ml double cream and 250ml custard

Decoration
ratafias **or** fresh fruit **or** whipped cream

Purée the fruit (see above), sweeten to taste, and leave to cool. If using cream, whip it until it holds its shape. Fold first the custard, if used, and then the cream into the fruit purée. Turn into a serving bowl and chill before serving. Decorate with ratafias, fresh fruit or whipped cream.

Note Some fruits especially soft berry fruits can be combined to make up the given weight, but as a rule the pure flavour of a single type of fruit is more attractive than mixed flavours.

Rhubarb and Banana Fool

6–8 helpings

500g rhubarb, preferably forced rhubarb
6 bananas

sugar
250ml thick pouring custard (p276) **or** double cream

Decoration
ratafias **or** whipped cream

Cook and purée the rhubarb (see above). Peel and mash the bananas or purée in a blender. Blend the two purées together and sweeten to taste. Whip the cream, if used, until it just holds its shape; fold either the custard or the cream into the fruit purée. Turn into a serving bowl and decorate with ratafias or piped whipped cream.

Fruit Salad

Always try to include a good selection of fruit with different colours, textures and flavours. Fresh fruit has the most vital flavour, and a portion should always be included, but frozen, canned, and even a few cooked, dried fruits can be added for bulk or variety. Allow about 150g fruit per person and 100ml fruit syrup.

The recipe below is for a basic fruit syrup which can be varied by adding more lemon juice, or sherry, Kirsch, brandy, port, Cointreau, Grand Marnier, white rum etc, to taste.

Basic Fruit Syrup
pared rind and juice of 1 lemon   75g sugar
500ml water

Put the lemon rind and juice into a pan with the water and sugar. Heat gently until the sugar has dissolved, then bring to the boil, and continue boiling until the syrup has been reduced by about half. Remove from the heat, strain, and leave to cool.

Fresh fruit is prepared according to kind as follows:

Apples: Cut into quarters and remove the cores; peel if wished, but if the skins are not too thick they provide an attractive contrast of colour. Cut into thin slices and dip quickly in lemon juice to preserve the colour, or put straight into the fruit syrup if it contains plenty of lemon juice.

Apricots: Cut in half and remove the stones. Cut each half into 2 or 3 pieces and add to the syrup. The stones of the apricots can also be split in half, the kernel removed and added to the fruit salad.

Bananas: Peel the bananas and cut into slices. Dip quickly in lemon juice to preserve the colour, then add to the fruit syrup. Only a few bananas should be added to a fruit salad and they should not be added too long before serving; this is because, even if coated with lemon juice, they will tend to discolour; this also happens if they are chilled in a refrigerator.

Cherries: Stone, cut in halves or leave whole, then add to the syrup.

Chinese gooseberries (kiwi fruit): Peel and cut into slices, and add to the syrup.

Grapes: Cut in half and remove the pips; if wished, grapes can also be peeled, although they provide attractive colour if left unpeeled.

Loganberries: Hull, and add to the syrup shortly before serving. Like other soft fruit they may go soggy or disintegrate if left in the syrup for long, especially if frozen.

Lychees: Peel, halve, remove the stones, and add to the syrup.

Mangoes: Peel, cut into slices and discard the stone, and add to the syrup.

Melons: Cut ripe melons in half, remove the seeds, then cut into cubes or balls with a melon scoop; discard all the peel. Add to the syrup.

Nectarines: As for peaches; the skin may be left on.

Oranges: Using a sharp knife, peel the oranges, removing all the white pith. Carefully cut between the segment skins to remove the flesh alone; do this over a plate to catch any juice and squeeze out all the juice from the remaining pulp. Add to the fruit syrup, together with the juice.

It is easier to remove all the pith if the oranges are put into boiling water for 2 minutes, cooled for another 2 minutes, then peeled while still hot.

Peaches: As for apricots, but cut each half into smaller pieces, or slice thinly.

Pears: Peel and core, then cut into thin slices, or cubes. Dip quickly in lemon juice to preserve the colour, then add to the fruit syrup, or put quickly into the fruit syrup if it contains plenty of lemon juice.

Pineapple: Peel the pineapple, and remove all the eyes. Cut in half or quarters lengthways and cut out the hard core. Cut the fruit into small pieces. Add to the syrup.

Plums: Halve, remove the stones, and cut into quarters, if large. Add to the syrup.

Raspberries: Hull, and add to the syrup shortly before serving.

Strawberries: Hull, and add to the syrup shortly before serving.

Serve fruit salad either in a large serving bowl, preferably glass, to emphasize the varied colours of the fruits, or in a scooped-out pineapple or melon.

To scoop out the fruit, remove the top third crossways. Keeping the case intact, cut or scoop out the flesh from the rest of the fruit, leaving about a 1cm rim. Remove the core from the pineapple. Cut the fruit into small pieces, or into balls if using a melon, and add to the rest of the fruit salad. Fill the scooped-out fruit with the salad.

Alternatively, the fruit can be presented in the form of a basket. Prepare as follows:

If using a pineapple, cut off and discard the green leafy tuft from the top. Keeping the fruit upright, and leaving about a 2cm piece intact in the centre for the handle, cut 2 equal-sized wedges from either side of the top half. Carefully cut out the flesh from the handle, leaving a 1cm rim. Scoop out the flesh from the lower half and continue as above.

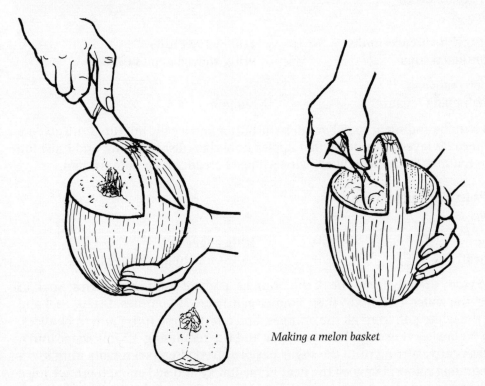

Making a melon basket

Note A pineapple container can also be prepared as for Sweet Pineapple Salad with Kirsch (p307).

Apple Snow (2)
6 helpings

4 large baking apples (750g approx)	2–3 eggs
juice and pared rind of 1 lemon	50g caster sugar
100g sugar (approx)	1 × 5ml spoon cornflour **or** arrowroot
250ml milk	4 individual sponge cakes

Decoration
glacé cherries

Bake and purée the apples (p303). Add the lemon juice to the purée, sweeten to taste, and leave to cool.

Put the lemon rind into a small pan with the milk and heat gently for 15 minutes, then strain. Separate the eggs and blend the yolks and sugar together with the cornflour or arrowroot. Add the lemon-infused milk. Cook, stirring all the time, in a saucepan for 20–30 minutes or until the custard coats the back of the spoon. Cool.

Split the sponge cakes in half and arrange them in the bottom of a glass dish. Pour the custard over them. Whisk the egg whites until they form stiff peaks, then fold into the apple purée. Pile the mixture on top of the custard and decorate with the glacé cherries.

Danish Apple Cake
4–6 helpings

150g dry white breadcrumbs	100–125g butter
75g granulated sugar	900g stewed apples (p302)

Decoration (optional)

300ml whipping cream	red jam

Mix the crumbs and sugar together. Melt the butter and fry the mixture until golden. Place alternate layers of crumbs and apples in a glass dish, starting and finishing with the crumbs. Decorate, if liked, with whipped cream and a little red jam.

Oranges in Caramel Sauce
4 helpings

6 oranges	200g sugar
250ml water	25–50ml chilled orange juice

Pare the rind carefully from one of the oranges, and cut it into thin strips. Soak in 125ml of the water for 1 hour, then simmer gently for 20 minutes. Drain. Peel and remove the white pith from all the oranges, and cut the flesh into 7mm thick slices. Place in a glass serving dish. Put the sugar and the remaining 125ml water into a pan. Heat gently, stirring until the sugar has dissolved, then boil rapidly until it is a golden caramel colour. Draw off the heat immediately and add enough orange juice to give the consistency of sauce required. Replace over the heat, stir until just blended, then add the orange rind. Pour the caramel sauce over the oranges and chill for at least 3 hours before serving.

Summer Pudding
6–8 helpings

1kg soft red fruit, eg black and red
    currants, blackberries, raspberries,
    and bilberries
100–150g caster sugar

1 strip lemon rind (optional)
8–10 slices day-old white bread
    (5mm thick)

Pick over and clean the fruit, put into a bowl with sugar to taste and the lemon rind, if used, and leave overnight. Turn the fruit and sugar into a pan, discarding the lemon rind, and simmer for 2–3 minutes until very lightly cooked. Remove from the heat. Cut the crusts off the bread, Cut a circle from 1 slice to fit the bottom of a 1.25 litre pudding basin. Line the base and sides of the basin with bread, leaving no spaces. Fill in any gaps with small pieces of bread. Fill with the fruit and any juice it has made while cooking. Cover with bread slices. Place a flat plate and a 1kg weight on top, and leave overnight, or longer if refrigerated.

    Serve turned out, with chilled whipped cream, sweetened if liked.

Sweet Pineapple Salad with Kirsch
4 helpings

2 small pineapples
100g black grapes
1 banana
1 pear

1 × 15ml spoon lemon juice
2–3 × 15ml spoons Kirsch
sugar

Cut the pineapples in half lengthways. Cut out the core, then scoop out the flesh, using first a knife, then a spoon, but taking care to keep the pineapple cases intact. Discard the core, and chop the flesh. Put into a bowl, together with any pineapple juice. Halve and de-pip the grapes. Peel and slice the banana; peel, core, and slice the pear, and toss both fruits in the lemon juice, before adding to the other fruit in the bowl. Mix all the fruit together, pour the Kirsch over them, and sweeten to taste with the sugar. Pile the fruit back into the pineapple cases and chill until required.

Uncleared Jellies

1) Choose a large non-aluminium saucepan as the liquid jelly will rise during making. A thick enamel saucepan is ideal.
2) Use 2 × 10ml spoons powdered gelatine to 500ml water for general purposes, but when a slightly firmer 'set' is required use 3 × 10ml spoons gelatine to 500ml water. The larger amount of gelatine will be required:
   a) in hot weather
   b) if no refrigerator is available
   c) when pieces of fruit are to be set in the jelly and the mould turned out
   d) if the jelly is to be used for lining a mould or chopped for decoration.
3) Always make sure that gelatine is completely dissolved before adding it to other ingredients. Gelatine will dissolve easily if it is sprinkled on to cold water or liquid to soften first. Put the liquid into a small heatproof container, add the gelatine

and leave for 5 minutes. Place the container in a saucepan of hot water over low heat and stir, especially round the sides, until the gelatine has completely dissolved.

4) Do not use milk to dissolve gelatine as it will curdle.

5) Do not add a hot gelatine solution to a really cold mixture. It will not mix properly but will set in globules and 'string' as soon as it comes into contact with the cold mixture. The mixture should be at room temperature, tepid, or, ideally, at the same temperature as the gelatine. In any case, the dissolved gelatine should be blended in quickly and thoroughly to prevent it setting in blobs.

6) If the mixture has to be strained, strain through scalded, well-washed, damp butter muslin. The muslin may be held up in a sieve.

7) A jelly mould may be made of glass, china, metal or plastic. When gelatine is included in a recipe, a sharp clean outline to the turned-out shape will be obtained if a metal mould is used. Tin-lined copper moulds are costly but ensure a perfect finish to the jelly. All moulds must be scrupulously clean and rinsed out or wetted with cold water before use. They should be wet inside when the jelly is poured in, although there should be no free water in the bottom.

8) To turn out a jelly, run the tip of a knife or finger round the top of the mould. Dip the mould into hot water for a few seconds, remove, and dry it. Wet a serving plate and place upside-down on top of the mould. Hold the plate and mould together firmly and turn both over. Shake gently and carefully remove the mould.

9) If using fresh pineapple juice in making a jelly, it must first be boiled for 2–3 minutes. It contains an enzyme, which, if left untreated, destroys the setting power of gelatine.

Blackcurrant Jelly
2 helpings

125ml blackcurrant syrup   1 × 10ml spoon gelatine
25g sugar   125ml cold water

Heat together the syrup and sugar until the sugar has dissolved. Cool. Soften the gelatine in the water in a small heatproof container. Stand the container in a pan of hot water and stir until dissolved. Pour into the cooled syrup. Pour into wetted individual moulds and leave for about 1 hour to set.

Blackcurrant Whip
4 helpings

375ml blackcurrant juice   2 × 10ml spoons gelatine
25–50g sugar   3 × 15ml spoons cold water

Put the blackcurrant juice and sugar into a saucepan and heat until the sugar has dissolved. Leave to cool. Soften the gelatine in the water in a small heatproof container. Stand the container in a pan of hot water and stir until dissolved, then add to the saucepan. Pour into a basin and whisk well until thick and foamy. Pile quickly into individual serving dishes and leave for about 45 minutes to set.

Mrs Beeton's Dutch Flummery
4–6 helpings

25g gelatine	4 eggs
125ml cold water	500ml dry sherry
juice and grated rind of 1 lemon	50g caster sugar

Soften the gelatine in the water in a small heatproof container. Stand the container in a pan of hot water and stir until dissolved, then make up with cold water to 500ml. Strain the lemon juice into the gelatine and add the grated rind. Beat the eggs, sherry, and sugar together and add to the mixture. Pour into the top of a double boiler and cook slowly over low heat, stirring all the time, until the mixture coats the back of the spoon. Do not let the mixture boil. Strain the mixture into a wetted 1.5 litre mould and leave for 2–3 hours to set before turning out.
Note Make the day before using if possible.

Fresh Lemon Jelly
2 helpings

pared rind and juice of 2 lemons	1 × 10ml spoon gelatine
175ml water	2 × 10ml spoons caster sugar

Put the lemon rind into a saucepan with half the water and simmer for 5 minutes. Cool. Soften the gelatine in the remaining water in a small heatproof container. Stand the container in a pan of hot water and stir until the gelatine has dissolved. Add the lemon juice and sugar. Pour into individual wetted moulds and leave for about 1 hour to set.
VARIATION
Fresh Orange Jelly
Use 2 oranges instead of lemons and only 1 × 10ml spoon of sugar.

Milk Jelly
2 helpings

250ml milk	1 × 10ml spoon gelatine
1 × 15ml spoon caster sugar	4 × 15ml spoons cold water
grated rind of 1 lemon	

Heat the milk, sugar, and lemon rind until the sugar has dissolved. Cool. Soften the gelatine in the cold water in a small heatproof container. Stand the container in a pan of hot water and stir until dissolved. Stir the gelatine into the cooled milk, then strain into a basin. Stir from time to time until it is the consistency of thick cream. Pour into a wetted mould and leave for about 1 hour to set.
VARIATIONS
The jelly can be flavoured with vanilla, coffee or other essence, if liked. If coffee essence is used, substitute orange rind for the lemon. Omit the rind if peppermint flavouring is used.

Cleared Jellies

Scald the saucepan, whisk, jelly bag, basins, and jelly mould before use, as the merest trace of grease may cause cloudiness in the finished jelly.

Whisk the egg whites lightly and crush the egg shells before adding to the mixture in the saucepan.

Heat the mixture and whisk constantly until a good head of foam is produced. It should be hot but not boiling. The correct temperature is about 70°C, when the foam begins to set or 'crust'. Care must be taken not to break up the 'crust' by whisking too long. Remove the whisk but continue to heat the liquid until the 'crust' has risen to the top of the saucepan; the gelatine must *not* boil.

Remove from the heat and let the contents of the saucepan settle in a warm place, covered, for 5–10 minutes.

Strain the settled, clear jelly through a jelly bag into a basin below, while the bag is still hot from scalding. Replace this basin of jelly with another basin and re-strain the jelly very carefully by pouring through the foam 'crust' which covers the bottom of the bag, acting as a filter.

If the jelly is not clear when a little is looked at in a spoon or glass, the filtering must be carried out again.

Filtering is most easily carried out using a jelly bag and stand, but if these are not available, the 4 corners of a clean cloth can be tied to the legs of an upturned stool.

Repeated filtering will cool the jelly, and, if done too often, can result in a poor yield of clear jelly as it will tend to solidify in the cloth.

Note Use lump sugar whenever possible for making clear jelly; it will give a more brilliant jelly than powdered sugar.

Lining and Decorating a Mould

Pour in just enough jelly to cover the base and sides of the mould, and leave to set completely. If canned fruit is being used, drain well before putting into the mould. Cut pieces of fruit to fit the shape of the mould, and place in a decorative pattern over the set jelly. Each piece of fruit can be dipped in a little liquid jelly, if liked, before being arranged in the mould. Carefully spoon a little liquid jelly over the decoration and allow to set before any other filling is added.

Filling the Mould

Moulds should be filled to the top; this prevents the shape of the mould being broken when it is shaken out. In the case of a cream mixture, liquid jelly may be used to fill the space if there is insufficient mixture.

Note If a jelly is to be set in layers, keep it in a warm place to avoid it setting.

Chopping Jelly for Decoration

Clear jelly should be quite firm. It should be coarsely chopped with a wet knife on wet greaseproof paper, so that the light is refracted from the cut surfaces as from the facets of a jewel.

Clear Lemon Jelly
6 helpings

4 lemons
750ml water
150g sugar
4 cloves

1 × 2cm piece cinnamon stick
40g gelatine
whites and shells of 2 eggs

Pare the rind from three of the lemons and squeeze the juice from all four. Make up the juice to 250ml with water, if necessary. Put the rind, juice, water, sugar, cloves, cinnamon stick, and gelatine into a large saucepan. Whisk the egg whites lightly, and crush the shells. Whisk over low heat until just below boiling point. Remove the whisk and allow the liquid to heat until it reaches the top of the pan. Simmer for 5 minutes. Remove from the heat and leave to stand for 5–10 minutes. Strain the liquid carefully through a jelly bag. Pour into a wetted mould and leave for 1–2 hours to set.

Note 2 × 15ml spoons of sherry may be added to the liquid just before filtering.

Fruit Jelly
6 helpings

fruit eg banana, grapes, cherries,
    tangerines, apricots, pineapple

750ml clear lemon jelly

Decoration
125ml chopped jelly (see **Note**)

Prepare enough fruit to decorate the sides of the mould and to make 3–4 layers of fruit in it.

Rinse a mould out with cold water. Pour in just enough jelly to cover the bottom of the mould and allow to set. Cut pieces of fruit to fit the shape of the mould; dip each piece in liquid jelly and place in the mould. Leave to set, then carefully cover the fruit with a little more liquid jelly. Leave to set again and repeat with layers of fruit and jelly, ensuring that each layer is set before the next layer is added, until the mould is full, finishing with a layer of jelly. Leave for about 2 hours to set, then turn out and decorate with chopped jelly.

Note For the decorative chopped jelly, choose a colour and flavour which suits the fruit, eg if using tangerines and grapes, use tangerine jelly.

Soufflés, Mousses and Creams

Lemon Soufflé (Milanaise Soufflé) *Basic recipe*
4 helpings

1 × 15ml spoon gelatine
3 × 15ml spoons water
3 eggs

grated rind and juice of 2 lemons
100g caster sugar
125ml double cream

Decoration
finely chopped nuts **or** cake crumbs
whipped double cream (optional)

crystallized lemon slices
angelica

Prepare a 500ml soufflé dish (p197). Soften the gelatine in the water in a small heatproof container. Stand the container in a pan of hot water and stir until dissolved. Cool slightly. Meanwhile, separate the eggs. Put the yolks, lemon rind and juice, and sugar into a heatproof basin and stand it over a pan half-full of hot water over low heat. Do not let the water boil or touch the basin. Whisk the mixture for 10–15 minutes until thick and pale. Remove from the heat and continue whisking until cool. Fold a little of the yolk mixture into the cooled gelatine, then whisk this into the yolk mixture. Put in a cool place until the mixture begins to set.

Whip the cream until it just holds its shape but is still soft. Using a large metal spoon, fold into the mixture until evenly mixed. Whisk the egg whites until stiff, and fold in until evenly blended. Tip the soufflé gently into the dish, and leave to set in a refrigerator for about 2 hours.

Remove the paper carefully, and decorate the sides of the soufflé with chopped nuts or cake crumbs. Pipe whipped cream on top, if liked, and decorate with crystallized lemon slices and small pieces of angelica.

VARIATIONS
In each of the variations below, omit the lemon rind and juice:

Chocolate Soufflé

Whisk the egg yolks with 2 × 15ml spoons water and 75g caster sugar. Melt 75g grated plain chocolate over a pan of hot water. Add to the yolk mixture with the dissolved gelatine and whisk well.

Coffee Soufflé

Dissolve 2 × 10ml spoons instant coffee in a little hot water, then add more water to make 100ml strong coffee. Whisk with the egg yolks. Decorate with grated chocolate, chopped walnuts, and cream.

Orange Soufflé

Whisk the egg yolks with the finely grated rind and juice of 2 oranges and use 75g caster sugar only. Add 2 × 15ml spoons Grand Marnier or orange curaçao, if liked. Dissolve the gelatine in 1 × 15ml spoon water and 2 × 15ml spoons lemon juice. When set, decorate the soufflé with crystallized orange slices, nuts, and cream.

Praline Soufflé

Prepare 75g praline (p400) and crush it. Dissolve 1 × 5ml spoon instant coffee in 2 × 15ml spoons hot water, and add 2 × 15ml spoons cold water. Whisk the liquid with the yolks. Add 50g crushed praline to the mixture with the whipped cream. Decorate with the remaining praline and cream.

Sherry Soufflé

Add 100ml sweet sherry, 1 × 15ml spoon lemon juice, and 75g caster sugar only to the egg yolks. Decorate with mimosa balls, angelica, coconut, and cream.

Blackcurrant Mousse *Basic recipe using purée*
4 helpings

250g fresh blackcurrants	2 × 15ml spoons water
50g caster sugar	125ml double cream
1 × 10ml spoon lemon juice	2 egg whites
1 × 10ml spoon gelatine	

Decoration

whipped double cream   blackcurrant jam (optional)

Save a few whole blackcurrants for decorating the mousse, if liked; sieve the rest. Make the purée up to 150ml with a little water, if necessary. Put the purée, sugar, and lemon juice in a bowl. Soften the gelatine in the water in a small heatproof container. Stand the container in a pan of hot water and stir until completely dissolved. Cool. Mix in a little of the purée, then stir this mixture into the main purée. Leave in a cool place until beginning to set.

Whip the cream until it just holds its shape, and fold into the mixture using a metal spoon. Whisk the egg whites until fairly stiff and fold in. Make sure that the mixture is fully and evenly blended but do not overmix it. Pour gently into a 500ml dish or wetted mould, or into individual glasses. Leave to set in a refrigerator for 1–2 hours. Turn out, if liked. Decorate with whirls of whipped cream and with either the reserved fruit or jam.

Note Canned or bottled blackcurrants in syrup can also be used; in this case substitute 3 × 15ml spoons of the syrup for the sugar and water. Frozen fruit can also be used; it must be well thawed and drained, and any sugar added must depend on the type and strength of sweetening (if any) used when freezing the fruit.

VARIATIONS
1) Fresh, frozen or canned fruits can be used, eg strawberries, raspberries, blackberries, gooseberries, cherries, apricots or bananas. The amount of sugar will vary according to the sweetness of the purée.
2) Omit the gelatine; pour the mixture into the ice trays and freeze it.

Chocolate Mousse (1)
4 helpings

150g plain chocolate
2 × 15ml spoons water

4 eggs
vanilla essence

Decoration
whipped double cream

chopped walnuts

Break up the chocolate or grate it. Put it into a large heatproof basin with the water and stand over a pan of hot water. Heat gently until the chocolate melts. Remove from the heat and stir until smooth. Separate the eggs. Beat the yolks and a few drops of vanilla essence into the chocolate. Whisk the egg whites until fairly stiff, and fold gently into the mixture until evenly blended. Pour into 4 individual dishes and leave for 1–2 hours to set.

Serve decorated with cream and walnuts.

VARIATIONS

Mocha Mousse
Dissolve 1 × 5ml spoon instant coffee in 2 × 15ml spoons hot water and stir this liquid into the chocolate with the egg yolks and vanilla essence.

Choc-au-Rhum Mousse
Add 1 × 15ml spoon rum to the mixture, or use brandy, Grand Marnier or Tia Maria.

Chocolate Mousse (2)
4 helpings

100g plain chocolate
4 × 15ml spoons water
1 × 10ml spoon gelatine

3 eggs
vanilla essence
100ml double cream

Decoration
whipped double cream

coarsely grated chocolate

Break up the chocolate or grate it. Put it into a large heatproof basin with the water. Sprinkle in the gelatine and stand the basin over a pan of hot water. Heat gently until the chocolate has melted and the gelatine dissolved. Remove from the heat and stir until smooth. Separate the eggs. Beat the yolks and a few drops of vanilla essence into the chocolate. Whip the cream until it just holds its shape and fold it into the mixture. Whisk the egg whites until fairly stiff and fold in gently until evenly blended. Pour into a 750ml wetted mould or a deep serving bowl and chill for about 2 hours until set.

If moulded, turn out on to a flat plate. In either case, decorate with the whipped double cream and coarsely grated chocolate.

Velvet Cream *Basic recipe*
4 helpings

fresh lemon jelly (p309) (optional)
glacé cherries (optional)
angelica (optional)
3 × 15ml spoons water
1 × 10ml spoon gelatine

50g caster sugar
2 × 15ml spoons sherry **or** a few drops
  vanilla essence
250ml double cream
250ml single cream

If the velvet cream is to be set in a mould, line a 750ml mould with some of the jelly. Cut the cherries into quarters and the angelica into leaf shapes and decorate the mould as described on p310. Chill the remaining jelly and use to decorate the mould.

To make the cream, put the water into a heatproof container, sprinkle in the gelatine and leave to soften. Stand the container in a pan of hot water and stir until the gelatine dissolves. Add the sugar and sherry or vanilla essence, and stir until the sugar dissolves completely. Put to one side.

Put the double and single cream into a bowl and whip lightly. Fold the flavoured gelatine into the cream and pour carefully into the prepared mould. Leave to set for about 2 hours.

Turn out on to a flat, wetted plate. Chop the chilled fresh lemon jelly (p310), and arrange on the plate around the cream.

Note Instead of being poured into a lined mould, the velvet cream can be poured into 4 individual glasses. A thin coating of lemon jelly can then be poured on top and decorated. Leave to set for about 1 hour.

VARIATIONS
In each of the variations below, omit the sherry or vanilla essence:

Almond Cream
Flavour with 1 × 2.5ml spoon almond essence.

Chocolate Cream
Flavour with 75g melted plain chocolate.

Coffee Cream
Flavour with 1 × 15ml spoon instant coffee dissolved in 1 × 15ml hot water. Add 1 × 15ml spoon rum, if liked.

Raspberry Cream
Use 375ml double cream and fold in 125ml sieved raspberry purée instead of the single cream.

Strawberry Cream
Make as for Raspberry Cream substituting strawberries.

Vanilla Bavarian Cream (Vanilla Bavarois) *Basic recipe*
4 helpings

200ml fresh lemon jelly (p309)	1 × 2.5ml spoon vanilla essence
angelica (optional)	4 × 15ml spoons water
250ml milk	1 × 10ml spoon gelatine
4 egg yolks **or** 1 whole egg and 2 yolks	125ml double cream
50g caster sugar	125ml single cream

Line a 750ml mould with lemon jelly, cut the angelica into leaf shapes, if used, and decorate the mould as described on p310. Chill the remaining jelly.

To make the cream, mix the eggs and sugar together until fluffy and pale. Warm the milk, but do not let it boil; slowly stir in the milk. Strain the custard back into the saucepan or into a double boiler or basin held over hot water. (Make sure the water does not touch the upper pan.) Cook over very low heat, unti it thickens. Do not let the custard boil.

Strain the thickened custard into a bowl, stir in the vanilla essence, and leave to cool.

Put the water into a heatproof container, sprinkle in the gelatine and leave to soften. Stand the container in a pan of hot water and stir until the gelatine dissolves. Cool until tepid and add to the custard. Leave in a cool place until it thickens at the edges, stirring from time to time to prevent a skin forming.

Put the double and single cream into a bowl and whip lightly. Fold into the custard mixture, and pour into the prepared mould. Leave to set for about 2 hours. Chop the chilled jelly (p310) and use to decorate the cream. Turn out on to a flat, wetted plate.

VARIATIONS
In each of the variations below, omit the vanilla essence:

Caramel Bavarois
Dissolve 100g granulated sugar in 1 × 15ml spoon water and heat until the syrup turns a rich brown colour. Add 4 × 15ml spoons hot water, remove from the heat, and stir until all the caramel dissolves. Stir into the custard.

Chocolate Bavarois
Grate 100g plain chocolate and add with the milk. It will melt in the warm custard. Add 1 × 5ml spoon vanilla essence.

Italian Bavarois
Infuse thin strips of rind from 1 lemon in the milk. Add the strained juice of the lemon to the custard with 1 × 15ml spoon brandy, if liked.

Neapolitan Cream
Line the whole mould with raspberry jelly. Divide the cream into 4 portions: flavour one with vanilla, the second with ratafia essence, colour it green, flavour the third with coffee, and the fourth with strawberry essence, colour it pink. Pour the vanilla cream into the mould and leave it to set, then add the others, allowing each layer to set first.

Apricot Custard Cream *Basic recipe*
4 helpings

oil for greasing
500g fresh apricots **or** 2 × 425g cans
   apricots
200ml milk
3 egg yolks **or** 1 whole egg and 1 yolk
50g sugar

lemon juice (optional)
4 × 15ml spoons water
1 × 10ml spoon gelatine
100ml double cream
100ml single cream

Oil a 750ml mould lightly. Poach fresh fruit in a little water and sugar if it needs cooking. Process any fruit in an electric blender when tender, or sieve it if it contains seeds (eg berries or currants). Make the purée up to 200ml, if necessary, with a little fruit juice, fruit syrup or water.

Warm the milk, but do not let it come near the boil. Mix together the eggs and 25g of the sugar until fluffy and pale, and slowly stir in the milk. Strain the custard back into the saucepan or into a double boiler or basin held over hot water. (Make sure the water does not touch the upper pan.) Cook over very low heat for 15–20 minutes, stirring all the time, until it thickens. Do not let it come near the boil. Strain the custard into a bowl and leave to cool. Blend together the fruit purée and the cooled custard. Taste, and add more sugar and a little lemon juice if required.

Put the water into a heatproof container, sprinkle in the gelatine and leave to soften. Stand the container in a pan of hot water and stir until the gelatine dissolves. Cool until tepid, and add to the custard. Leave in a cool place until it begins to set, stirring from time to time to prevent a skin forming.

Put all the cream into a bowl and whip lightly. Fold into the setting mixture, and pour gently into the mould. Leave to set for about 2 hours. Turn out on to a flat, wetted plate. Decorate as desired.

VARIATIONS
Blackcurrants, blackberries, damsons, gooseberries, peaches, raspberries, or strawberries also make delicious fruit creams.

Quick Fruit Cream (using custard powder)
4 helpings

1 × 127g pkt orange jelly
100ml water
50ml orange juice

2 × 15ml spoons custard powder
250ml milk
125ml double cream

Chop the jelly tablet roughly. Heat the water, add the jelly, and stir until dissolved. Add the juice and leave to cool. Meanwhile, blend the custard powder with a little of the milk. Heat the rest of the milk until it boils. Pour it slowly on to the blended custard powder, stirring all the time. Return to the pan, bring to the boil and boil for 1–2 minutes, stirring all the time, until the custard thickens. Cool slightly and stir into the jelly. Cool until beginning to set. Whip the cream until it leaves a trail and fold into the setting mixture. Pour into individual glasses and chill for about 1 hour. Decorate as desired.

Trifles, Charlottes and Syllabubs

Mrs Beeton's Tipsy Cake or Brandy Trifle

4–6 helpings

1 × 15cm sponge cake (p375)
redcurrant jelly (optional)
65–75ml brandy **or** white wine and
   brandy
50g whole blanched almonds

375ml milk
125ml single cream
8 egg yolks
75g caster sugar

Put the cake in a glass bowl or dish 16cm in diameter and as deep as the cake. Spread the cake thinly with jelly, if used. Pour over as much brandy or brandy and wine as the cake can absorb. Cut the almonds into spikes lengthways and stick them into the top of the cake all over. Mix the milk and cream. Beat the yolks until liquid, and pour the milk and cream over them. Add the sugar. Cook gently in the top of a double boiler for about 10 minutes or until the custard thickens, stirring all the time. Let the custard cool slightly, then pour it over and around the cake. Cover and chill. When cold, decorate with small spoonfuls of redcurrant jelly.

Mrs Beeton's Traditional Trifle

6 helpings

4 individual sponge cakes
raspberry or strawberry jam
6 macaroons
12 ratafias
125ml sherry
25g blanched shredded almonds

grated rind of ½ lemon
25ml thick hot custard (p278)
125ml double cream
1 egg white
25g caster sugar

Decoration
glacé cherries

angelica

Cut the sponge cakes in half and spread one half of each with jam. Sandwich together and arrange in a glass dish. Crush the macaroons and ratafias and put them into the dish. Pour the sherry over them. Sprinkle with the almonds and lemon rind. Cover with the custard and leave for about 30 minutes to cool. Cover with damp grease-proof paper to prevent a skin forming. Whip together the cream, egg white, and sugar until stiff and spread over the dish. Decorate with cherries and angelica.

Mrs Beeton's Charlotte Russe
6 helpings

24 sponge fingers (p375)
2 × 15ml spoons white glacé icing
  (p387)
3 × 5ml spoons gelatine
3 × 15ml spoons water

500ml single cream
3 × 15ml spoons any sweet liqueur
1 × 15ml spoon icing sugar or to taste
1 × 15cm round sponge cake (p375)
  or Genoese sponge (p376), 1cm thick

Cut 4 sponge fingers in half, and dip the rounded ends in icing. Line a 15cm soufflé dish with the halved fingers, placing them like a star, with the non-sugared sides uppermost and the iced ends in the centre. Dip one end of each of the remaining biscuits in icing. Line the sides of the dish with them, sugared sides outward, iced ends at the bottom. Trim the biscuits to fit the rim of the dish. Soften the gelatine in the water in a small heatproof container. Stand the container in a pan of hot water and stir until it dissolves. Remove from the heat and whisk together with the cream, liqueur, and sugar until frothy. Stand the mixture in a cool place until it begins to thicken. Fill the charlotte with the mixture, and cover it with the round of sponge cake. Leave in a cool place for 8–12 hours, until firm. Loosen the biscuits from the sides of the dish with a knife, carefully turn out the charlotte on to a plate, and serve.

Wine Syllabub
4 helpings

200ml double cream
2 egg whites
75g caster sugar

juice of ½ lemon
100ml sweet white wine or sherry

Decoration
crystallized lemon slices

Whip the cream until it just holds its shape. Whisk the egg whites until they form soft peaks. Fold the sugar into the egg whites, then gradually add the lemon juice and wine or sherry. Fold this mixture into the whipped cream. Pour into glasses and chill in a refrigerator for about 2 hours. Remove 20 minutes before serving. Serve decorated with the lemon slices.

Note The lemon juice and wine will settle in the bottom of the glasses, leaving a frothy top.

Gâteaux, Cheesecakes and Meringue Desserts

Black Forest Cherry Gâteau (Schwarzwälderkirschtorte)
10–12 helpings

1 × 20cm round chocolate sandwich
   cake (p374), using 3 eggs
250ml double cream
125ml single cream

1 × 540g can Morello cherries
Kirsch
25g plain chocolate

Cut the cake into 3 layers. Whip together the double and single cream until stiff. Drain and stone the cherries. Reserve the juice and 11 whole cherries. Halve the rest. Gently fold the halved cherries into half the cream. Put to one side. Strain the reserved cherry juice and mix it with Kirsch to taste. Prick the cake layers and sprinkle with the cherry juice and Kirsch until well saturated. Sandwich the layers together using the whipped cream and cherries. When assembled, cover with the remaining cream and use the whole cherries to decorate the top. Grate the chocolate and sprinkle it over the cream.

Chocolate Profiteroles
8 helpings

choux pastry (p408) using 100g flour
250ml (approx) Chantilly cream,
   confectioners' custard or chocolate
   butter cream (p398)

200g chocolate or coffee
   glacé icing (p388)

Use the choux pastry to pipe 24–30 small choux about 2cm in diameter (see p424). When cooked, open them at the bottom, remove any uncooked paste, and leave to dry out and cool completely. When cold, fill with the desired cream. Glaze the tops with glacé icing, reserving some for assembling the dish. Let the icing harden, then arrange the choux in a pyramid (if possible against the sides of a conical mould). Stick them together with small dabs of icing.

   Serve 3 or 4 choux per person, with hot chocolate sauce (p227).

Mille-Feuille Gâteau
6–8 helpings

375g prepared puff pastry (p412)
flour for rolling out
250ml double cream or confectioners'
   custard (p398)

100g raspberry jam (optional)
glacé icing (p387) using 100g icing
   sugar

Roll out the pastry on a lightly floured surface 2mm thick and cut into six 15cm rounds. Place on baking trays, prick well, and bake in a very hot oven at 230°C, Gas 8, for 8–10 minutes until crisp and golden-brown. Lift the rounds off carefully and cool them on a wire rack. Whip the cream until thick, if used. Sandwich each layer of pastry together lightly with the jam and cream or confectioners' custard. (If using custard, the jam can be omitted.) Cover the top layer of pastry with the icing.

Gâteau St Honoré
10–12 helpings

Base

150g prepared shortcrust pastry
(p407)
flour for rolling out

2 beaten eggs for glazing
choux pastry (p408) using 200g flour

Pastry Cream

3 eggs
50g caster sugar
35g plain flour
25g cornflour
a few drops vanilla essence

250ml milk
125ml double cream
50g granulated sugar
3 × 15ml spoons water

Decoration

glacé cherries

angelica

To make the base, roll out the shortcrust pastry on a lightly floured surface into a 20cm round and place on a baking tray. Prick the pastry well and brush with beaten egg. Using a 1cm nozzle, pipe a circle of choux paste round the edge of the pastry. Brush with beaten egg. Use the remaining choux to pipe 18–20 small choux buns separately (p424). Place the circle and buns on a greased baking tray, and brush with beaten egg. Bake in a fairly hot oven at 200°C, Gas 6, for 15 minutes, then reduce to fairly hot, 190°C, Gas 5, for a further 10–15 minutes, or until the choux ring is well risen and golden-brown. Cool on a wire rack.

To make the pastry cream, separate 2 of the eggs. Beat together the yolks, whole egg, and the caster sugar. Stir in the flour, cornflour, and vanilla esence. Heat the milk and gradually beat it into the egg mixture. Return the mixture to the pan, bring to the boil, stirring all the time. and boil for 2–3 minutes. Put the mixture into a clean basin, cover with buttered paper and leave until cold.

Whip the cream until stiff and pipe into the choux buns. Put the sugar and water into a small saucepan, heat until the sugar has dissolved, then boil until a light straw colour. Remove from the heat. Dip the bottom of each bun quickly in the syrup and arrange on the choux round. Spoon a little syrup over each choux bun. Whisk the 2 remaining egg whites until stiff and fold into the pastry cream, with any leftover whipped cream. Fill the centre of the gâteau with the pastry cream. Decorate the buns with glacé cherries and angelica.

Note This gâteau is the traditional birthday cake in France.

Savarin
6–8 helpings

Basic Mixture

75ml milk

15g fresh yeast **or** 1 × 10ml spoon
   dried yeast

150g strong white flour

$\frac{1}{4}$ × 5ml spoon salt

1 × 10ml spoon sugar

75g butter

3 eggs

oil for greasing

Rum Syrup

75g lump sugar

125ml water

2 × 15ml spoons rum

1 × 15ml spoon lemon juice

Glaze

3 × 15ml spoons apricot jam

2 × 15ml spoons water

Warm the milk until tepid. Blend in the fresh yeast or sprinkle on the dried yeast. Stir in 25g of the flour and leave in a warm place for 20 minutes. Sift the rest of the flour, the salt, and the sugar into a bowl. Rub in the butter. Add the yeast to the mixture, then add the eggs and beat until well mixed. Oil a 20cm ring mould (a savarin mould). Pour the mixture into the tin, cover with a large, lightly oiled polythene bag, and leave in a warm place until the mixture has almost reached the top of the tin. Bake in a fairly hot oven at 200°C, Gas 6, for about 20 minutes or until golden-brown and springy to the touch.

To make the rum syrup, put the sugar and water in a pan and heat until the sugar has dissolved. Bring to the boil and boil steadily for 8 minutes. Add the rum and lemon juice. Turn the warm savarin on to a serving dish, prick all over with a fine skewer, and spoon the rum syrup over it.

To make the glaze, sieve the apricot jam into a saucepan, add the water and bring to the boil, stirring all the time. Brush the glaze all over the soaked savarin.

VARIATIONS

The basic savarin is used for a number of French desserts and cakes. Instead of soaking it in rum syrup it can be filled with various mixtures, such as flavoured whipped cream or fruit purée mixed with rum.

Rum Babas
Makes 12

Make the basic mixture as above but add 50g currants. Grease 12 baba tins. Half fill the tins with the mixture. Place in a large, lightly oiled polythene bag and leave in a warm place for about 20 minutes or until the tins are two-thirds full. Bake in a fairly hot oven at 200°C, Gas 6, for 10–15 minutes or until golden-brown and springy to the touch. While still warm, soak with rum syrup as above.

Coffee Cheesecake
10–12 helpings

Base

50g butter **or** margarine
50g caster sugar
1 egg

50g self-raising flour
1 × 2.5ml spoon baking powder

Filling

75g butter
100g caster sugar
2 × 15ml spoons instant coffee
1 × 15ml spoon boiling water
1 × 15ml spoon orange juice
2 × 15ml spoons brandy

1 egg
50g plain flour
75g sultanas
500g full-fat soft chesse
250ml double cream

Beat together all the ingredients for the base until smooth. Spread the mixture over the base of a deep loose-bottomed 20cm cake tin.

To make the filling, cream together the butter and sugar until light and fluffy. Dissolve the coffee in the boiling water and orange juice, and leave to cool. Beat it into the creamed mixture with the brandy and egg. Fold in the flour and sultanas. In a separate bowl, beat the cheese until smooth. Gradually beat in the cream. Fold the cheese mixture carefully into the butter mixture and pour into the prepared tin. Bake in a warm oven at 160°C, Gas 3, for $1\frac{1}{4}$–$1\frac{1}{2}$ hours or until firm. Cool. Remove from the tin and serve cold.

Curd Cheesecake
4 helpings

Base

shortcrust pastry (p407) using
   125g flour

flour for rolling out

Filling

curds from 500ml milk (75g approx)
   or 75g curd cheese
50g butter
1 egg
a pinch of salt

100g sugar
25g currants
grated nutmeg
1 × 5ml spoon baking powder

Roll out the pastry on a lightly floured surface and use it to line an 18cm flan ring. Break down the curds with a fork or, if very firm, rub them through a sieve. Melt the butter. Beat the egg until liquid. Mix the butter, egg, salt, sugar, currants, and a little grated nutmeg thoroughly into the curds. Add the baking powder last of all. Put the mixture into the flan case. Bake in a fairly hot oven at 190°C, Gas 5, for 25–30 minutes until the pastry is lightly browned and the filling set. Serve warm or cold.

Lemon Cheesecake

8 helpings

Base

100g digestive biscuits

50g butter

25g caster sugar

Filling

200g full-fat soft cheese

75g caster sugar

2 eggs

125ml soured cream

15g gelatine

50ml water

grated rind and juice of 1 lemon

Decoration

whipped cream

crystallized lemon slices

To make the base, crush the biscuits finely with a rolling pin. Melt the butter and mix in the crumbs and sugar. Press the mixture on to the base of a 17cm loose-bottomed cake tin. Put in a cool place to set.

To make the filling, beat the cheese and sugar together. Separate the eggs, and beat the yolks into the cheese mixture. Stir in the soured cream. Soften the gelatine in the water in a small heatproof basin. Stand the basin in a pan of hot water and stir until the gelatine dissolves. Stir the lemon rind, juice, and gelatine into the cheese mixture. Whisk the egg whites until stiff and fold carefully into the mixture. Pour into the prepared tin and chill for 45 minutes–1 hour until firm. Remove from the tin and decorate with whipped cream and crystallized lemon slices.

Raspberry Yoghurt Cheesecake

8–10 helpings

Base

50g butter

50g caster sugar

1 × 15ml spoon golden syrup

25g walnuts

50g puffed rice cereal

fat for greasing

Filling

1 × 15ml spoon gelatine

50ml cold water

300g cottage cheese

125ml raspberry flavoured yoghurt

1 × 15ml spoon lemon juice

3 eggs

250g caster sugar

250ml double cream

1 × 175g can raspberries

Glaze (optional)

syrup from canned raspberries

water

1 × 10ml spoon arrowroot

a few drops red food colouring

Melt the butter, sugar, and syrup together in a saucepan. Chop the walnuts, and add with the puffed rice cereal to the pan. Stir well and press the mixture on to the base of a greased 20cm loose-bottomed cake tin. Chill for 10 minutes.

Soften the gelatine in the water in a small heatproof basin. Stand the basin in a saucepan of hot water and stir until the gelatine dissolves. Sieve the cottage cheese, add the yoghurt and lemon juice and beat until smooth. Separate the eggs. Mix the yolks and 150g of the sugar in a pan, and cook over low heat, stirring all the time, until the mixture thickens. Remove from the heat, add the gelatine, mix well, and allow to cool until the mixture is beginning to thicken.

Stir the yoghurt and cheese mixture into the cooled gelatine. Whisk the egg whites until stiff, then gradually whisk in the remaining sugar. Whip the cream until it just holds its shape. Fold the whites and cream into the main mixture, and pour it carefully into the prepared tin. Chill for at least 4 hours. If leaving the cake unglazed, remove from the tin, drain the syrup from the can of raspberries and arrange the fruit on top. Chill before serving.

If glazing the cake, make up the syrup to 125ml with water and blend it into the arrowroot in a small saucepan. Bring to the boil, stirring all the time, and simmer for 2–3 minutes until the sauce thickens and clears. Add a few drops of red colouring. Arrange the fruit on top and coat with the glaze. Chill before serving.

Cooked Meringue (Meringue Cuite)
Makes 4 cases or baskets or 16–20 × 2cm cases for petits fours

4 egg whites
250g icing sugar

2–3 drops vanilla essence

Whisk the egg whites and sugar together in a basin over a pan of gently simmering water until the mixture is very thick and holds its shape. Flavour with vanilla essence. Bake in a very cool oven at 110°C, Gas $\frac{1}{4}$, for 1–1$\frac{1}{2}$ hours.

To make meringue baskets, line a baking tray as when making a meringue case and make up the meringue mixture. Spoon the meringue on to the tray into 4 portions. Keep them well apart. Hollow out the centres to make neat nest-like shapes.

Alternatively, use a small star vegetable nozzle to make 4 small basket shapes. Bake as for a meringue case.

Make very small meringue cases for use as petits fours in the same way. Make circles 2cm across and hollow out with the tip of a pointed spoon. Then proceed as for meringue baskets. The small cases will, however, dry in 45minutes–1 hour.

Italian Meringue

200g granulated sugar
2 × 15ml spoons water

4 egg whites

Put the sugar and water into a small, thick-based saucepan and heat slowly until the sugar has dissolved completely. Stir once or twice to make sure that every grain has dissolved. Increase the heat slightly and continue heating the syrup, without stirring, until it reaches 140°C. Keep the syrup warm. Whisk the egg whites until stiff. Pour the syrup on to the egg whites slowly and steadily, without a pause, while still whisking. (It is easier to get someone else to pour the syrup.) Continue whisking until the meringue is thick and cold. Bake in a very cool oven at 110°C, Gas $\frac{1}{4}$, for 1–1$\frac{1}{2}$ hours.

Use for a vacherin or to cover cold desserts.

Swiss or Chantilly Meringue (for shells, toppings, and cakes)

Makes 12–16 medium-sized shells, 24–30 small shells; covers 1 × 20–22cm flan or tart; makes 1 × 20cm case

4 egg whites
a pinch of salt
200g caster sugar

$\frac{1}{2}$ × 2.5ml spoon baking powder (optional)

Cream filling (see Method)
125ml double cream
$\frac{1}{2}$ × 2.5ml spoon vanilla essence

1 × 5ml spoon caster sugar

Separate the whites from the yolks very carefully. No trace of yolk must be left, for the fat in them prevents the whites whisking properly. For the same reason the bowl and whisk must be absolutely clean and dry.

Put the whites into a large bowl with the salt. Whisk the whites until they are very stiff and standing up in points. They must be absolutely dry or the meringues will break down in baking. Gradually add half the caster sugar, 1 × 15ml spoonful at a time. Whisk very thoroughly after each addition until the mixture regains its stiffness. The sugar must be blended in very thoroughly or it forms droplets of syrup which brown, and may make the meringues sticky and difficult to remove from the paper. Sprinkle the remaining sugar all at once over the surface together with the baking powder (if used). Fold in very lightly using a metal spoon.

To make the cream filling, whip the cream with the essence and sugar until it just holds its shape.

For *meringue shells*, line a baking sheet with greaseproof paper and rub it lightly with cooking oil, or use vegetable parchment.

Put the meringue mixture into a forcing bag with a 1–2cm nozzle and pipe into rounds on the paper; or shape the mixture using 2 wet dessertspoons – take up a spoonful of the mixture and smooth it with a palette knife, bringing it up into a ridge in the centre. Slide it out with the other spoon on to the tray, with the ridge on top.

Dust the meringues with caster sugar and dry off in a very cool oven at 110°C, Gas $\frac{1}{4}$, for 3–4 hours until they are firm and crisp, but still white. If they begin to brown, prop the oven door open a little. When crisp on the outside, lift the meringues off the tray gently with a palette knife. Turn them on their sides and return them to the oven until their undersides are dry. If the meringues are large, press in the soft centres to dry them out completely.

Put the meringues on a cooling tray until absolutely cold. Sandwich them together with the sweetened flavoured cream not more than 1 hour before they are to be used, or they will go soft. Alternatively, use without the filling to decorate a cold dessert.

For *meringue topping*, use only 25–40g of sugar per egg white. Whisk the whites until stiff and fold the sugar in lightly. Pile the mixture on top of the pudding a few minutes before the end of the cooking time, and spread it out to cover the whole surface. It is more attractive if flicked up into small peaks.

By covering the pudding, the meringue seals it from the heat so that it does not dry out. Sprinkle the top of the meringue with caster sugar. Bake in a very cool oven at 140°C, Gas 1, for 30–40 minutes; or in a hot oven at 220°C, Gas 7, for about

10 minutes. In either case the meringue will be crisp and lightly coloured on the outside, but remain soft inside.

For *meringue cases* draw a 20cm circle on a sheet of greaseproof paper or vegetable parchment. Put the paper on a baking sheet. Oil the greaseproof paper very lightly.

Make up the meringue mixture as for shells. Spread some of the meringue all over the circle to form the base of the case. Put the rest of the mixture into a forcing bag and, using a large star vegetable nozzle, pipe it round the edge of the ring in a border 5–6cm high, or use a spoon to make the rim. Bake low down in a very cool oven at 110°C, Gas ¼, for 3–4 hours, or until quite dry. Leave to cool on a rack, remove the paper and fill the case with fruit and sweetened whipped cream.

Note If really dried out, meringue shells will keep for 1–2 weeks in an airtight tin.

Raspberry Vacherin *Basic recipe*
4 helpings

3 egg whites
a pinch of salt
150g caster sugar
300g fresh raspberries

250ml double cream
1 × 5ml spoon caster sugar
Kirsch

Decoration
a few angelica leaves

Line 2 baking trays with greaseproof paper or vegetable parchment. Draw a 15cm circle on each one and very lightly oil the greaseproof paper, if used.

Make up a cooked or Italian meringue mixture (p325) from the egg whites, salt, and 150g caster sugar. Put the meringue into a forcing bag with a 1cm plain nozzle. Starting from the middle of one circle, pipe round and round to form a coiled, flat round 15cm in diameter. Pipe a similar round on the other tray. Use any remaining mixture to pipe small meringue shells. Bake in a very cool oven at 110°C, Gas ¼, for 1–1½ hours. Leave to cool.

Pick over the raspberries, and leave on a plate for 30 minutes. Clean and pat dry. Reserve a few choice berries for decoration. Whip the double cream until it is thick and stands in firm peaks, then stir in the 1 × 5ml spoon caster sugar and Kirsch to taste.

Place one of the meringue rounds on a serving plate, spread with some of the cream, and arrange half the raspberries on it in a flat layer. (Do not make the cream layer too thick or the vacherin will be difficult and messy to eat and serve.) Put the second meringue on top of the raspberries, arrange the rest of the raspberries in the centre, and pipe rosettes or a decorative edge of cream round the berries. Decorate the sides of the vacherin with the small meringues and angelica leaves.

Serve cut in wedges like a cake, using a flat cake slice to lift the meringue on to the plates.

Hazelnut Meringue Gâteau
4 helpings

75g hazelnuts	2–3 drops vanilla essence
3 egg whites	125ml double cream
150g caster sugar	1–2 × 5ml spoons caster sugar
2–3 drops vinegar	

Reserve a few hazelnuts for decorating the gâteau and bake the rest in a moderate oven at 180°C, Gas 4, for 10 minutes. Rub off the skins. Chop the nuts very finely or process briefly in an electric blender or coffee mill.

Line 2 baking trays with greaseproof paper or vegetable parchment. Draw a 15cm circle on each one and very lightly oil the greaseproof paper, if used.

Make up a cooked or Italian meringue mixture (p325) from the egg whites and caster sugar. Add the vinegar, vanilla essence, and chopped nuts. Spread the meringue inside the marked circles or put the meringue into a forcing bag with a 1cm plain nozzle. If using a forcing bag, start from the middle of one circle and pipe round and round to form a coiled, flat round 15cm in diameter. Pipe a similar round on the other tray. Bake in a moderate oven at 180°C, Gas 4, for 35–40 minutes, until crisp and lightly browned. Leave to cool.

Whip the double cream until it stands in firm peaks, and stir in 1–2 × 5ml spoons caster sugar. Put one of the meringue rounds on a serving plate and spread with most of the cream. (Do not make the cream layer too thick or the gâteau will be difficult and messy to cut and serve.) Put the second meringue round on the cream layer and decorate with the rest of the cream and the reserved hazelnuts.

ICES AND FROZEN DESSERTS

Ices can be frozen in either a freezer or the ice-making compartment of a refrigerator. Whichever method is used, all equipment should be chilled before use.

Freezer

The dial should be set to 'fast freeze' about 1 hour before freezing. Except for *granités*, which are not beaten during freezing, any mixture should, if possible, be packed in a container in which it can be beaten. The mixture is beaten once or twice during freezing to break down the ice crystals and incorporate air. After beating, the mixture is put into its mould, if used, and frozen firm for immediate use, or storage at the freezer's normal temperature. Ices for storage must be sealed, or overwrapped and labelled. For details of storage life for ices, see p435.

Ice-making Compartment

The dial should be set at the coldest setting at least 1 hour before putting in the ice mixture. If there is room, the mixture should be frozen in a container, as in a home freezer, and beaten in the same way. If there is no room in the compartment, the mixture can be frozen in ice trays with the dividers removed or in similar containers, and either put into another container for beating, or whisked in the trays with a fork.

After beating, the ice is returned, covered, to the ice-making compartment until frozen firm, and the dial is then returned to its normal setting.

Electric Ice Cream Maker or Sorbetière
This appliance is placed in the ice-making compartment of a refrigerator, or a home freezer, and beats the mixture steadily until it is frozen, when it ceases automatically; it gives a very smooth texture and more bulk than when the mixture is hand beaten. A spare electric point near the refrigerator or freezer is needed to plug in the sorbetière. Electric churns for use outside the refrigerator are also available; they operate on the same principle as the hand churns described below, and need extra ice and salt to operate.

Churn Freezer
A churn freezer consists of a metal container for the ice cream mixture, placed in an outer churn packed with crushed ice and salt. A 1 litre capacity freezing container needs 3.25kg crushed ice and 1kg common salt or freezing salt (obtainable from most large department stores and fishmongers), for the churn.

Containers
The governing factors in choosing containers must be the size of the freezing space available, and the freezing time you can allow. A deep bowl or box, for example, may not fit into the ice-making compartment of the refrigerator, and a solid block of ice cream takes much longer to freeze than a shallow layer in an ice tray. The larger the quantity of ice mixture the more slowly it freezes, and since quick freezing is generally desirable to prevent the formation of large ice crystals, it is wise to freeze ices in single quantities of 1 litre or less. If it is necessary to freeze more than this amount, use two containers. Rigid plastic, stainless steel, or any similar containers can be used, provided they have lids or can be covered securely with foil. If space allows, it is easier to use rigid plastic bowls with lids to freeze ice mixtures before beating; they can then be beaten in the bowl and transferred to the container in which they are to be served or stored for the final freezing.

Moulds
Large ice cream moulds are exactly like decorative jelly moulds, but have lids. Individual ice creams can be frozen in small fluted jelly moulds which hold about 100ml. Moulds without lids should be covered with foil while the mixture is freezing.

   Bombes should be frozen in bell-shaped moulds, or in pudding basins. Use refrigerator ice trays or oblong foil trays for making a *biscuit glacé* or Neapolitan ice cream. Round, flat layers of ice cream for gâteaux can be frozen in deep cake tins, or in sandwich tins or foil dishes.

Other Equipment
An electric or rotary beater makes beating ice mixtures much easier both before and during freezing. A nylon (not metal) sieve for puréeing fruit is also necessary. Fruit can be processed in an electric blender, but fruits such as raspberries or grapes, with pips and skin, have to be sieved to make a really smooth purée. An ice cream scoop

for serving individual portions of ice cream or water ices, or for shaping ice cream into small balls for a *plombière* is a useful, though not essential, piece of equipment.

Water Ices, Granités and Sorbets

1) After pouring the mixture into a suitable container, chill if a hot syrup has been used, cover closely, and half freeze unless otherwise directed.
2) Beat the half-frozen mixture thoroughly, scraping off any crystals. Re-cover and freeze completely; label and store.

Note The recipes in the Water Ice section below can be served as *granités*;they should be frozen completely and the beating omitted.

Syrup (1)
Makes 1 litre (approx)

1kg caster sugar
750ml water

3 × 2.5ml spoons liquid glucose (optional)

Put the sugar and water in a strong saucepan and dissolve the sugar over gentle heat, without stirring. Bring the mixture to the boil and boil slowly for about 10 minutes or to a temperature of 110°C. Remove the scum as it rises. Strain, cool with a lid on the pan, add the liquid glucose, if used, and store in a glass bottle for use as required. If the syrup is to be used hot, re-heat in a covered pan, and keep covered during any waiting period.

Syrup (2)
Makes 500ml (approx)

200g lump sugar

500ml water

Make as for Syrup (1).

Lemon Water Ice
6 helpings

6 lemons
2 oranges

375ml hot syrup (1)

Pare the rind very thinly from the fruit, and put into a basin. Add the hot syrup, cover, and leave to cool. Add the juice of the lemons and oranges to the syrup mixture. Strain through a nylon sieve into a container, chill, and freeze as described above.

VARIATION
Orange Water Ice
Use 6 oranges and 2 lemons, and reduce the syrup quantity to 250ml.

Raspberry or Strawberry Water Ice
6 helpings

450g ripe strawberries, raspberries
   or loganberries

250ml cold syrup (1) (p330)
juice of 2 lemons

Rub the fruit through a nylon sieve, or process in an electric blender and sieve to make a smooth purée. Add the cold syrup and lemon juice, and mix well. Pour into a suitable container and freeze as described on p330.

Lemon Sorbet
6–8 helpings

2 × 5ml spoons gelatine
250ml water
150g caster sugar

1 × 2.5ml spoon grated lemon rind
250ml lemon juice
2 egg whites

Soften the gelatine in a little of the water over a pan of hot water. Boil the remaining water and sugar together for 10 minutes. Stir the dissolved gelatine into the syrup, add the lemon rind and juice, and leave to cool. Pour into a suitable container, cover, and freeze for 1 hour. Whisk the egg whites until they hold stiff peaks, beat the half-frozen ice mixture thoroughly, and fold the egg whites into it. Re-cover, and continue freezing for a further 2 hours.

Note This ice will not freeze hard.

Ice Creams, Puddings and Drinks

1) Cool hot custard unless required hot.
2) After turning the mixture into a container, chill until thoroughly cold, cover closely and half freeze unless otherwise directed.
3) Beat the mixture well and add any cream, if it has not been added before. Re-freeze until firm; label and store.

Note Ice creams made with an electric ice cream maker are prepared somewhat differently, and the manufacturer's directions should be followed.

Plain Custard (1)
Makes 500ml (approx)

2 × 15ml spoons custard powder
500ml milk

100g caster sugar

Blend the custard powder with a little of the milk. Heat the remaining milk to boiling point and pour on to the blended mixture. Return to the pan and simmer, stirring all the time, until the mixture thickens. Add the sugar, cover, and use hot or cold as required.

Plain Egg Custard (2)
Makes 500ml (approx)

500ml milk
3 eggs

100g caster sugar

Heat the milk until almost boiling. Beat the eggs and sugar together and add the hot milk, stirring well. Return the mixture to the pan and cook, without boiling, until the custard coats the back of a wooden spoon. Stir all the time. Strain, cover, and use as required.

Standard Custard (3)
Makes 500ml (approx)

500ml milk
8 egg yolks

2 eggs
100g caster sugar

Heat the milk until almost boiling. Beat the yolks, eggs, and sugar together until thick and white, and add the hot milk, stirring well. Return the mixture to the pan and cook, without boiling, until the custard thickens, stirring all the time. Strain, cover, and use as required.

Rich Custard (4)
Makes 500ml (approx)

8 egg yolks
100g caster sugar
500ml single cream

vanilla essence, ground spice, liqueur
or other flavouring

Beat the yolks and sugar together until very thick. Put the cream in a saucepan and bring slowly to the boil. Pour the cream over the yolks and sugar, stirring well. Return the mixture to the pan and cook, without boiling, until the custard thickens. Stir all the time. Strain, add a few drops of vanilla essence or other flavouring, cover, and use as required.

Vanilla Ice Cream
6 helpings

125ml double cream
500ml cold custard (1) (p331)

1 × 5ml spoon vanilla essence

Whip the cream until semi-stiff. Add the cold custard and vanilla essence. Turn into a suitable container, chill, and freeze as described on p331, beating once while freezing.

Rich Vanilla Ice Cream
6 helpings

250ml double cream
250ml cold custard (2) (p332)

1 × 5ml spoon vanilla essence
50g caster sugar

Whip the cream until semi-stiff. Add the cold custard, vanilla essence, and sugar. Turn into a suitable container, chill, and freeze as described on p331, beating once while freezing.

Rich Chocolate Ice Cream
6–8 helpings

100g plain chocolate
65ml water
250ml hot custard (3) **or** (4) (p332)

125ml double cream
1 × 5ml spoon vanilla essence

Break up the chocolate roughly and melt it in the water, either in a double saucepan or in a basin over hot water. Add the melted chocolate to the hot custard, and leave to cool. Whip the cream until semi-stiff and fold it into the custard mixture with the vanilla essence. Turn into a container, chill, and freeze as described on p331, beating once while freezing.

Lemon Ice Cream
6 helpings

8 egg yolks
200g caster sugar

juice of 2 lemons
250ml double cream

Beat the egg yolks until very thick, add the sugar, and beat again. Stir in the lemon juice. Whip the cream until semi-stiff, and add carefully to the egg and sugar mixture. Turn into a suitable container, chill, and freeze for 30 minutes. Beat thoroughly, and finish freezing as described on p331.

Strawberry or Raspberry Ice Cream
6 helpings

125ml milk
250ml double cream
2 egg yolks
150g caster sugar

400g strawberries **or** raspberries
1 × 15ml spoon granulated sugar
1 × 5ml spoon lemon juice
red food colouring

Put the milk and cream in a saucepan and bring almost to boiling point. Beat together the yolks and caster sugar, add to the milk and cream, and return to low heat, stirring all the time, until the mixture thickens. Rub the strawberries or raspberries through a nylon sieve. Fold the granulated sugar into the purée. Mix with the custard, and add lemon juice and a few drops of red food colouring. Turn into a suitable container, chill, and freeze as described on p331, beating once while freezing.

Baked Alaska
6–8 helpings

3 egg whites
150g caster sugar
1 × 20cm round Genoese **or** other
   sponge cake

500ml vanilla ice cream (p332)

Heat the oven to very hot, 230°C, Gas 8. Whisk the egg whites until very stiff, gradually whisk in half the sugar and fold in the rest. Alternatively, use the whites and sugar to make an Italian meringue (see p325).

Place the sponge cake round on an ovenproof plate and pile the ice cream on to it, leaving 1cm sponge uncovered all round. Cover quickly with the meringue, making sure that both the ice cream and the sponge are completely covered. Put in the oven for 3–4 minutes until the meringue is just beginning to brown. Serve immediately.
Note The ice cream must be as hard as possible.

Banana Split
6 helpings

6 bananas
500ml vanilla ice cream (p332)

250ml Melba sauce (p228)
50g chopped walnuts

Decoration
125ml double cream
sugar

6 maraschino cherries

Split the bananas in half lengthways and place in small oval dishes. Place 2 small scoops or slices of ice cream between the banana halves. Coat the ice cream with Melba sauce, and sprinkle with the chopped nuts. Whip the cream until stiff and sweeten to taste. Decorate with the cream and cherries.

Coupe Jacques
6 helpings

50g grapes
1 banana
1 peach
50g raspberries

2 × 15ml spoons Kirsch
250ml lemon water ice (p330) **or**
   vanilla ice cream (p332)
250ml strawberry ice cream (p333)

Decoration
125ml double cream

sugar

Chop and mix the fruit; soak in the Kirsch for 4 hours. Place one portion of each ice in each of 6 sundae glasses. Cover with the soaked fruit. Whip the cream until soft and sweeten to taste. Decorate each portion with the cream.

Knickerbocker Glory
6 helpings

1 × 500ml pkt yellow jelly
1 × 500ml pkt red jelly
200g canned peaches
200g canned pineapple chunks
150ml double cream

1 × 5ml spoon caster sugar
1 litre vanilla ice cream (p332)
500ml Melba sauce (p228)
50g chopped mixed nuts

Decoration
6 maraschino cherries

Make the jellies according to the directions on the packet. Leave until set. Drain the peaches and pineapple chunks, chop them, and mix the fruit together. Whip the cream until stiff, and sweeten with the caster sugar. Chop the set jellies with a fork until well broken up.

Put 1 × 15ml spoon of fruit in each of 6 sundae glasses. Cover with 1 × 15ml spoon of yellow jelly, add a scoop of ice cream, and coat with the Melba sauce. Repeat the process using the red jelly. Sprinkle with the chopped nuts, and pipe a rose of whipped cream on top. Decorate each portion with a maraschino cherry.
Note Tall wine glasses can be used instead of sundae glasses.

Neapolitan Ice
6 helpings

250ml double cream
250ml cold custard (3) (p332)
125ml strawberry **or** raspberry purée
75g caster sugar
red food colouring (optional)

$\frac{1}{2}$ × 2.5ml spoon almond **or** ratafia
essence
green food colouring
2 × 5ml spoons vanilla essence

Whip the cream until semi-stiff and fold into the cold custard. Divide this mixture into 3 equal portions. Mix the fruit purée with one-third of the mixture, and add 25g sugar and a few drops of red food colouring, if necessary. Add the almond or ratafia essence to another third of the mixture with a further 25g sugar and enough food colouring to tint it a bright but not vivid green. Add the vanilla essence and the last 25g sugar to the remaining third of the mixture. Cover, and freeze in separate trays until almost firm; then pack in layers in a suitable square or oblong mould. Cover and freeze until required. Serve cut in slices.

Peach Melba
6 helpings

500ml vanilla ice cream (p332)
6 canned peaches

250ml Melba sauce (p228)
125ml double cream

Place a scoop or slice of ice cream in each of 6 sundae glasses. Cover each portion with a peach half. Coat with the Melba sauce. Whip the cream until stiff, and pipe a large rose on top of each portion.

Poire Belle Hélène
4 helpings

4 firm ripe pears
250ml vanilla ice cream (p332)

250ml chocolate sauce (p227)
125ml double cream

Decoration
25g crystallized violets

Peel the pears, cut them in half, and remove the cores. Place a scoop or slice of ice cream in each of 4 dishes. Top with the pear halves and mask with chocolate sauce. Whip the cream until stiff, and pipe a large rose on top of each portion. Decorate with the crystallized violets.

Strawberry Ice Cream Layer Gâteau
8–10 helpings

1 litre strawberry ice cream (p333)
1 litre lemon ice cream (p333)
125g digestive biscuits
50g chopped mixed nuts
75g butter

25g soft light brown sugar
250g strawberry jam
4 × 15ml spoons Kirsch
200ml double cream
icing sugar

Decoration
whole strawberries

Line an 18cm loose-bottomed, deep cake tin with vegetable parchment. Soften both ice creams. Crush the digestive biscuits with a rolling-pin. Put 25g crumbs aside with 25g of the nuts. Melt the butter, and mix in the rest of the crumbs and nuts, and the brown sugar. Press the mixture into the lined cake tin, and chill until firm.

Sieve the jam, and mix with 1 × 15ml spoon of the Kirsch. Mix the strawberries for the decoration with 1 × 15ml spoon Kirsch and a little icing sugar, if liked. Chill for at least 1 hour.

Cover the chilled biscuit crumb base with half the strawberry ice cream, and spread the top with a third of the jam. Sprinkle with one-third of the remaining crumbs and chopped nuts. Freeze until the ice cream is firm. Repeat the process with half the lemon ice cream, then with the rest of the ingredients until alternate layers of ice cream and jam, crumbs, and nuts have been formed. Freeze until each layer of ice cream is firm before adding the next.

Whip the cream until stiff with the remaining Kirsch, and icing sugar to taste. Remove the gâteau from the cake tin, and peel off the vegetable parchment. Put on to a suitable plate, and cover the top layer of lemon ice cream with the whipped cream. Decorate with the strawberries, chill again, and serve.

Note It is easier not to try and detach the crumb base from the bottom of the cake tin; simply put the gâteau on the plate with the bottom of the tin still in place.

Chocolate Profiteroles (p320)

LEFT
Christmas Pudding (p289)
with Brandy Butter (p233)

BELOW
Mrs Beeton's
Tipsy Cake (p318)

RIGHT
Raspberry Yoghurt
Cheesecake (p324)

BELOW RIGHT
(back)
Hazelnut Meringue
Gâteau (p328)
(front)
Lemon Soufflé (p312)

Knickerbocker Glory (p335)

RIGHT (clockwise from top) Baked Alaska
(p334), Lemon Sorbet (p331), Strawberry Ice
Cream Layer Gâteau (p336), and Peach
Melba (p335)

LEFT Different types of Pastry

At the back, a raised pie (p410), in front, large, small and cocktail-sized vol-au-vent cases (p413)

RIGHT Cream Horns (p424) and Maids of Honour (p427)

BELOW Treacle Tart (p422)

Breads and Rolls (clockwise from top) Basic White Bread (p339), Rye Cobs (p344), Dinner Rolls (p342), Wholemeal Rolls (p343), Bridge Rolls (p342) and Bread Plait (p341)

Ice Cream Soda *Basic recipe*
4–6 helpings

200ml fresh fruit purée (p303)
150ml milk
50g caster sugar **or** to taste (depending
    on the sweetness of the fruit)

150g ice cream, suited to the fruit
    flavour used
250ml soda water

Process the fruit purée, milk, and sugar in an electric blender at medium speed until smooth. Add the ice cream and blend for a further 30 seconds. Pour into 4–6 glasses, and top up with the soda water.
Note Use a well-flavoured fruit purée.

Milk Shake *Basic recipe*
2 helpings

500ml milk
2 × 10ml spoons concentrated fruit
    juice **or** fruit syrup

2 scoops ice cream, suited to the fruit
    flavour used

Either simply stir the fruit flavouring into the milk, chill, and add the ice cream just before serving; or, mix all the ingredients together and chill well. Then just before serving, whisk thoroughly, or process briefly in an electric blender. Serve while still frothy.

VARIATION
Coffee Milk Shake
Substitute 1 × 10ml spoon coffee essence for the fruit flavouring. Use vanilla, chocolate or coffee ice cream.

BREADS, CAKES, BISCUITS, ICINGS, FILLINGS AND DECORATIONS

BREADS

Yeast Breads

The fermentation method of raising dough involves the use of yeast, which is a living organism. Whenever it is used, twice as much fresh yeast is needed as dried yeast; in other words, 50g fresh yeast = 25g dried yeast.

Fresh Yeast is quick and easy to use but is not always easily obtainable, especially in urban areas. It should be creamy in colour, have a slightly beery smell, be cool to the touch and easy to break. It will store in a polythene bag in a refrigerator for up to a week and will freeze, if well wrapped, for up to 1 month. Fresh yeast should always be blended into a warm liquid rather than creamed with sugar, which tends to give yeasty 'off' flavours in the finished bread.

Dried Yeast, available in packets and tins, has a shelf-life, unopened, of up to 1 year. Once opened, however, it keeps for only 2–3 months, and must be stored in an airtight container.

Before use, dried yeast must be reconstituted. 1 × 5ml spoon of sugar is dissolved in a warm liquid (usually water and/or milk at a temperature of 38°C, ie hand-hot). The dried yeast is sprinkled on the liquid and left in a warm place for 10–15 minutes, or until the yeast has fully dissolved and the mixture is frothy. (This may take longer when using all milk.) If after 30 minutes the mixture has not frothed, the yeast is stale and should be thrown away.

Kneading

Most doughs must be worked after mixing in order to strengthen and develop them and to make them rise well. Very soft doughs are beaten; all others are kneaded.

To hand knead: On a floured surface, fold the dough towards you, then push down and away from you with the heel of your hand. Give the dough a quarter turn and repeat the folding and pushing action, developing a rocking rhythm. Continue until the dough feels firm and elastic and is no longer sticky.

To knead in an electric mixer: Follow the manufacturer's directions for using a dough hook. Place the yeast liquid in the mixer bowl first, then add the dry ingredients. Turn the machine to minimum speed and mix for 1 minute to form the dough. Increase the speed slightly and mix for a further 2 minutes. It may be necessary to hand knead the dough into one piece when it is removed from the mixer bowl.

Rising

All yeast doughs must rise at least once before baking. Generally, a dough gives a better flavour and texture if it rises twice, but raising it once makes quite acceptable bread if time is limited. (The second rising is generally called *proving*.)

Rising times vary according to the type of dough and the temperature of the rising place; the warmer the place, the quicker the rise. The rising place must not, however, be too warm or the finished loaf will be dry and will quickly become stale. The dough may also be over-stretched by the yeast working too actively. The bread may collapse in the oven, and the loaf may smell yeasty or sour. As a rough guide, the dough should have risen enough when it has doubled in bulk.

The dough can be left to rise overnight in a refrigerator. In this case, return it to room temperature before shaping. Do not, however, leave rolls to rise in this way. All doughs should be covered during rising to prevent the surface drying out and a skin forming. The most convenient, efficient, and hygienic form of covering is a large polythene bag which has been lightly oiled inside to prevent it sticking to the dough and spoiling the surface of the shaped bread. The dough should only be covered loosely when it is put in the bag; ie some air space should be left above it so that it can rise unimpeded.

Unrisen dough can also be frozen (see p438).

Basic White Bread
Makes two 800g loaves

800g strong white flour
1 × 10ml spoon salt
1 × 10ml spoon sugar
25g lard
25g fresh yeast **or** 1 × 15ml spoon
   dried yeast

500ml warm water
flour for kneading
fat for greasing
beaten egg **or** milk for glazing

Sift together the flour, salt, and sugar into a large bowl. Rub in the lard. Blend the fresh yeast into the warm water or reconstitute the dried yeast. Add the yeast liquid to the flour mixture and mix to a soft dough. Turn on to a floured surface and knead for about 8 minutes or until the dough is smooth, elastic, and no longer sticky. Place the dough in a large, lightly oiled polythene bag and leave in a warm place for about 1 hour or until the dough has doubled in size. Knead the dough again until firm. Cut into 2 equal portions and form each into a loaf shape. Place the dough in 2 greased 23 × 13 × 7cm loaf tins and brush the surface with beaten egg or milk. Place the tins in the polythene bag and leave in a warm place for about 45 minutes or until the dough has doubled in size. Bake in a very hot oven, 230°C, Gas 8, for 35–40 minutes until the loaves are crisp and golden-brown and sound hollow when tapped on the bottom.

VARIATIONS
Fancy Roll Shapes
Makes 26
Divide the risen Basic White Bread dough into 50g pieces and shape as over (p340).

Small Plaits

Divide each piece of dough into 3 equal portions; then shape each of these into a long strand. Plait the 3 strands together, pinching the ends securely.

Small Twists

Divide each piece of dough into 2 equal portions, and shape into strands about 12cm in length. Twist the 2 strands together, pinching the ends securely.

'S' Rolls

Shape each piece of dough into a roll about 15cm in length, and form it into an 'S' shape.

Cottage Rolls

Cut two-thirds off each piece of dough and shape into a ball. Shape the remaining third in the same way. Place the small ball on top of the larger one and push a hole through the centre of both with one finger, dusted with flour, so joining the 2 pieces firmly together.

Huffkins

Shape each piece of dough into an oval about 12mm thick, then make a hole in the centre with one finger, dusted with flour.

Single Knots

Shape each piece of dough into a roll about 15cm in length and tie it into a knot. Place the shaped rolls, spaced well apart, on to greased baking sheets. Brush the surface of each with beaten egg or milk. Place the sheets in a large, lightly oiled polythene bag and leave in a warm place for about 25 minutes or until the rolls have almost doubled in size. Bake as for Basic White Bread (p339) but reduce the cooking time to 10–15 minutes.

Lardy Cake
Makes 18–20 slices

¼ recipe of risen Basic White Bread dough (p339) (350g approx)	100g caster sugar
flour for rolling out	100g sultanas **or** currants
125g lard	1 × 5ml spoon mixed spice

Glaze

1 × 10ml spoon caster sugar   1 × 15ml spoon water

On a floured surface, roll out the dough to a strip 2cm thick. Place a third of the lard in small pats over the surface of the dough. Sprinkle one-third of the sugar, dried fruit, and spice over it. Fold the dough into three. Repeat the rolling and folding twice more, using the remaining ingredients. Roll out to fit a 20cm square slab cake or baking tin. Score diamond shapes in the surface of the dough with a sharp knife. Place the tin in a large, lightly oiled polythene bag and leave in a warm place for about 45 minutes or until the dough has risen by half. Bake in a fairly hot oven, 200°C, Gas 6, for 40 minutes until crisp and golden-brown.

To make the glaze, boil together the sugar and water until syrupy, and brush over the surface of the warm cake.

Enriched Bread
Makes two 800g loaves

800g strong white flour	100g butter **or** margarine
1 × 10ml spoon sugar	2 eggs
400ml milk	flour for kneading
25g fresh yeast **or** 1 × 15ml spoon	fat for greasing
dried yeast	milk for glazing
1 × 10ml spoon salt	

Sift about 75g of the flour and all the sugar into a large bowl. Warm the milk until hand-hot, then blend in the fresh yeast or stir in the dried yeast. Pour the yeast liquid into the flour and sugar and beat well. Leave the bowl in a warm place for 20 minutes. Sift the remaining flour and salt into a bowl. Rub in the fat. Beat the eggs into the yeast mixture and stir in the flour and fat. Mix to a soft dough. Turn on to a lightly floured surface and knead for about 6 minutes or until the dough is smooth and no longer sticky. Place the dough in a large, lightly oiled polythene bag and leave in a warm place for about 1 hour or until it has doubled in size. Knead again until firm. Cut it into 2 equal portions and form each into a loaf shape. Place in 2 greased 23 × 13 × 7cm loaf tins and cover with the polythene bag. Leave in a warm place for about 30 minutes or until the dough has doubled in size. Brush the surface with milk and bake in a hot oven, 220°C, Gas 7, for 35–40 minutes until the loaves are golden-brown and sound hollow when tapped on the bottom.

VARIATIONS
Bread Plait
Make as for Enriched Bread. Cut the risen dough into 2 equal portions. Cut one of these into 3 equal pieces. Roll each piece into a strand 25–30cm long and plait the strands together. Repeat, using the second portion. Place the plaits on a greased baking tray, cover, rise, and bake as for Enriched Bread.

Fruit Bread
Make as for Enriched Bread but add 200g sultanas, currants or raisins to the dough when kneading for the second time.

Nut Bread
Make as for Enriched Bread but add 200g chopped nuts (walnuts, peanuts, etc) to the dough when kneading for the second time.

Poppy Seed Bread
Make as for Enriched Bread but sprinkle poppy seeds thickly over the dough before baking.

For further **variations**, see over.

Bridge Rolls

Makes 34–38

Make as for Enriched Bread (p341) but cut the risen dough into 50g pieces. Roll each piece into a finger shape about 10cm long. Place on a greased baking tray so that the rolls almost touch each other. Dust the surface of the rolls with flour, cover, and leave to rise for about 20 minutes or until the rolls have joined together. Bake as for Enriched Bread but reduce the cooking time to 12–15 minutes.

Dinner Rolls

Makes 34–38

Make as for Enriched Bread (p341) but cut the risen dough into 50g pieces. Shape each piece into a ball. Place on a greased baking tray 5–8cm apart. Brush with beaten egg, cover, and leave to rise for about 20 minutes or until the rolls have doubled in size. Bake as for Enriched Bread but reduce the cooking time to 12–15 minutes.

French Bread

Makes 2 French sticks

350g plain white flour (see **Note**)
50g cornflour
1 × 5ml spoon salt
15g fresh yeast **or** 1 × 10ml spoon
   dried yeast

250ml warm water
flour
beaten egg for glazing

Sift the flours and salt into a large bowl. Blend the fresh yeast into the warm water or reconstitute the dried yeast. Stir the yeast liquid into the flours and mix to a firm dough. Turn the dough on to a floured surface and knead for about 4 minutes or until it is smooth and no longer sticky. Place the dough in a large, lightly oiled polythene bag and leave in a warm place for about 1 hour or until it has doubled in size. Cut it into 2 equal portions. On a floured surface, roll out 1 piece to an oval 40cm in length. Roll it up like a Swiss roll and place on a well-floured baking sheet. With a sharp knife, slash the top surface at intervals. Brush the surface with beaten egg. Repeat with the other piece of dough. Leave both, *uncovered*, in a warm place for about 30 minutes or until doubled in size.

Meanwhile, place a pan of hot water in the bottom of the oven and heat the oven to hot, 220°C, Gas 7. This is to provide steam to make the French bread expand fully before using dry heat to form the typical crisp crust. Bake the loaves for 15 minutes, remove the pan of water, and continue baking until they are very crisp and well browned.

Note The dough is left uncovered to rise for the second time, so that the surface dries out and a very crisp crust is obtained after the loaf has been 'blown up' by steam heat in the oven. This can be done only when the volume of dough is as small as it is here, otherwise the bread splits open on baking.

Strong flour is not suitable for this bread.

Cooking time 30–35 minutes

Wholemeal Bread
Makes two 800g loaves

800g wholemeal flour
1 × 10ml spoon sugar
1 × 15ml spoon salt
25g lard
25g fresh yeast **or** 1 × 15ml spoon
   dried yeast

500ml warm water
flour for kneading
fat for greasing
salted water

Mix together the flour, sugar, and salt in a large bowl. Rub in the lard. Blend the fresh yeast into the warm water or reconstitute the dried yeast. Add the yeast liquid to the flour mixture and mix to a soft dough. Turn on to a lightly floured surface and knead for about 4 minutes or until the dough is smooth and elastic and no longer sticky. Place in a large, lightly oiled polythene bag and leave in a warm place for about 1 hour or until the dough has doubled in size. Knead again until firm. Cut it into 2 equal portions and form each into a loaf shape. Place the dough in 2 lightly greased 23 × 13 × 7cm loaf tins and brush the surface with salted water. Place the tins in the polythene bag and leave in a warm place for about 45 minutes or until the dough has doubled in size. Bake in a very hot oven, 230°C, Gas 8, for 30–40 minutes until the loaves are golden-brown and crisp and sound hollow when tapped on the bottom.

VARIATION
Wholemeal Rolls
Make as for Wholemeal Bread but shape into balls or fancy roll shapes as described on pp339–40. Bake for 10–15 minutes only.

Wheatmeal Bread
Makes two 800g loaves

400g wholemeal flour
400g strong white flour
1 × 10ml spoon salt
1 × 10ml spoon sugar
25g lard
25g fresh yeast **or** 1 × 15ml spoon
   dried yeast

500ml warm water
flour for kneading
fat for greasing
salted water

Mix together the flours, salt, and sugar in a large bowl. Rub in the lard. Blend the fresh yeast into the warm water or reconstitute the dried yeast. Add the yeast liquid to the flour mixture and mix to a soft dough. Turn on to a floured surface, and knead for about 4 minutes or until the dough is smooth and no longer sticky. Cut it into 2 equal portions and form each into a loaf shape. Place the dough in 2 greased 23 × 13 × 7cm loaf tins, and brush the surface with salted water. Place the tins in a large, lightly oiled polythene bag and leave in a warm place for about 50 minutes or until the dough has doubled in size. Bake in a very hot oven, 230°C, Gas 8, for 30–40 minutes until the loaves are golden-brown and crisp and sound hollow when tapped lightly on the bottom.

Granary Bread

Makes two 800g loaves

800g granary flour **or** meal
1 × 10ml spoon salt
1 × 10ml spoon molasses
500ml warm water
25g fresh yeast **or** 1 × 15ml spoon
   dried yeast

1 × 10ml spoon corn oil
flour for kneading
fat for greasing
salted water
1 × 15ml spoon cracked wheat

Mix together the flour and salt in a large bowl. Stir the molasses into the water, and when dissolved, blend in the fresh yeast, or reconstitute the dried yeast. Add the yeast liquid and the oil to the flour, and mix to a soft dough. Turn on to a floured surface and knead for about 4 minutes or until it is smooth, elastic, and no longer sticky. Place in a large, lightly oiled polythene bag and leave in a warm place for about $1\frac{1}{4}$ hours or until doubled in size. Knead the dough again until firm. Cut into 2 equal portions, and form each into a loaf shape. Place the dough in 2 greased 23 × 13 × 7cm loaf tins, brush the surface with salted water, and sprinkle with the cracked wheat. Place the tins in the polythene bag and leave in a warm place for about 45 minutes or until the dough has doubled in size. Bake in a very hot oven, 230°C, Gas 8, for 30–40 minutes until the loaves are browned and crisp and sound hollow when tapped on the bottom.

Rye Cobs

Makes 4 loaves

900g strong white flour
25g fresh yeast **or** 1 × 15ml spoon
   dried yeast
250ml warm water
450g coarse rye flour
500ml skimmed milk (from dried milk
   powder and water)

4 × 5ml spoons salt
4 × 15ml spoons molasses
4 × 15ml spoons cooking oil
flour for kneading
fat for greasing
warm water

Sift the white flour into a large bowl. Blend the fresh yeast into the warm water or reconstitute the dried yeast. Mix the rye flour into the white flour, then add the yeast liquid, skimmed milk, salt, molasses and oil, and knead to a soft dough. Place the mixing bowl inside a large, lightly oiled polythene bag and leave in a warm place for $1\frac{1}{2}$–2 hours until the dough has doubled in size. (Rye bread is slow to rise.) When risen, shape into 4 round loaves. Place on a lightly greased baking sheet or press into 4 greased 15cm sandwich tins. Place again in the polythene bag and leave to rise for 30–45 minutes. Sprinkle with warm water, and bake in a fairly hot oven, 190°C, Gas 5, for about 40 minutes until the loaves sound hollow when tapped on the bottom.

Brioches
Makes 22 brioches

400g strong white flour
1 × 5ml spoon salt
1 × 10ml spoon sugar
50g butter
25g fresh yeast **or** 1 × 15ml spoon
  dried yeast

4 × 10ml spoons warm water
2 eggs
flour for kneading
fat for greasing
beaten egg for glazing

Sift the flour, salt, and sugar into a large bowl. Rub in the butter. Blend the fresh yeast into the warm water or reconstitute the dried yeast. Beat the eggs into the yeast liquid and stir into the flour to form a soft dough. Turn on to a floured surface and knead for about 5 minutes or until the dough is smooth and no longer sticky. Place in a large, lightly oiled polythene bag and leave in a warm place for about 45 minutes or until doubled in size. Grease twenty-two 7cm brioche or deep bun tins. Knead the dough again until firm and cut into 22 equal pieces. Cut off one-quarter of each piece used. Form the larger piece into a ball and place in a tin. Firmly press a hole in the centre and place the remaining quarter as a knob in the centre. Place the tins on a baking sheet and cover with the polythene bag. Leave in a warm place for about 30 minutes or until the dough is light and puffy. Brush with beaten egg and bake in a very hot oven, 230°C, Gas 8, for 15–20 minutes until golden-brown.

Grissini
Makes 45 sticks (approx)

400g strong white flour
1 × 5ml spoon salt
1 × 5ml spoon sugar
25g margarine
50ml milk
200ml warm water
15g fresh yeast **or** 1 × 10ml spoon dried
  yeast

flour for kneading
fat for greasing
beaten egg white **or** milk for glazing
sesame seeds, poppy seeds **or** salt
  (optional)

Sift together the flour, salt, and sugar into a large bowl. Rub in the margarine. Warm the milk until hand-hot. Add to the warm water and blend in the fresh yeast or reconstitute the dried yeast. Add the yeast liquid to the flour and mix to a soft dough. Turn on to a lightly floured surface and knead for about 5 minutes or until smooth and no longer sticky. Place in a large, lightly oiled polythene bag and leave in a warm place for about 1 hour or until the dough has doubled in size. Knead again until firm. Cut into 15g pieces. Roll each piece into a strand 32cm long. Place the strands on a greased baking sheet, brush the surface of each with beaten egg white or milk, and sprinkle, if liked, with the seeds or salt. Place the baking sheet in the polythene bag and leave in a warm place for 10 minutes. Bake in a hot oven, 220°C, Gas 7, for 10–15 minutes until golden-brown and very crisp.

Croissants
Makes 12

400g strong white flour
1 × 5ml spoon salt
100g lard
25g fresh yeast **or** 1 × 15ml spoon
   dried yeast
200ml warm water

1 egg
flour
75g unsalted butter
beaten egg for glazing
fat for greasing

Sift the flour and salt into a large bowl. Rub in 25g of the lard. Blend the fresh yeast into the warm water or reconstitute the dried yeast. Beat the egg until liquid. Stir the egg and yeast liquid into the flour and mix to a soft dough. Turn on to a lightly floured surface and knead for about 8 minutes or until the dough is smooth and no longer sticky. Place the dough in a large, lightly oiled polythene bag and leave at room temperature for 15 minutes.

Meanwhile, beat together the rest of the lard and the butter until well mixed; then chill. On a lightly floured surface, roll the dough carefully into an oblong 50 × 20cm. Divide the chilled fat into three. Use one-third to dot over the top two-thirds of the dough, leaving a small border clear. Fold the dough into three by bringing up the plain part of it first, then bringing the top, fat-covered third down over it. Seal the edges together by pressing with the rolling-pin. Give the dough a quarter turn and repeat the rolling and folding twice, using the other 2 portions of fat. Place the dough in the polythene bag and leave in a cool place for 15 minutes.

Repeat the rolling and folding 3 more times. Rest the dough in the polythene bag in a cool place for 15 minutes. Roll it into an oblong 24 × 36cm and then cut it into six 12cm squares. Cut each square into triangles. Brush the surface of the dough with beaten egg and roll each triangle loosely, towards the point, finishing with the tip underneath. Curve into a crescent shape. Place on a greased baking sheet and brush with beaten egg. Place the sheet in the polythene bag again and leave in a warm place for about 30 minutes or until the dough is light and puffy. Bake in a hot oven, 220°C, Gas 7, for 15–20 minutes until golden-brown and crisp.

Bath Buns
Makes 12

400g strong white flour
1 × 5ml spoon sugar
125ml milk
75ml warm water
25g fresh yeast **or** 1 × 15ml spoon
   dried yeast
1 × 5ml spoon salt
50g butter

50g caster sugar
150g sultanas
50g chopped mixed peel
2 eggs
fat for greasing
beaten egg for glazing
50g sugar nibs **or** lump sugar, coarsely
   crushed

Sift about 75g of the flour and the 5ml spoon sugar into a large bowl. Warm the milk until hand-hot. Add the water to the milk and blend in the fresh yeast or sprinkle on the dried yeast. Pour the yeast liquid into the flour and sugar and beat well. Leave the bowl in a warm place for 20 minutes. Sift the rest of the flour and the salt into a bowl. Rub in the butter. Add the caster sugar and dried fruit. Beat the eggs into the frothy yeast mixture and add the flour, fat, and fruit mixture. Mix to a very soft dough. Beat with a wooden spoon for 3 minutes. Cover the bowl with a large, lightly oiled polythene bag and leave in a warm place for about 45 minutes or until the dough has almost doubled in size. Beat the dough again for 1 minute. Place 15ml spoonfuls of the mixture on a greased baking sheet leaving plenty of space between them. Place the sheet in the polythene bag and leave in a warm place for about 20 minutes or until the buns have almost doubled in size. Brush the surface of each with beaten egg and sprinkle with the sugar nibs or lump sugar. Bake in a hot oven, 220°C, Gas 7, until golden-brown.

Cooking time 15–20 minutes

VARIATIONS

Hot Cross Buns
Make as for Bath Buns but substitute 100g currants for the sultanas and use only 1 egg. Add 3 × 2.5ml spoons mixed spice, 1 × 2.5ml spoon ground cinnamon, and 1 × 2.5ml spoon grated nutmeg to the flour. After mixing to a soft dough, knead for about 5 minutes on a lightly floured surface until the dough is smooth and no longer sticky. Place in a large, lightly oiled polythene bag and leave to rise for about 1 hour until the dough has almost doubled in size. Knead again until firm. Cut into 12 equal pieces and shape each into a round bun. Place on a floured baking sheet. With a sharp knife, slash a cross on the top of each bun, or make crosses with pastry trimmings or a fairly stiff flour and water paste. Cover with polythene and leave for about 35 minutes until the dough has doubled in size. Bake as for Bath Buns.

Glaze the hot buns by boiling together 2 × 15ml spoons milk, 2 × 15ml spoons water, and 40g caster sugar for 6 minutes and brushing the surface of each with the glaze.

Bun Loaf
Makes one 800g loaf
Make as for Hot Cross Buns but bake the mixture in a greased 23 × 13 × 7cm loaf tin. Increase the cooking time to 30–40 minutes.

Chelsea Buns
Makes 16

400g strong white flour
1 × 5ml spoon sugar
200ml milk
25g fresh yeast **or** 1 × 15ml spoon
    dried yeast
1 × 5ml spoon salt
50g butter
1 egg

flour
1 × 15ml spoon butter
150g currants
50g chopped mixed peel
100g soft brown sugar
fat for greasing
honey for glazing

Sift about 75g of the flour and the 5ml spoon of sugar into a large bowl. Warm the milk until hand-hot and blend in the fresh yeast or sprinkle on the dried yeast. Pour the yeast liquid into the flour and sugar and beat well. Leave the bowl in a warm place for 20 minutes. Sift the remaining flour and the salt into a bowl. Rub in the 50g butter. Beat the egg into the frothy yeast mixture and add the flour and fat. Mix to a soft dough. Turn on to a lightly floured surface and knead for about 6 minutes or until smooth and no longer sticky. Place the dough in a large, lightly oiled polythene bag and leave in a warm place for about 1 hour or until the dough has doubled in size. On a floured surface, roll the dough into a 50cm square. Melt the 15ml spoon of butter and brush it all over the surface of the dough. Sprinkle with the dried fruit and sugar. Roll up the dough like a Swiss roll. Cut the roll into 16 equal pieces. Place the buns, about 3cm apart, on a greased baking sheet with the cut side uppermost. Place the baking sheet in the polythene bag and leave in a warm place for about 30 minutes or until the buns have joined together and are light and puffy. Bake in a hot oven, 220°C, Gas 7, for 20–25 minutes until golden-brown. While still hot, brush the buns with honey.

Cornish Splits
Makes 14

400g strong white flour
50g sugar
125ml milk
125ml water
15g fresh yeast **or** 1 × 10ml spoon
    dried yeast

1 × 5ml spoon salt
50g butter
flour for kneading
fat for greasing

Sift about 75g of the flour and 1 × 5ml spoon of the sugar into a large bowl. Warm the milk and water until hand-hot. Blend the fresh yeast into the liquid or sprinkle on the dried yeast. Pour the yeast liquid into the flour and sugar and beat until well mixed. Leave the bowl in a warm place for 20 minutes. Sift the rest of the flour and sugar and the salt together. Rub in the butter. Stir into the frothy yeast mixture and mix to form a soft dough. Turn on to a lightly floured surface and knead for about 6 minutes or until smooth and no longer sticky. Place the dough in a large, lightly oiled polythene bag and leave in a warm place for about 1 hour or until it has doubled in size. Knead the dough again until firm. Divide it into 50g pieces and form each into a round bun. Place the buns on a greased baking sheet. Place the sheet in the polythene bag and leave in a warm place for about 30 minutes or until the buns have doubled in size. Bake in a hot oven, 220°C, Gas 7, for 15–20 minutes until golden-brown.

Serve cold, split, and spread with cream and jam.

Crumpets
Makes 10–12

200g strong white flour	15g fresh yeast **or** 1 × 10ml spoon
1 × 2.5ml spoon salt	dried yeast
1 × 2.5ml spoon sugar	a pinch of bicarbonate of soda
100ml milk	1 × 15ml spoon warm water
125ml water	fat for frying

Sift together the flour, salt, and sugar into a large bowl. Warm the milk and water until hand-hot. Blend the fresh yeast into the liquid or reconstitute the dried yeast. Add the yeast liquid to the flour and beat to a smooth batter. Cover with a large, lightly oiled polythene bag and leave in a warm place for about 45 minutes or until the dough has doubled in size. Dissolve the bicarbonate of soda in the 15ml spoon warm water and beat into the batter mixture. Cover and leave to rise again for 20 minutes. Grease a griddle or thick frying pan and heat until a bread cube browns in $\frac{1}{4}$ minute. Grease metal rings, poaching rings or large plain biscuit cutters, about 8cm in diameter. Place the rings on the hot griddle. Pour about 1 × 15ml spoonful of batter into each ring so that the batter is about 3mm deep. Cook until the top is set and the bubbles have burst. Remove the ring and turn the crumpet over. Cook the other side for 2–3 minutes only until firm but barely coloured. Crumpets should be pale on top. Repeat until all the batter has been used up.

Serve toasted, hot, with butter.

VARIATIONS
Welsh Crumpets
These are cooked without rings on a buttered griddle or frying pan. Pour 3–4 × 15ml spoonfuls batter on to the hot surface, and cook the first side until small holes appear on the surface; turn and cook the second side until just golden.

Serve with bacon and chipolata sausages or butter and brown sugar or honey. These griddle cakes are more like small pancakes or thin pikelets.

Pikelets
Pikelets are cooked without rings like Welsh Crumpets. Some experts use double the amount of yeast and slightly more water (about 50ml) than in the basic crumpet batter, but no bicarbonate of soda.

Most pikelets are thinner than crumpets, cook more quickly, and are more like small pancakes. However, in some areas, they can be as thick as muffins. In Yorkshire, Lancashire, and parts of Derbyshire, pikelet is another name for crumpet.

Ring Doughnuts (1)
Makes 12

200g strong white flour
1 × 2.5ml spoon salt
150g caster sugar
2 eggs
50g butter
15g fresh yeast **or** 1 × 10ml spoon
   dried yeast

2 × 10ml spoons warm water
flour
oil for deep frying
1 × 2.5ml spoon ground cinnamon
   (optional)

Sift the flour, salt, and 50g of the sugar into a large bowl. Beat the eggs until liquid. Melt the butter and leave to cool slightly. Blend the fresh yeast into the warm water or reconstitute the dried yeast. Stir the eggs, butter and yeast liquid into the flour and mix to a soft dough. Turn on to a lightly floured surface and knead for about 5 minutes or until the dough is smooth and no longer sticky. Place the dough in a large, lightly oiled polythene bag and leave in a warm place for about 1 hour or until the dough has almost doubled in size. On a floured surface, roll out the dough to 1cm thickness. Cut into rings, using a 7cm plain cutter for the outside and a 4cm one for the inside. Place on a floured tray and cover with the polythene bag. Leave in a warm place for about 15 minutes or until the dough is light and puffy. Deep fry in hot oil (p11) until crisp and golden-brown, turning frequently. Drain on soft kitchen paper. Toss in the rest of the sugar or in the sugar and cinnamon mixed.

VARIATION
Jam Doughnuts
Cut the rolled-out dough into circles using a 7cm plain cutter. Place a little stiff jam in the centre of each circle and pinch up the edge of the dough to form a ball. Leave to rise, and fry as above.

Muffins
Makes 20

400g strong white flour
1 × 5ml spoon salt
25g butter **or** margarine
225ml milk
15g fresh yeast **or** 1 × 10ml spoon
   dried yeast

1 egg
flour
fat for frying

Sift together the flour and salt into a large bowl. Rub in the fat. Warm the milk until hand-hot. Blend the fresh yeast into the milk or reconstitute the dried yeast. Beat the egg into the yeast liquid. Stir the liquid into the flour to make a very soft dough. Beat the dough with your hand or a wooden spoon for about 5 minutes or until smooth and shiny. Put the bowl in a large, lightly oiled polythene bag and leave in a warm place for 1–2 hours, or until the dough has almost doubled in size. Beat again lightly. Roll out on a well floured surface to 1cm thickness. Using a plain 8cm cutter, cut the dough into rounds. Place the rounds on a floured tray, cover with polythene, and leave to rise at room temperature for about 45 minutes or until puffy. Lightly grease a griddle or heavy frying pan and heat until a bread cube browns in $\frac{1}{4}$ minute. Cook the muffins on both sides for about 8 minutes until golden-brown.

To serve, split open each muffin around the edges almost to the centre. Toast slowly on both outer sides so that the heat penetrates to the centre of the muffin. Pull apart, butter thickly, put together again, and serve hot.

Sally Lunn
Makes two 15cm Sally Lunns

400g strong white flour	15g fresh yeast **or** 1 × 10ml spoon
1 × 5ml spoon salt	dried yeast
1 × 5ml spoon sugar	1 egg
50g butter	fat for greasing
150ml milk	

Glaze

1 × 15ml spoon water	1 × 15ml spoon caster sugar

Sift together the flour, salt, and sugar into a large bowl. Rub in the butter. Warm the milk until hand-hot. Blend the fresh yeast into the milk or reconstitute the dried yeast. Beat the egg into the yeast liquid and stir into the flour mixture to form a very soft dough. Beat well. Pour the mixture into 2 greased 15cm round cake tins. Place the tins in a large, lightly oiled polythene bag and leave in a warm place for about $1\frac{1}{4}$ hours or until the dough has doubled in size. Bake in a hot oven, 220°C, Gas 7, for 20–25 minutes until golden-brown.

To make the glaze, boil together the water and sugar until syrupy. Brush the hot glaze over the top of the Sally Lunns.

To serve, split each Sally Lunn crossways into 3 rounds and toast each piece lightly on both sides. Butter thickly or fill with clotted cream, re-form the cake, and cut into slices or wedges.

Quick Breads

Basic Quick Bread
Makes 2 bun loaves

400g self-raising flour **or** a mixture
  of white and brown self-raising
  flours **or** 400g plain flour and
  2 × 10ml spoons baking powder
1 × 5ml spoon salt

50g margarine **or** lard
250ml milk **or** water **or** a mixture as
  preferred
flour for kneading
fat for greasing

Sift the flour, baking powder (if used), and salt into a large bowl. Rub in the fat. Mix in enough liquid to make a soft dough. Turn on to a floured surface, and knead lightly for 1 minute. Shape the dough into 2 rounds and place them on a greased baking sheet. Make a cross in the top of each with the back of a knife. Bake in a fairly hot oven, 200°C, Gas 6, for 30–40 minutes. Cool on a wire rack.

VARIATIONS

Wholemeal Quick Bread
Substitute 400g wholemeal flour for the plain flour in the basic recipe. Note that wholemeal flour will give a closer-textured loaf.

Nut Bread
Make Wholemeal Quick Bread; add 75g chopped nuts and 50g sugar to the dry ingredients, and add 1 beaten egg to the liquid.

Apricot and Walnut Loaf
Make the basic Quick Bread Mixture but use butter as the fat. Add 100g dried and soaked chopped apricots and 50g chopped walnuts to the dry ingredients, and add 1 beaten egg to the liquid.

Basic Soured Milk Quick Bread
Makes 2 loaves

400g plain flour
1 × 5ml spoon salt
1 × 10ml spoon bicarbonate of soda
1 × 10ml spoon cream of tartar

250ml soured milk **or** buttermilk
  (approx)
fat for greasing

Sift the flour, salt, bicarbonate of soda, and cream of tartar into a large bowl. Mix to a light spongy dough with the milk. Divide the dough into 2 equal pieces and form each into a round cake. Slash a cross on the top of each loaf with a sharp knife. Place on a greased baking sheet and bake in a hot oven, 220°C, Gas 7, for about 30 minutes until golden-brown. Cool on a wire rack.

Note The keeping quality of this bread is improved by rubbing 50g lard into the sifted flour.

Almond Bread

Makes 12 slices (approx)

75g almonds
250g plain flour
2 × 10ml spoons baking powder
a pinch of salt
2 eggs
100g granulated sugar

6 × 15ml spoons oil
a few drops almond **or** vanilla essence
flour
fat for greasing
50g caster sugar

Blanch and skin the almonds and chop them coarsely. Sift the flour, baking powder, and salt. Beat the eggs and granulated sugar lightly together in a large bowl. Add the oil, flavouring, flour, and almonds, and mix to form a dough. With floured hands, form into a long roll about 8cm wide. Place on a greased and floured baking sheet and bake in a moderate oven, 180°C, Gas 4, for about 30–40 minutes or until lightly browned. Leave until nearly cold, then cut slantways into slices about 1cm thick. Sprinkle lightly with caster sugar and return to a cool oven, 150°C, Gas 2, for about 50–60 minutes, until dry and lightly browned.

American Coffee Bread

Makes 12 slices (approx)

200g plain flour
100g light soft brown sugar
2 × 5ml spoons baking powder
1 × 5ml spoon salt
2 × 15ml spoons butter

1 egg
200ml milk
75g chopped walnuts
fat for greasing

Sift together the dry ingredients into a large bowl. Melt the butter, add it to the flour mixture with the egg, milk and walnuts, and beat thoroughly. Spread the mixture in a greased 23 × 13 × 7cm loaf tin, level the top, and bake for about 1 hour in a moderate oven, 180°C, Gas 4. Cool on a wire rack.

VARIATIONS

Orange Nut Coffee Bread

Reduce the milk to 100ml. Instead of sugar, use 250g orange marmalade.

Banana Nut Coffee Bread

Reduce the milk to 100ml; add 3 ripe medium-sized bananas, well mashed.

Date and Walnut Loaf
Makes 20 slices (approx)

275g plain flour
50g cornflour
150g caster sugar
1 × 5ml spoon salt
50g walnuts
225g cooking dates

2 × 15ml spoons oil
1 large egg
2 × 5ml spoons bicarbonate of soda
250ml boiling water
fat for greasing

Sift the flour, cornflour, sugar, and salt into a bowl. Chop the walnuts and dates and add to the dry ingredients. Whisk together the oil and egg and add to the flour, fruit, and nuts. Dissolve the bicarbonate of soda in the boiling water, and stir into the other ingredients. Beat well to a soft consistency. Pour into a greased 23 × 13 × 7cm loaf tin and bake in a moderate oven, 180°C, Gas 4, for about 1 hour until firm to the touch. Leave to cool slightly before turning out of the tin.

Date or Raisin Bread
Makes 12 slices (approx)

200g plain flour
1 × 15ml spoon baking powder
1 × 5ml spoon salt
$\frac{1}{4}$ × 2.5ml spoon bicarbonate of soda
100g dates **or** seedless raisins
50g walnuts **or** almonds, whole **or**
  chopped

25g lard
50g black treacle
50g dark Barbados sugar
150ml milk
fat for greasing

Sift the flour, baking powder, salt, and bicarbonate of soda into a large bowl. Chop the fruit and nuts finely if necessary, and add them to the dry ingredients. Warm the lard, treacle, sugar, and milk together. The sugar should dissolve, but do not over-heat it. Add the liquid to the dry ingredients, and mix to a stiff batter. Pour into a lined and greased 19 × 13 × 8cm loaf tin and bake in a moderate oven, 180°C, Gas 4, for 1½ hours. Cool on a wire rack. When cold, wrap in foil, and store for 24 hours before cutting.

Malt Bread
Makes 12 slices (approx)

400g self-raising flour
1 × 10ml spoon bicarbonate of soda
100g sultanas **or** seedless raisins
250ml milk

4 × 15ml spoons golden syrup
4 × 15ml spoons malt extract
2 eggs
fat for greasing

Sift the flour and bicarbonate of soda into a large bowl. Add the dried fruit. Warm together the milk, syrup, and malt extract, in a saucepan. Beat in the eggs. Stir the mixture into the flour. Put it into a greased 23 × 13 × 7cm loaf tin and bake in a fairly hot oven, 190°C, Gas 5, for 40–50 minutes until a skewer pushed into the bread comes out clean. Cool on a wire rack.

Scones

Important points to remember when making scones:

1) Because the basic mixture has only a small proportion of fat to flour, it should be mixed to a soft, slightly sticky dough and handled quickly and lightly.

2) Scones are baked in a hot, preheated oven to ensure maximum rising; the top should be brown and the texture open.

3) Cool baked scones on a wire rack so that they are crisp outside. Griddle scones and dropped scones are best cooled in a clean tea-towel so that they keep their traditional softness.

4) Raising ingredients
   When plain flour is used, add either baking powder
   or
   bicarbonate of soda and cream of tartar
   or
   bicarbonate of soda, cream of tartar, and soured milk or buttermilk.
      The exact quantities of the raising ingredients required are given in the recipes.

5) Using a griddle
   Grease or flour the griddle lightly, according to the recipe used, and place over heat until a faint blue haze rises or until the griddle feels comfortably warm if the hand is held about 2cm above it. If the griddle is too hot, the scones brown on the outside before being cooked through to the centre.
      Most griddle scones take about 5 minutes to cook on each side.

Plain Scones (1) *Basic recipe using* plain *flour*
Makes 10–12

200g plain flour
½ × 2.5ml spoon salt
50g butter **or** margarine
and *one of the following raising agents:*
1 × 5ml spoon bicarbonate of soda
1 × 10ml spoon cream of tartar
125ml fresh milk
or
4 × 5ml spoons baking powder
125ml fresh milk

or
1 × 5ml spoon bicarbonate of soda
1 × 5ml spoon cream of tartar
125ml soured milk **or** buttermilk
and
flour for rolling out
fat for greasing
milk **or** beaten egg for glazing
   (optional)

Heat the oven to hot, 220°C, Gas 7. Sift together the flour and salt into a large bowl. Rub in the fat. Sift in the dry raising agents and mix well. Add the milk and mix lightly to form a soft spongy dough. Knead very lightly until smooth. Roll out on a floured surface to 1.5–2cm thickness and cut into rounds, using a 5cm cutter. Re-roll the trimmings, and re-cut. Place the scones on a greased baking sheet and brush the tops with milk or beaten egg, if liked. Bake for 7–10 minutes until well risen and golden-brown. Cool on a wire rack.

Note If preferred, the mixture can be divided into 2 equal portions, each half rolled into a round, 1.5–2cm thick, and each round marked into 6 wedges.

VARIATIONS

Cheese Scones

Add 75g grated cheese to the dry ingredients before mixing in the milk. Cut into finger shapes or squares.

Fruit Scones

Add 50g caster sugar and 50g currants, sultanas or other dried fruit to the basic recipe.

Griddle Scones

Add 50g sultanas to the basic dough. Roll out to 5mm–1cm thickness, then cut into 6cm rounds. Cook on a moderately hot, lightly floured griddle or heavy frying pan for 3 minutes or until the scones are golden-brown underneath and the edges are dry. Turn over and cook for about another 2 minutes until golden-brown on both sides. Cool in a linen tea-towel or other similar cloth.

Nut Scones

Add 50g chopped nuts to the basic recipe.

Potato Scones

Use 100g flour and 100g sieved cooked mashed potato. Reduce the milk to 60–65ml.

Syrup or Treacle Scones

Add 2 × 10ml spoons light soft brown sugar, 1 × 2.5ml spoon ground cinnamon or ginger, 1 × 2.5ml spoon mixed spice, and 1 × 15ml spoon warmed golden syrup or black treacle to the basic recipe. Add the syrup or treacle with the milk.

Wheatmeal Scones

Use half wholemeal flour and half plain white flour to make the dough.

Plain Scones (2) *Basic recipe using* self-raising *flour*
Makes 12

200g self-raising flour	flour for kneading
1 × 2.5ml spoon salt	fat for greasing
25–50g butter **or** margarine	milk **or** beaten egg for glazing
125ml milk	(optional)

Heat the oven to hot, 220°C, Gas 7. Sift together the flour and salt into a large bowl. Rub in the fat and mix to a soft dough with the milk, using a round-bladed knife. Knead very lightly on a floured surface until smooth. Roll out to about 1.5cm thickness and cut into rounds, using a 6cm cutter, or divide into 2 equal portions as described for Plain Scones (using plain flour) (p355). Re-roll the trimmings, and re-cut. Place the scones on a lightly greased baking sheet, and brush the tops with milk or beaten egg, if liked. Bake for 10–12 minutes. Cool on a wire rack.

Cream Scones
Makes 12 (approx)

200g plain flour
$\frac{1}{2} \times 2.5$ml spoon salt
1 × 5ml spoon bicarbonate of soda
1 × 10ml spoon cream of tartar
75g butter **or** margarine

65ml milk
4 × 15ml spoons single cream
flour for rolling out
fat for greasing

Heat the oven to hot, 220°C, Gas 7. Sift together the dry ingredients 3 times. Rub in the fat and mix to a soft dough with the milk and cream. Knead lightly and roll out on a floured surface to just over 1cm thick. Cut into rounds, using a 6cm cutter. Re-roll the trimmings, and re-cut. Place the scones on a greased baking sheet and bake for 10–12 minutes.

Serve warm or cold, buttered or filled with thick cream and jam.

Dropped Scones (Scotch Pancakes)
Makes 24 (approx)

200g plain flour
1 × 5ml spoon salt
25g caster sugar
1 × 10ml spoon cream of tartar

1 × 5ml spoon bicarbonate of soda
1 egg
175ml milk
fat for greasing

Sift together the dry ingredients 3 times. Add the egg and milk gradually and mix to a smooth thick batter. Heat a lightly greased griddle or a very thick frying pan. Drop 10ml spoonfuls of the mixture on to the griddle or pan. Tiny bubbles will appear and when these burst, turn the scones over, using a palette knife. Cook the underside until golden-brown; then cool the scones in a clean tea-towel on a rack. The scones will take about 3 minutes to cook on the first side and about 2 minutes after turning.

CAKES AND BISCUITS

Preparing Tins for Baking

The best fats to use for greasing are lard, cooking fat or oil. If butter or margarine is used, it must be clarified (p232) first to remove any salt and water which it may contain.

There are 4 principal ways of preparing the insides of cake and bun tins, and the surface of baking sheets for biscuits.
1) Bun and patty tins, and baking sheets for biscuits should be greased; for some biscuits, sheets should be dusted with flour after greasing.
2) For rubbed-in cakes, grease the tin and line the base with greased greaseproof paper or non-stick vegetable parchment.
3) For creamed mixtures, it is advisable to line both the sides and the base of the tins with greased greaseproof paper or vegetable parchment, particularly when the baking time is more than 1 hour. Cake tins for gingerbread should also be lined and greased.

4) For sponge cakes, brush the tin with fat, then coat it with equal quantities of flour and caster sugar, sifted together.

Note Where preparation differs from the above, this is indicated within the recipe in question.

Cake tins, bun tins, and baking sheets are available with special non-stick finishes which do not usually need greasing. Consult the manufacturer's instructions as to whether you need grease the tin or not.

Round and Square Tins

A square tin holds the same amount of mixture as a round tin about 2cm larger in diameter, eg a recipe calling for an 18cm square tin can equally well be baked in a round 20cm tin, provided the tins are the same depth.

The length of time needed for cooking any cake depends on the depth of the mixture. If a smaller tin than specified is used, increase the baking time, and vice versa for a larger tin.

To line a tin – round or square

1) Measure and cut a single or double piece of paper to fit the base of the tin; ensure that it is not bigger than the base or it will spoil the shape of the cake.
2) Measure and cut a strip, single or double, long enough to line the sides of the tin, allowing for a slight overwrap. Make the strip 5cm deeper than the height of the tin.
3) Make a 2cm fold along the bottom of the strip and snip diagonally at 1cm intervals up to the fold.
   Paper for a square tin need only be snipped at the corners.
4) Grease the tin and place the strip round the sides of the tin with the cut edge lying flat against the base. Fit in the round. Grease the lined tin.

To line a Swiss roll tin

1) Cut a piece of paper large enough to fit both the base and sides of the tin. Do not make it higher than the sides of the tin as this may prevent the heat from browning the top.
2) Place the tin on the paper and make a cut on each corner of the paper from the edge to the corner of the tin.
3) Place the paper in the greased tin, folding the corners to give a neat fit. Grease the lined tin.

Storing Cakes and Biscuits

Wrap very rich cakes and wedding cakes in greaseproof paper and a clean tea-towel. Store in a cool, dry place. Biscuits and other cakes may be stored in a tin but should be used as soon as possible. The prepared dough can be frozen for 2 months (see p437).

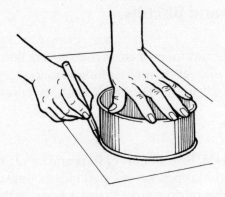

Measuring paper to fit the base of the tin

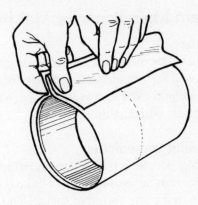

Measuring a strip to fit the sides of the tin

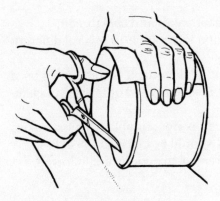

Cutting a strip of paper 5cm deeper than the rim

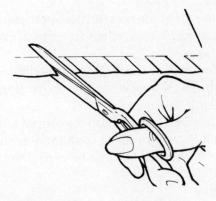

Snipping along the bottom edge of the strip towards the fold

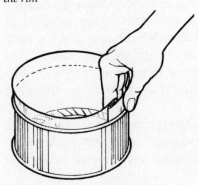

ABOVE *Placing the strip in the tin*

RIGHT *Lining a Swiss roll tin*

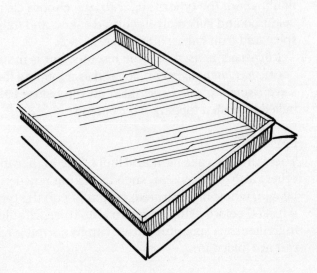

Main Ingredients for Making Cakes and Biscuits

Flour

General purpose household flour gives better results in most cases than strong flour, as used for breadmaking. Most flours are fine enough to make sifting unnecessary, unless it is used as a method of mixing several dry ingredients such as spices, cocoa, and salt with the flour.

Raising Ingredients

Baking powder is the raising agent most often used. Bicarbonate of soda and cream of tartar can be used instead of baking powder in the proportion of 1 part bicarbonate of soda to 2 parts cream of tartar. The most suitable raising agent to use is given in the individual recipes.

Fats

Butter gives the best flavour, particularly to rich fruit cakes and shortbread.

Margarine is excellent for general everyday use and is available in several different textures.

Lard which is 100% fat, contributes little colour or flavour; it is sometimes used with spices, treacle, and syrup for gingerbread but is seldom used otherwise in cake-making.

Dripping, being highly flavoured with meat juices, is not suitable for most cakes, but it is used for a few traditional regional ones. It should be clarified (p94) first.

Other special fats can be used if the manufacturers' instructions are followed.

Sugar

As a general rule, *granulated sugar* is used for rubbed-in and melted mixtures, and *caster sugar* is used for cakes prepared by the creaming method, whisking method, and all-in-one method. Generally, a recipe specifies the most suitable type of sugar to use when it is important for texture or flavour. *Soft dark brown sugar* gives a dark crumb, for instance, to some Christmas and wedding cakes, and to gingerbreads. If in doubt about the type of sugar to use, choose caster rather than granulated for light-coloured and delicately flavoured cakes, and light rather than dark brown sugar for spicy and fruit cakes, and gingerbreads.

Icing sugar is used in some biscuits, but is mainly employed for icings and fillings.

Crushed lump sugar can be used as a topping for some yeast buns. Some cakes may have *Demerara sugar* sprinkled on top before baking; it can also be used to make a baked or grilled topping after baking.

Eggs

These make a cake light and fluffy. The higher the proportion of eggs, the less of any other raising ingredient, such as baking powder, will be needed. Eggs may be added beaten, whole or separated, depending on the type of mixture. Separated egg whites, whisked before being added to a mixture, should be folded in lightly after the other ingredients. A spoonful or two can be stirred into the mixture to lighten it before the rest are folded in.

Dried Fruit

If fruit needs washing, do this well ahead of using it and dry thoroughly. If *glacé cherries* are very sticky or moist, wash and dry them before use, and toss in a little of the weighed flour.

Nuts

Almonds can be bought in their skins or already blanched. Blanched nuts can be bought whole, flaked, split, kibbled (lightly crushed) or as nibs (chopped).

Almonds bought in their skins need blanching for almost all cake recipes. Unless bought ready blanched, use the following procedure: place the almonds in a saucepan with plenty of cold water, bring just to boiling point, drain in a sieve under a running cold tap, pinch off the skins and dry on soft kitchen paper. If the almonds are required split, as for the top of a Dundee cake, do this with a small, sharp knife while the nuts are still warm from blanching.

Browned (or roasted) almonds are often used. They can be browned on a baking tray in a cool oven, or under the grill. If using the oven, almonds should be turned over once or twice during baking. If the grill pan is used, it should be shaken frequently to turn and move the nuts and to prevent dark scorch spots.

Desiccated coconut is used in many cakes, puddings, and biscuits. It can also be used as a decoration on top of jam or icing on a cake. It can be coloured or toasted (see p397).

Hazelnuts need skinning for most cakes. Place the nuts on a baking tray in the oven, and bake until the skins can be removed by rubbing in a cloth or in a paper bag. Rub off the skins. Alternatively, toast gently under the grill, shaking the pan to turn them over. Chop coarsely, or grind in a nut mill, coffee grinder or in an electric blender, or use whole as a decoration.

Peanuts: skin as for hazelnuts.

Pistachios: skin as for hazelnuts.

Walnuts do not need blanching. They can be bought whole or as roughly chopped pieces.

Brazils, pecans, and other nuts such as *unsalted peanuts* can be used for some cakes, buns, and cookies. Treat pecans like walnuts. *Chopped mixed nuts* are also available in packets. They are a useful substitute for chopped hazelnuts or walnuts.

How to Test when a Cake is Cooked

When fully baked a cake should be evenly browned and have come away from the sides of the tin slightly. If the top crust is pressed very lightly with the finger, the mixture should spring back or, in the case of fruit cakes, feel firm. If a fruit cake feels spongy, cover loosely with greaseproof paper and return to the oven for a short time. Re-test before taking the cake out of the oven.

Another way of testing rich cakes is to insert a thin, warmed poultry skewer or thin-bladed knife into the centre of the cake. If it comes out clean the cake is done; if there are crumbs or wet mixture sticking to it, return the cake to the oven for a short time. Re-test before taking the cake out of the oven.

How to Turn a Cake on to a Rack to Cool

If the cake tin has been lined, lift out the paper with the cake in it, place on a cooling rack and peel off the paper. Leave the cake to become quite cold. If the tin is unlined, place it on its side and gently ease out the cake. Turn it on to its base on the cooling rack.

Plain Cake *Basic recipe*

fat for greasing	50–100g margarine **or** other fat
200g self-raising flour **or**	75g sugar
200g plain flour and 1 × 10ml spoon	2 small eggs
baking powder	125ml milk (approx)
½ × 2.5ml spoon salt	

Grease a 15cm cake tin and line the base with greased paper. Mix the flour and salt together, cut the fat into small pieces in the flour, and rub in until the mixture resembles fine breadcrumbs. Add the baking powder, if used, and the sugar. Beat the egg with some of the milk and stir into the mixture. Add a little more milk if necessary, to give a consistency which just drops off the end of a wooden spoon. Put the mixture into the cake tin and smooth the top. Bake in a moderate oven, 180°C, Gas 4, for 1–1½ hours.

VARIATIONS

Cherry, Currant or Sultana Cake

Add 100g fruit, cut up if necessary, with the sugar.

Countess or Spice Cake

Use 100g flour, 100g cornflour, 1 × 2.5ml spoon ground ginger, 1½ × 2.5ml spoons ground nutmeg, and 1½ × 2.5ml spoons ground cinnamon. Add 50g currants and 50g seedless raisins after adding the milk.

Lemon or Orange Cake

Add the grated rind of 1 lemon or orange with the sugar. Replace some of the milk with the juice of the fruit.

Date and Walnut Cake

fat for greasing	75g dates
200g self-raising flour **or**	25g walnuts
200g plain flour and 1 × 10ml spoon	75g soft light brown sugar
baking powder	2 small eggs
a pinch of ground nutmeg	125ml milk (approx)
75g margarine	

Grease a 15cm tin and line the base with greased paper. Mix the flour and nutmeg together, and rub in the fat. Chop the dates and walnuts and add to the flour with the sugar and baking powder, if used. Beat the eggs and milk together and mix into the dry ingredients. Bake in a moderate oven, 180°C, Gas 4, for 1¼–1½ hours.

Dripping Cake

fat for greasing
200g self-raising flour
a pinch of salt
$\frac{1}{2} \times 2.5$ml spoon mixed spice
100g beef dripping (see **Note**)

75g granulated sugar
75g seedless raisins
50g currants
1 egg
100ml milk

Grease a 15cm round cake tin and line the base with greased paper. Mix the flour, salt, and spice together. Rub in the dripping, and add the sugar and dried fruit. Beat the egg with the milk and add to the dry ingredients; stir in, then beat until smooth. Put into the tin and smooth the top level. Bake in a moderate oven, 180°C, Gas 4, for 1 hour 10 minutes. Cover the top with greaseproof paper after 1 hour if the cake is already brown enough.

Note Use clarified dripping (p94) which does not have too strong a flavour. If it has been kept in the refrigerator, allow it to come to room temperature.

Plain Buns *Basic recipe*
Makes 12–14

200g self-raising flour **or**
    200g plain flour and 1×10ml spoon
    baking powder
$\frac{1}{2} \times 2.5$ml spoon salt
75g margarine

75g sugar
1 egg
milk
fat for greasing

Decoration (optional)
glacé icing (p387)

Heat the oven to fairly hot, 200°C, Gas 6. Sift or mix the flour and salt together. Cut the margarine into small pieces in the flour, and rub in until the mixture resembles fine breadcrumbs. Stir in the baking powder, if used, and the sugar. Beat the egg until liquid and add enough milk to make up to 125ml. Add the liquid to the dry ingredients and mix with a fork to a stiff consistency. This produces a sticky mixture which supports the fork. Divide the mixture into 12–14 portions and form into rocky heaps on a well-greased baking sheet, allowing about 2cm space between each. Bake above the centre of the oven for 15–20 minutes until firm to the touch on the underside.

Coat, if liked, with a spoonful of glacé icing when cool.

Note When small buns are baked in paper cases or greased patty tins, the consistency should be softer than when the buns are put on a baking sheet. Use 1 egg and 125ml milk, or enough to allow the mixture to drop off the spoon with a slight shake. The number of buns obtained will be 14–16, using the same quantity of flour.

VARIATIONS

Chocolate Buns

Add 50g cocoa to the flour and 1×5ml spoon vanilla essence with the milk.

For further **variations**, see over.

Coconut Buns
Add 75g desiccated coconut with the flour and an extra 2 × 5ml spoons milk.

Lemon or Orange Buns
Add the grated rind of 1 lemon or orange with the flour.

Raspberry Buns
Form the mixture into 12–14 balls with lightly floured hands. Make a deep dent in the centre of each ball and drop 1 × 5ml spoon raspberry jam inside each. Close the mixture over the jam. Brush with egg or milk and sprinkle with sugar.

Rock Buns
Add $\frac{1}{2}$ × 2.5ml spoon ground nutmeg to the flour and 75g mixed fruit (currants, peel, etc, according to taste) with the sugar.

Seed Buns
Add 1 × 15ml spoon caraway seeds with the sugar.

Spice Buns
Add an extra 1 × 5ml spoon mixed spice or 1 × 2.5ml spoon ground cinnamon and 1 × 2.5ml spoon ground nutmeg to the flour.

Ring Doughnuts (2)
Makes 12 (approx)

200g plain flour	1 egg
$\frac{1}{2}$ × 2.5ml spoon salt	4 × 15ml spoons milk (approx)
a pinch of ground cinnamon **or** nutmeg	flour for rolling out
3 × 2.5ml spoons baking powder	fat **or** oil for deep frying
40g butter **or** margarine	caster sugar
3 × 15ml spoons sugar	

Sift the flour, salt, spice, and baking powder into a bowl. Rub in the fat. Stir in the sugar. Beat the egg lightly. Make a well in the centre of the dry ingredients and add the egg. Gradually work it into the dry ingredients, adding enough milk to make a soft dough. Roll out the dough 1cm thick on a floured board. Heat the fat (p11). Cut the dough into rings using a 6cm and a 3cm cutter. Re-roll and re-cut the trimmings. Fry 1 or 2 doughnuts in the hot fat until light brown underneath; turn and cook the second side. Lift the doughnuts out and drain well. Put some caster sugar in a large paper bag and put in the doughnuts while still hot. Toss them gently until coated. Leave on soft kitchen paper dusted with sugar. Continue until all the doughnuts are fried. Bring the fat back to the correct temperature between each batch.

Serve warm or cold the same day.

Gingerbread *Basic recipe*

fat for greasing
200g plain flour
$\frac{1}{2}$ × 2.5ml spoon salt
2–3 × 5ml spoons ground ginger
1 × 2.5ml spoon bicarbonate of soda
50–100g lard

50g brown sugar
100g golden syrup **or** black treacle (**or**
  a mixture)
1 egg
milk

Grease a 15cm square tin and line with greased paper. Sift together the flour, salt, ginger, and bicarbonate of soda into a bowl. Warm the fat, sugar, and syrup in a saucepan until the fat has melted. Do not allow the mixture to become hot. Beat the egg until liquid and add enough milk to make up to 125ml. Add the melted mixture to the dry ingredients with the beaten egg and milk. Stir thoroughly; the mixture should run easily off the spoon. Pour into the tin and bake in a warm oven, 160°C, Gas 3, for $1\frac{1}{4}$–$1\frac{1}{2}$ hours until firm to the touch.

Rich Cake *Basic recipe*

fat for greasing
200g plain flour
$\frac{1}{2}$ × 2.5ml spoon salt
1 × 2.5ml spoon baking powder

4 eggs
150g butter **or** margarine
150g caster sugar
1 × 15ml spoon milk

Grease a 15cm round cake tin and line with greased paper. Sift together the flour, salt, and baking powder. Beat the eggs in a basin and stand it in tepid water (or make sure you use eggs at room temperature). Beat the fat until very soft, add the sugar, and cream well together until light and fluffy. Add the eggs gradually, beating well after each addition. If the mixture shows signs of curdling, add a little flour. Fold in the dry ingredients lightly but thoroughly. Add the milk if too stiff. Put into the tin, smooth the top and make a hollow in the centre. Bake in a moderate oven, 180°C, Gas 4, for 30 minutes, reduce the heat to warm, 160°C, Gas 3, and bake for a further 50 minutes or until firm to the touch.

VARIATIONS

Cherry Cake
Add 125g quartered glacé cherries with the flour.

Cornflour Cake
Use 100g cornflour and 100g plain flour.

Fruit Cake
Add 100g dried fruit (currants, seedless raisins, sultanas), 50g chopped glacé cherries, and 50g cut mixed peel. Bake in a 17cm tin.

Ginger Cake
Add 1 × 5ml spoon ground ginger with the flour and stir in 100g crystallized ginger.

For further **variations**, see over.

Ground Rice Cake

Use 150g flour and 50g ground rice.

Lemon or Orange Cake

Add the grated rind of 2 lemons or oranges and use fruit juice instead of milk.

Seed Cake

Add 3 × 5ml spoons caraway seeds with the flour.

Birthday Cake

200g mixed dried fruit
65ml milk **or** brandy
fat for greasing
100g butter **or** margarine
100g soft light brown sugar
35g golden syrup
3 eggs
150g plain flour **or** 125g plain flour
  and 25g cocoa

1 × 2.5ml spoon salt
1 × 5ml spoon baking powder
1 × 5ml spoon mixed spice
50g cut mixed peel **or** coarse-cut
  marmalade
75g glacé cherries
milk

Coating and Icing (optional)
almond paste (p392)   royal icing (p395)

Soak the dried fruit in the brandy, if used, for 2 hours before making the cake. Grease and line a 16cm round cake tin. Cream the fat, sugar, and syrup together thoroughly. Beat the eggs lightly. Sift together the flour (or flour and cocoa), salt, baking powder, and spice. Mix 25–50g of the flour with the dried fruit and peel, if used. Chop the glacé cherries and marmalade, if used. Mix the eggs and the flour alternately into the creamed mixture, beating well between each addition. Mix in lightly the floured fruit, cherries, and peel or marmalade. Mix in just enough milk to make a soft dropping consistency. Turn the mixture into the cake tin and bake in a moderate oven, 180°C, Gas 4, for 25 minutes, reduce the heat to cool, 150°C, Gas 2, and bake for another 2–2½ hours. Coat with almond paste and decorate with royal icing, if liked.

Christmas Cake

fat for greasing
200g plain flour
$\frac{1}{2} \times 2.5$ml spoon salt
1–2 × 5ml spoons mixed spice
200g butter
200g caster sugar
6 eggs
2–4 × 15ml spoons brandy **or** sherry

100g glacé cherries
50g preserved ginger
50g walnuts
200g currants
200g sultanas
150g seedless raisins
75g cut mixed peel

Coating and Icing
almond paste (p392)

royal icing (p395)

Grease and line a 20cm cake tin with doubled greaseproof paper and tie a strip of brown paper round the outside.

Sift the flour, salt, and spice together. Cream the butter and sugar together until light and fluffy. Gradually beat in the eggs and the brandy or sherry. Cut up the cherries, chop the ginger and walnuts, and stir with the dried fruit, peel and the flour into the creamed mixture. Put into the tin and make a slight hollow in the centre. Bake in a warm oven, 160°C, Gas 3, for 45 minutes, reduce the heat to cool, 150°C, Gas 2, and bake for a further hour. Reduce the heat to very cool, 140°C, Gas 1, and continue cooking for 45 minutes–1 hour until firm to the touch. Cool in the tin. Cover with almond paste and decorate with royal icing.

Devil's Food Cake

fat for greasing
plain flour for dusting
100g butter
350g granulated sugar
1 × 5ml spoon vanilla essence
3 eggs

275ml cold water
250g plain flour
50g cocoa
3 × 2.5ml spoons bicarbonate of soda
1 × 5ml spoon salt

Filling and Decoration
Seafoam Frosting (p390)

Grease and lightly flour three 20cm sandwich tins. Cream the butter with 225g of the sugar until light, then add the vanilla essence. Separate the eggs, and add the yolks, one at a time, to the creamed mixture alternately with the water, beating well after each addition. Beat in the flour, cocoa, soda, and salt. Whisk the egg whites until soft peaks form; add the remaining sugar and continue whisking until stiff peaks form again. Fold the egg whites into the creamed mixture, lightly but thoroughly. Gently pour one-third of it into each sandwich tin. Bake in a moderate oven, 180°C, Gas 4, for 30–35 minutes or until the cakes are firm in the centre, and have shrunk from the sides of the tins. When cold, fill and frost with Seafoam Frosting.

Dundee Cake

fat for greasing
200g plain flour
1 × 2.5ml spoon baking powder
½ × 2.5ml spoon salt
150g butter
150g caster sugar
4 eggs
100g glacé cherries

150g currants
150g sultanas
100g seedless raisins
50g cut mixed peel
50g ground almonds
grated rind of 1 lemon
50g blanched split almonds

Grease and line an 18cm cake tin. Sift together the flour, baking powder, and salt. Cream the butter and sugar together well, and beat in the eggs. Cut the cherries into quarters. Fold the flour, dried fruit, peel, and ground almonds into the creamed mixture. Add the lemon rind and mix well. Put into the tin and make a slight hollow in the centre. Bake in a moderate oven, 180°C, Gas 4, for 20 minutes, when the hollow should have filled in. Arrange the split almonds on top. Return the cake to the oven, bake for a further 40–50 minutes, then reduce the heat to warm, 160°C, Gas 3, and bake for another hour.

Madeira Cake

fat for greasing
150g butter **or** margarine
150g caster sugar
4 eggs
200g plain flour

2 × 5ml spoons baking powder
a pinch of salt
grated rind of 1 lemon
caster sugar for dredging
2 thin slices candied **or** glacé citron peel

Grease and line a 15cm cake tin. Cream the fat and sugar together until light and fluffy. Beat the eggs until liquid and add gradually to the creamed mixture, beating well after each addition. Sift the flour, baking powder and salt together, and fold into the creamed mixture. Mix in the lemon rind. Mix well. Turn into the tin. Dredge the top with caster sugar. Bake in a moderate oven, 180°C, Gas 4, for 20 minutes, then lay the slices of peel on top. Bake for a further 45–50 minutes.

Mrs Beeton's Nice Useful Cake

fat for greasing
100g butter **or** margarine
100g caster sugar
300g plain flour
2 × 5ml spoons baking powder

3 eggs
200ml milk
1 × 2.5ml spoon almond essence
50g flaked almonds

Grease and line a 15cm cake tin. Cream the fat and sugar until light and fluffy. Sift together the flour and baking powder. Beat the eggs until liquid with the milk. Add the dry ingredients to the creamed mixture in 3 parts, alternately with the egg and milk. Beat well after each addition. Lightly mix in the almond essence and the flaked almonds. Turn lightly into the tin, and smooth the top level. Bake in a warm oven, 160°C, Gas 3, for $1\frac{1}{4}$–$1\frac{1}{2}$ hours.

Simnel Cake

Dundee Cake mixture (p368)

Decoration
double quantity of almond paste
   (p392) **or** 450g prepared marzipan
apricot jam
1 egg

white glacé icing (p387) using
   50g icing sugar
Easter decorations

Prepare the Dundee cake recipe. Put half the mixture into the lined 18cm tin. Cut off one-third of the almond paste and roll it into a 17cm round about 1cm thick. Place it on the cake mixture lightly, and put the remaining cake mixture on top. Bake in a moderate oven, 180°C, Gas 4, for 1 hour, reduce the heat to warm, 160°C, Gas 3, and bake for a further $1\frac{1}{2}$ hours. Cool in the tin, then turn on to a wire rack.

    Warm, then sieve the apricot jam. When the cake is cold, divide the remaining almond paste into 2 equal portions. Roll one-half into a 17cm round. Brush the top of the cake with the apricot jam and press the almond paste lightly on to it. Trim the edge neatly. Beat the egg until liquid. Make small balls from the remaining paste (11 is the traditional number), and place them round the edge of the cake. Brush the balls with beaten egg and brown under the grill. Pour glacé icing into the centre of the cake and decorate with chickens and Easter eggs.

Three Tier Wedding Cake

If possible, prepare the 3 tiers together, using a very large bowl. Cream the butter and sugar, and mix in the other ingredients by hand. Few ovens are large enough to bake the 3 cakes at the same time; leave the cake(s) awaiting baking in a cool place, overnight if necessary.

Make the cakes at least 2 months before covering and icing them with almond paste and royal icing. For instructions on icing and decorating the cakes, see pp391–95.

If liked, the outside of each un-iced cake can be pricked with a skewer when cooled and sprinkled with a little extra brandy.

To store, wrap the cakes in clean greaseproof paper and a clean tea-towel, and keep in a cool, dry place.

If the top tier of a wedding cake is to be kept for some time (for instance to be used as christening cake), fresh almond paste and royal icing should be applied when it is used.

Small tier

fat for greasing
125g currants
100g sultanas
100g seedless raisins
50g glacé cherries
25g blanched whole almonds
25g cut mixed peel
grated rind of 1 small orange
25ml brandy

100g plain flour
$\frac{1}{2} \times 2.5$ml spoon salt
1×2.5ml spoon mixed spice
1×2.5ml spoon ground nutmeg
1×15ml spoon treacle
100g butter
100g soft dark brown sugar
2 large eggs
25g ground almonds

Grease and line a 15cm round or 13cm square cake tin with doubled greaseproof paper and tie a strip of doubled brown paper round the outside.

Pick over the dried fruit, removing any stalks. Chop the cherries and almonds coarsely. Put in a bowl with the peel, orange rind, and dried fruit, add the brandy, and stir well. Cover and put to one side while preparing the rest of the cake mixture.

Sift the flour, salt, and spices together in a mixing bowl. Put the opened treacle tin in a pan of hot water to make measuring easier. Cream the butter and sugar well together until pale and fluffy. Beat the eggs until liquid and add one-quarter at a time, together with a little flour, to the creamed mixture; beat well after each addition. Beat in the treacle. Add the rest of the flour, the ground almonds, and the fruit in brandy, and stir until evenly mixed. Put the mixture in the tin and make a slight hollow in the centre. Bake in a very cool oven, 140°C, Gas 1, for $2\frac{3}{4}$–3 hours, until firm to the touch. Cover with ungreased greaseproof paper after $1\frac{1}{2}$ hours. Cool in the tin. Leave for 24 hours before turning out.

Middle tier

250g currants
200g sultanas
200g seedless raisins
100g glacé cherries
50g blanched whole almonds
50g cut mixed peel
grated rind of 1 large orange
50ml brandy
200g plain flour

1 × 2.5ml spoon salt
1 × 5ml spoon mixed spice
1 × 5ml spoon ground nutmeg
2 × 15ml spoons treacle
200g butter
200g soft dark brown sugar
4 large eggs
50g ground almonds

Make as for the small tier. Bake in a prepared 20cm round tin or 18cm square tin, in a very cool oven, 140°C, Gas 1, for 4–4½ hours. Cover the top with ungreased greaseproof paper when the cake is sufficiently brown. Cool as for the small tier.

Large tier

625g currants
500g sultanas
500g seedless raisins
250g glacé cherries
125g blanched whole almonds
125g cut mixed peel
grated rind of 2 large oranges
125ml brandy
500g plain flour

1 × 5ml spoon salt
1 × 10ml spoon mixed spice
1 × 10ml spoon ground nutmeg
75ml treacle
500g butter
500g soft dark brown sugar
10 large eggs
125g ground almonds

Line a 28cm round or 25cm square cake tin with doubled greaseproof paper. Tie at least 3 bands of brown paper round the outside of the tin. Make the cake as for the small tier. Bake in a very cool oven, 140°C, Gas 1, for about 5½ hours. After 2 hours cover the top with doubled greaseproof paper, and give the tin a quarter turn, gently. Turn again after each 30 minutes to avoid overbrowning. Cool as for the small tier.

Small Rich Cakes (Fairy Cakes) *Basic recipe*
Makes 12–14

100g self-raising flour
a pinch of salt
100g butter **or** margarine

100g caster sugar
2 eggs
fat for greasing

Heat the oven to moderate, 180°C, Gas 4. Mix the flour and salt. Cream the fat and sugar together until light and fluffy. Beat the eggs until liquid, then beat into the mixture gradually. Stir in the flour and salt lightly. Divide the mixture evenly between 12–14 paper cases or greased bun tins, and bake for 15–20 minutes.

VARIATIONS

Cherry Cakes
Add 50g chopped glacé cherries with the flour.

Chocolate Cakes
Add 2 × 15ml spoons cocoa with the flour and add 1 × 15ml spoon milk.

Coconut Cakes
Add 50g desiccated coconut with the flour and 1–2 × 15ml spoons milk with the eggs.

Coffee Cakes
Add 2 × 5ml spoons instant coffee, dissolved in 1 × 5ml spoon water, with the eggs. Add cold.

Queen Cakes
Add 100g currants with the flour.

Apricot Baskets
Makes 12–14

basic Small Rich Cakes mixture

Decoration
1 × 425g can apricot halves
¼ × 500ml pkt lemon jelly
1 × 15cm piece angelica

1 × 142ml carton double cream
1 × 5ml spoon caster sugar

Make and bake the cakes in bun tins as directed in the basic recipe, then cool.

Meanwhile, drain the apricots and heat 125ml of the syrup to boiling point. Pour it on to the jelly cubes and stir until dissolved. Leave to cool. Soak the angelica in a little hot water until pliable, drain, and pat dry on soft kitchen paper. Cut into strips 5mm wide. Whip the cream and sugar until stiff.

When the cakes are cold and the jelly is just starting to set, place half an apricot on the top of each cake, rounded side uppermost. Coat each apricot with jelly. Using a forcing bag with a small star nozzle, pipe stars of cream around the apricots. Arch the angelica over the cakes to form handles, pushing them into the sides of the cakes.

Butterfly Cakes
Makes 12–14

basic Small Rich Cakes mixture (p372)

Decoration

1 × 5ml spoon caster sugar
½ × 2.5ml spoon vanilla essence

1 × 142ml carton double cream
icing sugar for dusting

Make and bake the cakes in bun tins as directed on p372, then cool.

Meanwhile, add the caster sugar and the vanilla essence to the cream and whip until stiff. Transfer to a forcing bag with a large star nozzle.

When the cakes are cold, cut a round off the top of each and cut these in half. Pipe a star of cream on each cake. Place the two halves of each round upright, cut side down, in the cream to resemble wings. Dust lightly with icing sugar.

Brownies
Makes 9 (approx)

fat for greasing
150g margarine
150g caster sugar
2 eggs

50g plain flour
2 × 15ml spoons cocoa
100g chopped walnuts

Grease and line a shallow 15cm square tin. Cream the fat and sugar until light and fluffy. Beat in the eggs. Sift together the flour and cocoa, and fold in. Chop the walnuts finely, and add half of them to the mixture. Spread evenly in the tin and bake in a moderate oven, 180°C, Gas 4, for 10 minutes; then sprinkle the rest of the walnuts all over the surface. Bake for a further 15 minutes. Cool in the tin. When cold, cut into squares.

Note The texture of Brownies should be the same as that of a fruit cake. When cooked, the top crust should just be firm to the touch, the inside soft or moist.

Victoria Sandwich Cake

fat for greasing
150g butter **or** margarine
150g caster sugar
3 eggs
150g self-raising flour **or** plain flour
and 1 × 5ml spoon baking powder

a pinch of salt
raspberry **or** other jam for filling
caster sugar for dredging

Grease and line two 18cm sandwich tins. Cream the fat and sugar together until light and fluffy. Beat the eggs until liquid, and add them gradually, beating well after each addition. Sift together the flour, salt, and baking powder, if used. Stir into the mixture, lightly but thoroughly, until evenly mixed. Divide between the tins and bake in a moderate oven, 180°C, Gas 4, for 25–30 minutes. When cold, sandwich together with jam, and sprinkle the top with caster sugar.

For **variations**, see over.

VARIATIONS
The cake can be baked in a 20cm tin for 40 minutes, cooled, then split and filled. This gives a softer centred cake. All loose crumbs must be brushed off the cut sides before filling. Too moist a filling will seep into the cake.

Chocolate Sandwich Cake
Use 125g self-raising flour and 25g cocoa, and add a few drops of vanilla essence with the eggs. Fill with chocolate butter icing (p389).

Coffee Sandwich Cake
Add 1 × 15ml spoon instant coffee dissolved in 1 × 10ml spoon water. Fill with coffee butter icing (p389).

Orange or Lemon Sandwich Cake
Add the grated rind of 1 orange or lemon to the creamed fat and sugar. Fill with orange or lemon butter icing (p390).

Small Victoria Sandwich Cake
Make the cake in two 15cm sandwich tins. Use only 100g fat, 100g sugar, 2 eggs, 100g self-raising flour, and a pinch of salt.

Feather-Iced Sandwich Cake

1 × 20cm Victoria Sandwich Cake (p373)

Decoration

white butter icing (p389) using 50g butter	glacé icing (p387) using 150g icing sugar
browned cake crumbs	food colouring

Coat the sides of the cake with the butter icing and roll in the browned crumbs, pressing them into place. Decorate the cake with Feather Icing (p387).

Battenburg Cake

fat for greasing	2 eggs
100g self-raising flour	pink food colouring
a pinch of salt	apricot glaze (p396)
100g butter **or** margarine	200g almond paste (p392)
100g caster sugar	

Decoration (optional)

glacé cherries	angelica

Grease and line a Battenburg tin, 22 × 18cm, which has a metal divider down the centre; or use a 22 × 18cm tin and cut double greaseproof paper to separate the mixture into 2 parts. Mix the flour and salt together. Cream the fat and sugar together until light and fluffy. Add the eggs, one at a time with a little flour, stir in, then beat well. Stir in the remaining flour lightly but thoroughly. Place half the mixture in one half of the tin. Tint the remaining mixture pink, and place it in the other half of the tin. Smooth both mixtures away from the centre towards the outside of the tin. Bake in a fairly hot oven, 190°C, Gas 5, for 25–30 minutes. Leave the cakes in the tin for a few minutes, then transfer them to a wire rack and peel off the paper. Leave to cool completely.

To finish the cake, cut each slab of cake into 3 strips lengthways. Trim off any crisp edges and rounded surfaces so that all 6 strips are neat and the same size. Arrange 3 strips with 1 pink strip in the middle. Brush the touching sides with the glaze and press together lightly. Make up the other layer in the same way, using 2 pink with 1 plain strip in the middle. Brush glaze over the top of 1 layer and place the other on this.

Roll out the almond paste thinly into a rectangle the same length as the strips and wide enough to wrap round them. Brush it with glaze and place the cake in the centre. Wrap the paste round the cake and press the edges together lightly. Turn so that the join is underneath; trim the ends. Mark the top of the paste with the back of a knife to make a criss-cross pattern. Decorate with glacé cherries and angelica, if liked.

Sponge Cake *Basic recipe*

fat for greasing	75g caster sugar
flour for dusting	75g plain flour
caster sugar for dusting	a pinch of salt
3 eggs	a pinch of baking powder

Grease an 18cm round cake tin or two 15cm sandwich tins. Mix small equal quantities of sifted flour and caster sugar and use to dust the sides and base of the tins.

Whisk the eggs and sugar together in a bowl over a pan of hot water, taking care that the base of the bowl does not touch the water. Continue whisking for 10–15 minutes until thick and creamy. Remove the bowl from the pan. Whisk until cold. Sift and fold in the flour, salt, and baking powder, using a metal spoon. Do this lightly, so that the air incorporated during whisking is not lost. Pour the mixture into the prepared tins. Bake in a moderate oven, 180°C, Gas 4, for 40 minutes in an 18cm tin, or for 25 minutes in two 15cm tins. Leave the sponge in the tins for a few minutes, then turn on to a cooling rack and leave until cold.

Note If an electric mixer is used, there is no need to place the bowl over hot water. Whisk at high speed for about 5 minutes until thick. Fold in the flour by hand.

VARIATION

Mrs Beeton's Savoy Cakes or Sponge Fingers

Prepare a baking sheet by greasing and then dredging with caster sugar and flour. Make the sponge mixture and put it in a forcing bag with a 1.5cm plain nozzle. Pipe out about 14 fingers, 8–9cm long. Dredge with caster sugar and bake in a moderate oven, 180°C, Gas 4, for 7–10 minutes.

Note Special sponge finger tins can be used, prepared as above. Fill three-quarters full, dredge with sugar and bake for 10–12 minutes.

Swiss Roll

fat for greasing	75g plain flour
3 eggs	a pinch of salt
75g caster sugar	jam **or** butter cream (p397)
1 × 2.5ml spoon baking powder	caster sugar for dusting

Heat the oven to hot, 220°C, Gas 7. Grease and line a Swiss roll tin 20 × 30cm. Whisk the eggs and sugar together in a bowl over a pan of hot water, taking care that the base does not touch the water. Whisk for 10–15 minutes until thick and creamy. Remove from the pan and whisk until cold. Sift the baking powder with the flour and salt, and fold in lightly. Pour into the prepared tin and bake for 10 minutes. Meanwhile, warm the jam, if used.

When the cake is cooked, turn it on to a large sheet of greaseproof paper dusted with caster sugar. Peel off the lining paper. Trim off any crisp edges. Spread the cake with the warmed jam and roll up tightly. Dredge with caster sugar and place on a cooling rack with the cut edge underneath.

Note If the Swiss roll is to be filled with butter cream, cover with greaseproof paper and roll up tightly with the paper inside. Cool completely. When cold, unroll carefully, spread with the filling, and re-roll. Dust with caster sugar.

VARIATION

Chocolate Swiss Roll

Use the recipe for Swiss roll but substitute 1 × 15ml spoon cocoa for 1 × 15ml spoon of flour. When cooked, roll up with greaseproof paper inside. When cold, prepare chocolate butter icing (p389). Unroll carefully, spread with just over half the butter icing and roll up. Spread the remainder over the top and, if liked, mark with a fork to resemble a log.

For a Yule log, put a robin or sprig of holly on top of the roll.

Genoese Sponge or Pastry (1)

fat for greasing	4 eggs
100g plain flour	100g caster sugar
1 × 2.5ml spoon salt	
75g clarified butter (p232) **or** margarine	

Grease and line a 20 × 30cm Swiss roll tin. Sift together the flour and salt, and put in a warm place. Melt the fat without letting it get hot. Put to one side. Whisk the eggs lightly, add the sugar, and whisk over hot water for 10–15 minutes until thick. Remove from the heat; the fat should be as cool as the egg mixture. Remove from the heat and continue whisking until at blood-heat. Sift half the flour over the eggs, then pour in half the fat in a thin stream. Fold in gently. Repeat, using the remaining flour and fat. Turn gently into the tin, and bake in a moderate oven, 180°C, Gas 4, for 30–40 minutes.

Genoese Sponge or Pastry (2)

Make as for Genoese Sponge (1), using 75g flour, a pinch of salt, 50g clarified butter or margarine, 3 eggs, and 75g caster sugar. Bake in an 18cm square or 15 × 25cm oblong cake tin.

French Cakes or Iced Petits Fours
Makes 18–24

Genoese Sponge (1) **or** (2) baked in
   an oblong tin

Filling
jam, lemon curd **or** butter icing (p389)
   using 50g butter

Icing
glacé icing (p387)   food colouring

Decoration
crystallized violets, silver balls,
   glacé fruits, angelica, chopped nuts,
   etc

Cut the cold sponge through the centre crossways; spread with the chosen filling and sandwich together again. Cut the cake into small rounds, triangles or squares, and place these small cakes on a wire rack over a large dish. Brush off any loose crumbs. Make up the icing to a coating consistency which will flow easily. Tint some of it with different colourings. Using a small spoon, coat the top and sides of the cakes with the icing or, if preferred, pour it over the cakes, making sure that the sides are coated evenly all over. Place the decorations on the tops and leave to set. The cakes can be served in paper cases.

Rubbed-in Biscuits *Basic recipe*
Makes 24–26

200g plain flour   1 × 5ml spoon baking powder
½ × 2.5ml spoon salt   1 egg yolk
75–100g butter **or** margarine   flour for rolling out
50g caster sugar   fat for greasing

Heat the oven to moderate, 180°C, Gas 4. Mix the flour and salt together. Rub in the fat, stir in the sugar and baking powder. Bind to a stiff paste with the egg yolk. Knead well and roll out just under 1cm thick on a lightly floured surface. Cut into rounds with a 5cm cutter. Re-roll and re-cut any trimmings. Place on a greased baking sheet. Prick the top of each biscuit in 2 or 3 places. Bake for 15–20 minutes or until firm to the touch and pale golden-brown. Leave to stand for a few minutes, then cool on a wire rack.

   For **variations**, see over.

VARIATIONS
Plain Chocolate Biscuits
Add 50g powdered drinking chocolate and 2 × 5ml spoons instant coffee dissolved in 3 × 2.5ml spoons water.

Plain Cinnamon or Spice Biscuits
Add 1 × 5ml spoon ground cinnamon or mixed spice to the flour. When cold, sandwich 2 biscuits together with jam, and dredge with icing sugar.

Plain Coconut Biscuits
Use 150g flour and 50g desiccated coconut. As soon as the biscuits are cooked, brush with warm jam glaze (p396) and sprinkle with coconut.

Almond Fingers
Makes 14 (approx)

150g plain flour	1 × 5ml spoon baking powder
50g ground almonds	1 egg yolk
½ × 2.5ml spoon salt	flour for rolling out
75–100g butter **or** margarine	fat for greasing
50g caster sugar	

Topping

1 egg white	50g nibbed almonds
75g icing sugar	raspberry jam

Heat the oven to moderate, 180°C, Gas 4. Mix together the flour, ground almonds, and salt. Rub in the fat, stir in the sugar and baking powder. Bind to a stiff paste with the yolk. Knead well and roll into a strip 8cm wide. Prick the surface well. Transfer to a greased baking sheet and pinch the long edges to decorate. Bake for 15 minutes.

Meanwhile, make the topping. Whisk the egg white until it stands up in peaks, and fold in the sugar and almonds. Remove the baked base from the oven and spread with raspberry jam. Spread the topping over the jam, and bake for 7–10 minutes, until the meringue is set and lightly browned. Cut into fingers while still warm.

Catherine Wheel Biscuits
Makes 24 (approx)

150g plain flour	a few drops vanilla essence
½ × 2.5ml spoon salt	25ml water
1 × 5ml spoon baking powder	1 × 5ml spoon cocoa
75g butter	flour for rolling out
75g caster sugar	fat for greasing

Sift together the flour, salt, and baking powder into a mixing bowl. Rub in the butter, and stir in the sugar. Make the mixture into a pliable paste with the essence and water. Divide the paste into 2 equal portions. Put 1 portion back in the mixing bowl. Sprinkle the cocoa over it and work it in evenly, using a fork.

Roll out the plain paste on a lightly floured surface into a rectangle 18 × 22cm. Put to one side. Roll out the chocolate paste to the same size and place it on top of the plain piece. Roll lightly with the rolling-pin to make them stick together. Roll up both pieces from the long side, like a Swiss roll, keeping the join underneath. Chill until firm.

Heat the oven to moderate, 180°C, Gas 4. Cut the paste into slices 1cm thick. Reshape into neat rounds with the hands and place on a greased baking sheet, spaced well apart. Bake for 15–20 minutes until the plain biscuit mixture is golden-brown.

Coffee Kisses
Makes 12 pairs (approx)

75g butter **or** margarine
150g self-raising flour
50g caster sugar

1 egg yolk
1 × 5ml spoon liquid coffee essence
fat for greasing

Filling
coffee butter icing (p389)

icing sugar for dusting (optional)

Heat the oven to fairly hot, 190°C, Gas 5. Rub the fat into the flour, then stir in the sugar. Mix the egg yolk with the coffee essence and use to bind the dry ingredients together to a stiff paste. Roll the mixture into balls about the size of a walnut and place on a greased baking sheet. Bake for 10 minutes. When cooked, leave to cool on a wire rack.

Use the coffee butter icing to sandwich the biscuits together in pairs. If liked, dust with icing sugar.

Digestive Biscuits
Makes 12 (approx)

75g wholemeal flour
25g plain white flour
25g fine **or** medium oatmeal
1 × 2.5ml spoon baking powder
$\frac{1}{2}$ × 2.5ml spoon salt

1 × 15ml spoon soft light brown sugar
50g butter **or** margarine
2 × 15ml spoons milk
flour for rolling out
fat for greasing

Heat the oven to moderate, 180°C, Gas 4. Mix all the dry ingredients, sifting the sugar if it is lumpy. Rub in the fat and mix to a pliable dough with the milk. Knead lightly on a floured board and roll out just under 5mm thick. Cut into rounds with a 6cm round cutter, place on a greased baking sheet and prick with a fork. Bake for 15 minutes.

Jumbles
Makes 20

50g plain flour
a pinch of salt
50g caster sugar
40g butter **or** margarine

1 × 10ml spoon beaten egg
flour for rolling out
fat for greasing

Heat the oven to warm, 160°C, Gas 3. Mix the flour, salt, and sugar together. Rub in the fat lightly. Stir in the egg and mix to a soft paste. Roll out with the hands on a floured surface to a long sausage shape about 2cm thick. Divide into 20 pieces, and roll each into an 8cm long sausage. Form into an S shape and place well apart on a greased baking sheet. Bake for 12–15 minutes. Allow the jumbles to cool for a few seconds, then slip a palette knife under each and place on a wire rack to finish cooling.

Oatmeal Biscuits
Makes 22–24

100g medium oatmeal
100g self-raising flour
1 × 2.5ml spoon salt
a pinch of sugar
100g butter **or** margarine

2 × 15ml spoons beaten egg
2 × 15ml spoons water
flour for rolling out
fat for greasing

Heat the oven to moderate, 180°C, Gas 4. Mix all the dry ingredients together and rub in the fat. Mix the egg with the water and use this to bind the dry ingredients together into a stiff paste. Roll out on a lightly floured surface to just under 1cm thick. Cut into rounds with a 5–6cm cutter. Prick the surface of the biscuits with a fork and place on a greased baking sheet. Bake for 15–20 minutes.

Shortbread
Makes 8 wedges

100g plain flour
½ × 2.5ml spoon salt
50g rice flour, ground rice **or** semolina

50g caster sugar
100g butter
fat for greasing

Mix all the dry ingredients together. Rub in the butter until the mixture binds together to a paste. Shape into a large round about 1cm thick. Pinch up the edges to decorate. Place on an upturned greased baking sheet, and prick with a fork. Bake in a moderate oven, 180°C, Gas 4, for 40–45 minutes. Cut into 8 wedges while still warm.

VARIATION
Shortbread Biscuits
Roll out the paste on a lightly floured surface to just under 1cm thick. Cut into rounds with a 5–6cm cutter. Prick the surface in several places with a fork. Bake for 15–20 minutes.

German or Spice Biscuits
Makes 12 (approx)

125g plain flour
50g caster sugar
½ × 2.5ml spoon mixed spice

75g margarine
flour for rolling out
fat for greasing

Heat the oven to warm, 160°C, Gas 3. Mix the flour, sugar, and spice together. Rub in the margarine until the mixture binds together and makes a pliable paste. Roll out on a floured board to 5mm thick, and cut into rounds with a 6cm round cutter. Place on a greased baking sheet. Bake for about 20 minutes until very pale golden-brown.

Creamed Biscuits *Basic recipe*
Makes 26–30

200g plain flour
½ × 2.5ml spoon salt
100–150g butter **or** margarine
100–150g caster sugar

1 egg yolk **or** ½ beaten egg
flour for rolling out
fat for greasing
caster sugar for dredging (optional)

Heat the oven to moderate, 180°C, Gas 4. Mix the flour and salt together. Beat the fat until soft, add the sugar, and cream until light and fluffy. Beat the egg into the creamed mixture. Fold in the flour, using a knife and then the fingers. On a lightly floured surface, knead lightly and roll out to 5mm–1cm thick. Cut into rounds with a 6cm cutter. Re-roll and re-cut any trimmings. Prick the surface of the biscuits in 2 or 3 places with a fork. Place on a well-greased baking sheet. Bake for 15–20 minutes. Leave on the baking sheet for 5 minutes before transferring to a cooling rack. Dredge with caster sugar, if liked.

VARIATIONS

Almond Biscuits
Use 150g plain flour and 50g ground almonds instead of 200g flour. When cold, sandwich the biscuits together in pairs with jam and dredge with icing sugar.

Dover or Easter Biscuits
Mix 1 × 2.5ml spoon ground cinnamon with the flour and salt, and add 50g currants. Brush with beaten egg white, and sprinkle with caster sugar 5 minutes before removing from the oven.

Lemon or Orange Biscuits
Add the grated rind of 1 lemon or 1 orange to the flour.

Shrewsbury Biscuits
Use 200g self-raising flour or 200g plain flour and 1 × 5ml spoon baking powder. Omit the salt and use only 100g fat and 100g sugar. Add 1 × 5ml spoon grated lemon rind to the yolk. Bake in a warm oven, 160°C, Gas 3, for 30–40 minutes.

Bourbon Biscuits
Makes 14–16

50g butter **or** margarine
50g caster sugar
1 × 15ml spoon golden syrup
100g plain flour

15g cocoa
1 × 2.5ml spoon bicarbonate of soda
flour for rolling out
fat for greasing

Filling
75g icing sugar
50g butter **or** margarine
1 × 15ml spoon cocoa

1 × 5ml spoon coffee essence **or**
1 × 2.5ml spoon instant coffee
dissolved in 1 × 5ml spoon water

Heat the oven to warm, 160°C, Gas 3. Cream the fat and sugar together very thoroughly; beat in the syrup. Sift the flour, cocoa, and soda together, and work into the creamed mixture to make a stiff paste. Knead well, and roll out on a lightly floured surface into an oblong strip about 5mm thick. Cut into two 6cm fingers. Place on a greased baking sheet covered with greased greaseproof paper. Bake for 15–20 minutes. Cut into equal-sized fingers while still warm. Cool on a wire rack.

Prepare the filling. Sift the icing sugar. Beat the fat until soft, add the sugar, cocoa, and coffee. Beat until smooth. Sandwich the cooled fingers with a layer of filling.

Melting Moments
Makes 16–20

100g margarine **or** 50g margarine and
   50g white cooking fat
75g caster sugar
25ml beaten egg
125g self-raising flour

a pinch of salt
rolled oats for coating
fat for greasing
4–5 glacé cherries

Heat the oven to moderate, 180°C, Gas 4. Cream the fat and sugar until pale and fluffy. Add the egg, a little flour, and the salt, and beat again. Stir in the remaining flour and shape the mixture into 16–20 round balls with the hands. Place the rolled oats on a sheet of greaseproof paper and toss the balls in them to coat them evenly all over. Place on 2 greased baking sheets. Place a small piece of glacé cherry in the centre of each. Bake for about 20 minutes until pale golden-brown. Leave to cool for a few minutes on the trays, then cool on a wire rack.

Piped Almond Rings
Makes 24 (approx)

175g butter
125g caster sugar
1 egg
250g self-raising flour

50g ground almonds
1–2 drops vanilla essence
2 × 5ml spoons milk (approx)
fat for greasing

Cream the butter and sugar together until light and fluffy. Beat the egg until liquid and add it to the creamed mixture, beating thoroughly. Blend in the flour and ground almonds gradually. Add the vanilla essence and enough milk to give a piping consistency. Leave the mixture to stand for about 20 minutes in a cool place.

Heat the oven to fairly hot, 200°C, Gas 6. Put the mixture into a forcing bag with a medium-sized star nozzle, and pipe small rings on to a well-greased baking sheet. Bake for 10 minutes.

Note These biscuits can be served as petits fours.

Princess Cakes
Makes 10 pairs

100g butter **or** margarine
25g caster sugar
a pinch of salt

100g self-raising flour
grated rind of $\frac{1}{2}$ orange
fat for greasing

Filling
orange butter icing (p390) using
    25g butter

Heat the oven to moderate, 180°C, Gas 4. Cream the fat and sugar well together. Work in the salt, flour, and orange rind. Place the mixture in a forcing bag with a large star nozzle, and pipe 9cm lengths on to a greased baking sheet, making 20 biscuits. Bake for 15 minutes. Cool on the sheet.

When cool, sandwich together in pairs with orange butter icing.

Brandy Snaps
Makes 14–18

50g plain flour
1 × 5ml spoon ground ginger
50g margarine
50g soft dark brown sugar

2 × 15ml spoons golden syrup
2 × 5ml spoons grated lemon rind
1 × 5ml spoon lemon juice
fat for greasing

Heat the oven to warm, 160°C, Gas 3. Sift the flour and ginger. Melt the margarine in a small saucepan. Add the sugar and syrup and warm gently but do not allow to become hot. Remove from the heat. Add the sifted ingredients, the lemon rind and juice, and mix well. Put small spoonfuls on to greased baking sheets, spaced well apart to allow the mixture to spread. Do not put more than 6 spoonfuls on a 20 × 25cm baking sheet. Bake for 8–10 minutes.

Remove from the oven and leave to cool for a few moments until the edges begin to firm. Lift with a palette knife and roll loosely round the handle of a greased wooden spoon. Leave to cool before removing the spoon handle. (Several spoon handles will be needed.)

Note If the brandy snaps are to be served at a party or as a dessert, fill at the last moment with fresh whipped cream, confectioners' custard (p398) or a similar filling. Use either a small spoon or a forcing bag with a large star or rose nozzle.

Ginger Snaps
Makes 56 (approx)

200g self-raising flour
a pinch of salt
1 × 5ml spoon ground ginger
100g soft light brown sugar

75g margarine
100g golden syrup
1 egg
fat for greasing

Heat the oven to warm, 160°C, Gas 3. Sift together the flour, salt, ginger, and sugar. Melt the margarine and syrup in a medium-sized saucepan. Beat the egg until liquid. When the fat has melted, add the dry ingredients and egg alternately and beat until smooth and thick. Using 2 teaspoons, place rounds of mixture on to well-greased baking sheets, spaced well apart to allow the mixture to spread. Bake for 15 minutes. Leave on the sheets for a few moments, and finish cooling on a wire rack.
Note The mixture will thicken as it cools. If necessary, wash the sheets for the second and later batches, regrease them and shape the mixture into small balls in the hands. Place on the sheets and bake as before. If the biscuits become too crisp to remove from the sheets easily, put back in the oven for a minute or two.

Flapjacks
Makes 20 (approx)

50g margarine
50g soft light brown sugar
2 × 15ml spoons golden syrup

100g rolled oats
fat for greasing

Melt the margarine, add the sugar and syrup, and warm gently. Do not boil. Remove from the heat and stir in the oats. Press into a greased 28 × 18cm tin. Bake in a warm oven, 160°C, Gas 3, for 25 minutes or until firm. Cut into fingers while still warm and leave in the tin to cool.

Oatcakes
Makes 16 (approx)

50g bacon fat **or** dripping
100g medium oatmeal
1 × 2.5ml spoon salt
$\frac{1}{2}$ × 2.5ml spoon bicarbonate of soda

boiling water
fine oatmeal for rolling out
fat for greasing

Melt the fat and stir in the dry ingredients. Add enough boiling water to make a stiff paste. Knead well. On a surface dusted with fine oatmeal, roll out into a round 5mm thick and cut into wedge-shaped pieces. Place on a greased baking sheet and bake in a warm oven, 160°C, Gas 3, for 20–30 minutes.

Canadian Crispies
Makes 12–14

100g plain block chocolate
50g crisp rice cereal

25g seedless raisins **or** sultanas

Break the chocolate into small pieces and put it in a basin over hot (not boiling) water until it melts and is liquid. Stir in the cereal and the dried fruit. Place in rough heaps in paper cases and leave to cool and set.

Florentines
Makes 20–24 (approx)

oil for greasing
25g glacé cherries
100g cut mixed peel
50g flaked almonds
100g chopped almonds

25g sultanas
100g butter **or** margarine
100g caster sugar
2 × 15ml spoons double cream
100g plain **or** couverture chocolate

Heat the oven to moderate, 180°C, Gas 4. Cover 3–4 baking sheets with oiled grease-proof paper. Cut up the glacé cherries and chop the mixed peel a little more finely if necessary. Mix with the flaked and chopped almonds and the sultanas. Melt the fat in a small saucepan, add the sugar, and boil for 1 minute. Remove from the heat and stir in the fruit and nuts. Whip the cream and fold it in. Place small spoonfuls of the mixture on to the baking sheets, leaving room for spreading. Bake for 8–10 minutes. After the biscuits have been in the oven for about 5 minutes, neaten the edges by drawing them together with a plain biscuit cutter. Leave the biscuits to firm up slightly before removing the paper, then cool completely on a wire rack.

To finish, melt the chocolate in a basin over hot water and use to coat the flat underside of the biscuits. Mark into wavy lines with a fork as the chocolate cools.

Mrs Beeton's Almond Macaroons
Makes 16–20

fat for greasing
2 egg whites
150g caster sugar

100g ground almonds
1 × 10ml spoon ground rice
split almonds **or** halved glacé cherries

Heat the oven to warm, 160°C, Gas 3. Grease a baking sheet and cover with rice paper. Whisk the egg whites until frothy but not stiff enough to form peaks. Stir in the sugar, ground almonds, and ground rice. Beat with a wooden spoon until thick and white. Place small spoonfuls of the mixture 5cm apart on the paper or pipe them on. Place a split almond or halved glacé cherry on each. Bake for 20 minutes or until pale fawn.

VARIATION

Ratafias
Make as above, but only 2cm in diameter. Omit the almond. Ratafias are used in trifles, to decorate desserts, and as petits fours.

Mrs Beeton's Coconut Pyramids
Makes 12

fat for greasing
2 egg whites

150g caster sugar
150g desiccated coconut

Grease a baking sheet and cover with rice paper. Whisk the egg whites until stiff, then fold in the sugar and coconut, using a metal spoon. Divide the mixture into 12 portions and place in heaps on the rice paper. Using a fork, form into pyramid shapes. Bake in a very cool oven, 140°C, Gas 1, for 45 minutes–1 hour until pale brown in colour.

ICINGS, FILLINGS AND DECORATIONS

Glacé Icing

Points for use: The correct consistency is stiff enough to coat the back of a wooden spoon thickly, otherwise it will run off the surface of the cake.

Glacé icing should be used immediately. If left to stand, even for a short while, it should be covered completely with damp greaseproof paper. Any crystallized icing on the surface should be scraped off before use.

Decorations: Decorations must be put on before the icing sets or it will crack. Do not use decorations liable to melt, run or be damaged by damp. Crystallized flower petals, chocolate decorations and some small sweets should not be used.

To Coat a Cake, Gâteau or Pastries with Glacé Icing
Top: If only the top of a cake or gâteau is to be iced, tie a band of doubled greaseproof paper round it which rises about 1cm higher than the top. This will prevent the icing spilling over the sides.

Top and sides: If the sides as well as the top are to be iced, omit the band, and place the cake, gâteau or pastries on a revolving cake stand (a turntable), on an upturned plate, or on a wire cooling rack with greaseproof paper underneath. Brush any loose crumbs off the surface, using a soft pastry brush.

Pour the icing on to the top of the cake, gâteau or pastries from the centre outwards; spread it lightly if necessary with a hot, wetted palette knife. Tilt the cake or gâteau so that the icing runs down the sides. Spread extra icing over any bare patches.

Decorations: Quickly put on any decorations and leave, undisturbed, to set. Trim off any icing round the base with a sharp knife, and transfer to a serving plate, using a cake slice or fish servers.

A trickling technique called fricking is used mostly for decoration; a coloured coating, eg chocolate, is trickled over a cake on which a white or pale glacé icing coating has been applied to the top and sides and allowed to set. The trickled icing drips over the edges of the cake to contrast with the base coating. Use a thin glacé icing which will spread easily.

Other methods: Very small pieces of Genoese Sponge (or similar cake), when used for petits fours are stuck on skewers and dipped in icing. They should be put immediately on to a wire rack, decorated and left undisturbed to dry.

Glacé icing can also be trickled over pastry desserts such as filled choux. No attempt is made to cover them completely. Éclairs, cream buns, and other dessert pastries are also only partially covered with a single line or cap of icing.

Glacé icing can also be used as a second coat over a base coat of royal icing.

Feather Icing
Enough to coat the top of one 18cm cake

Make up some white glacé icing, using 150g icing sugar. Remove 2 × 15ml spoons and tint it with a few drops of food colouring. Brown is the colour usually chosen as it shows up well.

Coat the top of the cake with the white icing. Place the tinted icing in a piping bag fitted with a fine writing pipe, and pipe parallel lines over the white icing; do this quickly before the coating sets. Then run a cocktail stick or fine skewer lightly across the cake in parallel lines, backwards and forwards at right angles to the piping. Allow to set firmly before cutting.

Feather icing is used on sponge and sandwich cakes, and on some gâteaux.

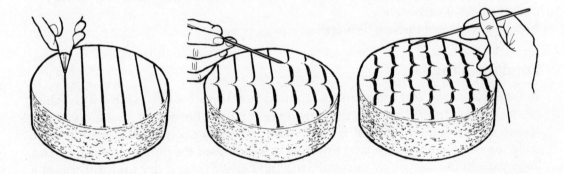

Glacé Icing
Enough to cover the top of one 18cm cake

100g icing sugar
2 × 10ml spoons water (approx)

1 × 2.5ml spoon strained lemon **or**
  orange juice (optional)
colouring (optional)

Sift the icing sugar. Put 1 × 15ml spoon water into a small non-stick or enamel saucepan with the icing sugar. If a mild lemon or orange flavour is required add the juice at this stage. Warm very gently, without making the pan too hot to touch on the underside. Beat well with a wooden spoon. The icing should coat the back of the spoon thickly. If it is too thick, add the extra 5ml water; if too thin add a very little extra sifted icing sugar. Add colouring, if liked. Use at once.

Note Icing sugars vary in the amount of liquid they will absorb.

For **variations**, see over.

VARIATIONS
Coffee Glacé Icing

Dissolve 1 × 5ml spoon instant coffee in the water.

Lemon or Orange Glacé Icing

Substitute strained lemon or orange juice for the amount of water used.
Note Other fruit flavours can be achieved by using a small quantity of flavouring essence.

Liqueur-flavoured Glacé Icing

Substitute 1 × 10ml spoon liqueur for 1 × 10ml spoon of the water.

Chocolate Glacé Icing
Enough to coat the top of one 18cm cake

50g plain chocolate	2 × 5ml spoons butter
1 × 15ml spoon water	100g icing sugar

Grate the chocolate into a small, heavy-based pan. Add the water and butter. Warm very gently, stirring thoroughly until the mixture is smooth and creamy. Sift the icing sugar and stir it in a little at a time, adding a little extra water if necessary to make a coating consistency.
Note The icing will thicken as it cools.

Fondant Icing

To use fondant icing: Put the quantity required in a heatproof bowl with a little water or stock syrup (p389) and set the bowl over a pan of hot water. Using a wooden spoon, stir the fondant until it is of a creamy spreading consistency, adding more water or syrup if necessary, and any flavouring. Spread the fondant quickly over a large cake in the same way as royal icing (pp393–95). Let it dry undisturbed on a wire rack. Any fondant which drips off can be scraped up after the cake is dry, moulded into a ball and stored, provided it has no crumbs in it. Fondant icing stores well if kept in an airtight jar, covered with waxed paper and a lid.

Fondant Icing
Enough to cover one 18–20cm cake

450g caster **or** lump sugar	2 × 10ml spoons liquid glucose
150ml water	

Put the sugar and water into a heavy-based saucepan which is absolutely free from grease. Heat gently until all the sugar has completely dissolved. Stir very occasionally. Wipe any crystals which form on the sides of the pan with a wet pastry brush. When the sugar has dissolved, add the glucose, and boil to 115°C without stirring. Keep the sides of the pan clean by brushing with the wet brush when necessary. Remove from the heat and allow the bubbles to subside.

Pour the mixture slowly into the middle of a wetted marble slab and allow to cool a little. Work the sides to the middle with a sugar scraper to make a smaller mass. Using a wooden spatula in one hand and the scraper in the other, make a figure-of-eight with the spatula, keeping the mixture together with the scraper. Work until the mass is completely white. Break off small amounts and knead well, then re-knead the small pieces together into one mass. Store in a jar, preferably of stoneware. Cover with waxed paper and a lid.

Stock Syrup (for diluting fondant)

150g granulated sugar   125ml water

Dissolve the sugar in the water in a saucepan. When it has dissolved, boil without stirring for 3 minutes. Remove any scum as it rises, with a spoon. Allow to cool and strain into a jar with a lid. Store for future use if not required immediately.
Note This syrup can also be kneaded into commercially made almond paste to make the paste more pliable.

Butter Icing

Points for use: The icing must be soft in texture so that it spreads easily or it may drag off loose crumbs which will make the icing look speckled. The butter should be at room temperature and must be softened thoroughly before the sugar is added. If the final consistency is too stiff, place the bowl containing the icing over a pan of warm water and beat well.

   Storage: Butter icing hardens as it sets. It can be stored in a refrigerator, but must be returned to room temperature and beaten well before it is used on a cake. Cakes filled or covered with butter icing can be frozen (see p438).

Butter Icing
Enough for 2 layers in one 18–20cm cake

250g icing sugar   1 × 15ml spoon liquid, eg milk, water
100g softened butter   **or** fruit juice

Sift the icing sugar and add gradually to the butter with the liquid, beating until the icing is smooth and of a soft spreading consistency.
VARIATIONS
Chocolate Butter Icing (1)
Grate 50g plain block chocolate. Put in a basin over hot water with 1 × 15ml spoon milk, stir until dissolved, then cool. Use instead of the liquid in the plain butter icing.

Chocolate Butter Icing (2)
Dissolve 1 × 15ml spoon cocoa in 1 × 15ml spoon hot water. Cool before use. Use instead of the liquid in the plain butter icing.

Coffee Butter Icing
Dissolve 1 × 5ml spoon instant coffee in 1 × 15ml spoon hot water. Cool before use. Use instead of the liquid in the plain butter icing.

Lemon or Orange Butter Icing
Use 1 × 15ml spoon juice and a little grated rind.

Vanilla Butter Icing
Add 1 × 2.5ml spoon vanilla essence with the milk.

Walnut Butter Icing
Add 25g finely chopped walnuts with the milk.

Frostings and Toppings

American Frosting
Enough to cover one 15–18cm cake

225g granulated sugar
4 × 15ml spoons water
a pinch of cream of tartar

1 × 2.5ml spoon vanilla essence **or**
 a few drops lemon juice (optional)
1 egg white

Have the cake standing ready to be iced, on a turntable, upturned plate, or wire cooling rack with paper spread underneath. Heat the sugar, water, and cream of tartar gently until the sugar dissolves. Add the flavouring if liked. Heat, without boiling, to 120°C, stirring all the time. Remove the syrup from the heat and leave to cool slightly until it stops swirling. Meanwhile, whisk the egg white until stiff. Pour the syrup on to the egg white in a thin stream, beating with a spoon all the time. Continue beating until the icing is of the required consistency. When thick enough, pour it over the cake and swirl with a round-bladed knife.

Seafoam Frosting
Enough to cover the top, sides, and fill one 20cm sandwich cake

2 egg whites
350g soft light brown sugar
$\frac{1}{2}$ × 2.5ml spoon cream of tartar

125ml cold water
a pinch of salt
1 × 5ml spoon vanilla essence

Put all the ingredients, apart from the essence, into the top of a double boiler or heatproof bowl. Beat until blended. Place over boiling water: do not allow the bottom of the top pan or bowl to touch the water. Cook, beating all the time, for about 7 minutes, until the frosting forms soft peaks. Do not overcook. Remove from the boiling water, add the vanilla essence, and beat the frosting for about 2 minutes until of spreading consistency.

Grilled Nut Topping
Enough to cover two 15cm square cakes

50g butter **or** margarine
100g soft light brown sugar

3 × 15ml spoons single cream
100g chopped mixed nuts

Cream the fat and sugar together, then beat in the cream. When fully blended, stir in the nuts. Spread the topping on the cake while still warm or just after cooling. Place under gentle grill heat, and grill for 2–3 minutes until the topping is light gold and bubbling. Remove from the heat at once. Leave to cool completely before cutting the cake.

Note Use on plain and light fruit cakes instead of icing.

VARIATION

100g finely chopped walnuts can be used instead of the mixed nuts.

Almond Paste and Marzipan

To Coat a Cake with Almond Paste or Marzipan

Always level the top of the cake first. If it has risen to a peak in the centre, do not cut it off. Cut out a thin strip of paste and put it round the edge to level the top. Roll it flat.

Brush the cake free of any loose crumbs, then brush it with warm apricot glaze (p396) or warmed apricot jam. Let it cool. If covering only the top of the cake with paste, do not coat the sides unless you want to cover them with crumbs or chopped nuts (p396).

To cover the top of a cake only: On a surface lightly dusted with icing sugar, roll out the almond paste or marzipan into a round or square of the required thickness, and 5mm larger than the top of the cake all round. Invert the cake on to the paste. Hold the cake down with one hand and, using a knife, mould and press the paste into the sides of the cake, to give a neat, sharp edge.

Turn the cake the right way up, and roll the top lightly with a rolling-pin dusted with icing sugar. If not level, make it so by rolling, then invert it again and press the excess paste into place on the sides.

To cover the top and sides of a round cake: Roll out the almond paste or marzipan into a circle of the required thickness, and 3–4cm larger than the top of the cake all around. On a cake of average height, this should give an almond paste coating for the sides about half as thick as on top. (If the cake is more than 8cm high, make the circle a little thicker or larger.)

Invert the cake on to the paste, placing it in the centre of the circle. Using the palms of both hands, mould and press the paste on to the sides of the cake, working it

upward to cover them. Press it on firmly and evenly. Press down on the cake to get a sharp edge between the top and sides. Then roll a straight-sided bottle or jar all round

Smoothing the sides of a cake coated with almond paste or marzipan

the cake to make the paste on the sides an even thickness. Turn the cake the right way up, and check that it is level.

To cover the top and sides of a square cake: Cover the sides first. Divide the paste into 2 parts and put 1 aside for the top. Cut the other part into 4 pieces, and roll each into a strip to fit one side of the cake. Lay them on a surface lightly dusted with icing sugar. Up-end the cake, and press each side in turn on to a strip of paste. Trim the edges of the paste with a knife if necessary.

Cover the top of the cake exactly as when covering the top only.

Leave any cake covered with almond paste or marzipan for at least 72 hours, or if possible, a full week, before icing it, to prevent any risk of almond oil from the paste seeping through the icing and staining it.

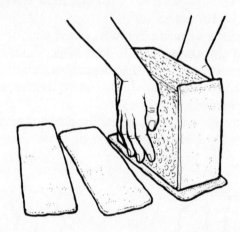

Almond Paste *Basic proportions*

100g ground almonds
100g icing sugar **or** 50g icing sugar
   and 50g caster sugar
1 egg yolk **or** 1 egg white **or** $\frac{1}{2}$ beaten
   standard egg

One of the following flavourings:
1 × 15ml spoon lemon juice **or**
   1 × 2.5ml spoon vanilla essence
   or 1 × 2.5ml spoon almond essence
   or 1 × 5ml spoon brandy

Work all the ingredients together to make a pliable paste. For a sweeter paste, increase the quantities of icing and caster sugar equally to give $1\frac{1}{2}$ times the weight of the almonds in sugar; eg when using 100g ground almonds as above, use 75g icing sugar and 75g caster sugar, giving 150g sugar in all.

Note When making almond paste, handle it as little as possible, as the warmth of the hands draws out the oil from the ground almonds.

Quantities to use

For the top only of an 18cm cake, use the basic proportions of ingredients as above.

For the top only of a 20 or 23cm cake, use 150g ground almonds, 150g sugar, enough egg (white, yolk or whole egg) to bind, and flavouring to taste.

For the top only of a 25cm cake, use 200g ground almonds, 200g sugar, $1\frac{1}{2}$–2 egg whites or yolks or 1 egg, and flavouring to taste.

For the top and sides of an 18cm cake, use 200g ground almonds, 200g sugar, $1\frac{1}{2}$–2 egg whites or yolks or 1 egg, and flavouring to taste.

For the top and sides of a 20 or 23cm cake, use 300g ground almonds, 300g sugar, 2 egg whites or yolks or $1\frac{1}{2}$ eggs, and flavouring to taste.

For the top and sides of a 25cm cake, use 400g ground almonds, 400g sugar, 3–4 egg whites or yolks or 2 eggs, and flavouring to taste.

Use the almond paste for covering cakes before applying icing, and for covering or filling some other cakes such as Simnel cake (p369). If the paste is not to be covered by icing, use egg yolk for binding; it is less brittle, and less likely to flake or crack when dry. The egg whites can be used for making royal icing if they can be stored on the bottom shelf of a refrigerator or a cool place in the larder for 2 days, or in a freezer until the almond paste has dried out.

Marzipan can be used, if preferred.

Marzipan *Basic proportions*

200g icing sugar
1 egg
1 egg white

200g ground almonds
flavourings as for almond paste (p392)

Sift the icing sugar. Whisk the egg, egg white, and sugar in a heatproof basin over hot water until thick and creamy. Add the ground almonds with the flavourings and mix well. Work in more flavourings if necessary. Knead until smooth.

Royal Icing

This classic icing cannot be applied directly to a cake, since it will drag crumbs off the surface. When it is spread on a cake coated with almond paste or marzipan, it should be the consistency of thick cream.

To Ice a Cake with Royal Icing

If an electric mixer is used for beating royal icing, leave the icing to stand for 2–3 hours afterwards, to let any air bubbles escape. Whenever it is left to stand, either during preparation or when fully prepared, cover it with a clean, damp cloth to prevent the surface drying out and forming a crust.

First coat: Put the cake, covered with well-dried almond paste or marzipan, on an upturned plate or on an icing turntable. Take just under half of the icing and put it in the middle of the cake top. Smooth it all over the top quickly with a spatula or palette knife. If necessary, dip the knife into a deep jug of very hot water, shake off surplus water and smooth the surface of the cake with the hot knife.

Smooth the rest of the icing over the sides, lifting a little at a time from the bowl, using a hot wetted knife. Have a fine skewer ready to prick any bubbles gently before the surface sets. See that the top edge is sharp and clean. Do not overwork the icing or it will lose its gloss. Allow the cake to dry, away from dust, for 24 hours.

Second coat: Once the first coating is completely dry, a second, thinner coat of icing can be poured over the cake if the first coat is not perfectly smooth. This second coat should be thick enough to need a little help with a knife to make it flow gently over the top and sides. Extra egg white can be added to make a coating with a very smooth finish. Alternatively, glacé icing (p387) can be used for this second coat.

Snow scene surface: For a 'snow scene', ie a coating with peaks and swirls, flick up the icing with a knife, making small peaks. If desired, sprinkle the icing, when dry, with sifted icing sugar to represent newly fallen snow.

To Decorate a Cake with Piped Royal Icing

The icing which coats the cake must be completely dry and hard before decorations are applied.

Decorative piping: Icing required for star or rose pipes (see diagram below) needs a little extra sifted icing sugar added so that it is slightly stiffer. When pulled up with a spoon, a 1cm point of icing should hold its shape; the stars will flatten if the icing is too thin. For writing pipes, the icing should be only slightly stiffer than icing for coating a cake, and should pull up into soft points. Beat it very thoroughly before use or it may break in the middle of a line or letter.

A design can be pricked out directly on the cake, using a long clean pin, eg a decorator's pin. However, if the design is to be geometrical or if writing is to be used, it is wise to draw the design on a piece of paper first. If this is done to scale, the paper can be placed on top of the cake and the design pricked through the paper on to the cake with a long clean pin.

To make a paper icing bag or cone: Use greaseproof paper or vegetable parchment. Cut a square about 25cm in diameter, and cut it into 2 triangles, following the diagrams below.

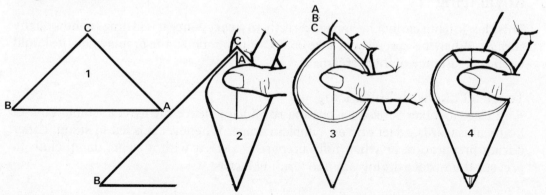

Take 1 triangle and fold A over C as shown. Wrap B round to A and C, and fold in the ends. Cut about 1 cm off the point and insert the pipe to be used. Repeat the process, using the other triangle, if a second bag is required.

Greaseproof paper cones can only be used once, but vegetable parchment ones can be wiped and re-used. The same applies to bought nylon icing bags.

Note Metal or plastic syringes can be bought and used for icing.

To fill the bag: After inserting the pipe required, place the bag in a clean jar with the piping tube or nozzle resting on the base of the jar. This will prevent loss of some of the contents while filling. Half fill the bag with icing, using a dessertspoon. Fold over the broad end, and tuck in the sides of the bag. Do not fill the bag more than half full.

For easier filling, the top half of a nylon bag can be folded back before filling; it prevents smears of icing on the part of the bag to be folded over.

Icing pipes to use: Use pipes 1, 2, and 3 (fine, medium, and thick) for straight lines, dots, and writing. These are called writing pipes.

Star or rose pipes may have 5, 6, 8 or more points. They are used for scrolls, shell edgings etc, as well as for rosettes and stars. The size of the decoration will depend on the amount of icing forced through the pipe.

Petal and leaf pipes for flowers and leaves, ribbon pipes for basket work, and many other decorative pipes are also available.

General hints on piping: Practise first on an upturned plate. If the icing is scraped off before it hardens, it can be re-used.

If possible, place the cake to be decorated on a turntable; it makes turning the cake easier and safer. The end of the pipe should be free of icing before starting. Begin close to, but not touching, the surface to be decorated. Exert an even pressure while forcing icing through the pipe, and stop pressing before lifting the pipe.

Start decorating in the centre of a cake and work outwards. When writing, work from left to right.

Allow all piped-on decorations to dry thoroughly before adding other decorations.

Keep some icing aside for attaching decorations. Cover with a damp cloth to prevent a crust forming.

Royal Icing

450g icing sugar   1 × 5ml spoon lemon juice
2 egg whites   1 × 5ml spoon glycerine

Sift the icing sugar. Put the egg whites and lemon juice into a bowl and, using a wooden spoon, beat just enough to liquefy the whites slightly. Add half the sugar, a little at a time, and beat for 10 minutes. Add the rest of the sugar gradually, and beat for another 10 minutes until the icing is white and forms peaks when the spoon is drawn up from the mixture. Add the glycerine while mixing.

Quantities to use
The quantities above will cover the top and sides of a 20cm cake. Use half quantities for the top only.

For a 25cm cake, double the quantities above, to cover the top and sides.

Glazes, Coatings, Fillings and Decorations

Apricot Glaze
Enough to coat the top and sides of one 15–18cm cake

200g apricot jam   2 × 15ml spoons water

Heat the jam and the water gently in a saucepan until smooth. Sieve the mixture and return to the cleaned saucepan. Bring slowly to the boil and heat gently until thick. **Note** The glaze is used to cover a cake before applying marzipan, almond paste, or a coating of ground or chopped nuts or crumbs. It is slightly thinner than jam used on its own, spreads more easily over a cake, and is therefore less likely to drag crumbs off the surface. It can be stored in a refrigerator for at least 2 weeks.

Sweet Coating Glaze for Flans and Tartlets
Enough to cover one 18cm fruit flan or 12–16 tartlets

1 × 5ml spoon arrowroot   1–3 drops food colouring
125ml fruit syrup from canned **or**   lemon juice
   bottled fruit **or** 125ml water and
   15–25g sugar

Blend the arrowroot with a little of the cold fruit syrup or water. Heat the remaining fruit syrup, or water and sugar, to boiling point in a small pan. Pour on to the blended arrowroot, stirring gently. Return to the pan and heat just to boiling point, stirring very gently, to avoid air bubbles (which cloud the glaze). Remove from the heat, add the colouring and lemon juice to taste. Pour or spoon the hot glaze carefully over the flan or tart. Leave to cool and set before serving.

To Apply Coatings over Jam Glaze or Butter Cream
Make sure that any coatings, ie nuts, crumbs or praline are finely crushed or ground, and that the coconut shreds are separated, otherwise they will not stick on the cake. Scatter the coating evenly across a sheet of greaseproof paper. Have ready a fine pastry brush for putting loose crumbs in place.

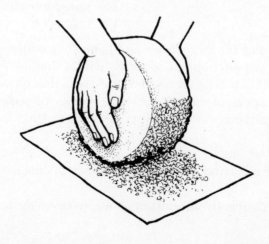

Using jam glaze: Brush any loose crumbs off the cake. Brush the sides with a warm apricot glaze (p396). Hold the cake on end between your palms, and roll the sides in the coating, pressing gently. Transfer the cake to a plate or wire rack and brush off any surplus crumbs. Brush the top with glaze and distribute the coating evenly over the surface. Use the fine brush to put loose crumbs, nuts, etc in place. Lay a piece of greaseproof paper over the top, and press lightly to make the coating stick.

Using butter cream: The butter cream should be soft enough to spread easily, and should be applied thinly. Proceed as when applying coatings to a jam glaze.

Glacé icing or whipped cream top: If the sides of a cake are to be coated with butter cream or jam glaze, and the top with glacé icing or whipped cream, ice and coat the sides first. Allow to set before applying the glacé icing. If using butter cream, mould it into a small ridge round the top of the cake to stop the icing spilling over the edge.

Coconut for Coating or Decoration

To colour: Place the coconut in a small bowl, and add a few drops of food colouring. Stir briskly until evenly coloured. Spread the coconut out on a baking tray, and leave to dry in a very cool oven, 120°C, Gas ½. Shake the pan and turn the coconut over to dry it evenly.

To toast: Spread the coconut on the grill pan under very low heat. Shake the pan and turn the coconut over to brown it evenly.

To Coat a Cake, Gâteau or Dessert with Whipped Cream

Flavour the cream and add food colouring, if liked. Whip the cream until very stiff. For a really firm coating, eg if the completed cake, gâteau or dessert must stand in a warm place for a time before being served, add a very little dissolved and cooled gelatine to the cream when whipping; about half the usual setting quantity is enough. Work quickly.

Place the cake on a turntable, an upturned plate or a wire rack. Smooth the whipped cream on the sides first, with a palette knife; then cover the top.

If liked, the cream can be flicked up with a knife, making a 'snow scene' surface like that used for Christmas cakes.

The cake, gâteau or dessert should be coated or decorated before the cream becomes too firm. Avoid decorations which may be spoiled by damp. If possible, chill the cake, gâteau or dessert until required for use.

Butter Cream

Enough for 2 layers in one 18cm cake

200g icing sugar	100g butter
2 egg whites	flavouring and colouring as required

Sift the icing sugar. Whisk the egg whites until stiff. Add the icing sugar, a third at a time, whisking between each addition until the mixture forms peaks. Cream the butter until fluffy and gradually beat in the meringue mixture. Flavour and colour as required.

For **variations**, see over.

VARIATIONS

Chocolate Butter Cream (1)

Grate 50g plain block chocolate into a saucepan. Heat gently until the chocolate melts, then cool. Use to flavour the butter cream.

Chocolate Butter Cream (2)

Dissolve 1 × 15ml spoon cocoa in 1 × 15ml spoon hot water, then cool. Use to flavour the butter cream.

Coffee Butter Cream

Dissolve 1 × 5ml spoon instant coffee in 1 × 15ml spoon hot water, then cool. Use to flavour the butter cream.

Chantilly Cream

4 helpings

250ml double cream   vanilla essence
25g caster sugar

Chill the cream for several hours. Whip it lightly. Just before serving, whip in the sugar and a few drops of vanilla essence to taste.

Confectioners' Custard

Makes 250ml (approx)

1 egg   25g plain flour
1 egg yolk   250ml milk
50g caster sugar   a few drops vanilla essence

Put the egg, egg yolk, and sugar in a basin and beat with a wooden spoon until light and fluffy. Add the flour and stir in gently. Mix in the milk gradually, keeping the mixture smooth. Transfer to a saucepan, and bring the mixture to the boil, stirring all the time. Add the vanilla essence, pour into a basin, and cover with damp grease-proof paper to prevent a skin forming. Leave to cool.

When cold, use as a filling for cakes, small pastries, and tartlets.

VARIATIONS

Chocolate-flavoured Confectioners' Custard

Dissolve 25g grated chocolate in the milk.

Crème St Honoré

Whisk 4 egg whites until stiff with 1 × 15ml spoon caster sugar. Fold into the hot confectioners' custard. Use as a filling for choux puffs or as an alternative to whipped cream.

Crème Frangipane

Beat 40g melted butter into the hot confectioners' custard, then add 75g crushed almond macaroons or ground almonds and a few drops of almond essence. Use as a tartlet or pancake filling.

Coconut Filling
Enough to fill 1 layer in one 15–18cm cake

50g icing sugar

1 egg yolk

1 × 15ml spoon lemon juice

25g desiccated coconut

Sift the icing sugar into a heatproof bowl, add the egg yolk and lemon juice and mix to a smooth paste. Place the bowl over a saucepan of hot water over low heat. Cook for 5–7 minutes until thick, stirring all the time. Remove from the heat and stir in the coconut. Leave to cool before using.

Crème Fraîche
Enough to fill 2 layers, or to fill and coat one 20cm sponge cake

250ml double cream

2 × 5ml spoons buttermilk

Pour the cream into a small basin or glass jar. Gently stir in the buttermilk. Cover, and leave it to stand at 25°C for 6–8 hours. Stir, and chill until needed.

This French cream has a slightly sharp taste, and is delicious served with rich desserts or gâteaux.

Mock Cream
Enough to fill 2 layers in one 18cm cake or gâteau

2 × 5ml spoons cornflour

125ml milk

50g softened butter

50g icing **or** caster sugar

$\frac{1}{2}$ × 2.5ml spoon vanilla essence

Blend the cornflour with the milk, bring to the boil in a small saucepan, and cook for 4–5 minutes, stirring all the time, until thick. Cover with damp greaseproof paper, and cool until tepid.

Cream the butter and sugar until it is the same consistency as the cornflour sauce. Add the sauce, a spoonful at a time, beating well after each addition. Beat in the essence and use as required.

Mrs Beeton's Sherry or Liqueur-flavoured Whipped Cream
4 helpings

grated rind and juice of $\frac{1}{2}$ lemon

1–2 × 15ml spoons sweet sherry **or**
  brandy-based liqueur (see **Note**)

2 × 15ml spoons caster sugar

250ml double cream

1 egg white (optional)

Put the lemon rind, juice, sherry or liqueur, and sugar into a bowl. Stir until the sugar is dissolved. Add the cream and whip lightly, gradually increasing speed until the cream is firm but not very stiff. Whisk the egg white, if used, until it holds soft peaks, and fold it gently into the cream.

Note A fruit-flavoured liqueur should be used, eg apricot brandy or Grand Marnier. Alternatively, brandy or a strong sweet white wine give a good flavour.

Chocolate Curls or Scrolls
Makes enough scrolls to decorate one 20cm cake

200g plain chocolate   1 × 15ml spoon salad oil

Break up the chocolate and put it on a heatproof plate. Place the plate over a pan of simmering water. When the chocolate has melted, work in the salad oil. Remove from the heat and leave to cool slightly, then spread out thinly on the plate. Leave until cold and almost firm. With a round-ended knife held almost parallel with the plate, scrape off bands or curls of chocolate, as wide or narrow as you wish. Place them on soft kitchen paper as you make them, since they are very fragile.

Praline
Makes 200g (approx)

100g caster sugar   100g browned **or** toasted nuts (p361)
½ vanilla pod   eg almonds, hazelnuts, walnuts
1 × 15ml spoon water   oil for greasing

Heat the sugar, vanilla pod, and water until the sugar is light golden-brown. Stir in the nuts. Turn the mixture immediately on to an oiled marble slab or metal surface, and leave to harden. When hard, crush with a pestle in a mortar, or process in an electric blender. Crush very finely if wanted for flavouring; leave more coarsely crushed for coating or decorating.

Use for flavouring, coating, and decorating cream desserts, ice creams, mousses, soufflés, and gâteaux.

Note Praline powder keeps well in an airtight jar.

PASTRY MAKING AND PASTRY GOODS

General Hints

1) Work in a cool place, if possible on a stone slab, and keep your hands cool.
2) Always sift the flour and salt after measuring, since this helps to lighten the pastry.
3) When rubbing the fat into the flour, use the finger-tips and lift the hands up from the bowl so that air is trapped as the flour falls back into the bowl.
4) Use cold water and a round-bladed knife for mixing. Flours vary in the amount of water which they absorb, so the quantities given in the recipes can only be approximate. It is important not to use too much water or the pastry will be hard.
5) Lemon juice strengthens the gluten or protein in flour and helps give a lighter and crisper result when making flaky, puff, or rough puff pastry.
6) Handle the pastry as little and as lightly as possible. Work quickly.
7) Chill the pastry, or leave in a cool place for 15–30 minutes after making and before rolling out.
8) Roll the pastry lightly, quickly, and evenly with short strokes, lifting the rolling-pin between each stroke. Do not roll off the edge of the pastry or the air will be pressed out.
9) Always roll away from yourself, never from side to side, and do not turn the pastry over.
10) Use very little flour for rolling out and remove any surplus flour with a pastry brush.
11) Use the rolled side of the pastry for the outside of a pie case, tart shell or crust.
12) Most pastries are baked in a fairly hot oven; the richer the pastry, the hotter the oven required for cooking. A high temperature is necessary to create steam within the dough and to make the pastry light. It also makes the starch grains burst; the starch then absorbs the fat. Unless the heat is high enough to act on the flour in this way, the melted fat runs out and leaves the pastry heavy and tough, and less rich.

Note Hot water crust and choux pastry are exceptions to these rules.

To Keep Pastry

Pastry which must be kept for several hours or overnight before baking should be wrapped closely in greaseproof paper and kept in a refrigerator or cool place.

Using Pastry

Open Tarts

Open tarts are usually baked on ovenproof glass or enamel plates. Sweet tarts can be filled with cooked or uncooked fruit, or with jam, syrup or treacle, mincemeat or a custard mixture. For an 18cm plate, pastry using 125g flour will be needed.

Shape the pastry into a ball or round bun shape. Then roll it out into a circle 2cm bigger than the plate all round, and about 2mm thick. Fold the pastry loosely over the rolling-pin and lift it on to the plate. Smooth it carefully with the fingers so that no air is trapped between the pastry and the plate. Take care not to stretch the pastry as it will shrink back during baking, leaving an uneven edge.

If the pastry shell is baked without a filling, prick the bottom well with a fork all over before baking, or bake blind (see p404).

Flans

A flan may be baked in a flan ring, which is a circular, often fluted, hoop of metal without a base. The ring is placed on a flat baking sheet during baking. After baking, the ring is lifted off the set pastry shell, which is then transferred to a serving plate.

Alternatively, a flan can be baked in an ovenproof ceramic or metal flan case, like a shallow sandwich tin but with fluted sides. In this case the flan is served from the dish.

To line a flan ring 18cm in diameter, pastry using 125g flour will be needed. Place the flan ring on a baking sheet. Roll the pastry into a round at least 5cm larger than the flan ring and 2mm thick. Lift the pastry with a rolling-pin to prevent it stretching, and lay it in the flan ring. Press the pastry gently down on the baking sheet so that no air bubbles are trapped. Working from the centre outward, press down lightly all over the base. Press the pastry right into the angle where the sides meet the base. Then work up the sides, making sure that the pastry fits into the flutes, and is of even thickness all round. Trim off any surplus pastry with a sharp knife, or roll across the top of the ring with the rolling-pin to cut off the pastry cleanly.

Line a ceramic flan case in the same way.

Double Crust Plate Pies or Tarts

Double crust pies or tarts can be made in ovenproof glass, enamel, metal or foil plates with a raised flat rim or border. A 20cm plate will need pastry made with 225g flour.

Divide the pastry into two portions, form each into a round shape, and roll one portion into a round 2cm larger than the plate and about 2mm thick. Fold it over the rolling-pin and lift on to the plate; smooth to fit the plate without stretching the pastry. Trim off any surplus pastry with a sharp knife. Put in a layer of filling, sprinkle with sugar if required, and cover with another layer of filling. Do not add any extra liquid or the pastry will become soggy.

Roll the remaining piece of pastry into a round slightly larger than the plate. Dampen the edge of the pastry lining the plate with cold water. Lift on the cover and ease it into position without stretching the pastry. Press the edges together firmly and knock up with the back of a knife. Make a small hole in the centre to allow steam to escape.

Deep Pies or Tarts

These can be made with a single top crust or with a double crust. A 750ml pie dish will need pastry made with 150g flour for the top crust. Allow slightly more than double this quantity if the dish is to be lined as well.

Either sweet or savoury fillings, eg stewed fruit, steak and kidney or vegetable, can be used. About 600g filling will be needed for a 750ml pie dish. If the filling is likely to shrink during cooking, or if there is not enough to fill the dish, place a pie funnel or inverted ceramic egg cup in the centre of the dish.

If using fruit, place half of it in the dish, sprinkle with sugar and any flavouring used, then add the remaining fruit, piling it high in the centre. Sugar should not be sprinkled on top of the fruit because it will dissolve and make the top crust soggy. Wet fruit can be dredged lightly with flour, if liked.

If making a double crust pie, line the pie dish in the same way as for a plate pie; then dredge the bottom crust lightly with flour or rolled oats before adding the filling if it is very moist.

For the top crust roll out the pastry 2mm thick and at least 2cm larger than the dish. If the dish has not been lined, cut off a strip of pastry the width and length of the rim of the dish. Dampen the rim of the dish with water, and place the strip of pastry on it. Join the cut ends by pressing them firmly together. Brush the strip of pastry with water.

Lift the pastry lid with the rolling-pin, and lay it over the dish, taking care not to stretch it. Press the two layers of pastry together firmly, trim off any overhanging pastry with a sharp knife, and knock up the edge with the back of the knife. Make a small hole in the centre to allow steam to escape.

Note To line a basin with suet crust pastry, see p287.

Guide to Shortcrust Pastry Quantities

1) To line a flan ring or make a top or bottom crust for a plate pie:
   18cm – pastry made with   125g flour
   20cm   ,,   150g flour
   23cm   ,,   175g flour
   25cm   ,,   200g flour
2) To make a double crust plate pie:
   18cm   ,,   200g flour
   20cm   ,,   225g flour
   23cm   ,,   250g flour
3) To make a top crust for a deep oval pie dish:
   500ml   ,,   125g flour
   750ml   ,,   150g flour
   1 litre   ,,   200g flour
   Use double these quantities to make a double crust deep pie.
4) Tartlets:
   Pastry made with 100g flour will make approximately twelve 7cm tartlets.

Note To make a puff or flaky pastry cover for a 1 litre oval pie dish, use 100g flour.

Baking Blind

In many cases, a tart, flan or patty case must be cooked empty or 'blind' before the filling is added. A partially cooked case is used if the filling will need cooking at a low temperature or for a short time only; a fully baked case is used if the filling will need only brief re-heating or will not be cooked at all.

To bake a case empty or blind, prick the bottom of the case well with a fork. Cover the base with a piece of greaseproof paper, then fill the case with dried beans, bread crusts or rice. Bake the case at the usual temperature for the type of pastry used, for 8–12 minutes if a partially cooked case is needed, ie until the pastry is set, or for 20–30 minutes if a fully cooked case is required. In either case, remove the paper and dry filling, and return the case to the oven for 5–7 minutes to dry out the inside. The dry filling can be stored and re-used many times.

The times given above are based on an average cooking temperature of 190°–200°C, Gas 5–6, for shortcrust or similar pastry. The time will however vary with the size of the case and the depth of the dry filling used. Tartlet cases may cook in a shorter time, large tart or flan cases may take a little longer if the dry filling is dense. With partially baked cases, care must be taken that the walls or sides of the case are of uniform thickness all round and are adequately firm before the dry filling is removed, or they may collapse while drying out.

If the top rim of the pastry case is already browned when the dry filling is removed, the case should be dried out at a lower temperature than that used for setting or cooking the pastry.

Pastry Decorations for Flans, Tarts, etc, Baked Blind

Cut out the required shapes in pastry, glaze if liked, and bake beside the main pastry. Cover loosely with foil or remove from the oven if they are cooked and brown before the main pastry.

Greasing Containers

It is not necessary to grease tins, baking sheets, etc when making pastry, unless choux pastry, pâte sucrée or suet crust pastry are used.

If using a container (jam jar, etc) to mould a raised pie, this should be greased and floured.

Finishes and Decorations

For Deep Pies or Double Crust Tarts (using shortcrust, rough puff, flaky or puff pastry)

Edges

Line the edge of a pie dish with a pastry strip, cover, and trim with a sharp knife held at an angle away from the dish to allow for shrinkage during baking. Knock up the edges with the back of a knife.

To flute (scallop) edges: Pressing the top with the thumb, draw the edge towards the centre of the pie for about 1cm using the back of a knife. Repeat round the pie edge. For savoury pies, leave about 2cm between the cuts and for sweet pies about 5mm.

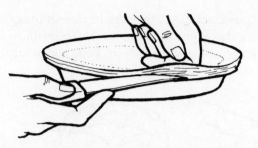

ABOVE *Knocking up the edges with the back of a knife*

RIGHT *Fluting the edges*

To fork edges: Press the back of a fork into the edge of the pie with the prongs pointed towards the centre. Repeat all round the pie edge.

To crimp edges: Pinch the edge between the thumb and first finger of both hands, then twist slightly in opposite directions.

Forking the edges   *Crimping the edges*

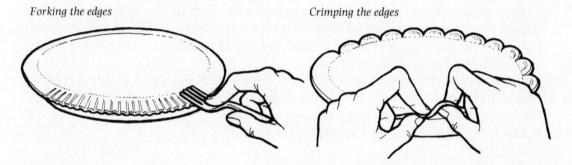

Tops

Make a small hole in the centre of any top pie crust to let the steam out. Decorate savoury pies with pastry leaves, a tassel or a rose. Dampen the shapes lightly before putting them in place.

To make leaves: Roll out a strip of pastry 2–3cm wide. Cut into diamond-shaped pieces. Mark veins on each leaf with the back of a knife. Pinch in one end for a stalk.

To make a tassel: Roll out a strip of pastry 2 × 15cm. Make 1–2cm cuts every 5mm along the strip. Roll up, place in the centre of the pie, and spread the ends into a fan shape.

LEFT *Making pastry leaves*

BELOW *Making a pastry tassel*

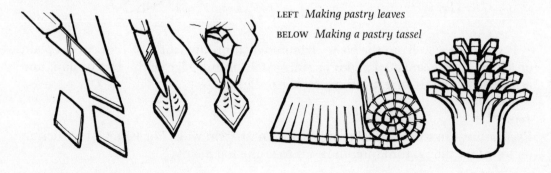

To make a rose: Make a ball of pastry and 2 pastry circles. Place the circles on top of each other and wrap round the ball, pressing the edges together under the ball, to seal. Cut a cross in the top of the ball through the circles with a sharp knife. Open out and turn back the segments to form petals.

For Open Tarts and Flans (using shortcrust pastry)

Edges
Use any of the finishes suggested for double crust tarts on pp404–5, or one of the following:

Twist: Roll pastry trimmings into a long thin strip. Trim to 2cm wide. Moisten the edge of the pastry. Press one end of the strip on to the edge of the tart or flan to secure it, then twist the strip with the right hand and press down gently between the twists with the index finger of the left hand.

Braid: Roll pastry trimmings thinly into a long strip and cut 2 pieces the same length and about 1cm wide. Moisten the edge of the tart or flan. Keeping the strips flat, secure the ends together on the edge, then interweave, pressing the plait down lightly with the finger-tip on the edge of the pastry.

Making a pastry twist   *Making a pastry braid*

Pastry shapes: Roll out the pastry trimmings thinly and cut into 1cm circles, plain or fluted, or into small triangles or stars. Moisten the edge of the tart or flan, and arrange the shapes on it, overlapping them slightly.

Tops
Plain lattice: Cut thinly rolled pastry strips 5mm–1cm wide. Place in a lattice design on top of the filling, trimming the ends to fit the top neatly.

Making a plain lattice

Twisted lattice: Make as above but twist the strips before laying them on the filling.

Pastry shapes: Cut pastry trimmings into shapes as described on p406. Use to mark a tart or flan into serving portions or to make a lattice design.

To Glaze Pastry

Meat pies, patties, sausage rolls, etc are usually brushed with well beaten egg before or during baking. If a deeper glaze is desired, the yolk alone is used. If milk or water is beaten with the egg or egg yolk to increase the quantity, the glaze is called an *egg wash*. Salt or sugar in the proportion of 1 × 2.5ml spoon per egg should be added to make the egg easier to brush on evenly.

Fruit tarts, puffs, etc may be brushed with cold water and dredged with caster sugar before baking. If a thin coating of icing is required, the pastry may be brushed with well whisked egg white and dredged with caster sugar when almost baked.

Shortcrust Pastry (1) (for pies, tarts, etc)
Makes 350g (approx)

200g plain flour
1 × 2.5ml spoon salt
100g fat, eg 50g lard and 50g butter
   or margarine

3 × 15ml spoons cold water
flour for rolling out

Sift together the flour and salt into a bowl. Rub the fats into the flour until the mixture resembles fine breadcrumbs. Mix to a stiff dough with cold water. Roll out on a lightly floured surface, and use as required.

Bake in a fairly hot oven, 200°C, Gas 6, until set, then reduce the heat to cook the filling ingredients, if necessary.

Shortcrust Pastry (2) (for pies, tarts, etc)
Makes 350g (approx)

200g plain flour
1 × 2.5ml spoon salt
1 × 5ml spoon baking powder

75g lard **or** clarified fat (p232)
4 × 15ml spoons cold water
flour for rolling out

Sift together the flour, salt, and baking powder into a bowl. Rub in the fat until the mixture resembles fine breadcrumbs. Mix to a stiff paste with cold water. Roll out on a lightly floured surface, and use as required.

Bake in a very hot oven, 230°C, Gas 8, until set, then reduce the heat to cook the filling ingredients, if necessary.

Sweet Paste or Pâte Sucrée (for sweet flans, tarts, and tartlets)
Makes 400g (approx)

200g plain flour
$\frac{1}{2}$ × 2.5ml spoon salt
125g butter
50g caster sugar

1 egg yolk
1 × 15ml spoon cold water
flour for rolling out

Sift together the flour and salt into a bowl. Cut the butter into small pieces and rub into the flour until the mixture resembles fine breadcrumbs. Mix in the sugar, then the egg yolk, and enough cold water to make a stiff dough. Roll out on a lightly floured surface, and use as required.

Bake in a fairly hot oven, 200°C, Gas 6, until set, then reduce the heat to cook the filling ingredients, if necessary.

Note In warm weather very little water is required.

Suet Crust Pastry (for meat puddings, dumplings, fruit puddings, and roly-poly puddings)
Makes 400g (approx)

200g plain flour
1 × 2.5ml spoon salt
1 × 5ml spoon baking powder

75g shredded suet
125ml cold water

Sift together the flour, salt, and baking powder into a bowl and mix in the suet. Mix to a firm dough with cold water. Bake, boil or steam as directed in the recipe.

Rich Suet Crust Pastry (for meat and fruit puddings and roly-poly puddings)
Makes 600g (approx)

200g plain flour
1 × 2.5ml spoon salt
1 × 5ml spoon baking powder

75g soft white breadcrumbs
125g shredded suet
175ml cold water

Sift together the flour, salt, and baking powder into a bowl and mix in the breadcrumbs and suet. Mix with cold water to form a dough which is firm but soft enough to roll out easily. Bake, boil or steam as directed in the recipe.

Note This makes a very light, easily digested pudding, but the pastry is liable to break if turned out of the basin.

Choux Pastry (for cream buns, cream puffs, éclairs, etc)
Makes 450g (approx)

100g plain flour
250ml water
50g butter **or** margarine

a pinch of salt
1 egg yolk
2 eggs

Sift the flour. Put the water, fat and salt in a saucepan, and bring to the boil. Remove from the heat and add the flour all at once. Return to the heat and beat well with a wooden spoon until the mixture forms a smooth paste which leaves the sides of the pan clean. Remove from the heat, cool slightly, add the egg yolk, and beat well. Add the other eggs, one at a time, beating thoroughly between each addition. Use as required.

Bake in a fairly hot oven, 200°C, Gas 6.

Note This pastry rises better if used while still warm, but if this quantity is not all required at once, raw pastry or baked shells can be successfully frozen (see p438).

Cheese Pastry (for savoury pies and canapés)

Makes 450g (approx)

200g plain flour
a pinch of dry mustard
a pinch of salt
a pinch of Cayenne pepper
100–125g butter (see **Note**)

100g finely grated cheese
1 egg yolk
1–2 × 15ml spoons cold water
flour for rolling out

Sift together the flour and seasonings into a bowl. Rub in the butter until the mixture resembles fine breadcrumbs. Add the cheese, egg yolk, and enough cold water to form a stiff dough. Roll out on a lightly floured surface and use as required.

Bake in a fairly hot oven, 200°C, Gas 6, until set, then reduce the heat to cook the filling ingredients, if necessary.

Note Use the smaller quantity of fat if the cheese is fatty and crumbly, the larger if it is fine and dry.

Potato Pastry (for covering meat or vegetable pies)

Makes 500g (approx)

200g freshly cooked potatoes (see **Note**)
200g plain flour
25g lard **or** dripping
25g butter

$\frac{1}{2}$ × 2.5ml spoon salt
1 × 5ml spoon baking powder
2 × 5ml spoons beaten egg
2 × 15ml spoons warm milk
flour for rolling out

Mash the potatoes, or rub them through a fine metal sieve. Leave until cold.

Sift the flour. Rub the fats lightly into the flour and add the cold potatoes, salt, and baking powder. Add the beaten egg and enough milk to mix to a smooth dough; the amount of milk needed depends on the type of potato used. Roll out on a lightly floured surface and use as required.

Bake in a fairly hot oven, 200°C, Gas 6, until set, then reduce the heat to cook any filling ingredients, if necessary.

Note Freshly made-up instant potato can be used to make this pastry.

Hot Water Crust Pastry (for pork, veal and ham, and raised game pies)

Makes 350g (approx)

200g plain flour
1 × 2.5ml spoon salt

75g lard
100ml milk **or** water

Sift the flour and salt into a warm bowl, make a well in the centre, and keep the bowl in a warm place. Meanwhile, heat the lard and milk or water together until boiling, then add them to the flour, mixing well with a wooden spoon until the pastry is cool enough to knead with the hands. Knead thoroughly and mould as required.

Bake in a hot oven, 220°C, Gas 7, until the pastry is set, then reduce the heat to moderate, 180°C, Gas 4, until fully baked.

Note Throughout the mixing, kneading, and moulding, the pastry must be kept warm, otherwise moulding will be extremely difficult. If the pastry is too warm, however, it will be so soft and pliable that it will not retain its shape or support its own weight.

To Mould a Raised Pie

Makes one 13cm diameter pie

hot water crust pastry using
200g flour

fat for greasing
flour

The pastry must be raised or moulded while still warm (see **Note** above).

Reserve one-quarter of the pastry for the lid and leave in the bowl in a warm place, covered with a greased polythene bag. Roll out the remainder to about 5mm thick, in a round or oval shape. Shape the pie gently with the hands. If this proves too difficult, use a jar, round cake tin or similar container, as a mould: grease and flour the sides and base of the mould, invert it, lay the pastry over it, and mould the pastry round the sides, taking care not to pull the pastry and making sure that the sides and base are of an even thickness. Leave to cool. When cold, remove the pastry case from the mould and put in the filling. Roll out the pastry reserved for the lid, dampen the rim of the case, put on the lid, and press the edges firmly together. Tie 3 or 4 folds of greaseproof paper round the pie to hold it in shape during baking and to prevent it becoming too brown.

LEFT *Flouring a greased jar*

ABOVE *Moulding the pastry round the sides of the jar*

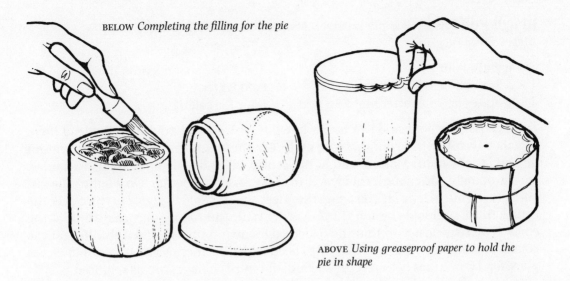

BELOW *Completing the filling for the pie*

ABOVE *Using greaseproof paper to hold the pie in shape*

Note If the pie is raised without using a jar, moulding is made easier by firmly pressing some of the filling into the lower part of the pie when it has been raised to the required shape and thickness.

Alternatively, line a hinged raised pie mould with the pastry and bake in the container.

Flaky Pastry (for pies, tarts, and tartlets)
Makes 450g (approx)

200g plain flour
$\frac{1}{2}$ × 2.5ml spoon salt
125g butter **or** 75g butter and 50g lard

1 × 2.5ml spoon lemon juice
125ml cold water
flour for rolling out

Sift together the flour and salt into a bowl. If butter and lard are used, blend them together evenly with a round-bladed knife. Divide the fat into 4 equal portions. Rub one-quarter of the fat into the flour. Mix to a soft dough with lemon juice and cold water. On a lightly floured surface roll the pastry into an oblong strip, keeping the ends square. Divide another quarter of the fat into small knobs, and place them at intervals on the top two-thirds of the pastry. Fold the bottom third up on to the fat and fold the top third down over it. With the rolling-pin, press the edges lightly together to prevent the air escaping. Turn the pastry so that the folded edges are on the left and right. Press the rolling-pin on the pastry at intervals, to make ridges and to distribute the air evenly. Cover the pastry with greaseproof paper and leave to rest in a cool place for 10 minutes. Repeat the rolling and folding 3 more times; the last rolling will be without fat. Leave the pastry to rest between each rolling. Use as required.

Bake in a hot oven, 220°C, Gas 7, until set, then reduce the heat to cook any filling ingredients, if necessary.

Rough Puff Pastry (for pie crusts, tarts, tartlets, sausage rolls)
Makes 500g (approx)

200g plain flour
½ × 2.5ml spoon salt
150g butter **or** 75g butter and 75g lard

1 × 2.5ml spoon lemon juice
cold water
flour for rolling out

Sift together the flour and salt into a bowl. If butter and lard are used, blend them together evenly with a round-bladed knife. Cut the fat into pieces the size of a walnut and add to the flour. Make a well in the centre of the flour, mix in the lemon juice, then gradually add enough cold water to make an elastic dough. On a lightly floured surface, roll into a long strip keeping the edges square. Fold the bottom third over the centre third, and fold the top third over it. With the rolling-pin, press to seal the edges. Turn the pastry so that the folded edges are on the left and right. Repeat the rolling and folding until the pastry has been folded 4 times. Allow it to rest in a cool place for 10 minutes between the second and third rollings. Use as required.

Bake in a hot oven, 220°C, Gas 7, until set, then reduce the heat to cook any filling ingredients, if necessary.

Puff Pastry (for pies, tarts, tartlets, bouchées, vol-au-vents, patties, etc)
Makes 500g (approx)

200g plain flour
½ × 2.5ml spoon salt
200g butter

1 × 2.5ml spoon lemon juice
100ml cold water (approx)
flour for rolling out

Sift together the flour and salt into a bowl and rub in 50g of the butter. Add the lemon juice to the flour and mix to a smooth dough with cold water. Shape the remaining butter into a rectangle on greaseproof paper. Roll out the dough on a lightly floured surface into a strip a little wider than the butter and rather more than twice its length. Place the butter on one half of the pastry, fold the other half over it, and press the edges together with the rolling-pin. Leave in a cool place for 15 minutes to allow the butter to harden. Roll out into a long strip. Fold the bottom third up and the top third down, press the edges together with the rolling-pin, and turn the pastry so that the folded edges are on the right and left. Roll and fold again, cover, and leave in a cool place for 15 minutes. Repeat this process until the pastry has been rolled out 6 times. Finally, roll out as required and leave in a cool place for 20 minutes before cooking.

Bake in a hot oven, 220°C, Gas 7. Do not open the oven door until the pastry has risen and become partially baked, since a current of cold air may make it collapse.

To Make Vol-au-vent Cases
Makes twenty-four 5cm or twelve 7cm bouchées or eight 9cm or
two 15cm vol-au-vent cases

puff pastry (p412) using 200g flour   beaten egg for glazing
flour for rolling out

Heat the oven to hot, 220°C, Gas 7. Roll out the pastry about 2cm thick (1cm thick
for bouchées) on a lightly floured surface and cut into round or oval shapes as liked.
Place on a baking sheet and brush the top of the pastry with beaten egg. With a
smaller, floured cutter, make a circular or oval cut in each case, to form an inner
ring, cutting through about half the depth of the pastry. Bake until golden-brown
and crisp. When baked, remove the inner circular or oval lid, and scoop out the soft
inside while still warm.
Note For a better appearance a separate piece of pastry can be baked for the lid
instead of using the centre portion of the case.

To Make Patty Cases
Makes twelve 7cm cases

puff (p412) **or** flaky (p411) pastry using   flour for rolling out
   200g flour   beaten egg **or** milk for glazing

Heat the oven to hot, 220°C, Gas 7. Roll out the puff or flaky pastry about 3mm thick
on a lightly floured surface and cut into rounds with a 7cm cutter. Remove the
centres from half these rounds with a 3cm or 4cm cutter to use as lids. Moisten
the uncut rounds with water and place the rings neatly on top. Prick the centres.
Place both cases and lids on a baking sheet and leave to stand for at least 10 minutes
in a cool place. Brush the cases and the lids with beaten egg or milk, and bake for
10–15 minutes.

Crumb Crusts
Biscuit crumbs or similar fine dry crumbs can be used to make a plate pie, flan or tart
shell. The method is quick and easy, and is popular for making cheesecakes.
   The crumbs should be prepared by crushing the biscuits with a rolling-pin in a
polythene bag. Care should be taken to see that the crumbs are fine and even. The fat
is melted gently with the sugar if used, cooled slightly, and mixed thoroughly with
the crumbs. The mixture is then pressed firmly into the plate, ring or tin. The rim
should be levelled by running a sharp knife round it (or over its surface if thick) and
any loose crumbs should be brushed off.
   The crust can then either be chilled until firm and used as required for a cold
filling; or it can be baked in a moderate oven, 180°C, Gas 4, for about 15 minutes
until firm, then chilled before filling. A baked case can be rebaked if the filling requires
it.
   Rolled oats are sometimes used in the same way as biscuit crumbs, and crushed
cornflakes can also be used, with a slightly higher proportion of fat and sugar.

Savoury Dishes using Pastry

Bacon Pasties
6 helpings

potato pastry (p409) using 100g flour
flour for rolling out
200g raw minced steak
150g streaky bacon, without rinds
100g lamb's kidney

1 large onion
salt and pepper
1 × 5ml spoon Worcestershire sauce
beaten egg for glazing

Roll out the pastry on a lightly floured surface and cut out six 18cm rounds. Put the steak into a bowl. Chop the bacon finely. Skin and core the kidney, and chop it finely. Skin and chop the onion. Mix all these ingredients with the steak, and season with salt, pepper, and Worcestershire sauce. Put a spoonful of mixture in the centre of each pastry round, dampen the edges, and fold up the pastry to form pasties. Crimp the tops with the thumb and forefinger and seal the edges firmly. Brush the pasties with the egg to glaze, place on a baking sheet and bake in a hot oven, 220°C, Gas 7, for 15 minutes. Reduce the temperature to moderate, 180°C, Gas 4, and bake for a further 45 minutes. Serve hot or cold.

Cheese Flan
4–6 helpings

cheese pastry (p409) using 150g flour
flour for rolling out
75g Cheddar cheese
2 eggs

200ml milk
a pinch of salt
Cayenne pepper

Roll out the pastry on a lightly floured surface and use it to line a 20cm flan ring about 2cm deep. Bake blind until set, then cool.

Meanwhile, grate the cheese for the filling. Whisk together with the eggs, milk, and seasonings. Pour into the flan shell, and bake in a fairly hot oven, 190°C, Gas 5, for 25–35 minutes or until firm in the centre and golden-brown.

Cheese and Onion Pie
6–8 helpings

3 small onions
shortcrust pastry (p407) using
    225g flour
flour for rolling out

2 × 10ml spoons plain flour
salt and pepper
100g Cheddar cheese
3 × 15ml spoons milk

Skin and parboil the onions. Roll out the pastry on a lightly floured surface and use half of it to line a 20cm pie plate. Season the flour with the salt and pepper. Slice the onions, toss them in the seasoned flour, and spread the slices over the base of the lined plate. Grate the cheese and sprinkle it over the onion. Sprinkle with 2 × 15ml spoons of the milk. Dampen the edges of the pastry, and use the remaining pastry to cover the dish, sealing the edges well. Knock up the edge and decorate, if liked. Brush the pastry lid with the remaining milk. Bake in a fairly hot oven, 200°C, Gas 6, for about 40 minutes.

Note If preferred, make the pie as an open tart, using pastry made with 150g flour. Reduce the cooking time to about 30 minutes.

Chicken Vol-au-vent (using cooked meat)
4 helpings

150g cooked chicken meat	a pinch of nutmeg
50g cooked ham **or** tongue	salt and pepper
50g button mushrooms	one 15cm vol-au-vent case (p413)
250ml Béchamel sauce (p207)	

Garnish
parsley sprigs **or** mustard and cress

Dice the chicken and the ham or tongue. Clean and slice the mushrooms thinly. Add to the Béchamel sauce, and heat thoroughly, stirring all the time. Add the nutmeg and seasoning.

Meanwhile, re-heat the vol-au-vent case in a warm oven, 160°C, Gas 3, for 10 minutes. Fill with the hot mixture, and serve at once, garnished with parsley or mustard and cress.

Note Small vol-au-vent or patty cases (p413) can be used instead of the large case. This quantity of filling is enough for twelve 7cm cases. Make as above, heating the baked cases for 6–9 minutes before filling.

Gougère (Choux Pastry with Cheese)
6 helpings

fat for greasing	salt and pepper
freshly prepared choux pastry (p408)	150g Gruyère cheese
using 150g flour	1 egg yolk

Lightly grease a shallow 18cm pie plate or sandwich tin. Season the pastry well with salt and pepper, and keep it in a warm bowl. Cut half the cheese into 5mm dice and grate the rest. Reserve about 25g of each, and put to one side. Mix the rest lightly into the pastry. Using a small round or oval spoon, place large spoonfuls of the mixture side by side in a circle all round the dish. Make a second circle just inside the first, and repeat until the dish is full. Make the last central choux rather bigger than the rest. Beat the egg yolk with a little water and brush the tops of the choux with it. Sprinkle with the reserved cheese. Bake in a fairly hot oven, 190°C, Gas 5, for 30–35 minutes, until risen and golden-brown. Serve hot or cold.

Note This is the traditional *gougère*. Quite often, the pastry is now used to line a soufflé dish, and is then filled with diced chicken or game in a savoury sauce.

Quiche Lorraine (Bacon and Cream Tart)
4–6 helpings

shortcrust pastry (p407) using
   125g flour
flour for rolling out
6 rashers streaky bacon, without rinds
3 eggs

300ml single cream
1 × 2.5ml spoon salt
a grinding of black pepper
a pinch of grated nutmeg
25g butter

Roll out the pastry on a lightly floured surface. Use it to line an 18cm flan ring placed on a baking sheet. Bake blind for 10 minutes until the rim of the pastry is slightly browned but the base still soft.

Cut the bacon rashers in strips 2cm × 5mm. Blanch in boiling water for 3 minutes. Drain well and scatter the strips over the pastry base. Press in lightly. Beat together the eggs, cream, seasoning, and nutmeg until fully mixed. Pour the mixture into the shell, and dot with flakes of butter. Bake in a fairly hot oven, 190°C, Gas 5, for 30 minutes. Serve at once.

Sausage Rolls
Makes 8

200g prepared puff **or** rough puff
   pastry (p412)
flour for rolling out

8 sausages **or** 200g sausage-meat
1 egg yolk

Roll out the pastry on a lightly floured surface and cut it into 8 equal-sized squares. Skin the sausages if required, or divide the meat into 8 equal portions. Form each portion into a roll the same length as a square of pastry. Place 1 roll of sausage-meat on each pastry square, dampen the edges of the pastry, and fold the pastry over so that they meet. Seal the joined edges and turn the rolls over so the joints are underneath. Leave the ends of the rolls open. Make 3 diagonal slits in the top of each roll. Brush the rolls with egg yolk. Bake in a very hot oven, 230°C, Gas 8, for 10 minutes or until the pastry is well risen and brown. Reduce to moderate, 180°C, Gas 4, and continue baking for 20–25 minutes. Cover loosely with greaseproof paper if the pastry browns too much.

Tomato and Mushroom Patties
Makes 6

300g tomatoes
200g mushrooms
1 small onion
25g butter **or** margarine
salt and pepper

1 × 5ml spoon chopped basil (optional)
shortcrust pastry (p407) using
   200g flour
flour for rolling out

Skin and slice the tomatoes. Clean and slice the mushrooms. Skin and chop the onion. Melt the fat in a frying pan and fry the onion gently for 5 minutes. Add the mushrooms and cook for a further 10 minutes, then add the tomatoes and cook for a further 5 minutes. Season to taste and add the basil, if liked. Leave to cool.

Roll out the pastry on a lightly floured surface and cut into six 18cm rounds. Drain the vegetable mixture and place in heaps covering half of each pastry round. Dampen the edges, fold the other half over, and pinch the edges together. Place on a baking tray and bake in a fairly hot oven, 190°C, Gas 5, for 20–30 minutes. Serve hot.

Desserts and Other Sweet Pastry Dishes

Apple Amber (2)
6–7 helpings

shortcrust pastry (p407) using
   150g flour
flour for rolling out
600g cooking apples
2 × 15ml spoons water

grated rind of 1 lemon
2 eggs
50g butter **or** margarine
75g brown sugar
50g caster sugar

Decoration (optional)
glacé cherries

angelica

Roll out the pastry on a lightly floured surface and use it to line a 750ml pie dish. Peel, core, and slice the apples. Put into a saucepan with the water and lemon rind, and stew until soft. Sieve, or process in an electric blender. Return the apple to the pan and re-heat slightly. Separate the eggs and add the yolks, fat, and brown sugar to the apple. Mix well. Put the mixture into the lined pie dish and bake in a moderate oven, 180°C, Gas 4 for about 30 minutes or until set. Whisk the egg whites until stiff and fold in the caster sugar. Pile on top of the apple mixture and decorate, if liked, with pieces of glacé cherry and angelica. Bake in a very cool oven, 140°C, Gas 1, for 30–40 minutes or until the meringue is golden-brown. Serve hot or cold.
Note For extra flavour, a good pinch of ground cinnamon and ground cloves can be added to the apples when stewing.

Apple Pie (basic deep fruit pie or tart)
6 helpings

shortcrust pastry (p407) using
   300g flour
flour for rolling out
600g cooking apples
100g sugar

6 cloves **or** 1 × 2.5ml spoon grated
   lemon rind
cold water for glazing
caster sugar for dredging

Roll out the pastry on a lightly floured surface and use just over half to line a 750ml pie dish. Peel, core, and slice the apples. Place half in the dish, add the sugar and flavouring, and pile the remaining fruit on top. Cover with the rest of the pastry and seal the edges. Brush the pastry with cold water and dredge with caster sugar. Bake in a fairly hot oven, 200°C, Gas 6, for 20 minutes, then reduce the temperature to moderate, 180°C, Gas 4, and bake for another 20 minutes or until the pastry is golden-brown. Dredge with caster sugar and serve hot or cold.
Note The pastry can be brushed with egg white and sprinkled with sugar before cooking, if liked.

Apricot Pudding
6 helpings

shortcrust pastry (p407) using
   150g flour
flour for rolling out
250ml milk
50g bread **or** plain cake crumbs

1 × 375g can apricots
25g sugar
grated rind of 1 lemon
2 eggs
75g caster sugar

Roll out the pastry on a lightly floured surface and use it to line a 750ml pie dish. Put the milk in a pan and bring to the boil. Pour it over the bread or cake crumbs. Drain the apricots and sieve, or process in an electric blender. Stir the apricot purée into the milk mixture with the sugar and lemon rind. Separate the eggs and beat the yolks into the milk mixture. Pour the mixture into the pie dish, and bake in a fairly hot oven, 200°C, Gas 6, for 25–30 minutes or until the pastry is golden-brown and the filling is set. Whisk the egg whites until stiff and fold in the caster sugar. Spread the mixture over the filling. Return to a very cool oven, 140°C, Gas 1, and bake for a further 30 minutes or until the meringue is crisp and golden.

VARIATIONS

Chester Pudding

Make as for Apricot Pudding, but increase the sugar to 100g and use 2 × 15ml spoons ground almonds instead of the apricots.

Gooseberry Pudding

Make as for Apricot Pudding, but use gooseberry purée instead of apricot purée.

Basic Fruit Flan
5–6 helpings

shortcrust pastry (p407) using
   125g flour
flour for rolling out
1 × 375g can fruit **or** 300g fresh fruit
   (strawberries, pears, pineapple,
   cherries, apricots, peaches, etc)

25g sugar (optional)
1 × 5ml spoon lemon juice
1 × 5ml spoon arrowroot

Decoration (optional)
125ml whipped cream

Roll out the pastry on a lightly floured surface and use it to line an 18cm flan ring. Bake blind, then leave to cool. If fresh fruit is used, prepare it, put in a saucepan with 1 × 15ml spoon water, cover, and stew gently until tender. Make up the stewed fruit to 125ml with water. Canned fruit and some fresh fruit, eg strawberries, do not need cooking. Drain the fruit and arrange it in the cold pastry shell. Return most of the liquid to the saucepan, add the sugar, if used, and the lemon juice, and simmer for a few minutes. Blend the arrowroot with the remaining liquid and add it to the hot syrup, stirring all the time. Cook for 3 minutes, still stirring. Cool slightly, and spoon the liquid over the fruit. When cold, decorate with piped whipped cream, if liked.

Coconut Custard Pie
5–6 helpings

shortcrust pastry (p407) using
   175g flour
flour for rolling out
3 eggs

100g sugar
$\frac{1}{2} \times$ 2.5ml spoon salt
75g desiccated coconut
375ml milk

Roll out the pastry on a lightly floured surface and use it to line a deep 23cm pie plate. Beat the eggs until liquid and add the rest of the ingredients. Pour into the pastry case and bake in a hot oven, 220°C, Gas 7, for 10 minutes, then reduce the temperature to moderate, 180°C, Gas 4, and bake for another 25–30 minutes or until set.

Hampshire Pudding
6–7 helpings

puff pastry (p412) using 150g flour
flour for rolling out
2 × 15ml spoons jam
2 eggs

1 egg yolk
75g butter
75g caster sugar

Roll out the pastry on a lightly floured surface and use it to line a deep 20cm pie plate. Spread the jam over the bottom. Beat the eggs and extra yolk together in a heatproof basin until frothy. Melt the butter in a saucepan. Gradually add the sugar and melted butter to the eggs. Place the basin over a pan of hot water and whisk the mixture until thick. Pour it over the jam and bake in a fairly hot oven, 200°C, Gas 6, for 30 minutes or until firm and golden-brown. If necessary, reduce the heat to moderate, 180°C, Gas 4, after 15–20 minutes to prevent the pastry browning too quickly. Serve hot.

Jam Tart
6 helpings

shortcrust pastry (p407) using
   150g flour **or** puff pastry (p412)
   using 150g flour
flour for rolling out

4–6 × 15ml spoons any firm jam
  (see **Note**)
beaten egg **or** milk for glazing
  (optional)

Heat the oven to hot, 220°C, Gas 7. Roll out the pastry on a lightly floured surface and use it to line a 20cm pie plate. Decorate the edge with any trimmings. Fill with jam, and glaze the uncovered pastry with beaten egg or milk, if liked. Bake for about 15 minutes or until the pastry is cooked. Serve hot or cold.

Note The larger quantity of jam will be needed if a whole fruit jam is used. Thin syrupy jams containing whole fruits are not suitable for a jam tart. Very firm jams should be lightly covered with greaseproof paper while cooking to prevent scorching.

Lemon Chiffon Pie
4 helpings

Pie Shell

100g digestive biscuits
50g butter

25g caster sugar

Filling

100g caster sugar
1 × 10ml spoon gelatine
3 eggs

50ml water
juice and grated rind of 2 lemons

To make the pie shell, crush the biscuits with a rolling-pin. Melt the butter and mix in the crumbs and sugar thoroughly. Line an 18cm shallow pie plate with the mixture; press it firmly in an even layer all over the base and sides. Put into a cool place to set.

To make the filling, mix 50g of the caster sugar with the gelatine. Separate the eggs. Blend the yolks, water, and lemon juice in a pan or basin over a pan of hot water, or in a double boiler. Stir in the gelatine and sugar mixture. Cook over very gentle heat for about 10 minutes, stirring all the time, until the custard thickens. Do not let it boil. Pour into a cold basin, cover with damp greaseproof paper, and chill until on the point of setting.

Stir the lemon rind into the cooled mixture. Whisk the egg whites until foamy, gradually whisk in the remaining sugar and continue whisking until stiff and glossy. Fold the lemon custard mixture into the meringue, pile into the pie shell and chill for at least 1 hour until set.

Lemon Meringue Pie
6 helpings

shortcrust pastry (p407) using
    175g flour
flour for rolling out
300g granulated sugar
3 × 15ml spoons cornflour
3 × 15ml spoons plain flour
a pinch of salt

300ml water
2 × 15ml spoons butter
1 × 5ml spoon grated lemon rind
75ml lemon juice
3 eggs
75g caster sugar

Roll out the pastry on a lightly floured surface and use it to line a 23cm pie plate. Bake blind until golden-brown, then cool.

Meanwhile, mix the sugar, cornflour, plain flour, and salt in the top of a double boiler. Boil the 300ml water separately, and add it slowly to the dry mixture, stirring all the time. Bring the mixture to the boil, stirring all the time; then place the top of the double boiler over hot water, cover, and cook gently for 20 minutes. Draw the pan off the heat. Add the butter, lemon rind, and lemon juice. Separate the eggs. Beat the yolks until just liquid, and add a little of the cooked mixture. Mix into the cooked ingredients. Replace over heat and cook, stirring all the time, until the mixture thickens. Remove from the heat and leave to cool. Whisk the egg whites until stiff and fold in the caster sugar. Pour the lemon custard into the baked pastry case and top with the meringue, making sure that it covers the top completely. Bake in a moderate oven, 180°C, Gas 4, for 12–15 minutes, until the meringue is lightly browned. Cool before cutting.

Mrs Beeton's Bakewell Pudding
4–5 helpings

shortcrust pastry (p407) using
   125g flour
flour for rolling out
jam
50g butter
50g caster sugar

1 egg
50g ground almonds
50g fine plain cake crumbs
a few drops almond essence
icing sugar for dusting

Roll out the pastry on a lightly floured surface and use it to line an 18cm flan ring. Spread over it a good layer of any kind of jam. Beat together the butter and sugar until pale and fluffy. Beat in the egg. Add the almonds, cake crumbs, and essence. Beat until well mixed, then pour the mixture into the flan shell, over the jam, and bake in a fairly hot oven, 200°C, Gas 6, for 30 minutes or until the centre of the pudding is firm. Sprinkle with icing sugar, and serve hot or cold.

VARIATION

Bakewell Tart

Make as for Bakewell Pudding, but use raspberry jam, and only 25g breadcrumbs or cake crumbs and 25g ground almonds. Bake for 25 minutes.

Mrs Beeton's Flan of Apples
6–7 helpings

6 dessert apples
4 cloves
3 × 15ml spoons medium-dry sherry
shortcrust pastry (p407) using
   175g flour

flour for rolling out
2 × 15ml spoons soft light brown sugar
3 egg whites
5 × 15ml spoons caster sugar

Peel and core each apple, and cut it into 8 sections. Place the sections in a heatproof bowl, add the cloves and sherry, cover closely and stand in a deep pan containing boiling water. Cook for about 20 minutes or until the apple sections are tender but not soft enough to break easily.

Meanwhile, roll out the pastry on a lightly floured surface and use it to line a 23cm flan case. Bake blind until the pastry is set. Fill the case with the apple sections arranged in a neat layer, strain 2 × 15ml spoons of the cooking juice over them, and sprinkle with the brown sugar. Whisk the egg whites until stiff with 2 × 5ml spoons of the caster sugar, and spread lightly over the apples. Sprinkle with the remaining caster sugar, and bake in a very cool–cool oven, 140°–150°C, Gas 1–2, for 1 hour. Serve either hot or cold.

Treacle Tart

6 helpings

shortcrust pastry (p407) using
   150g flour
flour for rolling out
3 × 15ml spoons golden syrup

50g soft white breadcrumbs
1 × 5ml spoon lemon juice **or** a good
   pinch of ground ginger

Roll out the pastry on a lightly floured surface and use most of it to line a 20cm pie plate, reserving a little for decoration. Warm the syrup in a saucepan until melted. Stir in the breadcrumbs and lemon juice or ground ginger, and pour the mixture into the pastry case. Roll out the remaining pastry into an oblong, and cut into 1cm strips. Arrange the strips in a lattice on top of the tart. Bake in a fairly hot oven, 200°C, Gas 6, for about 30 minutes.

Note If preferred, the tart may be baked as a double crust tart (p402). Use double the amount of pastry and bake for 50 minutes.

   Crushed cornflakes can be substituted for the breadcrumbs, if liked.

Small Pastries and Tartlets

Banbury Cakes

Makes 14

rough puff **or** puff (p412) **or**
   flaky (p411) pastry using 200g flour
flour for rolling out
25g butter **or** margarine
3 × 10ml spoons plain flour
½ × 2.5ml spoon ground nutmeg **or**
   ground cinnamon

100g currants
2 × 10ml spoons cut mixed peel
50g brown sugar
2 × 15ml spoons rum
1 egg white
25g caster sugar

Heat the oven to hot, 220°C, Gas 7. Roll out the pastry 5mm thick on a lightly floured surface and cut into rounds using a 7cm pastry cutter.

   To make the filling, melt the fat in a saucepan and stir in the flour and spice. Cook for 2 minutes. Remove from the heat, and add the fruit, brown sugar, and rum. Place a spoonful of filling in the centre of each pastry round. Dampen the edges of each round with water and gather them up to form a ball; turn the ball over so the join is underneath. Roll or pat each ball into an oval shape, approximately 10 × 6cm. With a sharp knife make 3 cuts in the top. Put the cakes on a baking sheet and bake for 15–20 minutes or until golden-brown.

   Whisk the egg white lightly and brush over the hot cakes; dust immediately with caster sugar. Return to the oven for a few minutes to frost the glaze.

Beatrice Tartlets
Makes 20

pâte sucrée (p408) using 150g flour
flour for rolling out
butter for greasing
3 bananas
juice of 1 lemon

1 × 15ml spoon caster sugar
50g chopped walnuts
125ml double cream
50g plain chocolate

Roll out the pastry on a lightly floured surface and use it to line 20 lightly greased 7cm patty tins. Bake blind, then cool. Chop the bananas and mix with the lemon juice and sugar. Stir the walnuts into the bananas. Pile the mixture into the pastry cases. Whip the cream until stiff, and pipe a large rosette on top of each tartlet. Grate the chocolate finely and sprinkle it over the cream.

Cherry Tartlets
Makes 12

shortcrust pastry (p407) using
    100g flour
flour for rolling out
1 × 375g can red cherries in syrup
25g lump sugar

1 × 5ml spoon arrowroot
1 × 10ml spoon lemon juice
a drop of red food colouring (optional)
125ml double cream

Roll out the pastry on a lightly floured surface and use it to line twelve 7cm patty tins or small boat-shaped moulds. Bake blind, then cool. Drain and stone the cherries, reserving the syrup. Place a layer of cherries in the pastry cases. Make up the syrup to 125ml with water. Heat the liquid and dissolve the sugar in it, bring to the boil, and boil for 5 minutes. Blend the arrowroot to a smooth paste with the lemon juice and add to the syrup, stirring all the time. Boil for 2 minutes until the syrup is clear and thick. Add the red colouring, if liked. Cool slightly, then pour a little of the glaze over the cherries. Leave to set. Whip the cream until stiff, and pipe a large rosette on each tartlet.

VARIATIONS
Blackcurrant Tartlets
Replace the cherries with 400g blackcurrants stewed in 2 × 15ml spoons water and 4 × 15ml spoons sugar. Omit the food colouring.

Strawberry or Raspberry Tartlets
Fill the tartlets with fresh strawberries or raspberries. Make the glaze using 125ml water instead of fruit syrup.

Cream Eclairs
Makes 10–12

choux pastry (p408) using 100g flour
fat for greasing
250ml whipping cream
25g caster sugar and icing sugar,
  mixed

3–4 drops vanilla essence
chocolate **or** coffee glacé
  icing (p388)

Make the pastry and use it while still warm. Put it in a forcing bag with a 2cm nozzle, and pipe the mixture in 10cm lengths on to a lightly greased baking sheet. Cut off each length with a knife or scissors dipped in hot water. Bake in a hot oven, 220°C, Gas 7, for 30 minutes. Do not open the oven door while baking. Reduce the heat to moderate, 180°C, Gas 4, and bake for a further 10 minutes. Remove the éclairs from the oven, split them, and remove any uncooked paste. Return to the oven for 5 minutes if still damp inside. Cool completely on a wire rack.

Meanwhile, whip the cream until it holds its shape, adding the mixed sugars gradually. Add the vanilla essence while whipping. Fill the éclairs with the cream, close neatly, and cover the tops with glacé icing.

VARIATIONS
Instead of vanilla-flavoured whipped cream, the éclairs can be filled with Chantilly Cream (p398) or with chocolate-flavoured confectioners' custard (p398) mixed with an equal quantity of whipped cream.

Cream Buns
Pipe the pastry in 5cm balls, use any of the fillings described above, and sift icing sugar over the tops instead of glacé icing.

Cream Horns
Makes 8

puff pastry (p412) using 100g flour
flour for rolling out
beaten egg and milk for glazing
3 × 15ml spoons sieved raspberry jam
4 × 15ml spoons liqueur-flavoured
  whipped cream (p399)

2 × 15ml spoons finely chopped nuts
  (preferably pistachios) **or**
  green-tinted desiccated coconut
  (p397)

Heat the oven to hot, 220°C, Gas 7. Roll out the pastry 5mm thick on a lightly floured surface and cut into strips 35cm long and 2cm wide. Moisten the strips with cold water. Wind each strip round a cornet mould, working from the point upward, keeping the moistened surface on the outside. Lay the horns on a dampened baking tray, with the final overlap of the pastry strip underneath. Leave in a cool place for 1 hour. Brush with beaten egg and milk, and bake for 10–15 minutes or until golden-brown. Remove the moulds and return the horns to the oven for 5 minutes.

Cool completely on a wire rack. When cold, put a very little jam in the bottom of each horn. Fill the horns with the cream. Sprinkle with the chopped nuts or desiccated coconut.

Note Chantilly Cream (p398) or 2 × 15ml spoons confectioners' custard (p398) and 2 × 15ml spoons stiffly whipped cream can also be used to fill Cream Horns.

Cream Slices
Makes 8

puff pastry (p412) using 100g flour
flour for rolling out
royal icing (p395) using 100g icing
  sugar

2 × 15ml spoons smooth seedless jam
125ml sweetened whipped cream
white glacé icing (p387) using
  100g icing sugar

Heat the oven to hot, 220°C, Gas 7. Roll out the pastry 1cm thick on a lightly floured surface into a neat rectangle. Cut it into 8 oblong pieces 10 × 2cm. Place on a baking sheet and spread the tops thinly with royal icing. Bake for 20 minutes or until the pastry is well risen and the icing is slightly browned. Leave to cool completely. When cold, split in half crossways. Spread the top of the bottom half with jam, and the bottom of the top half with cream; then sandwich the halves together again. Spread a little glacé icing on top of each slice, over the browned royal icing.

VARIATION
Vanilla Slices
Make as for Cream Slices but without the royal icing. When the slices are cold, fill with vanilla-flavoured confectioners' custard (p398) instead of cream. Ice the tops with white glacé icing.

Custard Tartlets
Makes 12

shortcrust pastry (p407) using
  100g flour and 1 × 5ml spoon caster
  sugar
flour for rolling out

1 egg
1 × 15ml spoon caster sugar
125ml milk
a pinch of grated nutmeg

Roll out the pastry on a lightly floured surface and use it to line twelve 7cm patty tins. Beat the egg lightly and add the sugar. Warm the milk and pour it on to the egg. Strain the custard into the pastry cases and sprinkle a little nutmeg on top. Bake in a moderate oven, 180°C, Gas 4, until the custard is firm and set. Leave to cool before removing from the tins.

VARIATION
Custard Meringue Tartlets
Make as for Custard Tartlets, but omit the nutmeg and bake for 15 minutes only. Whisk 2 egg whites until stiff and fold in 75g caster sugar. Pile the meringue on to the tartlets and bake in a very cool oven, 140°C, Gas 1, for about 30 minutes or until the meringue is crisp and very slightly browned.

Eccles Cakes
Makes 12–14

flaky (p411) **or** rough puff (p412)
   pastry using 200g flour
flour for rolling out
25g butter **or** margarine
1 × 15ml spoon sugar

75g currants
25g cut mixed peel
$\frac{1}{2}$ × 2.5ml spoon mixed spice
$\frac{1}{2}$ × 2.5ml spoon ground nutmeg
caster sugar for dusting

Heat the oven to hot, 220°C, Gas 7. Roll out the pastry 5mm thick on a lightly floured surface and cut into rounds using a 10cm pastry cutter. Cream together the fat and the sugar, add the currants, peel and spices, and place spoonfuls of the mixture in the centre of each pastry round. Gather the edges of each round together to form a ball. With the smooth side uppermost, form into a flat cake. Make 2 cuts in the top of each cake with a sharp knife. Brush with water and dust with caster sugar. Put on a baking sheet and bake for 20 minutes or until golden-brown.

Fruit or Jam Turnovers
Makes 8

shortcrust pastry (p407) using
   150g flour **or** flaky (p411),
   rough puff **or** puff (p412)
   pastry using 100g flour

flour for rolling out
100g stewed fruit **or** 2 × 15ml spoons
   jam
1 × 15ml spoon caster sugar

Heat the oven to fairly hot, 200°C, Gas 6. Roll out the pastry 3mm thick on a lightly floured surface and cut into rounds using a 10cm cutter. Place spoonfuls of fruit or jam in the centre of each pastry round. Moisten the edges with water and fold the pastry over the filling. Press the edges well together and crimp or decorate with a fork. Place the turnovers on a baking sheet, brush with water, and dredge with the caster sugar. Bake for about 20 minutes or until golden-brown.
Note These turnovers are called Coventry Turnovers when raspberry jam is used for the filling.

Mrs Beeton's Jam Tartlets

puff pastry (p412) trimmings
flour for rolling out

jam **or** marmalade

Heat the oven to fairly hot, 200°C, Gas 6. Roll out the pastry 5mm thick on a lightly floured surface and use it to line 7cm patty tins or foil tartlet cases. Bake blind for 7–10 minutes. Dry the empty cases in the oven for another 3–4 minutes. Cool, then fill with jam or marmalade.

Lemon Cheesecakes
Makes 12

shortcrust pastry (p407) using
   100g flour
flour for rolling out

3 × 15ml spoons lemon curd
25g whole candied peel

Heat the oven to fairly hot, 200°C, Gas 6. Roll out the pastry on a lightly floured surface and use it to line twelve 7cm patty tins. Half fill each pastry case with the lemon curd. Cut the candied peel into fine strips and use to decorate. Bake for about 20 minutes or until the pastry is golden-brown.

Maids of Honour
Makes 20

puff pastry (p412) using 200g flour
flour for rolling out
200g ground almonds
100g caster sugar

2 eggs
25g flour
4 × 15ml spoons single cream
2 × 15ml spoons orange flower water

Heat the oven to fairly hot, 200°C, Gas 6. Roll out the pastry on a lightly floured surface and use it to line twenty 7cm patty tins. Mix together the ground almonds and sugar. Add the eggs, and mix in the flour, cream, and orange flower water. Put the mixture into the pastry cases and bake for about 15 minutes or until the filling is firm and golden-brown.

Mince Pies
Makes 12

shortcrust pastry (p407) using
   300g flour **or** flaky (p411),
   rough puff **or** puff (p412)
pastry using 200g flour

flour for rolling out
250g mincemeat
25g caster **or** icing sugar for dredging

Heat the oven to very hot, 230°C, Gas 8. Roll out the pastry 2mm thick on a lightly floured surface, and use just over half to line twelve 7cm patty tins. Cut out 12 lids from the rest of the pastry. Place a spoonful of mincemeat in each pastry case. Dampen the edges of the cases and cover with the pastry lids. Seal the edges well, brush the tops with water, and dredge with the sugar. Make 2 small cuts in the top of each pie. Bake for 15–20 minutes or until golden-brown.

Palmiers

puff pastry (p412) trimmings   caster sugar
flour for rolling out

Heat the oven to hot, 220°C, Gas 7. Roll out the pastry on a lightly floured surface into a long strip about 30cm wide for large palmiers, 10–12cm wide for petits fours. Sprinkle well with caster sugar. Roll up the pastry from one long side to the centre of the strip. Then roll up, from the other long side so that the two rolls meet in the centre. Chill until firm, then cut the roll in slices; for petits fours, cut thin slices. Sprinkle the slices with more sugar, and place them, sugared side up, on a dampened baking sheet. Bake for 10–12 minutes, depending on the thickness of the slices. Lift off the sheet with a palette knife, and cool on a wire rack.

Serve large palmiers as afternoon tea biscuits, very small ones as petits fours.

Sly Cakes
Makes 16–20

rough puff pastry (p412) using   25g cut mixed peel
   200g flour   50g sugar
flour for rolling out   1 × 10ml spoon mixed spice
25g butter **or** margarine   beaten egg **or** milk for glazing
1 apple   caster sugar for dusting
200g currants

Heat the oven to hot, 220°C, Gas 7. Divide the pastry in half, and roll out each piece on a lightly floured surface into a 15cm square about 2mm thick. Melt the fat. Peel, core, and chop the apple and mix it with the currants, peel, sugar, spice, and melted fat. Spread the mixture on one piece of pastry, lay the other piece on top and seal the edges well. Mark the top into squares or oblongs with the back of a knife, without cutting through the pastry. Glaze with beaten egg or milk. Put on a baking sheet and bake for 20–30 minutes until golden-brown. Cut into squares or oblongs and dust with caster sugar.

HOME FREEZING

Nearly all fresh foods, and many cooked foods, freeze well, but there are a few items to avoid entirely, or to freeze only with great care. There are also a few foods which cannot be frozen and then eaten raw, although they can be used for cooking.

Foods Not to Freeze
1) hard-boiled eggs (including Scotch eggs, eggs in pies and in sandwiches)
2) soured cream, single cream (less than 40% butterfat), and half-cream which separate
3) yoghurt
4) cottage cheese; this becomes watery
5) custards (including tarts); the custard mixture of eggs and milk can be frozen uncooked, but there is little point in this
6) soft meringue toppings
7) mayonnaise and salad dressings
8) milk puddings
9) royal icing and other icings and frostings without fat; they crumble and chip in the freezer
10) salad vegetables with a high water content, eg lettuce, watercress, radishes
11) old boiled potatoes (potatoes can be frozen mashed, roast, baked or as chips)
12) stuffed poultry
13) food with a high proportion of gelatine
14) whole eggs in shells which will crack

Foods to Freeze with Care
1) Cooked onions, garlic, spices, and herbs. They sometimes get a musty flavour in cooked dishes in the freezer, and recipe quantities should be reduced in such dishes as casseroles; they can be adjusted during re-heating. Careful packing will help to prevent these strong flavours spreading to other foods, but a short time in storage is recommended.
2) Rice, spaghetti, and potatoes should only be frozen without liquid. They become mushy in liquid and should not be frozen in soups or stews.
3) Sauces and gravy are best thickened by reduction, or with a vegetable purée. If flour is used, the sauce or gravy must be re-heated with great care, preferably in a double boiler, to avoid separation. Cornflour can be used but gives a glutinous quality. Egg and cream thickening should only be added after freezing.

4) Apples, pears, avocados, melons, and bananas cannot be successfully frozen whole to eat raw. They can be prepared and frozen for use in various other ways (although pears are never very satisfactory). Bananas are not worth freezing as they are in season at a reasonable price throughout the year.

5) Cabbage cannot be frozen successfully to eat raw, and is not really worth freezing since it occupies a lot of freezer space. Red cabbage may be worth freezing, as it has a short season and is never very plentiful.

6) Celery and chicory cannot be frozen to eat raw. They are useful frozen in liquid to serve as vegetables. Celery can be used in stews or soups.

7) Tomatoes cannot be frozen to eat raw, but are invaluable frozen as purée or juice or to use in soups, stews, and sauces.

8) Milk must be homogenized and packed in waxed cartons. However, it is hardly worth freezing since several types of milk can be stored without refrigeration.

Labelling and Recording

All items should be labelled carefully with the contents, weight, date of freezing, and any special instructions for thawing or re-heating. All packs should be recorded on a board or in a book, and a note made when items are used.

Thawing

Thawing speeds up the chemical reactions which have been halted by freezing. It therefore encourages rapid deterioration, so that food is best thawed in a cold atmosphere such as a refrigerator. It must be eaten or cooked immediately after thawing.

Remove food from its wrappings before thawing if possible, unless otherwise directed.

Frozen cooked food must never be thawed and then refrozen. Raw materials should not be thawed and refrozen, but can be made into cooked dishes and then frozen.

Freezing Methods

Meat, Poultry, and Game

If buying a whole carcass, it is best to ask the butcher to freeze this quantity of meat, because it will take 3 or 4 days in a home freezer. Smaller quantities of meat, poultry, and game can be frozen successfully at home. Meat must be frozen quickly and the fast-freeze switch should be turned on well ahead of freezing time so that the cabinet is at the lowest setting.

It is best to freeze meat in the way in which it will be used, such as cubed or minced, as this will save many hours' thawing and preparation time. Poultry should be plucked, drawn, and jointed if necessary. Most game must be hung for the required time, then plucked or skinned, and drawn. Surplus fat should be removed, and the meat will take up less space if boned and rolled. Any bones should be padded with a twist of foil or paper before the meat is packed in polythene. Pack chops, steaks, and sausages in small quantities, separated by clingfilm. Remember that salted meats have a limited storage life since fat and salt react together in the freezer to cause rancidity.

Type of meat, poultry, and game	Preparation for freezing	High quality storage life	Thawing instructions
Cubed meat	Pack in small quantities in polythene, pressing together tightly	2 months	Thaw in refrigerator for 3 hours
Ham and bacon	Vacuum packed ham or bacon should be frozen sliced or in joints	1 month (sliced) 3 months (joints)	Thaw in wrappings in refrigerator
Offal	Wash and dry well, remove blood vessels and cores. Wrap in polythene, separating pieces with clingfilm	2 months	Thaw in wrappings in refrigerator for 3 hours
Joints	Trim, bone, and roll, if possible. Pack in polythene	12 months (beef) 9 months (lamb and veal) 6 months (pork)	Thaw in refrigerator allowing 4 hours per 500g
Minced meat	Use lean mince and pack in small quantities. Wrap in polythene	2 months	Thaw in refrigerator for 3 hours. If cooked while still frozen, mince may be tough
Sausages and sausage-meat	Pack in small quantities in polythene	1 month	Thaw in refrigerator for 2 hours
Steaks, chops or sliced meat	Pack in small quantities, separating pieces with clingfilm. Wrap in polythene	6–12 months (according to meat)	Cook slowly from frozen, or thaw in refrigerator
Chicken, guinea-fowl or turkey	Hang, pluck, and draw, if neccessary. Truss or cut in joints. Chill for 12 hours, pack in polythene bags, excluding giblets. Do not stuff	12 months	Thaw in wrappings in refrigerator. Must be totally thawed before cooking
Giblets	Clean, wash, dry, and chill. Pack in polythene bags	2 months	Thaw in refrigerator for 2 hours
Duck and goose	Hang, pluck, and draw, if necessary. Chill for 12 hours and pack in polythene bags, excluding giblets	6 months	Thaw in wrappings in refrigerator. Must be completely thawed before cooking
Grouse, partridge, pheasant, pigeon	Hang as liked after removing shot and cleaning wounds. Pluck, draw, and truss, and pad bones. Pack in polythene bags	6 months	Thaw in wrappings in refrigerator
Plover, quail, snipe, woodcock	Prepare as other game but do not draw	6 months	Thaw in wrappings in refrigerator
Hares	Clean shot wounds and hang, bleeding the animal and collecting the blood. Paunch, skin, clean, and cut into joints. Separate joints with clingfilm and pack in polythene bags. Pack blood separately	6 months	Thaw in wrappings in refrigerator
Rabbits	Paunch, skin, clean, and prepare as for hare	6 months	Thaw in wrappings in refrigerator
Venison	Clean, and hang before jointing. Skin, then pack in polythene bags	12 months	Thaw in a marinade in refrigerator

Fish

Only freshly caught fish should be frozen, and this should be done very quickly. Fish bought from a shop is not suitable for freezing. Clean and prepare fish completely and pack in polythene. Separate steaks or fillets with clingfilm, but avoid making packs deeper than 5cm so that fish is frozen quickly. To keep the flavour and colour of white fish, add the juice of a lemon to the water in which it is washed.

Plainly frozen fillets and whole fish (ie uncoated), should be thawed before cooking. Do not place the fish in water or hold it under a tap as this will wash away the natural moisture.

Commercially frozen breaded fish or fish in batter can be fried straight from the freezer, bearing in mind that the temperature of the fat will be reduced by the frozen fish, and this must be allowed for in the overall timing.

Type of fish	Preparation for freezing	High quality storage life	Thawing instructions
Crab, crayfish, and lobster	Cook and cool. Remove flesh and pack in polythene bags or rigid containers	1 month	Thaw in container in refrigerator and serve cold, or add to cooked dishes
Mussels	Scrub and clean thoroughly. Put in a large pan over medium heat for 3 minutes to open. Cool, remove from shells, and pack in rigid containers with juices	1 month	Thaw in container in refrigerator before adding to dishes
Oily fish (eg herring, mackerel, salmon)	Clean well, fillet, cut in steaks or leave whole. Separate pieces of fish with clingfilm. Wrap in polythene, excluding air carefully	2 months	Thaw large fish in refrigerator, but cook small fish from frozen
Oysters	Open and reserve liquid. Wash fish in brine (1 × 5ml spoon salt to 500ml water). Pack in rigid containers in own liquid	1 month	Thaw in container in refrigerator and serve cold, or add to cooked dishes
Prawns and shrimps	Cook and cool in cooking liquid. Remove shells and pack in polythene bags or rigid containers. Shrimps may be covered in melted spiced butter	1 month	Thaw in container in refrigerator and serve cold, or add to cooked dishes
Smoked fish	Pack in polythene bags, wrapping individual fish in clingfilm	2 months	Thaw in refrigerator to eat cold, or cook haddock and kippers from frozen
White fish (eg cod, sole)	Clean, fillet or cut in steaks, or leave whole. Separate pieces of fish with clingfilm. Wrap in polythene, excluding air carefully	3 months	Thaw large fish in refrigerator, but cook small fish from frozen

Vegetables

All vegetables for freezing should be young, fresh, and clean, and they should be frozen as soon as possible after picking. Grade vegetables for size and prepare in small quantities (ie 500g is the largest quantity which should be blanched at one time). All vegetables must be blanched by being cooked briefly in boiling water to retard enzymic action and retain colour, flavour, and nutritive value. Use a wire blanching basket in a large saucepan which will hold 4 litres water and has a lid. Vegetables should be put into the boiling water, and the water returned to boiling point as quickly as possible. Timing must be accurate, as under-blanching results in colour change and loss of nutritive value while over-blanching causes loss of flavour and crispness.

After blanching, vegetables must be cooled rapidly in water chilled with ice cubes, not under running tap water which is not cold enough. It should take as long to cool as to blanch each vegetable, and then the vegetables must be well-drained. They may be spread out on open freezing trays and frozen before packing, or packed directly into polythene bags or rigid containers. Vegetables with strong smells, eg onions and garlic, may need overwrapping.

After freezing, vegetables need little cooking. Most vegetables should be put straight into a small quantity of boiling water and cooked until just tender. Vegetables can also be cooked in butter, without any water, in a covered casserole or heavy saucepan, either in the oven or over heat.

Type of vegetable	Preparation for freezing	Blanching time	High quality storage life	Cooking instructions
Artichokes (globe)	Remove outer leaves, stalks, and chokes. Add lemon juice to blanching water	7 minutes	12 months	Cook in boiling water for 10 minutes
Artichokes (Jerusalem)	Peel and slice. Cook in chicken stock and purée	—	3 months	Heat purée and add milk or cream
Asparagus	Clean and grade. Cut in 15cm lengths	2 minutes (thin) 3 minutes (medium) 4 minutes (large)	9 months	Cook in boiling water for 5 minutes
Aubergines	1) Peel and cut into 2cm slices	4 minutes	1) 12 months	1) Place in boiling water for 5 mins
	2) Coat in batter and deep fry	—	2) 2 months	2) Heat in warm oven or fry
Avocado pears	Mash pulp with lemon juice (1 × 15ml spoon juice to each pear)	—	2 months	Thaw for 3 hours in refrigerator
Beans (broad)	Shell small young beans	1½ minutes	12 months	Cook in boiling water for 8 minutes
Beans (French)	Top and tail young beans. Leave whole or cut into 2cm chunks	3 minutes (whole) 2 minutes (cut)	12 months	Cook in boiling water for 7 minutes (whole) 5 minutes (cut)
Beans (runner)	Cut in chunks; do not shred	2 minutes	12 months	Cook in boiling water for 7 minutes
Beetroot	Cook very young beet, under 3cm diameter. Peel and leave whole or dice	—	6 months	Thaw for 2 hours, and add dressing

Type of vegetable	Preparation for freezing	Blanching time	High quality storage life	Cooking instructions
Broccoli	Trim stalks and soak in brine for 30 minutes (1 × 15ml spoon salt to 4 litres water). Wash before blanching	3 minutes (thin) 4 minutes (medium) 5 minutes (thick)	12 months	Cook in boiling water for 8 minutes
Brussels sprouts	Grade and wash well	3 minutes (small) 4 minutes (medium)	12 months	Cook in boiling water for 8 minutes
Cabbage	Shred crisp young cabbage	1½ minutes	6 months	Cook in boiling water for 8 minutes (do not use raw)
Carrots	Use very young carrots. Wash and scrape. Leave whole, dice or slice	3 minutes	12 months	Cook in boiling water for 8 minutes
Cauliflower	Wash and break into florets. Add lemon juice to blanching water	3 minutes	6 months	Cook in boiling water for 10 minutes
Celery	Scrub crisp young stalks and cut into 2cm slices	2 minutes	6 months	Cook in stock, or add to soups and stews (do not use raw)
Corn on the cob	Use fresh tender corn and grade for size. Remove husks and silks	4 minutes (small) 6 minutes (medium) 8 minutes (large)	12 months	Thaw in wrappings. Cook in boiling water for 10 minutes
Herbs	Wash and pack whole sprigs or chop into ice cube trays, freeze, and wrap frozen cubes	—	6 months	Thaw and drain, or add herb cubes to dishes
Leeks	Clean and cut into rings	2 minutes	12 months	Cook in boiling water for 8 minutes or add to soups and stews
Marrows and courgettes	1) Cook and mash marrows and freeze purée 2) Cut courgettes into 1cm slices without peeling	3 minutes	2 months	1) Re-heat from frozen in double boiler 2) Fry in oil and season well
Mushrooms	Wipe but do not peel. Pack into bags without blanching	—	3 months	Thaw and cook as fresh
Onions	Skin and chop or slice. Wrap well	2 minutes	2 months	Add to dishes while frozen
Parsnips, turnips, and swedes	Peel and dice	2 minutes	12 months	Cook in boiling water for 15 minutes
Peas	Shell young sweet peas	1 minute	12 months	Cook in boiling water for 5 minutes
Peppers	Remove seeds and membranes	3 minutes (halves) 2 minutes (slices)	12 months	Thaw for 1 hour (halves) or add frozen slices to dishes
Potatoes	Cook and mash, or make into croquettes. Jacket, baked and roast potatoes can be frozen. Slightly under-cook new potatoes, and freeze in bags which can be boiled for re-heating. Fry chips for 4 minutes but do not brown	—	3 months	Re-heat mashed or croquette, roast or jacket potatoes. New potatoes should be kept in bag and heated in boiling water for 10 minutes. Fry chips while frozen

Type of vegetable	Preparation for freezing	Blanching time	High quality storage life	Cooking instructions
Spinach	Remove any thick stalks and wash leaves very well. Press out moisture after blanching	2 minutes	12 months	Re-heat gently in butter
Tomatoes	Wipe, grade and pack in bags	—	12 months	Thaw for 2 hours (skins will drop off). Do not use raw

Cooked and Other Prepared Dishes

Make dishes to standard recipes, observing one or two special details. Thicken sauce or gravy by reducing, or by adding vegetable purée or cornflour; this is to prevent curdling during re-heating. Add rice, pasta or potatoes to liquid dishes only when re-heating, since they become too soft during freezing. Use onions, garlic, herbs, and spices with care, as flavours can deteriorate during freezing.

Pack cooked foods in freezer containers, or in ordinary dishes which will withstand freezing and heating. Label carefully if additional ingredients have to be included during re-heating. Use cooked foods within 2 months to retain high quality.

Type of dish	Preparation for freezing	High quality storage life	Thawing/re-heating instructions
Casseroles and stews	Slightly undercook vegetables. Do not add rice, pasta or potatoes. Remove surplus fat	2 months	Heat in double boiler, or thaw and bake in casserole in a moderate oven, 180°C, Gas 4 for 1 hour
Flans (sweet and savoury)	Prepare and bake. Open freeze and wrap in foil or polythene	2 months	Thaw at room temperature for 3 hours. Re-heat if required
Ices – fresh fruit purée	Fully prepare	3 months	Serve straight from freezer
– ice cream	Fully prepare	3 months	Allow to soften slightly in refrigerator before serving
– sorbets and water ices	Fully prepare	3 months	Serve straight from freezer
– bombes and other moulded desserts	Wrap in foil	3 months	Unmould on to chilled plate, using cloth wrung out in hot water to release ice cream. Wrap in foil and return to freezer for one hour before serving
– ice cream gâteaux	Pack in rigid containers or wrap in foil	3 months	Place on plate and serve at once. Slice with knife dipped in boiling water

Chart continues over

Type of dish	Preparation for freezing	High quality storage life	Thawing/re-heating instructions
Meat	Do not freeze cooked joints or grilled meats which can become tough, rancid, and dry 1) Slice cooked meat thinly and separate with clingfilm. Pack tightly in rigid or foil containers 2) Slice meat and pack in gravy or sauce in rigid or foil containers	2 months	Thaw in wrappings in refrigerator for 3 hours. Bake in a moderate oven, 180°C, Gas 4, for 40 minutes
Meat pies	1) Bake and cool. Wrap in foil or polythene	1) 2 months	1) Thaw in refrigerator for 6 hours to eat cold, or bake in a fairly hot oven, 190°C, Gas 5, for 1 hour
	2) Cook meat filling. Cool and cover with pastry. Wrap in foil or polythene	2) 2 months	2) Bake from frozen in a fairly hot oven, 200°C, Gas 6, for 1 hour
Mousses	Prepare in freezer-tested serving dishes	1 month	Thaw in refrigerator for 8 hours
Pancakes	Cool and pack in layers with clingfilm. Wrap in greaseproof paper, foil or polythene	2 months	Thaw at room temperature and separate. Heat in cool oven, 150°C, Gas 2, or on a plate over steam, covered with a cloth
Pasta	Slightly undercook, drain well, cool, and pack in polythene bags	1 month	Put into boiling water, bring back to the boil, and cook for 2–3 minutes until tender
Pasta dishes	Pack pasta and sauce in foil dish with lid	1 month	Remove lid and bake in a fairly hot oven, 200°C, Gas 6, for 45 minutes
Pâté	Cool completely and wrap in foil or polythene. Pâté may also be prepared in freezer-tested dishes	1 month	Thaw in refrigerator for 6 hours
Pizza	Prepare, using fresh herbs, not dried. Do not add anchovies. Bake. Cool and wrap in polythene	1 month	Unwrap and thaw at room temperature for 1 hour. Top with anchovies and bake in a fairly hot oven, 190°C, Gas 5, for 20 minutes
Rice	Slightly undercook, drain well, cool, and pack in polythene bags	1 month	Put into boiling water, bring back to boil, and cook for 2–3 minutes until tender
Rice dishes	Cook completely, but avoid adding hard-boiled eggs. Pack into bags or rigid containers	1 month	Heat in double boiler, stirring well and adding additional ingredients

Type of dish	Preparation for freezing	High quality storage life	Thawing/re-heating instructions
Sauces (savoury)	Prepare completely, but season sparingly. Pack in rigid containers, leaving headspace. Do not freeze sauces thickened with eggs or cream	1 month	Heat in double boiler and re-season if required
Sauces (sweet)	1) Fresh or cooked fruit sauces should be packed in rigid containers, leaving headspace 2) Thicken pudding sauces with cornflour and pack in rigid containers, leaving headspace	1) 12 months 2) 1 month	1) Thaw in refrigerator for 3 hours to serve cold, or heat in double boiler 2) Heat in double boiler
Soup	Use standard recipes but avoid flour for thickening. Do not include rice, pasta, barley, potatoes, milk or cream. Pack in rigid containers, leaving headspace	2 months	Heat in double boiler, adding additional ingredients
Steamed and baked puddings	Steam or bake puddings in foil containers. Cool and cover with lid, or pack in polythene bag	2 months	Thaw at room temperature for 2 hours, and steam for 45 minutes, or bake from frozen in a fairly hot oven, 190°C, Gas 5, for 45 minutes

Cakes, Pastry, and Breads

Use very fresh ingredients when baking for the freezer. Use butter for good flavour, but margarine for a light texture. Margarine is especially suitable for strongly flavoured cakes such as chocolate and coffee.

Icings and fillings made from fat and sugar can be frozen separately or on cakes. But do not attempt to freeze icings made without fat. Fruit or jam fillings in cakes become soggy after thawing, and are better added just before serving. Decorations are also better added then, since they absorb moisture during thawing and may stain the cake. Sweetened whipped cream can be frozen like a cake filling. Pack cakes carefully to avoid crushing during storage. It is better to open freeze iced cakes before packing to avoid smudging the surfaces.

Type of cake, pastry or bread	Preparation for freezing	High quality storage life	Thawing/baking instructions
Biscuits	Form dough into 2cm diameter roll. Wrap in foil or polythene. **Note** Baked biscuits are best stored in tins without freezing	2 months	Thaw in refrigerator for 45 minutes. Cut in slices and bake in a fairly hot oven, 190°C, Gas 5, for 10 minutes
Bread	Pack in polythene bags. Crusty bread quickly loses its crispness in the freezer	1 month	Thaw at room temperature for 4 hours
Breadcrumbs (plain)	Pack in polythene bags	3 months	Thaw in wrappings at room temperature, or sprinkle directly on food to be cooked

Type of cake, pastry or bread	Preparation for freezing	High quality storage life	Thawing/baking instructions
Bread dough	Knead dough and put in greased polythene bag without proving	2 months	Unseal bag and tie loosely to allow space for rising. Thaw at room temperature for 6 hours. Knock back, shape, prove, and bake
Brioches and croissants	Pack in rigid containers to prevent crushing, immediately after baking and cooling	1 month	Thaw at room temperature for 30 minutes and heat in oven or under grill
Cakes (uniced)	Cool completely and wrap in foil or polythene	4 months	Thaw at room temperature for 2–3 hours
Cakes (iced)	Fill and ice cake but do not add decorations. Open freeze on tray, and pack in a rigid container	4 months	Thaw at room temperature for 3 hours
Cheesecakes	Make baked or refrigerated variety in cake tin with removable base. Open freeze and pack in rigid container	1 month	Thaw for 8 hours in refrigerator
Choux pastry	Bake but do not fill or ice. Pack in polythene bags or boxes	1 month	Thaw in wrappings at room temperature for 2 hours. Fill and ice
Crumpets and muffins	Pack in polythene bags	1 month	Thaw in wrappings at room temperature for 30 minutes before toasting
Danish pastries	Bake but do not ice. Pack in foil trays with lids, or in rigid containers	2 months	Thaw at room temperature for 1 hour. Heat if liked
Fruit pies	Brush bottom crust with egg white to prevent sogginess. 1) Bake, cool, and pack 2) Use uncooked fruit and pastry, open freeze, and pack	1) 4 months 2) 2 months	1) Thaw to serve cold, or reheat 2) Bake from frozen in a fairly hot oven, 200°C, Gas 6, for 1 hour
Pastry cases	Freeze baked or unbaked, using foil containers	4 months	Bake frozen cases at recommended temperatures for type of pastry. Re-heat baked cases, or fill with hot filling
Sandwiches	Do not remove crusts. Spread thickly with butter or margarine. Do not use salad fillings, mayonnaise or hard-boiled eggs. Separate sandwiches with clingfilm and pack in foil or polythene	1 month	Thaw at room temperature and remove crusts, or toast under grill while still frozen
Scones and drop scones	Pack in small quantities in polythene bags	2 months	Thaw in wrappings at room temperature for 1 hour. Alternatively, bake frozen scones in a moderate oven, 180°C, Gas 4, for 10 minutes

Dairy Produce

Most cheeses can be frozen successfully but tend to crumble after being frozen. They should be frozen in small pieces, and cut when still slightly hard. Cream cheese tends to separate on thawing. It is best blended with heavy cream before freezing and used as a dip. Cottage cheese tends to separate and should not be frozen. Only homogenized milk in waxed cartons should be frozen, and then only in small quantities which can be used quickly. The texture of frozen cream can be heavy and grainy, but light beating will improve it. If used in hot coffee, the oil will rise to the surface. Only really good thick cream responds well to freezing. Eggs should be very fresh. They should be washed and then broken into a dish to check for quality. They should be frozen already beaten or separated, in rigid containers, and sugar or salt added in the proportions below to prevent coagulation.

Dairy produce	Preparation for freezing	High quality storage life	Thawing instructions
Butter and margarine	Overwrap in foil or polythene	6 months (unsalted) 3 months (salted)	Thaw enough for 1 week's use in refrigerator
Cheese – hard	Cut in 200g pieces and wrap in foil or polythene. Pack grated cheese in polythene bags. Pack blue cheeses in polythene and overwrap well	3 months	Thaw in open wrappings at room temperature for 3 hours. Cut while slightly frozen to avoid crumbling
– cream	Blend with heavy cream	3 months	Thaw in container in refrigerator overnight. Blend with fork to restore smoothness
Cream	Freeze all creams in cartons. Do not freeze single, soured or half-cream	6 months	Thaw in carton at room temperature and stir with a fork to restore smoothness
Whipped cream	Sweeten with 2 × 10ml spoons sugar to 500ml cream. Freeze in containers, or open freeze piped rosettes	6 months	Thaw in container at room temperature. Rosettes thaw in 15 minutes at room temperature
Eggs	Do not freeze in shell. 1) Mix yolks and whites, adding 1 × 5ml spoon salt or 1 × 10ml spoon sugar to 5 eggs 2) Mix yolks, adding 1 × 5ml spoon salt or 1 × 10ml sugar to 5 yolks 3) Put whites in containers with no addition	12 months	Thaw in refrigerator but bring to room temperature before use
Milk	Only homogenized milk can be frozen. Leave 2cm headspace	1 month	Thaw at room temperature and use quickly

Fruit

Freeze only fresh, top-quality fruit. Fruit can be frozen dry and unsweetened, with sugar, in syrup, or as purée, and in cooked dishes.

Note As in bottling, white sugar is normally used because it does not colour or flavour the fruit. Other sugar can be used, but Barbados sugar or molasses may develop an unpleasant flavour in storage, and colour the fruit.

Dry Unsweetened Pack

This is best for fruit to be used in pies, puddings, and jams, and for berries and currants to be eaten raw. Do not use it for fruit which discolours badly, since sugar helps to retard the action of the enzymes which cause darkening. Clean any fruit well and open freeze on trays, or pack into bags or rigid containers.

Dry Sugar Pack

Use 1 part sugar to 4 parts fruit, mixing lightly before packing. Sugar draws out juices, and some fruit, eg berries, can become over-soft during thawing.

Sugar Syrup Pack

Use this for non-juicy fruits and those which discolour easily. Make a syrup with white sugar and water, dissolving the sugar completely in boiling water and chilling before use. Three syrup strengths are generally used:

Light syrup	175g sugar to 500ml water
Medium syrup	275g sugar to 500ml water
Heavy syrup	400g sugar to 500ml water

Vitamin C helps to retard discoloration of fruit, and the juice of 1 lemon should be added to each litre of syrup for fruit such as apricots and peaches.

Cover the fruit completely in syrup and crumble a piece of greaseproof paper or clingfilm in the headspace to prevent the fruit rising above the syrup and discolouring.

Fruit Purée

Prepare purée from raw raspberries or strawberries, but cook other fruit in a little water first. Sweeten to taste before freezing and pack with 1.5cm headspace to allow for expansion.

Fruit Juices

Prepare fruit juice and freeze in trays. Wrap frozen cubes individually in foil and store in polythene bags. Apple juice will ferment quickly and should only be stored for a month. Other fruit juices will be at their best for 9 months.

Type of fruit	Preparation for freezing	Method of freezing	High quality storage life	Thawing/cooking instructions
Apples	Peel, core, and slice	1) Dry sugar 2) Medium syrup 3) Cooked purée	12 months 4 months	Cook in puddings or pies, or re-heat purée
Apricots	Skin and cut in halves or slices. Add lemon juice to pack	1) Dry sugar 2) Medium syrup 3) Raw purée	12 months 4 months	Thaw for 4 hours in covered pack in refrigerator

Type of fruit	Preparation for freezing	Method of freezing	High quality storage life	Thawing/cooking instructions
Blackberries and raspberries	Clean and hull	1) Unsweetened 2) Dry sugar 3) Raw or cooked purée	12 months 4 months	Thaw for 3 hours at room temperature
Blueberries	Wash and drain. Crush slightly to soften skins	1) Unsweetened 2) Dry sugar 3) Heavy syrup	12 months	Cook in puddings, pies or jam
Cherries	Chill in water for 1 hour and stone	1) Dry sugar 2) Medium syrup for sweet fruit 3) Heavy syrup for sour fruit	12 months	Thaw for 3 hours at room temperature. Use cold or cook
Cranberries	Wash and drain	1) Unsweetened 2) Cooked whole or purée	12 months 4 months	Cook while frozen, or thaw purée or cooked fruit for 3½ hours at room temperature
Currants (red, white, and black)	Strip fruit from stems	1) Unsweetened 2) Dry sugar 3) Medium syrup 4) Cooked purée	12 months 4 months	Thaw for 2 hours at room temperature
Damsons	Wash, drain, and stone	1) Heavy syrup 2) Cooked purée	12 months 4 months	Thaw for 3 hours at room temperature or cook while frozen
Dried fruit (dates, figs, raisins, currants, sultanas)	Pack in polythene bags	—	12 months	Thaw for 2 hours at room temperature and use in recipes
Figs	Wash ripe figs and remove stems. Do not bruise	1) Unsweetened 2) Light syrup if peeled	12 months	Thaw for 3 hours at room temperature. Eat raw or cooked in syrup
Gooseberries	Clean, top, and tail	1) Unsweetened 2) Medium syrup 3) Cooked purée	12 months 4 months	Thaw for 3 hours at room temperature, or cook while frozen
Grapefruit	Peel, remove pith, and divide into segments	1) Dry sugar 2) Heavy syrup	12 months	Thaw for 3 hours at room temperature
Grapes	Pack seedless grapes whole. Skin, de-seed, and halve large ones	Light syrup	12 months	Thaw for 3 hours at room temperature
Greengages and plums	Cut in half and stone	Medium syrup	12 months	Thaw for 3 hours at room temperature
Lemons and limes	Peel and slice, or slice without peeling and pack for drinks	Light syrup	12 months	Thaw for 1 hour at room temperature, or put in drinks while frozen
Melons	Peel and cut in cubes or shape into balls. Toss in lemon juice	Light syrup	12 months	Thaw for 3 hours in covered pack in refrigerator
Oranges	Peel, remove pith, and divide into segments, or slice	1) Dry sugar 2) Light syrup	12 months	Thaw for 3 hours at room temperature
Peaches and nectarines	Skin, cut in halves or slices, and brush with lemon juice. Alternatively, make a raw purée with 1 × 15ml spoon lemon juice to 500g fruit	1) Medium syrup 2) Raw purée	12 months 4 months	Thaw for 3 hours in covered pack in refrigerator

Type of fruit	Preparation for freezing	Method of freezing	High quality storage life	Thawing/cooking instructions
Pears	Peel, quarter, and remove cores. Dip pieces in lemon juice. Poach in medium syrup for 1½ minutes, drain, and cool before packing in syrup	Medium syrup	12 months	Thaw for 3 hours at room temperature
Pineapple	Peel and cut in slices or chunks	1) Dry sugar 2) Light syrup	12 months	Thaw for 3 hours at room temperature
Rhubarb	Wash in cold water and trim sticks	1) Unsweetened 2) Medium syrup 3) Cooked purée	12 months 4 months	Thaw purée at room temperature. Cook raw fruit while frozen
Strawberries	Clean and grade for size	1) Unsweetened 2) Dry sugar 3) Medium syrup 4) Raw purée	12 months 4 months	Thaw for 2 hours at room temperature

INDEX

Note All recipe entries are in italic, eg *Bakewell tart 421*

Accompaniments 47–59
Acorn squash 267
Aduki beans 238
Agro-dolce 213
Aïoli 219
Almond(s) 361
  coating cake with
    almond paste 391–2
  Bakewell tart 421
  – biscuits 381
  – bread 353
  Chester pudding 418
  – cream 315
  crème frangipane 398
  – fingers 378
  florentines 385
  maids of honour 427
  Mrs Beeton's Bakewell
    pudding 421
  Mrs Beeton's – macaroons
    385
  Mrs Beeton's nice useful
    cake 369
  – paste 392–3
  piped – rings 382
  roast chicken with honey
    and – 177
  – sauce 225
  – soufflé 283
  – soufflé ambassadrice 283
  trout with – 87
Ambrosia mould 301
American frosting 390
Anchovy:
  – butter 231
  – fillets as garnish 47
  salad niçoise 24
  – sauce 201
Apple(s):
  freezing 440
  – amber 294, 417
  baked – 296
  – batter pudding 294
  boiled – dumplings 288
  Brown Betty 297
  – charlotte 295
  – crumble 296
  Cumberland pudding 290
  Danish – cake 306
  Eve's pudding 294
  – fritters 297
  fruit curry sauce 218
  – in fruit salad 304
  fruit stuffing 187
  glazed – dumplings 297
  grilled pork chops with –
    slices 157
  ham slices with – 167

Apple(s) *– cont.*
  Mrs Beeton's bachelor's
    pudding 292
  Mrs Beeton's flan of – 421
  – pancakes 285
  – pie 417
  pork and – hot pot 158
  prune and – stuffing 45
  – pudding 289
  – purée 303
  – sauce 213
  – slices (fried) 47
  – snow 278, 306
  – soufflé 283
  stewed – 302
  stewed sliced – rings 302
Apricots:
  freezing 440
  – baskets 372
  – batter pudding 295
  – custard cream 317
  – fritters 298
  – in fruit salad 304
  – glaze 394
  ham slices with – 167
  – omelet 284
  – pancakes 285
  – pudding 418
  – soufflé 283
  spiced – 59
  stewed – 302
  stewed dried – 302
  – stuffing 43
  – and walnut loaf 352
Arbroath smokies 67
Arrowroot:
  – cereal sweet 301
  – pudding 275
  – pudding with eggs 276
  sweet – sauce 226
Artichokes, **see** Globe
  artichokes, Jerusalem
  artichokes
Asparagus 235–6
  freezing 433
  – points (tips) 236
  – soufflé 197
Aspic jelly 47
Aubergines 236–7
  freezing 433
  deep-fried – 237
  ratatouille 270
Aurora sauce 208
Avocado pear(s):
  freezing 433
  dressed – 14
  – with prawns 15
  – royale 15

Avocado pear(s) *– cont.*
  – vinaigrette 14
Azuki beans 238

Bacon:
  cooking 163–4
  cuts 162–3
  freezing 431
  grilling and frying times
    93
  boiled – 165
  – chops with fruit 167
  – and cream tart 416
  crumbled cooked – 48
  fried – 164
  grilled – 164
  lamb's liver and – 139
  – omelet 195
  – pasties 414
  – rashers as garnish 48
  – rolls (fried or grilled)
    48
  Yorkshire rarebit 199
Baked Alaska 334
Bakewell pudding: Mrs
  Beeton's – 421
Bakewell tart 421
Banana(s):
  Beatrice tartlets 423
  – custard 279
  – fritters 298
  fruit curry sauce 218
  – in fruit salad 304
  – nut coffee bread 353
  – pancakes 285
  rhubarb and – fool 303
  – split 334
Banbury cakes 422
Barley cereal sweet 300
Bath buns 347
Battenburg cake 374
Batter:
  apple pancakes 285
  apple – pudding 294
  apricot pancakes 285
  apricot – pudding 295
  baked – pudding 191
  banana pancakes 285
  basic thin – 191
  beef pancakes 192
  beer – 189
  cheese pancakes 193
  chicken pancakes 193
  chocolate pancakes 285
  coating – 190–1
  cream pancake – 192
  currant pancakes 285
  curried turkey pancakes 193

Batter *– cont.*
  dried fruit – pudding 295
  – for fish 77
  individual Yorkshire
    puddings 192
  jam pancakes 285
  layered pancakes 286
  lemon pancakes 285
  plain pancakes 192
  rich pancake – 192
  savoury pancakes 192–3
  smoked haddock pancakes
    193
  spinach pancakes 193
  surprise pancakes 285
  sweet pancakes 285–6
  toad-in-the-hole 189
  waffles 286
  Yorkshire pudding 191
Bavarois:
  caramel – 316
  chocolate – 316
  Italian – 316
  vanilla – 316
Bean sprouts 240
Beans:
  see also French beans,
    Runner beans, etc
  dried – 239
Béarnaise sauce 214
Beatrice tartlets 423
Béchamel sauce 207
  sauces based on – 207–9
Beef:
  carving 96–7
  cuts 102–5
  roasting times 92
  steak grilling and frying
    chart 107
  boeuf bourguignonne 113
  boiled – with vegetables
    and dumplings 116
  – broth 27
  brown stew 114
  brown stock 25
  carbonnade of – 112
  consommé 31
  consommé brunoise 31
  consommé frappé 32
  consommé Julienne 31
  consommé with rice 32
  consommé royale 32
  Cornish pasties 118
  cottage pie 122
  – creole 115
  – croquettes 122
  Exeter stew 115
  fillet of – en croûte 106

Beef – *cont.*
fondue bourguignonne
110
fried steaks 108
– galantine 121
grilled steak 107
hamburgers 120
iced consommé 32
marinated roast – 106
minced – 119
moussaka 139
Mrs Beeton's – à la mode
111
Mrs Beeton's steak pie
117
mulligatawny soup 37
– olives 112
– pancakes 192
pork brawn 161
potted – 22
roast – 105
sea pie 119
shepherd's pie 122
spaghetti bolognese 121
steak and kidney pie 117
steak and kidney pudding
118
steak and mushroom pie
117
steak au poivre 108
steak and potato pie 117
steak pudding 118
– stroganoff 114
– tea 28
tournedos Rossini 109
Beer batter 189
toad-in-the-hole 189
Beetroot 240–1
freezing 433
Bercy sauce 212
Beurre:
noir 85, 151, 214
– noisette 214
Beverages, see Drinks
Bigarade sauce 210
Bilberries: summer
pudding 307
Birthday cake 321, 366
Biscuits:
freezing 437
main ingredients 360
raising ingredients 360
storing 358
almond – 381
almond fingers 378
Bourbon – 382
brandy snaps 383
Canadian crispies 385
Catherine wheel – 378
coffee kisses 379
creamed – 381
– crumb crusts 413
digestive – 379
Dover – 381
Easter – 381
flapjacks 384
florentines 385
German – 381
ginger snaps 384
jumbles 380
lemon – 381
melting moments 382
Mrs Beeton's almond
macaroons 385

Biscuits – *cont.*
Mrs Beeton's coconut
pyramids 386
oatcakes 384
oatmeal – 380
orange – 381
piped almond rings 382
plain chocolate – 378
plain cinnamon – 378
plain coconut– 378
plain spice – 378
Princess cakes 383
ratafias 385
rubbed-in – 377
shortbread 380
shortbread – 380
Shrewsbury – 381
spice – 381
Bisque: prawn – 38
Bitter-sweet sauce 213
Black butter 85, 151, 214
Black cap pudding 295
Black Forest cherry gâteau
320
Blackberries:
freezing 441
– custard cream 317
summer pudding 307
thickened fruit sauce
228
Blackcurrants:
freezing 441
– custard cream 317
– jelly 308
– mousse 313
stewed – 302
summer pudding 307
– tartlets 423
– whip 308
Black-eyed peas 239
Blanching 433
Blancmange 301
Bloaters 67
Blueberries:
freezing 441
thickened fruit sauce 228
Boeuf bourguignonne 113
Bombes: mould for 329
Bordelaise sauce 204
Borlotti beans 239
Boston roast 240
Bouquet garni 25
Bourbon biscuits 382
Brains:
– in black butter 151
– sauce 201
– on toast 141
Brandy:
– butter 233
choc-au-rhum mousse
314
Mrs Beeton's – trifle
318
– sauce 225
– snaps 383
Brawn: pork – 161
Brazil nuts 361
Bread(s):
freezing 437–8
kneading 338
using 339
yeast breads 338
almond – 353
American coffee – 353

Bread(s) – *cont.*
apricot and walnut loaf
352
banana nut coffee – 353
basic quick – 352
basic soured milk quick –
352
basic white – 339
Bath buns 347
bridge rolls 342
brioches 345
brown – pudding 290
bun loaf 347
– and butter pudding 279
cabinet pudding 279
châpon 270
Chelsea buns 348
Cornish splits 348
cottage rolls 340
crescents of fried – 48
croissants 346
– croûtons 48
date – 354
date and walnut loaf 354
dinner rolls 342
enriched – 341
fairy toast 51
fancy roll shapes 339–40
French – 342
fruit – 341
granary – 344
grissini 345
Hot Cross buns 347
huffkins 340
lardy cake 340
malt – 354
Melba toast 51
nut – 341, 352
orange nut coffee – 353
– plait 341
poppy seed – 341
pulled – 51
quick – 352–4
raisin – 354
rye cobs 344
– sauce 215
sippets 48
toasted croûtons 48
wheatmeal – 343
wholemeal – 343
wholemeal quick – 352
wholemeal rolls 343
yeast – 338–51
Breadcrumbs: making 42
Bream 65
Bridge rolls 342
Brill 65
– and potato mornay 78
Brioches:
freezing 438
basic recipe 345
Brisling 69
Broad beans 237
freezing 433
Broccoli 241–2
freezing 434
Brochet: quenelles de – 83
Broth:
beef – 27
calf's foot – 30
chicken – 28
Scots (Scotch) – 29
veal – 30
Brown beans 239

Brown Betty 297
Brown butter 214
Brown stew 114
Brownies 373
Brussels sprouts 242
freezing 434
Bubble and squeak 268
Buck rarebit 199
Buckling 67
Buns:
Bath – 347
Chelsea – 348
chocolate – 363
coconut – 364
Cornish splits 348
cream – 424
Hot Cross – 347
lemon – 364
– loaf 347
orange – 364
plain – 363
raspberry – 364
rock – 364
seed – 364
spice – 364
Butter(s):
freezing 439
anchovy – 231
black – 85, 151, 214
brandy – 233
bread and – pudding 279
brown – 214
chocolate – cream 398
chocolate – icing 389
clarified – 232
coffee – cream 398
coffee – icing 389
– cream 397
garlic – 232
herb – 232
– icing 389–90
lemon – icing 390
maître d'hôtel – 232
meunière – 214
Mrs Beeton's fairy – 233
orange – icing 390
ravigote – 232
rum – 233
vanilla – icing 390
walnut – icing 390
Butter beans 239
– soup 33
Butterfly cakes 373

Cabbage 243–4
freezing 434
stuffed – leaves 244
Cabbage, red 243, 244
roast goose with fruit
stuffing and – 187
Cabinet pudding 279
Cake(s):
see also Gâteau(x)
coating with almond
paste or marzipan
391–2
coating with glacé icing
386
coating with whipped
cream 397
cooling 362
decorating with piped
royal icing 394–5
freezing 437–8

Cake(s) – *cont.*
  icing with royal icing 393–4
  main ingredients 360–1
  preparing tins 357–8, 359
  raising ingredients 360
  storing 358
  testing when cooked 361
  apricot baskets 372
  Banbury – 422
  Battenburg – 374
  Birthday – 366
  brownies 373
  butterfly – 373
  cherry – 362, 365, 372
  chocolate – 372
  chocolate sandwich – 374
  chocolate Swiss roll 376
  Christmas – 367
  coconut – 372
  coffee – 372
  coffee sandwich – 374
  cornflour – 365
  countess – 362
  currant – 362
  Danish apple – 306
  date and walnut – 362
  devil's food – 367
  dripping – 363
  Dundee – 368
  Eccles – 426
  fairy – 372
  feather-iced sandwich – 374
  fillings 397–9
  French – 377
  fruit – 365
  Genoese sponge (pastry) 376, 377
  ginger – 365
  ground rice – 366
  lardy – 340
  lemon – 362, 366
  lemon sandwich – 374
  Madeira – 368
  Mrs Beeton's nice useful – 369
  Mrs Beeton's savoy – 375
  Mrs Beeton's sponge fingers 375
  Mrs Beeton's tipsy – 318
  orange – 362, 366
  orange sandwich – 374
  pineapple upside-down – 298
  plain – 362
  queen – 372
  rich – 365
  seed – 366
  simnel – 369
  sly – 428
  small rich – 372
  spice – 362
  sponge – 375
  sultana – 362
  Swiss roll 376
  Victoria sandwich – 373, 374
  wedding – 370
  Yule log 376
Calabrese 241

Calamares 74
Calf's brains:
  – in black butter 151
  – on toast 141
Calf's foot:
  – broth 30
  – jelly 153
Calf's head:
  carving 100
  boiled – 142
Calf's liver:
  braised – 159
  – pâté 19
  – with savoury rice 152
  – soup 36
Canadian crispies 385
Canary pudding 291
Cannelloni: basic cooking method 272
Caper sauce 202, 205
Capon:
  carving 174–5
  roasting 171–2
Cappellini: basic cooking method 272
Caramel:
  – bavarois 316
  – custard 280
  – custard sauce 227
  oranges in – sauce 306
Caraway seed:
  – buns 364
  – cake 366
Carbonnade of beef 112
Carp 65
Carrots 244–5
  freezing 434
Carving:
  meat 94–102
  poultry 174–6
Casseroles and stews:
  freezing 435
  baked celery casserole 252
  baked leek casserole 252
  beef creole 115
  beef olives 112
  boeuf bourguignonne 113
  boiled beef with vegetables and dumplings 116
  boiled leg of lamb or mutton with caper sauce 137
  braised chicken with chestnuts and sausages 179
  braised lamb or mutton provençale 136
  braised oxtail 126
  braised pig's liver 159
  braised pork 157
  braised veal sweetbreads 152
  brown stew 114
  carbonnade of beef 112
  chicken casserole 180
  coq au vin 181
  curried lamb 135
  Exeter stew 115
  Irish stew 135
  Lancashire hot pot 134
  liver hot pot 123
  Mrs Beeton's beef à la mode 111

Casseroles and stews – *cont.*
  pork and apple hot pot 158
  pork fillets stuffed with prunes 157
  poultry hot pot 182
  stewed rolled breast of veal 147
  stuffed breast of veal 147
Catfish 65
Catherine wheel biscuits 378
Cauliflower 245–6
  freezing 434
  – cheese 246
Celeriac 247
  – in mustard dressing 15
Celery 247–8
  freezing 424
  baked – casserole 252
  – curls 48
  – sauce 215
Cereal sweets 300–1
Chantilly:
  – cream 398
  – meringue 326
Châpon 270
Charlotte(s):
  apple – 295
  Mrs Beeton's – russe 319
Chaudfroid of chicken 184
Chaudfroid sauce:
  brown – 219
  fawn – 219
  green – 219
  tomato – 219
  white – 218
Cheek: Mrs Beeton's stewed ox – 124
Cheese:
  freezing 439
  buck rarebit 199
  cauliflower – 246
  choux pastry with – 415
  – flan 414
  grated hard – as garnish 51
  macaroni – 193
  mixed vegetables with – 269
  – omelet 195
  – and onion pie 414
  – pancakes 193
  – pastry 409
  pizza con mozzarella 194
  Roquefort salad cream 223
  – sauce 201
  – scones 356
  – soufflé 197
  Swiss – fondue 198
  Welsh rarebit 199
  Yorkshire rarebit 199
Cheesecakes:
  freezing 438
  coffee – 323
  curd – 323
  lemon – 324
  raspberry yoghurt – 324
Chelsea buns 348
Cherry(ies):
  freezing 441
  Black Forest – gâteau 320

Cherry(ies) – *cont.*
  – cakes 362, 365, 372
  – in fruit salad 304
  – tartlets 423
Chester pudding 418
Chestnut(s):
  braised chicken with – and sausages 179
  – sauce 216
  – stuffing 44, 179
Chicken:
  accompaniments 173
  carving 174–5
  freezing 431
  roasting 171–2
  braised – with chestnuts and sausages 179
  – broth 28
  – casserole 180
  – chasseur 180
  chaudfroid of – 184
  consommé frappé 32
  coq au vin 181
  cream of – soup 34
  galantine of – 185
  giblet soup 35
  – giblet stuffing 44
  grilled – joints 177
  iced consommé 32
  – Kiev 178
  – mayonnaise 185
  Mrs Beeton's – pie 183
  – omelet 196
  – pancakes 193
  – rissoles 184
  roast – 176
  roast – with honey and almonds 177
  – soufflé 197
  spatchcocked – 178
  – stock 26
  stuffed – legs 183
  – vol-au-vent 415
Chicory 248–9
Chilli peppers 259
Chinese gooseberries: in fruit salad 304
Chips:
  deep fat frying temperatures 10
  basic recipe 261
  game – 261
Choc-au-rhum mousse 314
Chocolate:
  – bavarois 316
  – buns 363
  – butter cream 398
  – butter icing 389
  – cakes 372
  Canadian crispies 385
  choc-au-rhum mousse 314
  – cream 315
  – curls 400
  – custard sauce 227
  – flavoured confectioners' custard 398
  – glacé icing 388
  – mousse 314
  – pancakes 285
  plain – biscuits 378
  – profiteroles 320
  – pudding 292
  rich – ice cream 333

Chocolate – cont.
  – sandwich cake 374
  – sauce 225, 227
  – scrolls 400
  – soufflé 312
  – sponge 293
  – Swiss roll 376
Choux pastry:
  basic recipe 408
  – with cheese 415
Chowder: white fish – 39
Christmas cake 367
Christmas pudding 289, 290
Churn freezer 329
Cider: court bouillon 75
Cinnamon: plain – biscuits
  378
Coatings 396–400
  applying over jam glaze
    or butter cream
    396–7
  coconut 397
  using whipped cream
    397
  sweet – glaze for flans and
    tartlets 396
Cockle 70
Coconut:
  for coating or
    decoration 397
  – buns 364
  – cakes 372
  – custard pie 419
  desiccated – 361
  – filling 399
  Mrs Beeton's – pyramids
    386
  pink – mould 301
  plain – biscuits 378
  – sponge 293
Cod 66
  freezing 432
  fish cakes 80
  golden grilled – 78
  – à la maître d'hôtel 79
  – mousse 79
Cod roe: taramasalata 24
Coffee:
  American – bread 353
  banana nut – bread 353
  – butter cream 398
  – butter icing 389
  – cakes 372
  – cheesecake 323
  – cream 315
  – glacé icing 388
  – kisses 379
  – milk shake 337
  mocha mousse 314
  orange nut – bread 353
  – sandwich cake 374
  – sauce 226
  – soufflé 283, 312
Coley 66
  fish cakes 80
  white fish chowder 39
Confectioners' custard 398
  chocolate-flavoured – 398
Consommé:
  canned 32
  basic recipe 31
  – brunoise 31
  – frappé 32
  iced – 32

Consommé – cont.
  – julienne 31
  – with rice 32
  – royale 32
Convenience foods:
  storage life 12
Cookware: sizes 8–9
Coq au vin 181
Coquilles St Jacques mornay
  90
Corn, see Sweetcorn
Cornflake(s):
  – crusts 413
  treacle tart 422
Cornflour:
  – cake 365
  – cereal sweet 301
  – pudding 275
  pudding with eggs 276
  sweet – sauce 325
Cornish pasties 118
Cornish splits 348
Cornmeal:
  – pudding 275
  – pudding with eggs 275
Cottage pie 122
Cottage rolls 340
Countess cake 362
Coupe Jacques 334
Courgettes 249
  freezing 434
  ratatouille 270
Court bouillon 75
Coventry turnovers 426
Cow-heel soup 34
Crab 70–1
  cooking 71
  freezing 432
  picking and dressing 71
  – au gratin 88
Cranberry(ies):
  freezing 441
  – sauce 215
Crayfish: freezing 432
Cream:
  coating cake etc 397
  freezing 439
  almond – 315
  apricot custard – 317
  bacon and – tart 416
  – buns 424
  caramel bavarois 316
  Chantilly – 398
  chocolate – 315
  chocolate bavarois 316
  coffee – 315
  cold horseradish – 49
  creamed rice 300
  crème fraîche 399
  cucumber in soured – 16
  – éclairs 424
  – horns 424
  Italian bavarois 316
  mock – 399
  Mrs Beeton's sherry or
    liqueur-flavoured
    whipped – 399
  Neapolitan – 316
  – pancake batter 192
  pastry – 321
  quick fruit – 317
  raspberry – 315
  Roquefort salad – 223
  – salad dressing 220

Cream – cont.
  savoury – sauce 209
  – scones 357
  – slices 425
  soured – dip for crudités
    16
  soured – dressing 224
  strawberry – 315
  vanilla Bavarian – 316
  velvet – 315
Creamed biscuits 381
Crème:
  – anglaise 227, 278
  – brûlée 280
  – fraîche 399
  – frangipane 398
  – St Honoré 398
Crêpes Suzette 286
Croissants:
  freezing 438
  basic recipe 346
Crookneck squash 267
Croûtons:
  bread – 48
  toasted – 48
Crudités 16
  soured cream dip for – 16
Crumb crusts 413
Crumble:
  apple – 296
  fruit – 296
Crumpets:
  freezing 438
  basic recipe 349
  pikelets 349
  Welsh – 349
Cucumber 250
  épicurean sauce 220
  sliced – 49
  – in soured cream 16
Cumberland mutton pies
  138
Cumberland pudding 290
Cumberland sauce 216
Curd cheesecake 323
Currants, black, see
  Blackcurrants
Currants, dried, see Dried
  fruit
Currants, red, see
  Redcurrants
Currants, white, see White
  currants
Curry(ied):
  accompaniments 50
  fruit – sauce 218
  – lamb 135
  – mayonnaise 222
  – mixed vegetables 269
  – turkey pancakes 193
Custard:
  apricot – cream 317
  baked – 277
  banana – 279
  boiled – 276
  caramel – 280
  caramel – sauce 227
  chocolate – sauce 227
  chocolate-flavoured
    confectioners' – 398
  coating – 276
  coconut – pie 419
  confectioners' – 398
  crème brûlée 280

Custard – cont.
  cup or 'boiled' – 276
  egg – sauce 227
  – meringue tartlets 425
  plain – for ice cream 331,
    332
  pouring – 276
  – puddings 276–82
  rich – 276
  rich – for ice cream 332
  royale – 32
  simple – 277
  standard – for ice cream
    332
  steamed – 277
  – tart 281
  – tartlets 425
  thick – 278
  zabaglione 282
Custard marrow 267
Custard powder:
  – pudding 275
  – pudding with eggs 276
  – sweet 301

Dab 66
Dairy produce:
  deep fat frying
    temperatures 11
  freezing 439
Damsons:
  freezing 441
  – crumble 296
  – custard cream 317
  stewed – 302
  thickened fruit sauce 228
Danish apple cake 306
Date(s):
  – bread 354
  – and walnut cake 362
  – and walnut loaf 354
Deep fat frying
  temperatures 10–11
Demi-glace sauce 211
Desserts:
  see also Puddings
  coating with whipped
    cream 397
  cold – 300–28
  frozen – 328–37
  fruit – 294–9, 302–7
  hot – 274–99
  ice cream – 332–6
Devil's food cake 367
Digestive biscuits 379
Dips: soured cream – for
  crudités 16
Dogfish 66
  preparing 64
Doughnuts:
  deep fat frying
    temperatures 11
  jam – 350
  ring – 350, 364
Dover biscuits 381
Dover sole 69
  – Colbert 86
Dried fruit:
  in cakes and biscuits
    361
  freezing 441
  Banbury tarts 422
  – batter pudding 295
  birthday cake 366

Dried fruit – *cont.*
 black cap pudding 295
 brown bread pudding 290
 Christmas cake 367
 Christmas pudding 289,
  290
 countess cake 362
 Cumberland pudding 290
 currant cake 362
 currant pancakes 285
 Dundee cake 368
 Eccles cakes 426
 fruit bread 341
 fruit cake 365
 fruit roly-poly pudding
  288
 griddle scones 356
 lardy cake 340
 Mrs Beeton's bachelor's
  pudding 292
 queen cakes 372
 raisin bread 354
 raisin sauce 218
 rock buns 364
 – scones 356
 Simnel cake 369
 sly cakes 428
 spice cake 362
 spotted dick 288
 stewed – 302
 sultana cake 362
 wedding cake 370
Drinks:
 beef tea 28
 coffee milk shake 337
 ice cream soda 337
 iced – 337
 milk shakes 337
Dripping 94
 – cake 363
Dropped scones 357
Dublin Bay prawns 73–4
Duchesse potatoes 57
Duck:
 accompaniments 174
 boning 188
 carving 176
 deep fat frying
  temperatures 11
 freezing 431
 roasting 172
 English roast – 187
 roast – with orange 188
 stuffed boned – 188
Dumplings:
 basic recipe 50
 boiled apple – 288
 glazed apple – 297
 herb – 50
 meat – 51
 soya – 51
 suet – 116
Dundee cake 368

Easter biscuits 381
Eccles cakes 426
Eclairs: *cream –* 424
Eel 66
 preparing 64
Egg(s):
 in cakes and biscuits
  360
 freezing 439
 grading systems 11

Egg(s) – *cont.*
 almond soufflé 283
 apple snow 278, 306
 apple soufflé 283
 apricot soufflé 283
 asparagus soufflé 197
 bacon omelet 195
 baked Alaska 334
 baked custard 277
 banana custard 279
 'boiled' custard 276
 buck rarebit 199
 caramel custard 280
 Chantilly meringue 326
 cheese omelet 195
 cheese soufflé 197
 chicken omelet 196
 chicken soufflé 197
 chocolate soufflé 312
 chocolate-flavoured
  confectioners' custard
  398
 coating custard 276
 coconut custard pie 419
 coffee soufflé 283, 312
 cold soufflés 312–13
 confectioners' custards
  398
 cooked meringue 325
 – Courtet 17
 crème anglaise 227, 278
 crème brûlée 280
 crème St Honoré 398
 cup or 'boiled' custard
  276
 – custard for ice cream
  332
 custard meringue tartlets
  425
 – custard sauces 227
 custard tart 281
 custard tartlets 425
 custards 276–9
 filled omelets 195
 fish omelet 195
 fruit custard cream 317
 ham omelet 195
 ham soufflé 198
 ham and tongue soufflé
  198
 hard-boiled – as garnish
  52
 hazelnut meringue gâteau
  328
 Italian meringue 325
 large grain milk puddings
  with – 274
 lemon ice cream 333
 lemon meringue pie 420
 lemon soufflé 283, 312
 mayonnaises 222–3,
  224–5
 medium and small grain
  puddings with – 275
 meringue baskets 325
 meringue cases 327
 meringue cuite 325
 meringue shells 326
 meringue topping 326
 meringues 325–8
 mimosa salad 52
 mushroom omelet 195
 omelets 194–6
 omelette fines herbes 195

Egg(s) – *cont.*
 omelette provençale 195
 onion omelet 195
 orange soufflé 312
 pineapple soufflé 283
 plain – custard for ice
  cream 332
 plain omelet 194
 pouring custard 276
 powdered grain puddings
  with – 276
 praline soufflé 283, 313
 prawn and mushroom
  omelet 196
 queen of puddings 281
 raised veal, pork and – pie
  149
 raspberry soufflé 283
 raspberry vacherin 327
 – rémoulade 17
 rich chocolate ice cream
  333
 rich custard 276
 rich custard for ice cream
  332
 rich vanilla ice cream 333
 royale custard 32
 salmon soufflé 198
 savoury soufflé 196
 Scotch – 199
 sherry soufflé 313
 simple custard 277
 smoked haddock soufflé
  198
 smoked salmon soufflé
  198
 soufflé ambassadrice 283
 soufflé harlequin 283
 soufflés 196–8, 282–4,
  312–13
 stacked omelets 196
 standard custard for ice
  cream 332
 steamed custard 277
 strawberry soufflé 284
 stuffed Russian – 17
 sweet omelets 284–5
 Swiss meringue 326
 thick custard 278
 tomato omelet 196
 tomato soufflé 198
 tongue omelet 195
 vanilla ice cream 332
 vanilla soufflé 282
 zabaglione 282
Eggplant, **see** Aubergines
Endive 250
English foundation sauces
 200–7
English salad dressing 220
Epicurean sauce 220
Espagnole sauce 210
 sauces based on –
  210–11
Evaporated milk dressing
 221
Eve's pudding 294
Exeter stew 115

Faggots 160
Fairy cakes 372
Fairy toast 51
Fats:
 for cakes and biscuits 360

Fats – *cont.*
 clarifying 94
 meat-flavoured 94
 rendering 94
 temperature testing 11
 temperatures for deep
  frying 10–11
Feather-iced sandwich cake
 374
Feather icing 387
Fennel 250–1
Figs:
 freezing 441
 stewed dried – 302
Fillings for cakes 397–9
First-course dishes:
 artichoke salad 14
 avocado pears with
  prawns 15
 avocado pears vinaigrette
  14
 avocado royale 15
 celeriac in mustard
  dressing 15
 crudités 16
 cucumber in soured cream
  16
 dressed artichoke bases or
  fonds 14
 eggs Courtet 17
 eggs rémoulade 17
 grapefruit 18
 herring rolls 18
 kipper mousse 19
 liver pâté 19
 melon 20
 melon with Parma ham
  20
 mixed hors d'oeuvre
  wheel 21
 Mrs Beeton's dressed
  whitebait 21
 platter of pork meats 22
 potted beef 22
 potted prawns 22
 potted shrimps 22
 prawn cocktail 23
 Russian salad 23
 salad niçoise 24
 smoked mackerel pâté 24
 soups 25–41
 soured cream dip for
  crudités 16
 spiced grapefruit 18
 stuffed Russian eggs 17
 taramasalata 24
Fish:
 see also Cod, Haddock,
  etc
 boning 63
 cleaning 60
 cooking times 64–5
 deep fat frying
  temperatures 10
 filleting 62–3
 freezing 432
 preparing 60–4
 scaling 60
 skinning 61–2
 types 65–70
 baking – 76
 – cakes 80
 court bouillon 75
 deep frying – 77

Fish – cont.
　fisherman's hot pot 35
　– forcemeat 45
　frying – 77
　grilling – 75
　– à la meunière 77
　– mousse 79
　– omelet 195
　poaching – 76
　shallow frying – 77
　steaming – 76
　– stock 26
　white – chowder 39
Fisherman's hot pot 35
Flageolet beans 239
Flake 66
Flaky pastry:
　quantities 403
　basic recipe 411
　patty cases 413
Flans:
　see also Pies and Tarts
　freezing 435
　lining tins 402
　basic fruit – 418
　cheese – 414
　Mrs Beeton's – of apples
　　421
　sweet coating glaze for –
　　396
Flapjacks 384
Fleurons of puff pastry 51
Florentines 385
Flour:
　for cakes and biscuits
　　360
　– panada 45
Flummery: Mrs Beeton's
　Dutch – 309
Fondant icing:
　general points 388
　basic recipe 388–9
Fondue(s):
　– bourguignonne 110
　Swiss cheese – 198
Fool(s):
　fruit – 303
　rhubarb and banana –
　　303
Forcemeat(s):
　see also Stuffings
　basic herb – 43
　crumbed – balls 44
　fish – 45
　glazed – balls 44
　nut – balls 44
Foundation sauces, see
　Sauce(s)
Fowl (boiling):
　galantine of chicken 185
　Mrs Beeton's – pie 182
　poultry hot pot 182
Freezing:
　foods not to freeze 429
　foods to freeze with care
　　429–30
　labelling items 430
　methods 430–42
　recording items 430
　thawing foods 430
French beans 237–8
　freezing 433
　salad niçoise 24
French bread 342

French cakes 377
French dressing 221
French foundation sauces
　207–12
Fricadelles of veal 150
Fritters:
　deep fat frying
　　temperatures 11
　fruit – 297–8
　gooseberry – 298
Frosting:
　American – 390
　seafoam – 390
Frozen desserts 328–37
Fruit:
　see also Apples, Pears,
　　etc
　freezing 440–2
　basic – flan 418
　coupe Jacques 334
　– crumble 296
　– curry sauce 218
　– desserts 294–9,
　　302–7
　– fools 303
　– fritters 297
　ham slices with – 167
　– jelly 311
　poached fresh – 302
　– puddings 290, 294–9
　– purées 303
　quick – cream 317
　– salad 304
　salads with – 271
　stewed dried – 302
　stewed fresh – 302
　– stuffing 187
　summer pudding 307
　– syrup 304
　thickened – sauce 228
　– turnovers 426
Fry:
　faggots 160
　fried pig's – 160
　lamb's – 140
　savoury ducks 160

Game:
　freezing 430–1
　– stock 26
Game birds: boning 188
Gammon:
　carving 102
　cooking 163–4
　cuts 162–3
　grilling and frying times
　　93
　boiled – 166
　– slices with fruit 167
　– steaks with marmalade
　　168
Garlic:
　aïoli 219
　– butter 232
Garnishes 47–59
Gâteau(x):
　coating with glacé icing
　　386
　coating with whipped
　　cream 397
　Black Forest cherry –
　　320
　hazelnut meringue – 328
　mille-feuille – 320

Gâteau(x) – cont.
　– St Honoré 321
　strawberry ice cream
　　layer – 336
Genoese sponge (pastry)
　376, 377
German biscuits 381
Gherkin fans 52
Giblet(s):
　freezing 431
　preparing 173
　chicken – stuffing 44
　– gravy 229
　– soup 35
　turkey – stuffing 45
Ginger:
　– cake 365
　– sauce 226
　– snaps 384
Gingerbread 365
Glacé icing:
　general points 386–7
　basic recipe 387
　chocolate – 388
　coffee – 388
　lemon – 388
　liqueur-flavoured – 388
　orange – 388
Glazes:
　apricot – 396
　– for cakes 396
　meat – 55
　– for pastry 407
　sweet coating – 396
Globe artichokes 234
　freezing 433
　dressed – bases or fonds
　　14
　– salad 14
Golden syrup:
　– pudding 291
　– scones 356
Goose:
　carving 176
　freezing 431
　roasting 172
　giblet soup 35
　roast – with fruit stuffing
　　and red cabbage 187
Gooseberry(ies):
　freezing 441
　– crumble 296
　– custard cream 317
　– fritters 298
　– pudding 418
　– sauce 83
　stewed – 302
Gooseberry(ies), Chinese:
　– in fruit salad 304
Gougère 415
Goujons of plaice 84
Grain:
　– cereal sweets 300–1
　large – milk puddings 274
　large – milk puddings
　　with eggs 274
　medium and small – milk
　　puddings 275
　medium and small – milk
　　puddings with eggs
　　275
　powdered – puddings 275
　powdered – puddings with
　　eggs 276

Granary bread 344
Grand Marnier:
　choc-au-rhum mousse
　　314
　crêpes Suzette 286
Granités 330
Grapefruit:
　freezing 441
　basic recipe 18
　– baskets 53
　spiced – 18
Grapes:
　freezing 441
　– in fruit salad 304
Gravy(ies):
　giblet – 229
　lamb – 131, 229
　thickened – 230
　thin – 229
　vegetable – 230
Green salads 270
Greengages:
　freezing 441
　stewed – 302
Grey mullet 66
Griddle scones 356
Grissini 345
Ground rice, see Rice
Grouse: freezing 431
Guard of Honour 131–2
Gudgeon 66
Guinea-fowl:
　freezing 431
　roasting 172
Gurnard 66
Gurnet 66

Haddock 66–7
　freezing 432
　finnan – 67
　fish cakes 80
　fisherman's hot pot 35
　kedgeree 80
　– mousse 79
　smoked – 67
　smoked – pancakes 193
　smoked – soufflé 198
Hake 67
　freezing 432
　fisherman's hot pot 35
　– with sweet and sour
　　sauce 81
Halibut 67
　freezing 432
　scalloped – 81
Ham:
　carving 102
　cooking 163–4
　cuts 162–3
　freezing 431
　boiled – 166
　honey-glazed – with
　　pineapple 166
　melon with Parma – 20
　– omelet 195
　– slices with fruit 167
　– soufflé 198
　split pea and – soup 33
　– stuffing 43
　– and tongue soufflé 198
　veal and – pie 148
　veal and – pudding 150
Hamburgers 120
Hampshire pudding 419

Hare: freezing 431
Haricot beans 239
  Boston roast 240
  – soup 33
Hazelnut(s) 361
  – meringue gâteau 328
Head:
  boiled calf's – 142
  boiled sheep's – 142
  pork brawn 161
Heart: baked stuffed ox –
  123
Herb(s):
  freezing 434
  basic – stuffing 43
  – butter 232
  – for garnishing 52
  – dumplings 50
  omelette fines herbes 195
  ravigote butter 232
  – sauce 202
Herring 67
  boning 63
  freezing 432
  – with mustard sauce 82
  rollmops 67
  – rolls 18
Hollandaise sauce 217
  mousseline – 217
Holstein Schnitzel 146
Honey:
  – glazed ham with
    pineapple 166
  roast chicken with – and
    almonds 177
Hors d'oeuvre: mixed –
  wheel 21
Horseradish:
  cold – cream 49
  hot – sauce 202
Hot Cross buns 347
Hot pot:
  see also Casseroles and
    Stews
  fisherman's – 35
  Lancashire – 134
  liver – 123
  pork and apple – 158
  poultry – 182
Hot water crust pastry 410
Hotch potch 29
Hubbard squash 267
Huffkins 340
Huss 66

Ice cream:
  baked Alaska 334
  banana split 334
  coupe Jacques 334
  custards for – 331–2
  knickerbocker glory 335
  lemon – 333
  Neapolitan – 335
  peach Melba 335
  poire belle Hélène 336
  raspberry – 333
  rich chocolate – 333
  rich vanilla – 333
  – soda 337
  strawberry – 333
  strawberry – layer gâteau
    336
  surprise omelet 285
  surprise pancakes 285

Ice Cream – cont.
  vanilla – 332
Ice cream maker, electric
  329
Iced petits fours 377
Ices 328–37
  see also Ice Cream
  equipment for making
    328–30
  freezing 435
  blackcurrant mousse 313
  lemon water – 330
  loganberry water – 331
  orange water – 330
  raspberry water – 331
  strawberry water – 331
  syrup for water – 330
  water – 330–1
Icing(s):
  using royal icing 393–5
  American frosting 390
  butter – 389–90
  chocolate butter – 389
  chocolate glacé – 388
  coffee butter – 389
  coffee glacé – 388
  feather – 387
  fondant – 388–9
  glacé – 386–8
  lemon butter – 390
  lemon glacé – 388
  liqueur-flavoured glacé –
    388
  orange butter – 390
  orange glacé – 388
  royal – 395
  seafoam frosting 390
  vanilla butter – 390
  walnut butter – 390
Ink fish 74
Irish stew 135
Italian bavarois 316
Italian meringue 325
Italian sauce 124, 205,
  208
Italian tomato soup 41

Jam:
  baked – roll 293
  – doughnuts 350
  Mrs Beeton's – tartlets
    426
  – omelet 284
  – pancakes 285
  roly-poly pudding 288
  – sauce 228
  – sponge 293
  – tart 419
  – turnovers 426
Jelly(ies):
  chopping for decoration
    310
  cleared 310–11
  uncleared 307–9
  aspic – 47
  blackcurrant – 308
  blackcurrant whip 308
  calf's foot – 153
  clear lemon – 311
  cleared – 311
  fresh lemon – 309
  fresh orange – 309
  fruit – 311
  knickerbocker glory 335

Jelly(ies) – cont.
  milk – 309
  Mrs Beeton's Dutch
    flummery 309
  uncleared – 308–9
Jelly mould:
  filling 310
  lining and decorating
    310
Jerusalem artichokes 235
  freezing 433
Julienne vegetables 52
Jumbles 380

Kedgeree 80
Kidney(s):
  grilling and frying times
    93
  fried pig's – 161
  – in Italian sauce 124
  Lancashire hot pot 134
  sautéed – 140
  – soup 36
  steak and – pie 117
  steak and – pudding 118
Kidney beans, **see** Red
  kidney beans
Kippers 67
  · grilled – 82
  jugged – 82
  – mousse 19
  poached – 82
Kirsch:
  crêpes Suzette 286
  sweet pineapple salad with
    – 307
Kiwi fruit: – in fruit salad 304
Knickerbocker glory 335
Knives: sharpening 94–5
Kohlrabi 251

Lamb:
  carving 97–100
  cuts 127–8
  grilling and frying times
    93
  roasting times 92
  boiled leg of – with caper
    sauce 137
  boiled – tongues 143
  brains on toast 141
  braised – liver 159
  braised – provençale 136
  crown roast of – with
    saffron rice 130
  curried – 135
  – cutlets en papillotes
    129
  fried – cutlets or chops
    133
  – fry 140
  – gravy 131, 229
  grilled – cutlets or chops
    132
  Guard of Honour 131–2
  hotch potch 29
  Irish stew 135
  Lancashire hot pot 134
  – liver and bacon 139
  liver soup 36
  moussaka 139
  noisettes of – jardinière
    134
  – pie 137

Lamb – cont.
  – pudding 137
  roast leg of – 128
  – roll 138
  sautéed kidneys 140
  – shish kebab 133
  stuffed roast shoulder of –
    129
  sweetbreads bourgeoise
    141
Lancashire hot pot 134
Lardy cake 340
Leek(s) 251–2
  freezing 434
  baked – casserole 252
  hot vichyssoise cream
    soup 40
  iced vichyssoise 40
Lemon(s):
  freezing 441
  – baskets 53
  – biscuits 381
  – buns 364
  – butter icing 390
  – butterflies 53
  – cake 362, 366
  – cheesecake 324, 427
  – chiffon pie 420
  clear – jelly 311
  crimped – slices 54
  fresh – jelly 309
  – glacé icing 388
  – ice cream 333
  – jellies 309, 311
  – meringue pie 420
  Milanaise soufflé 312
  – omelet 284
  – pancakes 285
  – pudding 291
  rich – sauce 226
  – sandwich cake 374
  – sauce 226
  savoury – sauce 203
  – sorbet 331
  – soufflés 283, 312
  – sponge 293
  – twists 54
  – water ice 330
Lemon sole 69
  fillets of – bonne femme
    86
  – Véronique 87
Lentils 252–3
  – soup 33
  spiced – 253
Lettuce 253–4
Lima beans 239
Limes: freezing 441
Ling 67
  fisherman's hot pot 35
Liqueur(s):
  – flavoured glacé icing
    388
  Mrs Beeton's – flavoured
    whipped cream 399
Liver:
  grilling and frying times
    93
  braised calf's – 159
  braised lamb's – 159
  braised pig's – 159
  calf's – with savoury rice
    152
  faggots 160

Liver – cont.
  – hot pot 123
  lamb's – and bacon 139
  – pâté 19
  savoury ducks 160
  – soup 36
Lobster 71–2
  boiling 71
  dressing 72
  freezing 432
  – thermidor 88
Loganberry(ies):
  – in fruit salad 304
  – water ice 331
Lychees: – in fruit salad 304

Macaroni: basic cooking
    method 272
  – cheese 193
  – au gratin 193
Macaroons: Mrs Beeton's
    almond – 385
Macédoine of vegetables 54
Mackerel 68
  boning 63
  freezing 432
  – with gooseberry sauce
    83
  kippered – 68
  smoked – 68
  smoked – pâté 24
Madeira cake 368
Madeira sauce 211
Maids of Honour 427
Main courses:
  fish and shellfish –
    75–90
  meat – 105–68
  poultry – 176–89
  miscellaneous – 189–99
Maître d'hôtel butter 232
Maître d'hôtel sauce 202
Malt bread 354
Mange-tout peas 258
Mango(es):
  – in fruit salad 304
  – purée 303
Margarine: freezing 439
Marinade(s):
  – for beef 106
  cooked red wine – 231
  – for fish 81
  – for lamb 133
  uncooked red wine – 231
  uncooked white wine –
    230
Marmalade: gammon steaks
    with – 168
Marrow, see Vegetable
    marrow
Marrow bones:
  Mrs Beeton's boiled –
    126
Marzipan:
  coating cake 391–2
  basic recipe 393
Mayonnaise 222
  chicken – 185
  cooked – 222
  curry – 222
  green – 223
  rémoulade sauce 223
  Roquefort salad cream
    223

Mayonnaise – cont.
  tartare sauce 224
  Thousand Island dressing
    225
  tomato – 223
Measures 7–9
  metric/imperial
    equivalents 13
Meat:
  see also Lamb, Pork, etc
  boiling 94
  braising 93
  carving 94–102
  casseroling 93
  deep fat frying
    temperatures 10
  freezing 430–1
  freezing after cooking
    436
  frying 93
  grilling 92, 93
  methods of cooking
    91–4
  pot-roasting 93
  roasting 91–2
  roasting chart 92
  stewing 93
  bubble and squeak 268
  – dumplings 51
  – glaze 55
Megrim 68
Melba sauce 228
Melba toast 51
Melon 20
  freezing 441
  – basket 305
  – in fruit salad 304
  – with Parma ham 20
  – purée 303
Melting Moments 382
Meringue:
  apple snow 278
  baked Alaska 334
  – baskets 325
  – cases 327
  Chantilly – 326
  cooked – 325
  – cuite 325
  custard – tartlets 425
  hazelnut – gâteau 328
  Italian – 325
  lemon – pie 420
  Queen of puddings 281
  raspberry vacherin 327
  – shells 326
  Swiss – 326
  – topping 326
Metric/imperial equivalents
    13
Meunière butter 214
Milanaise soufflé 312
Milk:
  freezing 439
  basic soured – quick bread
    352
  cereal sweets 300–1
  coffee – shake 337
  confectioners' custards
    398
  custards 276–9
  evaporated – dressing
    221
  – jelly 309
  large grain – puddings 274

Milk – cont.
  large grain – puddings
    with eggs 274
  medium and small grain –
    puddings 275
  medium and small grain –
    puddings with eggs
    275
  mock cream 399
  powdered grain –
    puddings 275
  powdered grain –
    puddings with eggs
    276
  – puddings 274–82
  – sauces 225–6, 227
  – shake 337
Mille-feuille gâteau 320
Mimosa salad 52
Mince pies 427
Minestrone 37
Mint sauce 56
Mirepoix of vegetables 111,
    136, 269
Mocha mousse 314
Mock cream 399
Monkfish 68
  preparing 64
Mornay sauce 208
Moules marinière 89
Moussaka 139
Mousse:
  freezing 436
  blackcurrant – 313
  chocolate – 314
  fish – 79
  kipper – 19
  mocha – 314
Mousseline hollandaise
    sauce 217
Mousseline sauce:
  cold – 219
  green – 219
Mozzarella: pizza con – 194
Mrs Beeton's (recipes):
  – almond macaroons 385
  – bachelor's pudding 292
  – bakewell pudding 421
  – beef à la mode 111
  – boiled marrow bones
    126
  – brandy trifle 318
  – charlotte russe 319
  – chicken or fowl pie 182
  – coconut pyramids 386
  – dressed whitebait 21
  – Dutch flummery 309
  – fairy butter 233
  – flan of apples 421
  – jam tartlets 426
  – nice useful cake 369
  – roast turkey 186
  – savoy cakes 375
  – sherry or liqueur-
    flavoured whipped
    cream 399
  – sponge fingers 375
  – steak pie 117
  – stewed ox cheek 124
  – tipsy cake 318
  – traditional trifle 318
Muffins 350
  freezing 438
Mulligatawny soup 37

Mushroom(s) 254–5
  freezing 434
  – omelet 195
  prawn and – omelet 196
  – sauce 202
  – slices 56
  steak and – pie 117
  tomato and – patties 416
Mussels 72–3
  freezing 432
  moules marinière 89
Mustard:
  – dressing 15
  – sauce 82
Mutton:
  carving 97–100
  cuts 127–8
  grilling and frying times
    93
  roasting times 92
  boiled leg of – with caper
    sauce 137
  braised – provençale 136
  Cumberland – pies 138
  fried – cutlets or chops
    133
  grilled – cutlets or chops
    132
  hotch potch 29
  Irish stew 135
  Lancashire hot pot 134
  mulligatawny soup 37
  – pudding 137
  roast leg of – 128
  – roll 138
  Scots (Scotch) broth 29
  stuffed roast shoulder of –
    129

Neapolitan cream 316
Neapolitan ice cream 335
Nectarines:
  freezing 441
  – in fruit salad 304
Nut(s):
  see also Walnuts,
    Almonds, etc
  in cakes and biscuits
    361
  banana – coffee bread
    353
  – bread 341, 352
  – forcemeat balls 44
  grilled – topping 390
  – mince 269
  orange – coffee bread 353
  praline 400
  praline soufflés 283, 313
  – scones 356

Oatcakes 384
Oatmeal:
  – biscuits 380
  – cakes 384
  – pudding 275
  – pudding with eggs 275,
    276
Oats: rolled – crusts 413
Ocean perch 65
Offal:
  see also Brain, Liver,
    Kidney, Fry, Head,
    Tail, etc
  freezing 431

Omelet(s) (Omelettes):
apricot – 284
bacon – 195
cheese – 195
chicken – 196
filled – 195–6
– fines herbes 195
fish – 195
ham – 195
jam – 284
lemon – 294
mushroom – 195
onion – 195
plain – 194
prawn and mushroom – 196
– provençale 195
rum – 284
stacked – 196
strawberry – 285
surprise – 285
sweet soufflé – 284
tomato – 196
tongue – 195
Onion(s) 255–6
deep fat frying temperatures 10
freezing 434
cheese and – pie 414
fried – rings as garnish 51
– omelet 195
ratatouille 270
raw – rings as garnish 51
sage and – stuffing 46
– sauce 203, 205
soubise sauce 209
tomato and – pie 266
tripe and – 127
Orange(s):
freezing 441
– baskets 53
– biscuits 381
– brandy pancakes 286
– buns 364
– butter icing 390
– cake 362, 366
– in caramel sauce 306
fresh – jelly 309
– fritters 298
– in fruit salad 304
– glacé icing 388
– jelly 309
Mrs Beeton's fairy butter 233
– nut coffee bread 353
roast duck with – 188
– sandwich cake 374
– sauce 226, 227
– soufflé 283, 312
– sponge 293
– twists 54
– water ice 330
Oysters: freezing 432
Ox cheek: Mrs Beeton's stewed – 124
Ox heart: baked stuffed – 123
Ox kidney:
– in Italian sauce 124
– soup 36
steak and – pie 117
steak and – pudding 118

Ox liver:
– hot pot 123
– soup 36
Oxtail:
braised – 126
– soup 38
Ox tongue: boiled – 125

Palmiers 428
Panada: flour – 45
Pancakes:
freezing 436
apple – 285
apricot – 285
banana – 285
basic thin batter for – 191
beef – 192
cheese – 193
chicken – 193
chocolate – 285
cream – batter 192
currant – 285
curried turkey – 193
jam – 285
layered – 286
lemon – 285
orange brandy – 286
plain – 192
rich – batter 192
savoury – 192
Scotch – 357
smoked haddock – 193
spinach – 193
surprise – 285
sweet – 285–6
Parsley:
deep fat frying temperature 10
fried – 56
– sauce 203
savoury – balls 115
thyme and – stuffing 43
Parsnips 256–7
freezing 434
Partridge: freezing 431
Pasta:
cooking 271–2
freezing 436
– as garnish 56
salad with – 271
Pasties and patties:
bacon – 414
Cornish – 118
tomato and mushroom – 416
Pastries:
coating with glacé icing 386
Banbury cakes 422
cream buns 424
cream éclairs 424
cream horns 424
cream slices 425
Eccles cakes 426
fruit turnovers 426
jam turnovers 426
palmiers 428
sausage rolls 416
sly cakes 428
vanilla slices 425
Pastry:
see also Puff pastry, Shortcrust pastry, etc

Pastry – cont.
baking blind 404
decorations for tarts etc 404, 405–6, 406–7
finishing edges 404–5, 406
freezing 437–8
general hints 401
glazing 407
keeping 401
using 402–3
Pâté:
freezing 436
weighting and cooling 20
liver – 19
smoked mackerel – 24
Pâte sucrée 408
Patties, see Pasties and patties
Patty cases 413
Pea(s) 257–8
freezing 434
cream of green – soup 40
green – soup 40
Pea(s), dried 258
– soup 33
Pea(s), split 258
pease pudding 259
split – and ham soup 33
Peach(es):
freezing 441
– condé 301
– custard cream 317
fried pork chops with – 156
– in fruit salad 304
– Melba 335
– purée 303
spiced – 59
stewed – 302
stewed dried – 302
stuffed fresh – 299
Peanuts 361
Pear(s):
freezing 442
– crumble 296
– fritters 298
– in fruit salad 305
poire belle Hélène 336
spiced – 59
stewed – 302
Pease pudding 259
Pecans 361
Pepper(corns):
– sauce 206
steak au poivre 108
Peppers (sweet) 259
freezing 434
ratatouille 270
stuffed peppers 269
Perch 68
Petits fours, iced 377
Pettitoes: fricasséed – 162
Pheasant: freezing 431
Pies and tarts:
finishing edges 404–5, 406
freezing 436, 438
moulding raised pie 410–11
open tarts 402
pastry decorations 405–6, 406–7

Pies and tarts – cont.
using pastry 402–3
apple amber 417
apple pie 417
apricot pudding 418
bakewell tart 421
bacon and cream tart 416
Beatrice tartlets 423
blackcurrant tartlets 423
cheese and onion pie 414
cherry tartlets 423
Chester pudding 418
coconut custard pie 419
Cumberland mutton pie 138
custard meringue tartlets 425
custard tart 281
custard tartlets 425
gooseberry pudding 418
Hampshire pudding 419
jam tart 419
lamb pie 137
lemon cheesecakes 427
lemon chiffon pie 420
lemon meringue pie 420
maids of honour 427
mince pies 427
Mrs Beeton's bakewell pudding 421
Mrs Beeton's chicken or fowl pie 182
Mrs Beeton's jam tartlets 426
Mrs Beeton's steak pie 117
pot pie of veal 149
quiche Lorraine 416
raised pork pie 158
raised veal, pork and egg pie 149
raspberry tartlets 423
sea pie 119
steak and kidney pie 117
steak and mushroom pie 117
steak and potato pie 117
strawberry tartlets 423
sweet coating glaze for tartlets 396
tomato and onion pie 266
treacle tart 422
veal and ham pie 148
Pig, suckling: carving 102
Pigeon: freezing 431
Pig's brains on toast 141
Pig's fry:
faggots 160
fried – 160
savoury ducks 161
Pig's head: pork brawn 161
Pig's kidneys: fried – 161
Pig's liver:
braised – 159
faggots 160
– pâté 19
savoury ducks 160
Pig's trotters: fricasséed – 162
Pike 68
– quenelles 83
Pikelets 349
Pimentos 259

Pineapple:
　freezing 442
　– basket 305
　– fritters 298
　– in fruit salad 305
　ham slices with – 167
　honey-glazed ham with –
　　166
　– soufflé 283
　sweet – salad with Kirsch
　　307
　– upside-down cake 298
Pinto beans 239
Piquant sauce 206
Pistachios 361
Pizza:
　freezing 436
　– con Mozzarella 194
Plaice 68
　goujons of – 84
　– portugaise 84
　stuffed whole – 84
Plover: freezing 431
Plum(s):
　freezing 441
　– crumble 296
　– in fruit salad 305
　– with port 299
　stewed – 302
　thickened fruit sauce 228
Poire Belle Hélène 336
Poivrade sauce 206
Poppy seed bread 341
Pork:
　carving 101–2
　cuts 153–4
　grilling and frying times
　　93
　roasting times 92
　– and apple hot pot 158
　braised – 157
　– brawn 161
　– fillets stuffed with
　　prunes 157
　fried – chops 156
　fried – chops with peaches
　　156
　glazes for – crackling 55
　grilled – chops 156
　grilled – chops with apple
　　slices 157
　platter of – meats 22
　raised – pie 158
　raised veal, – and egg pie
　　149
　roast – 155
　roast savoury loin of –
　　153
　– sausage-meat 159
Port: plums with – 299
Potato(es) 259–61
　deep fat frying
　　temperatures 10
　freezing 434
　brill and – mornay 78
　chips 261
　cottage pie 122
　duchesse – 57
　game chips 261
　– as garnish 56–7
　hot vichyssoise cream
　　soup 40
　iced vichyssoise 40
　jacket – 260

Potato(es) – cont.
　– parisienne 56
　– pastry 409
　– puffs 261
　– ribbons 261
　– scones 256
　shepherd's pie 122
　steak and – pie 117
Potted beef 22
Potted prawns 22
Potted shrimps 22
Poultry:
　see also Chicken, Duck,
　　etc
　accompaniments 173–4
　boning 188
　carving 174–6
　deep fat frying
　　temperatures 10
　freezing 430–1
　jointing 170–1
　preparing for cooking
　　168–71
　roasting 171–3
　roasting in foil 172–3
　skinning 171
　trussing 168–70
　– hot pot 182
Praline 400
　– soufflés 283, 313
Prawns 73
　freezing 432
　avocado pears with – 15
　– bisque 38
　– cocktail 23
　– as garnish 57
　– and mushroom omelet
　　196
　potted – 22
　– stuffing 44
　sweet and sour – 89
Princess cakes 383
Profiteroles: chocolate – 320
Provençale sauce 136
Prune(s):
　– and apple stuffing 45
　fruit stuffing 187
　pork fillets stuffed with –
　　157
　stewed – 302
Pudding(s):
　freezing 437
　apple – 289
　apple batter – 294
　apricot – 418
　apricot batter – 295
　arrowroot – 275
　arrowroot – with eggs
　　276
　baked – 287–8
　baked batter – 191
　baked jam roll 293
　baked sponge – 293
　basic thin batter for –
　　191
　black cap – 295
　boiled – 287–8
　bread and butter – 279
　brown bread – 290
　cabinet – 279
　Canary – 291
　Chester – 418
　chocolate – 292
　chocolate sponge 293

Pudding(s) – cont.
　Christmas – 289, 290
　coconut sponge 293
　cold – 300–28
　cornflour – 275
　cornflour – with eggs 276
　cornmeal – 275
　cornmeal – with eggs 275
　Cumberland – 290
　custard – 276–82
　custard powder – 275
　custard powder – with
　　eggs 276
　dried fruit batter – 295
　Eve's – 294
　fruit – 290, 294–9
　fruit roly-poly – 288
　golden syrup – 291
　gooseberry – 418
　ground rice – 275
　ground rice – with eggs
　　275, 276
　Hampshire – 419
　hot – 274–82
　ice-cream – 334–6
　individual Yorkshire –
　　192
　jam sponge 293
　lamb – 137
　large grain milk – 274
　large grain milk – with
　　eggs 274
　lemon – 291
　lemon sponge 293
　medium and small grain
　　milk – 275
　medium and small grain
　　milk – with eggs 275
　milk – 274–82
　Mrs Beeton's bachelor's –
　　292
　Mrs Beeton's Bakewell –
　　421
　mutton – 137
　oatmeal – 275
　oatmeal – with eggs 275,
　　276
　orange sponge 293
　powdered grain – 275
　powdered grain – with
　　eggs 276
　queen of – 281
　rice – 274
　rice – with eggs 274
　roly-poly – 288
　sago – 274, 275
　sago – with eggs 274,
　　275
　semolina – 275
　semolina – with eggs 275
　spicy sponge 293
　spotted dick 288
　steak – 118
　steak and kidney – 118
　steamed – 287–8
　steamed sponge – 291
　suet – 288
　summer – 307
　tapioca – 274
　tapioca – with eggs 274
　veal and ham – 150
　Yorkshire – 191
Puff pastry:
　quantities 403

Puff Pastry – cont.
　basic recipe 412
　fleurons of – 51
　patty cases 413
　vol-au-vent cases 413
Pulses:
　see also Peas, Lentils,
　　etc
　salad with – 271
Pumpkin 262
Purées: fruit – 303

Quail: freezing 431
Queen cakes 372
Queen of puddings 281
Quenelles:
　– de brochet 83
　pike – 83
Quiche Lorraine 416

Rabbit:
　freezing 431
　mulligatawny soup 37
Radish(es):
　– roses 58
　– water lilies 58
Rainbow trout, see Trout
Raising ingredients for
　cakes and biscuits 360
Raisins, see Dried fruit
Raspberry(ies):
　freezing 441
　– buns 364
　– cream 315
　– crumble 296
　– custard cream 317
　– in fruit salad 305
　– ice cream 333
　Melba sauce 228
　– purée 303
　– soufflé 283
　summer pudding 307
　– tartlets 423
　thickened fruit sauce 228
　– vacherin 327
　– water ice 331
　– yoghurt cheesecake 324
Raspings 42
Ratafias 385
Ratatouille 270
Ravigote butter 232
Ravigote sauce (hot) 212
Ravioli: basic cooking
　method 272
Red cabbage 243, 244
　roast goose with fruit
　　stuffing and – 187
Red fish 65
Red kidney beans 239
Redcurrants:
　freezing 441
　Cumberland sauce 216
　stewed – 302
　summer pudding 307
Reform sauce 206
Remoulade sauce 223
Rhubarb:
　freezing 442
　– and banana fool 303
　– crumble 296
　stewed – 302
Rice:
　cooking 272
　freezing 436

Rice – cont.
 boiled – (brown) 273
 boiled – (white) 272
 calf's liver with savoury –
  152
 – cereal sweet 300
 consommé with – 32
 creamed – 300
 – as garnish 57
 ground – cake 366
 ground – cereal sweet
  301
 ground – pudding 275
 ground – pudding with
  eggs 275, 276
 kedgeree 80
 peach condé 301
 – pudding 274
 – pudding with eggs
  274
 saffron – 130
 – salad 271
 – stuffing 46
Rice breakfast cereal:
 Canadian crispies 385
Rigatoni: basic cooking
  method 272
Rissoles: chicken – 184
Robert sauce 207
Rock buns 364
Rock-fish 65
Roe: taramasalata 24
Rollmops 67
Roly-poly puddings 288
Roquefort salad cream 223
Rough puff pastry 412
Royal icing:
 general points 393–5
 basic recipe 395
Royale custard 32
Rum:
 – babas 322
 – butter 233
 choc-au-rhum mousse
  314
 – omelet 284
 – sauce 226
 – syrup 322
Runner beans 238
 freezing 433
Russian eggs, stuffed 17
Russian salad 23
Rye cobs 344

Saffron rice 130
Sage and onion stuffing 46
Sago:
 – cereal sweet 300
 – pudding 274, 275
 – pudding with eggs 274,
  275
Saithe 66
Salad(s):
 artichoke – 14
 cooked vegetable – 270
 fruit – 304
 – with fruit 271
 green – 270
 mimosa – 52
 mixed vegetables 268
 – niçoise 24
 with pasta 271
 with pulses 271
 rice – 271

Salad(s) – cont.
 Russian – 23
 sweet pineapple – with
  Kirsch 307
Salad dressing(s):
 aïoli 219
 cold mousseline sauce
  219
 cooked mayonnaise 222
 cream – 220
 curry mayonnaise 222
 English – 220
 Epicurean sauce 220
 evaporated milk – 221
 French – 221
 green mayonnaise 223
 green mousseline sauce
  219
 mayonnaise 222
 mustard – 15
 remoulade sauce 223
 Roquefort salad cream
  223
 soured cream – 224
 tartare sauce 224
 Thousand Islands – 225
 tomato mayonnaise 223
 vinaigrette sauce 221
 yoghurt – 224
Sally Lunn 351
Salmon 68–9
 freezing 432
 grilled – steaks 85
 poached – 85
 smoked – 68–9
 smoked – soufflé 198
 – soufflé 198
Salmon trout 69
Salsa pomodoro 217
Salsify 262–3
Sandwich cake:
 chocolate – 374
 coffee – 374
 feather-iced – 374
 lemon – 374
 orange – 374
 small Victoria – 374
 Victoria – 373
Sandwiches: freezing 438
Sardines 69
Sauce(s):
 all-in-one method 200
 beurre manié method
  200
 freezing 437
 roux method 200
 agro-dolce 213
 aïoli 219
 almond – 225
 anchovy – 201
 apple – 213
 aurora – 208
 based on béchamel –
  207–9
 based on espagnole
  210–11
 based on foundation
  brown – 204–7
 based on foundation
  white – 201–4
 based on velouté –
  211–12
 basic egg and oil – 222
 béarnaise – 214

Sauce(s) – cont.
 béchamel – 207
 bercy – 212
 bigarade – 210
 bitter-sweet – 213
 black butter 85, 151,
  214
 bordelaise – 204
 brain – 201
 brandy – 225
 bread – 215
 brown butter 214
 brown chaudfroid – 219
 caper – 202, 205
 caramel – 306
 caramel custard – 227
 celery – 215
 chaudfroid – 218–19
 cheese – 201
 chestnut – 216
 chocolate – 225, 227
 chocolate custard – 227
 coating consistency 200
 coffee – 226
 cold mousseline – 219
 cooked mayonnaise 222
 cranberry – 215
 cream salad dressing 220
 crème anglaise 227
 Cumberland – 216
 curry mayonnaise 222
 demi-glace – 211
 egg custard – 227
 English foundation –
  200–7
 English salad dressing
  (cream) 220
 Epicurean – 220
 espagnole – 210
 evaporated milk dressing
  221
 fawn chaudfroid – 219
 foundation brown – 204,
  210
 foundation white – 200,
  207
 French dressing 221
 French foundation –
  207–12
 French foundation brown
  – 210
 French foundation fawn –
  211
 French foundation white
  – 207
 fresh tomato – 216
 fruit – 228
 fruit curry – 218
 giblet gravy 229
 ginger – 226
 gooseberry – 83
 gravies 229–30
 green chaudfroid – 219
 green mayonnaise 223
 green mousseline – 219
 herb – 202
 hollandaise – 217
 horseradish – 202
 hot horseradish – 202
 Italian – 124, 205, 208
 jam – 228
 lamb gravy 131, 229
 lemon – 226
 Madeira – 211

Sauce(s) – cont.
 maître d'hôtel – 202
 mayonnaise 222
 Melba – 228
 meunière butter 214
 mint – 56
 mornay – 208
 mousseline – 219
 mousseline hollandaise –
  217
 mushroom – 202
 mustard – 82
 onion – 203, 205
 orange – 226, 227
 parsley – 203
 pepper – 206
 piquant – 206
 poivrade – 206
 pouring consistency –
  200
 provençale – 136
 raisin 218
 ravigote – (hot) 212
 Reform – 206
 remoulade – 223
 rich – 226
 rich lemon – 236
 Robert – 207
 Roquefort salad cream
  223
 rum – 226
 salad dressings 219–25
 salsa pomodoro 217
 savoury cream – 209
 savoury lemon – 203
 sharp – 58
 sorrel – 203
 soubise – 209
 soured cream dressing
  224
 suprême – 212
 sweet – 225–8
 sweet arrowroot – 226
 sweet cornflour – 225
 sweet and sour – 81
 sweet spice – 226
 sweet white – 225
 tartare – 209, 224
 thickened fruit – 228
 thickened gravy 230
 thin gravy 229
 Thousand Islands dressing
  225
 tomato – 216, 217
 tomato chaudfroid – 219
 tomato mayonnaise 223
 vanilla – 226
 vegetable gravy 230
 velouté – 211
 vinaigrette – 221
 white chaudfroid – 218
 white wine – 204
 yoghurt dressing 224
Sausage(s)
 (sausage-meat):
 freezing 431
 grilling and frying times
  93
 braised chicken with
  chestnuts and – 179
 pork – 159
 – rolls 416
 Scotch eggs 199
 – stuffing 46

Sausage(s) – *cont.*
  toad-in-the-hole 189
Savarin 322
Savoury cream sauce 209
Savoury ducks 160
Savoy cakes: *Mrs Beeton's –*
  375
Scallops 73
  coquilles St Jacques
    mornay 90
Scampi 73–4
  fried – 90
Schwälderkirschtorte
  320
Scones 355–7
  freezing 438
  cheese – 356
  cream – 357
  dropped – 357
  fruit – 356
  griddle – 356
  nut – 356
  plain – 355, 356
  potato – 356
  syrup – 356
  treacle – 356
  wheatmeal – 356
Scorzonera 362–3
Scotch (Scots) broth 29
Scotch eggs 199
Scotch pancakes 357
Sea pie 119
Sea trout 69
Seafoam frosting 390
Seed:
  – buns 364
  – cake 366
Semolina:
  – cereal sweet 300
  – pudding 275
  – pudding with eggs 275
Shallots: *aïoli 219*
Sharp sauce 58
Sheep's brains:
  – sauce 201
  – on toast 141
Sheep's head: baked – 142
Sheep's kidneys:
  Lancashire hot pot 134
  sautéed – 140
  steak and – pie 117
  steak and – pudding 118
Sheep's liver and bacon 139
Sheep's tongues: *boiled –*
  143
Shellfish:
  see also Shrimps,
    Prawns, etc
  deep fat frying
    temperatures 10
  freezing 398
  types 70–4
Shepherd's pie 122
Sherry:
  Mrs Beeton's – flavoured
    whipped cream 399
  – soufflé 313
Shish kebab: lamb – 133
Shortbread 380
  – biscuits 380
Shortcrust pastry:
  quantities 403
  basic recipe 407
Shrewsbury biscuits 381

Shrimps 74
  freezing 432
  potted – 22
  – stuffing 44
Simnel cake 369
Sippets 48
Skate 69
  preparing 63–4
  – in black butter 85
Sly cakes 428
Snipe: *freezing 431*
Sole 69
  freezing 432
  – Colbert 86
  fillets of – bonne femme
    86
  – Véronique 87
Sorbet: *lemon – 331*
Sorbetière 329
Sorrel 263
  – sauce 203
Soubise sauce 209
Soufflés:
  preparing dish 197
  almond – 283
  – ambassadrice 283
  apple – 283
  apricot – 283
  asparagus – 197
  cheese – 197
  chicken – 197
  chocolate – 312
  coffee – 283, 312
  ham – 198
  ham and tongue – 198
  – harlequin 283
  lemon – 283, 312
  milanaise – 312
  orange – 283, 312
  pineapple – 283
  praline – 283, 313
  raspberry – 283
  salmon – 198
  savoury – 196
  sherry – 313
  smoked haddock – 198
  smoked salmon – 198
  strawberry – 284
  sweet – omelet 284
  tomato – 198
  vanilla – 282
Soup(s):
  freezing 437
  beef broth 27
  beef tea 28
  butter bean – 33
  calf's foot broth 30
  chicken broth 28
  consommé 31
  consommé brunoise 31
  consommé frappé 32
  consommé Julienne 31
  consommé with rice 32
  consommé royale 32
  cow-heel – 34
  cream of chicken – 34
  cream of green pea – 40
  cream of vegetable – 39
  dried pea – 33
  fisherman's hot pot 35
  giblet – 35
  green pea – 40
  haricot bean – 33
  hot vichyssoise cream – 40

Soup(s) – *cont.*
  hotch potch 29
  iced consommé 32
  iced vichyssoise 40
  Italian tomato – 41
  kidney – 36
  lentil – 33
  liver – 36
  minestrone 37
  mulligatawny – 37
  oxtail – 38
  prawn bisque 38
  Scots (Scotch) broth 29
  split pea and ham – 33
  thick – 33–41
  thin – 25–32
  veal broth 30
  vegetable – 39
  white fish chowder 39
Soya beans 239
Soya dumplings 51
Spaghetti:
  basic cooking method 272
  – bolognese 121
Spaghettini: *basic cooking*
  method 272
Spatchcocked chicken 178
Spice(d)(s):
  – apricots 59
  – biscuits 381
  – buns 364
  – cake 362
  – grapefruit 18
  – lentils 253
  – peaches 59
  – pears 59
  plain – biscuits 378
  – sponge 293
  sweet – sauce 226
Spinach 263–4
  freezing 435
  green mousseline sauce
    219
  – pancakes 193
Split pea and ham soup 33
Sponge:
  baked – pudding 293
  – cake 375
  chocolate – 293
  coconut – 293
  Genoese – cakes 376,
    377
  jam – 293
  lemon – 293
  Mrs Beeton's – fingers
    375
  orange – 293
  spicy – 293
  steamed – pudding 291
Spoon measures 8
Spotted Dick 288
Sprats 69
Squash 267
Squid 74
Starters, **see** First-course
  dishes
Steak:
  grilling and frying times
    107
  fried – 108
  grilled – 107
  – and kidney pie 117
  – and kidney pudding 118
  Mrs Beeton's – pie 117

Steak – *cont.*
  – and mushroom pie 117
  – au poivre 108
  – and potato pie 117
  – pudding 118
  tournedos Rossini 109
Stews **see** Casseroles and
  stews
Stock(s):
  brown – 25
  chicken – 26
  fish – 26
  game – 26
  general household – 25
  vegetable – 27
  white – 26
Stock syrup 389
Strawberry(ies):
  freezing 442
  – cream 315
  – custard cream 317
  – in fruit salad 305
  – ice cream 333
  – ice cream layer gâteau
    336
  – omelet 285
  – purée 303
  – soufflé 284
  – tartlets 423
  – water ice 331
Stuffing(s) 42–6
  apricot – 43
  basic herb – 43
  chestnut – 44, 179
  chicken giblet – 44
  fruit – 187
  ham – 43
  prawn – 44
  prune and apple – 45
  rice – 46
  sage and onion – 46
  sausage-meat – 46
  shrimp – 44
  thyme and parsley – 43
  turkey giblet – 45
Suckling-pig: carving 102
Suet:
  rendering 94
  – dumplings 116
  – puddings 288
Suet crust pastry:
  lining a basin 287
  basic recipe 408
  rich – 408
Sugar: for cakes and
  biscuits 360
Sultanas, **see** Dried fruit
Summer pudding 307
Suprême sauce 212
Surprise omelet 285
Surprise pancakes 285
Swedes 264
  freezing 434
Sweet paste 408
Sweet and sour prawns 89
Sweet and sour sauce 81
Sweetbreads:
  – bourgeoise 141
  braised veal – 152
Sweetcorn 264–5
  freezing 434
Swiss cheese fondue 198
Swiss meringue 326
Swiss roll 376

Swiss roll – cont.
  lining tin 358
  chocolate – 376
Syllabub: wine – 319
Syrup:
  fruit – 304
  golden – pudding 291
  rum – 322
  – scones 356
  stock – for diluting
    fondant 389
  – for water ices 330

Tagliatelle: basic cooking
  method 272
Tail:
  braised ox – 126
  ox – soup 38
Tapioca:
  – cereal sweet 300
  – pudding 274
  – pudding with eggs 274
Taramasalata 24
Tartare sauce 209, 224
Tartlets, see Pies and tarts
Tarts, see Pies and tarts
Temperatures 9–11
Thawing frozen foods 430
Thousand Islands dressing
  225
Thyme and parsley stuffing
  43
Tia Maria: choc-au-rhum
  mousse 314
Tins:
  dimension and capacity
    8–9
  preparing for baking
    357–8, 359
Tipsy cake: Mrs Beeton's
  – 318
Toad-in-the-hole 189
Tomato(es) 265
  freezing 435
  – chaudfroid sauce 219
  eggs Courtet 17
  fresh – sauce 216
  – as garnish 59
  Italian – soup 41
  – lilies 59
  – mayonnaise 223
  – and mushroom patties
    416
  – omelet 196
  – and onion pie 266
  ratatouille 270
  – sauce 216
  – sauce (salsa pomodoro)
    217
  – soufflé 198
Tongue(s):
  carving 97
  boiled lamb's – 143
  boiled ox – 125
  boiled sheep's – 143
  ham and – soufflé 198

Tongue(s) – cont.
  – omelet 195
Tope 66
  preparing 64
Topping(s);
  grilled nut – 390
  grilled walnut – 391
Tournedos Rossini 109
Treacle:
  – scones 356
  – tart 422
Trifle(s):
  Mrs Beeton's brandy –
    318
  Mrs Beeton's traditional
    – 318
Tripe and onion 127
Trotters: fricasséed pig's –
  162
Trout (rainbow) 69, 70
  boning 63
  – with almonds 87
Tuna: salad niçoise 24
Turbot 70
Turkey:
  accompaniments 173
  carving 174–6
  freezing 431
  roasting 171–2
  curried – pancakes 193
  giblet soup 35
  – giblet stuffing 45
  – loaf 186
  Mrs Beeton's roast – 186
Turnip greens 267
Turnips 266–7
  freezing 434

Vacherin: raspberry – 327
Vanilla:
  – Bavarian cream 316
  – bavarois 316
  – butter icing 390
  – ice cream 332
  praline 400
  rich – ice cream 333
  – sauce 226
  – slices 425
  – soufflé 282
Veal:
  carving 100–1
  cuts 143–4
  grilling and frying times
    93
  roasting times 92
  braised – sweetbreads
    152
  – broth 30
  escalopes of – 146
  fricadelles of – 150
  fried – cutlets 145
  grilled – cutlets 145
  – and ham pie 148
  – and ham pudding 150
  Holstein Schnitzel 146
  mulligatawny soup 37

Veal – cont.
  Parisian – 146
  pot pie of – 149
  raised –, pork and egg pie
    149
  roast – 144
  steamed – 148
  stewed rolled breast of –
    147
  stuffed breast of – 147
  white stock 26
  Wiener Schnitzel 146
Vegetables 234–71
  blanching 433
  deep fat frying
    temperatures 10
  freezing 433–5
  bubble and squeak 268
  cooked – salads 270
  cream of – soup 39
  crudités 16
  curried mixed – 269
  fisherman's hot pot 35
  – gravy 230
  hotch potch 29
  Julienne – 52
  macédoine of – 54
  minestrone 37
  mirepoix of – 111, 136,
    269
  mixed – 268
  mixed – with cheese 269
  – soup 39
  – stock 27
Vegetable marrow 267
  freezing 434
  stuffed – 269
Velouté sauce 211
  sauces based on –
    211–12
Velvet cream 315
Venison: freezing 431
Vermicelli: basic cooking
  method 272
Vichyssoise:
  hot – cream soup 40
  iced – 40
Victoria sandwich cake 373
  feather-iced – 374
  small – 374
Vinaigrette sauce 221
Vol-au-vent:
  – cases 413
  chicken – 415

Waffles 286
Walnut(s) 361
  American coffee bread
    353
  apricot and – loaf 352
  banana – coffee bread 353
  Beatrice tartlets 423
  brownies 373
  – butter icing 390
  date and – cake 362
  date and – loaf 354

Walnut(s) – cont.
  grilled – topping 391
  orange – coffee bread 353
Water ices:
  equipment for making
    328–30
  freezing 435
  lemon – 330
  loganberry – 331
  orange – 330
  raspberry – 331
  strawberry – 331
  syrup for – 330
Watercress: – as garnish 59
Wedding cake: three-tier –
  370
Welsh crumpets 349
Welsh rarebit 199
Wheatmeal:
  – bread 343
  – scones 356
Whelks 74
White currants:
  freezing 441
  stewed – 302
Whitebait 70
  Mrs Beeton's dressed –
    21
Whiting 70
  fisherman's hot pot 35
Wholemeal:
  – bread 343
  – quick bread 352
  – rolls 343
Wiener Schnitzel 146
Wine:
  cooked red – marinade
    231
  court bouillon 75
  – syllabub 319
  uncooked red – marinade
    231
  uncooked white –
    marinade 230
  white – sauce 204
Winkles 74
Wolf-fish 65
Woodcock: freezing 431

Yeast:
  types 338
  – breads 338–51
Yeast dough:
  kneading 338
  rising 339
Yoghurt:
  – dressing 224
  raspberry – cheesecake
    324
Yorkshire pudding 191
  individual – 192
Yorkshire rarebit 199
Yule log 376

Zabaglione 282
Zucchini, see Courgettes